JAPANESE WAR CRIMINALS

JAPANESE WAR CRIMINALS

The Politics of Justice
After the Second World War

SANDRA WILSON, ROBERT CRIBB,
BEATRICE TREFALT, AND
DEAN ASZKIELOWICZ

Columbia University Press
New York

Columbia University Press
Publishers Since 1893
New York   Chichester, West Sussex
cup.columbia.edu

Library of Congress Cataloging-in-Publication Data
Names: Wilson, Sandra, 1957– author. | Cribb, R. B., author. |
Trefalt, Beatrice, author. | Aszkielowicz, Dean, author.
Title: Japanese war criminals : the politics of justice after
the Second World War / Sandra Wilson, Robert Cribb,
Beatrice Trefalt, and Dean Aszkielowicz.
Description: New York : Columbia University Press, [2017] |
Includes bibliographical references and index.
Identifiers: LCCN 2016028052 | ISBN 9780231179225
(cloth : alk. paper) | ISBN 9780231542685 (e-book)
Subjects: LCSH: War crimes—Japan. | War crime trials—Japan. |
War criminals—Japan. | World War, 1939–1945—Atrocities.
Classification: LCC KZ1181 .W55 2016 | DDC 341.6/90268—dc23
LC record available at https://lccn.loc.gov/2016028052

Columbia University Press books are printed on permanent
and durable acid-free paper.

Printed in the United States of America

Jacket design: Noah Arlow

CONTENTS

ACKNOWLEDGMENTS

W e would like to thank the many people and institutions who have assisted us in the completion of this project.

The project was supported financially by the Australian Research Council (DP110100582) and by smaller grants from Murdoch University, the Australian National University, Monash University, and the National Library of Australia (Japan Study Grant). These institutions also provided facilities and general support.

Valuable assistance was provided by the staff of the following archives and libraries: Archives New Zealand, Wellington; Mitchell Library, Sydney; National Library of Australia, Canberra (especially Mayumi Shinozaki); National Archives of Australia, Canberra and Melbourne; Australian National University Library, Canberra; Australian War Memorial, Canberra; Monash University Library, Melbourne; Murdoch University Library, Perth; National Archives of Japan, Tokyo; Diplomatic Archives of Japan (Gaikō shiryōkan), Tokyo; National Diet Library, Tokyo; Filipinas Heritage Library (Ayala Museum), Manila; American History Center, Ateneo de Manila University, Manila; Lopez Memorial Library and Museum, Manila; Jose P. Laurel Library and Museum, Manila; Magsaysay Library, Manila; Public Record Office, Hong Kong; Arsip Nasional Republik Indonesia, Jakarta; National Archives of Singapore; Arkib Negara Malaysia, Kuala Lumpur; National Archives of Myanmar, Yangon; Archives du Comité international de la Croix-Rouge, Geneva; NIOD Institute for War, Holocaust, and Genocide Studies, Amsterdam; Universiteitsbibliotheek, University of Leiden; Nationaal Archief, The Hague; Archives diplomatiques, La Courneuve; Archives nationales d'outre-mer, Aix-en-Provence; Archives nationales, Paris; Service historique de la défense, Vincennes; National Archives, Kew, London; Imperial War Museum, London; and National Archives and Records Administration, College Park, MD (especially Eric Van Slander).

We greatly appreciated the support of the University of Heidelberg in receiving us as visiting researchers in 2014, and thank, in particular, Kerstin von Lingen of the Cluster of Excellence "Asia and Europe in a Global Context." We also thank Barak Kushner of Cambridge University for inviting us to the 2014 conference "Breakdown of Japanese Empire"; Wada Hideho, Mike Lan, and Barak Kushner for inviting us to the 2012 conference in Kumamoto on Taiwanese war criminals; and Franziska Seraphim, Kerstin von Lingen, Wolfgang Form, and Barak Kushner for inviting us to the 2015 conference "Contested Visions of Justice: Allied War Crimes Trials in a Global Context, 1943–1958" in Dublin.

We are grateful to Professor Wolfgang Form for granting us access to the magnificent trials database of the Forschungs- und Dokumentationszentrum für Kriegsverbrecherprozesse (ICWC) at the University of Marburg.

We thank Anne-Marie Medcalf for assistance in gaining access to the French archives.

Our project has benefited greatly from discussions with colleagues and from their help on particular points: we thank Neil Boister, Nick Cheesman, Georgina Fitzpatrick, Wolfgang Form, Higurashi Yoshinobu, Andreas Hilger, Sarah Kovner, Barak Kushner, Mike Lan, Kerstin von Lingen, Suzannah Linton, Matsuda Kōichirō, Takeshi Moriyama, Narrelle Morris, Nagai Hitoshi, Sakamoto Kazuto, Franziska Seraphim, Carolyn Strange, Yuma Totani, and David Wells. We also acknowledge the helpful comments of the three anonymous reviewers of this manuscript. We thank our copy editor, Margaret B. Yamashita, for her close and helpful reading of the final text.

NOTE ON NAMES, SPELLING, AND TERMINOLOGY

In general we follow the Japanese convention for Japanese personal names, placing the surname before the given name. In some Western-language documents, including trial records, the form of names is not reliable. We therefore have preserved the spelling and order of personal names as they are used in the documents and have not attempted to insert macrons, except in the text when we discuss prominent people whose names appear in reference works. Thus we refer to Tōjō Hideki rather than Hideki Tojo.

As a general rule, we have referred to places in the terms and with the spellings that were current at the time. Thus we refer to Batavia, which was under effective Dutch control at the time, rather than to Jakarta, as the city was named by the Indonesian Republic, and to Tjipinang, rather than Cipinang. For Chinese place-names, however, we have used pinyin spelling conventions.

ABBREVIATIONS

ACICR	Archives du Comité international de la Croix-Rouge, Geneva
AD	Centre des Archives diplomatiques de la Courneuve
ADM	Admiralty (UK)
ALFSEA	Allied Land Forces, South East Asia
Alg. Sec.	Algemene Secretarie (Netherlands)
AM	Filipinas Heritage Library (Ayala Museum), Manila
AMSSO	Air Ministry Special Signals Office
AN	Archives nationales, Paris
ANM	Arkib Negara Malaysia
ANOM	Archives nationales d'outre-mer, Aix-en-Provence
ANZ	Archives New Zealand
ARNAS	Arsip Nasional, Jakarta
BAS	British Army Staff
BE	British Embassy
BuZa	Buitenlandse Zaken (Netherlands)
CAB	Cabinet (UK)
CINC, C in C	Commander in Chief
CO	Colonial Office (UK)
COMGENCHINA	Commanding General, US Forces, China Theater

CPB	Clemency and Parole Board for War Criminals (US)
CRO	Commonwealth Relations Office (UK)
DAG	Deputy Adjutant General
DO	Dominions Office (UK)
EA	External Affairs (Australia)
FARELF	Far Eastern Land Forces
FEC	Far Eastern Commission
FEPSC	Far Eastern and Pacific Sub-Commission
FO	Foreign Office (UK)
GDR	German Democratic Republic
GHQ	General Head Quarters
GSK	Diplomatic Archives (Gaikō shiryōkan), Tokyo
HK	Hong Kong
HMSO	His (Her) Majesty's Stationery Office
HQ	Headquarters
ICWC	International Research and Documentation Centre for War Crimes Trials (Forschungs- und Dokumentationszentrum für Kriegsverbrecherprozesse)
IMTFE	International Military Tribunal for the Far East
IOR	India Office Library and Records
JAG	Judge Advocate General
JSM	Joint Staff Mission
JSP	Japanese Surrendered Personnel
LCO	Lord Chancellor's Office
LM	Lopez Museum and Library, Manila
MEPO	Metropolitan Police (UK)
NA (NL)	Nationaal Archief, Netherlands
NA (UK)	National Archives, United Kingdom
NAA	National Archives of Australia
NAJ	National Archives of Japan
NAM	National Archives of Myanmar
NARA	National Archives and Records Administration, United States
NCO	noncommissioned officer
NEI	Netherlands East Indies
NMT	Nuremberg Military Tribunals

POW	prisoner(s) of war
PRC	People's Republic of China
PRO (HK)	Public Record Office, Hong Kong
QPP	Quirino Presidential Papers
RBNO	Regeringsbureau tot Nasporing van Oorlogsmisdrijven
ROC	Republic of China
SACSEA	Supreme Allied Commander, South East Asia
SCAO	Senior Civil Affairs Officer
SCAP	Supreme Commander for the Allied Powers
SEAC	South East Asia Command
SJS	Sensō jukeisha sewakai (Japan)
TS	Treasury Solicitors (UK)
UK	United Kingdom
UNWCC	United Nations War Crimes Commission
US	United States
WO	War Office (UK)

JAPANESE WAR CRIMINALS

INTRODUCTION

n July 1945 the leaders of the United States and Britain, freshly victorious in the war against Nazi Germany, along with the president of
China, issued a proclamation at Potsdam, outside Berlin, insisting on
unconditional surrender by Japan and foreshadowing "stern justice" for
war criminals in the Asia-Pacific theater. Already the Allied powers had
begun to gather information and evidence concerning war crimes committed by Japanese military personnel in the course of hostilities and
during the occupation of conquered territories. In May 1946, the prosecution opened its case against twenty-eight Japanese political and military
leaders at the International Military Tribunal for the Far East (IMTFE)
in Tokyo. The defendants were charged with planning and carrying out
aggressive war and with being responsible for atrocities committed during the hostilities. A much larger number of defendants—about 5,700—
appeared before courts in fifty or so venues in the Asia-Pacific region,
charged with what were then called "conventional war crimes," especially
acts of brutality against and neglect of prisoners of war (POWs) and civilians in occupied regions. Whereas the Japanese leaders were tried in a single, international courtroom, the other suspects faced separate national
courts set up by seven governments in a loosely coordinated system con-
sisting of six wartime allies—Australia, China, France, the Netherlands,
the United Kingdom, and the United States—together with the newly
independent Philippines. The last of these trials was concluded in 1951.

The majority of the defendants—about 4,000—were found guilty. Some were condemned to death and executed, but most were sentenced to prison terms. The Soviet Union and the People's Republic of China also prosecuted Japanese military personnel whom they designated as war criminals, though these trials took place outside the system created by the other wartime Allies.

The crimes for which Japanese military personnel were prosecuted had been committed in the course of Japan's invasion and occupation of parts of China, Southeast Asia, and numerous islands in the Pacific. Japan and China had been intermittently engaged in military conflict since 1928, with full-scale war breaking out in 1937. Japanese troops seized key areas of eastern China, and a brutal conflict continued for the next eight years. In 1940, Japanese forces moved into northern Indochina in an uneasy partnership with the French colonial authorities, who were affiliated with the Vichy French allies of Nazi Germany. The United States responded with an embargo on aviation fuel and scrap metal. Japan then occupied southern Indochina, prompting the United States to freeze Japanese assets in America, effectively preventing all shipments to Japan, including oil. These actions placed great pressure on the Japanese leadership. Then in December 1941, Japanese forces suddenly launched a military assault on parts of Southeast Asia, in concert with an attack on the U.S. Navy at Pearl Harbor in Hawai'i. During the next six months, Japanese forces overran British, Dutch, American, and Portuguese colonies in Southeast Asia. In the process, they humiliated both the colonial armies and the Australian and Indian forces that had been sent at the last minute to face the Japanese advance, and the Japanese forces took tens of thousands of POWs. Most Western civilians living in the region were interned. Japanese troops also pushed well into the Pacific. By mid-1942, Japan controlled an empire that stretched from the India–Burma border in the west to the Aleutian and the Gilbert Islands in the east. At that point, however, the tide of war began to turn against Japan. The United States recovered its naval ascendancy in the Pacific, defeating the Japanese forces at Midway Island in June 1942 and at Guadalcanal after bitter fighting between August 1942 and February 1943. Thereafter, the Allied forces gradually recovered territory occupied by the Japanese military, especially in the Pacific. The U.S. Navy severely disrupted Japanese lines of supply and communication at sea, and from late 1944, American aircraft systematically bombed Japanese cities. By early August 1945, Japanese forces had lost control of virtually all the Pacific islands, the Philippines, and Burma, but they still occupied the rest of Southeast Asia and large parts of China. In that month, United States aircraft dropped atomic bombs on Hiroshima and Nagasaki, and the Soviet Union declared war on Japan and attacked Japanese forces in Manchuria and Korea. Japan surrendered on August 15, 1945.

Japanese troops had committed crimes against both POWs and civilians, including massacres, individual murders, torture and beatings, cannibalism, forced marches, neglect of the detainees' health and welfare, rape, theft, and pillage. No adequate explanation of these crimes has yet been offered. The scale on which they took place, however, was strongly influenced by the circumstances of the Japanese imperial venture. Japan's empire had expanded rapidly, with little practical planning for the administration of the occupied regions or for dealing with the large numbers of POWs, with the even larger numbers of European and Chinese civilians resident in Southeast Asia, or with local populations in general. As the war went on, moreover, Japanese forces faced local insurgencies in many parts of Southeast Asia, which they attempted to suppress. In addition, Japan's war plans required the construction of major infrastructure, including railways and airfields, in remote and inhospitable places where the labor supply was inadequate, disease was rife, and food and medicines were in short supply.

The Japanese military personnel who were given prison terms for war crimes received sentences ranging from one day to life. Those with short sentences were released at the end of their term and, if held outside Japan, joined the massive repatriation of Japanese military personnel and civilians from Asia and the Pacific region that lasted into the 1950s. The prosecuting authorities had at first expected that the remaining prisoners would serve out their terms in full, mostly in or near the places where they had been convicted. In fact, by the end of August 1953, all surviving prisoners except those prosecuted by the Soviet Union and those held by the People's Republic of China for future trial had been transferred to Sugamo Prison in Tokyo. The prosecuting governments, however, retained control over their sentences. Over the next five years, all those tried under the system of national courts created by the former Allies were released, along with the surviving war criminals convicted at the IMTFE. All but a few of the prisoners convicted by the People's Republic of China in 1956 were released as well, along with thousands of former Japanese soldiers deemed to be war criminals by the Soviet government. With the exception of a handful who remained incarcerated in China until 1964, the last war criminals left Sugamo in May 1958 and were released unconditionally in December 1958.

———— ❧ ————

This book traces the processes by which Japanese war crimes were identified, investigated, prosecuted, and punished. It examines the decisions regarding war criminals that were negotiated between Japan and the prosecuting powers after the trials ended. The book also considers the part played by Japanese social and political forces in bringing about the repatriation and release of war criminals. All these processes were driven from beginning to end by concerns about justice, but justice in relation to war criminals was never conceived in absolute, static, or straightforward terms. Rather, at their core, perceptions of justice were a tangle of often conflicting moral, legal, and political considerations.

The prosecuting powers wanted to achieve what we would now call "substantive justice" for war crimes committed by Japanese military personnel. Substantive justice differs from procedural justice in that it focuses on outcomes and takes a pragmatic approach to procedural matters. It is considered to have been achieved if the right crime has been investigated, the right person prosecuted, the right verdict reached, and the right sentence handed down. It also requires that sentences be properly carried out or justly mitigated. In substantive justice, law and legal proceedings are tools for achieving justice, not an end in themselves. Emphasizing substantive justice implies that procedure should not be allowed to get in the way of pronouncing the guilt of those who truly are guilty. By contrast, proponents of procedural justice argue that guilt can be determined most reliably by following the correct procedure. The presumption of innocence and restrictions on what kind of evidence can be presented are characteristic concerns in procedural justice.[1]

There was and is no consensus on what would have constituted substantive justice for Japanese war crimes. The fact that Japanese military personnel committed many acts of violence against POWs and internees is indisputable. There is, however, a wide range of opinion on exactly which actions went far enough beyond acceptable wartime behavior to warrant prosecution. A difficult problem hovered over the questions of whether individual Japanese actions were criminal and, if so, how seriously they should be regarded; that is, the issue of whether acts of military violence by the Allied forces, in the Second War or in earlier conflicts, might also be considered criminal. If Allied actions were potentially criminal, how could substantive justice be served by prosecuting only Japanese defendants?

Complex questions of legal culpability also arose. Some judgments in the war crimes trials identified only a few excesses by particular individuals, while others inculpated the whole of the Japanese armed forces, and some politicians, in serious criminal activity. Japanese military violence had been committed mostly by individuals embedded in the intricate hierarchy of the Japanese armed forces. Did culpability lie with the ordinary soldiers who had beaten, killed, or starved captured enemies, or with the noncommissioned officers and junior officers who had issued the commands that directly led to the atrocities? Did it lie with the senior officers who had placed their men in circumstances and under general orders that made atrocities likely, or with the military commanders and political leaders who had managed the war? Did it lie with the Japanese emperor as the head of state and commander in chief of the armed forces? Did it lie with Japan and the Japanese people as a whole? Or did it implicate a combination of some or all of these levels of authority? It was far from clear, furthermore, just how courtroom practice should be calibrated to achieve substantive justice. Lack of time, shortage of resources, and difficulties with evidence made it impossible to replicate faithfully the standard procedures that were intended to ensure fairness in peacetime criminal courts. The expedited procedures made necessary by postwar circumstances brought significant risk of both wrongful conviction and mistaken acquittal.

These uncertainties over substantive and procedural issues meant that the Allied legal reckoning with Japanese war crimes was more than usually open to influence from nonlegal factors, including political considerations. It would be wrong, however, to say that politics trumped justice in Allied dealings with Japanese war criminals. Political calculation was seldom straightforward, and political considerations concerning war criminals often conflicted with one another. By the mid-1950s, for example, international politics suggested that the Western powers should free all the remaining prisoners who had been convicted of war crimes. The governments of the victorious powers, however, also feared that releasing war criminals would produce its own political repercussions, in the form of backlash from metropolitan and colonial publics who, they believed, still required revenge for wartime atrocities. Even though all these were political considerations, they grew directly out of conflicting ideas of substantive justice: that is, the different political stances arose from different views of how the correct outcomes were to be achieved. Politics and justice, therefore, were not separate and incompatible but were highly interdependent at every stage of the war crimes trial process. Casting the two as opposing forces oversimplifies and thereby misrepresents Allied thinking on war crimes at the time and also warps our contemporary understanding of the legacy of the trials.

Nonetheless, it was clear from the beginning that the prosecutions of Japanese defendants for war crimes, as well as subsequent events, were not driven solely and directly by considerations of justice. Politics played a conspicuous part. Realization of this fact provided scope for cynicism among contemporary and later observers and also led to sustained criticism of the trial program and the unraveling of its intended results. Much of the negative comment on the trials focused on procedural matters: whether evidence was properly marshaled and presented, whether the defense counsel was competent, and whether the judges were biased. These issues—summed up in the question of whether or not the trials were "fair"—are important in themselves. Concern over procedural justice in the war crimes trials, however, was often a stalking horse for concerns about substantive justice. It is much less likely that doubts about procedure would have been raised if observers had been satisfied with the outcomes of the prosecutions, that is, if they believed substantive justice had been achieved. Complaints about procedure reflected deeper misgivings about the legitimacy of the entire project of prosecuting and detaining suspected Japanese war criminals. Those fundamental doubts, however, were often poorly articulated.

Some of the questions about where responsibility for war crimes lay were reflected in the labels given to the different crimes prosecuted in the trials. The charter of the IMTFE, which was issued in January 1946 and set the framework for the Tokyo trials, distinguished among three categories of offense—crimes against peace, war crimes, and crimes against humanity—that had first been set down at the Conference on Military Trials in London in June 1945. That conference, convened mainly to plan for the Nuremberg trials of Nazi war criminals, differentiated these three categories using the letters A, B, and C.[2] Despite having little direct relevance to the Tokyo trial process, the three letters soon took on a life of their own because they were increasingly used to denote "classes" of accused war criminal. The defendants arraigned before the Tokyo tribunal were routinely referred to as "Class A" suspects and as "major war criminals." Those tried in courts set up under the seven national jurisdictions that operated loosely as a group came to be called "Class B/C" suspects and were referred to as "minor war criminals." Trials run by the Soviet Union and the People's Republic of China took place outside this framework, and the two governments divulged little or no information about them until the verdicts had been reached. The use of the labels A, B, and C in the other trials led to three enduring misconceptions.

The first was that the Tokyo defendants were charged only with "Class A" crimes (crimes against peace). In fact, as we shall see, the IMTFE indictments and verdicts included conventional war crimes.[3] The second misconception was that the Allies regarded conventional war crimes as "minor" in comparison with the crimes of Japan's leaders. The term "major" initially referred only to the political standing of the defendants in the Tokyo trial; as cabinet members and leading military figures, they had been among the most prominent government figures of their day. Very quickly, however, the adjective "major" was seen to encompass the crimes as well as the accused. A perception arose in Japan and elsewhere that the IMTFE defendants had been "major" in their iniquity and that the defendants in other trials warranted lesser condemnation, even though the individual actions that came to light in the smaller courts were often more awful than the remote culpability of the accused in Tokyo.[4] A third misunderstanding arose in the very early days of the Allied Occupation of Japan (1945–1952), before policy was widely understood and then entered popular usage among both American and Japanese observers. U.S. Occupation authorities communicated to the Japanese authorities the explanation that "B" would be applied to military officers who had formal responsibility for atrocities and that "C" would refer to soldiers who had actually carried out the criminal acts. This interpretation persisted in Japan and achieved a life of its own— perhaps, comments Higurashi Yoshinobu, because it fitted with Japanese sensitivity to hierarchy—although it never corresponded to the formal U.S. definition of Class B and C crimes and was not used by the American authorities at an official level.[5]

Even after the courts delivered their verdicts, governments and groups in civil society continued wrestling with problems of moral responsibility and equity, with issues of procedural fairness and legal integrity, and with questions concerning the social and political consequences of continued incarceration. Over more than a decade, the relative salience of the different elements in the conception of justice relating to war crimes and war criminals changed. On the whole, the preoccupation of officials, politicians, and others shifted away from retribution and from preventing Japanese war criminals from reoffending. They began to concentrate instead on restoring offenders to mainstream society and on collective restitution through a strong Japanese contribution to the tasks of national and international reconstruction. They also displayed greater recognition of the trying circumstances in which individuals had originally committed war crimes.

The prosecution of Japanese war criminals raised complex issues of justice relating to the ethics of warfare, the locus of guilt, procedural fairness, and comprehensiveness. Incarceration, too, challenged the Allied authorities with legal puzzles and ethical conundrums. Could the sentences survive the expiration of the mandates of the military courts that had handed down convictions? Who should bear the ongoing cost of imprisonment? And in a question whose salience increased as time passed, just what purpose was served by continuing to detain convicted war criminals as the conflict itself receded steadily into the past? The justice issues that had bedeviled the decision to prosecute also forced the Allies to contemplate the possibility of releasing the convicted men early. The outcome was a complex negotiation over which elements of the idea of justice should be given primacy.

For several governments, domestic considerations played a strong role in determining policies toward war criminals, not only before and during the trials, but also after the prosecutions had ended. In countries that had directly experienced Japanese occupation, such as Malaya and the Philippines, large sections of the population had bitter memories of Japan's wartime actions and a corresponding desire to punish war criminals. Resentment was also deep in countries that had not been occupied by Japan but whose soldiers or civilians had been imprisoned or interned in large numbers, especially Australia and the Netherlands. Electorates, the press, and grassroots organizations, including veterans' associations, at times vociferously demanded a hard line against Japanese war criminals. It was not always possible for governments to judge whether these opinions were limited to a vocal minority, but they could not risk ignoring articulate and potentially powerful views. In Japan, public opinion was

also a major influence shaping policy on war criminals. Reforms introduced during the Allied Occupation greatly expanded democratic rights
and the suffrage. Post-Occupation Japanese governments therefore were
responsive to public opinion to an unprecedented extent. From the early
1950s, popular demands for the repatriation and release of war criminals put significant pressure on the Japanese authorities to negotiate these
issues with the foreign governments that retained control of the prisoners
and their sentences.

Foreign governments could not long ignore Japanese pressure. From
1947 onward, most U.S. leaders were convinced that they should cultivate
Japan as a Cold War ally rather than continuing to punish it as a wartime enemy. The growing likelihood of a Communist victory in China and
then the outbreak of the Korean War in June 1950 made this calculation
even more persuasive. Furthermore, Japan was becoming an important
industrial and trading power, quickly recovering much of its prewar economic strength in Asia. The U.S. government was therefore more willing
to take account of and respond to Japanese concerns. Partly under American influence and partly out of consideration of their own interests, the
United States' allies gradually adopted the same approach.

In addressing issues relating to continued detention, Allied planners
and prosecutors inevitably traded some definitions of justice for others.
Individual accountability for criminal acts was traded for the collective
rehabilitation of the Japanese people through participation in the community of democratic nations. Desire for revenge was traded for willingness to allow rehabilitation. Preoccupation with the past was traded for
hopes for the future. Throughout the years in which Japanese war criminals were held in custody, the tension among these different conceptions
of justice prompted passionate and idealistic argument over what to do
with the prisoners. Deliberations about justice were also enmeshed with
a wide-ranging debate over practical politics. Public pressures in different countries, economic relations between Japan and other parts of the
world, and Japan's strategic place as a Cold War ally of the Western powers all generated pragmatic reasons either to keep prisoners in jail or to
release them. For and against every policy option—continued incarceration overseas, transfer to Japan, or various forms of release—there was a
complex set of idealistic and practical arguments.

The process of deciding what to do with war criminals was not always
fair to individual prisoners, who became commodities in global struggles

over the future strategic and economic place of Japan and over reckoning with the past in general. In the postwar world, war criminals stood for Japan as an adversary of the Western powers in Asia and the Pacific region. They also stood for human evil in a broad sense. Allied governments traded war criminals—units of guilt as it were—to achieve effective legal outcomes that would help exorcise both these threats. They also traded war criminals to allay domestic anxieties and to secure political and economic advantage.

Existing scholarship on the trials of Japanese military personnel suspected of war crimes has focused above all on two issues: whether the trials dealt appropriately with Japanese war guilt and whether they were procedurally fair. The answers to both questions have ranged from resoundingly negative to resoundingly affirmative, with many carefully qualified judgments spread across the middle ground.[6] In this volume, we have not sought to participate directly in these debates or to adjudicate among the answers given so far. Our view is that Japanese war guilt is real and deep. There is no doubt that Japanese military personnel committed terrible crimes, and the impulse to hold them accountable for those crimes was both justified and correct, in the moral, political, and legal senses. Problems of historical context and of comparison, however, make a straightforward verdict on the adequacy and the fairness of the trials impossible, no matter how much additional attention is paid to individual trials. Japanese war crimes were committed in complex wartime circumstances that limited and shaped the options of military personnel, whether commanders, ordinary soldiers, or prison camp guards. Japan's accusers, moreover, also committed war crimes and crimes against humanity, for which they were not held accountable.

In this book we have chosen an approach of historical analysis in which we accept the indisputable reality of Japanese wartime atrocities but take the collective guilt of the Japanese people and of any individual as a perception rather than a given. The Allied belief in Japanese war guilt prompted an unprecedented and extraordinarily ambitious Allied attempt to achieve justice. This effort had its immediate roots in the relatively uncomplicated wartime desire of the Allies for a postwar reckoning with Nazi Germany and with Japan. Almost immediately, however, it encountered the challenges inherent in reconciling competing, often contradictory, aspects of the idea of justice. At every point in the justice process that stretched from 1945 to 1958, Allied planners faced taxing moral and legal dilemmas. John Dower, the eminent historian of mid-twentieth-century Japan, utterly misunderstands the issues at stake when he writes of the release of uncharged "Class A" suspects in December 1948: "Ordinary people unversed in the subtleties of international law could be excused for failing to comprehend exactly where justice left off and political whimsy began."[7] In fact, the contrast was never between justice and politics. Rather, every competing notion of justice, harsh or mild, was embedded in domestic and international politics, and every political stance on the war criminals, moderate or extreme, drew power from its enmeshment with concepts of justice.

The problem of achieving justice for Japanese war crimes arose well before the days and weeks during which the different parties confronted each other in the courtroom, and it continued long after sentencing. From the very start of the Pacific War in 1941, the Western Allies grappled with the problem of how to respond to reports of Japanese atrocities. This problem remained just as acute after verdicts had been brought down and sentences pronounced. It persisted until the last Japanese war criminal was released in 1958, and it lingers today.

1

DEFINING WAR CRIMES
AND CREATING COURTS

W hen Japan attacked British Malaya, the Philippines, and Pearl Harbor on December 7/8, 1941, the U.S. president, Franklin D. Roosevelt, famously declared that the date of the attack would "live in infamy." Nonetheless, even though knowledge of Japanese brutality in China was widespread when Japanese forces rapidly occupied large tracts of Southeast Asia and the Pacific, the Allied powers seem to have expected Japan's occupation of the region to be marked at least by the reasonable treatment of Westerners. British officers who knew the Japanese army well in the 1920s and 1930s did not anticipate that Japanese soldiers would show anything other than normal courtesy toward Western prisoners in the Pacific.[1] On December 18, 1941, ten days after the first of the sudden Japanese attacks, the U.S. Secretary of State, Cordell Hull, sent a memo through the neutral Swiss to the Japanese Foreign Ministry expressing his hope that Japan would abide by the provisions of the Third Geneva Convention of 1929 on the treatment of prisoners of war, even though it had not ratified that convention, and asking for a statement of Japanese intentions.[2] This overture, however, seems to have been precautionary rather than based on an apprehension of the scale of atrocities that would be committed in the Asian and Pacific theater over the next three years. The Japanese government responded that it would observe the convention *mutatis mutandis*.[3] This expression, meaning "changing what has to be changed," implied that Japan would follow the spirit of the convention but that the exigencies of war and resulting variation in what food and clothing could be provided to prisoners might not allow it to follow the convention to the letter.[4]

By the time Japanese forces attacked Southeast Asia and Pearl Harbor, the Allies had already begun to consider pursuing war criminals in response to German atrocities in Europe. On October 25, just weeks before the Japanese launched their opening attack on Southeast Asia and the Pacific, British prime minister Winston Churchill issued a statement declaring that "retribution must henceforward take its place among the major purposes of the war [in Europe]."[5] On January 13, 1942, the representatives of nine European governments-in-exile met in London to issue an Inter-Allied Declaration (sometimes known as the St. James Declaration), which identified as a principal aim of the war "the punishment, through the channel of organised justice, of those guilty of or responsible for these crimes, whether they have ordered them, perpetrated them or participated in them." Representatives of the Chinese Republic quickly announced that China would "apply the same principles to the Japanese occupying authorities in China when the time comes."[6]

By the end of 1945, the Allied powers firmly intended to bring accused Japanese war criminals to justice in a complex array of courts and had already begun to do so. The trials rested on half a century's work by legal specialists and politicians in defining what was—and was not—a war crime. The pace of this work had accelerated greatly in the final years before the end of the Second World War, conditioned by Allied anticipation of the kinds of problems that would arise in prosecuting Japanese and German war crimes suspects. Important legal innovations had been established to facilitate difficult prosecutions, and care had been taken to protect Allied interests. Although Allied planners were undoubtedly sincere in seeking justice through the war crimes trials, such planning eventually prepared the way for a highly politicized series of court proceedings.

THE CRIMES

As the tide of war turned against Japan in the latter part of 1942, the Western Allies fighting in the Asia-Pacific theater began to consider how to deal with Japanese war crimes. The extremity of Japanese brutality in China was well known, especially through reports on the Nanjing massacre of 1937–1938.[7] Soon, however, information in the press and in intelligence reports based on intercepted Japanese documents began to provide evidence of brutality by Japanese forces elsewhere that went far beyond normal expectations of wartime conduct.[8] Thereafter, a stream of accounts confirmed a disturbing pattern of Japanese cruelty toward POWs and civilians—Western, Chinese, and local—in Asia and the Pacific. As time passed, specific episodes took on a special, exemplary character in the Western imagination. Shortly before the British surrender in Singapore in February 1942, for instance, Japanese troops entered the Alexandra Barracks Hospital, where they bayoneted dozens of patients and medical staff. A few days later, other Japanese troops herded hundreds of Chinese into the water off Singapore and shot them at close range in what became known as the *sook ching* massacre.[9] Twenty-one captured Australian nurses who had survived a shipwreck while fleeing from Singapore were murdered on the shore of Bangka, off Sumatra, in February 1942.[10] Two months later, Japanese forces in the Philippines finally defeated the American and Philippine forces that had earlier retreated to the Bataan Peninsula west of Manila. The captured servicemen, numbering around 78,000, of whom 85 percent were Filipino, were then marched under armed guard to a neighboring province. Weakened by the privations of the war, hurried along by their captors, and with insufficient food, rest, or medical care, the prisoners died in large numbers. Japanese guards beat and killed stragglers. By the end of the "Bataan death march," 5,000 to 10,000 Filipinos and 650 Americans were dead.[11] Another forced march from Sandakan in North Borneo in early 1945 killed more than a thousand Australian prisoners.[12] Throughout Asia, Allied POWs and internees reported crowded, unhealthy, humiliating conditions in the camps.[13]

Thousands of Allied POWs and Asian laborers working on the Thailand–Burma Railway died from ill treatment and overwork in the difficult environment.[14] In many parts of the empire, the Japanese military police, the Kenpeitai, tortured local people and Westerners who were suspected, often on flimsy grounds, of carrying out espionage or sabotage on behalf of the Allies. In Manchuria, Japan, and elsewhere, Japanese doctors conducted gruesome medical experiments on living human subjects, including vivisection, infection with diseases, injection with chemicals, and exposure to extreme conditions.[15] In February 1945, Japanese troops indiscriminately shot thousands of civilians and destroyed countless buildings during their unsuccessful defense of Manila.[16] In July 1945, Japanese troops and members of the Kenpeitai massacred around six hundred people in the village of Kalagon near Moulmein in Burma for failing to provide information on the movement of British troops in the area.[17] The postwar release and repatriation of Allied POWs and internees generated more accounts of atrocities. Gratuitous cruelty, senseless killing, vindictive retaliation, spiteful torture, and brutal disregard for human welfare appeared to be the hallmark of Japanese treatment of the peoples under their control.[18]

The atrocities carried out by Japanese forces have often been attributed to aspects of a presumed Japanese national character that allegedly inclined Japanese soldiers toward brutality or a casual disregard of human life.[19] In fact, rather than displaying generalized cruelty, Japanese wartime atrocities fell largely into three distinct categories: murder of inconvenient captives, brutal and neglectful treatment of inmates of prison and internment camps and of forced laborers and military prostitutes, and punitive investigation and suppression of local resistance movements and suspected spy rings. Although Japanese soldiers were tried for other crimes, including cannibalism, inhumane medical experiments, and the judicial murder of downed Allied flyers, these crimes were less common. Ethnic cleansing and genocide in the precise sense also were absent: the Japanese authorities did not attempt to eradicate any specific category of person or to empty land systematically of its original inhabitants for settlement by others. There was no Asian equivalent of the extermination campaigns launched by Nazi Germany against Jews, Sinti, Roma, and others;[20] this absence is especially notable in view of the comprehensive detention of Westerners, which would have made an extermination campaign feasible.

More detailed research has begun to cast doubt indirectly on the scale and extent of Japanese atrocities. Even though the most extreme cases were, by definition, not typical of Japanese action in general, such cases were especially prominent in Western reports. As John Dower demonstrated, wartime representations of Japanese atrocities in the U.S. media were designed to exacerbate the image of Japanese barbarity.[21] In addition, statistics were sometimes presented in a way that distorted the record of Japanese behavior. For example, the verdict of the International Military Tribunal for the Far East (IMTFE) stated that 35,756 Western prisoners of war had died, out of 132,134 in Japanese captivity.[22] Gavan Daws showed, however, that fully one-third of these deaths were a consequence of "friendly fire" at sea. Moreover, an even higher proportion died in the special, terrible circumstances of the Thailand–Burma Railway, where starvation, disease, and overwork were the dreadful result of mismanagement rather than of systematic torture.[23] These facts suggest that brutal Japanese behavior was less widespread than the IMTFE judgment implied. Some of the outrage was underpinned by cultural differences. Westerners commonly regarded execution by beheading as barbarous—execution "by normal shooting" was held to be better—whereas some Japanese portrayed beheading as a relatively honorable form of death (figure 1.1).[24] The indignation of Westerners living in Asia, moreover,

FIGURE 1.1 Execution of an Australian prisoner of war. This image was widely reproduced as evidence of Japanese brutality.

Sergeant Leonard Siffleet was a member of an Australian special unit operating behind Japanese lines in New Guinea. He was captured near Aitape and was summarily executed on October 24, 1943, by Yasuno Chikao on the order of Vice Admiral Kamada Michiaki. The photograph was found on the body of a dead Japanese soldier and was published in *Life* magazine on May 14, 1945. Kamada was subsequently tried by a Dutch court for war crimes in Flores and Borneo and was executed in October 1947. Available at http://www.awm.gov.au/collection/101099/ (accessed July 13, 2014).

arose partly from the loss of privilege that they experienced under Japanese occupation. Around 150,000 European residents in the Netherlands Indies were interned. Many suffered great hardship, and their resentment was increased by the experience of being reduced to "native" standards of living.[25] Undeniably, however, Japanese forces committed atrocities on a scale that had not been seen in Southeast Asia since the colonial wars of the late nineteenth and early twentieth centuries or in China since the mid-nineteenth-century Taiping Rebellion. In any case, the combination of truth and exaggeration in news reporting created a powerful appetite in Western and Asian publics for a reckoning.

ANTICIPATING PROSECUTION

As the war proceeded, Allied leaders increasingly foreshadowed legal action against those Japanese personnel considered responsible for war crimes. In February 1944, reacting to newly released information on the Bataan death march, Secretary of State Cordell Hull formally drew the Japanese government's attention to evidence of appalling treatment of American POWs, presenting his message unambiguously as a warning that these acts contravened international law.[26] On July 26, 1945, the leaders of the United States, Britain, and Republican China laid down further grounds for war crimes trials in a "proclamation defining terms for Japanese surrender" issued from Potsdam, near Berlin. The proclamation, which insisted on Japan's unconditional surrender, also noted: "We do not intend that the Japanese shall be enslaved as a race or destroyed as a nation, but stern justice shall be meted out to all war criminals, including those who have visited cruelties upon our prisoners."[27] Although the proclamation did not clarify who would dispense such justice, acceptance of this declaration by Japan in its instrument of surrender on September 2, 1945, was thereafter taken by the Allies and the Japanese government to mean that Japan accepted the legitimacy of war crimes trials.

Devising the "channel of organised justice" envisaged in the 1942 St. James Declaration as a means of bringing war criminals to account was a formidable challenge. Although rules for the conduct of war had a long pedigree, only twice before had a specific attempt been made to prosecute politicians and soldiers who had violated those rules. In 1919–1920, partly under pressure from the Allies, Ottoman military courts in Istanbul had prosecuted some two hundred people on charges related to the genocide of Armenians and Greeks during the First World War. Three junior officials were sentenced to death and subsequently executed, while more senior leaders were sentenced to death in absentia, having been allowed by the Ottoman authorities to flee the country. These latter sentences were never carried out. When the Ottoman authorities abandoned prosecution of other cases, the Allies turned to the idea of an international tribunal, detaining 145 generals, politicians, and intellectuals in Malta while they gathered evidence for a prosecution. In the end, all were released without trial and later received amnesty under an annex to the 1923 Treaty of Lausanne.[28] The victorious Allies had also proposed international trials for suspected German war criminals after the end of the First World War but eventually allowed the cases to be heard in German domestic courts. In 1921, the German Supreme Court in Leipzig tried seventeen men on charges related to atrocities in the European theater. Seven were acquitted, and the remainder were sentenced to prison terms ranging from a few months to four years.[29] The acquittals and apparently lenient sentences in Leipzig were strongly influenced by a German perception that the trials constituted what would later be called "victors' justice," that is, a vindictive attempt to punish an enemy nation rather than an impartial application of the laws of war.[30] The perception that Germany had been unilaterally blamed for the war, along with the imposition of heavy reparations and other burdens, was widely considered in the 1940s to have stimulated the resurgence of right-wing German nationalism and thus to have contributed to the outbreak of the Second World War.[31] With the memory of Leipzig vivid in their minds, the Allied governments of the 1940s in the Asia-Pacific theater faced the challenge of working out how to slake their populations' thirst for vengeance—which they themselves had fostered—by delivering a more comprehensive arraignment of suspected war criminals while avoiding the risk that such action might encourage a new round of Japanese militarism.[32]

An apparent answer to this conundrum came from Robert H. Jackson, U.S. representative at the International Conference on Military Trials, which began in London on June 26, 1945, six weeks after the German surrender, and which was attended by representatives of Britain, France, the Soviet Union, and the United States. The delegates set down the terms by which an international military tribunal would judge Nazi leaders at Nuremberg. Jackson, who subsequently became the chief prosecutor at the Nuremberg Tribunal, proposed a process that would concentrate the burden of guilt on individual perpetrators:

> What shall we do with [suspected war criminals]? We could, of course, set them at large without a hearing. But it has cost unmeasured thousands of American lives to beat and bind these men. To free them without a trial would mock the dead and make cynics of the living. On the other hand, we could execute or otherwise punish them without a hearing. But undiscriminating executions or punishments without definite findings of guilt, fairly arrived at, would violate pledges repeatedly given, and would not set [sic] easily on the American conscience or be remembered by our children with pride. The only other course is to determine the innocence or guilt of the accused after a hearing as dispassionate as the times and the horrors we deal with will permit, and upon a record that will leave our reasons and motives clear.

Jackson argued that the cruelties of the Nazis and the Japanese military were self-evidently criminal and that "through these trials we should be able to establish that a process of retribution by law awaits those who in the future similarly attack civilization."[33]

In adding the argument of deterrence to the case for war crimes trials, Jackson echoed a practical consideration already expressed by Allied wartime planners. As evidence emerged during the hostilities of Japanese brutality toward Allied POWs, the American, British, and Australian authorities had begun to see the threat of postwar trials as a potential means of deterring Japanese forces from further atrocities. In October 1944, upon landing in the Philippines, the commander of Allied forces in the Southwest Pacific, General Douglas MacArthur, warned Japanese commanders that he would hold them personally responsible for the treatment of POWs and civilians.[34] In June 1945, the United States government warned Japan through Swiss intermediaries that it already possessed evidence of war crimes committed against Allied prisoners and that it "firmly intended to bring to judgment anyone who had any part in these acts."[35] Nonetheless, the U.S. authorities kept secret the work of their war crimes investigation team until the end of the war in order to avoid the risk of reprisals.[36]

THE POLITICAL AIMS OF PROSECUTION

War crimes trials were aimed at three different audiences: the Japanese public, local populations in areas occupied by Japanese forces during the war, and domestic constituencies in the home countries of the prosecuting powers, especially military veterans and their supporters. Addressing each audience required different strategies and suggested different priorities.

In Japan, U.S. policies for the defeated enemy went far beyond consolidating victory and inflicting punishment for wartime aggression. As the dominant player in the Allied Occupation of Japan, which lasted from September 1945 until April 1952, the U.S. government was determined to bring about a far-reaching transformation of Japanese society through a program whose aims came to be characterized as demilitarization and democratization.[37] The pursuit of war criminals had two purposes. First, the trial, conviction, and punishment of specific war criminals would prevent their participation in postwar society. Many Americans and Asians believed that prominent Japanese militarists were waiting for an opportunity to subvert democratic reforms and to resume their old militarist ways.[38] The trials at Tokyo, in particular, would remove some of the men who had led Japan to war and so would alter the balance in Japanese society in favor of peace. Second, the public revelation of Japanese cruelties abroad and the conviction of perpetrators, it was hoped, would further contribute to the rehabilitation of Japan by showing the Japanese people what their armed forces had done, establishing the illegality of such actions, and providing a lesson to Japan about the consequences of militarism.[39]

The local populations in colonial territories in Asia and the Pacific constituted a second audience for the trials. Local populations sometimes spurred and assisted the Allied authorities to take action against war criminals. British investigations in Singapore, in particular, were prompted by a local Chinese community eager to take revenge for the *sook ching* massacres of Chinese people at the start of the occupation.[40] When General Yamashita Tomoyuki, the Japanese commander in Malaya at the time of the massacre, formally surrendered in the Philippines on September 3, 1945, a street banner in Singapore called for him to be tried in Singapore, and the Manila press called for his execution as a war criminal on account of his alleged crimes in the Philippines, specifically for his alleged responsibility for the Rape of Manila.[41] Postwar films and other forms of popular culture fed the perception, already encouraged by wartime propaganda, that Japanese troops had been exceptionally cruel (figure 1.2).[42]

Some scholars have suggested that prosecutors gave priority to cases involving Western victims,[43] and it is true that Westerners were overrepresented in view of their small proportion of the region's total population. An overwhelming majority of cases heard in the U.S. courts in Yokohama and Shanghai related to the mistreatment of American and other Allied POWs. Overall, however, the trial records suggest that around half of all Allied cases involved local victims. The Japanese defendants who were brought before French courts were accused of crimes against local people as well as Europeans and American POWs.[44] American courts in the Philippines, as well as British, Australian, and Dutch courts elsewhere, heard many cases involving local victims. Courts run by the governments of the Philippines and Nationalist China tried only the perpetrators of crimes against their own citizens.[45]

The choice to prosecute crimes against local victims does not indicate a Western intention to use the war crimes trials as a major means of reasserting colonial authority. The Western powers had suffered a serious loss of prestige in Asia as a result of their defeat by Japan. In the chaotic circumstances of postwar Asia, however, restoring civil order, defeating insurgents, and developing plans to retreat from, or at least to reframe, colonialism were far more important to winning the support of local people than any retrospective reckoning with Japanese war criminals. The colonial powers were aware that they would be criticized if they failed to conduct trials, but there was little positive advantage for them in the trial process. In some respects, moreover, prosecuting Japanese military personnel for crimes against local civilians was politically risky, especially if the offenses related to brutal Japanese counterinsurgency measures, because the prosecutions could remind local populations that the colonial powers had sometimes used similar techniques in suppressing nationalist rebellion and dissent.[46] When British and Dutch planners met in Singapore in December 1945, they agreed they should avoid giving the trials what they called a "political dimension."[47] While it is not clear what kind of political dimension they had in mind, their comment indicates that they thought it unwise to expand the significance of the war crimes trials beyond their immediate objectives.

FIGURE 1.2 Sensationalist postwar advertisement for the 1943 U.S. film *Behind the Rising Sun. Manila Times*, January 22, 1946, 8.

Prosecutions were potentially dangerous for another reason, too: they were inextricably connected with the issue of local residents' wartime collaboration with Japanese occupation forces. Japanese forces in Southeast Asia in 1941–1942 had made strong efforts to present themselves as liberators and were successful in recruiting support from local nationalists. Some collaborators had passionately shared Japan's public vision of "Asia for the Asians" or felt an affinity with the corporatist, collectivist ideologies promulgated by occupation authorities; some needed to make a living or relished the new employment and commercial and political opportunities that arose with the removal of Western and other anti-Japanese authorities. Others saw it as their duty to serve their government and people as well as they could in difficult times, or chose collaboration because they realized that the Japanese authorities might suspect them of subversion if they kept their distance. For many, the impulse to work with the occupation authorities had arisen from a complex combination of circumstances: rather than deciding at a key moment to collaborate with Japanese forces, they had been drawn gradually into a partnership from which eventually they could not extricate themselves.[48] Western governments, however, regarded collaborators as despicable betrayers of their own people.[49] The British in Singapore prosecuted those who had been directly engaged with the Kenpeitai.[50] U.S. authorities instructed the postwar Philippines government to establish a "People's Court," which convicted around 150 collaborators.[51] In the U.S. Pacific territories of Guam and Kwajalein, collaboration trials were mixed with war crimes trials, and 17 of the 144 defendants were local people accused of collaboration.[52] The Chinese authorities were just as concerned with collaboration as were their Western counterparts. The venom of both the Guomindang authorities and their Communist Party rivals was directed far more against those who had worked for the collaborationist Wang Jingwei government than against Japanese military personnel.[53]

The war crimes trials' association with collaboration endangered the basic aims of the European colonial powers in Southeast Asia. Already in the prewar period, the imperialist powers had begun to plan for decolonization, drawing away from the tight relationship of colonial dominance that had characterized the first decades of the twentieth century. They now aimed to hand political power to friendly, modern local elites that would accept that their interests were tied to the West's continuing economic presence in Southeast Asia. The underlying strategy was to do a deal with the moderates to isolate the extremists. In this context, the project of prosecuting Japanese military personnel for war crimes was also a veiled indictment of those who had worked for or sympathized with Japanese rule, who might include some of the very people the imperialist powers were now trying to cultivate. In the Netherlands Indies, the first efforts to achieve a rapprochement between progressive colonial authorities and the new Indonesian Republic, proclaimed in 1945, were overturned by the vehemence of Dutch conservative hostility to the republic for its Japanese connections. The Indonesian Republic, they asserted, was "made in Japan," and its leaders had "Japanese souls in Indonesian bodies."[54] In Burma, British authorities deliberately held back on their pursuit of Japanese war criminals because of the risk that the program would entrammel their main political partner, Aung San, who had collaborated with the Japanese authorities until March 1945.[55]

Staging war crimes trials would not restore the damaged and always limited legitimacy of colonial authorities, but a failure to prosecute Japanese war criminals would have been perceived as a dereliction of duty. The prosecutions were in part a response to the argument from local nationalists that the Western powers had forfeited their sovereign rights by failing to defend their colonial subjects against Japanese brutality.[56] Rejecting this argument was particularly important to the French, since their colonial authorities in Indochina had been formally allied with Japan until March 1945,[57] but it was also important to the Dutch, whose loss of authority in the Indies had been humiliating. The trials thus reasserted the capacity and willingness of the Western imperialist powers to champion the interests of their subject peoples.

The third audience for the war crimes trials of Japanese suspects comprised former POWs and internees, their families, and the metropolitan communities in general. These groups often spoke or were expected to speak the language of revenge and had the potential to influence policy through their political representatives.[58] Newspapers in metropolitan centers fed their readers a steady diet of stories with titles such as "Enemy Tortured Dying Americans with Sadist Medical 'Experiments'"; "Japanese Cruelty Described by Nisei: Prisoners Used as 'Guinea Pigs' in Samurai Sword Practice, Former Sergeant Says"; "Jap Captain Charged with Deaths of 2390 Men"; "Japs Tried to Freeze Soldiers to Death"; and "The Grim Record of Japan's Brutal Gestapo."[59] The press reported that members of the public were demanding prompt and abundant executions.[60] "Mercy is not called for," wrote the *Adelaide News* in an editorial; "the Japanese, in any case, wouldn't understand the meaning of the word."[61] When seemingly lenient terms of punishment were given to Japanese military personnel convicted of war crimes in an Australian court in Darwin, the Australian press and public reacted so angrily that the government decided no more trials would be held on the Australian mainland.[62] Veterans' associations expressed astonishment at the sentencing;

one spokesman suggested that in future, courts should be presided over only by men who had directly experienced Japanese brutality.[63] The authorities in all the prosecuting countries remained attuned to the presumed sensitivity of their metropolitan audiences during every stage of the processes of investigating, prosecuting, sentencing, incarcerating, and releasing war criminals.

LEGAL QUESTIONS

Allied plans for the trials of alleged war criminals were based on principles of justice common to all modern judicial systems. Allied reasoning implied that the prosecutions would be comprehensive rather than exemplary, with the further implication that trials would take place on an unprecedented scale. Not dozens or hundreds but thousands, even tens of thousands, of cases would be investigated, and as far as possible, all perpetrators would be tried. Such reasoning also placed an emphasis on correct process. Guilt was not to be taken as self-evident but was to be proved in courts. These laudable legal intentions, however, set up for the Allied powers a complex set of legal and practical problems.

First, although it could be and was argued that the Potsdam Declaration and Japan's acceptance of it provided a sufficient foundation for the trial of alleged war criminals, the legal basis of the declaration itself was far from certain. International law had traditionally recognized a right of belligerency under which soldiers were immune from criminal or civil liability for acts carried out as part of military operations. Accordingly, a British authority on international law, A. Berriedale Keith, expressed the view in 1944 that individuals could not be held accountable for war crimes committed under their governments' orders.[64] The Japanese government, moreover, had not ratified the 1929 Geneva Convention, which gave protection to POWs. As Nagai Hitoshi showed, the Japanese government in fact had very little idea of what it was obliged to accept in terms of war crimes trials and, in the immediate postwar period, put considerable effort into attempting to establish the Allies' intentions.[65]

Just as important, there was no clear international legal agreement that belligerents should not commit atrocities against civilians. It was commonly believed that military necessity gave armies collectively, and soldiers individually, the right to do anything they judged essential to victory.[66] Although the 1899 and 1907 Hague Conventions appeared to restrict the claim of military necessity in relation to harming civilians,[67] legal opinion on the scope of the restrictions was deeply divided.[68] A committee working at the Versailles Conference of 1918–1919 prepared a list of actions against civilians that were to be regarded as war crimes, with thirty-two categories ranging from torture, rape, and the poisoning of wells to deportation and the debasement of currency.[69] This list, however, was not incorporated into the Versailles Treaty or any subsequent international agreement. To prosecute Japanese and German soldiers for brutalities against civilians, therefore, required a leap in legal doctrine, either by accepting that laws against such crimes could legitimately be made retrospective because they represented a kind of natural law that did not require prior formal codification to be valid, or by asserting that the extraordinary brutality of the offenses overrode objections to retrospectivity.[70] For the most part, the Allied powers endorsed both rationales. In ex post facto regulations drafted after the Second World War, they revived the Versailles list of acts of brutality against civilians and declared them—along with one or two additional acts—to be war crimes. This list of crimes, which then guided the postwar Allied prosecutions, was subsequently incorporated into the 1949 Geneva Convention on the protection of civilians in time of war.[71]

The expansion of the definition of war crimes was significant and unequivocal but nonetheless limited. It restricted, but did not overturn, the doctrine of military necessity. War crimes did not encompass, for instance, acts of brutality carried out against enemy soldiers in the course of hostilities. Thus, the incineration of Japanese soldiers in the tunnels of Corregidor in the Philippines by American forces during the battle for the island in 1945[72] could not be included. Nor were Japanese soldiers charged with war crimes if the acts in question had been carried out as a part of military operations during hostilities. Legal specialists were evidently mindful of Allied interests when they defined war crimes: they were wary of encompassing practices that were widely known to have been carried out not only by Japanese forces but by Allied forces as well. Most important was the killing of shipwreck survivors and enemy soldiers attempting to surrender. The strafing of lifeboats and survivors in the water lay on the shadowy boundary of the definition of war crimes. If survivors had the potential to return to combat on the enemy side, they might legally be killed, but if they were *hors de combat* (incapable of performing a military function), then they were protected by international law.[73] On a number of occasions early in the war, Japanese aircraft had strafed the survivors of sunken vessels, and in December 1945 a British admiralty official commented that he expected these events to give rise to "a number of prosecutions."[74] The Allies, however, had done similar things, most notably in the Battle of the Bismarck Sea in March 1943.[75] Newspaper reports in Allied countries openly boasted of a "convoy holocaust" after that battle: "All barges, lifeboats, and rafts still afloat were strafed and sunk and all the occupants killed or drowned."[76] In the war as a whole, Allied troops had been reluctant to take prisoners, and thousands of Japanese soldiers were shot at the point of surrender.[77]

The expansion of the definition of war crimes also stopped short of including what today is called "collateral damage," that is, the incidental killing of civilians in enemy territory in the pursuit of military goals. Neither the massive firebombing of Tokyo in March 1945 nor the dropping of atomic bombs on Hiroshima and Nagasaki in August of that year could be considered war crimes under the immediate postwar Allied definition, because those actions had been carried out as a military operation in which civilians were, at least notionally, not the main target. Rather, the new doctrine effectively defined as war crimes those cruelties committed by soldiers against people whom they had a formal duty to protect, whether conquered peoples or POWs. In the case of the Allied bombings of Japanese cities, the Japanese victims were neither conquered nor imprisoned and thus were not legally entitled to Allied protection. In practice, military necessity was considered a legitimate defense against some but not all of the charges made possible by the new rules.[78] Necessity, however, was constrained by the vague principle of proportionality, in which military advantage must be set against the scale of the harm that would be done.[79] Legal protection for civilians against collateral damage was not inscribed into international law until the 1977 Protocol Additional to the Geneva Conventions of August 12, 1949.[80]

A separate but related set of legal-political considerations arose in connection with the question of how to deal with the Japanese leaders who had launched and directed the war but who had not directly engaged in atrocities. Existing doctrine gave sovereign immunity to national leaders for actions taken according to their judgment of the national interest. It was therefore difficult to identify a formal basis for prosecuting the leaders of either Japan or Germany. According to one school of thought, certain leaders were self-evidently criminal, so no formal, legal basis for their punishment was necessary. In the later stages of the war, both Churchill and Roosevelt seriously considered drawing up a list of a hundred or so leaders who would be declared outlaws and shot summarily when they were captured.[81] Many on the Allied side, however, were disturbed by this approach, seeing it as an unacceptable form of arbitrary violence and fearing it would drive Axis leaders into desperate measures that might worsen the violence of the concluding stages of the war. A solution to the problem was provided by the 1928 Kellogg-Briand Pact, which was retrospectively identified by U.S. State Department officials as a watershed in international law.[82] The pact had been signed and ratified by most of the world's powers, including the United States, the United Kingdom, the Soviet Union, France, Japan, Germany, and Italy. Its ambitious aims were stated in its full title: General Treaty for Renunciation of War as an Instrument of National Policy.[83] Although the pact itself had not hinted at the personal liability of national leaders for violations, in June 1945 the International Conference on Military Trials in London decided that it would provide the legal basis for prosecuting Nazi and Japanese leaders for "crimes against peace."[84] In fact, international lawyers in the late 1920s had been uncertain just how much the Kellogg-Briand Pact in practice bound any state to renounce war, especially when national interest was at stake.[85] There was no attempt, however, to address these subtleties in 1945.

The Allied planners unilaterally decided that Japan's war had been aggressive, whereas their own had not. The Japanese government's actions in attacking Southeast Asia and Hawai'i in December 1941 had been based on an assessment of national interest. The American authorities' 1941 freezing of Japanese assets in the United States, and the consequent cessation of oil exports to Japan, had helped persuade Japanese leaders that they must go to war for their nation's survival.[86] Nonetheless, in prosecuting Japanese leaders after the war, Allied planners took the attacks on Malaya and Pearl Harbor and the ongoing conflict with China as unambiguous cases of aggression, despite the element of self-defense in Japan's military actions, at least from 1941 onward. Any consideration of whether Japan's actions had constituted illegal aggression would have raised serious questions about, for example, whether America's freezing of Japanese assets was itself an act of illegal aggression.

Crimes against humanity were distinguished from war crimes not by the nature of the offense but by the category of victim. In the technical sense, war crimes were defined as crimes committed by belligerents, in the context of war, against persons of nationalities other than their own. Crimes against humanity, by contrast, encompassed actions by perpetrators against persons of any nationality, including their own. The term "crime against humanity" had been used three decades earlier to identify the Ottoman massacres of Armenians and Greeks as a potential basis for international prosecutions. Allied planners subsequently revived it so they could prosecute Nazis for the persecution of Jewish and other Germans, who otherwise would not have been protected by the laws of war.[87]

To commence the work of prosecuting war crimes, the Allies established the United Nations War Crimes Commission (UNWCC) on October 20, 1943.[88] The commission took on three tasks: to refine the legal basis of the planned trials, to advise generally on the legal and political implications of decisions relating to the trials, and to begin the collection of evidence. Initially, the UNWCC's principal focus was Europe, with the Asian branch of the commission, called the Far Eastern and Pacific Sub-Commission (FEPSC), established in the provisional Chinese capital of Chongqing only in November 1944.[89]

The issue of obedience to military orders was crucial to refining the legal basis for trials. The obligation of soldiers to obey the orders of their commanders without question had been a cornerstone of discipline in all military forces. Indeed, immediately before the First World War, both Britain and the United States had amended their military manuals to identify superior orders as a full defense against war crime accusations.[90] The prospect of German and Japanese perpetrators in the Second World War escaping conviction on the basis of superior orders, however, galvanized Allied officials into reversing this provision. Most of the Allied powers altered their military manuals in 1943–1944 to remove the superior orders defense for cases in which the illegality of the ordered action was, or should have been, manifest.[91] Aware of these complexities, the UNWCC carefully examined the legal status of superior orders when war crimes were alleged to have occurred. As a consequence, the Allies produced a clear guide for the planned war crimes tribunals:

Neither the official position, at any time, of an accused, nor the fact that an accused acted pursuant to order of his government or of a superior shall, of itself, be sufficient to free such accused from responsibility for any crime with which he is charged, but such circumstances may be considered in mitigation of punishment if the Tribunal determines that justice so requires.[92]

In Japan, the Imperial Rescript to Soldiers and Sailors of 1882 was unambiguous in stating that soldiers must render total obedience to their superiors.[93] Defendants in the war crimes trials sometimes claimed that the penalty for disobeying orders in the Japanese military was death. The Army Penal Code (Rikugun keihō) of 1908 (revised in 1942), however, stipulated a range of penalties for resisting or refusing to obey an order. If a soldier was disobedient in battle, the penalty was death; otherwise, an offender was liable for imprisonment.[94] For example, according to army regulations, refusal to carry out an illegal execution in a POW camp should not have attracted the death penalty. It is not surprising, however, that soldiers feared being killed for disobeying an important order like a command to execute a prisoner. For decades, military training had aimed "to guarantee absolute obedience to a superior's orders and instill unquestioning compliance as a reflex or habit in the tractable soldier." Imperial symbols were increasingly used to reinforce the point, and soldiers were told that a superior's order was equivalent to an order from the emperor.[95] In practice, moreover, there was much room for interpreting army regulations,[96] and in wartime, there was less scope for supervising military discipline and monitoring penalties.

The mode of imposing discipline in the Japanese army had been very different from that in Western armies. Whereas British courts-martial during the Second World War convicted 210,029 British military personnel of infringements of military discipline, Japanese military courts in China punished only 9,000 Japanese soldiers for infractions of Japanese military law between July 1937 and November 1944.[97] The vast majority of disciplinary actions in the Japanese forces were performed executively by noncommissioned officers. An ordinary soldier would routinely be punished harshly for minor infractions, such as being slow to respond to a command or appearing with a fleck of dirt on his uniform. Punishments commonly included beating, slapping, and being required to stand still, often in the open, for long periods. Such punishments were never officially recorded.[98] The same kinds of punishment were inflicted by Japanese military personnel on POWs and internees during the Second World War.

The former Japanese military governor of Java, General Imamura Hitoshi, gave evidence at a trial on Manus Island in October 1950 that the Japanese military academy had provided solid training in international law until the outbreak of full-scale war in China in 1937, at which point the courses were severely curtailed because of the urgent need to supply soldiers to the front. Imamura claimed that Japanese officers recruited after 1937 would not have had sound knowledge of the laws of war and that expertise on legal matters was probably inadequate at the battalion level and below. According to Imamura's evidence, practices for supervising POWs would depend on orders from the commanding general rather than on a basic knowledge of legal obligations. Imamura added that the Japanese army ministry did not issue any directive on the treatment of POWs until August 1943.[99]

JURISDICTION

The UNWCC also paid close attention to the jurisdiction of the courts that would try accused war criminals.[100] Who might legitimately prosecute suspects? The question was complex because jurisprudence normally placed strict territorial constraints on the jurisdiction of any national court. A conventional interpretation would not have allowed the Allies in the Asia-Pacific theater to prosecute crimes that had taken place outside their prewar territories. In practice, politics, rather than legal principle, determined the distribution of authority to conduct war crimes trials in Asia.

In the Moscow Declaration of November 1, 1943, Roosevelt, Churchill, and Josef Stalin issued an emotional threat to German war criminals, promising that "they will be brought back to the scene of their crimes and judged on the spot by the peoples whom they have outraged."[101] The declaration was subsequently interpreted as having established the principle that most war criminals would be tried by national courts, with a few to have their fate determined jointly by the Allies, but that strict rules of territorial jurisdiction would not be enforced.[102] On August 29, 1945, the UNWCC's Far Eastern Sub-Committee recommended simply that any suspects not needed for projected international trials in Tokyo be "apprehended and sent back to the countries in which their abominable deeds were done or against whose Nationals crimes and atrocities were perpetrated."[103]

When the war ended, Allied territorial responsibilities in the Asia-Pacific region were reallocated. For the greater part of the war, Allied responsibility had been divided into four large command areas.[104] Then on August 17, 1945, two days after Japan surrendered, MacArthur rearranged these areas, abolishing one of them, the South-West Pacific Area (SWPA), in the process. The Philippines reverted to U.S. rule and eastern New Guinea to Australian rule. The South East Asia Command (SEAC), under the British admiral Lord Louis Mountbatten, now covered Sumatra, Malaya, Burma, the Indonesian archipelago, Thailand, Hong Kong, and the southern part of Indochina. Australian troops, formerly under the SWPA, took responsibility under SEAC for eastern Indonesia (including Dutch and British Borneo).[105] The China theater, headed by Chinese president Chiang Kai-shek, now covered the Chinese mainland, Manchuria, the northern part of former French Indochina, Hainan, and Taiwan. In addition, China had to accept the stationing of U.S. marines in north China and a U.S. command headquarters in Shanghai (see figure 1.3).[106]

The Combined Chiefs of Staff of the Allied forces had agreed that each command would be responsible for accepting the Japanese surrender within its territories; for providing humanitarian assistance—including the opportunity for repatriation—to Allied POWs and internees; and for restoring civil government. Although acceptance of the Japanese surrender in a particular territory and restoring the civil government there were assumed to encompass responsibility for the investigation and prosecution of war crimes, several obstacles to the rapid assumption of this responsibility remained. For the sake of Allied prestige, MacArthur ordered that no local Japanese surrenders take place until the formal surrender of the Japanese imperial government in Tokyo. Originally scheduled for August 28, that ceremony was delayed, partly by a typhoon, until September 2, 1945.[107] Although the Allies instructed local Japanese military commanders to maintain law, order, and the political status quo in their occupied territories, the interregnum gave an opportunity to Indonesian and Vietnamese nationalists to declare independence and to begin constructing national governments in what had formerly been Dutch and French colonies.[108] This development meant that Allied forces faced many more difficulties in recovering the former colonies than they had expected. Even without this delay, British forces in SEAC were

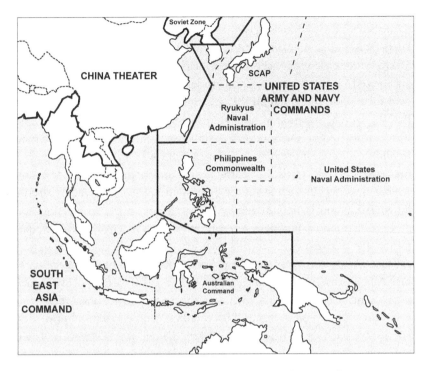

FIGURE 1.3 Allied military commands in Asia and the Pacific, December 31, 1945.

poorly prepared to take on the task of establishing military authority over so large an area. They had relatively few troops and little reliable intelligence about the regions to be reoccupied. Moreover, a significant proportion of their forces was drawn from the Indian army, and the British authorities were acutely conscious that Indians might be reluctant to take part in the suppression of Southeast Asian nationalist movements for the sake of European colonial powers.[109]

LEGISLATION AND COURTS

The balance between national and international interests among the prosecuting powers was delicate. Technically speaking, all the war crimes trials can be understood as "international" prosecutions except those run by the U.S. Navy in Guam and Kwajalein in the Pacific and those held under Soviet Russian jurisdiction and, much later, the jurisdiction of the People's Republic of China (PRC). The trials of major war criminals in Tokyo were self-consciously international. U.S. trials in Yokohama were authorized by the Supreme Commander for the Allied Powers (SCAP), who formally represented all the occupying nations.[110] Trials run by the British, Dutch, Australian, and French governments in Southeast Asia were authorized by the Southeast Asia Command, led by Mountbatten. In addition, often more than one government was interested in a particular case: in POW trials, for example, victims might come from several Allied countries. In such instances, judges and prosecutors might also be drawn from more than one country. In practice, however, the investigation and prosecution of Japanese war criminals quickly devolved to different national endeavors, each with its own incentives and capacity to pursue suspects. With the exception of the Soviet Union and the PRC, the separate Allied prosecution regimes kept one another informed of what they were doing and cooperated with one another when it suited them, but each had a distinct character and operated according to its own priorities. For a start, each set of trials was based on the relevant government's own national war crimes legislation or regulations, which had sometimes been specially drawn up and sometimes already existed. Although they were broadly similar, the law governing each prosecuting regime reflected the specific concerns of the relevant power.

In August 1944, the French authorities in Algiers in North Africa, acting in anticipation of the Axis defeat, had issued a war crimes ordinance that invoked the prewar French Code pénal to identify war crimes and established the principle that military tribunals could prosecute them.[111] The United Kingdom established the authority to try war criminals under a royal warrant (a form of executive decree) dated June 14, 1945, rather than by legislation. The royal warrant's Regulations for the Trial of War Criminals authorized the prosecution of any "violation of the laws and usages of war" in hostilities involving Britain since 1939. This formulation was based on only one category of crime, "war crimes," and technically prevented British courts from prosecuting either crimes against peace or crimes against humanity. Wary of the broader implications for themselves of extending international humanitarian law, given that they ran an empire, the British authorities wanted to keep the focus of the postwar trials in Asia as sharply as possible on Japanese military suspects,

avoiding both political figures and civilian collaborators in local populations.[112] The U.S. government prepared no formal legislation or regulation
concerning war crimes; rather, the American authorities took the position that international law had criminalized atrocities and violations of
the customs of war and that U.S. military commanders therefore already
had authority to try such crimes.[113] On December 4, 1944, the U.S. Navy
authorities in Guam convened a military commission to try both civil and
war crimes, issuing an indictment as early as April 26, 1945.[114] In the name
of the U.S. Army Forces Pacific Area, MacArthur also issued a set of regulations on September 24, 1945, authorizing war crimes trials. The regulations listed general categories of offenses, including crimes against peace
and against humanity as well as conventional war crimes. MacArthur's
document further alluded to the idea of "conspiracy" to commit crimes,
declaring that "leaders, organizers, instigators, accessories and accom-
plices participating in the formulation or execution of any such common
plan or conspiracy will be held responsible for all acts performed by any
person in execution of that plan or conspiracy."[115]

On December 5, 1945, after the first trials held by the U.S. Army had
been completed, these regulations were revised and reissued as "regulations governing the trial of accused war criminals." Then on January 21,
1946, similar regulations were issued covering the U.S. trials in the China
theater.[116]

The Australian War Crimes Act, passed in October 1945, incorporated
the thirty-two categories of crime that had been prepared after the First
World War and added crimes against peace as well as cannibalism and
mutilation of the dead. These latter offenses had been among the atrocities
reported from the Pacific theater of the war. Although the list was meant
to be indicative, not exclusive, the Australian authorities were determined
that these offenses would be unambiguously criminal.[117] The Netherlands
Indies authorities also decided that separate regulation was necessary to
criminalize wartime atrocities; as the colony was constitutionally distinct
from the Netherlands, Dutch metropolitan law did not apply there in the
way that French law commonly applied in French colonies. Not until June
1946, however, was the legal preparation complete in the Netherlands
Indies. The relevant colonial ordinance resembled Australia's in enumer-
ating specific crimes, incorporating the 1919 list, and adding crimes that
were of special concern in the Indies, notably the ill treatment of interned
civilians or POWs and the intentional withholding of medical supplies

from civilians. The list also included the "commission, contrary to the conditions of a truce, of hostile acts or the incitement thereto, and the furnishing of others with information, the opportunity or the means for that purpose," a provision intended specifically to allow the punishment of Japanese commanders who had aided Indonesian nationalists in the creation of their new republic in August 1945.[118] China did not pass its law governing the trial of war criminals until October 24, 1946. This law limited the scope of prosecution to crimes against China and Chinese people. It listed not only crimes against peace but also "malicious insults," "stupefying the mind and controlling the thought of its [China's] nationals," and "plundering of historical, artistic or other cultural treasures." It also specified that Taiwanese people accused of war crimes while Japanese subjects would be tried as enemy aliens, even though they had formally become Chinese citizens after the war.[119]

Although the Soviet Union was formally part of the alliance against Japan, it remained apart from the other Allies' broader, loosely coordinated trial effort. The Soviet Union had entered the war against Japan only on August 9, 1945, but it had quickly occupied Manchuria and northern Korea and had captured an estimated 575,000 Japanese military personnel. Large numbers of these prisoners were transported to the Soviet Union as laborers, and a significant number were later tried as war criminals.[120] Like France, the Soviet Union chose not to create a separate legal category of war crime but instead prosecuted suspects under the 1927 Soviet Criminal Code.[121] The People's Republic of China, too, retained large numbers of Japanese soldiers after its victory over the Nationalists in 1949. When the PRC finally embarked on war crimes trials of Japanese suspects in 1956, it did so on the basis of the Decision on the Handling of Japanese War Criminals Under Detention Who Committed Crimes During the Japanese Invasion War, which was adopted by the People's Congress in April 1956 and then issued by the Communist Party chairman, Mao Zedong. Article 2 provided that suspected war criminals would be tried by a special military tribunal set up by the Supreme People's Court.[122]

At the time of the Japanese attack in 1941, the Philippines had been an autonomous commonwealth under U.S. sovereignty, but after the war, the U.S. government resolved to transfer sovereignty rapidly and scheduled the Philippines' independence for July 4, 1946. Because it had not been an independent entity, the Philippines had not technically been part of the wartime alliance against Japan except as part of the United States, but postwar U.S. rhetoric treated the commonwealth very much as if it had been, and a Philippines representative was included on the Far Eastern Commission (FEC), a Washington body that nominally supervised the Allied Occupation of Japan. On August 16, 1945, the Philippine government issued an order creating the National War Crimes Office within the Philippine army, but this office acted under American direction, even after independence.[123] Like other U.S. jurisdictions, the Philippines had no formal definition of war crimes.

The complex politics of the former wartime alliance against Japan meant that hierarchy was embedded in the relations among the different prosecuting regimes. Mountbatten, the Supreme Allied Commander South East Asia, was formally equal in standing to MacArthur. The Dutch and French colonial authorities were subordinate to SEAC, but they were reluctant to brook any interference in what they regarded as their sovereign rights over war criminals. The Chinese government represented a separate command, nominally equivalent to the other two, but the political reality was that it depended on U.S. support in its battle with its Communist rivals. Not only did the government have to accept U.S. war crimes investigations within its territory; it also had little choice but to acquiesce in the U.S. military prosecution of Japanese war crimes suspects in Shanghai in 1946.[124] When the Australian authorities were operating in Southeast Asia and not in their own territories, they also were subject to the British command, but in general they were more energetic in pursuing war crimes cases, and the British were reluctant to stand in their way. Australia stationed an investigation team in Singapore, that is, outside its allocated territory, and also sent teams to Thailand and western Indonesia.[125] Even within the U.S. sphere, there were two jurisdictions, with the U.S. Navy War Crimes Commission undertaking trials on the Pacific islands of Guam and Kwajalein, albeit in close collaboration with the SCAP authorities in Japan.[126]

The courts that tried alleged Japanese war criminals had different names in the various jurisdictions that established them—the United States and the Philippines called them military commissions;[127] Nationalist China had military tribunals;[128] the Netherlands Indies had *temporaire krijgsraden* (temporary military courts);[129] and the French had *tribunals militaires*.[130] British and Australian tribunals were military courts,[131] and the court in Tokyo was an international military tribunal. Whatever their formal names, however, the courts functioned as military tribunals. Although this term is sometimes conflated with "court-martial," the two institutions are distinct. Whereas courts-martial try soldiers for alleged breaches of their own military law, military tribunals are convened under the authority of a military commander to try foreign citizens for hostile acts that are not protected by the rights of belligerency.[132] They are not judicial bodies in the formal sense of the word; rather, they are advisory bodies to the local military commander concerning the application of executive measures for maintaining military order. Military tribunals tend to be ad hoc and relatively short-term bodies established in response to particularly pressing circumstances rather than permanent institutions, and their staff are normally released from other employment or specially recruited for short-term duties. They are characterized by accelerated procedures that dispense verdicts quickly by limiting the opportunity of the accused to prepare a defense and by sidestepping at least some of the procedural protections against wrongful conviction that are normally present in both civilian criminal courts and courts-martial.[133] They are normally conducted by military personnel, to ensure that the proceedings are in the hands of people who understand the practicalities of military affairs. Nonetheless, military tribunals generally follow many of the procedures found in the corresponding civil courts, because these procedures are believed to be the most suitable or because they add to the tribunal's public legitimacy.

Some support could be found in both the Japanese public and the Japanese government for the idea that the Japanese government should hold its own trials. This suggestion was consistent with the Allied intention announced in the Potsdam Declaration to pursue only guilty individuals and not to punish the Japanese people as a whole: if some Japanese were guiltless, there was no reason the Japanese authorities could not prosecute their own war criminals. The leading daily newspaper, the *Asahi shinbun*, suggested as early as September 1945 that the Japanese people propose their own lists of defendants and possibly organize their own trials. A large number of readers agreed strongly with this stance.[134] In the final days of the war, perhaps in view of the Leipzig precedent, the Japanese military had argued in vain that Japan's right to conduct its own trials should be a condition of acceptance of the Potsdam Declaration, and in September 1945, the Higashikuni cabinet voted to investigate crimes and conduct its own trials. The emperor then intervened to say that he would not tolerate Japanese trials of his own loyal subjects, though in the end he was persuaded that Japanese trials would be preferable to prosecutions by foreigners.[135] Nonetheless, offering the lessons of Leipzig as an example—one 1944 U.S. military publication labeled the German trials a "fiasco"[136]—the early planners of the prosecutions were unwilling to allow Japanese individuals or institutions to hold trials.

The Japanese government did not give up easily, and between September 1945 and March 1946, it actually staged four separate trials, in which eight low-ranking military personnel were prosecuted for conventional war crimes and given relatively lenient sentences. The Japanese authorities appear to have concluded that the defendants could not then be charged in Allied courtrooms, but in fact all were retried in Allied courts and sentenced to heavy punishments.[137] In a few cases, military commanders in the field also took action against those considered responsible for war crimes. In September 1945 Japanese forces in Indochina conducted their own trial of Japanese troops who had murdered four Frenchmen on August 22 and 23, 1945. The crime had apparently been an angry retaliation for the victims' derogatory comments regarding Japan's defeat. The perpetrators were found guilty by a Japanese military tribunal and sentenced to prison terms ranging from three to fifteen years.[138] There is evidence of a similar trial in Thailand,[139] and an internment camp commander in Java, Sonei Ken'ichi, also claimed to have been punished by his superiors with ten days in detention for shaving the heads of Dutch women internees.[140] Just after Japan's surrender, Japanese military authorities on the Thailand–Burma Railway appear to have demoted Captain Noguchi Hideji to the rank of private for the maltreatment of a British officer, Captain William Drower.[141]

Some proposals for dealing with war criminals were aimed at giving the Japanese people a stake in postwar legal proceedings without allowing them to actually run trials. Joseph Keenan, the IMTFE's chief prosecutor, proposed including the Japanese government as a party to the indictment of wartime leaders, and the British Foreign Office toyed with the idea of allowing indictments for prewar domestic political crimes such as political assassinations, presumably in order to give the Japanese people a chance to seek justice for offenses that had damaged their own society.[142] These ideas were countered by Allied planners' perception that their publics required unequivocal revenge: Allied authorities did not believe that victims and their relatives would take seriously a trial process in which, for example, Japanese judges sat on the bench. It is likely that another reason for SCAP's reluctance to include Japanese people in the trial process was the fact that the main advocates of Japanese-held trials came from the Japan Communist Party. At the start of the Occupation, SCAP had released Communist leaders from jail and had legalized the party for the first time. In December 1945, party leaders convened the People's Assembly for the Prosecution of War Criminals.[143] Although SCAP initially wanted to demonstrate to the Japanese people that it favored political diversity and healthy political opposition, the Allied authorities were nevertheless deeply suspicious of Japanese Communists.

There was widespread acceptance on the Allied side that the appropriate complement to Allied national war crimes courts was an international court to try Japanese leaders in the way that the International Military Tribunal in Nuremberg was prosecuting Nazi leaders. MacArthur took direct responsibility for the complex process of assembling this court as the International Military Tribunal for the Far East. In the end, judges from eleven countries—Australia, Britain, Canada, China, France, India, the Netherlands, New Zealand, the Philippines, the Soviet Union, and the United States—sat on the tribunal, with the Australian judge Sir William Webb as its president.[144]

The Allied powers were thus firmly committed to prosecuting Japanese war criminals. They hoped to avoid imputing collective guilt to the Japanese people in a way that might encourage a postwar return to militarism, but they were determined to implement a comprehensive program of trials of individual perpetrators. They began with an agenda based on unimpeachable judicial principles, but the international law they had worked so hard to create gave an inescapable political cast to the proceedings that then unfolded. In practice, there was no possibility that Allied forces would be subject to prosecution. In principle, Allied leaders were immune because of the notion that only the Japanese had fought an aggressive war. Allied military personnel—and Japanese soldiers up to a point—were protected by the principle that actions taken out of military necessity were justified. Above all, the proceedings were unequal because it was the Allied authorities who decided who to prosecute and how to set up the courts. Before the trials could proceed, however, the Allies had to begin the daunting task of assembling evidence and indicting suspects.

2

INVESTIGATION AND ARREST

Complex though it was, the task of establishing a legal basis for prosecution was only a preliminary step in the postwar reckoning for offenses committed by Japanese military personnel. As soon as the state of hostilities made it possible, the Allied powers in the Asia-Pacific theater began to identify suspects and to collect documentary and testimonial evidence of war crimes. The process was challenging above all because of the scale of the investigation. More than 30,000 Allied prisoners of war had died in captivity, and unsubstantiated reports suggested that tens of thousands of local people, including Chinese and European settlers, had also been killed in Southeast Asia. The death toll in China was in the millions, though the extent of Japanese responsibility was made uncertain by the scale of death from famine, natural disaster, and atrocities carried out by Chinese forces against their own people.

Despite the Allied planners' goal of prosecuting all suspected war criminals, the size of the task of identifying suspects and collecting evidence made it immediately obvious that choices would have to be made. The question then arose of how to choose. Inevitably, an order of priority emerged. Practical considerations were necessarily overwhelming: what evidence could be found, and which suspects could be identified and located? There were many obstacles to an effective investigation and to arrest of suspected war criminals, from the destruction of written evidence to the need to rely sometimes on Japanese assistance. Investigation teams generally depended on Japanese interpreters for contact with Japanese detainees; one team was embarrassed to discover that a suspect for whom it had been searching had efficiently covered his tracks by working as their interpreter during the hunt![1] Other considerations also influenced what was investigated and who was arrested. Despite the firm ruling of the United Nations War Crimes Commission (UNWCC) against it, investigators from an early stage tacitly implemented a superior orders defense. Thus the junior soldiers with the least amount of independent responsibility for atrocities would usually be passed over in favor of middle-ranking or more senior personnel. Political considerations intruded, too. Western publics were believed to require justice for particular sorts of crimes, especially offenses committed against POWs and civilian internees, and governments were anxious to prosecute crimes committed in sensitive regions or against particular ethnic groups. The U.S. government, for example, gave high priority to investigating crimes against Filipinos, and the British authorities were careful to begin with a case in which the victims had been Indian, in order to counter Indian sympathy for Japanese war aims. The combination of practical, legal, and political factors affecting the investigation of war crimes and arrests of suspects highlighted the selective and even arbitrary nature of a process that had announced itself to the world as comprehensive and impartial. Ultimately, the process of selecting defendants and deciding on charges thus contributed to disillusionment with and criticism of the war crimes trials as a whole.

COLLECTING EVIDENCE, ARRESTING SUSPECTS

Australian authorities began to collect evidence concerning Japanese war crimes very early in the hostilities. In May 1942, an official court of inquiry reviewed evidence of massacres of Australian troops alleged to have taken place near Rabaul in New Guinea in January of that year.[2] Then in June 1943, the Australian government commissioned the chief justice of Queensland, Sir William Webb, who later presided at the Tokyo Trial, to prepare a secret report on Japanese atrocities in Australian New Guinea more generally. Webb interviewed both Australian troops and local people to create a dossier of a dozen or so incidents of Japanese cruelty in New Guinea and East Timor.[3] Between August and October 1944,

Webb headed a second commission to gather evidence in New Guinea as Australians and Americans gradually drove the Japanese off the island; the evidence was then transmitted to the UNWCC in London.[4]

Whereas the Australian authorities used a formal commission to gather evidence when the advancing front line permitted direct access to atrocity sites, British military forces reconquering Burma during 1944 and early 1945 allocated the task of investigating war crimes to district officers, the regional civilian officials who had been the linchpin of the colonial administration, in collaboration with the intelligence section of the British Twelfth Army Headquarters.[5] As a guide to adjudicating what might constitute a war crime, the officials were given a list of the thirty-two acts that had been identified in 1919.[6] Members of the Burmese public were invited, in public announcements, to give information to the investigators in order to hasten the identification of suspects.[7] In the areas of Southeast Asia that came under Britain's South East Asia Command (SEAC) only after the Japanese surrender, investigations could not commence until the postwar military administration was established. In most of these regions, the British authorities formed separate war crimes investigations teams, though in the Andaman Islands, where terrible atrocities were known to have occurred, the investigation took the form of a court of inquiry.[8]

Meanwhile, in October 1944, to begin collecting evidence, the U.S. Army opened a war crimes office in Washington, with a branch for the Pacific theater. A navy war crimes officer for the Pacific was appointed in April 1945, and an army investigations office was established in Manila in June.[9] The Philippine government established a national war crimes office in August 1945 to liaise with the American authorities.[10] But on August 9, 1945, the U.S. Coordinating Subcommittee for the Far East, drawn from the Departments of State, War, and Navy, urged that war crimes investigations not be made public until Japan had surrendered and all POWs and internees had been released.[11] The officials were evidently concerned that Allied personnel still in Japanese hands might be used as hostages by Japanese forces in exchange for concessions on war crimes.

The government of the Netherlands Indies was slower to begin its investigations because the terms of the Allied agreement for accepting Japan's surrender and restoring civil government gave the initial authority in their former colony to Britain's SEAC. Only in September 1945, after a formal agreement on the status of Netherlands Indies officials within SEAC, did the Netherlands Indies government-in-exile in Australia establish its

Regeringsbureau tot Nasporing van Oorlogsmisdrijven (RBNO, Government Bureau for the Tracing of War Crimes). This civil body came under the control of the colonial procureur-generaal (attorney general), but because the whole Netherlands Indies administration was technically a civil affairs branch of SEAC, the RBNO was subject to SEAC's authority.[12]

The position of the French authorities in Indochina was still more difficult. During the war, the colonial government had sided with the collaborationist Vichy regime, which was allied with Nazi Germany and thus also with Japan. Until March 1945, with the formal assent of the French authorities, Japanese troops had been stationed in Indochina. Although the Western powers in Europe had chosen to acknowledge France as an ally, the U.S. government had been reluctant to restore France to power in Indochina, and it was uncertain whether the Allies would recognize the French government's authority to conduct war crimes trials in a colony that had been allied with Japan. Accordingly, although the French authorities in Paris had created the Direction de la recherche des crimes de guerre (Department for Investigation of War Crimes) for Indochina by October 1945, it operated at first outside the formal framework of Allied war crimes investigations. Only after some weeks could it begin work as the Service des crimes de guerre (War Crimes Section) in Saigon.[13]

China appears to have left its initial investigations with the Far Eastern and Pacific Sub-Commission of the UNWCC, to the extent that other Allied investigators complained that they could get little cooperation from Chinese authorities in either obtaining affidavits or arresting suspects.[14] Later, however, the pace of Chinese investigations seems to have picked up. In October 1946, the national War Crimes Office claimed to have recorded 160,000 allegations, of which 30,000 had been used as the basis for serious charges, many of them presumably in the form of multiple charges against the same accused. The UNWCC reported that "70,000 [allegations] of a less serious nature had been dealt with directly by the Chinese authorities."[15]

National investigators all largely ignored both the UNWCC and its Chongqing subcommission. Although the commission's offices in Europe continued to receive detailed reports on investigations and other matters relating to war crimes from the Allied authorities in Asia and the Pacific, the idea that the UNWCC might function as a central coordinating body for the investigation and prosecution of war crimes rapidly receded. Even in relation to the investigation of Japanese crimes in China, the UNWCC subcommission in Chongqing became marginal to the investigative efforts of the Chinese authorities. The subcommission continued to issue lists of suspects and to prepare charges, but it had no authority to act on them and was obliged simply to hand its material to national jurisdictions.[16]

For the most part, the Allied investigators adopted three approaches in attempting to establish a comprehensive record of war crimes deserving prosecution. First, they gathered information from the tens of thousands of Westerners who emerged from POW and internment camps at the end of the war. Australian investigators collected 12,000 to 15,000 completed questionnaires from former detainees.[17] A 1949 U.S. report claimed that "every known former American prisoner of war from privates to General Jonathan Wainwright [commander of Allied forces in the Philippines at the time of surrender to the Japanese]" had been contacted for information. U.S. investigators took around 50,000 affidavits in the Tokyo area, 8,000 in Manila, and 6,000 in San Francisco, the port through which many former prisoners returned to the United States.[18] Investigators followed up the more promising questionnaire returns with interviews. If those interviews appeared to offer useful information, the former prisoners were asked to provide sworn statements that could later be presented in court.[19] In some venues, investigators organized identity parades, inviting victims to point out their persecutors. Photographs of suspects taken in one jurisdiction also could be circulated to others (figure 2.1).[20]

The investigators had to work fast. Their total staff was relatively small for the scale of the operation: the British investigative force consisted of about four hundred, evenly divided among officers, soldiers, and civilians.[21] In addition, the facilities in the Allied centers were cramped, and each batch of former POWs and detainees had to be moved on quickly to make room for the next. Most of the Western witnesses were eager to return home, with some leaving before they could be questioned.[22] The resulting lists of suspected war criminals therefore contained information of widely varying quality. Sometimes the precise nature, date, and location of the incident relating to a war crime were recorded, together with the names of the victims and perpetrators, but at other times the records were vague. The offense might be described only as "brutality," the victims as "natives" or "an Australian officer." Many perpetrators were identified only by a surname or a nickname ("Liverlips," "Oswald," "Boy Bastard," "the Tiger").[23] British war crimes investigators thus had to maintain a card index of nicknames in order to keep track of suspects.[24]

FIGURE 2.1 Identity parade in French Indochina. European former internees assembled as a group to determine which of their former jailers had been guilty of cruelty. "The Roles Are Changed in Indo-China," *West Australian*, March 19, 1946, 5.

Other suspects were simply labeled "Unknown." As new information came to light, the investigators would sometimes reconnoiter areas where crimes were alleged to have occurred or where a prisoner had disappeared with insufficient explanation, or they would inspect sites of air crashes and other possible gravesites.[25] Investigators faced particular problems in Thailand, which had been allied with Japan during the war. The Thai authorities were seeking to reposition their country, much as Austrian authorities had done in Europe, as a victim rather than accomplice of fascist militarism, and thus they promised the Allies "full assistance" in the prosecution of war criminals. Local Thai authorities, however, were often reluctant to assist foreign investigators.[26]

The second approach of war crimes investigators was to seek testimony from local witnesses, but this task often presented even greater difficulties. Many victims of Japanese brutality—including the tens of thousands of Asians forced to work on the Thailand–Burma Railway—had been dispersed long before the surrender. Others had fled as soon as they found out the Japanese had capitulated. There was no collection point at which the investigation teams could approach them, and the breakdown of law and order all across Southeast Asia made investigations difficult and sometimes dangerous outside the main towns.[27] Indeed, three Australian war crimes investigators were killed by Indonesian revolutionaries outside Bogor in West Java in April 1946.[28] Language was also a barrier, except in Indonesia, where Dutch officials could often speak Malay, and in China, where Chinese investigators questioned local people about war crimes. Investigation in Chinese, however, was made more difficult by the fact that Japanese personal names could be read with very different pronunciations in different Chinese languages. One SEAC list noted that the suspect identified as "Leng Meng Tong Choa" was probably Lieutenant Colonel Sugimoto.[29] The British in Malaya advertised for witnesses in the English-language press, encouraging local people to come forward with information, but of course these calls reached principally those who were literate in English. The result was that class, more than ethnicity, was sometimes the determinant of which Asian victims were heard in the investigation process.

As a third approach, the investigators also screened the surrendered Japanese troops who came into their hands as the investigators moved into formerly occupied territory, visiting the temporary detention camps that were scattered throughout the region and interrogating anyone whose rank or service history gave reason for suspicion.[30] According to the 1949 U.S. report on the war crimes trials, more than 100,000 Japanese personnel were questioned by U.S. teams.[31] Investigators sifted through Japanese documents to obtain lists of former detainees and prison camp staff, as well as summaries of the war service records of Japanese personnel. Some Japanese soldiers had kept diaries whose contents became incriminating evidence.[32] Investigators plied Japanese authorities at every level with questions intended to establish the circumstances in which crimes had been committed. In late November 1945, for instance, the Supreme Commander for the Allied Powers (SCAP) in Japan instructed the Japanese government to supply complete information about the military and administrative structures of the POW camps in Japan.[33] Because the Japanese authorities knew that this information was wanted for war crimes investigations, the Allied investigators often viewed the answers with suspicion. "It is impossible to give an estimate of when I will complete all cases," wrote an Australian investigator, "as investigation into these matters depends entirely on the veracity of the Japanese in the furnishing of corroborative evidence."[34]

As a matter of policy, the Allied authorities detained all Japanese military personnel who belonged to suspect categories. These categories were principally the Kenpeitai and Tokkeitai (military police and naval police, respectively), POW and internment camp guards and commanders, troops involved in the sea transport of Allied POWs, interrogation staff, and courtroom officials.[35] The investigators also interrogated specific suspects to obtain detailed testimony of the circumstances in which they had beaten or killed their victims. The aim was to establish just who, if anyone, had issued the order to beat or kill and whether the suspect, if prosecuted, might convincingly argue that the action had been consistent with the imperatives of war.[36] Some suspects cooperated with investigators because they were confident their actions did not warrant prosecution. Many others, however, were less forthcoming, asserting that they had not been present when an atrocity was carried out or that the order had come from elsewhere.

On September 11, 1945, General Douglas MacArthur ordered the arrest of forty people who were expected to be prosecuted for war crimes. At the head of the list was General Tōjō Hideki, who had been prime minister for much of the war and who was, apart from the emperor, the Japanese leader best known in the West. The list included other cabinet members and senior military commanders, as well as officials attached to POW camps in Japan; five Westerners accused of collaboration; and figures from the Japanese-sponsored wartime Republic of the Philippines.[37] By early December, the U.S. authorities had detained more than one hundred suspects.[38]

A list of suspects held under SEAC control in Bangkok's Bangkwang jail in mid-1946 has survived. Bangkwang was the principal SEAC assembly point for those suspected of war crimes on the Thailand–Burma Railway. The list indicates that nearly half the suspects were noncommissioned officers (including warrant officers; see table 2.1 and figure 2.2). Relatively few privates were on the list, which probably reflects, first, the practicalities of POW camp management. Reliable soldiers were needed on the front line. The comparatively undemanding task of guarding prisoners and internees was therefore not given to regular army privates but was largely delegated to Koreans, especially on the Thailand–Burma Railway and in Singapore and Java, and to Taiwanese personnel in Borneo and the Philippines. As colonized subjects, both groups served with the Japanese military. But they were less trusted than ethnically Japanese personnel.

TABLE 2.1 Suspected War Criminals Held in Bangkwang Prison,
Bangkok, July 1946

Rank	Number	Percentage of total
Senior officers	12	2
Junior officers	118	18
NCOs/warrant officers	298	46
Privates	69	11
Guards	52	8
Gunzoku	37	6
Interpreters	14	2
Civilians	40	6
Unspecified	1	
Total	641	

Source: "War Service Histories of War Criminal Suspects Held at Bangkwang Gaol, Bangkok,"
July 1946, 53, NA (UK), FO 371/57570.

The great majority of the Korean and Taiwanese guards, as well as colonial subjects working in other positions, especially as interpreters, were not technically military personnel but were civilian employees called *kōin*, *yōnin*, or *gunzoku*.[39] In May 1942, the Japanese authorities decided to form special units of Korean and Taiwanese personnel who would become camp guards, in response to the sudden detention crisis that the armed forces faced following the capture of so many prisoners in the preceding months.

Three thousand Korean recruits were briefly trained in Korea before being dispatched to Southeast Asia.[40] In the camps, the guards worked under the command of Japanese NCOs and junior officers. At one stage, for instance, the forced labor program on the Thailand–Burma Railway was supervised by 40 Japanese officers, 85 Japanese noncommissioned officers, and 1,280 Korean guards.[41] The guards occupied the lowest rungs of the Japanese military hierarchy and were themselves subject to harsh discipline if they failed to maintain order.[42] In many accounts from Allied

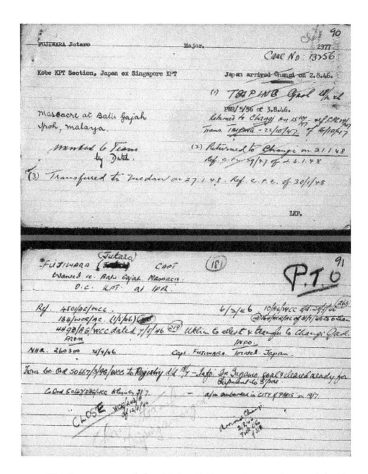

FIGURE 2.2 SEAC suspect card for Major Fujiwara Jutaro. Arrested in Japan, he was transferred to Changi, then to Taiping in Malaya, and back to Changi before being transferred to Medan for trial by Netherlands Indies authorities (NA [UK], WO 357/1). Reproduced by permission.

internees, Koreans were described as more inclined to brutality than were Japanese soldiers.[43] Reporting on the treatment of POWs on the Thailand–Burma Railway, the Brisbane *Courier-Mail* noted: "The guards, who were Koreans, almost invariably behaved with the utmost brutality, having learned their lesson from the way the Japanese had treated them."[44] As this comment implies, the brutal treatment of Koreans as colonial subjects of Japan was believed to have contributed to their own brutal behavior in the camps.[45]

Information is more readily available on Korean than on Taiwanese suspects, because Koreans appear on the Bangkwang list, whereas Taiwanese suspects from Borneo were more likely to have been sent to Changi in Singapore. The Bangkwang list identifies some seventy suspects as Koreans. Although half a dozen other detainees can be identified as Korean from other sources and there is circumstantial evidence that one hundred or so other Koreans may have been in Bangkwang earlier than July 1946, the numbers suggest that SEAC war crimes investigators had chosen not to detain significant numbers of these very junior personnel. From the start, investigators appear often to have accepted the defense of superior orders. Common soldiers and guards were not further investigated unless there were indications that they had exceeded the commands of their superiors in cruelty toward prisoners. Suspect cards assembled by SEAC investigators point to the same conclusion. Even though all cards carry a statement of the suspected crime, here and there the note is added: "admittedly carried out orders from superior."[46]

The investigation of crimes was impeded by wartime deaths and the massive movement of people around the region. After the war, the Japanese authorities estimated that 1,555,308 Japanese military personnel had died in battle and from illness during the conflict from 1941 to 1945;[47] many of them would have been suspects or potential witnesses if they had survived. Rear Admiral Shibazaki Keiji might have faced command responsibility charges for the massacre of New Zealand coast watchers in Tarawa in October 1942, but he had died in the Allied counterattack on the island a year later.[48] Also, a significant number of Japanese officers, like their German counterparts in Europe, committed suicide.[49] Japanese forces had moved frequently during the war years, so that soldiers who had committed crimes in Singapore might have ended up in Indochina, while soldiers present at the Bataan death march might have been moved to one of the smaller Pacific islands. As a result, it was often difficult to locate suspected perpetrators (figure 2.3).

Most of the 700,000 Japanese soldiers who had been stationed in Southeast Asia in August 1945 had been repatriated by 1947, though tens of thousands were retained by local Allied authorities as a convenient and tractable labor reserve or as a competent and useful military or technical force.[50] Repatriating troops to Japan who were not required for labor was a matter of urgency in order to limit the burden on local economies and their potential participation in emerging independence struggles.[51]

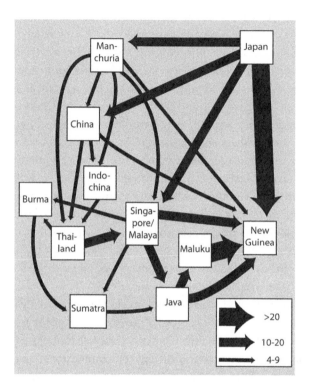

FIGURE 2.3 The Road to Hollandia: war service movements of Japanese personnel charged as war criminals in Hollandia, Netherlands Indies. Trajectories with fewer than four persons and service careers before final departure from Japan are not shown. Compiled from individual charge sheets in NA (NL), Vertegenwoordiging Japan, 1946–1954, 2.05.116, inv. nr. 531.

By the end of 1946, 19,050 Japanese military personnel and civilians had been repatriated from Hong Kong, 132,303 from the Philippines, 31,583 from Indochina, 138,167 from Australian-controlled territories, and 130,795 from Pacific islands.[52] War crimes suspects had somehow to be filtered out of this vast mass of defeated enemy personnel and resident civilians. With understaffed investigation teams, the process was likely to take months. Moreover, as an Australian memo noted,

Many of these [soldiers] have same surnames as those appearing in official lists of perpetrators or suspected criminals but the other information given in such lists is insufficient to establish definitive identity. As an example under serial no 1132 on SEAC Theatre list of suspects[,] no. 10 is given the name Yamamoto. There are 55 prisoners-of-war of this name [in Australian hands].[53]

Military authorities reported, too, that Japanese soldiers who had been captured before the surrender had provided false names, perhaps to avoid bringing shame on their families or to avoid prosecution.[54] The collection of evidence was further hampered by the fact that many Japanese units had destroyed documents upon hearing of the surrender,[55] partly as a normal military reaction to defeat and partly to obstruct the war crimes investigation.[56] American forces had done the same when the island of Corregidor fell to the Japanese in May 1942.[57] In 1948, Australian officials in Tokyo claimed to have uncovered "extensive evidence proving a planned policy by major Japanese army and navy commands to conceal war crimes from Allied investigators," by destroying records, fabricating evidence, and instructing subordinates to withhold evidence and lie about war crimes.[58]

Some Japanese suspects went on the run. The flamboyant Colonel Tsuji Masanobu, who was suspected of participating in massacres in Malaya and on the Bataan Peninsula, remained underground in Thailand, Vietnam, and China until 1949, when his name was removed from the arrest list and he was free to return to Japan.[59] Katō Tetsutarō, accused of the murder of an American POW in Japan, remained in hiding for three years, sheltered by friends and family and even at one time working for the Americans under an assumed name.[60] In Southeast Asia and China, some suspects joined the local nationalist or communist movements, though not all who did so were suspected of war crimes.[61] Some of those who were arrested managed to escape from custody; others committed suicide while in Allied hands. General Tōjō tried unsuccessfully to commit suicide as American military police surrounded his house, but he survived and was given intensive care so as to be available for his subsequent trial.[62] A few weeks later, former prime minister Konoe Fumimaro succeeded in killing himself before he could be detained as a suspect. The card files of the SEAC war crimes investigators tersely record dozens of other self-killings.[63] War crimes teams sought to keep suspects under guard, preferably in single cells, rather than leaving them in loosely supervised transit camps or allocating them to work units, to prevent them from committing suicide and thereby evading justice.[64] Keeping suspects apart was also intended to prevent them from colluding with one another, especially if they were expected to give evidence in trials other than their own.

The meaning of the term "suspect" changed over time. Before the end of the war, it referred primarily to a few thousand people named or otherwise identified in the lists held by the UNWCC of people who warranted investigation. Almost none of these suspects would have known that they had been identified as such. In the early stages of the postwar investigation, the term "suspect" included not only any Japanese person on whom suspicion had fallen, whether because of witness reports or because of his formal role in the Japanese military or political apparatus, but also potential witnesses who were not believed to have committed any crime. Some "suspects" were discharged; others were marked for prompt prosecution; and still others were sent back into detention to await the outcome of further investigation. Chaen Yoshio estimated that roughly 25,000 Japanese military personnel were arrested across all the prosecuting countries,[65] but the number under arrest at any one time was always less than this,[66] and it is likely that ten times this number came under at least fleeting suspicion. Many suspects, too, were simply detained without formal arrest, and the degree of suspicion attaching to an individual might ebb and flow. The war crimes investigation teams routinely issued instructions that specified Japanese personnel were no longer under suspicion and should therefore be released.[67] Many cases were immediately closed because of lack of reliable evidence or because key suspects were dead.[68] Some suspects were detained, then released for lack of evidence, and later arrested when new evidence became available.

As the investigations proceeded, the focus shifted from the general screening of all Japanese personnel who had some association with a suspected war crime to an approach that targeted those against whom there was a substantial prima facie case. The war crimes teams developed complex systems of card indexes, paper files, and lists that cross-referenced the personal details of Japanese suspects with evidence from questionnaires, affidavits, and interrogations and with information on the suspect's last known location. Lists that had been at first vague and brief, sometimes with no more than the name and rank of the suspects, were transformed into detailed specifications including place and date of birth, next of kin, service history, and a summary of the suspected crimes. These lists then made reference to dossiers that assembled the available evidence. As a suspect came increasingly into view as a prospective defendant, the investigators began to seek evidence to strengthen the case. War crimes teams in each jurisdiction exchanged thousands of messages asking for information or evidence concerning the Japanese suspects against whom they were building cases.[69]

Suspects were originally held in vast detention camps along with other military personnel. Ahlone Park on the outskirts of Rangoon, for example, had become a sea of tents.[70] After a time, however, suspects were increasingly concentrated in prisons that offered greater security than such barbed-wired camps. The U.S. authorities in Japan initially kept suspects in a holding camp at Ōmori in Tokyo. From November 1945 on, they were delivered to Sugamo Prison in Tokyo. Originally opened in 1895 as a civil prison, Sugamo had been transferred by the Japanese government to the U.S. Eighth Army in October 1945. It was then refurbished and opened on November 1 as a detention center for suspected war criminals.[71] Elsewhere, Rangoon Central Jail (also known as "110 POW Cage Rangoon"), Changi and Outram Road (Singapore), Pudu (Kuala Lumpur), Bangkwang (Bangkok), Luzon Prisoner of War Camp no. 1 (Manila), Saigon's Maison Centrale, and Hong Kong's Stanley Prison became the hubs in a regional system of detention and exchange.

As the suspect lists were refined, it became apparent that many alleged war criminals had simply joined the vast multitude of Japanese people being repatriated from formerly occupied regions, mainly during 1946. Most of them had simply returned to their former homes, if they still existed, and had rejoined their families and were attempting to rebuild their lives in the difficult circumstances of postwar Japan. To obtain custody of these men, the SCAP authorities worked through the Japanese government. Whereas the wartime Allies in Europe formally dissolved the German government and assumed all its powers to facilitate reconstruction of the country, SCAP preserved the Japanese government, which continued, for instance, to have a prime minister, national elections, and a functioning parliament throughout the Occupation. American police had arrested Tōjō in September 1945, but the manner of his arrest, and his attempted suicide at the time, caused such disquiet among the Japanese authorities that the Americans agreed to channel all future arrests through the Central Liaison Bureau (Chūō renraku kyoku), which in turn passed requests to the Japanese police.[72] SCAP also published lists of wanted men whose addresses were unknown. By September 1946, British and Australian authorities had requested delivery of 462 suspects for trial in

Southeast Asia; both governments maintained liaison officers in Tokyo to undertake interrogations and collect affidavits.[73] The U.S. authorities also transferred suspects to China and the Philippines, while the British sent suspects to China, Indochina, and the Netherlands Indies. In 1950, the Soviet Union transferred 971 suspects to the People's Republic of China to enable the new government there to cement its international status by holding trials.[74]

Some suspects turned themselves in, perhaps confident they would be exonerated or sensing they could not avoid capture.[75] Katayama Hideo had returned to Japan three weeks after the offenses on Ambon for which he was eventually convicted and had married and resumed civilian life. He turned himself in to the authorities upon seeing his name in a Japanese newspaper as a wanted criminal, only to be sent to Morotai for trial in an Australian court, convicted, and executed.[76] In the immediate post-surrender months, many Japanese people were ashamed of the record of wartime atrocities that was placed before them by the Occupation authorities, and some actively supported the war crimes investigations out of a sense of decency. In May 1946, a recently discharged sailor, Oka Harumitsu, arrived unannounced at the Osaka office of the United States War Crimes Team, prepared to testify concerning the beheading of Allied flyers at Seletar in Singapore.[77] Others feared that their friends or family members were being set up to take responsibility for the crimes of others and offered to implicate those they regarded as the truly guilty.[78]

Paired with the arrest process was the massive operation to collect sworn affidavits from Western witnesses who had returned to the United States, the United Kingdom, Australia, the Netherlands, and other places. As likely candidates for prosecution were identified, investigators consulted the original "Q" forms collected from former prisoners and asked police forces in their home countries to track down potential witnesses. Police would then ask these witnesses to identify suspects formally from photo sheets of Japanese soldiers, whose names were not usually revealed to the witnesses, and would accept or take down notarized statements that provided detailed evidence on the specific events to be presented in later trials (figure 2.4).[79]

Many Japanese suspects were wanted by more than one of the Allied powers, and it required both tact and a willingness to bargain on the part of the separate war crimes offices to have suspects transferred between jurisdictions.[80] Transfers often went smoothly, but most prosecuting

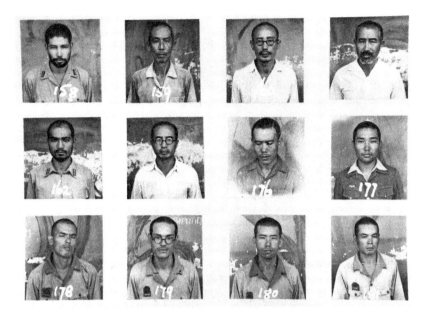

FIGURE 2.4 Witnesses providing affidavits in Britain, Australia, and elsewhere were shown pages of photographs of unnamed suspects and were invited to identify the perpetrators of the crimes they had reported (NA [UK], CN 4/10 [3]). Reproduced by permission.

powers were reluctant to hand over those they considered to be high-value figures. The Chinese authorities dearly wanted to prosecute General Matsui Iwane, one of the most senior Japanese commanders of troops who carried out the 1937–1938 massacre at Nanjing, but he had been arrested in Japan at the end of the war, and MacArthur insisted he be tried in Tokyo.[81] Chiang Kai-shek's Guomindang (Nationalist Party) in turn dragged its feet on transferring war crimes suspects to the French authorities in Indochina, especially General Tsuchihashi Yūitsu, the former commander of Japanese troops in Indochina.[82] When the French finally obtained custody of Tsuchihashi, they blocked Dutch plans to interrogate him.[83] The British authorities in Singapore efficiently located and transferred to Indochina the officers of the 226th Battalion, suspected of massacres at Hà Giang on the Tonkin–China border in March 1945, but declined to allow French investigators to interrogate General Terauchi Hisaichi, the former Japanese commander for all Southeast Asia.[84]

THE PROMISE AND PROBLEM
OF COMMAND RESPONSIBILITY

In tacitly accepting that superior orders mitigated, or even erased, the guilt of junior Japanese, Korean, and Taiwanese personnel who had actually carried out killings and beatings, the Allied investigators shifted their focus beyond the lower ranks of the Japanese military forces to encompass the midranking and senior officers who had had ultimate responsibility for atrocities. Given the destruction of documents and the generally chaotic circumstances in which many atrocities had been committed, the Allied prosecutors realized it would be difficult to demonstrate the direct complicity of senior officers in most cases. The charter of the International Military Tribunal for the Far East (IMTFE) identified the legal concept of conspiracy as a key device for making Japanese leaders responsible for war crimes committed far from Tokyo and without their direct knowledge.[85] The charge of conspiracy, however, was a blunt tool. Historically a means of repressing political and social dissent, it demanded only a common purpose and intent; it did not require the actual commission of a crime.[86] In this respect, conspiracy law was usefully fluid, but it required prosecutors to demonstrate actual connivance. This task was difficult, given the opacity and ambiguity of Japanese official documents, even those that had survived. A legal doctrine making it sufficient that the defendant had occupied a senior position in an organization that committed atrocities greatly simplified the task of prosecution.

To reach upward through the Japanese military hierarchy, prosecutors therefore employed the legal doctrine known as "command responsibility," which had barely been considered by wartime planners and the UNWCC. The doctrine of command responsibility had been articulated sporadically since the early twentieth century.[87] After the Second World War, it was used to hold senior officers to account for atrocities committed by their subordinates, but it did not make clear how far up the military chain of command or in what circumstances a superior might bear responsibility for the criminal actions of his subordinates. Although effective acceptance of the superior orders defense did not interfere with the fundamental aims of the war crimes trial program, it differed with command responsibility. The breadth and uncertainty of the principle seriously undermined the aim of comprehensiveness that was still at the core of that program. Several factors influenced whether and how command responsibility was applied; uneven use of the doctrine then exacerbated the sense that war crimes trials were arbitrary regarding whom they caught and how heavy the punishments were. As a result, deployment of the doctrine of command responsibility ultimately damaged the credibility of the war crimes trials.

The doctrine of command responsibility was the means by which U.S. prosecutors targeted Lieutenant General Yamashita Tomoyuki in the first major Allied trial, held in Manila between October 29 and December 7, 1945. During Yamashita's tenure as commanding officer of the Japanese Fourteenth Area Army in the Philippines from October 9, 1944, his forces had committed extensive atrocities against Allied prisoners and Filipino locals, including during the siege of Manila in January and February 1945. The prosecution alleged that Yamashita bore responsibility for those atrocities. Prosecutors did not attempt to establish what Yamashita actually knew, or even what he could have known in the chaotic conditions in the Philippines in 1944–1945, but instead alleged that the war crimes were so extensive that Yamashita should have known of them and that his responsibility as commander was to prevent them. Yamashita's defense team pointed out that U.S. military law established no such principle, noting that "no one would even suggest that the Commanding General of an American occupation force becomes a criminal every time an American soldier violates the law."[88] Defense lawyers showed not only that Yamashita had been unable to exercise effective command as a consequence of American military action but also that he had issued explicit instructions to his subordinate commanders to negotiate a peaceful withdrawal from Manila. Those subordinates had disobeyed his commands. The court decided, however, that the scale of atrocities was such that Yamashita should not have been ignorant of them and that he should have prevented them. Accordingly, Yamashita was found guilty and was executed on February 23, 1946.[89]

The Yamashita trial has often been interpreted as an act of vengefulness by MacArthur.[90] The precedent that had been established raised misgivings in Allied legal circles because of the implications of such a stringent ruling for their own military hierarchies.[91] The greater consequence of the precedent, however, was to enable the prosecution of Japanese commanding officers everywhere on similar charges of responsibility for atrocities, even if they had issued none of the relevant orders.[92] With the principle of command responsibility at their disposal, prosecution teams could try to indict both a senior officer, who could be charged with command responsibility, and relatively junior soldiers—most commonly noncommissioned officers—who had directly participated in the atrocity. At the same time, the scope of the IMTFE trials could legitimately be extended beyond the so-called Pearl Harbor Cabinet that had authorized the 1941 attacks to encompass senior and notorious military commanders such as General Matsui Iwane, who had commanded troops responsible for the rape of Nanjing, and General Kimura Heitarō, former commander of Japanese troops in Burma. Flexibility in identifying command responsibility was important, especially in cases of "notorious" war crimes, in which pressure to achieve a conviction was greatest. If the likely principal perpetrators had died during the war, prosecutors tended to seek out the most plausible survivor for trial, even if that person had not played the central role in the atrocity, and to charge him with command responsibility.

The Yamashita precedent was not always followed. In sharp contrast, Australian investigators chose not to prosecute Lieutenant Commander Baron Takasaki Masamitsu for the execution of four captured Australian airmen on Ambon in March 1944, even though he was the commander of the unit that ordered and carried out the executions and even though circumstantial evidence indicated he had ordered them. Takasaki's subordinate, Katayama Hideo, who led the squad, was tried and executed, along with two junior officers, one of whom had done no more than drive the truck that carried the victims to the place of execution. Takasaki, however, had evidently convinced the investigators that he had not ordered the execution. He may also have been protected by his aristocratic status and perhaps by wealth.[93] Decades later, this case still rankled in the Australian press and in popular culture because of its seeming unfairness to the more junior personnel and the unwarranted exculpation of the senior officer.[94] In July 1948, in a pretrial stage, the French court in Saigon dismissed command responsibility charges against Miyoshi Ichiro for the murder, pillage, torture, and rape committed by troops under Miyoshi's command, on the grounds that Miyoshi had not ordered his men to commit these acts and had shown his intention to maintain good behavior on another occasion by punishing one of his subordinates for attempted rape. The court also noted that the defendants were not properly identified in the indictment, meaning that it could not be certain that they were the right people to charge.[95]

Japanese officials may also have indirectly influenced Allied decisions concerning whether to deploy the principle of command responsibility. The internal organization of the Japanese imperial forces was complex, and wartime circumstances had routinely brought changes to practical command arrangements. Consequently, Allied officials sometimes had to rely on Japanese officials' accounts of their own military's command structure. On December 10, 1945, for instance, U.S. investigators preparing for the trial of Lieutenant General Honma Masaharu sternly instructed the imperial Japanese government "to furnish this headquarters with an official statement as to the scope or extent" of Honma's command in the Philippines.[96] Although the Japanese government complied with such requests, there was a lingering suspicion on the Allied side that information might have been managed in order to exonerate favored figures.

Moreover, the Allied military authorities themselves sometimes had strong reason to exercise discretion in favor of Japanese commanders if they were likely to be useful in Allied postwar plans. In several parts of Southeast Asia, Allied commanders turned to surrendered Japanese forces for military support in confronting insurgent nationalist movements, relying on them well into 1946.[97] In a memo to the British War Office on November 18, 1945, Mountbatten vehemently objected to the arrest of senior Japanese commanders from Southeast Asia on war crimes charges, on the grounds that he needed them to transmit orders to their subordinates, who were engaged in action on behalf of the British.[98] Even in 1948, there was pressure to delay the trial of Admiral Fukutome Shigeru because of his value as commander of the remaining Japanese forces in Singapore.[99] In Indonesia in the closing months of 1945, Japanese troops played a crucial role in keeping order on behalf of the Allies in the face of the emerging nationalist revolution. Japanese troops in Semarang in Java fought with Indonesian rebels in October 1945 in a battle in which dozens, perhaps hundreds, were killed.[100] In Indochina, French military authorities offered immunity from prosecution to the one thousand to two thousand Japanese troops who had joined the nationalist-communist Viêt Minh, on the condition that they present themselves for immediate repatriation to Japan, thus removing themselves from Indochina.[101] In China, Indonesia, and Indochina, Japanese commanders had some capacity to win concessions on war crimes accusations by promising cooperation. This bargaining potential, though never strong, was not insignificant, because the weakness of Allied forces in these regions meant that they depended on the continued willingness of the Japanese military to help maintain order. Hinting to Japanese commanders that their liability for past war crimes would be tempered if they cooperated in the present in maintaining law and order became a common tactic across the whole region. A British naval officer in Jakarta wrote a piece of doggerel referring to the Japanese military commander in Java, General Yamamoto Moichirō:

> General Yamamoto, information now received
> Says you've executed prisoners who should have been reprieved.
> No action will be taken while the Allies you can serve
> But later you'll receive the sort of treatment you deserve.[102]

China was the site of the most far-reaching accommodation between Allied authorities and Japanese potential war crimes defendants. The end of China's war with Japan marked an intensification of the civil war between the ruling Guomindang and the Chinese Communist Party. Both sides not only sought to acquire Japanese military equipment but also to selectively recruit or conscript Japanese personnel for their own war efforts. Guomindang authorities placed the commander of Japan's China Expeditionary Army, General Okamura Yasuji, under no more than house arrest, even though he was a prime candidate for prosecution for his counterinsurgency campaigns in China.[103]

The problem of arbitrariness also arose in the IMTFE. Before the tribunal was convened, American authorities wrote to their counterparts in other Allied military commands asking them to identify Japanese figures who would warrant trial before an international bench. Although the criteria for proposing defendants were not set out, the intent was clear. These trials would be of the big fish: high-level Japanese political and military leaders who would bear overall responsibility for Japanese aggression. Australia, China, the United Kingdom, and eventually the Soviet Union all responded. The draft list, repeatedly revised, grew from an original three defendants to seven to thirty-two, before shrinking to twenty-eight.[104] The most notable act of discretion, however, was the U.S. decision not to place the Japanese emperor on trial, even though he had been Japan's head of state during and before the war and even though some Japanese people called for his indictment.[105] The basis for this decision was the assessment that the emperor was a constitutional monarch who had had no practical capacity to influence government policy and who had been manipulated by his ministers.[106] In terms of the principle of command responsibility that had been established in the Yamashita case, this decision was difficult to defend. It is generally accepted, however, that the Allies feared that the Japanese people were so attached to the emperor that any attempt to remove him would lead to a mass uprising. A trial of the emperor (and the likely sentence of death) would thus hinder U.S. plans to entrench liberal democracy in postwar Japan.[107] This reasoning extended impunity to other members of the imperial family as well. The emperor's uncle, Prince Asaka Yasuhiko, had been the highest Japanese military commander in Nanjing at the time of the massacre there but was never charged.

SELECTION OF DEFENDANTS

When arranging the trials, investigators had no alternative but to choose among the thousands of potential defendants available to them. British authorities decided in early 1946 that they would not pursue cases against suspects who were likely to be sentenced to less than seven years in prison. But in November 1946 this limit was reduced to one year, and in practice British military courts delivered many sentences shorter than seven years.[108] This decision meant that most British courts heard cases involving murder and torture. Other prosecutors were inclined to cast the net more widely and to pursue, for instance, cases involving beatings or the withholding of food or medicines, but they, too, gave priority to cases regarded as serious. In line with the practice they had already adopted at the investigation stage, the war crimes teams quietly dropped many junior suspects who might be expected to offer a plausible defense of superior orders. Ordinary soldiers who, for instance, had clearly obeyed a command to shoot or behead a prisoner were seldom prosecuted. Korean guards on the Thailand–Burma Railway who had done no more than bully prisoners into working harder were rarely charged unless they were identified as individually vindictive. The corporals and sergeants who had issued orders to the guards were much more likely to be charged. In one high-profile Thailand–Burma Railway case, heard in Singapore in 1946, the charge explicitly referred to the beating of prisoners by Koreans, but no Korean personnel were arraigned.[109] In the February 1946 Katayama case mentioned earlier, an Australian court in Morotai prosecuted three men of second lieutenant rank but did not charge the lower-ranking soldiers who had executed the four Australian airmen by firing squad.[110]

Out of the substantial crowd of remaining potential defendants, and with command responsibility as an enormously flexible tool, the Allied investigation teams had to decide which suspects they should prosecute and on what charges. Some British authorities expected in October 1945 that around five hundred trials would be needed, but they still anticipated that the process could be completed by the end of July 1946.[111] U.S. authorities had similar expectations.[112] Very soon, however, the potential scale of the program became apparent. By early November 1945, British forces in Southeast Asia had a suspect list with 1,117 names, along with 925 names from other commands. By July 1946, the number of suspects in British custody had grown to about 7,600, presenting a formidable challenge of management.[113] U.S. Navy investigators in the Pacific assembled a list of 550 suspects.[114] Although the growing scale of the investigations and prosecutions did not prompt any formal reconsideration of overall plans, it did generate subtle pressure to move away from the initial emphasis on comprehensive proceedings, in which every war criminal would theoretically be punished, and toward holding a smaller—but still significant—number of exemplary trials.

In most cases, the Allies chose to begin with a high-profile case. American authorities tackled Yamashita first. Then in Manila in December 1945, they charged Lieutenant General Honma Masaharu with responsibility for war crimes committed by his forces in the Philippines, especially in the April 1942 Bataan death march. Ōta Seichi and Nagahama Akira, Kenpeitai commanders in the Philippines in the brutal closing stages of the war, were quickly brought to trial. U.S. authorities also pursued those responsible for the deaths of several of the so-called Doolittle flyers. These American airmen had bombed Tokyo and other locations on the Japanese main islands in April 1942 in order to demonstrate the United States' capacity to strike back after Pearl Harbor. Several flyers were captured after they crash-landed in Japanese-occupied China, and some of them were paraded through the streets in Hangzhou before being publicly strangled. A U.S. court in Shanghai sentenced to death both the perpetrators of this act and their commanding officer.[115] Others among the Doolittle flyers had been executed after a Japanese military tribunal found them guilty of war crimes for killing civilians. Another U.S. court in Shanghai tried the Japanese judges on the grounds that they had unlawfully caused the death of men who should have been treated as POWs. But it then found "unusually strong mitigating consideration" in the fact that the American flyers had received a proper trial, and so imposed prison sentences rather than the death penalty.[116] In Japan itself, in addition to opening the military tribunal at Yokohama, the U.S. authorities gave high priority to prosecuting Japanese political and military leaders in the IMTFE,[117] which was modeled on the International Military Tribunal at Nuremberg. General Douglas MacArthur proclaimed the establishment of this court on January 19, 1946. As previously noted, twenty-eight of the one hundred or so suspects arrested in the first sweeps of late 1945 were charged. Less senior figures such as midranking military officers and POW camp officials were soon transferred to the jurisdiction of American military courts.

For their first trial, which began at Wewak, New Guinea, in November 1945, the Australian authorities chose the high-profile case of Tazaki Takahiko, who was charged with cannibalism.[118] Britain's first trial, begun in Singapore in January 1946, was of Japanese military personnel who had maltreated Indian POWs aboard a ship and then on Babelthuap Island in Belau (Palau).[119] The case was chosen because a few months earlier, in November 1945, British authorities in India had commenced the so-called Red Fort Trials of British Indian troops who had fought on the Japanese side as members of the Indian National Army, with the avowed aim of liberating India from colonial rule. The Red Fort Trials aroused great controversy because many Indians saw the defendants as patriots, even though they had fought alongside Japanese soldiers.[120] It was thus politically useful for the British in India to begin their war crimes trials with a case in which the main victims had been Indian, to emphasize the point that Japanese soldiers had mistreated Indians and to show that the British authorities were seeking redress. The first war crimes trial in Rangoon, which opened in March 1946, prosecuted thirteen Japanese soldiers and their commander, Major Ichikawa Seigi, on charges of carrying out a massacre at the village of Kalagon, near Moulmein. An estimated six hundred villagers had been killed on July 7, 1945, because some of them had collaborated with British special forces operating in the region behind Japanese lines.[121]

In their first case, the Dutch authorities in Indonesia dealt with Captain Sonei Ken'ichi, commandant of an internment camp for women and children in Jakarta, who was infamous for maltreating his captives.[122] The French authorities first prosecuted Japanese military personnel who had killed a former resident-superior (effectively governor) of Annam, Jean Haelewyn, and two others, a few days after the surrender, apparently because Haelewyn had insulted a Japanese officer by saying that he refused to take orders from a member of a defeated army.[123] For the Chinese authorities, the most important "notorious" defendants were five Japanese officers prosecuted for their role in massacres of Chinese civilians and surrendered soldiers at Nanjing in December 1937 and January 1938. They included a senior Japanese commander, Lieutenant General Tani Hisao, and two second lieutenants, Mukai Toshiaki and Noda Tsuyoshi, who were accused of engaging in a contest to be the first to kill one hundred Chinese people.[124] The main exception to this pattern of beginning with high-profile cases was the U.S. naval jurisdiction in Guam, which opened the very first Allied war crimes trial of a Japanese suspect in September 1945. The defendant, former Kenpeitai sergeant major Hosokawa Akiyoshi, was charged with beating two local residents a year earlier. The two victims survived to testify at the trial, and Hosokawa was found guilty and sentenced to twelve months in prison.[125]

When trials began, it still appeared that prosecutors would pursue all or most suspected Japanese war criminals. At the IMTFE, the chief prosecutor, Joseph B. Keenan, initially envisaged a second tranche of prosecutions targeting industrialists, senior bureaucrats, and ideologues, including the industrialist Sasakawa Ryōichi and the politician Kishi Nobusuke.[126] These potential defendants were retained in custody in Sugamo, though all plans for prosecution were delayed until the trials of the top-level leaders were completed. Elsewhere, large numbers of suspects were retained for future trials. Already, however, the goal of comprehensiveness had proved vulnerable to political, economic, and practical considerations. Allied investigators, moreover, had revealed a willingness to look beyond the immediate perpetrators of the atrocities and to take account of a potential suspect's position in the military hierarchy, as well as the military circumstances of the crime. The next, perilous, step was to bring the defendants and the charges to court.

3

IN COURT

Indictment, Trial, and Sentencing

The drafting of national war crimes legislation and regulations, the investigations, the gathering of evidence, and the arrests of suspects culminated in court proceedings that stretched from late 1945 to mid-1951, except for the trials in the People's Republic of China (PRC), which took place in 1956. Especially during the early trials, prosecutors, defendants, and judges all were sensitive to their many audiences. The trials would establish a record and a precedent as well as delivering individual verdicts, and all participants were conscious that much was at stake.

Every judicial finding is a wager on the future. The court relies on society continuing to recognize the validity of the laws that the court enforces, continuing to respect the validity of the court and its procedures, and continuing to accept the court's judgment of the crime's seriousness as reflected in the sentence. War crimes trials after the Second World War were positioned on the uncertain frontier of legal innovation, where none of these assumptions was solidly based. Moreover, given the large number of trials and defendants, the different prosecuting authorities and the relatively long period over which prosecutions took place, it was never realistic to expect consistency in the court proceedings, verdicts, or sentencing. The whole enterprise of war crimes trials on this scale was new; it was placed in many different hands simultaneously; and it unfolded during a period of rapid, dramatic political and social change. As a result, initiatives taken in a genuine effort to secure justice could easily come to seem arbitrary or biased, undermining the perception that the Allied trials aimed to attribute blame impartially and universally.

INDICTMENTS

One by one, starting in April 1945, the Allied powers began to decide whether there was sufficient evidence to send individual suspects to trial and to prepare the formal indictments. In most cases, the indictments comprised several specified charges or counts, each charge linking a single individual with a single event or sequence of events. The number of charges against any individual varied from one to a dozen.

Around half the trials throughout the Asia-Pacific region involved more than one defendant. Sometimes all the defendants faced the same charges, though they might eventually receive different verdicts and sentences. Netherlands Indies and French law allowed the joint trial of members of a Kenpeitai or Tokkeitai unit that had engaged in atrocities—meaning that individuals could bear responsibility for group actions even if they had not participated personally—but in practice, the Dutch trials focused on individual defendants.[1] In many cases, multiple defendants were tried for different combinations of charges in a single court case.[2] The largest such trial was conducted by Australian authorities on Ambon and then Morotai in early 1946. Ninety-two Japanese officers and soldiers were prosecuted for various combinations of fifteen different charges of ill-treatment of Australian and Dutch prisoners at Tantoei Camp on Ambon.[3] The largest British trial in Singapore had forty-four defendants.[4] Mass trials were held partly to hasten the processing of suspects, but courts sometimes also used them as an opportunity to encourage defendants to implicate one another.[5] Very large trials were difficult to manage. While discussing a case heard in the Australian court on Manus Island[6] in April 1951, the judge advocate general noted that although the trial records documented one defendant's confession to the crime of murder, he was found not guilty, but at the same time, guilty verdicts were passed on other defendants in the same trial for similar crimes. It appears the court simply could not keep track of all the proceedings.[7]

The crimes that appeared in the charges varied widely. A large proportion can be placed in the following three categories. First were the brutalities carried out in POW and internment camps, during the transport of prisoners by sea and on work sites such as the Thailand–Burma Railway. These crimes consisted principally of imposing harsh and sometimes arbitrary discipline, including public humiliation, restricted access to food and medical assistance, beatings that led to death, and summary execution. Rape was also an element in this category as a consequence of the highly unequal power relationship between guards and female prisoners. Poor conditions contributed strongly to the crimes. Most prison camps were makeshift affairs because Japanese military planners had not anticipated dealing with around a quarter of a million POWs and internees.[8] Detainees, often sullen and resistant, outnumbered guards, and neither side had much facility in the other's languages. Partly because Japanese shipping had been disrupted by Allied submarine warfare, food, clothing, medical supplies, and basic tools were scarce everywhere in Japanese-occupied regions, and in addition, camp commanders commonly withheld access to such resources for disciplinary reasons.

A second category of war crime was the murder of POWs and civilians, especially in the immediate aftermath of capture or upon the fall of a city. The Nanjing and *sook ching* massacres were well-known instances, but indictments also covered the execution of downed Allied flyers and the slaughter of prisoners who were, for one reason or another, inconvenient for the Japanese forces to detain. Japan had not ratified the 1929 Geneva Convention, which was specifically intended to end this practice, but in any case, the military pressures to dispose of prisoners had not disappeared.[9]

A third prominent category of crime related primarily to the treatment of POWs and civilians who were suspected of spying or of otherwise assisting the Allies. Kenpeitai troops, who had principal responsibility for investigating such cases, were commonly accused of torturing suspects, sometimes to the point of death, both to obtain information and to create feelings of terror. Moreover, both Kenpeitai and regular troops carried out reprisals against civilians suspected of working with the Allies against the Japanese empire.[10] Less commonly specified in the indictments were the forced prostitution of women, the pillage or pilfering of goods, the conduct of medical experiments not warranted by current standards of medical care,[11] and the use of POWs as labor for military projects. In French Indochina and Guomindang China, a significant number of charges were economic, including theft and extortion. General Douglas MacArthur sought to insist that only the International Military Tribunal for the Far East (IMTFE), and thus not the various Allied national courts, could prosecute crimes against peace. The Chinese authorities, in fact, also asserted their right to prosecute suspects on these charges. Accordingly, in August 1946 a Chinese court tried a former Japanese commander, Sakai Takashi, for crimes against peace on the basis of his alleged role in fabricating grounds for Japan's military intervention in China.[12] This trial, however, was the only proceeding in a national tribunal to prosecute crimes against peace.

The Soviet Union conducted trials at the same time as the other Allies but did so separately from the legal understandings and practical cooperation shared by the other powers. Like the Allies in Southeast Asia, the Soviet Union had retained very large numbers of surrendered Japanese personnel as an unpaid labor force. From these hundreds of thousands of prisoners, the Soviet authorities tried just under fifteen hundred as war criminals in Siberia. The prosecutions appear to have begun in August 1949 and were conducted under the criminal code of the Russian Soviet Federal Socialist Republic as a constituent element of the Soviet Union.[13] The charges differed greatly from those levied in East and Southeast Asia, as table 3.1 indicates.

The only trial publicized by the Soviet authorities was held in Khabarovsk in eastern Siberia between December 25 and 31, 1949, to hear charges against twelve former Japanese military personnel for brutal biological warfare experiments conducted in Manchukuo by the notorious Unit 731 and the related Unit 100.[14] In this case, the indictment was comparable to those in U.S. and British trials for unwarranted medical experiments, though the American authorities chose not to prosecute the Unit 731 personnel they had captured.[15]

Whereas the Nuremberg tribunal considered only four charges, the IMTFE indictment had fifty-five,[16] although many, as we will see, were eventually dropped. The first charge in the IMTFE indictment resembled the first count at Nuremberg in accusing the defendants of conspiracy to wage war in violation of international law, but the next thirty-five charges specified Japanese aggression country by country and circumstance by circumstance. This proliferation appears to have been mainly a device to give space for each of the eleven prosecution teams to take charge during part of the procedure. By contrast, the Nuremberg trial was prosecuted and judged by only the United States, the Soviet Union, Britain, and France.

TABLE 3.1 Charges Recorded Against Japanese War Criminals Held in Khabarovsk Camp no. 16, May 1953

Charge	Number held
Crimes against the Soviet Union	22
Aid to the international bourgeoisie	177
Espionage	1,022
Armed attack on a Soviet command post	1
Theft of socialist and personal property	20
Wrecking	1
Terror	35
Sabotage	205
Unlawful release from custody	1
Counterrevolutionary agitation	3
Failure to give information	2
Counterrevolutionary sabotage	8
Banditry	4
Attempted murder	1
Contravention of camp rules	1
Maiming	1
Total	1,484

Source: V. A. Gavrilov and E. L. Katasonova, eds., *Iaponskie voennoplennye v SSSR 1945–1956* (Moscow: Demokratiia, 2013), 154.

IMTFE Charges 37–52 were categorized as "Murder." The defendants were accused of formulating and carrying out a plan "unlawfully to kill and murder" American and British victims "by initiating unlawful hostilities" in December 1941; of conspiring "to procure and permit" the wholesale murder of prisoners of war, members of enemy armed forces, civilians under Japanese control, and crews of ships "destroyed by

Japanese forces"; and of committing murders during the Japanese attacks on China and the Soviet Union between 1937 and 1945. Counts 53–55, "Conventional War Crimes and Crimes Against Humanity," included inhumane treatment of POWs and internees, rape of female prisoners, illegal use of POW labor, withholding of proper medical care, use of poison gas in battle, killing of surrendered enemy soldiers and survivors of shipwrecks, pillage of property, murder, torture, rape and enslavement of local populations, and "failure to respect family honor and rights." Other specifications were closely tied to the colonial interests of the Western powers: making prisoners work in Japan and elsewhere "for the purpose of exposing them to the insults and curiosity of the inhabitants" and compelling Allied officers to salute and to work under the command of Japanese noncommissioned officers.

None of these specifications referred to crimes against Japanese subjects, whereas count 4 of the Nuremberg indictment specifically referred to crimes inside Germany, including the destruction of German Jews, which were specified as crimes against humanity. A comparable count at the Tokyo Trial might have referred to crimes against Koreans who, as Japanese subjects, could not, in formal, legal terms, be the victims of war crimes carried out by Japanese troops. No such count, however, was included. No documentary evidence has yet appeared to explain this omission, but it appears that two factors were critical. First, the idea of crimes against humanity was developed in the postwar trials explicitly to permit the prosecution of Nazis who had taken part in the Holocaust. The concept was new, and there was much uncertainty as to how well grounded it was. Since the Holocaust had no obvious analogy in the Asia-Pacific theater, as there was no campaign of extermination against any ethnic or social group, Allied prosecutors had no interest in seeking out cases in Asia that could be tried under this heading. Second, there was no significant demand from Koreans themselves, in either Korea or Japan, for the military trial of Japanese suspects for their actions in Korea or against Koreans. Instead, Korean politics was focused on pursuing Korean collaborators with the Japanese colonial administration and on the intense ideological conflict between left and right.[17] Regardless of the reasons, the consequences of this decision were significant: no prosecutions took place in the IMTFE, or indeed in any of the postwar trials, for crimes committed against Korean or Taiwanese people, who had been legally subjects of Japan throughout the war.

COURTS

All across the former Japanese empire, except in Korea, Allied military tribunals convened to judge the suspects who had been selected as defendants in the extensive investigation process. Although there were no trials in Thailand, Portuguese Timor, or the Andaman and Nicobar Islands (India), offenses in these territories were investigated and, in some cases, prosecuted. Australian trials in Darwin and the Soviet trials in Siberia were the only proceedings to take place outside the former Japanese empire. U.S. Navy trials began in September 1945; the U.S. Army began its first proceedings in October. Australia started trials in November, Britain in January 1946, China in April 1946, the Netherlands Indies in August, and France in September. Trials under the authority of the Philippines did not begin until August 1947, after independence from the United States in July 1946 (figure 3.1).

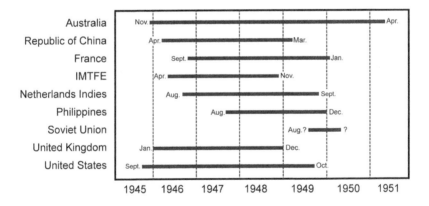

FIGURE 3.1 Date span of national trial programs and the IMTFE, 1945–1951.

The PRC's trials are omitted because they were held much later than the other national trials. Chaen identifies two French trials of individual Japanese suspects, both apparently civilians, in February 1946 but does not identify the men or the charges against them. The trial records of these men are not held with the others in the French archives. It is likely that they were tried on charges other than war crimes. See Chaen Yoshio, *BC-kyū senpan Chūgoku Fukkoku saiban shiryō* (Tokyo: Fuji shuppan, 1992), 274. The UNWCC's records suggest that Chinese trials had begun by March 1946. See UNWCC, Far Eastern and Pacific Sub-Commission, Minutes of the twenty-second meeting (March 8, 1946), PURL: https://www.legal-tools.org/uploads/tx_ltpdb /File_2826–2827_01.pdf.

Trials took place in fifty-three cities, towns, and camps, excluding proceedings run by the Soviet Union.[18] Most authorities chose to concentrate their trials in one or two places—the French in Saigon and the Philippines in Manila. The U.S. Navy held its trials in Guam and Kwajalein, and the U.S. Army in Shanghai, Manila, and Yokohama; British trials in Burma convened in just two locations, Rangoon and Maymyo, even though the offenses being prosecuted had been committed in many parts of the country. Within its own territory, Australia held most of its trials in Rabaul in New Guinea, though it also convened courts on Morotai in the Netherlands Indies,[19] at Labuan in British Borneo (for trials arising from the Sandakan death march) and in Singapore, Changi, and Hong Kong (including trials for offenses committed on the Thailand–Burma Railway). The last Australian trials were held on Manus Island.[20] The United States held trials in Shanghai to deal with crimes against American POWs in China. Singapore and Hong Kong became hubs for British trials of alleged war criminals whose offenses had been committed both locally and as far away as the Caroline Islands, New Britain, Japan, Taiwan, Cambodia, Sumatra, and the Andaman Islands (see figure 3.2). China, the Netherlands Indies, and the British authorities in Malaya, by contrast, convened courts in many centers. This practice reflected a desire to try alleged war criminals close to the scenes of their crimes in order to display Allied justice to local people. Whereas the British trials relating to the treatment of POWs were held in Singapore, charges of offenses against local people were heard in fourteen separate locations in Malaya, in addition to Singapore and Changi. A Kenpeitai sergeant major, Tanaka Hideo, for instance, was the only person tried in the small town of Raub in the hills of Pahang, on charges of killing two local Chinese civilians (see figure 3.3).[21]

The scale and grandeur of the courts varied enormously. The international military tribunal that convened in Tokyo in April 1946 to judge twenty-eight senior Japanese political and military leaders met in an imposing building in the district of Ichigaya that had previously been the headquarters of the Imperial Japanese Army. Britain held many of its trials in the similarly impressive Supreme Court building in Singapore. The high-profile trial of General Yamashita took place in the war-damaged ballroom of the former residence of the U.S. high commissioner in the Philippines. Trials in the Malayan town of Ipoh, by contrast, were held in the more modest circumstances of an old school building, and some of the Hong Kong trials took place in a converted

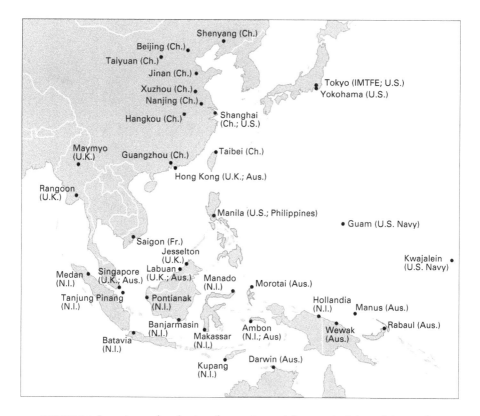

FIGURE 3.2 Location and authority of war crimes trial venues in Asia and the Pacific, 1945–1956 (excludes Soviet trials).

warehouse. Australian courtrooms in New Guinea and eastern Indonesia were often no more than makeshift buildings with corrugated iron roofs and open sides.

The heart of each court was the bench of judges, normally three in number, though there might be five in complex or high-profile cases and, as we have seen, there were eleven at the IMTFE (table 3.2). As a general rule in military courts, judges are expected to understand not just military law but also the realities of military practice. Moreover, military judges are usually expected to have a rank equal to or higher than that of the defendants. In many cases, however, one or the other of these conventions was relaxed. In China and the IMTFE, the judges were civilian, so that civil society could be better represented. Because senior officers were

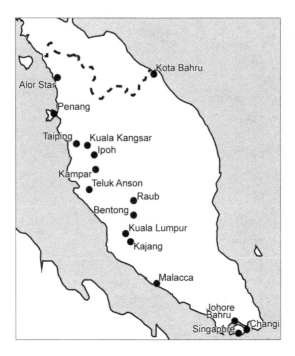

FIGURE 3.3 Trial locations in British Malaya.

needed elsewhere, judges in other courts seldom held a rank higher than lieutenant colonel, even when the court was arraigning Japanese generals.[22] In the prominent U.S. trial of General Yamashita Tomoyuki, all five judges were generals, but none had been commanders in the field. British and Australian authorities sometimes waived the formal requirement that at least one judge should have legal qualifications. In these cases, however, they normally ensured either that a junior legal official known as a judge advocate was present in the court to provide legal advice or that the judge had previous experience on the bench in war crimes trials. In U.S. courts, the judges never had legal training, but they were assisted by an additional "law member."

Some judges were potentially compromised by their immediate backgrounds. British judges were often drawn directly from the war crimes investigation teams; for example, the prosecutor in one trial might appear as a judge in another a few weeks later. The Philippine judge on the IMTFE,

TABLE 3.2 Number of Defendants and Trials by Prosecuting Authority (excluding the Soviet Union and the People's Republic of China)

Prosecuting authority	Jurisdiction	Number of trials	Number of defendants prosecuted
United States	Yokohama	372	1,061
	Philippines	97	215
	Pacific	47	123
	Shanghai	11	75
	Tokyo	2	2
	Total	529	1,476
Netherlands Indies	Ambon	49	77
	Balikpapan	20	88
	Bandjarmasin	10	30
	Batavia	171	419
	Hollandia	54	54
	Kupang	21	23
	Makassar	36	90
	Medan	59	136
	Manado	46	59
	Morotai	21	65
	Pontianak	19	36
	Tandjung Pinang	6	11
	Total	512	1,088
Australia	Rabaul	188	390
	Manus Island	26	113
	Morotai	25	148
	Singapore	23	62
	Labuan	16	145
	Hong Kong	13	42
	Darwin	3	22
	Wewak	2	2
	Total	296	924
United Kingdom	Singapore	130	466
	Malaya	67	165
	Hong Kong	47	126
	Burma	40	134
	Borneo	19	29
	Total	306	920
China (ROC)	Shenyang		136
	Beijing		115
	Taiyuan		11
	Jinan		24
	Xuzhou		35
	Nanjing		33
	Shanghai		181
	Hankou		162

(continued)

TABLE 3.2 (Continued)

	Taibei		16
	Guangzhou		170
	Total	605	883
France		40	
			233(including 53 in absentia)
Philippines		73	155
IMTFE		1	28
Total		2,362	5,707

Note: The first published work to present numbers of trials and defendants by prosecuting country was Hōmu daijin kanbō shihō hōsei chōsabu, *Sensō hanzai saiban gaishi yō* (Tokyo: Hōmu daijin kanbō shihō hōsei chōsabu, 1973), 266. This work, sponsored by the Japanese government in the mid-1950s as part of its effort to achieve the release of convicted war criminals, proposed an overall figure of 2,244 trials and 5,700 defendants. Despite its political intent (see Kushner, *Men to Devils, Devils to Men*, 231–32), its nation-by-nation figures have generally been accepted as reliable (e.g., by Hayashi Hirofumi, *BCkyū senpan saiban* [Tokyo: Iwanami shoten, 2005]). In 1979, Piccigallo reproduced the statistics from this work (Philip R. Piccigallo, *The Japanese on Trial* [Austin: University of Texas Press, 1979], 263–64, n. 10) but suggested different figures for the United States, Britain, and Australia based on other sources. The differences between the *Sensō hanzai saiban* and Piccigallo figures are not trivial. For instance, Piccigallo suggests there were 474 U.S. trials, whereas *Sensō hanzai saiban* has 456; Piccigallo suggests 1,409 defendants before U.S. courts, whereas *Sensō hanzai saiban* has 1,453. It is likely, however, that these differences reflect inconsistencies in record keeping by different authorities and technical matters of counting, rather than carelessness in either source: some trials were aborted because the defendants were ruled unfit for trial; a few were suspended and never resumed; some defendants were tried twice or three times for different crimes (sometimes by different jurisdictions); and a small number were retried for the same offense. In one or two cases, the surviving documents are ambiguous, allowing for different conclusions on the status of the trial. For a discussion of ambiguities in the British figures, see R. John Pritchard, "The Nature and Significance of British Post-War Trials of Japanese War Criminals, 1945–1948," *Proceedings* (British Association for Japanese Studies) 2 (1977): 280–81.

In this table we accepted as a starting point Piccigallo's figures and checked them against archival materials that we accessed directly (especially the National Archives [UK]) and the digital collection of the Forschungs- und Dokumentationszentrum für Kriegsverbrecherprozesse at the University of Marburg (hereafter cited as Marburg ICWC). These records suggest slightly different figures for the French trials and significantly larger figures for the U.S. trials in Yokohama (372 trials, 1,061 defendants, rather than Piccigallo's 319 trials, 916 defendants). For Philippines trials, we followed Sharon Williams Chamberlain, "Justice and Reconciliation" (PhD diss., George Washington University, 2010), 70. City-level figures for the Netherlands Indies are from Kōseishō hikiage engokyoku hōmu chōsashitsu hen, Tanaka Hiromi kaisetsu, *Sensō saiban to shotaisaku narabini kaigai ni okeru senpan jukeisha no hikiage* (Tokyo: Ryokuin shobō, 2011), 50–62. This work is a facsimile reproduction of a 1953 Ministry of Welfare report and may slightly understate the figures (Piccigallo has 448 trials and 1,038 defendants), but city-level data for the Netherlands Indies are otherwise unavailable because the trial files in the Nationaal Archief (The Hague) and the NIOD Institute for War, Holocaust, and Genocide Studies (Amsterdam) are still closed. The Batavia figures, however, have been corrected from L. F. de Groot, "De rechtspraak inzake oorlogsmisdrijven in Nederlands Indië (1947–1949)," *Militair Rechtelijk Tijdschrift* 78 (1985): 162. City-level figures for China are from Chaen Yoshio, *BCkyū senpan Chūgoku Fukkoku saiban shiryō* (Tokyo: Fuji shuppan, 1992), 5. In August 1948, the *Straits Times* reported that Chinese authorities had investigated 2,438 Japanese war crimes suspects and tried 1,455 ("War Criminals," *Straits Times*, August 16, 1948, 1). We could not, however, find corroboration for these figures. They may refer to summary trials by local authorities outside the central trials framework. Figures vary, but Iwakawa Takashi suggests that as many as 3,500 suspected war criminals may have been executed after "people's trials" (*Kotō no tsuchi to narutomo* [Tokyo: Kōdansha, 1995], 80).

Delfin J. Jaranilla, was a survivor of the Bataan death march; William Webb, president of the IMTFE, had investigated Japanese war crimes in New Guinea before the end of the conflict; Lieutenant Colonel R. C. Laming, who presided in British trials in Burma and Hong Kong, had been a prisoner on the Thailand–Burma Railway. Only in the Dutch courts was the defendant permitted to request that a judge disqualify himself on the grounds of personal involvement in the case.

Although trials took place under national regulations, British, American, Australian, and Dutch courts from time to time included judges from another jurisdiction if the offenses involved victims from that jurisdiction. Lieutenant Colonel Charles Monod de Froideville of the war crimes investigation branch of the Netherlands Indies army, for instance, sat as judge in several British courts in Singapore in which the defendants were accused of crimes against both British and Dutch POWs. An Australian brigadier, J. W. O'Brien, presided in the final U.S. trial at Yokohama, which acquitted Admiral Toyoda Soemu of responsibility for the rape of Manila.[23] The Nationalist Chinese government, however, declined to send its judges to other trials or to accept foreign judges in its own courts. With the sole exception of the United States in the Manila trials, the prosecuting powers never included local people with legal qualifications on the bench, although the British courts sometimes included Indian judges.[24]

The prosecution in most jurisdictions was run by the local war crimes investigation team. Assembled hastily at the end of the war, at a time when most personnel were hoping to return home, the teams were a mixed crew. Some had a legal or police background; others had no qualifications other than interest in the job. Raymond Plummer, heading one of the war crimes teams in Malaya, had no legal or police training at all.[25] Monod de Froideville had been a district officer in Indonesia's outer islands before the war. In a few British trials in Rangoon for the ill-treatment of American POWs, the prosecution was undertaken by Americans released from other duties,[26] and Canadian prosecutors appeared in some British and American trials involving crimes against Canadians.[27]

In the earliest cases, the defense counsel was also drawn from investigation teams;[28] soon, however, the courts began to use Japanese personnel with legal training, most of them former legal officers in the Japanese occupation administrations.[29] The Netherlands Indies authorities were forced into this arrangement because Dutch lawyers would not accept the brief to defend Japanese suspects.[30] Although they were spared the hard labor required of many other Japanese soldiers after the surrender, Japanese lawyers worked under difficult conditions, living in detention camps, receiving little or no payment for their work, and being banned from returning to Japan in the general repatriation of Japanese troops.[31] Still later, qualified lawyers were sent from Japan to take over defense cases.[32] The investigation teams also were responsible for providing interpreters. Initially the interpreters were drawn from the detainees, and most of them were former employees of Japanese firms operating in Southeast Asia. When it proved impossible to find enough such men—separate interpreters were needed for the defense and prosecution teams—they were recruited directly from Japan, with their wages paid by the Japanese government.[33]

PROCEDURES

In November 1945 Lord Louis Mountbatten, head of SEAC, commented that the trials of accused Japanese war criminals should be kept as concise as possible:

> The proceedings in court must be short and formal: I do not consider that any case of this nature need take longer than 30 minutes, including the time for interpretation. The sworn evidence as to the nature of the crime having been read out, it would only remain for the accused to be identified. He can then be pronounced guilty; and execution can take place within 24 hours of the termination of the case.[34]

The military legal authorities, however, quickly qualified this drastic approach, emphasizing the need for something more closely approaching normal procedure.[35] Accordingly, war crimes trials generally had a broad resemblance to civil criminal trials. Proceedings usually began with a statement of the charges and the identification of the accused. The prosecution made an opening speech outlining the case against the defendant(s) and then presented evidence. This evidence normally combined witness testimony, sworn affidavits, transcripts of interrogations of the accused made at the time of arrest, and documents, including unsworn testimony.[36]

The proportion of witnesses and affidavits varied greatly. Some Australian and American prosecutions for the ill-treatment of POWs rested entirely on documents. In such cases, no attempt was made to bring witnesses to Yokohama or Singapore, let alone to remote locations such as Rabaul or Labuan.[37] But the U.S. authorities would sometimes bring witnesses back to Asia from their American homes in order to provide direct testimony at the Yokohama trials, and the British authorities sometimes brought witnesses from their homes to Singapore. By contrast, prosecutions for crimes involving local people normally rested substantially on the testimony of witnesses who were examined and cross-examined in the courtroom, often through interpreters. Although some witnesses appeared eagerly, others were reluctant. In some cases, it seems, they simply wanted to put their wartime experiences behind them and did not relish the prospect of reliving them from the witness stand. Other potential witnesses recalled later that they had had misgivings about the war crimes trials in general, feeling that the narrow specification of the charges failed to take account of the extreme circumstances of war that Japanese soldiers had faced and that Japanese soldiers had behaved little differently from the way in which Western soldiers would have behaved—and, in some cases, had behaved—in comparable circumstances.[38] Japanese documents were seldom presented to court, partly because Japanese authorities had systematically destroyed prison camp records just after the capitulation.[39] Japanese documentation, moreover, was troublesome in that it had to be translated, and there was no pressing need to do so, given the admissibility of other kinds of evidence.

Westerners with legal knowledge often felt misgivings about the courts' substantive reliance on affidavits, because affidavit evidence could not be cross-examined, but Japanese defendants were more skeptical of witnesses, who, they believed, were willing to perjure themselves to ensure a conviction. In one case, it has been alleged that Australian soldiers perjured themselves in testifying against Japanese guards who were falsely accused of torturing and murdering an Australian soldier who had tried to escape.[40] Munemiya Shinji, who defended Japanese suspects in Ambon and Morotai, commented that former POWs were "inclined to exaggerate every ill-treatment they received; they are influenced by private considerations which are most harmful to fair justice." He was also skeptical of what he called the "caprice" of Indonesian witnesses: "They are, as is often the case with people who are under the influence of other nation [sic], intentionally or unintentionally, going to pick up and exaggerate the smallest wrong of the former influence (the Japanese Force) to curry favour of the present influence (the Australian Force)."[41] It would not be surprising if some Indonesian witnesses saw the war crimes courts as a tool of Australian power and did indeed judge that it was in their interest to testify against Australia's former enemies.[42] In another case, "a young officer of twenty-seven years of age was put into the empty cell next to mine," wrote war crimes suspect Fujii Hajime in the Philippines. "He was sentenced to be hanged owing to the usual false testimonies of thirteen Filipinos."[43] Owari Saburō, writing to his wife from prison in the Philippines, complained:

> I know of many people who died on the gallows because of the false testimonies against them. . . . In fact, practically all of the real perpetrators of the crimes have now gone home while those unlucky but honest persons who have a stronger sense of justice are left behind, made to shoulder and to die for the responsibility of others.[44]

The perception that witnesses had given false testimony later become one of the most important bases of Japanese claims that the trial process had been unfair.

Many defendants declined to testify or offered only an unsworn testimony, meaning that they could not be cross-examined.[45] This choice probably reflected assumptions in Japanese legal practice, in which evidence from the accused was normally understood as confession rather than as defense.[46] In fact, the practice in some war crimes courts converged with that of Japan: written interrogation records were sometimes deemed sufficient evidence against the defendant, and the defendant might be refused the opportunity to recant in court.

If the trial were straightforward—the facts of the matter were clear and the identity of the perpetrator appeared certain—then the proceedings might be over in a few days or even a couple of hours. The shortest U.S. trial lasted four hours, and one Australian trial in Rabaul lasted two hours.[47] More complex cases involving many defendants and multiple charges generally took longer. Proceedings that raised difficult issues could last longer still. The trial of Lieutenant General Sawada Shigeru and three others in Shanghai for the execution of the Doolittle flyers, for instance, lasted about six weeks. The U.S. prosecution of Sakaba Kaname and Suzuki Kunji in

1948 at Yokohama for command responsibility for crimes committed in POW camps in the Tokyo area lasted five and a half months, as did the U.S. prosecution in the same year of thirty former members of the Western Army Headquarters and staff of the Medical School of Kyūshū Imperial University for the murder by vivisection of eight or so American prisoners.[48] The defendants in this trial included a nurse, Tsutsui Shizuko, apparently the only woman prosecuted in the Asia-Pacific war crimes trials.

All the courts adhered to the expedited procedures that distinguished military tribunals from civil courts. Such procedures sometimes disadvantaged the prosecution, which had little time to prepare cases. The consequences for the defendants, however, were potentially far more severe. Affidavits and, in some cases, hearsay and unsworn evidence were permitted much more readily than they were in civil courts.[49] The choice of affidavits in the prosecution case was effectively in the hands of the prosecuting lawyers, drawn from the investigation teams, because they were the only ones who knew what material was available. It appears that they sometimes used this power to suppress evidence that might have favored the defendant. Moreover, the courts appear not to have taken account of the possibility that written confessions might have been obtained under duress. Whereas the prosecution could have witnesses delivered from other parts of the Allied detention system, the defense, if it called witnesses at all, generally had to make do with people who happened to be locally available. Defense lawyer Munemiya Shinji reported that Japanese troops were often reluctant to testify on behalf of their colleagues because they feared incriminating themselves.[50] Most accused were given little warning of when they were to be brought to trial, and the defense lawyers commonly had very little opportunity to discuss the case with the defendant.[51] It was rare, therefore, for fresh evidence to be presented to the court by the defense. The Rangoon trial of young prison medical officer Onishi Akio for neglect of POWs provides striking examples of the problems these procedures could produce.[52] Onishi's American prosecutor failed to present affidavits from three British doctors who had been held in the jail and who might have been in a position to comment positively on Onishi's actions.[53] Moreover, officials reviewing his case in 1954 concluded that Onishi's interrogation report had been obtained "by little short of 'third degree' methods."[54] He had not, moreover, been permitted to testify at his own trial. Onishi was originally condemned to death, though his sentence was commuted to life imprisonment.

In most procedural respects, the IMTFE in Tokyo differed from all other tribunals. First convened on April 29, 1946, it concluded its hearings nearly two years later on February 10, 1948, and handed down its verdict over four days, between November 9 and 12, 1948. Judges, prosecutors, and the twenty-eight defendants enjoyed the luxury of time. The court was supported by an impressive infrastructure that produced a daily account of proceedings amounting to 49,858 pages by the time the trial ended.[55] Indeed, the proceedings reportedly consumed one-quarter of all the paper used by the U.S. Occupation authorities in Japan at that time.[56] The defendants were provided with Japanese and American defense teams as well as interpreters and translators (though there were not enough of the latter) and had ample opportunity to muster their arguments.[57]

CASE FOR THE DEFENSE

Only a few of the accused meekly accepted the charges laid against them and pleaded guilty,[58] expressing remorse as they did so and appealing for mercy.[59] In some instances, senior officers accepted full responsibility for the crimes committed under their authority and urged the exoneration of their subordinates.[60] In the Philippines, Rear Admiral Furuse Takasue pleaded guilty to charges of ordering the massacre of civilians in Tayabas, insisting his subordinate bore "no responsibility whatever" for the crimes.[61] For those who pleaded not guilty, however, the defense generally depended on one or more of four categories of argument: weak evidence, ambiguities of responsibility arising from rank, military necessity (and thus lawfulness), and the Allied courts' lack of authority to conduct trials.

First, the defense commonly questioned the quality of evidence presented and its connection with the accused, pointing out imprecisions or contradictions in the accusations that made formal proof difficult, perhaps drawing attention to doubts over the identification of defendants, highlighting inconsistencies in the testimony of a single witness or among the testimonies of different witnesses, and emphasizing the problem of hearsay evidence.[62] When affidavit evidence was a significant part of the prosecution case, the defense sometimes complained about the impossibility of cross-examining it.[63] When the prosecution used the accused's own statements, the accused would often claim he had been misrecorded and sometimes that he had been tortured.[64] The accused sometimes presented evidence that he had not been on the spot at key moments.[65] Allied prosecutors believed that some Japanese suspects agreed among themselves to incriminate a particular person—preferably an officer who was dead, on the run, or already under sentence—as a means of escaping blame for command responsibility.[66] In the Philippines trial of Morishita Tsuneo, the defendant sought to blame Doi Kunio, whom he believed had been killed during the war. Not surprisingly, Morishita was disconcerted to be called as witness at the subsequent trial of Doi, who had been found safe and well in Japan.[67] A common form of the weak-evidence defense was that victims had been less harshly treated than was claimed in the indictment.[68] Defendants accused of cruelly beating captives routinely asserted that they had done nothing worse than strike the person with the flat of their hand[69] or that their striking or kicking of the victim had not been sufficient to produce the injuries claimed.[70] This defense was sometimes presented in cases involving the death of prisoners who may have been beaten but who were already in a weakened condition because of illness. It was sometimes stated that prisoners reported to have been killed had in fact survived. One defendant in a Thailand–Burma Railway case argued that conditions on the railway had been relatively good.[71]

Second, many defendants argued that their rank or place in the command structure freed them from culpability (table 3.3). Prison camp guards located responsibility for the welfare and discipline of prisoners with specific officers and asserted that it had not been their responsibility to intervene.[72] Similar arguments were presented in so-called hell-ship cases, in which strict lines of command and divisions of responsibility could be asserted.[73] Junior personnel offered the defense of superior orders, making strong claims regarding the harsh discipline imposed in the Japanese armed forces and the dire consequences of disobedience.[74] As we have seen, investigators had often implicitly accepted this defense in deciding who to indict, and knowledge of this fact may have encouraged Japanese defendants to use the defense of superior orders. Relatively few defendants, however, were ordinary soldiers or guards from whom absolute obedience might have been expected. More often, they were corporals, sergeants, and junior commissioned officers who, as in all armies, were expected to show at least some degree of initiative and independent judgment. Defendants of lower rank were generally in court because they were believed to have been cruel or brutal beyond the requirements of superior orders.

TABLE 3.3 Military Ranks of Japanese Personnel Tried
in Selected Jurisdictions

Rank	Australia (trials in Singapore and Hong Kong)	Britain (trials in Burma)	Philippines	Total
Senior officers	7	4	19	30 (8%)
Junior officers	38	37	54	129 (33%)
NCOs/warrant officers	30	86	47	163 (42%)
Privates	4	6	27	37 (9%)
Guards (Korean)	16	—	—	16 (4%)
Civilians	8	—	8	16 (4%)
Total	103	133	155	391

Note: In many cases, the defendants had been promoted in the time between the alleged commission of the offense and the trial; this table records rank at the time of trial. U.S. trial records do not consistently record ranks in the trial descriptions (though ranks can sometimes be determined from the trial proceedings).

Sources: British and Australian figures are calculated from archives in NA (UK) and NAA; Philippines figures are from Sharon Williams Chamberlain, "Justice and Reconciliation" (PhD diss., George Washington University, 2010), 71.

Similarly, in command responsibility cases, officers commonly argued that soldiers committing atrocities had acted without or even against orders.[75] General Sakai Takashi, arraigned because he had commanded troops who carried out atrocities in China, claimed they had acted without his knowledge.[76] Others asserted that they had had no control over the soldiers who actually carried out the war crime.[77] A sergeant, on trial for requiring two young women to kneel in the open all night, pleaded that he had told a subordinate to wake him at 10 P.M. in order to release them but that the subordinate had failed to do so.[78] One officer, accused of the neglect of prisoners leading to hundreds of deaths from disease, pleaded that he had instructed his men to treat the prisoners well.[79] Yamamoto Moichirō, the military governor of Java, was acquitted of responsibility for the ill-treatment of POWs and internees because not he but the commander of the Sixteenth Army was responsible for them.[80]

Third, many defendants argued that their actions had been consistent with military practice and military necessity and were thus lawful. Defendants accused of neglecting prisoners' welfare commonly maintained that the harsh conditions had been a consequence of the difficult circumstances of war and of tough physical conditions and thus were not proof of culpable neglect.[81] Tropical conditions in Southeast Asia and bitter winters farther north were beyond the control of the accused, and acute wartime shortages made conditions difficult for all.[82] Charged with brutality, defendants argued that the beating of insubordinate prisoners and internees was warranted as a means of summary punishment, especially given the absence of facilities such as provision for solitary confinement.[83] In some testimonies, the courts received a glimpse of the challenges faced by Japanese authorities in maintaining order within camps where bored, resentful men from different backgrounds were crowded together. Theft, rowdiness, extortion, swindling, brawling, and the lack of hygiene not only undermined Japanese authority in camps but also made life harder for the other detainees.[84] The punishment of offenders by Japanese authorities was not always unwelcome. Evidence presented in court occasionally indicates that senior Allied officers in camps consulted with Japanese staff over the punishment of recalcitrant or troublesome POWs.[85] Some Japanese defendants claimed they had given minor punishments to detainees in order to spare them formal disciplinary proceedings that would have been more stringent.[86]

The defense that punishment had been appropriate was especially important when POWs had been executed. In 1942, new Japanese regulations made the bombing and strafing of civilian targets a war crime,[87] meaning it was then legitimate under Japanese military law for commanders to order the prosecution and punishment of captured Allied personnel who had killed or injured civilians. Japanese authorities considered that captured Allied soldiers suspected of war crimes had forfeited their status as POWs and thus had no protection under international law.[88] A Japanese regimental commander in Burma issued the following order in February 1944:

Recently bombings in the Burma area have . . . become more intense[.] [T]argets of these attacks are not tps [troops] or military installations but the unfortunate inhabitants and non military establishments. One can realise the barbarism of these blind bombings. In view of existing conditions all captured enemy air personnel will not be treated as POW. Instead after having been searched for necessary information they will be handed over to the gendarmerie [Kenpeitai]. All of them will be dealt with severely by the area army excepting those who can be put to some spec[ial] use. They will be separated from other prisoners.[89]

Thus some Allied prisoners were executed after formal, if hasty, judicial proceedings.[90]

Defendants charged with killing civilians suspected of engaging in espionage or otherwise aiding the Allies often pleaded military necessity, sometimes pointing to harsh Allied military practice, including the dropping of the atomic bombs, as evidence that military necessity could lead to legitimate, albeit cruel, outcomes. Although the 1929 Geneva Convention gave significant protection to POWs, it gave no protection to spies or to guerrillas and other combatants not wearing uniforms.[91] Before the expansion of hostilities to Southeast Asia and the Pacific in the 1940s, Japanese troops had been engaged in counterinsurgency wars in Korea, Siberia, Manchuria, and China proper. In the Second World War they brought to newly conquered regions a strategic assumption that harsh measures were necessary and effective, and consequently they were ruthless in their treatment of local people whom they suspected of acting on behalf of the Allies.[92] In several cases, Japanese troops executed Allied soldiers operating out of uniform beyond the front line. Under international law such men, if captured, could legitimately be regarded as spies or saboteurs and thus were not protected as POWs even by the Geneva Convention.[93]

Finally, some defendants questioned the authority of the Allied court to judge them at all.[94] This defense sometimes cited the weak basis of the prosecution under international law: as we have seen, there was no formal international agreement protecting civilians, and Japan had not ratified the Geneva Convention protecting POWs.[95] The argument sometimes asserted the principle of *tu quoque* (you, too), declaring that brutalities carried out by the Allies deprived them of the moral authority to judge Japanese actions.[96] In some cases, the defense argument was based on the victims' status or situation. In December 1948, a U.S. judge advocate reviewed the case of twenty-one policemen accused of the brutal treatment of Chinese civilians held in jail in Osaka on suspicion of smuggling and other offenses. The judge advocate concluded that the beatings did not constitute a war crime because they did not occur as a result of the war but merely because the Chinese victims lived in Japan.[97] More complex was the prosecution of Takashima Shotaro and Asako Koichi for the ill-treatment of Indian laborers in New Britain. The Indians had been captured as soldiers in Singapore, had renounced their allegiance to the British Crown, and had sworn allegiance to the Japanese emperor. Prima facie, they thus came under Japanese legal authority and could not be the victims of war crimes. British law, however, did not permit the renunciation of allegiance to the Crown in wartime, meaning that the Indians' status might not have changed legally.[98] In a few cases, the defense that the Allies had no right to try the suspect rested on the claim by a defendant that he was actually an Allied subject and therefore not under the jurisdiction of war crimes legislation, which applied only to enemy subjects.[99]

VERDICTS, SENTENCES, AND REVIEW

After the evidence and the concluding arguments of defense and prosecution had been heard, the judges retired to consider their verdict. The time required for this step varied enormously. In one Australian trial, the bench retired for a mere five minutes before delivering a verdict of guilty.[100] The judges in the IMTFE required six months and produced a document of 1,781 pages, as well as dissenting opinions on specific issues from four of the judges and disagreement on virtually all points of the majority judgment from the Indian judge, Radhabinod Pal.[101]

Only sometimes does the written record provide insight into how the judges in military tribunals treated the evidence and argument that was placed before them. In British, U.S., and Australian trials, judges were not required to provide a detailed record of their reasoning.[102] We do not know whether judges applied any greater skepticism to affidavit evidence than, for instance, to witnesses who could be cross-examined. Occasionally a presiding judge explicitly repudiated the *tu quoque* argument as inadmissible in principle because the court could not hear objections to its own jurisdiction.[103] The IMTFE's procedure systematically excluded evidence that might indicate that the Allies, especially the Soviet Union, had engaged in aggressive war, ruling that illegal actions on the part of the Allies had no bearing on Japan's guilt.[104]

The Chinese, Dutch, and French systems required judges to provide grounds for their decisions, both to the court and in the written trial summaries, but the judges generally recapitulated the evidence rather than explaining their reasoning.[105] Their comments indicate that some courts took a coolly forensic approach to the evidence,[106] while others regarded the accused with bitter hostility. The Dutch judges in the trial of Sonei Ken'ichi, commander of the Tjideng (now Cideng) internment camp in Batavia, recorded fifteen considerations that led them to find the accused guilty of "systematic terrorism" and bad treatment of POWs and internees. Their reasoning includes the following:

> CONSIDERING that it was in the period of the Tjideng camp that the accused could for the first time really himself go thoroughly and make ardent and ample use of the opportunity to torment the internees confided to him, this period lasting for much longer than a year and being brought to a close by him on 20th June 1945 with the words: "All the women are going to die";
>
> CONSIDERING that although cowardliness has already been shown by beating and humiliating defenceless men in the 10th Battalion camp who had not been condemned to punishment, the cowardliness proper to sadists and brutes shown to weak, starving women and old people by striking them to the ground, brutally ill-treating them and humiliating them by cutting off their hair, resists every qualification.[107]

A British judge prefaced his sentence in one trial with similarly bitter words: "The time has now come for you to pay for the pain you have known so well how to inflict on helpless people. You are just brutes without any redeeming features."[108] Another addressed the defendant:

> Lieut. Kishi, the unanimous sentence of this Court . . . is that you will suffer death by hanging. The Court has taken into consideration the fact that you belong to a black race from which little or no decency is expected, but by no conceivable standard of conduct is there any excuse for what you did.[109]

Despite the advantages given to the prosecution, courts sometimes brought down verdicts of not guilty. Some cases were dismissed because witnesses were unconvincing or documents central to the prosecution turned out to be lost.[110] Some judges were persuaded during the proceedings that a defendant was the victim of mistaken identity. In some cases, the court accepted that the defendant's role in the crime was too minor to warrant conviction.

In the end, a total of 4,520 defendants, four out of every five who were prosecuted, were convicted of war crimes in the trials that followed the Second World War in Asia and the Pacific. The scale of acquittal is masked somewhat by the fact that most defendants faced more than one charge and were sentenced if found guilty on any of them. Every defendant in the IMTFE except Kimura Heitarō was acquitted of at least one charge, but none was exonerated of all charges. French courts marked those tried in absentia as guilty of contempt of court (*contumace*), and they were invariably found guilty on all charges, though the majority were never apprehended. Courts in most jurisdictions routinely dropped or at least amended charges found to be not viable.[111] The IMTFE judges ruled that they did not have jurisdiction to consider murder, so counts 37 through 52 were simply dropped during the trial. They also decided that another twenty-nine counts were redundant, so the verdict was eventually pronounced for ten charges only.[112] The conviction rates in the different jurisdictions varied from China's at 57 percent to the Netherlands Indies at 95 percent, but these figures are subject to so many qualifications that it is difficult to draw any firm conclusions from them (figure 3.4 and table 3.4). There is no strong pattern in the rate of acquittal among the different ranks across three sample jurisdictions or any obvious change in the likelihood of acquittal over time (table 3.5).

Before sentencing, the defendants could plead mitigating factors. A Japanese major found guilty of atrocities on the Thailand–Burma Railway was one of many who asked for mercy on the grounds of old age.[113] Others pleaded, like Nishi Yoshinobu, that they had a family to support.[114] A Japanese defense counsel argued that the death penalty was barbarous and would send the wrong message to backward countries.[115] One defendant pleaded his background of "sincereity [*sic*], punctuality, co-operation, earnestness and whole-heartedness" as a clarinetist in the prewar Penang Municipal Band.[116]

In considering mitigation, courts appear to have paid most attention not to health or family responsibilities but to evidence that the convicted man had behaved benevolently or honorably in other circumstances or, alternatively, had been manifestly ineffective. A guard at Sandakan in North

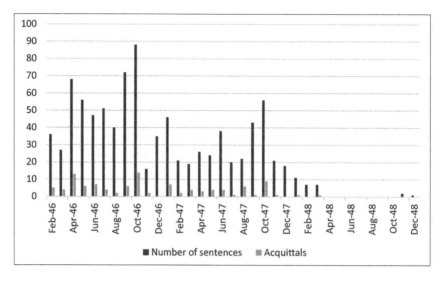

FIGURE 3.4 Trends in British war crimes courts: sentences and acquittals.

Borneo who had been ordered to execute five prisoners and who beheaded three of them received an eighteen-month sentence on the grounds that he had helped the other two escape.[117] The Philippines military commission that convicted Furuse Takasue altered his death sentence from hanging to "death by musketry"—considered a more honorable end for a soldier—in recognition of his public acceptance of command responsibility.[118] Colonel Banno Hiroteru, a senior commander of POW camps on the Thailand–Burma Railway, was described in courts as "an incompetent fatuous old man" and was sentenced to a mere three years.[119] It seems to have been difficult, however, for some defendants to assemble testimony that they had behaved well. In one case, a British former POW wrote to the authorities well after the event, asking whether he might send money to Sakamoto Shigeru, who had been convicted in the so-called Double Tenth trial involving the torture of Europeans in Singapore suspected of subversion. Sakamoto had been kind to him, but the former POW had not said so at the time, because of the "climate of public opinion."[120] In considering pleas for mitigation, judges sometimes acknowledged the harsh regime of the Japanese military and recognized that the perpetrators could have been victims of militarism just as the victims of war crimes were.

TABLE 3.4 Conviction Rates

Prosecuting authority	Number of defendants receiving a verdict	Number convicted
United States	1,409	1,229 (87%)
Netherlands Indies	1,024	969 (95%)
Australia	924	644 (70%)
United Kingdom	918[a]	811 (88%)
China	883	504 (57%)
France	233	204[b] (88%)
Philippines	155	138 (89%)
IMTFE	25	25 (100%)
Total (excluding Soviet Union)	5,571	4,524 (81%)
Soviet Union	2,883	1,690 (59%)
Total (including Soviet Union)	8,454	6,214 (74%)

[a] In fact, 920 defendants received verdicts in British courts, but the records of two trials have been lost, so the verdicts are unknown.
[b] Fifty-one defendants in the French courts were convicted of *contumace* (failure to appear, literally "insolence") rather than war crimes.

Note: The figures here refer to the number of defendants who received a verdict, thus excluding those who died or escaped during trial, who were ruled unfit for trial, or whose trials were not concluded. For instance, two of the original twenty-eight defendants in the IMTFE died during the trials, and one was ruled unfit for trial. The U.S. figures in this table differ from those in table 3.2 because we were unable to obtain the conviction figures that correspond to the revised Yokohama figures in this table. Note, too, that many defendants were tried on multiple charges and that those who were found guilty of one or more charges may have been acquitted on others.

Sources: Philip R. Piccigallo, *The Japanese on Trial: Allied War Crimes Operations in the East, 1945–1951* (Austin: University of Texas Press, 1979), 264; Sharon Williams Chamberlain, "Justice and Reconciliation" (PhD diss., George Washington University, 2010), 70; French records in Marburg ICWC; V. A. Gavrilov and E. L. Katasonova, eds., *Iaponskie voennoplennye v SSSR 1945–1956* (Moscow: Demokratiia, 2013), 17.

TABLE 3.5 Acquittal Rates by Rank in British, French, and Australian Trials

Rank	Britain		France		Australia	
	Total number receiving verdict	Number acquitted	Total number receiving verdict	Number acquitted	Total number receiving verdict	Number acquitted
Senior officers (lieutenant colonel and above)	48	5 (10%)	6	1 (17%)	7	—
Junior officers (lieutenant, captain, major)	218	36 (17%)	52	5 (10%)	38	4 (11%)
NCOs and warrant officers	401	50 (12%)	143	22 (15%)	30	9 (30%)
Privates	33	11 (33%)	20	1 (5%)	4	—
Guards/Koreans	64	3 (5%)	—	—	16	2 (13%)
Civilians Interpreters	28	5 (18%)	13	1 (8%)	8	1 (13%)
"Civilians"	81	9 (11%)				
Unspecified	38	2 (5%)				
Total	911	121 (14%)	234	30 (13%)	103	16 (16%)

Note: British figures are calculated from the slightly incomplete card index in NA (UK), WO 357/3. The actual number of verdicts in British courts was 920.

Except in the Chinese system, which prescribed a specific range of sentences for different offenses,[121] the war crimes tribunals received no guidance on consistency in sentencing. The Soviet Union abolished the death penalty in 1947, before the start of its trials, but reportedly still executed some convicted war criminals.[122] British authorities initially considered flogging as a penalty, even though it had long been abolished in both the British army and military prisons.[123] In the end the only sentences awarded by British courts were death or imprisonment, except in a single case, in which a fine was levied.[124] Some convicted war criminals received sentences as short as one year's imprisonment or less; in at least three cases, the sentence was to a single day of incarceration.[125] Courts routinely imposed a range of sentences even in joint trials in which the members of a unit were prosecuted on a single set of charges.[126] Even in the IMTFE, the rationale behind the sentences was hard to fathom. Despite the voluminous IMTFE trial records, there is no clear explanation for Hirota Kōki's death sentence. He was the only civilian to receive this penalty and had in fact been a leader of the antiwar faction until he was forced from office by the military in 1938. Although he had been the prime minister when Japan signed the Tripartite Pact with Germany and Italy, his engagement in the war had been minimal.[127]

In the Australian courts, a relatively high number of death sentences were passed against the earliest defendants: 120 out of a total of 148 possible death sentences were imposed (though not all these were carried out, as we will see) during the first six months. In most jurisdictions, however, the change in sentencing pattern over time was less marked.[128] The British courts imposed heavy sentences in the early period, followed by an interlude of lighter sentencing and a final, briefer period of heavy sentencing. The pattern suggests that prosecutors opened with the more serious cases, then turned to lesser offenses, before making a final attempt to resolve the remaining serious cases before the trial process ended (figure 3.5).

There is no evidence that sentences were systematically more lenient when the victims had been Asian, as has sometimes been alleged (table 3.6).[129] In fact, Arujunan Narayanan concluded that sentences in the Singapore trial for the 1942 *sook ching* massacre were more severe than usual because Chinese public opinion in the colony expected harsh penalties.[130] Although the proportion of death penalties imposed by the prosecuting powers varied substantially, it is difficult to attach meaning to these differences. The higher proportion of death penalties in the Philippines, for instance, may reflect the fact that Philippine courts tried a large number of murder and rape cases, whereas U.S. courts tried predominantly prison camp guards. Overall, however, there was a striking pattern in the distribution of punishment by rank. The more senior the rank of the convicted man, the more likely he was to get the death penalty and the longer his term of imprisonment was likely to be (table 3.7).

Because military tribunals were not formally judicial bodies but were advisory to the local military commander, every verdict and sentence had to be confirmed by the military commander, or his nominee, before it could be implemented.[131] Partly on these grounds, the United States

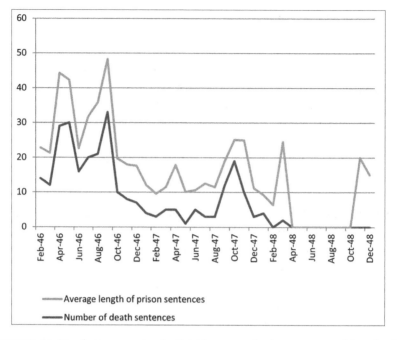

FIGURE 3.5 Trends in sentencing by British courts: death sentences and length of prison sentences. Data from R. John Pritchard, "The Nature and Significance of British Post-War Trials of Japanese War Criminals, 1945–1948," *Proceedings* (British Association for Japanese Studies) 2 (1977): 217.

Supreme Court refused to rule on the correctness of General Yamashita's conviction in 1945, as the proceedings had been part of the executive exercise of military government, not a court case that could be reviewed in legal terms.[132] Japanese soldiers convicted in French courts were permitted to appeal their sentence formally, though it appears that few did so; in other jurisdictions the convicted men had no direct legal means to contest their sentences.[133] But every jurisdiction had a process of review intended to prevent an inappropriate procedure or sentence. In the British, U.S., and Australian systems, a judge advocate, generally a junior officer with legal training, could, if it were deemed desirable, be appointed to sit in court and write a report on the legal validity of the proceedings that would be forwarded to the judge advocate general for consideration.[134] In the French system a government commissioner sat in court to play the same role.[135] Death sentences normally had to be

TABLE 3.6 Conviction Rates and Death Sentences

Prosecuting authority	Number convicted	Death sentences (death sentence as percentage of convictions)
United States	1,229	163 (13%)
Netherlands Indies	974	227 (23%)
United Kingdom	790	278 (35%)
Australia	644	148 (23%)
China	504	149 (30%)
France	203	63 (32%) or 26 (13%)[a]
Philippines	155	79 (51%)
IMTFE	25	7 (28%)
Total	4,513	1048 (23%)

[a] Thirty-seven of the French death sentences were pronounced in absentia; only twenty-six Japanese defendants who received this sentence were actually in French hands.

Sources: British figures are from nearly complete card files in NA (UK), WO 357/3; Philippines figures are from Sharon Williams Chamberlain, "Justice and Reconciliation" (PhD diss., George Washington University, 2010), 71; French figures are from Marburg ICWC; and Dutch figures are from Kōseishō hikiage engokyoku hōmu chōsashitsu hen, Tanaka Hiromi kaisetsu, *Sensō saiban to shotaisaku narabini kaigai ni okeru senpan jukeisha no hikiage* (Tokyo: Ryokuin shobō, 2011). Other national figures are from Philip R. Piccigallo, *The Japanese on Trial: Allied War Crimes Operations in the East, 1945–1951* (Austin: University of Texas Press, 1979), 264.

confirmed by the head of the national or colonial government (president, governor-general, or SCAP).

The convicted man was also permitted to submit a petition opposing the tribunal's finding, though this had to be done promptly and normally was done only in the case of death sentences.[136] U.S. and British military courts occasionally drew the attention of the officer whose duty it was to confirm sentences to procedural issues that had arisen during the trial, and at times the courts even recommended clemency for the sentenced war criminal.[137] Confirming officers sometimes overturned the verdict of a military tribunal altogether, quashing the verdict as unsafe. A review board in the Philippines commented that the court had "grossly

TABLE 3.7 Sentences According to Rank in British Trials

Rank		Total number tried	Death sentence	Life sentence	Average sentence (if defined)
Senior officers (lieutenant colonel and above)		48	24 (50%)	3 (6%)	11.7 years
Junior officers (lieutenant, captain, major)		218	87 (40%)	19 (9%)	8.25 years
NCOs and warrant officers		40	116 (29%)	22 (5)	7.9 years
Privates		33	4 (12%)	0	7.7 years
Guards/Koreans		64	11 (17%)	10 (16%)	9.0 years
Civilians	Interpreters	28	10 (36%)	1 (4)	7.8 years
	"Civilians"	81	18 (22%)	5 (6%)	7.3 years
	Unspecified	38	8 (21%)	1 (3%)	—
Total		911	278 (31%)	65 (7%)	—

Note: Calculated from card index in NA (UK), WO 357/5.

disregarded the evidence presented and superimposed in its stead a finding of their own which finds no basis in the trial record" and overturned the verdict.[138] In a handful of cases, confirming officers sent a convicted war criminal back for retrial.[139] They also altered sentences if they felt the proposed punishment was disproportionately harsh or if they identified mitigating factors. For example, in the cannibalism case tried by an Australian court at Wewak in November 1945, the defendant claimed he had consumed a dead body as his only possible form of sustenance. The confirming officer accepted his claim and reduced his sentence.[140]

The presence of a confirming officer, however, did not necessarily protect a convicted man, because confirming officers did not always overturn verdicts even if they felt uncomfortable with some aspect of the trial. The Australian judge advocate general, reviewing the trial of forty-six prison camp guards, most of them Korean, at Labuan in January 1946, for allegedly frequent assaults on prisoners between May 1942 and September 1945, commented:

> This trial is unsatisfactory. The great number of the accused tried jointly make it extremely difficult to follow and allocate evidence to the individual and in addition, the evidence for the prosecution consisted of wholly written documents a great deal of the contents of which was irrelevant, even taking into context the relaxed rules of evidence by the [War] Crimes Act and it is difficult to be sure that such irrelevant evidence did not have some effect on the members of the court.[141]

Nonetheless, he left the sentences unchanged. Even more significant was the fact that in the Australian system, the decision of the judge advocate general was not legally binding; rather, it constituted advice to the confirming officer. In many cases the judge advocate general's advice was not followed, for reasons that the confirming officer was under no obligation to explain.[142]

British confirming officers altered around 17 percent of the verdicts by reducing sentences or ordering the defendant to be released.[143] In all jurisdictions, a significant number of death sentences were commuted to prison terms.[144] In the Netherlands Indies, the confirming officer could make the sentence harsher, even requiring the death penalty when it had not originally been handed down. Unlike in other systems, however, the decision of the confirming officer had to be referred back to the judge for his assent.[145] At times, this process led to a long, confrontational negotiation between the two. In 1949, the Netherlands Indies confirming authority refused to approve sentences in six cases, including the acquittal of the former Java commander, Imamura Hitoshi. He reluctantly confirmed three of the outcomes, including Imamura's, only on December 24, 1949, on the eve of the end of Dutch colonial rule in Indonesia.[146] In China, the review process could not formally overturn the sentence, but Chinese authorities intervened to have General Okamura Yasuji found not guilty of war crimes at Nanjing so they could use him to recruit Japanese soldiers to the Guomindang cause against the Chinese Communist Party.[147] Verdicts and sentences from the IMTFE were confirmed by the Allied Council for Japan, the Tokyo-based body that theoretically oversaw the Occupation, and then by SCAP.[148] Once again, the pattern of clemency at review stage demonstrated the inclination of Allied authorities to recognize superior orders as a mitigating factor (table 3.8).

TABLE 3.8 British Trials: Commutation and Remission of Sentence at Time of Confirmation

Rank		Death sentence	Death sentence commuted at confirmation	Prison sentence remitted at confirmation
Senior officers (lieutenant colonel and above)		24 (50%)	0	1
Junior officers (lieutenant, captain, major)		87 (40%)	7 (8%)	6
NCOs and warrant officers		116 (29%)	7 (6%)	8
Privates		4 (12%)	1 (25%)	2
Guards/Koreans		11 (17%)	5 (4.5%)	12
Civilians	Interpreters	10 (36%)	0	3 (30%)
	"Civilians"	18 (22%)	11 (61%)	6 (33%)
	Unspecified	8 (21%)	2 (25%)	2 (25%)
Total		278 (31%)	33	40

Note: Calculated from card index in NA (UK), WO 357/5.

The final verdict of one court did not necessarily end the matter. Admiral Hara Teizō, for instance, was acquitted in a British court for crimes allegedly committed in the Andaman Islands, but he was subsequently arraigned by another court, found guilty, and sentenced to death.[149] Convicted men were sometimes transferred to face trial in other jurisdictions. General Tanaka Hisakazu, the last Japanese governor of Hong Kong, was tried by the United States in Yokohama and sentenced to death before being handed over to the Chinese authorities in Guangzhou. There he received the same sentence, which the Chinese authorities carried out on March 27, 1947.[150] Rear Admiral Hamanaka Kyoho was sentenced to fifteen years in prison by an Australian court in Morotai in January 1946 before being transferred to the Netherlands Indies authority for trial in Manado.[151] Shimojo Harukichi, sentenced by a British court in Singapore to four years' imprisonment in July 1946 for crimes on the Thailand–Burma Railway, was then handed to the Australian court there, where he received a death sentence (which was later commuted).[152] Nishimura Takuma was sentenced to twenty-one years in Singapore on April 2, 1947, but was transferred to the Australian authorities on March 21, 1950, and sent to Manus Island, where he was put on trial and condemned to death for the mistreatment of POWs. He was one of the last Japanese war criminals to be executed, on June 11, 1951.[153]

In describing the trials and the sentences, public rhetoric on the Allied side consistently repudiated the word "vengeance." According to Joseph Keenan in his opening address to the IMTFE: "Our purpose is one of prevention or deterrence. It has nothing whatsoever to do with the small meaner objects of vengeance or retaliation."[154] Nonetheless, the remainder of Keenan's speech announced precisely this object; in repudiating vengeance, he evidently meant only to repudiate disproportionate retaliation as well as to cloak himself in moral probity. Other goals of punishment also hovered in the background. Sometimes directly in sentencing, sometimes in the broader planning process, officials expressed their firm belief or pious hope that the trials would deter Japan from future excesses, that society would be better without the convicted man's presence, or that time in prison would enable war criminals to recognize the moral character of their deeds. A British judge in Singapore addressed Muneyuki Yasuo upon his conviction: "You will be given a long time to reflect on the fact that there are more manly pursuits for a man of 25 years than flogging an old man of 77 years."[155]

EXECUTION

War criminals whose sentence of death had been confirmed were generally executed promptly unless they were required to give evidence in other trials.[156] Most of the prosecuting powers were punctilious in the procedure to be followed between sentence and execution. The British military authorities in Malaya ruled that executions should take place within twenty-four hours of confirmation of sentence, though the interval later stretched to several weeks.[157] Regulations specified the means of execution, the witnesses who should be present, and the requirement to complete a death certificate. Occasionally the condemned man received a sedative before execution.[158] In the British, American, and Australian jurisdictions, those whose crimes were judged most heinous were hanged; shooting was considered a more honorable death for a military man.[159] In French Indochina, where shooting was the standard means of execution, an official carefully recorded the places on the corpse where the bullets had entered, including the "coup de grâce" to the temple. Newspapers reported the last minutes of the condemned men, their mostly unfaltering steps to the gallows and usually a final cry of "Tennō heika banzai" (Long live the emperor).[160] Nonetheless, there were occasional reports of botched executions. In June 1947, three witnesses at a hanging in Singapore alleged that the executed men were not in fact dead.[161]

In China, condemned men were sometimes paraded through the streets in front of jeering crowds before being shot publicly by firing squad.[162] The British commonly kept a photographic record of the condemned man's final steps and of the hooded body dangling from the rope. SCAP, in contrast, banned external witnesses and photographs when the seven IMTFE convicts were hanged on December 23, 1948.[163] The Soviet authorities are estimated to have executed three thousand Japanese captives as war criminals after summary proceedings, even though there was officially no death penalty.[164]

After the execution, in some cases a Japanese officer or priest was allowed to take from the body a strand of hair and fingernail cuttings to send to the dead man's family in Japan, to facilitate Buddhist ceremonies for the dead.[165] After executions in Saigon until late 1946, a Japanese officer was allowed to remove part of one of the dead man's fingers, for the same reason.[166] But then SCAP asked the French government to cease the practice, as "the policy in the cases of executed war criminals provides that no portion of the body will be preserved for possible later use in shrines to be erected commemorating war criminals."[167] The biographer of executed war criminal Hirota Kōki claims that despite SCAP's precautions to prevent the preservation of war criminals' remains, some of the ashes of the IMTFE convicts executed at Sugamo Prison were recovered in the middle of the night on Christmas Eve 1948 and preserved for later enshrinement at the Yasukuni Shrine, a major Shinto shrine in Tokyo that commemorates the Japanese dead of all wars.[168]

The rest of the body was generally buried with a simple marker. General Yamashita's grave was indicated by a plain white stake.[169] Authorities in

Hong Kong and Singapore sometimes burned the corpse or disposed of it at sea so that no grave might become a site for paying respect to a war criminal.[170] Relatives' requests for permission to collect the prisoners' remains were routinely refused, and they were sometimes not told where the executed prisoners were buried.[171] Only from the mid-1950s did Japanese authorities undertake the serious collection of the remains of executed war criminals if their graves could be located.[172]

The last known execution of a convicted Japanese war criminal by Chinese authorities took place in March 1947.[173] The seven men sentenced to death by the IMTFE on November 12, 1948, were hanged on December 23, 1948. The British authorities carried out their last executions in Singapore on January 16, 1948, and in Hong Kong on March 22, 1949.[174] The U.S. authorities executed the last batch of prisoners they had condemned in August 1949, having handed over to the Philippines in May 1947 responsibility for executing war criminals sentenced to death by the U.S. court in Manila before independence.[175] The Dutch authorities also carried out their last executions in August 1949.[176] The final executions took place in the Philippines in January 1951, in Indochina in March, and on Manus Island in June.[177]

The term "victors' justice" did not gain currency until the publication of Richard Minear's book of that title in 1971,[178] but fear that the courts were inherently illegitimate had hovered over the prosecutions from the start. Most acutely, it is hard to imagine that the judges who sat on tribunals prosecuting Japanese judges for the wrongful conviction of Allied flyers, shot down after bombing raids on Japanese territory, did not reflect at least in passing on the contingent nature of their own authority. Could they themselves have been arraigned in the unlikely event of a different outcome to the war? U.S. Supreme Court justice Frank Murphy foreshadowed an enduring public criticism of the trials when he described the procedures used in prosecuting General Honma as unconstitutional and as risking "a procession of judicial lynchings without due process of law."[179] In February 1946, Australian newspapers were relieved to report that the Japanese defense counsel on Morotai had formally thanked the Australian authorities for the fairness of the trials.[180] It was not only the verdicts, however, that were hostage to the future. The safety of the sentences, especially custodial ones, balanced precariously on the expectation that moral choices taken in the courtroom would remain viable indefinitely. It soon became evident that they would not.

4

DILEMMAS OF DETENTION
AND THE FIRST MISGIVINGS

Spread across a dozen jurisdictions in Asia and the Pacific and a turbulent half decade of postwar transformation, the war crimes trials delivered verdicts on a handful of civilian politicians and around 5,700 former personnel of the Japanese armed forces, of whom a little more than 1,000 were acquitted. Some died in the course of the trials; a few were discharged as insane; and the records of a few others were sourly annotated with the comment "insufficient evidence." Those who were not convicted had their files closed and then disappeared from the war crimes trials process. If they had been tried in the U.S. court at Yokohama, they were free to go home, providing a home existed in battered postwar Japan. If they were tried elsewhere, they were tipped back into the huge pool of Japanese surrendered personnel, prisoners of war, and expatriate civilians awaiting repatriation from Japan's former empire. The vast majority of convicted war criminals, however, now faced prison terms ranging from a few months to life.

Every sentence imposed by a war crimes tribunal bundled together a set of distinct, though interconnected, justice considerations: revenge, deterrence, prevention of further crime (or removal of the criminal), and rehabilitation. The sentencing process fused the intricacy of the individual crime and the vast complexity of the court's moral philosophy into a decision either to execute a prisoner who had been found guilty or to incarcerate him indefinitely or for a set number of days, months, or years. A custodial sentence expressed a rough estimate of the time that would be necessary to achieve the aims of punishment. Yet for each aim, the time needed in prison was different. Detention, moreover, produced new dilemmas. Many prisoners were incarcerated in areas of the former Japanese empire that had been heavily damaged or that faced new threats from independence movements. It soon became clear that carrying out the sentences imposed by the courts would not be straightforward. And as time passed, it became less certain that deterrence was relevant to war crimes or that rehabilitation was likely to be achieved at the level of the individual. As a result, the terms of incarceration began to be reconsidered: where should war criminals be imprisoned, who should bear the cost, and how long should they remain incarcerated? Decisions on these matters were shaped by political, economic, and legal pressures at every turn.

One important aim of the war crimes trials was achieved as soon as the sentences were publicly declared. In pronouncing death or life or some other term in prison, the judge expressed on behalf of society an assessment of the degree of the crime's iniquity and, at the same time, validated the system of laws and procedures that had produced this result. For many observers, the important fact was that the war criminals had been found guilty and would be punished, not that punishment should continue for any specific length of time. The significance of the declaration of guilt and of the sentence, however, quickly faded after the verdict had been reported in the press, the bodies of executed men had been quietly disposed of, and the rest had been consigned to their cells. The pronouncement of sentences stood in the public record and in public memory, but the implementation of sentences took place behind high walls, invisible to the vast majority of people.

Whereas their arrest, trial, and conviction had been based on extensive, if somewhat chaotic, legal preparation, hardly any thought had been given to the question of how those with custodial sentences might be managed after conviction. In a handbook sent to the South East Asia Command (SEAC) on May 19, 1946, the Legal Section of the Supreme Commander for the Allied Powers (SCAP) described the trial procedures in detail but touched on what came next in one sentence: "As a general policy a sentence of imprisonment will be served in the civil prison of the country in which the trial was held."[1] This simple statement masked both the legal complexities and the growing practical and political problems that eventually led to the transfer of all remaining convicted war criminals to Japan for incarceration in Sugamo Prison in Tokyo.

PRISONS

From December 1945 onward, Sugamo was the sole place in Japan where convicted war criminals were imprisoned. In Hong Kong, the British authorities requisitioned the civilian prison at Stanley for military detentions; in Singapore, they took over Changi and Outram Road jails and, in Rangoon, the Central Jail; and in Malaya they arranged to have the suspects housed in half a dozen jails that were still under civilian authority, but there they were kept separate from other prisoners. French authorities in Indochina used the newly constructed Maison centrale de Saigon (Chí Hòa Prison) and the penitentiary on Poulo Condore (Côn Sơn Island, off the coast of southern Vietnam), while the Netherlands Indies used Tjipinang (now Cipinang) Prison outside Batavia (Jakarta). Australia and the U.S. Navy lacked substantial prisons in their territories, so they resorted to specially built compounds at Wewak, Labuan, Morotai, Rabaul, Kwajalein, Guam, and, later, on Manus Island. War criminals convicted in the Australian courts in Singapore and Hong Kong served their sentences in Changi and Stanley.

Prison superintendents in the British colonies coped with war criminals by crowding other inmates, incarcerated for ordinary crimes, into the remaining space, but they became increasingly uneasy as more and more sentences were passed. "It is requested that you advise where these people can be incarcerated," wrote the government secretary in Malaya to the inspector of prisons in May 1946, "since it is feared that the War Crimes Courts may soon start sentencing war criminals to punishments other than death."[2] The British military authorities predicted that prison space would have to be found for around one thousand convicted war criminals in Malaya and Singapore alone by the end of 1946.[3] On June 1, 1948, after the U.S. authorities complained they were running out of space, the Philippine government agreed to transfer convicted prisoners from the U.S.-run Luzon Prisoner of War Camp no. 1 to New Bilibid Jail, a civilian prison in Muntinlupa on the outskirts of Manila.[4]

Crowding was also a problem in Sugamo. The commanding officer at the jail, Colonel Francis W. Grary, reported to SCAP that as of June 30, 1947, the prison held 1,040 prisoners, about half of them already convicted. Grary expected another 113 prisoners to arrive very soon from Manila.[5] Some prisoners in Sugamo were awaiting transfer to the courtrooms of other prosecuting governments, but they numbered only 130 or so.[6] Suspects might be released from Sugamo if it seemed they would not eventually be charged, and several high-profile suspects were indeed freed in August 1947,[7] but such releases were likely to be few at this stage. According to an Eighth Army report in October 1947, 55 suspects apprehended after the war had been held for nearly two years in anticipation of trials that had not yet been planned. Moreover, apprehension orders were current for 744 suspects yet to be taken into custody, so it appeared that in the short term at least, Sugamo's population was unlikely to shrink.[8] The fact that the Yokohama court sentenced convicted war criminals to prison terms with hard labor also led to practical problems. In November 1949, more than 1,000 prisoners were held in Sugamo on hard-labor sentences, but authorities could find jobs for only 599 of them.[9]

Although the 1946 SCAP directive had confidently stated that prison terms would be served "in the civil prison of the country in which the trial was held," this arrangement produced significant legal complications in some jurisdictions. As we have seen, the tribunals that convicted war criminals were not formally judicial bodies but were advisory to military commanders in the exercise of their executive power. This meant that strictly speaking, war criminals could be detained only on the continuing authority of a military commander exercising wartime powers.[10] The immediate postwar structure of Allied military authority in Asia and the Pacific, however, began to evaporate once the most urgent tasks associated with accepting the Japanese surrender had been completed. The British Military Administration in Burma was wound up on January 31, 1946, in Hong Kong on March 1, and in Malaya and Singapore on April 1, 1946; Australia handed civil responsibilities back to the Dutch in eastern Indonesia in February 1946.[11] Britain terminated its postwar mandate in Vietnam in March. The United States granted independence to the Philippines on July 4, 1946, while Burma became independent on January 4, 1948. France recognized the independent state of Vietnam on June 14, 1949, though it retained a significant degree of influence there, and the Netherlands transferred sovereignty to the Republic of Indonesia at the end of December 1949. In October 1949, after a long civil war, Mao Zedong proclaimed the inauguration of the People's Republic of China (PRC), and two months later, the government of Republican China withdrew to the island of Taiwan. Guam was transferred from the U.S. Navy to the U.S. Department of the Interior in August 1950. The most stable jurisdictions were Japan, where U.S. authority remained in place in the form of SCAP until April 1952, and New Guinea, where Australia's League of Nations mandate to govern the former German colony shifted seamlessly to a mandate to administer New Guinea as a United Nations trust territory.[12] None of the changes invalidated judgments that had already been passed, and indeed, trials continued in many jurisdictions even after new political arrangements had been made. Nonetheless, the new circumstances created uncertainty. In July 1946, officials in Hong Kong ordered a halt to the execution of Japanese war criminals who had been sentenced to death, so as to consider whether new legislation might be needed to validate the earlier sentences following the return to civilian rule.[13] Throughout the region, cautious bureaucrats began to allude to a new and increasingly pressing question: just who was responsible for the continued incarceration of convicted Japanese war criminals?

The prisoners in the most critical legal position were held under Australian authority on the British island of Labuan and the Netherlands Indies island of Morotai. With the restoration of civil rule on both islands, the military authority that had sustained the detentions expired, and Australia had no choice but to transfer the prisoners to another jurisdiction. Accordingly, they were sent to Rabaul in Australian New Guinea in January and February 1946. Japanese war criminals convicted by Australian courts remained, however, in prisons in Singapore and Hong Kong. A similarly acute problem arose in 1947 as the independence of Burma approached. Eighty-five convicted war criminals had been consigned to the Rangoon Central Jail by British courts, but it was far from clear that the Burmese government, due to assume sovereignty on January 4, 1948, could or would take over from SEAC the authority to continue to imprison war criminals. Relations between the departing British authorities and the incoming Burmese government were strained, and the colonial government had itself issued legislation granting amnesty for crimes committed during the war years by Burmese forces allied with Japan.[14] There appeared to be every chance that independent Burma might simply release the war criminals in its charge. The secretary of state for Burma therefore sternly reminded the governor of Burma that it would be Burma's responsibility as an independent nation to shoulder part of the collective burden of punishing war criminals.[15] One possibility was to shift the prisoners incarcerated in Rangoon to Singapore, but the British authorities in Singapore were unwilling to allow this, as Changi was already overcrowded. A compromise was reached by dividing the Rangoon convicts into those who had committed crimes against Burmese nationals and those who had committed crimes mainly against Allied POWs and internees. At the last minute—on December 11, 1947—the Colonial Office in London and the departing colonial authorities in Rangoon persuaded the nascent Burmese government to continue to imprison the convicts who had committed crimes against Burmese people on condition that the remainder would be shipped to Singapore.[16]

Even though SCAP had decreed that convicted criminals be jailed close to the scene of their crimes, the imprisoning authorities soon began to concentrate war criminals in a smaller number of centers where they could be more closely and consistently supervised. Prisoners tried by American courts on Guam and Kwajalein were dispatched to Sugamo Prison in Tokyo; the first group of 11 Japanese military personnel arrived at Sugamo on June 24, 1947.[17] The U.S. government ordered the transfer to Sugamo of 114 prisoners suspected or convicted of crimes against American nationals in the Philippines, with the last of them arriving in July 1947.[18] Prisoners of the Dutch were gradually shifted from other jails to Tjipinang Prison in Batavia. Prisoners concentrated by the Australian government in Rabaul were sent to Manus Island in March 1949. Manus, an isolated island under Australian administration north of New Guinea, about 811 square miles (2,100 sq km) in area, had been a U.S. base during the war. In early 1949 it was described in a press report as a "deserted junk heap overgrown by jungle." The Australian government, however, had plans to build a naval base there, using the convicted war criminals as a labor force.[19] The final transfers took place in February–March 1950, when SCAP, on behalf of the Australian government, transported 96 suspects from Sugamo Prison to Manus for trial.[20]

Concentrating war criminals imprisoned by the British authorities proved to be a difficult task because of the British Empire's complex constitutional arrangements. SEAC's command structure had not opposed the transfer of prisoners from one region to another. Indeed, the mobility of suspects had been crucial to prosecuting them in what was deemed to be the most appropriate venue in any particular case. During 1946, however,

SEAC's authority was reduced by the restoration of civil government in the British, Dutch, and French colonies it had previously managed. Then in November 1946, SEAC was abolished altogether. Henceforth, there was no overarching authority apart from the British government in London to coordinate relations among the colonies of Burma, Malaya, Singapore, Sarawak, North Borneo, and Hong Kong. In these circumstances, tension arose over the uneven distribution of prison responsibilities among the different colonies. In February 1947, the British judge advocate general's office clarified the status of Japanese convicts: "In our view, once sentence is passed on them by a military court, they cease to be members of the Japanese armed forces and become civil convicts subject to the prison regulations of the country in which they committed their offences and in which they were tried and sentenced."[21] The ruling meant that convicted war criminals should henceforth stay where they had been convicted until their sentences had expired.

Particularly for the small Crown colonies of Singapore and Hong Kong, this outcome was most unwelcome. Because they had relatively ample jails and relatively abundant facilities for hearing cases, these two colonies had hosted trials relating to many other parts of the region: most trials relating to the Thailand–Burma Railway, for example, were held in Singapore. Even though these jails had now been restored to civil authority, they still were encumbered with the prisoners previously deposited there.[22] As early as May 1946, British military forces noted that the Changi and Outram Road jails in Singapore held not only war criminals convicted for offenses on the Thailand–Burma Railway but also prisoners whose crimes had been committed elsewhere in Thailand and Burma, as well as in the Nicobar and Andaman Islands, New Britain, Sumatra, Batavia, French Indochina, the Riau archipelago to the south of Singapore, New Guinea, and Malaya. Of 232 prisoners, only 63 had actually committed their crimes in Singapore, while another 69 might have committed crimes elsewhere against people from Singapore.[23] Another 20 had not been convicted by the British at all, but by an Australian court in Singapore, principally for crimes committed on the Thailand–Burma Railway.[24]

In December 1947 the governor of Singapore, Sir Franklin Gimson, reminded the Colonial Office that things had not gone according to the initial plan. Japanese war criminals were originally supposed to serve their sentences in the country in which they had been tried, but instead, he noted tartly, Singapore "has been used as a dumping ground for prisoners from all over the Far East."[25] The Hong Kong authorities were also annoyed to find themselves holding war criminals on behalf of the Australian government; in November 1949, Stanley Prison's inmates included 29 who had been sentenced by Australian courts.[26] Perhaps not coincidentally, when the Australian government's lease on the building in which it held trials expired in November 1948, the government of Hong Kong refused an extension.[27] The Australian authorities had suggested to SCAP in mid-1948 that Australian trials might be shifted to Japan. The chief of SCAP's Legal Section, Alva C. Carpenter, ruled that the request be refused because it would undermine the principle of SCAP control over justice in Japan. He also pointed out that such trials would force SCAP to take responsibility for the custody of war criminals convicted by the Australian authorities, whereas each government "should make its own provisions for the continued confinement of such criminals."[28]

At the core of the concerns in Singapore and Hong Kong were the cost and inconvenience of holding war criminals. Both colonies were in financial difficulties after the war and had their own criminal populations to look after, so the extra burden of housing the war criminals was unwelcome. So, too, was the cost of repatriating them to Japan when their sentences expired. In the larger colonies of the French and the Dutch and in Burma, these costs do not seem to have been a concern.[29] While SEAC existed, it had taken responsibility for the repatriation war criminals who had completed their sentences, along with the massive transport of civilians and surrendered Japanese soldiers back to Japan. Once the SEAC mandate expired and because the prisoners were no longer considered military personnel, they were classified as illegal aliens on their release, and their deportation to Japan was another cost for local authorities to bear.[30] As the Colonial Secretariat in Hong Kong noted in June 1948: "It is of course absurd that we should be expected to dispose of these ex-convicts, many of whom were brought here for trial by the Army for crimes not committed in the colony."[31] A few months later, the governor of Hong Kong threatened to refuse custody of newly convicted war criminals at Stanley Prison unless the issue of the costs were resolved. This was not a trivial threat, because the trials in the high-profile Shanghai Bridge House case, in which Kenpeitai officers were held to account for prolonged torture of Western and Chinese civilians, were about to begin.[32] By 1950, the prison authorities in Hong Kong were carefully calculating the cost of maintaining prisoners. The estimated cost for each prisoner was HK$2.50

per day, and the total cost of maintaining Japanese war criminals up to March 31, 1950, was calculated as $267,172.50, or £16,702.[33] Although Gimson in Singapore pressed the Colonial Office to rule that Australia, the relevant colonies, and SCAP should be tapped to pay their share of the cost, the Colonial Office stubbornly resisted. In July 1948, Treasury in London ruled both that the amounts involved were too trivial to be bothered with and that the likely labor value of the Japanese war criminals to the Singapore and Hong Kong governments exceeded the cost of their maintenance.[34] Treasury added to the sting by ruling that Singapore and Hong Kong should also bear any costs involved in repatriating war criminals who had completed their sentences.[35]

Some colonial authorities were also concerned about the security risk presented by war criminals in their territory. The convicts often had significant military experience, and several groups were able to escape. In January 1946, seven Koreans escaped from British custody in Saigon, killing their British Indian guards.[36] Japanese prisoners escaped from Pudu Jail in Kuala Lumpur in August and October 1946.[37] On August 19, 1947, Sakaguchi Toshio and Furuichi Shigeo, both former Kenpeitai commanders, escaped from the Maison centrale prison in Saigon. Their escape was especially worrisome to the French authorities because the two had vowed revenge against the French and might contribute their military experience to "the Viet Minh rebellion."[38] In addition, the release into the local community of prisoners whose sentences had expired added yet another layer to colonial officials' concern about whose responsibility they should be. In Hong Kong, the colonial government urged the immediate deportation of released convicts for fear that their presence on the streets would incite lynching and mob violence.[39]

Not surprisingly, the convicted men and their supporters complained from time to time about the treatment they received in prison. Some of these complaints may simply have reflected an unfamiliarity with the harsh practices of prison life, such as regular body searches. Other complaints suggested revenge taking by the guards.[40] Prisoners who reached the end of their sentences in Southeast Asian jails and returned to Japan sometimes reported both casual brutality and systematic deprivation during their detention. In July 1947, Vice Admiral Shibata Yaichirō sent to Carpenter, head of SCAP's Legal Section, a long account of conditions in Netherlands Indies prisons. He reported what he called vindictive, vengeful treatment by guards who were former POWs of Japan, the theft of personal belongings, poor food, a prohibition on mosquito nets, hard labor, and meager medical care.[41] The Red Cross newspaper in Japan, *Ai no hikari* (*Light of Love*), reported in January 1952 that prisoners faced tough conditions on Manus Island, with tropical illnesses common. Most of the Japanese complaints about Manus, however, seem to have focused on its isolated location and the lack of information that filtered back to Japan about the prisoners held there.[42] Unpleasant as the circumstances in which Japanese war criminals found themselves may have been, they were probably typical of general prison conditions in the region at that time. In October 1949, an internal British investigation in Singapore concluded that there may have been some poor treatment of prisoners while they were under British military responsibility, but there was no evidence of bad conditions after the transfer of Singapore prisons to the civilian prison authorities.[43] A Japanese defense lawyer on Morotai described the island lyrically, referring to the "splendid view" from the camp and to "lovely birds in blue [that] sang their silvery songs of joy." He also commended the Australian authorities on their attention to hygiene.[44]

Reports by the International Committee of the Red Cross (ICRC) on the circumstances of convicted war criminals in British, French, and Dutch prisons indicated that conditions were generally acceptable.[45] The ICRC delegate who visited war crimes suspects in the Rangoon Central Jail in May 1946 reported that although the men were kept in single cells, they were allowed out for a daily bath at a pump in the yard; "they are well looked after as regards food and each man receives 10 cigarettes a week." By contrast, conditions in the crowded Japanese repatriation camps elsewhere in Burma were poor because of shortages of food, clothing, and accommodation caused by the hard-fought wartime campaign.[46] When the same Red Cross delegate visited the Rangoon Central Jail again at the end of 1946, he reported that the 1,460 inmates, who included 458 suspected or convicted war criminals, "were all housed in substantial two-storied buildings and were much better off as regards accommodation than the S.P. [Surrendered Personnel] in the camps": they had good water and adequate food, and all appeared healthy.[47] Another Red Cross official visited war criminals in Stanley Prison in Hong Kong on January 25, 1951, reporting that "treatment is fair and correct and no complaints were made [by prisoners] in this respect." Many of the prisoners had dental problems, and the Red Cross ended up paying a substantial amount for dental treatment for them. Food was plentiful and cells were "spotlessly clean." Although the prisoners wanted tofu as a substitute for cooking oil (a request that was denied by prison authorities) and a larger food ration, and expressed a wish to return to serve out their sentences in Japan, they otherwise had no complaints.[48]

Criticism was also leveled at Sugamo Prison in Tokyo. The prison was decades old when the U.S. Eighth Army took it over (figure 4.1). Although it had survived the war with little damage, a good deal of work was required to make it suitable as a major prison. The labor to refurbish the premises was provided by the war crimes suspects and, in time, by the convicted war criminals. The IMTFE convicts had their own section of the prison and reportedly asked for the door linking their section to the area occupied by common war criminals to be closed after incidents in which the high-ranking suspects had been abused by the others.[49] Conditions were harsh at first,[50] but probably not out of proportion to the difficulties of life in immediate postwar Japan. Moreover, the conditions for the prisoners gradually improved. They generally ate well, and after some months, they were permitted to borrow books from the Ueno library.[51] Across the road from the main gate of Sugamo, an office staffed by a member of the Japanese Foreign Ministry helped family members and other visitors apply to the U.S. Eighth Army for permission to visit.[52] In December 1951, former naval chief of staff

FIGURE 4.1 Gate of Sugamo Prison, March 1952. Mainichi shinbunsha, *Ichiokunin no Shōwashi: Nihon senryō 2* (Tokyo: Mainichi shinbunsha, 1980). Also available at https://commons.wikimedia.org/wiki/file%3AGate_of_Sugamo_Prison.jpg (accessed September 7, 2015).

Admiral Fukutome Shigeru told a parliamentary inquiry that Sugamo felt like a first-class hotel compared with the other jails he had seen and that it had better food and conditions than were available even to the average Japanese household.[53]

The concentration of prisoners in a few jails may have improved their conditions, but it also worsened the problem of equity. Transfers of prisoners exposed flaws in record keeping. Some convicts turned up at their new jails without trial records or associated documents. One set of documents was marked with the words "case canceled," which raised the disturbing possibility that the man had been wrongly imprisoned.[54] Moreover, as we have seen, there had been no real attempt to ensure parity of sentence across the whole war crimes trials system, and there was some indication that sentences had become more lenient as time passed. A consequence was that sentences might vary greatly for what was essentially the same category of offense. This disparity became more noticeable when prisoners from different regions were brought together. British officials became at least mildly uncomfortable at the situation.[55]

ENDING THE TRIALS

The ideal of comprehensiveness implied that the trial of alleged Japanese war criminals would continue until the very last one had been brought to justice. Because the Allies had detained many thousands of suspected war criminals in the early postwar period, the prosecutions could have gone on for a long time had there been a desire to continue.[56] Implicit, however, in the early acceptance by the war crimes prosecution teams that they should give priority to the worst cases was an understanding that their goals might be served just as well—or nearly as well—by a representative selection of cases and that the Allies were unlikely to be able to bring all possible cases to trial.

The earliest misgivings over the prospect of a trial process stretching far into the future were prompted, again, by the issue of cost. The prosecution of war crimes was expensive; it called on substantial human and material resources at a time when all the governments in the region were pressed for resources. First to show signs of breaking ranks was the Philippines. Because the Philippines had not been independent when the trials began, it had not initially taken a formal part in prosecutions, although a significant number of trials took place in U.S. courts in Manila. The Allies recognized that the Philippines had experienced the greatest physical destruction and the greatest loss of life in Southeast Asia as a consequence of Japanese aggression and that in the immediate aftermath of the war, Japanese people were deeply unpopular in the Philippines. The U.S. government therefore expected that the new Philippines government, independent as of July 4, 1946, would enthusiastically take over the trials process. This expectation turned out to be mistaken. The new government of President Manuel Roxas pleaded lack of funds and declined to take over trials until the United States promised to meet a large part of the cost. SCAP eventually did agree that the United States would meet the cost of detaining war criminals and of transferring any witnesses and equipment needed for the trials.[57] At much the same time, Allied planners started to feel that little might be served by bringing yet another prison camp guard before a tribunal. Many of the most notorious cases had been tried or else had been abandoned for lack of evidence or defendants.

The U.S. Occupation authorities in Japan and planners in Washington, moreover, were becoming more and more convinced that the trials were hindering their goal of engineering political and social change in Japan. If the trials continued, there might be a backlash among the Japanese people and a damaging division of opinion, conditions that were considered likely to favor the Communist cause in Japan.[58] These misgivings crystallized in March 1948 in a memorandum prepared by the director of the U.S. State Department's Policy Planning Staff, George F. Kennan. After commending the war crimes trials for their good intentions, Kennan announced baldly, "These trials were profoundly misconceived from the start and are working increasing injury to the Allied cause in Japan." He dismissed the validity of pursuing charges of waging aggressive war when the aggression had been the act of a state, and he scorned the capacity of those conducting the prosecution and defense to understand the implications of the trials for international relations. "These are political trials," he wrote. Kennan was disdainful of the fact that American lawyers for the accused would defend Japanese wartime policy, as he thought this practice sent a confused political message to the Japanese public and suggested hypocrisy on the part of the Americans.

And he attacked the fact that the trials continued long after the events that were being judged:

> It is a rule with peoples, as with individuals, that punishment, if it is to have any exemplary effect, must be swift and incisive and must follow immediately on the heels of the offense. A delayed and long-protracted punishment (and what else are these interminable trials?) loses its effect on both the victim and the public. The Japanese public has long since ceased to feel any reactions toward the trials other than one of sympathy for these fellow Japanese who are forced to sit through these endless and humiliating ordeals which have so little to do with anything that anyone in Japan can understand. It would have been much better received and understood if we had shot these people out of hand at the time of the surrender.[59]

Kennan's message had a powerful effect because it came in the context of broader decisions, with which Kennan himself was closely associated, to move from occupation and retribution toward restoring Japan's sovereignty and democracy. Narrower legal considerations were also important, especially in relation to the IMTFE. Further IMTFE trials had been envisaged by some, notably the chief prosecutor, Joseph Keenan, with arrest warrants issued for around one hundred suspects between September and December 1945. Consideration was also given to sending more "Class A" suspects to the military tribunals. In June 1947, fifty suspects remained in Sugamo in anticipation of a new IMTFE trial. Obtaining convictions and significant sentences in a second set of IMTFE processes, however, appeared likely to be a challenge. Potential defendants held in Sugamo were less clearly connected either with the decision to go to war or, by means of the principle of command responsibility, with actual atrocities. U.S. planners began to reconsider the value of embarking on a new round of trials. Budgetary issues in the Department of the Army, which was responsible for funding and managing war crimes trials, created further pressure to end the prosecutions.[60]

About half the IMTFE suspects were released without charge in two groups in August and September 1947.[61] Several others were evidently released individually in late 1947, either to freedom or, at least in the case of Kuroda Shigenori, to stand trial in national-level courts.[62] The IMTFE ceased its work after trying the first batch of twenty-eight suspects.

In December 1948 only nineteen potential suspects for the IMTFE remained in Sugamo. Two died in prison in December, and the remaining seventeen were released on the twenty-fourth and twenty-fifth of that month.[63] A public announcement stated that it was doubtful that the remaining suspects would have been found guilty of the charges leveled at the IMTFE. Furthermore, "the periods in office of the suspects investigated by Legal Section were of such limited duration as to render it unlikely that 'B' and 'C' charges would be supported on the basis of the responsibility of their official position." The upshot was that "after a thorough consideration of all the factors involved," it had been decided that no more trials for these men would be initiated.[64]

In fact the decision to wind up the Tokyo trials was not absolute. In October 1948, SCAP convened trials of two former IMTFE suspects, Lieutenant General Tamura Hiroshi and Admiral Toyoda Soemu. In a gesture to the former intention to try them before an international tribunal, the U.S. authorities appointed an Australian officer as president of each tribunal and installed a panel of seven judges, but the trials took place under SCAP authority rather than as a continuation of the IMTFE.[65] Tamura, former head of the Japanese government's Prisoner of War Information Bureau, was sentenced to eight years in prison. Toyoda, commander of all Japanese naval forces at the time of the battle for Manila in 1945, was tried on exactly the same charges as Yamashita Tomoyuki had been in October 1945. Although evidence was produced that Toyoda had been the one to issue the orders for Japanese forces to defend Manila at all costs, he was acquitted.[66]

U.S. authorities also began to reduce investigations into ordinary war crimes and to wind down the trials. In March 1949, the Far Eastern Commission, essentially endorsing what had been general SCAP policy for some time, formally recommended to all the Allied powers that they end their trials by September 30.[67] Toyoda's trial, which concluded on October 19, 1949, was the last to be conducted by the U.S. authorities. Some twenty-five suspects remained at large; they were never brought in for questioning, but their names were not deleted from the suspect list.[68]

The British authorities had decided early in 1948 that any case that had not been brought to court by March 31 would be abandoned. Affected by this decision was the case against two Kenpeitai staff, Lieutenant General Kinoshita Eiichi and Sergeant Yoshida Bunzo, who were allegedly two of the people responsible for horrific tortures of Western and Chinese civilians at the Kenpeitai headquarters in Bridge House in Shanghai. The case did not proceed, but the release and repatriation of Kinoshita and Yoshida caused a storm of protest in the local European press in China, and the issue was raised in the British Parliament. The authorities then relented, recovered the two suspects from Japan, and placed them on trial; Kinoshita was sentenced to life imprisonment.[69] Britain's final trial, prosecuting Kenpeitai Sergeant Major Yokohata Toshiro, who was also accused of torture in Bridge House, finished on December 20, 1948.[70] According to some reports, British authorities in Southeast Asia repatriated to Japan nine thousand suspects from whom the threat of prosecution had now been lifted.[71]

Authorities in the Republic of China had been forced to end their trials by the pressures of the civil war; the Netherlands Indies, by Indonesia's independence. The French authorities in Indochina finished their last trial in March 1950. Australia appeared to have ended its trials in December 1948 but resumed them in December 1949. In September 1949, SCAP had proposed releasing the 87 suspects still held in Sugamo on Australia's behalf, but the Australian government responded by making plans for more trials on Manus Island. Twenty-four trials were held, the last one concluding only in April 1951.[72] In July 1950, the Soviet Union transferred 971 Japanese suspects to the new People's Republic of China (PRC) for trial as war criminals on the grounds that their crimes had been committed on Chinese soil, but none of this cohort was prosecuted until 1956.[73] As Communist countries, the Soviet Union and the PRC did not work together with the other Allies on the war crimes trial process.[74]

TOWARD PAROLE AND RELEASE

Despite the Allies' original intent in 1945 to remain steadfast in their pursuit of Japanese war criminals, their commitment to sustaining the sentences passed by the courts started to weaken surprisingly quickly. U.S. authorities began to discuss sentence reduction on the basis of "good behavior" in August 1946, though apparently they took no steps to implement the idea as yet. As Higurashi pointed out, such initial impulses to modify sentences began before the more general change in Occupation objectives away from punishment and toward the rehabilitation of Japan became evident. By the end of 1948 at the latest, officials dealing with war criminals in the Department of the Army were considering ways of releasing and rehabilitating prisoners, partly in order to affirm the justice of the trial process and to show the democratic countries' high moral standard by demonstrating that they were concerned with more than simply trial and punishment.[75]

One initial sign of misgivings about sustaining the original sentences was that the Allied authorities began to justify their actions rather than taking them for granted. On March 13, 1946, the day after the first executions under British auspices, a member of SEAC's staff summed up the reasons for SEAC's participation in the war crimes trials. These reasons were "(a) our moral obligation to victims; (b) lively interest taken in trials by ex PW [POWs] and internees, their relatives, and general public; (c) necessity of upholding British prestige."[76] As is often the case, this reaffirmation of the reasons for continuing was the first sign of doubts. Such doubts, no more than niggling to begin with, focused especially on the consequences of delay in bringing suspects to justice. Judgment, verdict, and punishment had been swift in the initial trials: the first British executions took place in Kuala Lumpur on March 12, 1946, and were followed two days later by three more in Singapore.[77] Another fifteen condemned men awaited the Singapore hangman at this point; twenty had been sent to prison for long terms; and eight had been acquitted.[78] The executions and long sentences appeared to confirm the British authorities' determination to see justice done. Yet the small numbers of defendants whose cases had been decided by March 1946 signaled that the trials program would not achieve the initial goal of five hundred verdicts by the end of July 1946. Lord Louis Mountbatten had been anxious in October 1945 about delays in getting the prosecutions started,[79] and this concern was now compounded by slow progress in the early months.

The British deputy judge advocate general, Brigadier Henry Shapcott, declared in September 1947 that all war criminals convicted in British courts—both Japanese and Germans—should serve their sentences in their entirety and not be eligible for any reduction of their sentences, apart from those decided by the reviewing officer at the time of sentencing. Shapcott argued that if war criminals were released, they might endanger the security of the Allied Occupation forces. He also pointed out that the United States had made no provision for reducing the sentences of war criminals and suggested that Britain would do well to maintain a common policy with the United States.[80] Ironically, Shapcott's comments became a catalyst for the first British move toward clemency, in both Europe and Asia. They attracted the attention of British officials in the Legal Division and the Penal Branch in Germany, who were responsible for supervising incarcerated war criminals, by highlighting a serious contradiction within the broader Allied penal policy in Germany. Prisoners convicted of crimes against humanity, that is, crimes against German citizens, especially Jews, were eligible for remission of sentence for good conduct, whereas Germans convicted of conventional war crimes, many of whom were in the same prisons and had been sentenced to similar terms, were not. The Legal Division and the Penal Branch also refuted the contention that the war criminals were a threat to the Occupation.[81]

Thus, in principle at least, clemency was on the table for both the U.S. and the British authorities. In the legal thinking of that time, the term "clemency" referred to any reduction in or removal of sentence that was implemented after the confirmation of sentence, which marked the formal end of the trial process. Historically, clemency has taken many forms, including a reduction of sentence for good behavior or for testifying against others, an outright pardon for commemorative or political reasons, and an annulment of prison sentences in a time of emergency such as war or a natural disaster.[82] In the case of the Japanese war criminals, the only forms considered, with minor exceptions, were a reduction of sentence and, later, parole. In U.S. official thinking, clemency for war criminals referred to reduction of sentence only and was separate from parole, although a sentence reduction might be necessary in order to make a prisoner eligible for parole, as a prisoner earned eligibility after serving a certain proportion of the original or amended sentence. Parolees in the U.S. and other systems remained formally under sentence but were permitted to live outside prison under specific conditions, usually amounting to good behavior and regular reporting to local authorities. In theory, they could be returned to prison for infractions of their parole conditions. In practice, parole was simply used as a form of early release. Clemency was an administrative act undertaken by officials who had no formal judicial status. As we shall see, however, considerations of clemency for Japanese war criminals were always deeply embedded in the justice issues that had underpinned the original sentences.

Concentrating the convicted war criminals in a few selected prisons was not intended to be a step toward release. Nonetheless, the process of concentration prompted some of the convicting countries to reflect on whether it remained necessary to sustain the original sentences. In August 1948, the Netherlands Indies granted a standard eight months' remission to all war criminals whose sentences had been confirmed by that date; a further remission of three months was granted at the end of April 1949. The president of the colonial supreme court ruled in September 1949 that all sentences would be calculated from the first date of detention as a war crimes suspect, in most cases effectively reducing sentences by some months.[83] The governments of the United Kingdom and United States also counted the time spent in detention before trial.

In April 1948, the British judge advocate general, Sir Henry Foster MacGeagh; his deputy, Shapcott; the secretary of state for war, Emanuel Shinwell; and the undersecretary of state, T. J. Cash, had met and decided that war criminals should be eligible for some form of remission of sentence and, furthermore, that a comprehensive review should be carried out in order to standardize the sentences handed down at the trials. In the European theater there was substantial anecdotal evidence of wild discrepancies in sentencing, but the conference attendees nevertheless decided that a comprehensive review of all sentences at the completion of all the trials would be a better option than individual case reviews. Two boards of review were later created, one for convicted German war criminals and one for Japanese war criminals. The review boards would study the trial records and associated documents for each case, including any petition that the convicted man had submitted immediately after the trial.[84]

In January 1949, Shinwell appointed Brigadier E. F. Lynch as head of the No. 2 War Crimes Sentences Review Board (Far East). The board's mandate was to examine sentences and to recommend reductions to the secretary of state for war when they would improve the sentences' parity. The board was not authorized to consider the correctness of the guilty verdict in the light of the evidence, but only to examine the appropriateness of each sentence in relation to the circumstances of the crime. Shapcott nonetheless suggested to Lynch in March 1949 that the board might draw his attention to cases in which the verdict was problematic,[85] though it is unclear whether the board actually did so. The board firmly declined to view petitions from other people or groups in favor of the convicted criminals.[86] The board quickly developed a table that graded offenses into a hierarchy of seriousness and set them against the war criminal's individual responsibility for the act in question. Three levels of culpability—minor, intermediate, and major—along with the level of individual responsibility indicated to the board what kind of sentence should have been applied (table 4.1).[87] If it appeared that a sentence had been inconsistent with others of its kind, the board consulted the table to recommend an alteration.

The Lynch board recommended the alteration of 109 of the 441 sentences due to expire on or after September 30, 1949.[88] Life sentences were now to be fixed to specific terms, with a maximum of twenty-one years. Fifty-two life sentences were fixed at twenty-one years, while others were reduced to ten or fifteen years.[89] Another fifty-two sentences for terms up to twenty years were reduced as well. In addition, and apart from the review board's recommendations, the War Office determined that all convicted war criminals would be given one-third off their sentences for good conduct, which was assumed unless there was evidence to the contrary. This measure was a response to a comment from the staff at Werl Prison in Germany, where German war criminals convicted by Britain were held, that allowing the prisoners remission for good behavior and application to industry would help maintain discipline in the prison.[90] As a result of two simultaneous decisions, war criminals with life sentences thus found themselves serving no more than fourteen years.[91] The British government also accepted the Lynch board's recommendation that if a war criminal had been sentenced to prison terms for two different offenses, the sentences would run concurrently rather than consecutively.[92]

In setting out his opposition to sentence reductions in September 1947, Shapcott had correctly noted that the United States had no system of clemency for war criminals. On Christmas Day 1949, however, SCAP announced that sentences would be reduced for good behavior; in consequence, the remaining prison terms of nearly fifty convicted war criminals evaporated, and they were released on December 28.[93] On March 7, 1950, SCAP instituted a remission and parole system for war criminals.[94] There was also a provision for small-scale temporary releases in special circumstances.[95] The new rules allowed for remission on the basis of good conduct, on a scale of five days for every month served. For sentences of one to three years, the remission was six days per month, and the scale of remission increased up to sentences of ten years or more, in which a war criminal was eligible for ten days' remission per month served. All time in custody as a war criminal, including time served as a war crimes suspect,

TABLE 4.1 Table of Crimes and Responsibilities as Used by Review Board no. 2

Crime	Major responsibility[a]	Intermediate responsibility[b]	Minor responsibility[c]
1. Ill-treatment of prisoners of war or civilians causing death	Life	10 to 15 years	5 to 7 years
2. Gross and/or indecent torture	Life	10 to 15 years	5 to 7 years
3. Concerned in killing of prisoners of war or civilians	Life	10 to 15 years	5 to 7 years
4. Gross and/or prolonged ill-treatment of prisoners of war or civilians	Life	10 to 12 years	4 to 6 years
5. Unlawful arrest, trial, and execution	Life	10 to 12 years	3 to 5 years
6. Execution of alleged subversives without trial	Life	10 to 12 years	3 to 5 years
7. Inefficiency in control and/or administration causing death and/or acute suffering	14 to 16 years	8 to 10 years	2 to 3 years
8. Minor torture (e.g., beating, etc., not sufficient to cause severe injury)	3 to 5 years	1 to 2 years	—

[a] Those responsible for initiating and/or entering wholeheartedly into the commission of war crimes. (Note: any person who enters wholeheartedly into gross and/or indecent torture is normally guilty under this heading.)
[b] Persons of some status, e.g., officers, warrant officers, and senior NCOs, who on the orders of their superiors were concerned in the commission of war crimes.
[c] Persons of low status or intelligence who, on the orders of their superiors, were concerned in the commission of war crimes.

Source: Adapted from R. John Pritchard, "The Parameters of Justice: The Evolution of British Civil and Military Perspectives on War Crimes Trials and Their Legal Context (1942–1956)," in *International Humanitarian Law*, vol. 3, *Origins, Challenges and Prospects*, ed. John Carey, William V. Dunlap, and R. John Pritchard (Leiden: Brill, 2006), 311.

was used to calculate remission. The U.S. Eighth Army retained the right to revoke, at any time, remissions granted for good behavior in prison.

At the same time, SCAP also established a three-person board, chaired by George T. Hagen, to investigate and review applications from war criminals for early release on parole. Its task was to consider how well a prisoner had applied himself to work while in custody, his overall behavior as an inmate, the details of his trial, and any petition against his conviction or sentence. The board also considered the age, health, and financial situation of the prisoner and his family.[96] Applications were processed and prison records scrutinized, and the applicant then appeared before the board.[97] A war criminal became eligible for parole after serving one-third of his original sentence, or sentence as adjusted by remissions.

The SCAP parole system required effective mechanisms to supervise the prisoners who were released, necessitating a new level of cooperation between SCAP and the Japanese government. On May 31, 1949, the Japanese Diet (parliament) passed the Offenders' Prevention and Rehabilitation Law (Hanzaisha yobō kōsei hō) to allow for parole and remissions of sentences, which had previously not been permitted in the Japanese system. The National Offenders' Prevention and Rehabilitation Commission (NOPAR) was subsequently created as an independent section of the Japanese attorney general's office, responsible for managing prisoners' parole.[98] The SCAP Board of Parole then decided to use the NOPAR system to supervise war criminals on parole while reserving the right to modify it as necessary.[99] After the parole board recommended a prisoner for parole, the case went to SCAP for final approval; if approval were granted, the war criminal became the responsibility of NOPAR. Upon leaving prison, war criminals were required to proceed directly to the destination where they were to serve their parole and to report to their supervisor within eight days. After that, they were required to report monthly.[100] Parole supervisors generated monthly reports on each parolee.[101] War criminals on parole were bound to abide by the parole regulations set by SCAP Circular No. 5, including a requirement that the prisoner must not travel more than fifty miles (80 km) from his residence or leave his home for more than three days without the approval of his parole supervisor. If a parolee violated the regulations, the Parole Board had the power to revoke his release.[102]

Using NOPAR for parole supervision saved SCAP time and resources, but in some geographical areas, it was difficult or impossible for NOPAR to function. The NOPAR system was set up to supervise parole on main-land Japan; supervision on Okinawa was harder to arrange.[103] Moreover, NOPAR could not arrange supervision in Taiwan or Korea, and Taiwan-ese and Korean war criminals did not necessarily have homes or fami-lies in Japan that conformed with the requirements of parole. In the end, social welfare organizations catering to Taiwanese and Korean war crimi-nals appear to have accepted responsibility for those who were paroled.[104]

Altogether, the SCAP Parole Board received 1,184 applications for parole. By the time the Occupation ended, 892 war criminals had been granted parole, and only 19 applications had been denied. The board had reviewed but taken no formal action on 200 applications, by choice or through lack of time, and another 73 had been "administratively closed," perhaps because of the death of the applicant or the expiration of his sentence.[105]

FURTHER MISGIVINGS

As the sentences' initial value as a public declaration of war criminals' guilt receded into the past, other aims of punishment became more salient. These aims, however, were also subject to relentless pressure from the passage of time and changes in circumstances. A subsidiary objec-tive of the trials had been to remove from Japanese society a group of people who might be expected to stand in the way of SCAP's ambitious program to democratize and demilitarize their country. Whether or not there had ever been real danger that war criminals might sway postwar Japanese society, the possibility had largely disappeared by the end of the 1940s. In the second half of 1947, driven above all by the intensifying Cold War, SCAP began to wind back some of the more radical aspects of its reform program in Japan in a new policy that was later character-ized as the "Reverse Course." The new program limited the freedom of left-wing forces to operate in postwar Japan in order to forestall a poten-tial slide into Communism, and it recruited what were seen as strong ele-ments in pre-Occupation Japanese society in order to make the country more resilient in the face of Cold War pressures. Crucially, the Reverse Course included what was sometimes called the "depurge," a reversal of the purge from public office of thousands of politicians, military men, and others who, although usually not suspected of war crimes, had been judged early in the Occupation to be too sympathetic, as individuals or by virtue of their formal positions, to the war aims of the Imperial government.[106] In the changed environment, it was harder to maintain that war criminals should continue to be isolated from Japanese society. The force of arguments that the continued imprisonment of war criminals would deter future crime had also weakened: Japan was demilitarized, and the possibility that future generations could commit war crimes was remote. The guilty verdicts and subsequent sentences could still be brandished, as Robert Jackson had intended, as a standard to which all peoples would be held in the future. To do so, however, demanded a somewhat naive confidence in the willingness of the world to repeat the trial exercise.

The value of imprisonment in promoting rehabilitation, or even the simple remorse that was suggested by Muneyuki Yasuo's judge in 1946 ("You will be given a long time to reflect"), also turned out to be less convincing in practice than it had been in anticipation. Throughout 1948 and 1949, the Special Branch in Singapore monitored letters between Japanese convicts in Singapore and Malaya and their families. A report on this correspondence in June 1949 stated that "most of the prisoners never grow tired of telling their families that, far from being criminals, they are the pick of their countrymen, the chosen ones to expiate their country's defeat." Those convicted, the report went on, assured their families that their convictions were based on unfair trials. They complained that they were treated badly by their jailors and they resented being jailed with other criminals of Chinese, Indian, or Malay ethnicity, whom they considered inferior either because of their race or because they had been jailed for common criminal offenses, or both. The few who sympathized with the local prisoners did so because they saw them as political prisoners, fellow victims of British colonialism.[107] The Special Branch raised no hope that Japanese convicts would change: as a handwritten note attached to one of the reports stated, "It is increasingly evident that the leopard's spots are being continually refurbished."[108] Governor Gimson in Singapore commented morosely: "I have seen reports on the censored letters which have been sent by these prisoners to their relatives in Japan, from which it is clear that the prisoners show no sign of repentance. In fact they regard themselves as martyrs in the Japanese cause of freedom."[109] If anything, the Singapore reports suggested that the war criminals' distance from Japan, far from promoting remorse or rehabilitation, allowed them to avoid confronting the criminality of their acts.[110]

Some of the evidence regarding the war criminals' attitudes was more ambiguous. An Australian soldier on Morotai reported that a photograph of an Australian being beheaded (probably the Siffleet photo in chapter 1 of this book) had been pinned to the wall of the camp in which convicted and accused war criminals were held. "The Japs here don't like gazing upon this photo. . . . Most of them feel deeply ashamed and humiliated when they see [it] and, when asked about it, they just hang their heads and refuse to comment."[111] Although formulaic expressions of regret for war crimes were common in petitions against sentence ("The prisoner regrets his crime"), personal displays of remorse were rare and appeared halfhearted at best. A detainee in Changi expressed his repentance for participation in the *sook ching* massacres by offering a gift of S$5 to the Singapore Chinese community.[112]

Grounded in misgivings about the purposes that punishment was expected to serve, a new set of considerations was thus superimposed on the doubts about the underlying justice of the trials and their procedural fairness. Added to the cost of detention and other difficulties, these misgivings prompted the Allied planners to reconsider the rationale for imprisonment each time they faced new challenges. In formal terms, the Review Board convened under Brigadier Lynch in January 1949 was a response only to the issue of inequity in sentencing. It had no mandate to reconsider the purpose of punishment or to consider whether the punishment had been effective.[113] Yet the board initiated a wholesale reduction in the sentences imposed by British courts. The reduction was constructed so as to appear to be a routine bureaucratic process, but nevertheless it invited further review of the sentencing. By the end of the 1940s, too, there was a growing divergence of interest among the convicting powers. Whereas the French were losing interest in the war criminals they had convicted, the Netherlands Indies authorities continued to see them as a danger because of their alleged past and suspected future support for the Indonesian republic. The judges and confirming officers who pronounced sentences in the various national tribunals saw their actions as the end of a long process of identification, investigation, indictment, prosecution, and delivery of the verdict. In fact, the sentences were only the start of a new phase in applying justice to war criminals.

5

SHIFTING MOOD, SHIFTING LOCATION

Review of sentencing was on the table by the late 1940s. Utilitarian pressures to reduce the practical and financial burden of imprisoning convicted war criminals were strong, even after the work of the Lynch board and the Occupation parole system had begun to ensure that many prisoners were released before the expiration of their original terms. These practical pressures were joined by further considerations that nudged policymakers toward clemency, including a consciousness of inconsistency in sentencing. The impulse to continue punishing Japanese war criminals nevertheless remained strong. Authorities such as Sir Franklin Gimson, the governor of Singapore, held firmly to the principle of retribution: the crimes committed, they maintained, had been too awful to permit any form of clemency. Against this vengefulness, various groups in Japan launched an increasingly effective argument for clemency based on compassion. They did not argue directly in terms of guilt or the purposes of punishment but focused simply on the present-day suffering of the convicted men and their families. The new emphasis on compassion for the prisoners stimulated a Japanese push to have the war criminals who were incarcerated in other parts of Asia returned to Japan, to serve out the remainder of their sentences there. Political and economic factors, by contrast, began to persuade Allied planners that transferring the prisoners to Japan was a good idea.

APPEALING TO COMPASSION

The argument that convicted war criminals merited compassionate treatment began to take shape in 1947 in the context of the broader movement to facilitate the return to Japan of hundreds of thousands of soldiers and civilians still stranded overseas, including tens of thousands upon whom suspicion of war crimes had fallen, at least temporarily. During 1947, the repatriation of Japanese soldiers and civilians from Southeast Asia was largely completed. Return from the Soviet Union and China, however, had barely begun, and even basic information about the identities and whereabouts of Japanese subjects in those countries was patchy. In Japan, activists attempted to persuade the Japanese government, the Occupation forces, and the Western powers to use their influence to bring these exiles home.[1] In May 1947, various support groups for recent repatriates and for the families of those still overseas merged into a national organization, the Association of the Families of the Missing to Promote the Repatriation of Compatriots Overseas (Zaigai dōhō kikan sokushin rusu kazoku renmei). The new association concentrated predominantly on the tens of thousands who were still trapped in China and the Soviet Union.[2] In comparison, the number of war criminals in overseas prisons was small. Occupation propaganda, moreover, highlighted the atrocious nature of the crimes that had led to their trials. Not surprisingly, therefore, the families and supporters of convicted war criminals initially kept a low profile within the larger repatriation movement. Nevertheless, the broader campaign provided a means of supporting the war criminals' families in Japan and a channel and model both for delivering petitions to the imprisoning powers for the release of individual war criminals and for lobbying politicians.

Elected politicians regularly raised the issue of delayed repatriations and the status of overseas war criminals in the Japanese Diet (parliament), only to be reminded by Foreign Ministry officials that the Japanese government was subject to the Occupation authorities and thus was hampered in its ability to intervene on behalf of war criminals. It could only urge the International Commission of the Red Cross (ICRC) to monitor the prisoners' health and welfare.[3] Within the Japanese bureaucracy, former members of the Army and Navy General Staff, now operating as civilian bureaucrats in the First and Second Demobilization Bureaus respectively,[4] supported the families of war criminals by providing what information they could about their whereabouts and circumstances.[5] From late 1947 onward, politicians, bureaucrats, mutual assistance organizations, and individuals increasingly argued that prisoners should be brought back to Japan. The idea that war criminals should serve their sentences at home, where they would be held in better conditions and would be safe from civil wars and able to see their families, was gradually supplemented with the notion that their sentences should be reduced on humanitarian grounds and that forgiveness and mercy were now warranted. Even so, in the early stages of the campaign on behalf of Japanese soldiers and civilians stranded overseas, the broader issues of repatriation and welfare provision for repatriates continued to overshadow concerns about war criminals. In October 1947, only two petitions were presented to the Diet on behalf of the war criminals, compared with sixty-three demanding government action for Japanese overseas or the provision of repatriate welfare.[6]

In late 1947, a campaign began to emerge that dealt specifically with convicted war criminals. In its earliest stages, it combined an emphasis on the underlying humanity of the prisoners with an assertion of the defense of superior orders. As we have seen, the idea that following superior orders mitigated wartime offenses had already played a major role in determining who would be tried and who would receive the harshest sentences, but this trend among the investigators and prosecutors was not well known, and the public campaign implied that the defense of superior orders had been ignored. On November 27, 1947, the House of Representatives Committee for Foreign Affairs discussed a petition arguing that war criminals convicted by the Guomindang authorities in China should be repatriated. The petitioners claimed that war criminals were housed in a politically unstable part of Manchuria, in a jail with inadequate facilities and food, and that leaving them there with winter approaching was akin to giving them a death sentence. Moreover, few of the defendants had been in positions of responsibility during the war.[7] In February 1948, Socialist Party Diet member Shōji Hiko concisely presented the proposition that ordinary military personnel were not responsible for what they had been asked to do:

> Of course we hate their [the convicted war criminals'] crimes, and as their compatriots we have our own feelings about these things. However, we also need to think about their families. Leaving aside the issue of how

the war was planned, and whether this was a good or a bad thing, these soldiers, who had no responsibility for these decisions, were sent overseas and followed the orders of their superiors without asking questions, and it was this that set them on a collision course with war crimes trials.[8]

Here Shōji was arguing for repatriation rather than release, but the propositions that the majority of war criminals were simply loyal soldiers who had done their duty and that they deserved considerate treatment quickly became the twin central tenets of the release campaign as well.

Japanese families and friends of individual war criminals sent hundreds of petitions to Allied governments urging clemency for the convicted men. Yamamoto Kinuyo, for instance, petitioned the Netherlands Indies High Commissioner in August 1949 on behalf of her husband, Warrant Officer Yamamoto Torao, who had been sentenced to ten years' imprisonment by the military tribunal in Batavia. She listed the attributes that she evidently believed justified his release:

> First, he was a peaceful and generous man whose father died in his childhood. He was very kind and affectionate for us. He was a father and husband [who] never scolded us at home, intending to make [our] home peaceful and warm because he was not very happy in his childhood.
>
> Second, he was the most obedient son for my aged mother [or mother-in-law] and while he was serving at Kobe Custom-house, he sent her some money from his salary every month.
>
> Third, at home he would devote his leisure time to such peaceful taste as feeding birds, taking photo, or playing Japanese classic musical instruments.
>
> Fourth, he had a religious belief, worshipping at Buddhist temple on Mt. Futatabi in Kobe every day.[9]

Although the petition concluded with a comment that gently challenged the verdict of the trial—"we can't find it possible for him [Yamamoto] to have done such evils"—its central aim was to highlight the humanity of the convicted man and to provoke feelings of sympathy for him and his family.

Petitions to individual politicians triggered discussions in the Diet. Diet member Shōji Hikō pleaded for the repatriation of war criminals so that their family members could visit them. He was prompted, he said, by the many requests that had reached him from the public, though he was careful to add that his request that the government "do something" about war criminals overseas was made as a private citizen.[10] On February 20, 1948, a Foreign Ministry representative was asked to give information to a Diet committee about the conditions in which war criminals were held overseas, about the government's efforts to bring the prisoners back to Japan, and about the possibility of ensuring that any further trials were fair. Kojima Taisaku explained that the government was expending a great deal of effort talking with the Supreme Commander for the Allied Powers (SCAP) and the ICRC on behalf of the accused and the convicted. He also suggested that while there had been initial concerns about trial procedure, the Japanese government had noted improvements in the use of evidence and the selection of witnesses.[11] Questions about the trials' fairness nonetheless continued to be raised. On April 2, 1949, Diet member Wakamatsu Torao brought to the attention of the Committee on Foreign Affairs a petition he had received from the relatives of Shinnai Tatsuo, who had been condemned to death in the Philippines a year earlier in a group trial for rape and torture of civilians in Cebu. The petition, Wakamatsu explained, suggested that Shinnai was of gentle character and unlikely to have taken part in such a crime, that in any case he and several others of the accused had been in hospital at the time the crime had been committed, and that Shinnai had been condemned in place of the real criminal, his commander Higashinaka, who had died in battle. Wakamatsu added that the sentences handed down in the Philippines seemed especially harsh, and he asked what the government intended to do about this case. Other committee members raised concerns about alleged cases of mistaken identity in the war crimes trials.[12] Throughout 1949 and 1950, Diet members continued to call attention to the petitions sent to them by war criminals' families asking for repatriation, sentence reduction, and even for the relocation of trials to Japan as a way to ensure fairness.[13] At times, the topic of war criminals led to heated debates between politicians and bureaucrats, usually about whether the government was making sufficient progress in negotiating with foreign powers.[14]

In Germany, by contrast, advocates for convicted war criminals were much more likely to highlight the identity and status of the prisoners as soldiers, rather than to argue that they should be treated compassionately on humanitarian grounds. The problem of what to do with the large number of unemployed and impoverished former soldiers, who were initially

banned from taking other employment or from receiving welfare benefits, meant that the social reintegration of military personnel was already
a topic of public discussion in Germany in the late 1940s. From 1946
onward, former German army officers repeatedly called for the release of
"military prisoners," meaning both POWs and convicted war criminals.
There was a marked emphasis by former soldiers, as well as politicians and
other public figures, on the alleged need to restore the "honor" of German
soldiers, which had supposedly been damaged, not by their actions during
the war, but by the victorious Allies and their war crimes trials, by the negative views of the military that were frequently expressed in German public commentary in the early postwar period, and by discrimination against
former soldiers when they sought employment or in the workplace. Many
former soldiers, it was said, felt degraded and humiliated, and the continued incarceration of convicted war criminals greatly exacerbated such
feelings.[15] By the beginning of 1949, German public opinion in the western
occupation zones was strongly sympathetic to war criminals, in Norbert
Frei's assessment.[16] In Japan, it would have been more difficult to advocate
the restoration of the prisoners' military honor, given that the military
had been disbanded and that under the new constitution of 1946, Japan
had renounced war and the means of waging war.

Concern over the condition of Japanese war criminals in Allied prisons grew when reports of poor treatment circulated in Japan. In August
1950, former naval chief of staff Fukutome Shigeru, who had been convicted in February 1948 on command responsibility charges over the
1945 execution of downed Allied flyers in Singapore,[17] published an
article in the influential monthly magazine *Bungei shunjū* on the Changi
and Outram Road prisons in Singapore, complaining of overcrowding,
inadequate food, and the hard labor required of convicted war criminals
there. In an echo of the indignation expressed by European residents in
Southeast Asia, who complained that they had been interned by Japanese
authorities in what they contemptuously described as the natives' living
conditions, Fukutome wrote: "For us, the most painful thing was that we
were treated equally to the natives, or no, even worse, we were considered
even lesser."[18] Fukutome's description of the jail conditions in Singapore
struck a chord with the Japanese public because in a well-respected publication and as a member of the elite, he confirmed existing rumors about
conditions in Allied prisons overseas.[19] The British authorities gave such
complaints little credence. But in a sign that Japanese public opinion

was beginning to matter to the Allies, they were nevertheless concerned about the potential impact in Japan of adverse reports about the prisoners' circumstances.[20]

CHANGING PERCEPTIONS
OF JAPANESE SOLDIERS

In Japan, the attempt to evoke sympathy for the imprisoned men continued, and public reports increasingly cast doubt on their underlying guilt as well. A petition on behalf of Yano Kenzo, sentenced in the Medan military tribunal, put the position carefully:

> We have, of course, no intention at all to criticize the fair judgement in the sacred court. The only thing we desire to state as his intimate friends who are familiar with his character and activities in the past is that we believe he is not such a person of nature committing inhumane act or approving his staff to act.[21]

Thus, ostensibly at least, the petition did not repudiate the evidence underlying Yano's conviction but rather implied that he had acted in special and unusual circumstances that belied his essential character.

As we have seen, judges sometimes expressed sweeping assessments of the character of the war criminals at the time of sentencing: "You are just brutes without any redeeming features."[22] Members of the public in Western countries wrote to the press dismissing Japanese war criminals as savages.[23] Justice Radhabinod Pal, the Indian judge at the International Military Tribunal for the Far East (IMTFE), argued in his dissenting judgment that no defendants at the Tokyo Trial should have been found guilty. He considered the prosecution in the national tribunals of lower-level military personnel, however, to be proper.[24] In Western eyes, the legitimacy of the war crimes trials relied on the widespread acceptance of the idea that it was obvious where good and evil lay. The perception that Japan's attack on Pearl Harbor had been entirely unprovoked, together with early reports of Japanese atrocities and the detailed accounts of individual incidents that were presented to Western publics through reporting on the trials, reinforced this belief. Nearly four decades after the end of the Second

World War, the American oral historian Studs Terkel characterized the conflict as "the good war," from the point of view of U.S. perceptions.[25] By this term, he implicitly contrasted what appeared to be the Second World War's simple dichotomy between good and evil with the moral ambiguities and contradictions of the Vietnam War of 1961–1972.[26] Powerful though this perception was at the time and powerful though it has remained, all those on the Allied side who contemplated the moral issues surrounding the war in both Europe and the Pacific had to confront evidence that it had not been a just war but, as the clergyman Robert H. Hamill put it in a different context, just another war.[27]

Buried in the record is evidence that some Westerners who encountered defeated Japanese soldiers did not see them as unutterably evil. Military men, especially, could identify with their counterparts on the other side and felt the pull of a powerful shared military culture. They did not necessarily see the war, or all the soldiers on the other side, as exceptional. When the commander of the China Expeditionary Army, General Okamura Yasuji, surrendered to his Chinese counterpart, General He Yingqin, the atmosphere was described as "relaxed";[28] the two men had known each other since they were junior officers.

When British forces arrived in the Andaman Islands in September 1945 to accept the surrender of the Japanese garrison there, they reported on their meeting with Admiral Hara Teizō: "Hara was full of good humour and it was found difficult to remain 'coldly polite' as instructed by SACSEA [Supreme Allied Commander South East Asia]."[29] The British officers found Hara helpful in providing information to assist the British landing in the Andamans. They discovered that as a junior lieutenant during the First World War, Hara had worked with the other Allies convoying Australian troops across the Indian Ocean. In 1924 he had accompanied the then Japanese crown prince (who later became the emperor Hirohito) on an enjoyable visit to London.[30] Hara was subsequently tried twice in Singapore on command responsibility charges and was executed as a war criminal, but the British officers who first encountered him clearly saw him as a brother officer with the same military values as themselves. Such encounters were repeated time and again in the early stages of the Allied recovery of Southeast Asia. The interpreter Louis Levy (later known as Louis Allen), who had interviewed Japanese military personnel near Pegu in Burma as potential defendants or witnesses in war crimes trials, recalled that the work led him to see them as humans rather than as the savages of wartime propaganda.[31] Even former POWs sometimes reminded the broader public that Japanese people as a race were not evil.[32]

In the immediate aftermath of the war, observers were inclined to notice the placidity of many defeated Japanese soldiers. Typically they interpreted it as a sign of their inability to function effectively except under orders.

> I have come to the conclusion [wrote Private Ranford Cunningham after attending a number of Australian war crimes trials in Morotai] that the average Japanese soldier is a mixture of the animal and the child, and therefore is a dangerous menace when under the wrong kind of control. He is an uncalculating creature who will obey the commands of his master, no matter what those commands may be, and will carry out commands without question.
>
> When freed from any domination, he is a carefree, happy individual, quite content to live on the bare necessities of life, and to live in peace with his companions.[33]

Another Australian newspaper carried photos of convicted war criminals smiling and listening to one of their number play the *shakuhachi* (flute) (figures 5.1 and 5.2). Such reports may have chimed on one level with wartime descriptions of apparent Japanese fatalism and insouciance in the face of death—another soldier who knew the condemned men shown in the photograph commented: "Death sentences did not seem to mean a thing to them."[34] Nonetheless, such accounts also suggested an underlying humanity in the defeated soldiers. Nothing in the newspaper photograph conjured up the crime for which the men had been condemned. John L. Ginn, a member of the U.S. military staff at Sugamo Prison, reported:

> The Western mentality and morality found it extremely difficult to match the prisoners' personalities to their past records as soldiers or sailors in the Imperial Forces. The American guards found them to be intelligent, docile, interesting, and often humorous. Most of them wanted to learn English and had their own methods for getting the guards to talk to them.[35]

Basil Archer, an Australian interpreter with the Occupation forces, went to see the IMTFE trial in Tokyo and commented in his diary, "To see Tojo and his mates lined up, I would never have thought them capable of organising a baseball match let alone a war."[36] Elaine Fischel, a member of the

FIGURE 5.1 Japanese war criminals at work in a saw mill on Manus Island, ca. 1948 (http://www.awm.gov.au/collection/306750/).

FIGURE 5.2 "Jap War Criminals in Condemned Compound," *Daily News* (Perth), January 16, 1946, 5. The accompanying text reads: "Sentenced to death for ordering the execution of three R.A.A.F. prisoners of war in the Taland [Talaud] Islands, Japanese war criminals in the condemned compound at Morotai placidly await the result of their appeals."

U.S. defense team at the IMTFE, commented of the accused: "In the court-room, dressed in cast-off clothing or uniforms that sagged on their wasted bodies, they did not look particularly formidable. In fact, the majority of these defendants appeared rather docile."[37]

These impressions of individual Japanese suspects and war criminals as not especially dangerous raised the possibility that Japanese atrocities might have been a consequence, at least in part, of the difficult circum-stances of war rather than simply a reflection of savagery embedded in Japanese culture. The dropping of the atomic bombs on Hiroshima and Nagasaki in the last days of the war was the single most important exhibit in the emerging, albeit contested, argument that there was some element of moral equivalence between the two sides,[38] but much smaller incidents could also have a powerful effect. In March 1946, Australian authorities used the former Japanese destroyer *Yoizuki* to repatriate more than one thousand former POWs and internees, many of them Taiwanese, from Sydney. Conditions aboard the ship were appalling, and a number of passengers died. When reports reached Australia, the press immediately labeled the vessel a "hell-ship," the term used for vessels in which Japanese forces had transported Allied POWs, often in extremely poor conditions.[39] An Australian engineer, J. G. Reed, told the press that he had cabled Aus-tralian prime minister Ben Chifley with the message: "Demand you as head of Christian government institute proceedings [for] punishment [of] Belsen brained brutes responsible Yoizuki atrocity, failing which apologet-ically pardon Japanese war criminals awaiting execution."[40]

Australian ministers for the army and navy defended themselves by explaining that the nature of the vessel and the number of people to be placed on board had been determined by SCAP in Japan; a member of parliament scornfully commented that this was equivalent to the Japa-nese war criminals saying they had only acted under orders.[41] Reed's mes-sage was one of several that explicitly compared the West's willingness to prosecute Japanese suspects for war crimes and its failure to uphold high standards on its own side.[42] There was little chance that those on the Australian side who were responsible for the incident actually would be prosecuted. One effect of the message, therefore, was to suggest that the ordinary, incompetent men responsible for the *Yoizuki* affair might well have ordinary, incompetent counterparts on the Japanese side.

Just as encounters with Japanese war criminals suggested that the conflict could be interpreted as an ordinary war between ordinary armies, the *Yoizuki* affair, together with the Japanese petitions, highlighted the possibility that many atrocities for which Japanese military personnel had been convicted might have been unforeseen results of the extreme circumstances of war rather than the deliberate actions of evil individual perpetrators. This perspective had the potential to bring a dramatic change to moral evaluations of the war. It suggested that the Japanese military might have behaved in wartime much as all militaries behave: as a complex organism that acted above all as a tool of the national interest, making judgments in the field about military necessity that often involved harsh outcomes and in which obedience to superior orders was a central organizing principle.

In 1959, the British production company Hammer Films released *Yesterday's Enemy*, a film set during the British retreat from Burma in 1942. The commander of a British unit orders his troops to execute two innocent Burmese civilians in an attempt to persuade a collaborator to reveal information. He ignores remonstrations from some of his subordinates that this action constitutes a war crime, only for his unit to be subjected to the same treatment when it is later captured by Japanese forces. Such a comparison lay at the heart of an implied or stated rebuke to the war crimes trials process: that rather than setting standards for the civilized conduct of war, it had imposed what Richard Minear later called "victors' justice."[43] The essence of this critique was that the war crimes proceedings had applied laws to the losing side only, so that the trials and verdicts were unjust for two reasons: the standards for the losers were unreasonably high, and the standards for the victors were unreasonably low.

TRANSFER TO JAPAN

The 1929 Geneva Convention allowed for the repatriation of ill and injured POWs during a conflict on the condition that they would not return to arms, and it provided for the prompt repatriation of POWs after the end of hostilities. The transfer of civilian criminals, as the war criminals were now officially considered to be, however, had no real precedent.[44] Nevertheless, Allied planners began seriously to consider the repatriation of convicted war criminals to Japan. They were motivated not by compassion for the prisoners but by economic considerations and calculations of where the political advantage lay. It was costly to keep war criminals in detention. Moreover, the prisoners had become a factor in international and imperial relationships in the intensifying Cold War: in some cases, leaving them where they were entailed the risk that new governments would simply release them, and in other cases, it seemed likely that Allied governments could extract direct political advantage from the prisoners.

In late 1947, with the independence of Burma planned for January 4, 1948, British officials suggested to the SCAP authorities in Japan that before the change of sovereignty, Japanese war criminals convicted in Burma be transferred to incarceration in Japan. As we saw in the previous chapter, British officials feared that the independent Burmese government might simply release any remaining war criminals. At first, American officials in Japan rejected the British suggestion out of hand. The idea of repatriating Japanese war criminals grew in strength in 1948–1949, however, as it became clearer that removing them from Southeast Asian jails would suit the political and economic interests of the incarcerating authorities. Not surprisingly, the suggestion met with favor in Japan. In mid-April 1948, a Japanese government spokesman announced that the authorities were preparing to petition the Allies to allow war criminals to serve out their sentences in Japan.[45] Later that month, C. F. Aeschliman, the chief delegate of the ICRC, South East Asian Area, noted confidentially that the Red Cross was "actively working on a scheme for repatriation."[46] It is difficult to ascertain how much influence the ICRC was able to exert. The organization went on to push for the repatriation of all Japanese soldiers and civilians still outside Japan, including war criminals, through both its local representatives in Southeast Asia and the central body in Geneva, which lobbied Allied governments through the United Nations Organization There is no direct evidence, however, that the Red Cross's efforts were successful.[47]

In July 1949, the governments of Singapore and Malaya joined forces to recommend to the British government that the approximately 370 war criminals still in their jails be transferred to Japan as soon as possible "to complete their terms of imprisonment there." Officials argued that the prisoners were mostly "underlings" and emphasized the value of easing overcrowding in local jails, along with the additional advantage of "relieving the local Governments of maintenance charges which would then fall, as they properly should, on the people of Japan." The Hong Kong authorities reportedly approved the plan as well.[48]

As indicated by SCAP's reluctance to accept prisoners from Burma, the American authorities in Japan initially were unwilling to approve the transfer of convicted war criminals from outside their jurisdiction. But by early 1949, SCAP's views had changed. In March 1946, civil war had broken out in China between the Nationalist and Communist forces, and by the beginning of 1949, most of the north of the country was in Communist hands and the defeat of the Nationalists appeared certain. War criminals were caught in the cross fire. The Communists identified the Nationalist leader, Chiang Kai-shek, and other Guomindang leaders as "war criminals" and demanded that the Nationalists hand them over for trial as a condition of peace. They also demanded that Japanese war criminals who had been convicted in Nationalist courts be handed over as well, along with General Okamura Yasuji, who had been acquitted by the Nationalists by executive fiat in 1948 so that he could provide high-level military advice to the Guomindang forces.[49] The Nationalist authorities approached SCAP, claiming to fear that Japanese war criminals would be massacred by the Communist army if they remained in place. In late January 1949, SCAP hastily agreed to accept 251 of them for detention in Sugamo Prison.[50] The Chinese Communist Party described the transfer of war criminals to Japan as a "traitorous" act by the Guomindang and as evidence of the Nationalists' "insincere" approach to peace negotiations.[51]

The Netherlands Indies government, too, had become unexpectedly eager to ship its convicted war criminals to Japan because of its imminent withdrawal from its Southeast Asian colony. With the transfer of sovereignty to Indonesia due on December 29, 1949, the colonial authorities focused suddenly on the situation of the 680 Japanese war criminals who remained in their custody, all of them now in Tjipinang jail in Batavia. They were less concerned about the prisoners' formal legal status than about political considerations. Although the wartime Japanese occupation had destroyed infrastructure and cost numerous lives, Indonesian nationalists often credited Japan with creating the conditions for the 1945 declaration of independence. In turn, many Dutch officials continued to regard the Indonesian Republic, with which they had been fighting a civil war since 1945, as an artifact of Japanese machinations. They feared that the incoming Indonesian authorities, sympathetic to the Japanese, would simply release the war criminals in Tjipinang. A few weeks before the scheduled transfer of sovereignty, they approached General Douglas MacArthur with the idea of moving the prisoners to Sugamo. MacArthur was amenable, though he stipulated that the Dutch government would have to surrender all influence over the prisoners' subsequent fate. The convicts boarded ship on December 26, 1949, and arrived in Japan on January 23, 1950.[52]

The French government also moved to repatriate Japanese war criminals, in a move directly related to its own colonial struggle in Southeast Asia. In August 1948, former officers among the Japanese convicts in Indochina drew up a petition asking to be allowed to serve out their sentences in Japan. French military commander General Roger Blaizot suggested that repatriation could be offered if the highest ranking of the Japanese officers, General Tsuchihashi Yūitsu, persuaded the former Japanese soldiers now fighting on the side of the Việt Minh to surrender and leave Indochina.[53] Tsuchihashi, who had been imprisoned in Saigon on suspicion of war crimes, was released to help round up Japanese deserters, a task he performed with limited success.[54] Although records of the French government in Indochina are patchy, it can be concluded that the French authorities gradually decided that the war criminals were an unnecessary distraction in their ongoing conflict with the Việt Minh. In July 1949, the French president granted remissions of sentence to fifty-five prisoners to mark Bastille Day,[55] and in November of the same year the French government instructed its representative in Japan to find out whether SCAP would be willing to accept war criminals convicted in French courts. SCAP evidently agreed to do so. In early June 1950, eighty-two convicted war criminals, as well as thirty-five other repatriates—including war criminals whose sentences had expired, witnesses who had given evidence at the trials, and some recaptured Japanese deserters to the Việt Minh—were transported to Yokohama. Those with jail terms entered Sugamo Prison.[56] A handful who had been condemned to death were left behind in Saigon and were executed after their sentences were confirmed in March 1951.[57]

In July 1949 the British War Office and Foreign Office also began to pay serious attention to the idea of repatriation. Foreign Office officials, at least, were coming to the conclusion that the "balance of political advantage" lay in "getting these men back to Japan as soon as possible."[58] In Singapore, Governor Gimson combined practical and ideological concerns in his summary of the arguments:

> I consider that the proper course would be for these war criminals to be sent to Japan to serve out the rest of their sentences and thus, incidentally, relieve this Government of the cost of their custody. The criminals might

then be made to understand the true nature of their offences in respect of which they have brought disgrace on Japan itself.[59]

Approached by British officials in December 1949, MacArthur was entirely receptive to the idea of repatriating the war criminals to Japan, revealing that he had already agreed to transfers from China and was discussing a similar arrangement with the Netherlands. He warned, however, that transfer would depend on the availability of prison space in Japan and the willingness of the British government or its colonies to pay the repatriation costs.[60] About a week after MacArthur's assent to the proposal, the Foreign Office had lists of the prisoners ready to send to SCAP,[61] but the issue of cost seems to have caused unexpected delay. It took considerable effort for the British authorities to persuade the colonial governments that they would save themselves maintenance costs in the long term if they paid for the shipment of war criminals to Japan.[62] The repatriation proposal was complicated, moreover, by the continued presence of war criminals convicted by Australian courts in Singapore, Malaya, and Hong Kong.[63] Not until August 1950 did Britain ask the Australian government for its consent to repatriation. Although the Australian government delayed its response until December, it requested only that MacArthur be pressed for assurance that he would enforce the original sentences.[64] As we have seen, discussion of repatriation prompted the Australian authorities to transfer the prominent prisoner Nishimura Takuma from Singapore, where he had been tried by a British court, to Manus Island for a second trial in an Australian court, thus guarding against the possibility that he might slip out of their grasp before they could prosecute him.[65]

On January 18, 1951, the Foreign Office finally wrote to the British representative in Tokyo to report that all the governments concerned had agreed to repatriation and would provide details of the number of prisoners who would need to be accommodated in Sugamo (table 5.1). On February 23, 1951, MacArthur formally notified the Foreign Office that prison facilities were available and confirmed that he would uphold sentences, but he declared unambiguously that the prisoners would come under SCAP's "complete jurisdiction." He also insisted that no prisoner under sentence of death be transferred, presumably because he did not want SCAP to be forced to take responsibility for implementing or modifying death sentences handed down in other jurisdictions.[66] Prisoners in Hong Kong were repatriated in May 1951. Those in other British colonial

TABLE 5.1 Japanese War Criminals Reported in British Hands
and in Independent Burma, January 1951

Jurisdiction	Number of prisoners
Malaya	84
Singapore	147
North Borneo	15
Hong Kong	87
Burma	10
Total	343

Note: The Foreign Office commented that some figures might be too high. Burma, however, later was found to have thirty prisoners.

Source: FO to Tokyo, January 18, 1950, NA (UK), DO 35/2937.

jails were transferred to Singapore throughout the first half of 1951 before being repatriated to Japan aboard the *Tairea* on August 14.[67]

MacArthur emphasized the same point to every prosecuting power wishing to transfer its prisoners to Japan: SCAP would recognize the sentences imposed by the original court, but it would also assume full responsibility for implementing the sentences from the moment the prisoners arrived and were transferred to Sugamo. In other words, convicted war criminals would immediately come under SCAP's provisions for remission and parole.[68] When the Chinese representative on the Far Eastern Commission (FEC) questioned SCAP's authority to change a sentence imposed by the court of another government, SCAP replied that its complete authority in judicial matters in Japan had been established under FEC rules and that the provision of parole should not be mistaken for a reduction in sentence.[69] In fact, SCAP was less than punctilious in recognizing the precise terms of other governments' sentences. SCAP's Legal Section ruled, for instance, that all sentences be served concurrently, even when the prosecuting power had intended them to be consecutive. For sentences exceeding forty-five years, including life, parole applied after a flat fifteen years.[70] But SCAP was willing to allow a convicting power to make additional reductions to a sentence, as French president Vincent Auriol did on Bastille Day in 1951 as part of a general amnesty.[71]

Only the governments of the Philippines and Australia held out against the transfer of convicted war criminals to Japan. In Manila, responsibility for the custody of war criminals shifted from the United States to the Philippines in 1948. Sharon Chamberlain speculates that the Philippine government may have wished to keep custody of the war criminals as a bargaining chip in negotiations with Japan over reparations for wartime damage; Nagai Hitoshi cites the strength of anti-Japanese feeling in the Philippines as the more fundamental reason for not repatriating the prisoners.[72] In February 1951 the Philippine president, Elpidio Quirino, became the first authority to end the sentence of a Japanese war criminal, in this case Matsuzaki Hideichi, by means of a pardon. It was an unexpected step, given that parole and sentence reduction were by then the established mechanisms for releasing Japanese war criminals. It may have signaled Quirino's determination to set his stamp on Philippine policy in this area, or it may simply have been a device to avoid the likely complexity of setting up a body to administer parole in the Philippines. Only a few prisoners, however, received a presidential pardon.[73]

Australia permitted the repatriation of war criminals convicted in Australian courts in Singapore, Malaya, and Hong Kong. These prisoners, who had been held in colonial jails alongside their British-convicted counterparts, were sent to Japan in 1951 together with war criminals in British custody. But the Australian government was not ready to give up its control of convicted war criminals held on Manus Island or of other suspects it still intended to prosecute. In late 1949 SCAP had informed the Australian government that it would release the suspects it held on Australia's behalf in Sugamo if the Australian government did not soon take action to decide their fate. In response, the Australian government resumed its prosecutions after a hiatus in 1949–1950 and opened a new trial venue on Manus Island.[74] In early 1950, Australian authorities requested the transfer from Sugamo to Manus of around fifty suspects, including General Imamura Hitoshi, whose prosecution for war crimes had been a complicated and prolonged saga. Imamura had been the military governor in Java at the start of the Japanese occupation there and had later commanded the Japanese forces that surrendered at Rabaul in 1945. In May 1947 an Australian tribunal in Rabaul had sentenced him to ten years in prison on command responsibility charges. The Australian authorities had then transferred him to Java for trial by the Dutch authorities.[75] In one of the last Netherlands Indies trials, in March 1949, Imamura was acquitted of command responsibility charges, although the verdict was not confirmed until December 24, just days before the mass repatriation from Batavia. He arrived in Japan on January 23, 1950, but in February was shipped to Manus Island to continue the sentence originally imposed by the Australian court.[76] He was one of the two hundred or so Japanese war criminals under Australian control on Manus in the early 1950s.

The concentration and repatriation of convicted war criminals had been undertaken mainly for legal, practical, and economic reasons. The ambiguities of jurisdiction in the rapidly changing Asia-Pacific region had led the prosecuting powers to remove prisoners from locations where the legal basis for their detention might be questioned or where there might be political pressures for their release or their murder. In the small British colonies of Singapore and Hong Kong, and to some extent in Malaya, the issue of cost also intruded into the decision to repatriate. These considerations quickly came to overshadow the earlier principle that war criminals should be imprisoned as close as possible to the scenes of their crimes, in order to demonstrate to the victims that justice had been done. Two of the three detention locations that remained in mid-1951 were relatively safe from the threat of violence or political pressure. The New Bilibid Prison at Muntinlupa outside Manila, with 138 convicted war criminals, was in the territory of the sovereign Philippine Republic, while Manus Island was an Australian external territory in New Guinea that was untroubled by nationalist rumblings. The third place of detention, Sugamo Prison, which held by far the largest number of convicted war criminals, was in Japan, which was still securely under American occupation. Political change in Japan, however, soon precipitated major doubts about whether these prisoners should remain incarcerated.

FROM INDIVIDUAL GUILT TO NATIONAL RESPONSIBILITY

The slowly growing inclination in the West to reinterpret at least some of the Japanese war criminals as ordinary soldiers driven to desperate measures in difficult circumstances was paralleled in Japan. According to Higurashi Yoshinobu, in 1948 when the verdicts were handed down, all the major Japanese newspapers accepted the judgment of the Tokyo Trial as an affirmation of peace and democracy.[77] The Japanese press initially paid little attention to any of the war criminals once they had been convicted. Public opinion regarding their fate seems to have been largely indifferent, and sometimes negative.[78] According to later media reports, the families of war criminals had suffered social discrimination in the early years. For example, they were refused employment and did not fare well in marriage negotiations. Some local authorities apparently denied permission for the construction of graves for executed war criminals.[79] Nonetheless, members of the Japanese public who regarded the war as a mistake and who perhaps regretted the atrocities when they learned of them early in the Occupation did not necessarily regard the war as an actual crime. When General Yamashita Tomoyuki was sentenced to death, a reported two thousand Japanese people swamped a small stand in the Ginza district of Tokyo to sign a petition for clemency. A sign above the stand read "The Japanese nation has not been softened enough to remain inactive on Yamashita's behalf. Remember how we clapped hands when we saw movies showing Singapore's fall!"[80]

A broad argument emerged that individual war criminals were scapegoats who had been punished on behalf of all the Japanese people. Suzuki Katsuhiko, a chaplain who ministered to Japanese war criminals in Singapore, described meeting "Prisoner K.," who had been condemned to death. K. had initially been angry about having to expiate, in his view, the guilt of a whole nation and was anxious that his condemnation might lead to discrimination against his wife. But recently, according to Suzuki, K. had had a change of heart and had reached a great sense of calm. Facing death, he was now "sending his forgiveness to the Japanese people who had abandoned them [war criminals], the Japanese people who had thrown them and their families into the depths of hell, the Japanese people who had sent them into madness."[81]

Tsuji Yutaka, a special correspondent for the *Asahi shinbun*, wrote in February 1952 that the prisoners at Muntinlupa in the Philippines felt that their punishment was the penance they offered as individuals for wartime Japan's guilt, and they wanted acknowledgment at home of their sacrifice.[82] Tsuji calculated that a mere 200 men had borne the guilt of 400,000 Japanese military personnel who had fought in the Philippines. Could the Japanese people who sent them there, he asked, not share their responsibility?[83] The weekly *Shūkan asahi* reported a comment by an unnamed Sugamo prisoner in the same month: "There is a strong feeling [among the prisoners] that we have been made to shoulder the responsibility for the defeat." This prisoner went on to mention a celebrated speech in September 1945 by Prime Minister Prince Higashikuni, expressing contrition on behalf of the entire Japanese people for their overall conduct of the war. Higashikuni's expression of regret became publicly known as *ichioku sōzange,* or the "repentance of 100 million people." The unnamed prisoner continued: "The so-called 'repentance of 100 million people' was at some point transformed into [the narrower concept of] 'war responsibility' [*senso sekinin*], and the war criminals alone ended up being the victims of this version of national guilt."[84]

At one level, this argument simply called on the Japanese people to be generous and understanding toward those who were suffering punishment on their behalf. It quickly, however, conjured up the idea also that the war criminals were not being punished for individual crimes but were bearing the consequences of national guilt. This implication in turn generated the argument that forgiveness and mercy for war criminals were warranted because Japan had turned its back on war,[85] an assertion that directly contradicted the Allied version of the war crimes trials program. According to Allied logic, individuals were to be punished for the crimes that they themselves had committed or, at the least, that their units had committed. The courts had paid great attention to identifying the locus of guilt in complex cases with imperfect evidence. The trials were intended to separate the war criminals from the mass of the Japanese people, rather than to turn them into representatives of Japan. By February 1950, however, the public support for war criminals was sufficient to spur the Legal Section of the General Headquarters of the U.S. Occupation machinery to express concern about the political pressure being exerted in Japan on behalf of the prisoners. Legal Section warned that if the campaign continued, it would glorify war criminals and turn them into martyrs.[86]

Japanese concern was further aroused when the Australian government resumed its trials in June 1950 on Manus Island. Both the Labor government and its Coalition successor that came to power in December 1949 feared that abandoning the trial program would generate a significant public outcry in Australia, as well as the sense that war criminals had escaped punishment. They therefore insisted on the transfer to Manus of the suspects still held in Sugamo. Nonetheless, the Australian authorities wanted to limit the trials to the most serious offenses and to keep them as short as possible. In the event, 101 defendants were prosecuted in twenty-four trials at

Manus. Thirty-eight defendants were acquitted. Of the remainder, fourteen were condemned to death, but, acting on the advice of the judge advocate general, the Australian government commuted all but five of the death sentences.[87] The final trial concluded on April 9, 1951, when a court on Manus Island acquitted Miyazaki Jyosuke of charges of murdering an Australian POW at Kupang in 1942.[88]

On January 19, 1951, however, the news had reached Japan that fourteen war criminals had been executed at Muntinlupa in the Philippines. The executions galvanized public opinion and prompted a surge in public interest in the fate of Japanese war criminals overseas. According to the Japanese Ministry of Welfare, Muntinlupa and Manus became "two names known to even very young children" in this period.[89] Most of the attention focused on seventy war criminals under sentence of death who remained at Muntinlupa.[90] The jail's Japanese chaplain, Kagao Shūnin, not only broke the news in Japan about the January 1951 executions, but also fanned fears about further executions, linking them with fraught negotiations between the Philippines and Japan on war reparations. Kagao reported that anti-Japanese sentiment was worsening in the Philippines because of Japan's perceived reluctance to pay reparations. In his analysis, the Philippine government had ordered the executions to proceed as a way of applying diplomatic pressure on the Japanese government.[91] Kagao was probably mistaken: recent assessments indicate that confirmation of the death sentences had simply been delayed by a shortage of qualified legal personnel.[92] But the suggestion that Japanese citizens were being executed overseas as pawns in a game of diplomatic relations stunned the Japanese public. A headline in the major newspaper *Mainichi shinbun* read: "Please, no more executions."[93] In the Diet, politicians and bureaucrats condemned the executions and repeatedly acknowledged the many petitions for the repatriation of Japanese war criminals overseas, not just in the Diet's committees but also in its full sittings.[94] One typical petition, signed by 2,633 people in Nagano Prefecture, reiterated the idea that those in jails in Manus and Muntinlupa were expiating the guilt of the Japanese nation as a whole, urging the Diet to send a delegation to the Philippines to express the deep apologies of the people of Japan to the people of the Philippines and to ask the Philippine government to show clemency to the convicted.[95]

Japanese reaction to the executions in Muntinlupa in January 1951 marked the consolidation of a far-reaching change in prevailing ideas about what should happen to the convicted war criminals. In Japan, ambivalence about the status of the convicted men disappeared, at least in the dominant public discourse. The Japanese government and Japanese public opinion were convinced that the men should no longer be detained, and they had a formidable arsenal of arguments to support this stance. Those arguments referred to perceived unfairness in the trial process, to humanitarian regard for the prisoners and their families, and to what was seen as the special status of the prisoners as scapegoats for a collective Japanese war responsibility that was soon to be erased by the signing of a peace treaty between Japan and most of its wartime enemies. On the side of the imprisoning powers, too, deterrence, prevention, and rehabilitation had by this time lost force as justifications for continuing to detain the convicted men. The only argument to retain its vigor was that retribution was justified for what had been truly terrible crimes. In the negotiations over the peace treaty, however, the collision between retribution and reconciliation produced an unexpected outcome that was to keep Japanese war criminals in prison for years to come.

6

PEACE AND ARTICLE 11

I n 1947, the United States began serious planning for a peace treaty with Japan. American officials considered that the peace terms would be crucial to consolidating a postwar settlement in Asia that was favorable to U.S. interests and consistent with American ideals. The process of drafting the treaty accordingly prompted extensive internal debates over what should be asked of and conceded to Japan and, in addition, how far the interests and demands of America's allies should be accommodated. Drafts of a treaty began to appear as early as August 1947 and continued to appear until mid-1951. Initially punitive, these drafts gradually became more lenient, but the process was not linear; it reflected both wide-ranging discussions in U.S. policymaking circles and accommodation with the concerns of other powers, including Japan.[1]

Reparations and security were the crucial issues, dwarfing matters concerning war criminals. For all the prosecuting governments, however, the anticipated end of the Occupation prompted the question of what would become of the convicted war criminals when Japan regained its sovereignty. The conclusion of peace required a new approach, since the U.S. Occupation authorities, which controlled the great majority of the convicted war criminals, would depart when peace was formally declared. Moreover, the parole system set up in Sugamo by the U.S. military would cease to operate, as the Americans would no longer be in charge of the prison, and no new system had been devised to take its place. The release campaign in Japan was becoming more vociferous and was not balanced by any significant Japanese voices arguing that the sentences should be sustained. There thus seemed a distinct possibility that a sovereign Japanese government would simply release all the war criminals unless the Allied governments took specific action to prevent it from doing so. Once the Occupation ended, there might even have been a legal obligation to do so: in September 1951, a Japanese scholar of international law, Irie Keishirō, wrote that without the specific provision for war criminals that was included in the final draft of the treaty, the sentences would have lapsed when the formal peace came, since the war crimes trials had taken place as part of military action, and military action ceased with the peace treaty.[2]

The provision regarding war criminals in the eventual peace treaty had a tortuous history, reflecting not only competing views on how far Japan should continue to be punished but also the fluctuating postwar relations among the greater and lesser Western powers. Except for their deliberations in the International Military Tribunal for the Far East (IMTFE), it was the first time the Allies had been forced into sustained negotiations and trade-offs with one another over the future of Japanese war criminals. These dealings then began to reveal cracks in Allied solidarity on what should happen to war criminals and, more broadly, how Japan should now be treated.

EARLY TREATY DRAFTS

Despite considerable diplomatic friction over the terms of the peace between the United States and the governments of the People's Republic of China (PRC), after 1949, and the Soviet Union, the United States was generally acknowledged to be the leader in the peace negotiations.[3] For their part, officials in the Japanese Foreign Ministry's Treaty Bureau apparently considered the participation of other governments to be "purely academic" and were convinced that the United States was the only power that mattered.[4] Nevertheless, the negotiations were multilateral, especially in the initial stages, and in the late 1940s the Allies had competing goals and strategies in relation to Japan. Nor was there a unified official American view on the best way to deal with Japan, or any accepted overall policy.

Marked differences existed, especially at first, among the State, Defense, War, and Navy Departments and the Supreme Commander for the Allied Powers (SCAP), and in different sections of the State Department as well. Officials disagreed about what should be in a treaty and about whether a peace conference should be convened early so that Japanese sovereignty would be restored quickly, or delayed until Japan was politically and economically stronger.[5] In theory, the Japanese government had very little say over the treaty's content. The Japanese Foreign Ministry, however, set up an internal committee as early as November 1945 to plan for a settlement, and attempts to influence American decision makers began in the first half of 1947. By late 1950, the Foreign Ministry's Treaty Bureau was producing its own treaty drafts.[6] In the negotiations' later stages, U.S. officials encouraged the Japanese government to comment on provisions in the Allies' drafts, and the Treaty Bureau studied successive versions closely.[7] The discussions among the Allied powers, and the internal discussions in each of their policymaking centers, made it clear that the automatic release of convicted war criminals would not be acceptable. As we have seen, opinion concerning the character of the prisoners and the nature of their crimes had begun to shift in the West. Nevertheless, there still was a strong feeling that automatic release would call into question the underlying validity of the original trials and thus would undermine whatever good the complex and costly war crimes program had done. Many Allied planners also felt that indiscriminate early release would break faith with the victims and their families, and they were conscious of the potential for negative political reactions in the metropolitan constituencies. The question, therefore, was how to ensure that prisoners would not automatically be released.

Allied planners were convinced that any attempt to control future release would need to be set out in a binding agreement between Japan and the prosecuting governments. Concern over whether a former enemy could otherwise be trusted to ensure that the sentences were carried out was exacerbated by the Italian case. A small number of Italian war criminals had been tried and convicted in British and American military tribunals between 1945 and 1947. The Allies had decided, however, not to insert into the peace treaty with Italy, signed in February 1947, a clause requiring the continued punishment of the convicted men. The British and American authorities had been satisfied with an informal promise that the Italian government would honor the sentences imposed, and Britain had

also made a "gentlemen's agreement" with Italy that the British government would have the final say on any form of clemency.[8] Nonetheless, the
Italian government had allegedly proceeded to release the prisoners, "in
many cases on the flimsiest of excuses."[9] The Allied authorities feared
therefore that the Japanese government, under pressure from the growing
strength of public sympathy in Japan for convicted war criminals, would
release the prisoners once peace was restored unless a specific section in
the treaty prevented it.

The first draft treaty, produced in August 1947 by officials from the
U.S. State Department's Far Eastern Affairs section, led by the Japan specialist Hugh Borton, contained a whole chapter on war criminals. At this
early stage, when trials were still in full swing, provision was made for the
further apprehension and handing over of suspects, a concern that disappeared from later drafts as the peace settlement was further and further
delayed, and in the meantime, it became clear that trials would soon end.
Power over clemency, however, was already an issue in 1947. In the Borton
draft, this power was left with the Allies, with no role at all for Japan.
Article 20 stipulated that "Japan undertakes to execute fully the sentences
imposed." The right to vary sentences was given to the Council of Ambassadors for Japan, a body that was to represent the eleven nations then
sitting on the Far Eastern Commission (FEC) but that in fact was never
created.[10] Meanwhile, also in August–September 1947, representatives of
the British Commonwealth met in Canberra to discuss the Japanese treaty.
As Frederick Dunn commented, a prime aim of the Canberra conference
was to strengthen the Commonwealth's influence, especially that of Australia and New Zealand, over the future settlement.[11] Like Borton's group,
the Commonwealth favored a severe and restrictive treaty as the basis of
"a stable peace in the Pacific, free from the threat of Japanese aggression
in the future."[12] Britain, Australia, and New Zealand were not alone in
advocating a strong line against Japan: the Philippines, China, and Burma
also feared a resurgence of Japanese militarism, and pursued the question
of reparations.[13]

In the U.S. State Department and other branches of government, however, views of Japan had begun to change. Particularly influential was
the State Department's new Policy Planning Staff, which was led by the
Soviet specialist George Kennan, the major strategist of the emerging U.S.
policy of "containing" any Soviet plans for expansion. Kennan and his
small staff, along with Undersecretary of the Army William H. Draper Jr.

and Defense Secretary James V. Forrestal, worked to change American policy on Japan. Convinced that Japan was vulnerable to Soviet influence or even control, they insisted that the antidote was to strengthen Japan economically and politically, which meant ending democratic reforms that were disruptive to the Japanese economy or to political stability, abandoning the pursuit of a retaliatory peace and allocating significant economic aid to Japan. They also countered General Douglas MacArthur's attempts to engineer an early peace settlement, arguing that Japanese sovereignty should not be restored until a stable and strong Japanese government had been established and until it was clear that Japan would be friendly to the United States. In a long report on his visit to Tokyo in March 1948, Kennan advocated ceasing all elements of the reform agenda that might block Japanese economic recovery or undermine social stability, including war crimes trials, as noted earlier. Kennan's recommendations were supported in Washington, endorsed by the National Security Council and approved by President Harry S. Truman in October 1948. Meanwhile, Japan's weak economy and the demands of America's Cold War strategy against the Soviet Union meant that the desire for a more lenient approach to Japan had gradually spread, so that by the end of 1948, proponents of a punitive peace had no strong voice among U.S. decision makers. The new draft treaty produced in October 1949 therefore was based on the restoration of Japanese sovereignty with as few restrictions as possible.[14]

Other governments were slower to adopt the same position. But by the end of 1950, the British secretary of state for foreign affairs, Ernest Bevin, was in complete accord with the new emphasis in dealings with Japan, inviting his cabinet colleagues to agree that "His Majesty's Government's major objective in the Peace Treaty discussions should be to secure a treaty which will permit the development of a peace-loving Japan with a viable economy."[15] China's intervention in the Korean War in October 1950 had had a massive effect on assessments of the Cold War in Asia. In the official British view, it was now even more urgent to act "to prevent the absorption of Japan into the Communist orbit and to accomplish its definite commitment to the side and cause of the free world."[16] The British government now advocated a brief, liberal, nonrestrictive peace that would allow Japan to rearm quickly, with American aid, so that Japan could join in its own defense if necessary.[17] Bevin noted in his report to the UK cabinet, however, that the Australian and New Zealand governments disagreed with the rest of the Commonwealth about the security provisions that would be necessary in the peace settlement: they still wanted significant controls on Japan to prevent future aggression.[18] Bevin and his most senior officials had already informed the U.S. government that they wanted more attention paid to Commonwealth concerns in the negotiations; Bevin had also agreed to mediate between the Commonwealth and the U.S. government.[19]

Despite their new emphasis on leniency, the American authorities continued to be concerned with the issue of how to deal with the convicted war criminals. Although Occupation authorities were now releasing many people from the "purge," State Department officials told the Japanese government they would still seek to preserve war criminals' sentences after the formal restoration of peace.[20] In one of several treaty drafts produced in 1950, described as "liberal, general and brief" by its authors, Article 14 stated that Japan "undertakes to execute the sentences" of war criminals; the power to vary sentences would be exercised by Japan, but on the approval of the prosecuting governments.[21] On the face of it, this clause allowed latitude to Japan, and the Japanese role was certainly greater than it had been in the Borton draft. In practice, though, the requirement for the foreign governments' approval would greatly have curtailed Japan's freedom of action.

The commentary on the treaty draft suggests that this provision might have represented a compromise solution to the problem of what to do with the convicted war criminals. The document raised three questions. The first was whether arrests and trials should continue after the treaty had been signed; the writers concluded they should not. Trials scheduled by the U.S. authorities had ended in October 1949, and key officials now considered that "to perpetuate the stigma inevitably attaching to a requirement for the apprehension of possible further war crimes suspects would . . . run counter to the fundamental aims of the treaty draft."[22]

The second question was where the war criminals held in Japan when the treaty was concluded should serve their sentences. War criminals convicted by the United States and Britain in Italy, it was noted, had been transferred to Italian custody on signing of the peace treaty, and it seemed reasonable that Japanese war criminals would similarly be turned over to Japanese authorities. The only real alternative, according to these officials, was to move the prisoners to the United States. Such a course of action, however, would be costly, and it would introduce inequities because prisoners held in the United States would have better food and other conditions than would ordinary criminals incarcerated in Japan. Conversely, those in the United States would be separated from their families. Moreover, it would be problematic to mix Japanese with American criminals, even if prison space was available, and in any case it was doubtful that Japanese prisoners could legally be held in the United States. If Japanese war criminals were instead left under Japanese jurisdiction, the authorities could be asked for a guarantee that they would serve out their sentences. The same course of action was also contemplated for German war criminals.[23] In fact, the governments of the United States, Britain, and France did impose the same condition on West Germany in exchange for the transfer of prisoners to German custody. As there was no formal peace treaty with Germany, the arrangement was made through the Bonn Conventions with the Federal Republic of Germany of May 26, 1952, which terminated the Occupation of Germany.[24]

The third issue in the Japanese case was what procedures should be established for the exercise of clemency if the prisoners were left in Japan. U.S. officials believed the Allies should have a say:

> Considering that war crimes were committed against the Allies, whose military tribunals have after careful investigation and trial imposed the sentences now being served, it would seem logical and appropriate that with SCAP no longer present to approve or disapprove clemency actions such actions initiated after the coming into force of the treaty should require the approval of the government or governments which imposed the sentence in each instance.[25]

An Allied consensus thus began to take shape. The treaty drafters wanted to be assured that war criminals would not simply be released, but they also wanted to avoid the difficulties of removing prisoners from Japan in order to watch over them. As a compromise, they would extract a promise from the Japanese government and reinforce it by preventing the Japanese authorities from acting without the approval of the prosecuting governments. This strategy represented an advance on what had been done in Italy, where the Allies had decided not to insert a clause in the peace treaty guaranteeing the continued punishment of convicted war criminals. In the Japanese case, in view of the new value accorded to Japan as an important contributor to the democratic side in the Cold War, the insistence on retaining rights over convicted criminals was balanced rhetorically by giving the Japanese government the capacity to act, at least in theory. By September 1950, the draft wording indicated that the power to vary sentences would be exercised "jointly by Japan and the Government or Governments which imposed the sentence in each instance."[26]

Discussions between the United States and its allies over the peace treaty reached a peak in 1950 and 1951. In May 1950 President Truman had appointed John Foster Dulles, Republican adviser to the Department of State, to handle the negotiations. In the same month, British Commonwealth governments set up a working party in London to discuss the treaty, at which the principal concern was postwar security. Australia and New Zealand, unlike Britain, were still "more afraid of Japan than of Russia."[27] Toward the close of 1950, Dulles held informal bilateral discussions in New York and Washington with America's allies on the terms of the coming settlement. Talks with the other members of the FEC, and later with Indonesia and Ceylon as well, were based on a U.S. memorandum outlining seven general principles on the content of the treaty. To the apparent consternation of the governments of Australia, New Zealand, the Philippines, and Burma, this document did not seek to restrict Japanese rearmament, though U.S. officials concluded that Australia and New Zealand "would withdraw their objections in return for an adequate U.S. guarantee of their security" and that Burmese objections were "purely nominal."[28]

Dulles's broad approach to a settlement with Japan was in sympathy with the emphasis that had originated with Kennan and the State Department's Policy Planning Staff on the need to conclude a liberal agreement. Dulles considered Communism the greatest danger to world peace. Consequently, in talks with Australian diplomats in New York in September 1950, he emphasized what one Australian official described as "the expected line": "Japan must be denied to U.S.S.R. and kept on the side of Western democracies. To achieve this object, the Treaty should be designed so as not to engender Japanese resentment."[29]

Apart from the Cold War imperative, Dulles, a prominent lawyer who had been a member of the reparations commission at the Versailles Peace Conference, was highly conscious of the lessons of Versailles. The principal lesson was, he believed, "that justice, fair play, magnanimity, and humanity were the essential ingredients not only for a moral peace settlement, but also for one which in the long run would be safe and successful."[30] Thus he considered a generous peace as well as a strong Japan to be absolutely necessary, insisting that "restrictive provisions (e.g., prohibition of re-armament) . . . should not be imposed on Japan."[31] The British government agreed and, once again, indicated to U.S. officials that it would use its influence to persuade the Commonwealth governments also of the necessity of a short and lenient peace settlement.[32] Meanwhile, Japanese officials prepared a document setting out what they wanted in the treaty, in which war criminals would be granted a general amnesty unless they had committed crimes against common law. The request represented an ambit claim, advanced in the hope of encouraging the Allies to consider favorable conditions for convicted war criminals. The document went on to list more moderate alternatives to a general amnesty, principally the commutation of death sentences and generous reductions in other sentences—especially for prisoners who had been young and rash at the time of their offenses or who had committed crimes under the orders of their superiors—as well as the repatriation of those still held overseas.[33]

In 1951 Dulles visited the Philippines, Australia, and New Zealand to discuss the terms of the Japanese settlement. When he arrived in Canberra in February, he was confronted with a hostile Australian and New Zealand reaction to the U.S. proposal to share with Japan the responsibility for war criminals. The official Australian view was that the Japanese authorities should have no right at all to alter sentences: "Having regard to the strength of public opinion on the question of Japanese war atrocities, the power to alter war crimes sentences should be confined to the Allied nations." Although Dulles opposed the adoption of too restrictive a stance on war criminals,[34] he failed to convince the Australian officials. Their discussions on security fared better. During the Canberra talks, a new security treaty was drafted. The proposed Australia, New Zealand, and U.S. Security (ANZUS) Pact, eventually signed in San Francisco in September 1951, a week before the peace treaty, went a long way toward reassuring the Australian and New Zealand governments that any future threat from Japan would be countered with U.S. assistance.[35]

WAR GUILT AND "PARDON"

The Canberra talks also highlighted another point of difference between U.S. negotiators and some of their allies: whether the peace treaty should refer to Japan's responsibility for provoking the war. The issue was closely associated with the proposed provision on war criminals, since both related to war guilt. Avoiding a war guilt clause was very important to the U.S. government; in fact, it may have been more important to Dulles himself than any other aspect of accountability and responsibility in the treaty, probably because of his experience at Versailles and the widespread subsequent perception that the public blaming of Germany for the First World War had facilitated the later rise of the Nazis. At the end of 1950 and despite his commitment by then to a generous peace, British foreign secretary Bevin had made it clear that he favored including in the preamble to the treaty a reference to the Japanese regime's responsibility for provoking hostilities, along the lines of a passage in the settlement with Italy.[36] Other Commonwealth governments, as well as the Philippines, agreed. In a radio broadcast on August 15, 1951, Philippine president Elpidio Quirino cited an admission by Japan of its war guilt and recognition of the damage Japan had inflicted on the Philippines as the first of the Philippines' goals for the peace treaty.[37] American officials, however, firmly opposed including a statement of Japan's guilt.[38]

The British government nonetheless put its foot down, as did Australia, New Zealand, and the Philippines.[39] In turn, the U.S. authorities insisted that the request for a statement of war guilt was "inconsistent with the agreed objectives of the Treaty," that is, the aim to turn Japan into a viable and peace-loving nation. Furthermore, such a statement would be unlikely to achieve anything positive, and the Versailles experience suggested it might be dangerous. The U.S. authorities were also reluctant to agree to a war guilt clause because it was now more than five years since the end of the war and because of the "splendid co-operation given by all the people of Japan" to the United Nations in the Korean War.[40] In other words, in official American eyes, the Cold War had trumped the Second World War. As State Department officials told the New Zealand government, "It is known that the Japanese people feel that their [good] conduct since surrender makes this [a war guilt clause] inappropriate," and "undesirable repercussions are foreseeable." In any case, American officials felt that Japanese guilt for the war had been sufficiently addressed in the Potsdam Declaration and the judgments of the Tokyo Trial.[41]

The British government eventually accepted the United States' reasoning and gave up on the war guilt clause. As Foreign Secretary Herbert

Morrison advised the cabinet in April 1951, "Little is likely to be achieved at this stage either in Japan or in British possessions in South-East Asia by recording specifically Japan's misdeeds in the past."[42] Thanks to pressure from the Philippine government, a limited expression of Japanese guilt appeared in Article 14 of the final document, which begins: "It is recognized that Japan should pay reparations to the Allied Powers for the damage and suffering caused by it during the war."[43] But demands for a more general statement were shelved.

In the meantime, however, another matter had arisen, this time one that particularly vexed Britain and the Commonwealth. U.S. treaty drafts established conditions for granting war criminals not only parole or sentence reduction but also "pardon."[44] This term was anathema to the Commonwealth countries in any context relating to war criminals. The disagreement almost certainly arose because of different understandings of the term. It is difficult to determine precisely what "pardon" meant in the minds of American planners, because it was used to mean different things in different U.S. jurisdictions, and its meaning had also changed over time. In American usage, "pardon" might mean sentence reduction and did not necessarily imply removing the guilt of the pardoned person.[45] To the British government, however, the suggestion that war criminals could possibly be pardoned was "wholly unacceptable":

> The word may have a different meaning in American law, but in England it could only mean that a war criminal would not only be released but that his conviction would be set aside. . . . It would be most objectionable to provide in the Peace Treaty that any properly convicted war criminal could in any circumstances have his conviction reversed except by due process of law.[46]

In short, in the British authorities' eyes, a pardon would "wipe out" a war criminal's conviction,[47] making a mockery of all the efforts of those responsible for the trials and of the justice they had worked for. At this point the British government appeared to care much more about use of the word "pardon" than about any other matter connected with future dealings with war criminals. The New Zealand, Canadian, and Australian governments agreed with the British stance.[48]

THE FINAL DRAFTS

Dulles had decided that Britain should be invited to sponsor the treaty jointly with the United States. The two governments had agreed that each would produce a provisional draft as the basis for a subsequent joint version.[49] The British draft of April 1951 was much longer than the American version of the previous month, despite the UK government's commitment since late 1950 to a brief and general peace. Possibly it was designed in part "to prevent an impression that it [the British government] was not serious enough about Commonwealth interests."[50] The draft contained a new formulation relating to war criminals: the Japanese government would now "undertake to accept the judgments" of all the original tribunals, as well as "respecting convictions and sentences imposed upon Japanese nationals."[51] Higurashi Yoshinobu concluded that the requirement to "accept the judgments" of the Allied courts, a phrase that survived to be included in the final version of the treaty, was highly significant. He concluded that for the British Commonwealth, especially Australia and New Zealand, it was on a par with the war guilt clause as an attempt to ensure that Japan would not only carry out the sentences but would also acknowledge the legitimacy of the trials and the verdicts and thus, ultimately, Japan's responsibility for the war.[52] In this draft, the British government accepted the U.S. wording providing for "joint decision" by Japan and the Allied powers on future clemency for war criminals. The British foreign secretary now recommended that in view of the American government's attitude, the cabinet not pursue a war guilt clause. He reiterated, however, that Britain should in no circumstances back down on the matter of the "pardon."[53]

Talks between the UK and the U.S. governments ended on May 4, 1951. A joint treaty draft was produced the following month and publicly released in July.[54] In this version, both the war guilt clause and the word "pardon" were omitted, resolving what appears to have been the chief issue for each side. Britain's requirement that Japan "accept the judgments" of the tribunals was included in the draft's Article 11, probably in exchange for the loss of the war guilt clause and to please Australia and New Zealand.[55] Thus, the role of the Allied governments in approving variations to war criminals' sentences was promoted to the status of "decision," while that of Japan was reduced to "recommendation."

In what is fairly obviously an Anglo-American compromise, such variation could occur only "on the decision of the Government or Governments which imposed the sentence in each instance, and on recommendation of Japan." The practical effect may not have been very different if the previous wording had been preserved so that decisions either were made "jointly" or depended on Allied approval, but Japan's lack of authority in this matter was now highlighted.

The negotiating process that led to the change of wording is not explicit in the official documents, but it appears that Australia was chiefly responsible, with the New Zealand government solidly in agreement. Overall, the British authorities acknowledged that the Commonwealth's influence on the peace treaty had been significant. They noted that the joint U.S.–UK treaty draft contained substantial American concessions:

> The present agreed draft, compared with the original United States draft of March last, represents an improvement beyond all recognition, and roughly half of it has in fact been contributed by the United Kingdom. . . . That it has been possible [to have so much influence] is largely due to the constructive and open-minded attitude of Mr. Dulles himself and in particular to his realisation of the importance of our connections with the Commonwealth.[56]

Evidently Dulles had recognized that the British government was obliged to represent the interests of the Commonwealth. Moreover, by implication, the Commonwealth's views had been further than the British government's views from what the U.S. government wanted, as suggested by the reluctance of the Australian and New Zealand governments to embrace the shift to leniency in late 1950 and early 1951. A memorandum from the Australian Department of External Affairs confirms that Australia's role was crucial: in the negotiation process leading up to production of the final treaty draft, "Australian views were pressed in the question of war criminal sentences and the original article was eventually amended in a way that met Australian views as formulated at the time."[57]

Yet the Australian government was still not prepared to express satisfaction with the final version. In commenting on the U.S. draft at the end of May 1951, Australian officials continued to argue that the Japanese government should have no rights at all in the matter of war criminals.

U.S. officials responded in an internal document that did not go to the Australians: "Japan's rights and powers are now reduced simply to the right to recommend clemency to an Allied Power whose military tribunals convicted a war criminal imprisoned in Japan. It is difficult to see how Australia could maintain strong objection to this."[58] Australian officials seem to have been aware that their stance was extreme, but to them, the very idea of Japanese participation in decisions on war criminals was unacceptable. The minister for external affairs, Percy Spender, had apparently stated: "The introduction of any right of Japan to deal with this matter, though it might be said the article gives her no right except that which is consented to by other powers or majority of other powers, is objectionable."[59]

The former British cabinet secretary, Lord Hankey, was virtually a lone voice in objecting to Article 11 before the treaty was signed. Hankey tried hard to influence the British government to deal leniently with both Japanese and German war criminals; he had already published a book criticizing both the Nuremberg and the Tokyo Trials.[60] Hankey wrote in a letter to *The Times* in August 1951 that Article 11 "differs from any other article in the treaty in raising profoundly moving human issues—national pride and self-respect, patriotism and elementary human rights."[61] He considered the article to be "misconceived," unfair, and likely to cause trouble in Japan, but his views were rejected by the British government.[62]

JAPANESE RESPONSES

Japanese authorities made little or no comment on the restriction of their participation in posttreaty decisions on war criminals' sentences. They may have had no formal rights in the process of producing the text of the peace settlement, but Japanese officials were active negotiators all the same, and especially in the later stages of discussions, their American counterparts were prepared to seek and respond to their opinions. Officials from the Japanese Foreign Ministry and the Ministry of Justice commented on various draft provisions, engaging in vigorous discussion on questions of rearmament, reparations, and other matters. They sought amendments to draft provisions, some of which were granted. They discussed the issue of war criminals and studied the drafts of Article 11, asking the opinions of knowledgeable and sympathetic people on the Allied side, notably Major Benjamin Bruce Blakeney Jr., who had been a defense lawyer at the IMTFE.[63] They lobbied key figures, including Sir Robert Craigie, former British ambassador to Japan, and William Sebald, political adviser to General Douglas MacArthur (that is, the State Department's representative in Japan during the Occupation).[64] Yet the government appears to have made little attempt to soften the stance on war criminals taken in the San Francisco Peace Treaty, apart from the ambitious and probably disingenuous request for a general amnesty mentioned earlier. Otherwise, the government raised no open objections, even though the article became harsher in the drafting.[65] Japanese Foreign Ministry officials recorded that they had "no particular reason to object" to the revised provision in the joint U.S.–UK draft, in which Japan had to "accept the judgments" of all tribunals and in which Japanese rights over war criminals' sentences were downgraded to "recommending" variations.[66]

Given that the future of war criminals became a major public issue in Japan within a year of the signing of the peace treaty, this passivity by Japanese bureaucrats is, at first, surprising. Official opinion in Japan was by no means united, and the views of Treaty Bureau staff were not shared by everyone. For example, Foreign Ministry officials were much more likely to favor a cautious approach when dealing with their wartime enemies than were bureaucrats in the Justice Ministry. Foreign Ministry officials had the job of responding formally to the draft treaty provisions, and they had special reason to show caution in relation to war criminals. In 1951, when the final drafts of the treaty were being produced, the Philippines and Australia continued to hold convicted Japanese war criminals at Muntinlupa and on Manus Island, respectively. These prisoners' repatriation to Tokyo was not announced until mid-1953. Japanese officials and others, including the war criminals and their families, feared in 1951–1952 that strident demands on behalf of convicted war criminals might antagonize the Philippines and Australia and delay or even prevent those last repatriations.

More fundamentally, as Higurashi found, the Foreign Ministry officials respected international legal obligations and wanted Japan to be seen as a country that did so. They acknowledged Japan's obligation to carry out the sentences passed on war criminals on the grounds that Japan had accepted the Potsdam Declaration, with its warning that war criminals would be pursued. Thus they were not critical of Article 11 or, at least,

not of the part about honoring sentences. Some of them did have reser-
vations about "accepting the judgments" of the tribunals, because they
considered the trials to constitute what would later be called "victors'
justice,"[67] but under the circumstances they were reticent in expressing
such doubts and did not oppose the wording in this part of Article 11
either. In reality, the Japanese government had no choice but to accept
Article 11 in exchange for the restoration of peace. Especially for the British Commonwealth, a peace treaty without Article 11 was unlikely, and
out of realism, Japanese officials accepted the provision.[68]

Moreover, officials at the time do not seem to have been particularly
worried about the fact that Japanese authorities were to have no greater
role than "recommending" variations in sentences. Incarcerated war
criminals themselves were indignant and deeply disappointed by this provision. They had had great hopes that the treaty would free the prisoners, on the grounds that they had been tried by the Allies, not by Japan,
and that the treaty supposedly returned full sovereignty to Japan.[69] Some
Justice Ministry officials appear also to have expected clemency to accom-
pany the signing, the coming into effect, or the ratification of the treaty.[70]
Even when no clemency was granted, however, officials did not regard the
situation as hopeless, and in fact they were optimistic about the scope
allowed by Article 11.[71] For a start, it was possible to interpret the article
to mean that the Allies were willing to grant clemency, since they had
provided a framework within which it could be negotiated. According to
a Japanese official in late 1952, the Japanese public believed that "the gist
of the Article 11 of the Treaty of Peace connotates [sic] that the countries
concerned will be willing to agree to the recommendations of Japan for
clemency in the basic spirit of reconciliation and trust in which the Treaty
was written."[72]

Furthermore, Treaty Bureau officials expected that in practice, other
Allied countries would follow the U.S. lead in showing leniency. From
the beginning, Treaty Bureau officials had regarded the peace settlement
as a U.S. undertaking and had concluded that while Australia and other
countries might take a tough stance, those countries ultimately needed
U.S. protection, so American priorities would win out.[73] U.S. authorities
openly favored Japan by the time the treaty was signed, and prisoners
were being steadily released on parole from Sugamo under the system
instituted by the U.S. military in 1950. There was no reason to suppose
that the stream of releases would slow or stop. Sugamo's inmates believed

that Article 11 had become harsher because of intervention by "Britain" (presumably including the Commonwealth) and that the United States was at least somewhat more favorably inclined towards the prisoners' situation.[74] Treaty Bureau officials, too, probably overestimated the influence that U.S. authorities were likely to have over other governments' exercise of clemency, and they almost certainly overestimated the rate at which the American authorities themselves would continue to authorize releases.

THE JAPANESE PUBLIC AND WAR CRIMINALS

The final draft of the San Francisco Peace Treaty was released on August 15, 1951,[75] though the treaty did not come into effect for another seven and a half months. The war criminals themselves were deeply disappointed with Article 11, as we have seen. Thanks to press stories recording their comments—anonymously, because identifying them might have endangered their prospects of release—their disappointment became more widely known. Such stories promoted an image of convicted war criminals as men who had already paid a considerable price for their crimes and were now at the mercy of inscrutable foreign governments. As an unidentified prisoner wrote, "We were simply holding out for the peace treaty, and so were our families, only to find we are as badly off as ever now that it has come."[76] Despite the setback, many prisoners, along with some government officials, seem to have assumed there would still be some kind of general clemency when the treaty actually came into force in April 1952.[77] Even legal experts were taken by surprise. Japanese intellectuals were aware of the principle, established by President Abraham Lincoln after the U.S. Civil War of 1861–1865, that general amnesty might follow the end of a conflict.[78] As late as May 1952, an official in the Justice Ministry, Shimomaki Takeshi, was still expressing confidence that Article 11 would apply only to war criminals convicted in the IMTFE, whereas those convicted in national tribunals would soon be released under a general amnesty, as "the principle of amnesty exists in international law." Because he believed that the legal basis of judgments made before the peace treaty took effect would disappear with the end of the Occupation, Shimomaki predicted that a number of convicted war criminals would then be retried in Japanese courts, on charges he did not specify.[79]

Moreover, there were signs that the prospects for war criminals might not be as bad as they had seemed, despite Article 11. In October 1951, the ban on former military officers holding public office was lifted in a large number of cases, in what is known as the "depurge": of 122,000 career military personnel who had originally been "purged," 117,000 were released from restrictions by April 1952.[80] Former senior members of both services became conspicuously active in politics and in civil society at the local, prefectural, and national levels.[81] Tsuji Masanobu, until 1949 a fugitive from British justice in Singapore, was elected to the Diet in October 1952, and one-third of his fellow Diet members were men who had just been released from the purge.[82] Press commentary cautiously noted that senior military officers, who were generally considered responsible for the war, had returned to normal life and to public office, whereas those war criminals convicted in the national trials, who had mostly, they said, been more junior men, were still incarcerated. It was claimed that these convicted men had been found guilty and were now facing long prison terms simply because they had followed orders.[83] According to one report, the prisoners themselves considered that the crimes prosecuted in the national courts, as distinct from those prosecuted in the IMTFE, were on a par with the offenses committed by the purgees. It therefore was wrong, in this view, that MacArthur had shown benevolence to purgees but not to war criminals.[84] Then, in November 1951, the prisoners were encouraged to learn that four months earlier, the French president, Vincent Auriol, had reduced the life sentences for war criminals convicted in Indochina to ten or fifteen years, depending on the individual case. Because the information was initially sent to Indochina rather than to Japan, these sentence reductions were transmitted to the Japanese government only on November 20.[85]

Throughout the autumn of 1951, politicians in the Diet continued to raise the implications of Article 11 and to present petitions from the public for the war criminals' release.[86] In mid-November, the House of Councillors (the Upper House) established a subcommittee (Sensō hanzainin ni taisuru hōteki shochi ni kansuru shōiinkai) of the Committee on Legal Affairs to deal specifically with war criminals and to examine especially the implications for Japanese domestic law of their continued incarceration after the enactment of the peace treaty.[87] Ten elected politicians formed the subcommittee,[88] which met for the first time on November 21, 1951. The subcommittee organized meetings with the chief of SCAP's Legal Section, Alva C. Carpenter, and a fact-finding visit to Sugamo Prison. In addition, during ten sessions ending on April 24, 1952, the subcommittee formally sought the opinions of three groups: first, those with personal relationships to, or personal experience as, convicted war criminals; second, relevant bureaucrats of the Foreign Ministry; and third, lawyers who had defended the accused at the IMTFE.[89]

The formation of the Diet subcommittee signaled the politicians' growing recognition of the public's interest in war criminals. Its sessions provided those working on behalf of the prisoners in the broader society with direct access to government members and with an opportunity to present arguments to an official parliamentary inquiry. The first to testify was Imamura Hisako, whose husband, the former army general Imamura Hitoshi, was incarcerated at Manus. She spoke as a representative of the families of war criminals. Imamura was then asked to introduce several former convicts from Manus who had returned to Japan at the conclusion of their sentences. Of the four she presented, the most vocal was Katayama Fumihiko, who had returned from Manus in 1950 after serving a five-year term for his part in the murder of two men in New Britain. Also invited were the prominent former naval officers and released convicts Hara Chūichi and Fukutome Shigeru, and Sekiguchi Jikō, the head of the White Lotus Society (Byakurensha), a Buddhist sect whose organization provided chaplains to the convicts in Sugamo.[90]

The testimonies heard by the subcommittee reveal the arguments that had been marshaled by those supporting the release of war criminals: the convicted men were not criminals in the true sense of the word but were victims of circumstances; the trials had been unfair, and the conditions in overseas jails were atrocious; and at home, prisoners' families were suffering financially and psychologically in the absence of their loved ones. Katayama placed the repatriation of those at Manus and Muntinlupa in the context of the broader postwar repatriation, beginning his testimony by saying that prospects for "a bright, peaceful and democratic Japan" were blighted by "the serious problem of repatriation" from China, the Soviet Union, Manus, and the Philippines. Katayama then recited a litany of complaints about the Australian trials and the conditions on Manus. He described hellish labor conditions, accidental and work-related deaths, suicides, illness, lack of fresh food, and gratuitous violence by Australian military personnel. Although conditions on the remote island of Manus undoubtedly were tough, Katayama's claims are now very difficult to evaluate, especially as the specific incidents and names he cited have been blacked out from the Diet's records.[91] No other evidence has emerged to support his claims. Whether true or not, however, reports of Katayama's evidence strengthened the sense that Japanese war criminals were being unjustly treated by cruel captors seeking revenge rather than justice.

With similar rhetorical flourish, former Vice Admiral Fukutome claimed that the prisoners in jail for war crimes were not the perpetrators of the unspeakable horrors publicized by the Occupation authorities a few years earlier—the guilty ones had not been caught, and instead, people who had simply done their duty had ended up in prison. Thus, Diet members should not mistake those incarcerated at Sugamo for "common criminals."[92] An extension of this argument, offered by Sekiguchi of the White Lotus Society, was that their release was entirely warranted, since in contrast with common criminals, those convicted of war crimes were unlikely to offend again:

No such people as war criminals would exist, literally, if there hadn't been a war, and so these are not people who will offend again. What's more, if the coming treaty were to engender a general amnesty or some act of grace, these people would, without a doubt, as good citizens, lend their strength to the reconstruction of our country.[93]

Imamura Hisako emphasized the suffering of war criminals' families: left without their main breadwinner, elderly parents, wives, and children lived in pitiful poverty, she claimed, resulting in physical and psychological damage through overwork, hunger, and anxiety. She spoke eloquently of the plight of an elderly woman left to care for a grandchild with no means of support, her only remaining son in jail in Sugamo; of a woman desperate to scrape together a train fare for the long journey from Fukuoka in Kyūshū to Tokyo, so that her eleven-year-old daughter could meet her father for the first time; and of a schoolboy who first found out about his father's execution in the Philippines from neighbors, who had happened to read the father's name in the newspaper. According to Imamura, the only resolution to the welfare issues affecting the war criminals' relatives was to allow the return of the main breadwinner to his family.[94] The apparent willingness of politicians on the Diet subcommittee to accept such testimony encouraged the activists to continue hoping that once the peace treaty took effect and the Japanese government regained sovereignty, it would be free to determine its own domestic laws, despite Article 11, and would therefore be able to release war criminals. Even though the press cautioned against optimism, prisoners in Sugamo and their families were further encouraged by the November 1951 news of the French sentence reductions and by the increasing numbers of prisoners released by.the SCAP parole system.[95] Hopes for immediate release were, however, destroyed when the peace treaty came into force.

THE TREATY AND ARTICLE 11

On September 8, 1951, the United States, Japan, and forty-seven other countries signed a treaty at San Francisco that took effect on April 28, 1952. The treaty reestablished peace after six and a half years of occupation. U.S. forces would no longer run Sugamo Prison, but even though Japan regained sovereignty in most other ways, it did not recover control over the sentences of Sugamo's inmates. Article 11 of the treaty reserved to the prosecuting countries the ultimate decision regarding any significant variation in the sentences of convicted criminals.

Article 11 stated:

> Japan accepts the judgments of the International Military Tribunal for the Far East and of other Allied War Crimes Courts both within and outside Japan, and will carry out the sentences imposed thereby upon Japanese nationals imprisoned in Japan. The power to grant clemency, to reduce sentences and to parole with respect to such prisoners may not be exercised except on the decision of the Government or Governments which imposed the sentences in each instance, and on recommendation of Japan. In the case of persons sentenced by the International Military Tribunal for the Far East, such power may not be exercised except on the decision of a majority of the Governments represented on the Tribunal, and on the recommendation of Japan.[96]

Article 11 was the instrument by which the fate of war criminals once again became closely enmeshed with the separate though overlapping politics and diplomatic priorities of the individual prosecuting governments.

Between 1949 and 1951, all the convicting powers except Australia and the Philippines had sent war criminals back to Japan to serve out their sentences in Sugamo. The prisoners' fate was then controlled by the U.S. Eighth Army, which ran Sugamo Prison, and later by the SCAP Legal Section, which managed parole. Although the prisoners had been prosecuted under different jurisdictions, the SCAP parole system applied uniform rules to their sentences. From 1950 on, war criminals were paroled steadily if not quickly; 892 prisoners had been paroled by the time Japan regained its sovereignty. According to Japanese government figures, along with 313 prosecuted by American tribunals, 278 of those released on parole had been convicted by the Netherlands Indies, 140 by Britain,[97] 128 by China, 32 by France, and 1 by the IMTFE.[98] Thus, a single authority had decided on the future of the prisoners in Tokyo, and these decisions had come to reflect, broadly, the changes in official U.S. attitudes toward Japan, that is, the trend toward leniency. On the day the peace treaty came into effect, the United States had custody of all 927 prisoners in Sugamo. Only the 317 war criminals convicted by Australia and the Philippines who were still on Manus Island and in Muntinlupa, respectively, were covered by other regulations.[99] Under Article 11 of the peace treaty, however, this unified system had to be unraveled. The prisoners remained in Sugamo under a common prison regime, but responsibility for their release was transferred to the seven governments that had cooperated in conducting national trials and the eight governments that assumed the right to review the sentences passed down by the IMTFE.

Article 11 was the pivot on which all policy and all representations made on behalf of war criminals during the rest of the 1950s turned. It determined the institutions and the mechanisms that dealt with war criminals from then on, in Japan and in the countries whose governments had jurisdiction over the prisoners. Article 11 greatly complicated the practical situation of convicted war criminals, as well as the actions of the foreign governments, which increasingly sought to rid themselves of the problem of war criminals without undermining the validity of the original trials. Once peace was restored, prisoners housed in the same facility, Sugamo, and sentenced to roughly the same terms for similar crimes could be subject to markedly different rules on sentence reduction and parole. Prisoners with longer sentences were thus released according to widely varying timetables and procedures, with the first freed in 1952 and the last in 1958. In the prosecuting countries, responsibility for prisoners generally shifted from a department or ministry of defense or war to a department or ministry of foreign affairs. The change from military to civilian authorities meant that a new group of policymakers now had to grapple with the legal issues raised by the incarceration of war criminals.

Even though Article 11 compromised Japan's posttreaty sovereignty, in 1951–1952 the Japanese government did not see war criminals as an issue on which diplomatic pressure was possible or proper, or likely to be effective. Nor did Foreign Ministry officials, at least, see such pressure as necessary. The domestic campaign in support of war criminals was not yet strong enough to force the government to take significant notice; the SCAP parole system was working and led officials to believe that the releases would continue. It was thought, reasonably enough, that the United States favored Japan and was so influential in world affairs that other countries holding war criminals would follow its lead. Japanese officials could not be expected to foresee that even in the United States, a shift of responsibility for war criminals would completely change the dynamics of the process of reviewing applications for parole and recommending prisoners' release or continued detention. Within a short time, however, domestic pressure on behalf of war criminals increased significantly; influential figures closely associated with the prisoners assumed positions of political power; and diplomats and politicians began to seize the opportunity presented by Japan's new status in the Cold War world to take a stronger and more confident role in international relations and to insist that the war criminals be released.

7

JAPANESE PRESSURE MOUNTS

The San Francisco Peace Treaty altered the legal position of convicted war criminals because Article 11 distributed control of their sentences among the prosecuting powers. The treaty also changed the context in which war criminals were discussed. U.S. media censorship gradually relaxed, stopping completely with the end of the Occupation in April 1952, so the Japanese public could address the war and war crimes more openly. It became easier, too, for those who sympathized with war criminals to lobby publicly on their behalf. The coming of peace thus allowed the consolidation and expansion of existing activities on behalf of war criminals, as well as a more forceful articulation of public support. Engaging with the issue of what should happen to war criminals was one way in which the Japanese people, like the West Germans, could begin to draw a line under the Occupation years, to demarcate the present and future from the postwar period of foreign control, and to begin to assert their own view of what the war had meant, after years in which Allied views of the conflict had predominated. In the new conditions of post-Occupation Japan, a much more sympathetic public view of war criminals emerged. The prisoners prosecuted in the national tribunals, at least, were increasingly presented as ordinary men caught in difficult situations, rather than as exceptional wrongdoers. The continued incarceration of war criminals thus became a volatile and emotive issue in Japanese domestic politics.

In West Germany, the trend was similar. War criminals there had become an important political issue slightly earlier, however, because of the different circumstances of the Allied Occupation of Germany and the greater urgency with which the Allies sought to incorporate Germany into the Western defense alliance in the late 1940s. Whereas the Japanese government and the national Diet continued to function throughout the Occupation of 1945–1952, no German federal government or national legislature was operating between 1945 and 1949. Limited sovereignty returned to Germany only in May 1949, when the American, British, and French zones of occupation were combined to establish the Federal Republic of Germany. This "new beginning" greatly stimulated public discussion of war criminals in West Germany, just as the formal restoration of peace did in Japan in 1952. The Allies retained exclusive rights over clemency for the war criminals they had convicted, as they did in Japan, but the issue of war criminals became heavily politicized after 1949, and by September 1951 had become a "very irritating" question in political and diplomatic negotiations between Germany and its former enemies.[1] By 1952, West German journalists and church figures, as well as politicians, were vocal in their support of war criminals. In East Germany, by contrast, where the Soviet Union established the German Democratic Republic (GDR) in October 1949, press controls ensured there was no open and public discussion of the wartime past. Official rhetoric maintained that the GDR was heir to antifascist forces. The governing party was "highly uncomfortable with addressing issues of war crimes at all," attempted to distance the socialist GDR from Germany's Nazi past, and blamed war crimes on West Germans or on German POWs who remained captive in the Soviet Union.[2]

For Japanese war criminals and their supporters, 1952 was the crucial year, in which the fundamental dynamics relating to war criminals shifted in both Japan and the prosecuting countries. Sugamo Prison changed hands, and Americans no longer made the rules that governed prisoners' day-to-day lives. Even though the prosecuting governments retained control of sentences, Japanese priorities started to gain weight in the balance of interests that determined the prisoners' fate. In Japan the release campaign gathered strength to the point that it put the authorities under considerable pressure to do more for the war criminals. In turn, the Japanese government became more and more assertive in its representations to foreign authorities. The domestic and international implications of the public campaign were thus closely intertwined. Japanese officials quickly began to recommend clemency and parole in accordance with Article 11, and their counterparts in the prosecuting countries started to realize that they would have to respond. Japanese requests for clemency in themselves became a potent force, compelling the prosecuting governments to face up to the implications of their control of the sentences of Japanese war criminals. All the prosecuting governments, including that of the United States, which inherited SCAP's authority, had to work out how to deal with the prisoners: whether and when to repatriate them to Japan, in the case of the Philippines and Australia, and, in all cases, how long to keep them and how to respond to applications for clemency and parole.

IMMEDIATE RESPONSES TO THE PEACE AND ARTICLE 11

The war criminals and their supporters in Japan had been aware since mid-1951 that the peace treaty made no provision for their immediate release. The lack of any general clemency to mark the formal end of the Occupation redoubled their disappointment, anger, and frustration.[3] The long process of negotiating with individual foreign governments over the terms of continued incarceration then began. It took time for the separate governments to develop systems to decide on the clemency recommendations sent to them by the Japanese authorities. As a result, in the early posttreaty period, releases slowed dramatically, to the consternation of the prisoners and their supporters.[4]

The Netherlands government was the earliest to start discussing posttreaty clemency with the Japanese government—the subject was broached at the San Francisco Peace Conference in September 1951—but it signaled immediately that clemency would come at a price. The treaty made no provision to compensate the approximately 150,000 civilians with Dutch status who had been interned by the Japanese military during its occupation of the Netherlands Indies. Apart from the many deaths, the physical and financial losses suffered by the internees were a sensitive matter at home. The Netherlands government was also concerned that it might become legally liable for signing away the right of its citizens to obtain compensation from Japan.[5] At the peace conference, Foreign Minister

Dirk Stikker intimated to Prime Minister Yoshida Shigeru that clemency would not be extended to war criminals until compensation for internees' losses was paid. Yoshida exchanged correspondence with Stikker implying that an agreement could be reached,[6] but no progress was made, and the Dutch continued to hold out for compensation.[7]

Only the Republic of China (ROC) did as the war criminals and their supporters had hoped, marking the return of peace with Japan with an amnesty for the convicted prisoners. The ROC had not been invited to the peace conference because of the diplomatic difficulty over which China should be recognized as legitimate, the government in Taibei or the government in Beijing, but the Nationalist government signed a separate treaty with Japan in Taibei on April 28, 1952, the day the San Francisco agreement took effect. The treaty came into force on August 5, at which time the ROC government transferred to Japanese authority the ninety-one war criminals in Sugamo whom it had convicted, in effect authorizing a general release. On the day the treaty was ratified, the Japanese government freed all the prisoners except one, who had also been sentenced by the United States. The sentences of the eighty-six prisoners prosecuted by the Nationalist Chinese and since paroled by SCAP also were terminated.[8] The ROC was thus the first to show that even though the pursuit and punishment of war criminals had been a high priority immediately after the war, clemency was a different matter. Direct information about why the Taibei government released Japanese war criminals has not emerged, but the decision fits with the overall attitude toward Japan of Chiang Kai-shek's Nationalists in the immediate postwar period. Before and after their 1949 defeat by Mao Zedong's Communists, the Nationalists took a "benevolent" approach to relations with Japan.[9] In 1952 the Taibei government apparently concluded that it had more to gain by cultivating Japan as an anti-Communist ally than by continuing to pursue legal redress for war crimes. Japanese wartime crimes in China had been extensive and terrible, and doubtless the moment of sentencing in each case had been an important vindication of Chinese wartime suffering. The ready granting of clemency as part of the arrangement of a peace settlement, however, shows that the fate of Japanese war criminals could be negotiated afterward.

The prisoners held by the ROC were the first to be freed as a group before the completion of sentence and without making individual applications. The unexpected gesture greatly encouraged those working for the early release of convicted war criminals. According to the British ambassador in Tokyo, Sir Esler Dening, the mass release heightened the "tone of arrogance" that, he maintained, had increasingly come to characterize petitions submitted on behalf of other war criminals. The released prisoners, who were freer to express their views than were those still incarcerated, called on other Allied representatives in Japan to follow Taibei's example, as did some sections of the Japanese press.[10] In popular culture, the 1952 film *Sugamo no haha* (*Sugamo Mother*) featured a scene in which other war criminals looked longingly from the prison windows as their compatriots, lucky enough to have been convicted by the ROC rather than by other governments, walked out of the gates as free men.[11] In a long document asking foreign governments (unsuccessfully) to release war criminals to commemorate the November 1952 investiture of the emperor's son as crown prince, the Japanese authorities remarked that the war criminals' "hopeful expectation" of liberation "has been heightened by the release of the war criminals involved in the cases related to China."[12] Although the Japanese government continued to hope for a general release, no other governments authorized mass releases for a long time, and most prisoners had to take on the protracted bureaucratic process of applying for clemency to the government that had prosecuted them.

In fact, the remaining prisoners in Sugamo found that authorization of parole, which had been granted at a rapid rate in the last months of the Occupation, stopped entirely when the Occupation ended. The war criminals and their supporters complained bitterly about the suspension of parole.[13] Perhaps the most unfortunate case was that of Yagi Yoshika, who had been convicted by a U.S. military tribunal of mistreating prisoners as a civilian guard at a POW camp in Japan. His parole under SCAP, along with that of two codefendants from his trial, was approved on March 28, 1952. Though the other two were duly released, it proved more difficult to organize parole supervision for Yagi, whose home was in distant Okinawa. Arrangements could not be finalized before SCAP lost its authority on April 28, 1952, and so Yagi remained in prison until a new system could be put in place to handle applications for parole and clemency.[14]

One notable attempt was made to circumvent the provisions of Article 11 for a specific group of war criminals, those of Korean and Taiwanese ethnicity. In June 1952, an appeal for habeas corpus was lodged in the Tokyo District Court on behalf of the twenty-nine Koreans and one Taiwanese war criminal then held in Sugamo, on the grounds that the

Japanese government had no power to detain them after the peace treaty came into force, because they had lost their Japanese citizenship and Article 11 of the peace treaty required Japan to "carry out the sentences imposed . . . upon Japanese nationals imprisoned in Japan." The Japanese Supreme Court took over the case, "in view of its significance."[15] The appeal was rejected on July 30, 1952, on the grounds that the defendants had Japanese nationality at the time sentence was imposed and had been confined in Japan at the effective date of the peace treaty. Furthermore, "a later loss of or change in their nationalities shall not affect the obligation to be performed by Japan" under Article 11.[16] Korean and Taiwanese war criminals thus remained subject to the same regulations and processes as did all other "Japanese" war criminals convicted in Allied tribunals.

MANAGING ARTICLE 11

Once the Japanese authorities learned the provisions of the forthcoming peace treaty, they set about devising mechanisms to deal with the ruling on war criminals, conferring extensively with officials from SCAP's Legal Section as they did so.[17] When the Occupation ended, Sugamo Prison and responsibility for the day-to-day activities of its inmates were transferred to Japanese administration. On the same day, the Diet passed Law No. 103, or the Law Concerning the Enforcement of Sentences, the Granting of Clemency, Etc., in Accordance with the Provision of Article 11 of the Treaty of Peace.[18] The new law provided regulations for the management of Sugamo and also included a system of parole, which, on the advice of U.S. officials, was closely modeled on the one that had operated in Sugamo under the Americans.[19] The Japanese authorities had no independent control over parole, given the force of Article 11, so they were not free to stipulate how parole would work or even if parole should exist at all. But they had to institute a method for dealing with war criminals in the new conditions set by Article 11; the SCAP parole system had worked fairly well from everyone's point of view, and it was reasonable to assume that the same system might continue. Indeed, SCAP's Legal Section had intended to recommend that the U.S. government continue the Occupation-period system once peace was restored, though it did not manage to do so before SCAP was disbanded, on April 28, 1952.[20]

Article 16 of Law No. 103 stipulated that a convicted war criminal could apply for parole once he had served a third of his sentence. Articles 28 and 29 also provided that any convicted war criminal could apply for clemency, meaning reduction of sentence. Both forms of application were to be accompanied by a statement of "fact for which the applicant was convicted of war crime, relation with the accomplice and extenuating circumstance" (Articles 17 and 29), as well as a report on the prisoner's behavior in detention. With these provisions, the Japanese authorities accepted the path of individual review of cases, even though they still hoped for comprehensive releases on the Chinese model. Individual prisoners were to apply for parole or clemency through the prison governor to the National Offenders' Prevention and Rehabilitation Commission (NOPAR), an external agency of the Ministry of Justice. The parole application followed the same form as that used in the SCAP system. NOPAR then investigated the case. If it endorsed the application, NOPAR forwarded it to the embassy of the foreign government concerned, which in turn passed on the application, with its own recommendation, to the home government. If the relevant agency of the home government approved the application, the prisoner's release was authorized. In July 1952, the Japanese cabinet ruled that NOPAR make its requests to foreign governments through the Ministry of Foreign Affairs.[21] At the insistence of U.S. officials, the Japanese authorities had asked each government individually to approve two provisions of the new law: Article 9, allowing for confinement before trial to count as time served, and Article 11, providing that sentences could be reduced for good conduct.[22]

The U.S., Dutch, and French authorities accepted Law No. 103.[23] The British and Australians appear to have accepted it in general terms but did not consider themselves bound by its parole regulations. Britain had no system of parole for domestic criminals and did not intend to invent one to deal with Japanese war criminals. Likewise, the Australian states had no parole system, and the federal government was unwilling to allow parole for war criminals. Moreover, the Australian government worried that the parole provisions in Law No. 103 might somehow supersede Article 11 of the peace treaty.[24] The Philippine government does not appear to have been concerned about Law No. 103.

NOPAR began its work immediately, sending its first parole recommendations to foreign governments by the end of June 1952.[25] The Japanese authorities had apparently hoped that including a U.S.-style parole mechanism in Law No. 103 "would influence other governments concerned so that all prisoners would be under one system and would have the benefits thereof."[26] The prosecuting powers, however, never joined forces in a single combined body to deal with NOPAR, and the Japanese authorities faced very different situations among the sentencing powers. The need for a mechanism to respond to NOPAR's requests appears to have caught the foreign governments by surprise, and they took some months to put any institution or procedure in place, with the result that few early releases were authorized during the remainder of 1952. Apart from the mass release by the ROC, only the Americans freed Japanese prisoners during 1952, not counting normal discharges at the expiration of sentence, and even they did not begin to do so until six months after the Occupation ended.

Apart from the ROC, the prosecuting authorities formally rejected the idea of a blanket amnesty. The French government, however, did so only after consultation with the other powers, having previously given ambiguous responses to the Japanese government about a potential general amnesty to mark Bastille Day 1952.[27] In August 1952, the British secretary of state for foreign affairs ruled out "any *system* of clemency or . . . a general amnesty"; all applications for clemency would be decided individually and on merit.[28] U.S. authorities made the most detailed case against a general release, explicitly labeling general amnesty as a "political solution" and contrasting it with their insistence on a "judicial solution." Declining to recognize any sense in which legal matters were politically constructed, they maintained this distinction, at least in name, until the late 1950s. Justice, in this respect, was intended to take precedence over politics. Conrad E. Snow, a Department of State legal adviser who later became chairman of the Clemency and Parole Board, asserted in May 1952 that a "political" solution would "negative [*sic*] the principle of the Potsdam Declaration that stern justice shall be meted out to all war criminals." It would "arouse a storm of indignation in this country [United States]" among victims of Japanese cruelty and their families; it would "impugn the fairness of the trial . . . [and] the validity of the convictions"; and ultimately, it would "discredit the quality of American justice." Decisions about prisoners' fate should be based instead on "the accepted principles of clemency and parole" and thus must be based on facts, including mitigating circumstances, the prisoner's health and family situation, and his behavior in prison. To determine these facts and reach a decision, a board should be formed.[29]

On September 4, 1952, President Harry S. Truman authorized the establishment of the Clemency and Parole Board for War Criminals in Washington. The board had three members, one each from the Departments of State, Defense, and Justice, with the State Department representative, Conrad Snow, as chairman.[30] The Americans continued SCAP's parole system.[31] But now, the cases were reviewed by civilians, who made recommendations on parole and clemency (the latter meaning, in effect, sentence reduction) to the president. The first paroles were recommended on October 20, 1952. Yagi Yoshika, still in prison although his parole had been authorized seven months earlier, was one of the first two war criminals to be recommended for release by the new board.[32]

The board recommended paroles steadily over the next months, though the prisoners were not released as quickly as they had been under SCAP. Between the signing of the peace treaty in September 1951 and the formal end of the Occupation in April 1952, SCAP had paroled 567 prisoners at an average of 71 per month; in April 1952 alone, 136 prisoners had been paroled.[33] Posttreaty paroles were much slower, partly because of the time taken to process applications, and partly because the board's recommendations had to be approved by the president. By March 16, 1953, the board had received 85 parole applications from NOPAR, and the president had approved 37 of them. Seven more cases were awaiting Truman's decision, and 34 were being processed by the board. The president approved all cases put to him until mid-1953, when he refused a recommendation for the first time.[34] As clemency was a prerogative of the executive, the president did not have to give reasons for his action. By October 1954, Presidents Truman and Dwight D. Eisenhower had rejected nine recommendations for parole and another four for reduction of sentence;[35] clemency officials acknowledged in internal reports that these actions made them more conservative in evaluating prisoners' applications.[36]

The idea of a comprehensive release was not universally rejected, even within the U.S. establishment. Early in 1953, Roger Kent, a lawyer from the Office of Defense and a member of the Clemency and Parole Board, wrote to President Truman, offering his resignation from the board because he did not have faith in the procedure he had helped implement. In essence, Kent was seeking to disrupt the neat distinction between the "judicial" and the "political" solutions by pointing out that the legalities were politically constructed. Kent wrote that the existing system was both inadequate and detrimental to U.S. interests. He observed that the paroles authorized by the board were in fact "political releases," arguing that in accepting formulaic Japanese reports on the suitability of a prisoner for parole, which were always favorable, and in delegating supervision of paroled prisoners to Japanese officers, the U.S. authorities had effectively ceded control of parole to their Japanese counterparts. Kent thought it would make more sense to "extract political advantage from such political releases" rather than continuing a program that "seriously endangers the success of our basic policy of friendship with Japan." In other words, a mass release, and soon, would be the most effective method of dealing with the remaining war criminals in U.S. hands. Kent offered his resignation, which was accepted, "because I believe the present program is illusory as a parole program, impractical of fulfillment, and prejudicial to the best interests of the United States."[37] In a less formal communication to a colleague, he expressed himself more succinctly: "They [war criminals] should be hung, acquitted or given no more than five years, and if through lack of experience and foresight, we give them long terms which will cause nothing but continuing trouble, we should rectify our mistake right now."[38] Kent's argument had few supporters at this early stage. His two colleagues on the Clemency and Parole Board disagreed with him, and in a letter to Truman, they explained why:

A general amnesty, without reference to the enormity of the particular crimes committed, or to individual deserts of the war criminals, would derogate from the justice of the very convictions themselves, most certainly from the justice of the sentences imposed. . . . A general amnesty at this time . . . would nullify such progress in international law and morality as has been made by the war crimes trials that have followed World War II, both in Germany and in Japan. It might expose American and Allied prisoners of war, now in the hands of their enemies in Korea, or those who may be made prisoners in any future war, to cruelties similar to those practiced by both Japanese and Germans in World War II [because the perpetrators could assume they would not be properly punished, even if apprehended].[39]

Kent's view did not prevail. The president appointed a replacement for him on the Clemency and Parole Board, and the board maintained its case-by-case approach.

In Britain, clemency was the prerogative of the Crown. Until 1952, administrative responsibility for war criminals had been exercised by the secretary of state for war, but authority to administer Article 11 and to recommend clemency to the Queen was transferred to the foreign secretary soon after the peace treaty with Japan came into effect, as "the decisions reached must affect the United Kingdom's relations with Japan and other Asiatic countries and may involve liaison with other governments."[40] The British did not set up a separate authority to deal with clemency applications; instead, they conducted reviews within the Foreign Office. The War Office seemed only too glad to hand authority over war criminals to the Foreign Office,[41] but it nevertheless did not transfer the trial records until December 1952.[42] There was thus a considerable delay in examining NOPAR applications, but the British government had also been reluctant to begin reviewing cases for another reason: officials were furious at the treatment by the Japanese courts of a minor crime committed by two young British sailors in Kobe in August 1952. In the first case in which any Westerner had been sentenced by a Japanese court since Japan regained its sovereignty, the two drunk sailors were convicted of robbery with violence, for stealing a small amount of money from a taxi driver. The money was returned to the driver and no weapon was used in the assault, but the perpetrators were sentenced to two and a half years' imprisonment.[43] As one British official claimed, "Public opinion here [in Britain] would not tolerate the faintest possibility of any war criminals being released while the two sailors on a spree were still in jail!"[44] The British authorities refused even to inform the Japanese government of how they planned to deal with clemency applications until "a decent interval" had elapsed after the sailors' release in November 1952.[45] They did not begin to study clemency applications until the spring of 1953, by which time the Japanese authorities had sent eighty-two recommendations.[46] A senior official expressed the hope that all reviews could be completed within six months,[47] but in fact the process took more than three years.

Australia and the Philippines had not yet repatriated the prisoners in their custody to Japan, let alone begun any serious consideration of clemency. The French government reported that all applications for clemency were being considered by the French president.[48] By December 1952, the Dutch had received 167 parole applications but still had no process for considering them, partly because they had no record of the original trials on which to base any decisions.[49] The trial records were said to have been left behind in Indonesia on the transfer of sovereignty in December 1949 or possibly had been transferred to Dutch New Guinea, and not until May 1953 did the Dutch authorities obtain from the Americans copies of the records of sentence that the Netherlands Indies authorities had sent to SCAP at the end of 1949.[50]

In December 1952, the Japanese Diet amended Law No. 103 in an attempt to relax restrictions on convicted war criminals, but the move backfired. Article 24 of the law already allowed for "provisional parole" of five days in pressing circumstances such as the serious illness or death of a close family member, without the approval of the prosecuting government, and the relevant foreign authorities had accepted this provision. The amendment to Law No. 103, known as Law No. 4, extended the ruling on provisional parole to permit the release of prisoners in "special circumstances" for fifteen days, renewable for a further fifteen days, without limitation on the number of such paroles and again without approval by the prosecuting government. This attempt to exploit the latitude permitting the Japanese authorities to act on short-term releases prompted an angry reaction from the United States and other governments. As U.S. officials warned, implementation of the revised law might lead the American government prohibit any provisional parole without specific approval, and more broadly, the amendment "may very well give rise to apprehension concerning Japanese intentions towards Article 11 of the Treaty of Peace with Japan."[51] Evidently, even U.S. officials were not prepared to tolerate such a blatant attempt to free Japanese war criminals. In the face of such opposition, and conscious that intransigence might further delay the repatriation of convicted war criminals still held overseas and the release of others through established diplomatic channels, Japanese officials undertook not to use the new provision without first consulting the government concerned, and the issue quietly went away.[52]

For the most part, NOPAR's applications for clemency and parole did not impress the Allied authorities, because NOPAR appeared to endorse all applications routinely without adding any information on extenuating circumstances, except to reiterate arguments that had already been offered at the trial. British and American officials generally considered NOPAR's applications to be worthless.[53] As one British official commented: "The applications for release on parole are apt to be rather perfunctory. Many of them are limited to a description of the circumstances of the prisoner's family and to a statement that the prisoner himself is well-behaved, regrets his past misdeeds and is longing to rejoin his family."[54]

Nevertheless, NOPAR and its recommendations became a powerful force. The bureaucratic process associated with managing Article 11 developed a momentum of its own as the Japanese authorities embraced the little latitude they possessed under the treaty. NOPAR relentlessly sent application after application to foreign governments, asking them to parole war criminals. The authorities on the receiving end were forced not only to create new systems to deal with these applications but also to formulate statements and policies that could be sent to their ambassadors in Japan or given directly to visiting Japanese politicians or diplomats while taking care not to alienate their own electorates or, in the case of Britain, the populations of colonial territories.

ORDINARY MEN WITH AGING MOTHERS

With the end of the Allied Occupation, the press controls imposed by the Americans disappeared, allowing for a much greater range of public comment on and representation of convicted war criminals and of the war more generally. The prisoners' supporters could now campaign for their release without restriction. During the Occupation, the media had not been permitted to discuss themes deemed to be militarist, nationalist, or antiforeign.[55] In 1952 and 1953, in contrast, at least five popular movies were made portraying the prisoners favorably, and a steady stream of press articles demanded sympathy for the plight of those who had been convicted in the national tribunals.[56] The longing of war criminals for home and family was also narrated in heart-wrenching terms in popular songs.

The growth of the media in Japan was a major factor in the war criminals' rise to prominence as a political and social issue. Mass culture expanded rapidly in the early 1950s. The cinema was moving into its "second golden age," with movies providing "Japan's primary source of entertainment" until about 1960.[57] Weekly news magazines proliferated. In one 1952 survey of 6,700 households throughout Japan, 56 percent said they had bought a magazine in the last month, at a time when poverty was widespread; in the cities, the proportion was 63 percent.[58] The press and filmmakers naturally had an appetite for human interest stories, and they needed a lot of such stories because the mass media were expanding so rapidly. Journalists and filmmakers invited convicted war criminals to tell their stories or based their works on published collections of the war criminals' writings.[59] The resulting articles naturally ended up presenting the war criminals' version of events, whereas in earlier years their voices had rarely been heard. The demand for copy, with Occupation censorship no longer an issue, was responsible for the wide circulation of certain stock theses: that trial verdicts were unfair, that defendants had been mistakenly identified, that they had only been following orders, that punishments were disproportionate to offenses, and that relatively junior officers were made to suffer in place of their superiors. The dominant trend in the press was to report on war criminals as they supposedly were now—ordinary men, missing their homes and families and needed by those families—rather than to describe or reflect on what they had done during the war. The press was thus crucial to the moral reconfiguration of the war criminal in popular Japanese culture.

By 1952, the only convicted war criminals still in prison overseas were held by Australia on Manus Island and by the Philippines in Muntinlupa. Those on Manus remained out of reach of the press, and very little information about them leaked out. In contrast, the hundred or so war criminals in Manila, about sixty of whom had been sentenced to death, became celebrities.[60] Muntinlupa inmates presented immediate human interest. Their fate could readily be positioned as a nonpolitical issue belonging to the private realm: reporting concentrated on the suffering of the prisoners' families, the war criminals' homesickness and the anxiety felt by those awaiting execution, and the untiring efforts of people working to get prisoners released. The prisoners in Manila became an emotive focus of press coverage, and the imposing walls of Muntinlupa jail became one of the most distinctive symbols of the prisoners' plight, along with the gates of Sugamo Prison, with their English-language signs in the middle of Tokyo.

It was not difficult for journalists to write about war criminals because the prisoners could be made to fit neatly into standard tropes that were familiar from wartime. Media stories replicated themes from earlier Japanese propaganda and presumably had immediate resonance for that reason. The portraits in journalistic articles and in readers' responses reflect wartime stereotypes of fighting men and of their patriotic, grieving mothers and wives. Soldiers were said to have been convicted because in wartime they had "burned with patriotism" in carrying out their superiors' orders or in advancing national aims.[61] They now felt, it was suggested, that they were taking responsibility for Japan's defeat on behalf of the Japanese people, just as previously they had fought a war on behalf of the Japanese people.[62] The portrayal of this selfless soldier of 1952 or 1953 or later is not very different from that of the selfless propaganda soldier who had gone to war between 1937 and 1945 (figure 7.1). Meanwhile, those who suffered most from their absence apparently were their grieving mothers. Whereas the ubiquitous propaganda mother in wartime had stoically sent her son to war, in the early 1950s, she stoically awaited his return from prison; unlike in wartime, however, the media could now dwell on her suffering.

Supposedly factual, and heavily sentimental, accounts by Japanese journalists offered a classic type of story familiar from wartime and before, known as the "beautiful story," or *bidan*, focusing on such prototypical figures. A 1952 press article described a mother weeping beside the radio as she heard her son's voice for the first time in ten years, on

FIGURE 7.1 Girl visiting her father (?). Sugamo Committee, *A Factual and Statistical Survey of the Inmates at Sugamo* (November 1952). Copy available in Archives nationales (Paris), 4 AG663.

a program transmitting messages from prisoners in Muntinlupa.[63] In a story of a devoted wife based on an actual case, Ichinose Chiyuri, a young woman in poor health, finally receives news that her husband Ichinose Haruo, a former naval doctor, is alive and incarcerated in Manila. She springs from her bed and rushes off to Tokyo, where she ceaselessly petitions the authorities on his behalf until she collapses and is admitted to hospital. Many people come to her aid, and fortunately she survives until her husband's safe return.[64] Feature films presented the same kind of characters in avowedly fictional settings. The 1952 film *Sugamo Mother* begins with an elderly widow waiting patiently at the dock for the ship that will finally bring her son home from the war. She has already lost her other three sons in the conflict. But unfortunately, her surviving son is arrested as a suspected war criminal on his first night of freedom at home, even before he can taste the meal his mother has gone to great lengths to prepare for him. Without his support and because of her efforts to visit him in prison, the long-suffering mother is reduced to dire poverty and illness. At the end of the film, though, he is released from prison temporarily to attend her deathbed, and she dies happy thinking he has been freed permanently.

In other press reports, readers learned about key people who made heroic efforts to assist and comfort the war criminals. The thirty-year-old bureaucrat Ueda Shinkichi was presented as an ally working tirelessly from Tokyo on behalf of Japanese prisoners in Manila. He apparently swore he would not marry until the last prisoner had returned to Japan.[65] Numerous stories were written about "the saint of Muntinlupa," the Buddhist chaplain Kagao Shūnin, who ministered to the Japanese prisoners in Manila from 1949 to 1953. Kagao also became a major advocate for the convicted criminals, writing for the press and petitioning the authorities and influential people in both the Philippines and Japan on their behalf.[66] The combined effect of such "beautiful stories" was to suggest that loyalty, faithfulness, sincerity, hard work, and true religion were on the side of the convicted war criminals.

In addition to the frequent press coverage of the lives of war criminals in Muntinlupa, the prisoners' repatriation became the subject of a haunting tune on the radio. Muntinlupa chaplain Kagao encouraged two of his charges to write a song. "Montenrupa no yo wa fukete" (It's Getting Late in Muntinlupa), in which a son in Muntinlupa and his mother in Japan sing of their longing for each other, was recorded by popular wartime singer Watanabe Hamako. It became an enormous radio hit in 1952 and, with a spin-off movie, helped publicize the plight of war criminals in the Philippines.[67] *Sugamo Mother* did the same for those in jail in Tokyo. Both the Muntinlupa song and the Sugamo film, focusing on the loving relationship between mothers and sons and the tragedies caused by their separation, rehearsed the idea that war criminals constituted a domestic issue, a matter of personal tragedies created by circumstances that were barely alluded to.

A distinction was sometimes drawn between the prisoners convicted at the International Military Tribunal for the Far East (IMTFE) and those sentenced in national tribunals. In the posttreaty period, the press paid much less attention to the former, and public opinion about them appears to have been ambivalent. Some newspapers took up the cause of the "Class A" criminals,[68] but many people appear to have believed they had got what they deserved: they had started the war and had plunged the Japanese people into great hardship.[69] According to Takahashi Saburō, divisions between a reviled elite and the selfless and rational common soldier also characterized the many veterans' memoirs published in this period.[70] The idea that war crimes could be divided into "classes," even though in practice it was not adhered to in the courtroom, became a springboard for public exoneration of the majority of war criminals: those tried in Tokyo seemed self-evidently the worst, because they were labeled "Class A." In the Diet, Naruse Banji, of the Socialist Party's left faction, expressed "endless sympathy" for the "Class B and C" war criminals in July 1953 but insisted on the war guilt of those in "Class A."[71] In August 1954, the Diet debated an amendment to the Pension Law that was designed to allow the families of executed war criminals and those who had died in prison to receive the same level of financial support as the families of other deceased soldiers. Opponents of the measure in the Lower House were divided on whether Class B and C war criminals' relatives should benefit, but not on the question of Class A, as they thought it wrong to support those found guilty at the Tokyo Trial.[72]

Military personnel convicted in the national tribunals appeared to be more easily exonerated or forgiven. Press accounts, statements by activists, and fictional portrayals generally adopted one or more of three strategies: they suggested that the war criminals were not fundamentally guilty, that they were guilty but had made sufficient recompense, or that they were guilty and had repented.

A range of reasons supported the idea that the criminals convicted in national tribunals were not really guilty or were not very guilty. It was often asserted that individual war criminals were the victims of mistaken identity. Though courts occasionally did acknowledge that the wrong person had been charged with a crime and acquitted him,[73] there is no external evidence for the claim that many convicted criminals had been mistakenly identified. A 1952 press article reported on a particular group of prisoners in Manila who had been convicted because their unit had committed atrocities against Filipinos, but according to the article, these specific individuals had had nothing to do with the atrocity. One former soldier declared he had slept through the whole thing.[74] Another man was said to have been convicted of a separate offense solely, according to his mother, on the evidence that "a tall Japanese wearing glasses" from his unit had killed a Filipino.[75] In a survey of 731 inmates of Sugamo Prison in October 1952, 80 claimed to be the victims of mistaken identity; 114 claimed to have been arrested simply because they were Japanese; and 206 said they were victims of some kind of false testimony.[76] Such reports reached the public domain and achieved wide currency because there were so many organs of the press looking for and trading on human interest stories. Works of fiction presented similar cases.

Just as in Germany, it was often claimed in Japan that the war crimes trials had dealt harshly with subordinates while ignoring the highly placed.[77] The media often stated that Japanese personnel prosecuted in the national tribunals were lower-ranking soldiers who had merely followed the orders of their superiors and should therefore be considered innocent or less guilty than senior officers. In many cases, it was said that the superior officers had fled or had given false testimony, leaving their subordinates to take the blame for actions they had ordered.[78] The press did not acknowledge that the most junior soldiers had in fact been treated relatively leniently in the trial process but instead projected an image of hapless pawns who had been harshly punished. For example, two of the four main characters in Kobayashi Masaki's 1953 film *Kabe atsuki heya* (*The Thick-Walled Room*) had been victims of more senior officers. At other times, it was asserted that very minor offenses, like "slapping" prisoners, had attracted unreasonably heavy penalties. Sometimes it was argued that all soldiers did such things in wartime, but only the Japanese side, and only some Japanese at that, had been held accountable; therefore, the punishment was selective. Sometimes it was explicitly argued that war crimes had been politically constructed by the victors or that actions considered unremarkable in Japanese culture were condemned by the Allies. Thus, prisoners cited in one article maintained that actions that in Japan would have won the Order of the Golden Kite, an imperial award for military valor and leadership, were treated by the Allies as war crimes.[79] It could equally be observed, it was said, that polygamy is legal in some countries and illegal in others.[80] Conversely, slapping prisoners and subordinates was said to be routine in the Japanese military and therefore not a criminal action. In other cases, prisoners claimed to have been blamed for things that were beyond their control or beyond anyone's control. Typically, such objections related to provision of inadequate food and medical treatment to POWs.[81]

The media, political figures, and the prisoners themselves admitted that many convicted criminals were guilty. According to a 1953 press account, officials reinvestigating cases in order to make clemency recommendations found that one-third of the prisoners completely denied the facts of their alleged crimes and two-thirds admitted their guilt.[82] The Christian magazine Nyū eiji (New Age) published an article by Audrey Henty, a British missionary in Singapore, describing her experience a few years earlier of the last days of a war criminal condemned to death in Singapore for torture and murder. The former military police officer reportedly faced death with a mixture of terror and calm, clearly acknowledging his guilt. He found solace in conversion to Christianity a few days before his execution.[83] Despite such acknowledgment of war criminals' guilt, many people felt that enough was enough. The chairman of the Welfare Committee of the Diet's Lower House, Ōishi Buichi, commented in April 1952 that the prisoners awaiting execution in Muntinlupa might have committed terrible crimes but that seven years in jail was sufficient payment.[84] As another conservative politician remarked, the lenient peace treaty demonstrated that Japan had been forgiven as a nation; it was now time to forgive the war criminals, too.[85] Moreover, it was often asserted, prisoners who really had done terrible things had used their time in prison to reflect on their actions and had sincerely repented.[86] Only one of the four main characters in The Thick-Walled Room appeared to have participated willingly in the mistreatment of the captured enemy, in this case in China. He was so haunted by the memory that he hanged himself in his cell.

Not everyone was happy about the prisoners' high public profile. The issues of how to interpret war crimes and of the degree of war criminals' guilt remained fraught; some people worried that that they were being made into heroes, which presumably would turn Japanese society away from peace and democracy.[87] Continued reports that prisoners had difficulty in finding employment or suffered other forms of discrimination suggest that positive press coverage did not necessarily accurately represent the gamut of public attitudes.[88] In January 1953, former members of the Naval General Staff working for the Demobilization Bureau in the Ministry of Welfare were convinced that substantial negative feeling about war criminals remained, even though public sympathy had increased markedly since the end of the Occupation. Families of executed war criminals and those who died in prison, for example, still did not receive public support in the form of pensions.[89] These officials now rededicated themselves to wide-ranging efforts to encourage both public support and government action, advocating the manipulation of mass media, nongovernment organizations, and prefectural assemblies; the stimulation of the petition campaign; and attempts to influence Diet members. In their view, the essential task was to deepen the public consciousness that war criminals and their families were victims of the war, just as much as others were.[90] Despite any doubts about the real extent of public sympathy, by early 1953 press articles were claiming with increasing confidence that the public wanted to see the prisoners released or at least paroled.[91]

Once the Occupation had ended, the press sometimes acknowledged that the prisoners did not constitute a uniform body and did not always conform to the ideal types common in public discourse. Not everyone felt satisfaction at having served his country or his emperor in wartime. One of the most cynical comments on the situation of war criminals appeared in print with the title "I Want to Be a Shellfish." Katō Tetsutarō, convicted by a U.S. tribunal at Yokohama, wrote an essay under a pseudonym from inside Sugamo Prison in October 1952, which was published the following year in a collection of war criminals' writings. A fictional "Sergeant Akagi" leaves a note before his execution expressing his disgust at what has happened to him and his lack of respect for the emperor. Believing he was fighting the war for the sake of the emperor, Akagi had faithfully obeyed orders, no matter how distasteful they might have been, and never once neglected his military duty. Yet the emperor had not saved him from his current fate. The only things he had ever received from the emperor were seven or eight cigarettes on the China front and some cakes in the field hospital. The cigarettes proved to be very costly: he would eventually pay for them with his life, since serving the emperor in war had led to his conviction as a war criminal. He refused to be silenced any longer and considered his debt to the emperor canceled. If he should be reborn as a Japanese after his execution, Akagi insisted, he would never again be a soldier. In fact, he did not want to be a Japanese at all, or even a human being. Nor did he want to be a cow or a horse, as such animals were harassed by humans too. If he had to be reborn, he wanted to come back as a shellfish. A shellfish clings to a rock deep in the ocean without having to worry about anything. Because it knows nothing, it is neither happy nor sad. It feels neither pain nor itchiness, never gets a headache, is never taken as a soldier, never experiences war, and has no anxieties about wife or children.[92]

Interviews with prisoners sometimes underlined the point, presenting war criminals as a divided and resentful group, in reports highlighting hierarchical divisions within Sugamo and the inmates' political cynicism and alienation from normal society. In a report of a group interview published in the respected journal *Chūō kōron*, several well-educated soldiers described the attitudes of ordinary farmers and workers who had been conscripted into the military and then convicted as war criminals. Such enlisted men, they said, felt they had been fooled. They had fought hard for the emperor, only to find themselves on trial. Meanwhile, their superiors, who in many cases had ordered them to commit their crimes, had fled, and the emperor was apparently carefree and relaxed. Not surprisingly, they had lost respect for all forms of authority. They would never choose to be soldiers again and would never do anything for the sake of their country. They were even, it was claimed, sending letters to young men who joined the Public Security Force (Hoantai), predecessor of the Self-Defense Forces, asking them how they could be so stupid as to enlist.[93]

Katō's "Sergeant Akagi" complained that there were hardly any decent senior Japanese officers. They treated ordinary soldiers with contempt and did not hesitate to deceive them. At war crimes trials, they sacrificed their subordinates without a qualm.[94] An article in the weekly *Shūkan asahi* also pointed to the support expressed by convicts at Sugamo for the riotous demonstrators in the May Day parade of 1952 and to their hatred of both the Japanese and the American governments, their distrust of both right- and left-wing politicians, and their general sense of alienation from society.[95]

PUBLIC ADVOCACY

Organizations specifically representing war criminals emerged openly after the departure of the Occupation forces. Four days before the peace treaty took effect, an official support group, the Association to Support the War-Convicted (Sensō jukeisha sewakai), was formed with more than six hundred members under the guidance of former Vice Admiral Hara Chūichi, who had been convicted by the Americans on Guam and had served six years in Sugamo Prison.[96] Formally inaugurated on May 10, 1952, the association became a redoubtable civilian organization.

The campaign on behalf of war criminals came to wield significant political clout for at least two reasons. First, politicians quickly realized that war criminals could be exploited to win votes. Second, a considerable number of influential people had firsthand knowledge of the issues relating to war criminals. The prime group was former senior military men, who might themselves have been "purged," arrested as suspects but later released, or even imprisoned for short terms for war crimes, as Hara had been; or as military men, they might simply have empathized with the imprisoned war criminals, understood their situation, felt grateful or guilty that they were not in the same position, or felt responsible for the welfare of former subordinates now in prison. In the early 1950s, many military men were returning to public life and thus to influence.[97] Certain prominent civilians, too, had had a close association with the Allied reckoning with war criminals. Shigemitsu Mamoru, who was convicted at the IMTFE and paroled in 1950, became chairman of a new national political party, the Kaishintō, in 1952 and was appointed foreign minister for the fourth time in 1954; Kishi Nobusuke, detained in Sugamo as a potential IMTFE defendant but never charged, was elected to the Lower House in 1953. Wealthy and well-connected businessmen Sasakawa Ryōichi and Shōriki Matsutarō, too, had been imprisoned in Sugamo as possible IMTFE defendants. Some prominent individuals had been close to the trials in other ways. Kiyose Ichirō, former Prime Minister Tōjō's defense lawyer in the IMTFE, became secretary-general of Shigemitsu's Kaishintō after he was released from purge restrictions.

The Association to Support the War-Convicted was backed by powerful figures from across politics, business, and the legal world. Its list of directors was a who's who of wartime military and civilian elites, and many of them continued to be highly influential in postwar politics. It was headed by the prominent businessman and politician Fujiwara Ginjirō, who had been purged from public office during the Occupation. Kishi and Shōriki were among the executive directors. Also on the board were Kiyose, Nomura Kichisaburō, who had engaged in high-level negotiations in Washington with Secretary of State Cordell Hull in the lead-up to Pearl Harbor, and many other influential figures. Along with Hara, other former senior military officers among the membership included men who had been convicted as war criminals and sentenced to short periods in prison. Fukutome Shigeru, for example, was a former admiral who had served as chief of staff of the Combined Fleet; he had been convicted by the British in Singapore and released in 1950.[98] Among the directors were individuals already working actively for the welfare of war criminals and their families, including Imamura Hisako, the president of the Association of the Families of War Criminals (Sensō hanzainin kazoku kai) in Tokyo, whose husband continued to serve out his sentence on Manus Island.[99] By the end of 1952, branches of the Association to Support the War-Convicted, or similar organizations, had been established in thirty-two of Japan's forty-seven prefectures.[100]

The association formally took the view that the convicted war criminals had waged war for the sake of the nation and thus should be considered as victims, deemed criminal because Japan had been defeated. Therefore they and their families deserved moral and material support. Members began to exert pressure on the Diet, the Foreign Ministry, and the Justice Ministry to bring about the commutation of death sentences for prisoners in the Philippines, the repatriation of those still in Manila and on Manus, and, ultimately, the release of all war criminals from prison.[101] In the short term, they wanted to ensure both that conditions at Sugamo did not worsen after the transfer of the jail to Japanese administration and that employment and health and welfare assistance would be provided to former convicts. Another important aim was to look after the interests of the families of the war criminals and to ensure they had access to the same welfare provisions as did the relatives of people missing in China or the Soviet Union. The association also lent its support to an emerging movement to reinstate pensions for the families of fallen soldiers and veterans, which had been abolished by the Occupation forces in 1946. The members maintained that such pensions should also be made available to the families of war criminals who had been executed or who had died in jail.[102]

The Association to Support the War-Convicted worked actively with the families of war criminals, government ministries, and organizations working on behalf of war criminals in Tokyo, in regional areas and overseas, including religious groups, the YMCA, and groups within Sugamo itself. For its activities it relied on donations, which were plentiful. Prefectural governments, wealthy individuals, prominent businesses, and nongovernmental organizations contributed money, which the association distributed mainly as welfare to indigent families of war criminals, as monthly payments to those in jail, as grants to enable families in distant prefectures to travel to Sugamo, as pensions to the families of those executed, and also to cover the costs associated with dealing with foreign governments and with publishing and advertising. In September 1952 the association listed 478 companies as donors, including major banks, insurance companies, transport and construction companies, publishers, real estate brokers, and many others that together had by then donated more than ¥31 million. The allowance for a family visit to Sugamo was ¥3,000, and poor families were offered ¥5,000 per year as general welfare support.[103]

Public education was one of the association's basic aims. Within a month of the end of the Occupation, the association had produced a printed pamphlet of twenty-two pages, giving information on the war crimes trials, the governments that had sentenced prisoners, conditions in jails overseas and at home, the problems facing war criminals' families, and the implications of the peace treaty's Article 11. Personal accounts by war criminals were also included. Another, shorter, pamphlet produced in November 1952 urged readers to donate to the association, focusing especially on the plight of the families whose relatives were in jail overseas.[104] On July 3, 1953, the association held its first national meeting in Tokyo, a day-long gathering in which some eighty delegates from thirty-one prefectures and municipalities met to discuss strategy and to hear from two top bureaucrats from the Ministries of Foreign Affairs and of Justice, as well as Diet member Yamashita Harue. The meeting resolved to coordinate national petition drives, hold national rallies, and lobby the government to send elected representatives overseas to discuss war criminals with foreign governments (figure 7.2).[105]

Other groups also continued to act on behalf of the war criminals. In May 1952 the Japan Federation of Lawyers (Nihon bengoshikai) established a special committee on war criminals, whose members included several former defense lawyers from the Tokyo Trial. They complained

FIGURE 7.2 Public signing of petitions for the repatriation of prisoners held overseas, August 5, 1953. Kōseishō, *In Search of Peace*, August 5, 1953, Archives du Comité international de la Croix-Rouge (Geneva), B AG 210 000.

that the defense arguments at the IMTFE had been crushed, implying that the arguments in favor of the defendants had never been seriously considered and that the Japanese people had been stigmatized at the trial as aggressors. They now pressed the government, the Diet, and the media to take positive steps to secure the release of convicted war criminals.[106] Representatives of the lawyers' federation were reported to be the first civilians to get inside Sugamo to conduct a group interview, in April 1952.[107] At the end of that year they organized mass public rallies in Tokyo and Osaka calling for the war criminals' immediate release. Religious organizations continued to work for the prisoners, and not surprisingly, right-wing groups and individuals were also very active. The prominent rightist Sasakawa Ryōichi was said to have taken hundreds of politicians on individual visits to Sugamo.[108] Ultranationalist associations like the Kenseikai (Japan Sound Youth Association) and the Junkoku seinentai (National Martyrs Youth Corps) conducted petition campaigns, appealed to foreign embassies, and organized rallies.[109]

The Sugamo war criminals themselves also worked energetically for their own release and to get their compatriots repatriated from the Philippines and Manus. Their efforts were made more and more openly and aggressively until they were directly appealing to the Diet, prefectural governments, and other public bodies.[110] In November 1952 a telegram was sent in the name of all prisoners to the chief secretary of the Foreign Ministry, requesting that the government mark the occasion of the crown prince's investiture on November 10 by asking foreign governments to pardon the prisoners. In due course, the ministry formally notified the prisoners that it had done so.[111] Prisoners put their case to visiting politicians and commented on the Diet's deliberations about them. In December 1952 they discussed the prospects for the repatriation of war criminals held by the Australian government on Manus Island with Nishi Haruhiko, the first postwar Japanese ambassador to Australia, less than three weeks before he departed to take up his new post. In the same month, Sugamo's inmates were briefed by the chief secretary of the Foreign Ministry on the situation with regard to the countries that still held Japanese prisoners.[112] Around the same time, a big rally was held inside the prison, at which panelists demanded the repeal of Article 11, recommendations from the Japanese government to foreign governments for war criminals' release, and the protection of prisoners' livelihood once they were freed.[113] In early 1953, prisoners reportedly discussed a proposal to be put to the government and the Diet for special envoys to be sent to foreign countries to negotiate the release of war criminals.[114]

Prisoners in Sugamo were active in disseminating their views through publications in the outside world. In 1952 the Sugamo Legal Affairs Committee (Sugamo hōmu iinkai) published *Senpan saiban no jissō* (*True Facts of the War Crimes Trials*), an 852-page book intended to convince the public of the unfairness of the trials and to bring the national tribunals out from the shadow of the Tokyo trials. The book argued that the national-level prosecutions had been "a theatre of revenge in the garb of a trial." In Utsumi Aiko's assessment, it had a large impact on the government and Diet members.[115] Sugamo prisoners also published *Seiki no isho* (*Testaments of the Century*), a lavishly produced work containing 800 pages of last testaments of prisoners about to be executed.[116] Prisoners also wrote personal memoirs and press articles from inside the prison, using pseudonyms in order not to endanger their prospects of release.[117] Foreign governments and influential individuals overseas were the target

FIGURE 7.3 Petitions collected for the release of war criminals, in Sugamo Committee, *A Factual and Statistical Survey of the Inmates at Sugamo* (November 1952). Available at Archives nationales (Paris), 4 AG663.

of some Sugamo publications. At the end of 1952, for example, a group of Buddhist priests due to visit India was entrusted with materials on war criminals addressed to Indian Prime Minister Jawaharlal Nehru and Justice Radhabinod Pal.[118]

Outside the prison, the campaign to support war criminals not only courted political champions but also used highly visible strategies, including public demonstrations, sit-ins, hunger strikes, distribution of leaflets, and petition drives. During 1952 alone, according to Japanese officials, more than 10 million people signed petitions for the repatriation to Japan of convicted war criminals still held overseas and for sentence reduction for all prisoners.[119] A Sugamo Prison publication declared that 1.05 million of Gifu Prefecture's population of 1.5 million, that is, 70 percent, had signed petitions and that the All Japan Flower-Arranging Federation (Zen Nihon kadō) had collected a million signatures in three days.[120] Photographs of large piles of petitions with millions of signatures were regularly sent to the embassies of overseas countries and directly to foreign governments: the Ministry of Welfare claimed in 1953 that petitions for the repatriation of war criminals sent to President Elpidio Quirino in the Philippines contained five million signatures (figure 7.3).[121] Embassies of all the governments holding Japanese war criminals were inundated with petitions, and diplomats complained they could not cope with the workload, writing to their home governments, sometimes in urgent terms, asking them to do something about the war criminals because they were under such pressure in Tokyo. The U.S. embassy reported in October 1952 that "in addition to the petitions and letters, the Embassy receives at least four delegations a week from various parts of Japan who plead for the release of the 424 war criminals held by the United States."[122]

POLITICIANS, BUREAUCRATS, AND WAR CRIMINALS

The response of Japanese authorities to lobbying on behalf of the prisoners was uneven. Elected politicians understood the importance their constituents placed on the release of war criminals. Bureaucrats often professed sympathy. At the same time, many officials argued that public disquiet about war criminals, and the potential for unrest to result, damaged negotiations within the Japanese government and with foreign authorities and might affect the future treatment of war criminals by the foreign governments that retained control over their sentences. Undeniably, however, lobbying put strong pressure on the Japanese authorities to act.

After the peace treaty took effect, the Japanese government had little choice but to embark on a long series of representations to foreign governments for clemency. Opinion was divided, however, on what strategy to pursue. Assessments of eligibility for sentence reduction, parole, and any form of clemency fell within the jurisdiction of the Justice Ministry, while the Foreign Ministry liaised with the governments of the prosecuting countries. Along with the Demobilization Bureaus, with their staff of former military personnel, the Justice Ministry was impatient to see the war criminals freed and favored pressing the prosecuting governments for their rapid release. Justice Ministry officials considered convicted war criminals to be "leftovers" of war and occupation, asserting that there should be no foreign-convicted war criminals in an independent country.

The Demobilization Bureaus, meanwhile, provided resources and advice to nongovernment organizations that were active in the public campaign and urged politicians and other parts of government, particularly the Foreign Ministry and the Justice Ministry, to take action. Officials at the Demobilization Bureaus also made plans to stimulate foreign sympathy for Japanese war criminals, in order to put pressure on the governments that controlled their sentences. By contrast, the Foreign Ministry and Prime Minister Yoshida were conscious of foreign governments' sensitivities and their determined stance on war criminals and favored a gradualist approach. Even Yoshida, however, was forced to make concessions before elections: in June 1952, before the October general election, he instructed officials to expedite recommendations for parole under Article 11.[123]

Two months after Japan regained its sovereignty, the Diet started passing resolutions calling for the repatriation of prisoners still held overseas by the Philippines and Australia and urging the government to negotiate for parole for those held in Japan. On June 9, 1952, independent Diet member Okabe Tsune presented a bill to the House of Councillors proposing that the government negotiate with the foreign powers for clemency for those sentenced to death in the Philippines, for the rapid repatriation of those imprisoned in Manus and the Philippines, and for the adoption of benevolent measures for those in Sugamo, by which Okabe meant, as he explained, the reduction of sentences, parole, and pardons.[124] The proposal was accepted by a large majority: only Iwama Masao, for the Communist Party, registered his opposition, for which he was heckled by other members. Iwama explained that he was concerned about the impact that such a proposal would have on Japan's international relations generally and more specifically on the fate of Japanese civilians and former soldiers remaining in China and the Soviet Union.[125]

On December 9, 1952, a coalition of parties reiterated the same sentiments in the House of Representatives, arguing that the trials in general had little credibility and claiming that world opinion now favored the war criminals' release. As evidence, the bill's supporters referred to Lord Hankey, a former British cabinet secretary, who had advocated clemency for German and Japanese war criminals since at least 1951, and Justice Pal, who had issued a dissenting judgment at the Tokyo Trial. Supporters of the bill also pointed out that many in Sugamo proclaimed their innocence and cited numerous examples of hardship: war criminals found themselves divorced, and, after release, were refused employment and sometimes suffered mental illness as a result of their time in jail.[126] Left-wing parties opposed the resolution, denouncing the campaign to release war criminals as symptomatic of a reactionary trend in Japanese society, which, they said, was encouraged by the government in order to direct public attention away from the push to rearm Japan in the early postwar period. Critics expressing such views, however, were in a minority.[127]

Advocating leniency for war criminals became politically useful to politicians, many of whom cultivated direct connections with the prisoners. As in Germany, defending ordinary war criminals was a way of displaying patriotism in the hope of gaining electoral votes.[128] Opposition parties used the apparent lack of progress on leniency to criticize the Yoshida government, which remained in power until December 1954, and conservatives and socialists, though not the communists, agreed that war criminals convicted in the national tribunals should not be held personally accountable for war crimes. War criminals were an issue in the October 1952 election.[129] National elections were held in 1953 as well, and in both years, luxury cars reportedly lined up at the gates of Sugamo as politicians competed to make speeches of consolation and encouragement to the prisoners. "It's exactly as though this were a zoo," prisoners were said to have commented in August 1953: "Talking about the war is appealing to the masses. They [the politicians] come to Sugamo for material for their election speeches. There even seems to be a superstition that candidates who visit Sugamo will win, and those who don't come will lose."[130]

Though the fate of war criminals depended on decisions made in foreign countries, the main target of the public campaign was Japan's own government, as people all over the country attempted to persuade the authorities they had to do something to bring back the remaining prisoners from overseas jails and then to get them freed. Behind the scenes, activists lobbied politicians and bureaucrats.[131]

Some politicians and bureaucrats openly embraced the use of mass rallies and petitions. Ministry of Welfare officials, for example, often approved of such tactics.[132] Bureaucrats in the Foreign Ministry, by contrast, were more cautious: attuned to the sentiments of the powers that had convicted the war criminals, they endeavored to reassure foreign powers that the provisions of Article 11 were being observed. Foreign Ministry officials were particularly conscious that diluting the effect of Article 11 might harm the future of war criminals in the Philippines, especially those with death sentences, and the prospects of repatriation of those on

Manus Island. At the same time, the Minister of Foreign Affairs could, when convenient, use the alleged threat of potential domestic unrest in Japan over war criminals as a negotiating tool. Foreign Minister Okazaki Katsuo convinced French Ambassador Maurice Dejean shortly after the peace treaty came into effect that popular sentiment regarding war criminals was so strong that their continued incarceration might destabilize Japan's conservative government. Dejean accordingly told his government in July 1952 that a carefully timed reduction of sentences for war criminals convicted in Indochina would not only improve France's image in Japan but would also help keep in power Japan's conservative government, an important ally in the free world.[133] The British legation was more cynical and saw the hand of the Japanese government in the coordination of popular movements for the release of war criminals.[134]

Officials in other ministries had different concerns. The Ministry of Finance complained about the cost of incarceration at Sugamo, where the standard of prisoner welfare was so high that it cost nearly six times more to maintain an inmate there than in Fuchū Prison in Tokyo, which housed ordinary prisoners. According to an agreement with the departing U.S. authorities at the termination of the Occupation, however, the same conditions were to be maintained in Sugamo after the U.S. military left, so the standards could not simply be lowered.[135] Sugamo Prison itself became the center of a tussle among the different ministries once it was returned to Japanese administration in April 1952. The prison governor's position was distinctly uncomfortable. In an interview with a representative of the British embassy in early 1953, he reportedly complained that politicians came from far and wide to be seen with Sugamo inmates, only to agitate them with empty promises before leaving again; that officials of the Ministries of Foreign Affairs, Justice, and Finance fought over the cost and the administration of the prison and that he, the governor of Sugamo, was caught in the middle; that he was regularly insulted by visiting prefectural politicians and officials who heaped abuse on him for jailing fellow citizens; that he saw a conflict of interest in his current duties because he did not believe that Japanese citizens should have the responsibility of incarcerating Japanese war criminals; that his prison guards constantly talked of resigning because of the terrible reputation they had outside the jail and the fact that they were treated as servants by the convicts; and that should the Sugamo prisoners' association decide simply to walk out, no one would be willing or able to stop them—not the guards, the governor, or the public.[136] On February 12, 1953, high-profile lawyer and Diet member Onimaru Gisai, who had chaired the House of Councillors Special Committee on War Criminals in 1951 and 1952, filed a lawsuit against the prison governor requesting the release of all of Sugamo's inmates, whose incarceration, he argued, contravened domestic law by making it subordinate to international treaty.[137] Although the case was rejected by the Tokyo Court of Appeals on February 28, 1953, on the grounds that international treaties must be understood to override domestic law, it further destabilized the role of the prison's governor.[138] Meanwhile, politicians periodically castigated bureaucrats in the Diet. War criminals came up in Diet discussions several times a month from February to June 1953, and the Ministry of Foreign Affairs was regularly attacked for its perceived failures and its "ineptitude and inaction" (*munō muryoku*) on the question of their repatriation and release.[139]

By 1953, war criminals were firmly on the political agenda in Japan and on the diplomatic agenda in Japan's negotiations on the world stage. The perceived place of Japan in the Cold War world was changing rapidly, and the political capital of Japanese leaders consequently grew. In the West, the desire to cultivate new and more amicable relations with Japan, the conviction that concessions had to be made to keep Japan in the Western camp, and the possibility of commercial gain through a resumption or expansion of trade were among the factors prompting the governments holding war criminals to reconsider whether the costs of keeping them in prison outweighed the benefits. In this context, the constant missives from NOPAR, along with mountains of petitions from civic organizations and ordinary people throughout Japan, increasingly unsettled the foreign diplomats and politicians who dealt with war criminals. The Japanese government could not determine the fate of the prisoners. Because of the vigor of the public campaign and the relentless energy of NOPAR, however, Japan's influence came to exceed by a big margin the apparent bounds so carefully set by Article 11 of the peace treaty.

8

FINDING A FORMULA FOR RELEASE

I n 1953, six governments apart from the Soviet Union—Australia, Britain, France, the Netherlands, the Philippines, and the United States—were still responsible for Japanese war criminals convicted in national tribunals, and the prosecuting powers were jointly responsible for reviewing sentences passed by the International Military Tribunal for the Far East (IMTFE). There now was a wide gap between Japanese public opinion, which generally believed the prisoners to have been punished sufficiently, perhaps excessively, and Allied opinion, which generally maintained that the trials had been fair and that the sentences were appropriate or perhaps even lenient. On the Allied side, however, there was a growing willingness to set other issues alongside this acceptance of the trials' underlying validity. Policymakers had come to understand that continued detention of war criminals might no longer serve the political and economic interests of the imprisoning powers. The broader Western aims of the postwar settlement had largely been achieved: Japan was no longer a militarist threat to world peace but instead had become a peaceable democracy and a strategic Cold War ally of the United States, with increasing importance to the global economy. In these circumstances, it was hard to see that further incarceration of war criminals served any noble or useful purpose. Moreover, if the imprisoning governments continued to thwart Japanese public opinion, Western policymakers feared that Japan might drift diplomatically toward the Soviet bloc or China and that Western business interests might lose opportunities in Japan.

Such reasoning implicitly acknowledged that the trials had been conducted not only to punish individuals but also to signal the guilt of Japan as a nation. Throughout the trials, Japanese defendants, lawyers, and observers had complained of irregularities in the selection and identification of defendants and in the acceptance or rejection of evidence in court. Even before the peace treaty, these complaints had coalesced into a perception in Japan that the Allied authorities were not taking sufficient care to identify the right perpetrators. Individual war criminals thus seemed like scapegoats, imprisoned mainly to confirm that the nation as a whole had acted wrongly, not primarily because they themselves had committed a crime. On the Allied side, too, many people saw the convicted men as proxies for Japan. The growing willingness among the imprisoning powers to forgive what they perceived as Japan's war guilt often translated into a willingness to grant clemency to individuals. The challenge, however, was to devise a means that affirmed the integrity of the original sentences while allowing considerations in favor of release to prevail.

Each of the convicting powers perceived these issues and experienced their associated pressures in different ways. Nonetheless, they were bound together by their shared moral and political predicament as well as their joint control of prisoners from the IMTFE, which required them to agree by majority decision on any variations in sentencing. Between 1953 and 1956, all the imprisoning powers embarked on a path toward the release of the remaining war criminals. The governments of the Republic of China (ROC) and the Netherlands had already concluded that war criminals were a political issue and had essentially traded the prisoners they had convicted in military tribunals for political gain. The ROC had released them for Cold War advantage; the Netherlands authorities retained control of the prisoners they had convicted but had named their price, in the form of compensation for the losses incurred by Dutch wartime internees in the Netherlands Indies. But each of the governments still holding war criminals concluded that it could not simply go its own way on decisions about clemency, even when the national tribunals were concerned. It was not possible to ignore Japanese opinion, given the country's new status as a Cold War ally. It was also impossible, or at least highly inadvisable, to settle the future fate of the war criminals unilaterally or even in bilateral negotiations with Japan. Policy on war criminals became enmeshed with complex, high-level negotiations regarding Japan's reentry into global politics and with Cold War relations among the Allies themselves. The period from 1953 onward was accordingly marked by intense international diplomacy in decisions about war criminals, among the prosecuting powers and between each of them and Japan.

FURTHER RELEASES

At the end of May 1953, the Philippine government announced that it would release five prisoners from Muntinlupa to mark the Philippines' Independence Day on July 4. The lucky five included, for the first time, a prisoner originally sentenced to death. The Japanese press reported on the joyful responses of the men's families and then, in "continuous good news about releases," revealed that the French government was to free the prisoners convicted in Indochina.[1]

After the restoration of peace with Japan in April 1952, responsibility for Japanese war criminals convicted in Indochina had passed from the authorities there to the French government in Paris.[2] In the face of numerous petitions from Japan and recommendations from the National Offenders Parole and Rehabilitation Commission (NOPAR), the French government had meager interest in retaining control of Japanese war criminals. The French public cared little for Asian affairs, and the French authorities placed more emphasis on the need to keep Japan in the Western camp in the Cold War. As we have seen, the French ambassador in Tokyo had already advised his government in July 1952 that the restoration of peace provided an opportunity for France to make a gesture of clemency to war criminals in deserving cases.[3] By January 1953, other officials favored the immediate release of all thirty-eight war criminals still under French control, for reasons of international politics and also of pragmatism: French trial records commonly gave few details about the circumstances of the crime or the evidence presented during the proceedings, and officials commented that the files they had on Japanese war criminals did not provide enough information on their convictions or their current circumstances to facilitate any sound legal ruling on a case-by-case basis.[4] Although they may, between July and September 1952, have contemplated an early general release, the French authorities in the end fell into step with other governments in publicly committing themselves to considering individual cases for clemency rather than granting a blanket amnesty. The effect of a general amnesty was nevertheless achieved when the French government announced individual reductions of sentences to allow all war criminals to finish their prison terms on May 26, 1953. Two or three prisoners stayed in Sugamo until April 1954, as their status was unclear, apparently because while they were technically the responsibility of France, they had also been tried by China.[5] The French government probably released the prisoners as a political gesture aimed at improving relations with Japan. On June 1, 1953, upon receiving the good news, the Japanese government expressed its gratitude and did indeed pledge itself to work further to improve Japanese–French relations.[6] The French government thus became the second after that of the Republic of China to rid itself of the problem of what to do with Japanese war criminals convicted in its national tribunals.

The Netherlands government also began to release prisoners. Although the Dutch authorities were unwilling to make major concessions until the Japanese authorities agreed to provide compensation for wartime internees' losses, Cold War politics modified this stance. Dutch officials believed that "an early release of a number of war criminals might help to keep Japan in the Western orbit."[7] In mid-1953 the Dutch government paroled twelve war criminals as a gesture to mark the official visit of the Japanese crown prince, Akihito, to the Netherlands in July of that year.[8] By this action, the Netherlands became the second government after the United States to release Japanese war criminals on parole.

The first Dutch-convicted war criminal eligible for parole according to NOPAR rules was Hayashi Tetsuo. He had originally been sentenced to life imprisonment, in Ambon in April 1947, but NOPAR claimed to have evidence that the sentence had been reduced to ten years. NOPAR also applied a remission for good behavior to the supposed ten-year sentence and informed the Netherlands authorities that Hayashi would be released on July 3, 1953. For reasons that remain unclear, NOPAR then authorized Hayashi's release one month earlier, on June 3. The Dutch authorities were indignant and issued a stern warning to their Japanese counterparts, casting doubt on the evidence that the Japanese authorities had used to calculate the release date and demanding to be informed in advance of any future releases.[9] They became still more indignant when they could find no record in their files that Hayashi's sentence had ever been reduced to ten years. Internal Dutch correspondence accused the Japanese of bad faith and *boerenbedrog* (the deceitfulness of peasants). The Japanese authorities responded that they had calculated Hayashi's prison term in good faith. They were able to show that the mistake in record keeping was attributable to the American authorities in Sugamo, who had been in charge of Hayashi and all other prisoners in Tokyo until the peace treaty took effect. The Dutch authorities, however, doggedly insisted that Hayashi's sentence had been for life and that he should return to Sugamo.[10]

Hayashi became a cause célèbre. He had been informed in November 1953 that he should return to Sugamo. He agreed reluctantly in order, he said, to prevent any adverse effect on the remaining prisoners; the Netherlands authorities had indeed stated that there would be no further releases until Hayashi was back in prison. Nothing happened, however, until his story reached the press in February 1954 and a public campaign in his defense was launched. It was reported that 230,000 petitions were presented in his support.[11] Proceeding cautiously, the Japanese government then asked the Dutch government to make a formal request for Hayashi's reimprisonment. He returned to Sugamo on February 22, "leaving his wife, two sons and blind mother" (figure 8.1).[12] Dutch businesses in Japan were very unhappy about the bad publicity arising from the Netherlands government's

FIGURE 8.1 Hayashi Tetsuo returns to Sugamo, February 22, 1954. *Nippon Times*, February 23, 1954. Copy in NA (NL), BuZa Code-Archief 45–54, 2.05.117, inv.nr. 7836).

insistence on Hayashi's return to prison.[13] To salvage something from the damage, on March 3, 1954, the Dutch authorities accepted a NOPAR recommendation to reduce Hayashi's sentence from life to twenty years, making him eligible for immediate parole, after remission for good conduct in prison.[14] The parole paperwork then assembled by NOPAR showed him to have been an excellent worker in Sugamo, with a family outside that needed him. Moreover, in words attributed to Hayashi, "an extent of the torturing against the victims was not so severe, and I was held too heavy responsibility, I think, to control my men under the command."[15] Parole was formally granted on May 28.[16] Though they continued to insist on the compensation deal, Dutch officials periodically released further small groups of prisoners on parole, usually after one-third of the sentence had been served.[17] By the end of September 1955, the Dutch authorities had freed 100 prisoners by this method,[18] but another 117 remained incarcerated.

By this stage, NOPAR had taken on an advocacy role. In September 1953, it distributed a survey of what it called the "family situation" of the war criminals in Sugamo. Some 231 families were recorded as being in "extreme distress," with another 257 "precarious, but may be in extreme distress in 1954" (figure 8.2).[19] Beginning in November 1953, NOPAR sent a monthly statistical statement of the number of war criminals held under each jurisdiction,

TABLE 3. CONDITION OF FAMILIES	United States	Nether-lands	Britain	France	Aus-tralia	Total
Living conditions of families are:						
Extremely impoverished	79	54	32	4	6	175
Just managin to eke out existence	155	81	49	23	10	318
Uncertainty ahead	112	52	21	7	4	202
No worry at all	11	3	4	1	-	19
Conditions of impoverished families are:						
Protected by Livelihood Protection Law	41	10	8	3	1	63
Aided by relatives	166	80	43	12	6	307
Aided by persons other than relatives	49	10	3	1	-	63
Families that broke up	23	8	2	1	1	35
Being war criminals they were compelled to:						
Divorce	11	8	7	1	1	28
Break off engagements	17	15	7	2	-	41
Being families of war criminals they:						
Failed to get employed	6	9	4	2	1	22
Failed to get married	8	2	2	-	-	12
Social pressure brought to bear	31	12	9	-	4	56
Attempted suicide	6	4	-	2	-	12
Became insane	7	2	4	-	2	16
While serving prison terms their:						
parents died	94	53	27	8	4	186
Wife or children died	24	8	7	-	-	39
Other blood relations died	143	70	39	13	5	270
Separated from families for:						
Five years or more	237	24	24	5	7	297
10 years or more	75	133	70	23	6	307
15 years or more	11	35	12	5	1	64
20 years or more	2	3	1	-	-	6

Note: Survey made on the families of 731 out of 819 war criminals on October 18, 1952.

FIGURE 8.2 Results of Japanese survey of war criminals in Sugamo, October 1952. Copy in NA (NL), BuZa Code-Archief 45–54 (1945–1954), 2.05.117 inv.nr. 7707.

FIGURE 8.3 Photograph included in a petition to the U.S. authorities on behalf of Bunro Saiki, sentenced to 24 years' imprisonment. The prisoner's wife and 85-year-old mother await his return. Petition from Ungoro Uchigasaki, Chief Manager of War Criminals from Miyagi-ken [*sic*], to John Moore Allison, U.S. Ambassador to Japan, February 1954, NARA, RG220, Box 5, folder: Working Papers re A, B & C War Criminals 6/1/53–5/31/55 (2).

as well as any change in numbers or status, to the foreign governments concerned.[20] The purpose was evidently to encourage the more recalcitrant authorities to follow the example of the United States in proceeding steadily with releases or, better, to emulate China and France in releasing all the prisoners unconditionally. For the individual sentencing powers, NOPAR also prepared monthly reports on the conduct of the men in prison, including notes on their health ("His complete recovery is hopeless").[21]

NOPAR also continued to collect parole applications from prisoners and transform them into petitions that were intended to be persuasive and heartwarming (figure 8.3). The dossier supporting the application of Kasai Heijiro, for instance, noted:

He feels not only great difficulty in daily life but also is constantly exposed to fear of the loss of his life. Further he may be liable to haemorrhage . . . and the future condition of his illness is extremely bad. Under these circumstances, his continued prison life will cause great suffering to him, and we think, from a humanitarian point of view also, that such an infliction of suffering on him is too severe.

The petition went on to say that Kasai "hoped to devote the remainder of his life to praying for the souls of unfortunate war victims." Another convict, Mori Shohachiro, according to NOPAR, had been an interpreter at an internment camp in Sulawesi and had inadvertently been identified as camp commander, as a result of which he received a sentence of twenty years and had been serving his term "in grief" ever since. He, too, was ill, and "there is no prospect of its cure, it being beyond the knowledge of present medicine."[22]

THE LAST REPATRIATIONS

In the first half of 1953, some three hundred war criminals were still incarcerated outside Japan, about one hundred in Muntinlupa and about two hundred on Manus Island. With all other prisoners housed together in Sugamo, the insistence of the Philippine and Australian governments on keeping prisoners overseas looked increasingly anomalous.

A dramatic new development came on June 27, 1953, shortly after the first Dutch releases on parole. As an act of clemency to mark the Philippines' Independence Day on July 4, the president, Elpidio Quirino, suddenly announced that the prisoners at Muntinlupa would be repatriated to Japan. Furthermore, the sentences of those condemned to death would be commuted to life imprisonment in Sugamo, while the remainder would be freed as soon as they reached Japan. The president's action was not technically an amnesty, which would have required the approval of the Philippine congress, but a series of individual pardons.[23] At a ceremony on July 15 at New Bilibid Prison in Muntinlupa, 106 prisoners and the remains of 17 others who had been executed by the Philippines authorities, which had been recently exhumed and cremated, were handed over to the Sugamo Prison governor, Honda Seiichi, and the head of the Japanese mission in the Philippines, Nakayama Toru.[24] The *Hakusan Maru* sailed for Yokohama with the prisoners the next day, after Chaplain Kagao Shūnin had performed a shipboard Buddhist ceremony for the dead.[25] The Japanese press went into a frenzy of reportage: the popular affinity for the prisoners at Muntinlupa was such that on July 22, 1953, the day they arrived in Yokohama, 28,000 people reportedly thronged into the port to welcome the returning prisoners and the ashes of those who had been executed. This crowd was much larger, the press noted, than the one that had seen off Crown Prince Akihito on his first foreign trip, a world tour during which he was to represent Japan at the coronation of Queen Elizabeth II in London.[26] Press accounts of the return of the Muntinlupa prisoners focused on sentimental stories about encounters between fathers and children they had never met and other tearful family reunions.[27]

Quirino's pardon was widely reported as an act of Christian humanitarianism and kindness, rendered all the more poignant because his wife and three of his children had been killed by Japanese forces during the Battle of Manila in February 1945. Japanese Foreign Minister Okazaki Katsuo interpreted Quirino's move as "emanating from the sublime Christian spirit as well as motivated by friendly sentiments to restore more cordial relations between the two countries."[28] Quirino himself reportedly said of the pardons: "I am happy to have been able to make this spontaneous decision as the head of a Christian nation."[29] In hospital in the United States for treatment of a stomach ulcer, he declared:

> I should be the last one to pardon them [the war criminals], as the Japanese killed my wife and my three children and five other members of my family. I am doing this because I do not want my children and my people to inherit from me the hate for people who might yet be our friends for the permanent interest of the country. After all destiny has made us neighbors.[30]

Quirino's decision to repatriate and pardon the war criminals was not as spontaneous as he claimed. In early 1952, the Japanese government had directly contacted the president about repatriation, having made previous inquiries through intermediaries. There was, however, no immediate reply. According to historian Nagai Hitoshi, Quirino was reluctant to repatriate the prisoners principally because of the intense anti-Japanese feeling in the Philippines.[31] More than a million Filipinos had been wounded or killed during the Japanese occupation of their country; the capital had been destroyed; and Japanese forces had committed shocking atrocities against civilians, as evidence at the Tokyo Trial had graphically revealed.[32] In April 1952 Moises B. Bautista, a journalist for the *Philippine Herald*, had claimed in a prominent Japanese journal that Quirino had secretly decided to stop further executions of Japanese war criminals and to return all the prisoners to Japan but that he could not announce his decision because of the public backlash it would certainly cause.[33]

Any relaxation of the punishment of Japanese war criminals was thus fraught with difficulty in the Philippines, but there also were other issues at stake. Japanese and Filipino officials and the press in both countries believed that Quirino announced he would repatriate the prisoners because he hoped to influence the Japanese authorities to make decisions favorable to Manila on several pending questions, especially war reparations.[34] Compensation for wartime losses was a sensitive matter in the Philippines, so much so that Manila had pushed hard and successfully, against initial U.S. opposition, for including a war reparations clause (Article 14) in the peace treaty.[35] Discussions with Japan on reparations had been under way since 1951, but with no concrete result by 1953.

The idea that prisoners could be repatriated to Japan in return for a reparations deal was in the public domain well before Quirino's June 1953 announcement. Six months earlier, senators of the Nacionalista Party, the opponents of Quirino's Liberal Party, had reportedly indicated they would support a transfer of convicted war criminals to Japan "should the Tokyo government offer a satisfactory solution to the reparations impasse."[36] This offer to exchange prisoners for reparations was seemingly not well received in Japan; the *Nippon Times* expressed shock at the suggestion that human beings could be used as pawns by a noncommunist country.[37] After Quirino's apparently magnanimous announcement of June 1953, however, a reciprocal gesture by Japan was widely expected in both countries.[38] According to Nagai, Quirino's decision was a calculated political move, made when he was facing an imminent election defeat by a younger and more popular politician, Ramon Magsaysay. In this view, Quirino hoped that by pardoning Japanese war criminals, he would be able to demonstrate progress in the reparations negotiations before the November 1953 election.[39] If such hopes existed, they were not fulfilled. No agreement was reached on reparations until 1956, and Quirino lost the 1953 election to Magsaysay.

Then on December 29, 1953, came another dramatic announcement: as almost his last act before leaving office on December 30, Quirino pardoned the remaining fifty-two war criminals in Sugamo, whose death sentences had been commuted to life imprisonment four months earlier.[40] It was not an unexpected development for officials from Japan's Foreign Ministry, who had been quietly hoping for such an eventuality since the return of the prisoners in July. Foreign Ministry officials believed that the initial separation of the war criminals into two groups, with only one group receiving an immediate pardon, had been a concession to public opinion in the Philippines, especially to the sensitivities of war veterans, and did not necessarily represent the Quirino government's wishes.[41] Reports of the pardon were featured on the front page of all the newspapers in Japan.[42] With this announcement, the Philippines followed Nationalist China and France in settling the issue of Japanese war criminals convicted in national tribunals.

Parts of the Philippine press and some opposition political figures believed Quirino had accepted money in return for the pardons. The possibility that Japanese war criminals could be exchanged not for a reparations agreement but for direct monetary payment seems to have been acknowledged several years earlier. In 1948–1949, with President Quirino's Liberal Party short of funds and facing a 1949 election, the party's treasurer is said to have suggested that funds could be obtained through the Japanese prisoners. His comment was based on rumors that relatives would pay 6,000 pesos for the release of each war criminal. "Since their return was at the discretion of the President," the treasurer allegedly reasoned, "what a bonanza it would be for the Liberal Party if it could profit on the deal."[43] According to the official exchange rate at the time, 6,000 pesos were equivalent to 3,000 American dollars,[44] a sum representing about double the annual salary of a secondary school teacher or elementary school principal in the Philippines in 1953.[45] As for electioneering expenses, it has been estimated that the average candidate for the Lower House in the 1953 Philippines election spent 30,000 pesos on the campaign,[46] so if the rumor about how much Japanese relatives would pay was accurate, the going rate for one Japanese prisoner would have covered 20 percent of that cost. Elpidio Quirino's biographer, his nephew Carlos Quirino, stated, however, that the president firmly rejected the proposal to extract money from Japanese war criminals' relatives in exchange for repatriation.[47] In November 1952, Foreign Minister Joaquin

Miguel Elizalde informed President Quirino that he had received a request from the Japanese Foreign Ministry for clemency for war criminals and repatriation from Muntinlupa. Elizalde added: "It might be to our government's financial benefit if those war prisoners still in the Philippines not convicted of very serious crimes could be pardoned for the purpose of repatriating them to Japan."[48] There is no information about whether the money that Elizalde suggested might be forthcoming would take the form of reparations or direct payment.

After Quirino lost the election to Magsaysay in a bitter contest in November 1953, strong rumors surfaced about his exercise of the presidential pardoning power while in office. Between mid-1952 and the end of 1953, mostly without the recommendation of the Board of Pardons, Quirino had pardoned 323 criminals who had been convicted of treason—for crimes committed as wartime collaborators with the Japanese—and 114 Japanese war criminals.[49] In the last days of his administration, he pardoned 42 people convicted of crimes of treason committed in Cavite Province, including murder and illegal possession of firearms. They were pardoned less than two months after they had begun their sentences.[50] In March 1954, with Quirino out of power, the Senate resolved that a "Blue Ribbon Committee," that is, the Senate's Committee on Accountability of Public Officers and Investigations, should examine the circumstances in which the collaborators and the Japanese war criminals had been pardoned.[51] Rumors suggested that "some considerations figured in the granting of those pardons to the Japanese war criminals." One senator claimed that the president himself was not to blame: "I have information that there had been a racket on the part of individuals other than the President connected with this pardon."[52] In April 1954 the Blue Ribbon Committee asked Quirino to explain his last-minute executive clemency,[53] but Quirino declined the invitation, declaring: "I am answerable only to God and my own conscience, and I am not perturbed." After several hearings, the committee recorded its suspicion that in many cases, "the presidential power of pardon had been abused."[54] Soon after his election, President Magsaysay had announced his intention to nullify the Cavite pardons, but by this stage he had already dropped his plans to do so, on the grounds that the pardons had been legally valid.[55] Presumably, the same applied to the pardons of Japanese war criminals.

Although some commentators maintain that the president himself was personally honest, contemporary observers and later historians have branded the Quirino administration as a whole as particularly corrupt, lending credibility to the claim that Japanese war criminals might have been repatriated and pardoned in exchange for money. The 1949 national election, won by Quirino, was believed to have been rigged.[56] Quirino's political enemies claimed he was corrupt and called for his impeachment in 1949.[57] *Time* magazine opined, however, that the problem was not the president himself: "Filipinos generally regard him as personally honest, but much of his administration is corrupt and he is surrounded by politicians who cannot resist a chance to make a fast peso."[58] Corruption in the Quirino period is said to have "permeated the entire gamut of the Philippine bureaucracy, extending from the lowest level of the civil service to the top, except the President himself."[59] A cartoon in the *Manila Chronicle* suggested that on the matter of pardons for war criminals, Quirino was approached by a Japanese representative who was backed by a businessman (figure 8.4). There was no shortage of Japanese businessmen

FIGURE 8.4 Quirino (who suffered from gout) exchanges pardon for war criminals for money. *Manila Chronicle*, in Carlos Quirino, *Apo Lakay* (Manila: Total Book World, 1987), after 242.

sympathetic to war criminals, as the list of donors to the Association to Support the War-Convicted confirms.[60] One prominent example was Sasakawa Ryōichi, who was both wealthy and politically active, having been elected to the House of Representatives in 1942; had been imprisoned as a possible IMTFE defendant but never charged; and, after his release at the end of 1948, had energetically supported imprisoned war criminals.[61] Nagai's research suggests the strong possibility, however, that it was the Japanese Ministry of Foreign Affairs, working through the Association to Support the War-Convicted in Tokyo and a senior Japanese diplomat in Manila, that paid substantial "ransom" money (*minoshirikin*) to encourage the release of Japanese prisoners in Muntinlupa.[62]

When the war criminals were repatriated and pardoned, there was an outpouring of Japanese gratitude to the Philippines, and to Quirino specifically. Japanese groups and individuals continued to send gifts, letters of appreciation, and inquiries after Quirino's health for several years afterward.[63] Although the desired reparations deal did not follow the president's 1953 granting of clemency, it seems there were other benefits. In February 1954 Jinbo Nobuhiko, a former chief of staff of Japanese forces in Mindanao, wrote to Quirino proposing a joint enterprise between the Philippines and Japan to build a canning factory in Zamboanga, in Mindanao, for tuna and bonito. The Japanese side would provide the considerable sum of ¥250 million, or the equivalent of US$1.4 million, while Quirino was simply asked for his "cooperation." Jinbo also reaffirmed the Japanese people's gratitude for Quirino's clemency to war criminals.[64] The *Manila Chronicle*, moreover, suspected Quirino and his political allies of improperly starting an import-export business with Japan, presumably by taking advantage of unhealthily close past relations (figure 8.5).

The popular excitement at the return of war criminals to Japan increased when the Australian government, under pressure from the Philippines decision,[65] announced that prisoners would be repatriated from Manus Island to Sugamo early in August 1953. The Japanese government had been sending formal requests for repatriation and release of war criminals to the Australian government for more than a year, and Australian diplomats and officials, like their Dutch, British, and American counterparts, had also received many petitions for clemency. In September 1952, an official in the Australian embassy in Tokyo noted that seventeen had been received in that particular week, either by post or in person.[66] Though grassroots petitions appear to have had little direct

FIGURE 8.5 "The Apo" is Quirino, and "LP" refers to his Liberal Party. The banner at the top reads (in Japanese) "Mr. Quirino and Friend: Philippine–Japan Company." Carlos Quirino, *Apo Lakay* (Manila: Total Book World, 1987), after 242.

impact, representations from the Japanese government were more effective in persuading officials and politicians that Australia's tough stance on war criminals had to be modified. Australian officials were shifting to the view that the new circumstances of the Cold War, plus opportunities for postwar trade with Japan, were more important than retaining direct custody of war criminals. The Australian government also was aware that it was the last to repatriate prisoners to Japan, and it was reluctant to appear to have harsher policies for war criminals than its allies had. After discussion within the government and in the press in 1952–1953, the cabinet decided on repatriation, provided that the Japanese government undertook to carry out the prisoners' sentences faithfully. The prisoners disembarked in Yokohama on August 8, 1953.[67] No doubt mindful of the reception accorded to prisoners returning from the Philippines, the Australian embassy in Tokyo had reportedly asked that the Japanese press refrain from treating the returning war criminals as "heroes."[68]

The return of the prisoners from Muntinlupa and Manus marked a high point in the Japanese campaign for the war criminals' release and in the level of popular interest in them. The newspapers reported on war criminals almost every day in the weeks preceding and following their return. On September 9, 1953, a "mass rally to thank the people of the Philippines," organized by the Association to Support the War-Convicted, was held in Hibiya Hall in Tokyo. Signaling an appreciation of the political importance of the issue, Prime Minister Yoshida himself addressed the crowd and expressed the thanks of the Japanese people to President Quirino, promising also that the government would continue negotiating with foreign powers to achieve the release of those at Sugamo.[69] The Association to Support the War-Convicted continued its efforts to mobilize popular pressure. On November 11, 1953, the association participated in a mass rally at Ryōgoku Hall in Tokyo, which called for practical support for repatriates, progress in repatriations from the Soviet Union, and the release of war criminals from Sugamo.[70] The association claimed that more than 10,000 people had participated in the rally and that petitions to the prime minister and the leaders of both houses of the Diet had been signed by more than 30 million people (more than a third of Japan's population at that time).[71] The campaign for the release of war criminals continued into 1954, and a large number of petitions reached the government in the early months of that year.[72] But the activism gradually died down, for two main reasons.

First, discussion of the release of the Sugamo prisoners was eclipsed by news of the impending repatriation of Japanese "war criminals" from the People's Republic of China (PRC) and the Soviet Union. Because Japan did not have diplomatic relations with either of the Communist countries, negotiations regarding the repatriation of Japanese soldiers and civilians were handled by nongovernment organizations, principally the Red Cross. The PRC had allowed the return of 26,000 Japanese citizens between March and October 1953.[73] After Josef Stalin's death in 1953, the Soviet government began to free its own citizens held in the Gulag and to repatriate foreign prisoners as part of a general readjustment of its foreign policy.[74] Following negotiations with the Japan Red Cross in late 1953, the Soviet Red Cross announced that approximately 1,320 Japanese prisoners would be released, 420 of whom were convicted or pardoned war criminals, and about 900 of whom were "convicted civilians."[75] The Soviet authorities then repatriated two groups of prisoners said to be war criminals: 811 returned in December 1953 and 420 in March 1954 (to be followed by another group in March 1955), on the Red Cross ship the *Kōan Maru*, in events that were extensively covered by the Japanese and the international press.[76]

Even after the 1954–1955 repatriations, thousands of prisoners in the Soviet Union remained unaccounted for.[77] The fate of war criminals held by the PRC, meanwhile, remained unclear well into mid-1954, despite attempts by the Japan Red Cross to obtain information through its sister organization in the PRC.[78] Then the PRC's leaders evidently decided to release at least some Japanese prisoners in the interests of good political relations with Japan. In August 1954, the People's Revolutionary Military Commission of the PRC announced that Beijing would pardon and release 417 Japanese prisoners, referred to as "war criminals." Most of them had been investigated for war crimes, and all had confessed to their offenses, but they were released without indictment as a gesture of benevolence. On September 27, 1954, the *Kōan Maru* arrived in the port of Maizuru in western Japan with the 417 "war criminals" aboard. On October 12, in a joint statement with the Soviet Union, the PRC government announced its desire to normalize its relations with Japan.[79]

The second reason for the public campaign's lower profile was that in 1954–1955, the Association to Support the War-Convicted began to change its tactics, placing less emphasis on applying political pressure through large-scale public activities. Although numerous petitions for the release of war criminals were distributed overseas on the occasion of Prime Minister Yoshida's world tour late in 1954, such petitions seemed to have little effect. Shigemitsu Mamoru, foreign minister in the succeeding Hatoyama Ichirō government and a board member of the association, later explained the reason for this failure to association members: it was because the Japanese government had pushed for a "political" resolution when the Allied countries required a "legal" solution. It was by using legal principles to evaluate individual parole applications that foreign governments could best manage their own domestic opposition to the release of Japanese war criminals.[80] Although the association did not entirely abandon holding mass rallies, gathering petitions, and pressing media outlets to report on war criminals, it shifted its main attention to supporting the government in providing the necessary information for individual parole applications.[81] This approach, however, also produced limited results, as a 1955 meeting of the Association to Support the War-Convicted was told, since the prosecuting governments were slow to release prisoners even after they had received all the relevant paperwork. The association concluded that political measures were the best after all, but rather than exerting pressure through high-profile public activities, the only way to break through an apparent stalemate was to apply direct political and diplomatic pressure on foreign governments.[82]

This change of tactics, combined with the greater newsworthiness of repatriations from China and the Soviet Union, meant that the issue of war criminals gradually disappeared from the media and from the Diet's debates, although resolutions continued to be passed in the Diet and in prefectural assemblies. Release of the prisoners reverted to its former status as an issue that predominantly concerned the families of war criminals, prison authorities, bureaucrats in charge of parole applications, and Foreign Ministry officials. Advocacy of the release of war criminals became primarily a matter for diplomatic representations, which were frequent, and private pleas, as U.S. officials noted.[83] Politicians in the Diet still occasionally accused foreign ministers of being "as slippery as eels" on the release of war criminals,[84] and newspapers sporadically noted the parole of individual convicts. The odd editorial raised questions about the sluggishness of the parole process, although without finding satisfactory answers as to why some individuals were still in prison.[85] On December 18, 1956, in a small article on Sugamo, the *Asahi shinbun* noted that prisoners complained that nobody came to visit them any more, contrasting the focus on the returnees from the Soviet Union and China with the lack of attention to their own fate.[86]

CLEMENCY FOR THE IMTFE DEFENDANTS

The seven governments apart from the Soviet Union that had convicted war criminals in national tribunals were entitled to make their own, separate, decisions on what should happen to the prisoners, though they kept a close eye on one another. Under the provisions of Article 11 of the San Francisco Peace Treaty, however, decisions regarding the men convicted by the IMTFE had to be made jointly. There was a large scope for clash of perceived national interests. Cold War rivalries and other international tensions were sharply revealed in the discussions on the fate of the IMTFE prisoners, and by 1956, solidarity among the Allies on the subject of war criminals had been severely tested.

Agreement on which governments had the right to negotiate was not easily reached. After discussions in Washington and Tokyo in 1952–1953, representatives of the Allied powers decided that only those governments that had participated in the Tokyo tribunal and had also signed and ratified the peace treaty would be eligible. This ruling combined the provision of Article 11—which stated that power to vary the sentences of those convicted in Tokyo "may not be exercised except on the decision of a majority of the Governments represented on the Tribunal, and on the recommendation of Japan"—with the provisions of Article 25, which limited the benefits of the treaty to those governments that had signed and ratified it.[87] Although they had participated in the Tokyo tribunal, China, the Soviet Union, India, and the Philippines had not ratified the peace treaty and thus were ruled ineligible to review the sentences. Pakistan had not existed during the Second World War, having been established with the partition of India and independence from Britain in 1947. But it was ruled eligible because as part of the former British India, it was deemed to have acquired the position of a state formerly at war with Japan, had participated (as part of British India) in the IMTFE, and, unlike independent India, had signed and ratified the peace treaty.[88] The claims of India and Pakistan to join other Allied governments in deliberating on IMTFE sentence reviews, however, were not so readily settled.

The British authorities had asked the Indian government as early as April 1952 whether it wished to participate, and the Indian government had given the British to understand that it was not concerned with war criminals and wished to have as little as possible to do with them.[89] Nonetheless, in May 1953, Indian officials lodged a protest with the British and other governments over their country's exclusion.[90] But even though the Indian authorities formally objected to Pakistan's inclusion, it became clear that they did not actually want to participate in the discussions over clemency themselves and did not much mind if Pakistan did either. The Indian government's real focus was India's international position. Officials and politicians were deeply concerned that Pakistan might be considered a successor state to British India—not in the context of war criminals but because that principle, once established, "may be followed in other connexions with more serious consequences."[91] The British, left by the other Allies to deal with the question, assured their Indian counterparts that both India and Pakistan would have been eligible to join in if India had signed and ratified the peace treaty, but the Indian authorities were not mollified. Highly complex legal, political, and diplomatic discussion of the matter consumed an enormous amount of time and energy in 1952 and 1953.[92]

U.S. officials had originally reached a different legal interpretation of Articles 11 and 25 of the treaty, which concerned the right to review IMTFE sentences. The American authorities had advocated the inclusion of India (as well as Pakistan), the Soviet Union, and the Republic of China and had remarked that excluding the Philippines would be "embarrassing" to the United States and might prejudice the Philippine government against ratifying the treaty in the future.[93] The U.S. government wanted to include the Soviet Union on the assumption that it would probably oppose clemency, which "would provide useful propaganda in Japan"; that is, it would help turn the Japanese people away from the Soviet Union.[94] The British authorities agreed that inviting the Soviet Union to participate "would provide evidence of Western sincerity which would be useful propaganda." But they pointed out that it would then be "illogical and difficult" to leave out China. Considering China's claim, they noted, would only underscore the difference of opinion between Britain and the United States concerning which China was legitimate, since Britain diplomatically recognized Beijing rather than Taibei, whereas the United States did the opposite. Moreover, the Japanese people would probably resent an invitation to the Soviet Union and China to review decisions on IMTFE war criminals, especially because the Soviet Union still held hundreds of thousands of Japanese prisoners, about whom it divulged no reliable information.[95] Ruling out the Soviet Union and China would then require the exclusion of the Philippines as well.[96] Evidently, State Department's opinions on these matters were not very firmly held, and the United States gave way to the British view in each case, including that of India.[97] These issues were significant for more than their direct political import, as they potentially affected the balance of voting on clemency. On December 6, 1952, months before the Allied powers decided which countries were eligible to review sentences, the Japanese Foreign Office announced that the Indian and the Nationalist Chinese authorities had agreed (without consulting their allies) to parole the IMTFE war criminals.[98] Indian participation would presumably, therefore, contribute one additional vote to the majority required for approval of clemency. The British authorities, in particular, were anxious to avoid this situation.[99]

After the protracted negotiations over which governments had the right to review IMTFE sentences, eight countries became the joint arbiters: Australia, Canada, France, the Netherlands, New Zealand, Pakistan, Britain, and the United States. They were joined in the final deliberations by the Philippines after it ratified the San Francisco Peace Treaty in 1956. Collective decisions were reached at meetings in Washington by representatives of the eight governments, who acted on the instructions of their home governments.

A second procedural issue with broad political implications then arose, concerning the method by which majority decisions reached by the Allied powers should be communicated to the Japanese authorities. Again, much time and energy were expended on settling this question. After extensive discussion, Allied representatives decided that individual governments would not tell the Japanese authorities what reasons had given rise to majority decisions or how any individual country had voted. Instead, identical notes would be sent by the different governments on the same day, recording merely the decision that had been reached. The overriding concern was that the Japanese government should not be in a position to play off the Allied governments against one another. Moreover, if individual states were allowed to say what their own decisions had been, the Japanese authorities could add up the number of minority opinions, then perhaps add the states that had been excluded from the decision making—especially the Soviet Union, China, and India—thereby possibly enabling the Japanese authorities to claim that the decision had not been made by a genuine majority of the states represented at the Tokyo tribunal. Such a claim might then make it appear that the provisions of Article 11 of the peace treaty were not being properly observed.[100]

At first, the U.S. government was once again out of step with the British Commonwealth on these issues. The State Department wanted each government to have the discretion to communicate its individual view to the Japanese government. In internal correspondence, British officials were highly cynical about the Americans' reasons, assuming that the American authorities wanted simply "to be in a position to curry favour with the Japanese":

We can think of only one reason why the Americans should wish to communicate their individual decision to the Japanese, namely, to enable them to gain kudos with the Japanese for their humane attitude. If this is so, it means that political expediency is likely to count for more than judicial impartiality in arriving at a decision on applications for clemency.[101]

For Britain, which was supported on this point by Australia, New Zealand, the Netherlands, and France, to do as the State Department wanted would undermine the solid front that the Allies should present to the Japanese.[102] But the State Department refused to budge. In the end, the Allied representatives meeting in Washington agreed that each government could use its discretion on whether or not to transmit an individual decision. The Dutch and British governments had decided they would not exercise the privilege.[103] In practice, other governments did not do so either, but the threat to break ranks and communicate individually with the Japanese authorities remained powerful.

In late 1952, twelve men convicted by the IMTFE remained in Sugamo Prison, all sentenced to life terms. Of the original twenty-five convicted, seven had been executed, and five had died in prison. One, former (and future) foreign minister Shigemitsu Mamoru, had been sentenced to a seven-year term and was paroled by SCAP in 1950. In October 1952, NOPAR asked the Allied powers to grant clemency to all twelve in Sugamo,[104] but the various governments replied that individual applications would be necessary. Thereafter, a pattern was established that proved to be enduring: NOPAR applications were based on a humanitarian approach, with emphasis on age and infirmity. This tactic was largely successful. It was easy to justify applications for release for the IMTFE defendants on such grounds, especially as three of the prisoners were aged over seventy in 1952, and it was comparatively easy for the Allied powers to agree to free them on "special medical parole," without seeming to impugn the judgment of the war crimes trials and without releasing them unconditionally. Medical parole thus became a useful device. In April 1953, NOPAR recommended the release of the three aged over seventy—Araki Sadao, Hata Shunroku, and Minami Jirō—on the grounds of their age.[105] The eight governments reviewing sentences agreed unanimously in January 1954 that Minami—at nearly eighty, the oldest, and believed to be at death's door—should be granted special medical parole.[106] John Allison, U.S. ambassador in Japan, wrote in a telegram: "Medical report Minami cerebral arteriosclerosis, heart weak, mentally unsound, remaining days short. Politically wise expedite parole."[107] No government wanted Japanese war criminals, especially the elderly and infirm, to die in prison, as it would make the prosecuting powers look heartless and vengeful, and Minami was freed in a hurry. He survived, however, for almost two years after his release.

From the end of 1954 onward, pressure in and from Japan to negotiate the release of the IMTFE prisoners increased considerably. Although the mass campaign may have paid little attention to the "major" war criminals, focusing instead on soldiers convicted in the national tribunals, matters were different at the elite level. The national cabinet led by Yoshida, who was a gradualist on the release of war criminals and favored dependence on the United States in diplomacy, was replaced in December 1954 by the Hatoyama cabinet, which insisted on a policy of "independence," albeit still within the framework of United States–Japan cooperation. Hatoyama served as prime minister until December 1956. His cabinets appointed several people to influential positions who had close associations with the IMTFE. Shigemitsu, the first IMTFE prisoner to be released on parole, was foreign minister and deputy prime minister from 1954 to 1956, while Kiyose Ichirō, defense lawyer for Tōjō Hideki at the Tokyo tribunal, served as education minister from December 1955 onward. Tani Masayuki, a former foreign minister who had been arrested as a potential IMTFE defendant, became a powerful Foreign Ministry adviser and was appointed ambassador to the United States in 1956. Kishi Nobusuke, also arrested as a potential defendant in the Tokyo tribunal, became secretary-general of the ruling Democratic Party (Minshutō). For all these people, the release of the IMTFE prisoners was a personal issue, and under the Hatoyama administrations, pressure on other governments for the rapid release of all the prisoners strengthened.[108]

Diplomatic efforts to secure the release of war criminals redoubled after Shigemitsu's appointment as foreign minister.[109] Hatoyama and Shigemitsu also made the most of their personal contacts. As a 1955 article in the *New York Times* observed, the two politicians "keep the subject of the prisoners' release constantly alive in official contacts with Washington."[110] Shigemitsu, a career diplomat and former ambassador to China, the Soviet Union, and Britain who had served three times as foreign minister by the time he appeared before the Tokyo tribunal, displayed not the slightest embarrassment at being a convicted war criminal.

Within weeks of his fourth appointment as foreign minister, he had made a lengthy "personal appeal" for the release of war criminals to both U.S. Ambassador Allison and Admiral Arthur W. Radford, chairman of the U.S. Joint Chiefs of Staff, when Radford visited Tokyo. The Japanese ambassador in Washington also raised the matter at the Department of State in the same month.[111] In London, diplomats in the Japanese embassy included Shigemitsu's nephew, First Secretary Shigemitsu Akira, who visited the British Foreign Office (where many officials must have known Shigemitsu Mamoru) soon after his uncle again became foreign minister, to inquire about progress in speeding up the release of war criminals. The younger Shigemitsu remarked during the meeting that the subject of war criminals was "of particular interest" to his uncle, in view of his own incarceration in Sugamo. The British official who received him reported that "I gave him no encouragement," but minutes recorded by his colleagues make clear that they expected more such approaches: "We shall not be allowed to forget this one."[112] In August 1955, Kishi participated in a formal delegation to Washington, led by Foreign Minister Shigemitsu, to discuss United States–Japan relations. No more embarrassed at having been arrested as a suspected war criminal than was Shigemitsu, Kishi remarked in an "unofficial" meeting with State Department officials and diplomats that the continued detention of Japanese war criminals was one of the "major irritants" in bilateral relations. Urging the United States to take a "bold stand" and resolve the question comprehensively, Kishi added that "he and the Foreign Minister had spent some time in Sugamo Prison and could not but be emotionally concerned in obtaining the release of those still in prison as soon as possible."[113]

The Lower House of the Japanese Diet passed a resolution on July 19, 1955, calling on the government to urge the relevant foreign authorities to release war criminals and to take concrete measures to ensure a "general settlement" of the problem by August 15, 1955, the tenth anniversary of the end of the war. The resolution declared that "our national feeling towards the war crimes trial has reached such an extent that it no longer tolerates a further continuation of their [the prisoners'] confinement."[114] In his speech supporting the resolution, which was passed with no dissent, Nagayama Tadanori of the Liberal Party (Jiyūtō) asserted that international opinion questioned the validity of the war crimes trials and considered the atomic bombings to be inhumane. He also declared that the inability of the relevant governments to stage war crimes trials after the Korean War and the turmoil in French Indochina exposed the weak rationale of the tribunals.[115] Shortly after the Diet resolution was passed, NOPAR, again alluding to the tenth anniversary of the war's end, issued its own request to the relevant foreign governments for the release of all 579 prisoners remaining in Sugamo.[116] The request had no discernible effect.

Since Minami had been freed in January 1954, there had been a stalemate in deliberations among the eight governments reviewing IMTFE sentences. The specific issue was the release of Araki, the next case to be dealt with, and the first to be considered for ordinary parole or clemency rather than special medical parole. The United States, the Netherlands, France, and Pakistan favored immediate release of Araki and then presumably of the remaining prisoners. Britain, however, supported by the rest of the "old [British] Commonwealth," that is, Canada, Australia, and New Zealand, was initially prepared only to assess life terms at twenty-one years, as was the case with prisoners sentenced by national tribunals, and then to apply a one-third remission for good conduct. Prisoners would thus serve fourteen years, counted from the date of arrest, and would be eligible for release in 1959. When agreement could not be reached and in order to avoid a "politically undesirable" split, the British government proposed 1956 as a compromise, providing there was unanimous agreement. Although the Australian government wanted to hold out for 1959, and the Pakistani authorities wanted immediate release, the British authorities believed that the 1956 formula would be accepted. "At the last moment, however, the United States ratted,"[117] insisting that Araki be released during 1954. British officials then decided they could compromise no further, because of difficulties over public opinion in Japan as much as at home: "In our view firmness and not capitulation to political pressures commands respect from Japanese."[118]

At this point came a standoff. When the 1956 formula failed, the eight governments reverted to their original positions, meaning that they were evenly split, four against four, on Araki's release, and thus, no majority decision could be made unless at least one government changed its stance. U.S. officials felt themselves to be under serious pressure from Japan. The United States was committed to improving relations with Japan, and State Department officials also began to feel the burden of perceived leadership. The State Department knew that Japanese officials believed the United States dominated decisions on war criminals and that if the United States took a firm lead, the other countries would follow. In this Japanese view, it was therefore the Americans' fault that the prisoners had not yet been released, and they would be further blamed if Araki stayed in prison until 1956.[119] It became clear that if the four old Commonwealth countries blocked his immediate release, the Americans were prepared to revert to 1959 rather than agreeing to 1956. They were confident that the Japanese would then place "the blame and opprobrium" on the old Commonwealth, not the Americans, and in any case they were prepared to tell the Japanese that they, the Americans, had favored early release but had been blocked. As the New Zealand ambassador to Washington caustically commented:

> It is clear that they [the Americans] are almost entirely preoccupied with their political relationships with Japan rather than with any humanitarian feelings towards the individuals [war criminals] concerned. It would therefore suit their purposes better to have the prisoners retained until 1959 or even later with the blame definitely attributed to the Commonwealth countries rather than to share in the opprobrium of keeping them in custody until 1956. Their strong inclination is therefore, they informed us, to refuse to be party to the 1956 formula "and to let the chips fall where they may."[120]

The British authorities believed that the U.S. position was a bargaining stance, designed to induce one or more of the Commonwealth governments to change its view. In return, the British were prepared to threaten the Americans that if Araki ended up staying in prison until 1959 and Commonwealth countries were blamed, British officials might inform the Japanese that the U.S. side had rejected the 1956 compromise. This threat, too, was designed primarily to counter American pressure at the Washington meetings.[121]

The issue of the release of the IMTFE prisoners and, more broadly, the different priorities in the two governments' approaches to Japan, evidently were beginning to strain Anglo-American solidarity. The situation was saved when it turned out that the U.S. attitude was not as rigid as it had appeared to be. In March 1954, a State Department official suggested to a British diplomat in Washington that the best thing would be to defer taking a decision on Araki's case and that a majority in favor of immediate release might emerge if the matter were left "simmering" for some time.[122] The question was resolved in a different manner in June 1955. The eight governments, fearing that Araki might die in prison, an eventuality almost certain to provoke a hostile reaction in Japan, unanimously approved medical parole for him.[123] In fact, he lived until 1966.

The return of war criminals from Communist China and the Soviet Union, plus the promise of more repatriations, exerted additional pressure on the authorities reviewing clemency for prisoners held in Japan. Governments in the "free world" were afraid that the contrast between Communist clemency and Western reluctance to release war criminals would encourage leftism in Japan and turn the Japanese people away from support of the Western camp. In December 1953 and March 1954, as we have seen, a total of 1,231 "war criminals" were repatriated from the Soviet Union, with more returns promised, and in midyear, Beijing announced that 417 "war criminals" would be pardoned and returned to Japan.[124] Shigemitsu had already begun to play on the anti-Communist theme in his January 1955 meeting with Radford and Allison in Tokyo. Continued detention of war criminals, he said, not only "keeps alive war resentments, [and] hinders full and complete collaboration between our two nations which is so essential" but also "plays into hands of leftists and Communists who point to releases being made by Communist China and Soviets."[125] In October 1954 the French representative on the Washington committee reviewing IMTFE sentences expressed his government's concern that "the communist powers are willing for propaganda purposes, to get ahead of the western powers in granting clemency to the Japanese war criminals they hold." He urged the Washington committee to resume its discussions on release.[126]

By September 1954, NOPAR had recommended clemency for all the IMTFE war criminals.[127] In October, the eight governments agreed to release Hata Shunroku (who died in 1962) and Oka Takasumi (who died in 1973) on medical parole.[128] Former admiral Shimada Shigetarō, who survived until 1976, was released on medical parole in March 1955.[129] After Araki was released in June 1955, seven IMTFE prisoners remained in Sugamo. Apart from Shigemitsu in 1950, who had been unilaterally paroled by SCAP, no one had yet been freed except for medical reasons, and no agreement had been reached on how to release the IMTFE prisoners except on medical grounds.

In May 1954, New Zealand's Department of External Affairs had proposed to the British government that all the IMTFE prisoners be released on parole after ten years, pointing out that sticking to the 1956 proposal "in the present situation will be considered not so much as evidence of a desirable firmness towards the Japanese, but rather as an indication of a degree of inflexibility in dealing with our friends [i.e., the other Allied governments]."[130] In October, the U.S. government made the same suggestion. Under this proposal, all IMTFE war criminals would be released in 1955 or 1956.[131] France, the Netherlands, and Pakistan had always favored early clemency and were expected to support the U.S. proposal; only Australia and Britain now opposed such leniency.[132] After reviewing the individual cases of the remaining seven prisoners, British officials had earlier agreed on modest remissions of sentences, which would require the men to serve custodial terms of eleven to fourteen years, with the last releases in 1959. By the end of 1954, however, they expected only Australia to support this option and realized they would therefore be overruled by majority opinion among the eight governments.[133]

At this point, Foreign Office officials reached the view that their stance might no longer best serve Britain's interests. Their position had been based on not only a determination to review the merits of each individual case but also a commitment to take account of public opinion in the British Commonwealth, in Japan, and at home. Commonwealth opinion was now divided, with Canada and New Zealand (as well as Pakistan) favoring early release. Moreover, if a majority vote went against Britain, the United States might leak information about the decision to the Japanese, or allow others to leak it, so that the Japanese people would learn that Britain (and probably Australia) had opposed early release. Given the strength of Japanese feeling about war criminals, such a development was certain to damage Anglo-Japanese relations: "the other countries will get the credit and we shall get the odium."[134] At home, as Colin Crowe of the Foreign Office observed, public opinion seemed unlikely to obstruct release of the IMTFE prisoners. In Germany, Crowe argued, although the crimes of the major Nuremberg defendants—Goering, Doenitz, Hess, Streicher—were notorious, the public knew virtually nothing about the war criminals convicted in subsequent trials.[135] It was the opposite in regard to the Japanese war criminals, however. To the general public in Britain, and especially former POWs,

> a Japanese war-criminal is a Korean guard, a camp commandant or a prison warder, who needed no directives from his superiors in Tokyo to perpetrate acts of brutality. It is very doubtful if any members of the British public are aware even of the names of the Japanese major war

criminals—except TOJO, who was hanged. It therefore seems unlikely that there would be any strong adverse reaction in this country to earlier release of Class "A" Japanese war criminals.

Thus, for political reasons and to maintain unanimity with Britain's allies, Crowe suggested that Britain give way—but he was not yet prepared to embrace the ten-year option, instead advocating, in internal correspondence, yet another compromise between the two positions.[136] In the event, the State Department once again failed to pursue its proposal to free all IMTFE prisoners after ten years, perhaps partly because other sections of the U.S. government, including the Clemency and Parole Board, were less keen than the State Department to announce a comprehensive release. So medical parole once again became the favored method.[137] In these circumstances, the British Foreign Office decided that "our best tactics are to aid and abet the apparent State Department desire to let sleeping dogs lie."[138]

In April 1955 the Australian government, which had the reputation for being the toughest on Japanese war criminals, changed its stance. In accordance with a new policy to foster good relations with Japan, the government announced, for the first time, a parole system for war criminals. Under this system, prisoners would be eligible for parole after serving one-third of their sentences, or a maximum of ten years, providing the new policy did not contradict the regulations or practice of other Commonwealth countries.[139] Although the policy was not fully implemented, as we will see in the next chapter, the trend was clear to British officials, who realized they were now out of step with even the most recalcitrant of their allies. In July 1955 Britain, too, finally capitulated, in order to avoid a "dangerous isolation" from its allies, which in any case could overrule Britain, and to forestall criticism from the Japanese for being less lenient than others.[140] On July 28, 1955, the British cabinet approved the parole of IMTFE prisoners after ten years in custody.[141] At a meeting in Washington on September 7, the representatives of the relevant governments agreed on this principle to the parole of Hashimoto Kingoro, Kaya Okinori, and Suzuki Teiichi.[142] On December 6, 1955, parole was approved as well for Hoshino Naoki, Ōshima Hiroshi, and Kido Kōichi, who had also been in prison for ten years.[143] Satō Kenryō was the last to be released, on March 31, 1956 (table 8.1).

TABLE 8.1 Dates and Category of Release of IMTFE Prisoners, 1950–1956

Name	Penal term	Disposition	Date of parole	Remarks
Shigemitsu Mamoru	7 years	SCAP parole	November 21, 1950	
Minami Jirō	Life	Medical parole	January 3, 1954	Died on December 5, 1955
Hata Shunroku	Life	Medical parole	October 30, 1954	Under medical care
Oka Takasumi	Life	Medical parole	October 30, 1954	Under medical care
Shimada Shigetarō	Life	Medical parole	April 4, 1955	Under medical care
Araki Sadao	Life	Medical parole	June 18, 1955	Under medical care
Hashimoto Kingoro	Life	Parole	September 17, 1955	
Kaya Okinori	Life	Medical parole	September 17, 1955	
Suzuki Teiichi	Life	Medical parole	September 17, 1955	
Hoshino Naoki	Life	Medical parole	December 13, 1955	
Kido Kōichi	Life	Medical parole	December 16, 1955	
Oshima Hiroshi	Life	Medical parole	December 16, 1955	
Satō Kenryō	Life	Medical parole	March 31, 1956	

Source: Adapted from NOPAR, table attached to "Statistical Report on War Criminals in Sugamo Prison, Japan (as at 31 March 1956)," NAA 271958, 395.

NEW TRIALS

By 1956, the Netherlands, Australia, Britain, and the United States were struggling with the question of how to reach final decisions on Japanese war criminals. The People's Republic of China, however, had not yet even begun trials. In 1956, the PRC held 1,062 suspected Japanese war criminals in custody, including 969 who had originally been detained by Soviet forces in Siberia and then handed over to China on July 18, 1950. Another 140 had willingly or unwillingly fought for the Nationalists against the Communists at the end of the war instead of returning to Japan. Their trials had been delayed by the need to concentrate on reconstruction after the civil war of 1946–1949; by the PRC government's eagerness to prosecute the Nationalist Party enemy from the civil war, which exceeded its eagerness to prosecute the Japanese enemy from the earlier conflict; by the outbreak of the Korean War; and by careful calculations of when the best time would be to extract maximum political and diplomatic benefit from the prosecution and release of Japanese war criminals.[144]

In the mid-1950s, PRC leaders were extraordinarily lenient to the Japanese suspects in their custody, especially in comparison with the vehemently anti-Japanese discourse of the immediate postwar period, with its emphasis on the "sea of blood and grievances" that Japanese soldiers had left behind in China.[145] The PRC leaders' motives were directly political. They hoped, by generous treatment of Japanese war criminals, to accelerate the normalization of official ties between the two countries, distance Japan from the United States in the Cold War, and encourage Sino-Japanese trade. Moreover, to pass harsh sentences on war criminals so long after the conflict had ended, just as other prosecuting governments were releasing war criminals, would have risked international condemnation.[146] Of the 1,062 suspects, the PRC government pardoned 1,017 without trial. When the formal prosecutions finally began, only 45 people appeared in court.[147] Those who had been pardoned returned to Japan in three transfers in mid-1956, with the last departing in late August, again on the Red Cross ship the *Kōan Maru.*

The forty-five suspects selected for prosecution appeared in four trials in June and July 1956, held in the cities of Shenyang and Taiyuan. Some were convicted of antirevolutionary crimes as well as war crimes, committed while fighting the Chinese Communists after Japan's surrender.

Offenses included the usurpation of China's sovereignty, the destruction of towns and villages, murder, rape, spying, massacre of POWs, and the use of bacteriological weapons and poison gas.[148] Although the defendants were thus convicted of—and all had confessed to—the most terrible crimes, the penalties were comparatively light. None was condemned to death. Sentences ranged from eight to twenty years, with only four defendants receiving the heaviest term. Time spent in custody in the Soviet Union or China was taken into account, so that most of those convicted were freed within a few years. The Chinese government released the last three Japanese war criminals in 1964.[149] In June 1956, U.S. Ambassador Allison in Japan commented that Communist China's generosity might "arouse considerable emotional resentment against us for 'anti-Japanese' attitude."[150] It was all too easy to contrast Beijing's leniency with the apparent recalcitrance of some of the Western powers. Australia, the Netherlands, and Britain were already taking steps to put themselves on the other side of the ledger, leaving the United States the most vulnerable to Japanese criticism.

Events had moved rapidly between 1953 and 1956. By the end of 1953, all surviving war criminals convicted in the loosely coordinated national tribunals and still imprisoned overseas had been repatriated to Japan. In deliberations on clemency, two main approaches had emerged. Four of the six countries that still had control over prisoners convicted in national tribunals, as well as the group that collectively considered the IMTFE, sooner or later chose a broad political solution: they found ways to free war criminals more or less en masse, without a detailed review of the merit of individual cases. Even the Soviet Union and the PRC released a substantial number of the prisoners they held for war crimes, again for broadly political reasons. On the day that the last IMTFE prisoner, Satō Kenryō, was freed, however, 383 war criminals remained in Sugamo Prison, according to Japanese Ministry of Justice records.[151] The United States, in particular, was to have considerable difficulty in working out how to release them without courting political trouble.

9

THE RACE TO CLEAR SUGAMO

By the mid-1950s, it was clear that keeping Japanese war criminals in prison was an impediment to the closer political and economic relationship with Japan that the Western powers now either actively wanted or realized was inevitable. The United States and its allies had avoided the temptation to exact a punitive peace, had declined to use the peace treaty to blame Japan for the war, had allowed and encouraged Japanese rearmament, and had largely sidestepped the matter of war reparations. The U.S. government had also signed a separate defense agreement with Japan in 1951 at the same time as the peace treaty. In such an environment, the failure to release war criminals stood out as a seemingly anomalous reminder of the past conflict just when the Western powers were committing themselves to the escalating Cold War. By December 1954, a U.S. State Department memo noted, "The continued incarceration of Japanese war criminals" had become "an important source of political and psychological friction between this Government and Japan" and was "inconsistent with United States policies to develop a close political and security alignment with Japan." The issue "constitutes a residue of wartime and Occupation policies which it is necessary to liquidate in order to bring United States policy toward Japan in accord with existing international realities."[1] In a broader sense, there was an air of inevitability about freeing war criminals. A British comic poem, "Rhyming Prophecy for a New Year," written for 1956, began:

Fog and snow for New Year's greeting, ban on all domestic heating,
Russia leaves a UNO meeting, threat of war in Middle East.
Feb. Australian Test team chosen, everything but wages frozen,
Eggs at two pounds ten a dozen, all war criminals released.[2]

The prisoners who remained in detention were more and more clearly marked as relics of an immediate postwar reckoning that had ceased to be the most fitting way to deal with world affairs. Although the Western imperative to continue to avenge war crimes did not disappear, it was countered by the desire to establish good relations with Japan. In the 1950s, moreover, pressure on Allied governments to free the war criminals came not only from politicians, diplomats, and the public in Japan, but also from international Christian and pacifist organizations. Furthermore, it was increasingly evident that under Japanese administration, life in Sugamo Prison had relaxed considerably, to the extent that in Western eyes, it scarcely seemed like punishment. Several factors had constrained Western governments from simply ordering the prison doors to be opened. The different governments wanted to stay in step with one another if they could. More important was the Allies' reluctance to repudiate their own military tribunals. In these circumstances, fitting the length of sentence to the gravity of the crimes remained immensely difficult.

By the mid-1950s, however, the imperative to release the prisoners was overwhelming. No government now wanted to be left as the last one responsible for Japanese war criminals. The fact that each of the prosecuting powers was unwilling to be branded as the government with the harshest attitude indicates the large degree to which Western relations with Japan had changed: in stark contrast with the attitude of the immediate postwar years, the risk of offending the Japanese people was now considered a grave one, with potentially significant political consequences. When dealing with clemency for Japanese war criminals, the governments of Australia, the United Kingdom, the Netherlands, and the United States kept a closer eye on one another than they had at any other stage of the war crimes trial program, and they spent considerable time second-guessing what the other governments would do. In the end, each government raced to clear Sugamo of the prisoners it had convicted before its allies could do likewise, as long as it could be done in a seemly manner.

Administrative strategies were developed to accelerate release without implying any comment on the gravity of the crimes. No government wanted to revisit the original trials and verdicts, partly because it would be time-consuming and difficult but also because of two other considerations. Reviewing the evidence was certain to reveal embarrassing inconsistencies and, at worst, might expose miscarriages of justice. Revisiting the evidence would also highlight all over again the enormity of some of the crimes committed by Japanese military personnel, making it difficult to justify releases. The Netherlands and Australia found solutions to the problem of Japanese war criminals without such a reexamination of the evidence. Authorities in the United Kingdom and the United States, however, while processing applications for clemency as fast as they could, continued to insist that each case had to be decided on its merits and that no general measure was possible.

British and American officials clung firmly to the idea that the original verdicts had to be upheld because they genuinely believed it essential that the crimes be sufficiently punished; because they wanted to be seen to be adhering to principle rather than giving in to less worthy, political considerations; and because they believed their publics demanded it. Allied policymakers were often convinced that public opinion, in the metropoles and colonial territories, demanded the continued punishment of war criminals, and they wanted to keep faith with their publics. In practice, such a stance meant they had little choice but to revisit the trials and sentences, no matter how often they denied they were doing so. By the mid-1950s, this approach also meant that both governments were left with a core group of prisoners who had committed terrible crimes. Review of these difficult cases then prompted serious reconsideration of the basic assumptions about what constituted a war crime and what circumstances might mitigate such crimes.[3]

THE NETHERLANDS AND
AUSTRALIA FIND A WAY OUT

By September 1955, as we have seen, the Dutch authorities had released one hundred of the war criminals they had convicted, but it was clear they would continue to retain custody of prisoners until the Japanese government agreed to provide compensation for the significant losses incurred by wartime civilian internees in the Netherlands Indies. Japan's position on the matter was not simply obstructive. Although the Western signatories to the San Francisco Peace Treaty had given up their right to compensation, the Japanese authorities were engaged in complex reparations negotiations with Southeast Asian governments. The scale of the damage to be compensated for in Southeast Asia far exceeded the collective harm suffered by Dutch internees, and the Japanese authorities were reluctant to set a figure in dealing with the Dutch that might become the basis for a ruinously multiplied reparations sum for the Southeast Asian region as a whole. In November 1954, however, the Japanese government agreed to pay Burma US$200 million, deferred for ten years.[4] These terms, far more than any potential settlement with the Netherlands, set a baseline for other Southeast Asian reparations agreements, thereby freeing the Japanese authorities to open negotiations with the Netherlands. Serious talks began in October 1955, with the Netherlands government initially asking for US$27.5 million in compensation.[5] When agreement was finally reached at the end of January 1956, the Netherlands side settled for an indemnity of US$10 million, to be paid to 110,000 Dutch internees in installments over five years.[6]

Japanese sources said that the settlement of the claim would be followed by the release of the final 111 war criminals convicted by Dutch tribunals. The arrangement was reported to the Dutch parliament as a minor matter, buried among other issues, in the hope that no one would notice.[7] On April 5, 1956, 25 prisoners were released, and on May 16, the life sentences of another 27 were reduced to twenty years, thereby making them eligible for parole. Another 84 were released in three batches in June and July 1956. The last Dutch-convicted detainee, Misuzaka Takeo, was paroled on August 15, 1956, four months after the Japanese Diet had approved the compensation payment.[8] In the U.S. files, George Hagen recorded a comment, evidently reflecting a view that both the Philippine and Dutch governments had tried to trade war criminals for compensation, but that the Philippine government had failed. According to Hagen, the Dutch had "apparently learned from Phillipine [*sic*] incident . . . — make the deal before the release."[9] By mid-August, only Australia, Britain, and the United States continued to hold Japanese war criminals.

In April 1955 the Australian government had decided on a new parole system for war criminals, with the proviso that it not contradict the regulations or practice of other Commonwealth countries, which effectively meant Britain. Although Australian officials wished to be neither harsher nor more lenient than Britain, it was not easy to match the two systems: Britain had no parole, whereas Australia now did, but Britain recognized pretrial custody when calculating sentences, whereas Australia did not.

By the mid-1950s, no war criminals under British jurisdiction were serving less than fifteen years, so it was hard to decide on policy for Australian-convicted criminals with shorter sentences.[10]

In any case, partly because of the need to consult with British officials, Australia's 1955 system did not produce results quickly. The first three prisoners released on parole left Sugamo on September 27, 1955, five months after the new policy had been announced, and only seven were freed on parole in 1955, along with another seven whose sentences had ended.[11] In 1956, however, the pace accelerated: to the satisfaction of the Japanese authorities, thirty-four prisoners were paroled by May 10.[12] Nevertheless, Australian authorities calculated that at the current rate of release, they would probably still be responsible for eighty-eight war criminals at the end of 1956. The last would not be freed until 1961, given that several prisoners had commenced life sentences as late as 1951.[13] Meanwhile, British-convicted war criminals were steadily leaving Sugamo at the expiration of their sentences. Australian officials also believed that the Dutch and U.S. authorities would free all or most of their prisoners by the end of 1956, though in fact the Americans did not.[14] The Australian government realized that it might be left as the last to hold Japanese war criminals, a situation it would not welcome: "We cannot afford to allow a position to arise where the only war criminals detained in Japan are those sentenced by Australian courts."[15] The Australian government had formerly been well known for a stern resolve concerning Japanese war criminals. It had continued to place them on trial and to execute some of them after all the other prosecuting powers had stopped, and had been the last to repatriate prisoners to serve out their sentences in Japan. In 1953, a Sugamo prisoner reportedly asserted that whereas the United States and China were the least antagonistic to Japan, Australians were the "most stubborn" when war criminals were concerned and were "the most anti-Japanese than any other people [sic]."[16] Australian officials were aware in 1955–1956 that "everyone else is liberalising hard—except us."[17] If Australia were left as the last country holding Japanese war criminals, pressure for their release would increase, and "it may be charged that she [Australia] alone among the Allies of World War II is being unnecessarily vindictive."[18]

The Australian government announced a dramatic change on July 3, 1956: parole was abolished, and prisoners would have the remaining portion of their sentence remitted after serving one-third of it, or a maximum of ten years.[19] Those currently on parole would have their sentences terminated. When the decision was announced, 109 prisoners convicted by Australia were still in Sugamo, and 89 would be eligible for release under the new policy.[20] Release was not automatic: the Australian government was opposed to granting releases "in a sensational way,"[21] because "we would not want newspaper headlines about 'mass release.' "[22] Notionally, each case was considered individually,[23] but the records contain no evidence that officials closely examined the situation of eligible prisoners. Over the next twelve months, the authorities released the prisoners in batches small enough to avoid attracting adverse attention in Australia. The Melbourne *Argus* reported one such release with no hint of irony in a small article entitled "Japs Pay for War Crimes."[24] Officials agreed that the rate could be speeded up if all the other governments were to release the war criminals under their jurisdictions,[25] but in the end the Australian authorities were well ahead of the Americans. The last Japanese war criminal for whom Australia was responsible left Sugamo on July 4, 1957.[26]

The new policy came as something of a shock to Australia's allies[27] and, no doubt, to the Japanese government. The Japanese authorities called the change a "most gratifying step to cut the Gordian Knot of the war criminals problem," which would "have an excellent effect on the future relations between Australia and Japan."[28] For U.S. ambassador John Allison in Tokyo, the alteration to Australian policy was likely to exacerbate resentment of the United States in Japan: "Public knowledge Australia's new war criminal policy will add impetus to Japanese pressures [for] more liberal treatment U.S. convicted war criminals."[29] Headlines like one that appeared in the *Japan Times* would not have enhanced America's image: "Japanese Efforts Fail to Gain U.S. Clemency for War Felons." As the article noted, the White House was disinclined to offer executive clemency despite Japanese diplomatic pressure, and case-by-case review of applications would continue.[30] Even though Allison asked the State Department to give urgent consideration to matching the Australian releases,[31] this did not happen.

BALANCING MORAL PRESSURE
WITH PUBLIC OPINION

In the 1950s, pressure to grant clemency came from a large number of sources. As we have seen, in the absence of a formal appeal system,

convicted war criminals, their relatives and friends, prefectural governments, and organizations in Japanese civil society had, from the
beginning, petitioned for leniency. In internal correspondence, British
diplomats in Tokyo freely admitted that they treated the petitions with
disdain: "Our usual custom is not to send an acknowledgement and to
have the appeals burned with the confidential waste."[32] Appeals for clemency soon began to appear from outside Japan. Japanese politicians,
diplomats, intellectuals, and public figures were well connected internationally. Decades of experience of diplomacy and of distinguished
work in international organizations, including the League of Nations,
the International Red Cross, and the Institute of Pacific Relations, had
given them many Western allies. Christianity had strong roots in Japan,
and Japanese representatives were prominent in international Christian
organizations, including the YMCA, while Western missionaries also
were active in Japan. The U.S. Clemency and Parole Board, in particular,
received many letters from Christian organizations asking for leniency
for the Japanese prisoners.

Western advocates of amnesty for war criminals emphasized both
humanitarian and political arguments. The National Council for Prevention of War made a submission to the Clemency and Parole Board
in Washington in November 1952, asserting that further punishment of
war criminals and, by implication, of Japan as a whole, was unnecessary
now that peace had been restored, and that leniency would be a better
foundation for future relations with Japan.[33] In April 1954, W. P. Bradley,
associate secretary of the Washington-based General Conference of Sev-
enth Day Adventists, wrote to the board's chairman after a visit to Japan.
Bradley argued that whereas it was proper for prisoners convicted by the
International Military Tribunal for the Far East (IMTFE) to continue to
serve their sentences, the other war criminals should be released. He cited a
list of reasons. None of the remaining prisoners had committed an offense
grave enough to receive the death penalty; they had already undergone significant punishment; their families were suffering; the great majority were
not "career militarists" and so would do no harm if they were returned to
society; and release of the prisoners would constitute "a stroke of excellent diplomacy," whereas continuing to incarcerate them might increase
Japanese resentment of the United States. Bradley concluded: "Personally,
I would look on it as an act of Christian charity to end their imprisonment
and restore them to civilian life."[34]

In the United Kingdom, Lord Hankey and his associates continued to press for leniency for both German and Japanese war criminals.[35] Hankey insisted that the war crimes trials were not simply a matter of justice because they had always featured "a tremendous lot of politics." In the Cold War context, he argued, politics should now outweigh punishment. As he wrote to Lord Reading, minister of state for the Foreign Office:

> I feel . . . that something more than clemency in driblets, calculated on a strictly judicial basis, is required if we are to get our former enemies into a frame of mind where they are [likely] to become wholehearted Allies—and from a military point of [view] nothing less is of the slightest value.[36]

Hankey believed the issue of war criminals was so important in Japan that unless they were released, Prime Minister Yoshida Shigeru might lose his position and thus would be unable to continue his policy of countering Communism and keeping Japan in the Western camp.[37] Conservative member of Parliament Godfrey Nicholson, who had visited Japan as part of a parliamentary delegation the previous year, told the House of Commons in June 1955 that without strong Western support, Japan might, for economic rather than political reasons, be "lost as a strong and solid bastion" and could be "sucked into the Communist vortex, looking towards the mainland of Asia rather than to the outside world." Release of the eighty-seven remaining war criminals convicted by British national tribunals would have an "immense" effect in Japan, Nicholson said, "for it would prove to Japan that we really want friendship with her and are willing to make a new start."[38]

The Japanese authorities also sent their own high-powered emissaries to plead the cause of war criminals in Western countries. Cabinet members and diplomats used official visits to press for leniency, as we have seen, and representatives of other sections of society and politics appeared as well. In 1953 Arita Hachirō, a former foreign minister who had been elected to the Lower House of the Diet in 1953 after being released from purge restrictions, visited France, the Netherlands, the United Kingdom, and the United States to discuss clemency. Arita was accompanied by Mrs. Yamashita Harue, then a representative of the Kaishintō (Reform Party) in the Lower House and chair of a special investigative committee on welfare for repatriates and bereaved families

(Kaigai dōhō hikiage oyobi izoku engo ni kansuru chōsa tokubetsu iinkai).[39] Two months later, NOPAR's chairman, Tsuchida Yutaka, also visited Britain and the United States for discussions with officials handling clemency applications.[40]

It is not clear what effect, if any, such appeals had on the Western authorities. British officials noted that the case put forward by Arita and Yamashita was "highly unconvincing" but that the meetings with Tsuchida were "useful."[41] Arguments favoring early release were countered by a concern for public opinion, which was believed to demand continued incarceration. Officials in London were wary of offending the public both at home and in colonial territories. The Foreign Office's Colin Crowe believed that anti-Japanese feeling in Britain was perhaps stronger than anti-German feeling, "and nearly all the remaining . . . Japanese war criminals for whom we are responsible were convicted of crimes against British subjects, whereas less than half the Germans were."[42] His colleague J. A. Pilcher made the surely exaggerated claim that "there was not a village in this country which had not suffered from Japanese treatment of our prisoners-of-war."[43] He felt there was "considerable public feeling" in Britain against leniency for Japanese war criminals and that any reductions in sentence "may give rise to Parliamentary questions,"[44] an eventuality that officials worked hard to avoid. Another colleague, F. W. Marten, agreed: the treatment of war criminals was "a matter, which (since it involved brutality to our prisoners of war) is political dynamite in this country."[45] British diplomats in Tokyo did not concur. One complained that the British government's policy "[ratified] the spirit of revenge of a limited number of Britons" while "creating in the vanquished a sense of injustice and grievance which can be and is being exploited by our enemies."[46] The London view prevailed, even though one Foreign Office document conceded in early 1955 that "public opinion [in Britain] has in fact shown little or no interest up till now in the dates of release of Japanese war criminals."[47] Right up to the last releases, British officials were wary of possible opposition to leniency in the territories where the war criminals had committed their offenses, even though colonial governors almost always reported that no adverse reaction was expected. The Australian, Dutch, and U.S. governments, too, believed their publics demanded a tough approach.[48] H. F. McIntyre of Upper Darby, Pennsylvania, sent the following postcard to the U.S. Clemency and Parole Board in 1956:

Gentlemen—

Newspaper reports indicate you have paroled a Japanese sergeant who executed an American prisoner of war, Capt. Burton C. Thomson.

What can possibly be in your weak minds when you do such a thing? Can you possibly realize the enormity of the Japanese soldier's crime?[49]

HOTEL SUGAMO

The perception that incarceration in Sugamo was hardly a punishment also gained ground in the mid-1950s. As we have seen, conditions in Sugamo had been comparatively good since the late 1940s, and under Japanese administration, they improved further. Kidō Kōichi, the former Lord Privy Seal convicted at the IMTFE, later recalled that after 1952, Sugamo had been "much more comfortable than the Gakushūin dormitory," referring to the Peers' School, at which many children of the nobility had been educated.[50] Prisoners did not lack facilities for recreation and entertainment or contact with the outside world. In addition to a large number of politicians, a parade of comedians, dancers, and singers visited the jail: in 1952 alone, nearly 2,900 entertainers reportedly staged 114 performances for the prisoners.[51] Visitors conducted classes in flower arranging and tea ceremony; haiku and *tanka* experts came to speak to the prisoners' poetry associations; and Buddhist and Christian ministers visited. Prisoners could go to lectures, watch television, listen to the radio, and play baseball.[52] In one notorious episode, 640 war criminals were allowed out of the prison in November 1952 to watch a professional baseball game in Tokyo. The excursion was widely publicized, and Western diplomats and other officials were infuriated. Afterward, one British official noted with disgust, "Packages of fruit, candies and cigarettes were presented to all of them before they were conducted back to their centrally heated cells."[53] Moreover, under the system of temporary release, a prisoner could be granted a short period of leave in the case of the serious illness or death of a close relative or other pressing circumstance. The result, claimed a 1952 British report, was that "his relatives are placed on a planned rotation system of illness."[54]

War criminals were already able to leave the prison to further their "vocational training" as barbers or to attend a driving school as long as they restricted their daytime absences to once or twice a week.[55] Outside work expanded beyond these parameters from 1953 onward.[56] One convicted war criminal even went to a job at Yamaichi shōken (Yamaichi Securities) every day.[57] Another, serving a life sentence in Sugamo, worked as a doctor at Keiō University Hospital; a Western colleague was surprised to find out later that he was a war criminal.[58] Others worked in factories or lumber yards, allegedly drawing civilian rates of pay.[59] In October 1955, outside work, "long the subject of Tokyo gossip," made headlines.[60] The former army general Araki Sadao, convicted in the IMTFE, gave a press interview after his June 1955 release. The interview was published in the November issue of the prominent periodical *Bungei shunjū* but was released earlier to various embassies. Araki reportedly said that incarcerated war criminals "left the prison for work in the morning and returned there in the evening." According to one translation that circulated among Western diplomats, Araki stated that the prison "was nothing but an apartment house where they were [staying] only for sleep."[61] Some war criminals, he alleged, even ran bars or pinball (*pachinko*) parlors outside the prison. Araki maintained that the system of special leave was manipulated to allow prisoners to be absent on personal business for up to a month, instead of the few days intended by the Allied governments.[62] The statements attributed to Araki caused agitation in the Japanese press, foreign embassies, and diplomats' home governments.[63] The Japanese Foreign Ministry, doubtless alarmed at the damage such reports might do to the Allied governments' willingness to grant further clemency, told the press that Araki's comments were exaggerated and contrary to the facts.[64] The Justice Ministry later concluded that the government had been successful in its efforts to allay Western anxiety that Sugamo prisoners had an unreasonable amount of freedom.[65]

Despite suspicion that war criminals had an easy time in Sugamo, the prisoners still wanted to be released. There were a few exceptions, however. Life on the outside could be particularly difficult for Korean and Taiwanese war criminals, who might have extra trouble finding work and might not have families or supporters in Japan to assist them. Of the 753 prisoners in Sugamo in May 1954, 23 were Koreans and 44 were Taiwanese, according to the Association to Support the War-Convicted.[66] In January 1955 one former Korean guard, Arai Shoko, and six Taiwanese war criminals refused to leave prison, even though they had been granted parole. They declared that because they were ineligible as foreigners to receive public welfare support, they could not survive financially in Tokyo.[67] A British official noted cynically that Arai's desire "to stay in prison and to enjoy the good rations and easy regime of Sugamo" was understandable.[68] The Sugamo authorities were preparing to eject Arai by force, but at the last minute the Association to Support the War-Convicted, which regularly channeled funds from government agencies and other sources to support Korean and Taiwanese prisoners, contributed ¥20,000 to each of the prisoners, together with help in finding accommodation and work.[69] Arai and the six Taiwanese war criminals duly left the prison. The release of several other Korean prisoners was delayed in May 1955 for similar reasons.[70]

By this stage, the work of the Association to Support the War-Convicted was tapering off. Two major goals of earlier years—bringing about a cessation of the death penalty and ensuring the repatriation to Japan of all war criminals in overseas prisons—had been achieved. The association remained firmly committed to working for the release of the 646 prisoners who were still in Sugamo in April 1955. Members also continued a wide range of other activities, including visiting prisoners, providing employment advice and assistance for released prisoners, helping those hospitalized with serious illnesses, assisting in the collection of documentary materials to facilitate study of the trials, and putting pressure on the government to include war criminals and their families in arrangements for veterans' pensions—pressure that was largely successful. Apparently in accordance with the wishes of the war criminals' families, the association also negotiated to have deceased war criminals enshrined at Yasukuni Shrine along with the other war dead. Although the shrine administrators assented in 1954, war criminals were not enshrined until the 1960s, in the case of those convicted in the national tribunals, and 1978, for those convicted in the IMTFE.[71] Despite all this continuing activity, officials of the Association to Support the War-Convicted concluded in 1955 that they had achieved most of their goals, that the work was now more or less routine, that the number of the organization's administrative staff and the frequency of meetings could be reduced, and that donations from the public were drying up, so that future activities would have to be funded from existing reserves. In the mid-1950s they remained palpably frustrated, however, at the fact that progress on the release of war criminals was so slow.[72]

REVIEWING THE CASES

The British Foreign Office, as we saw in chapter 7, started reviewing clemency applications only in 1953. Case reviews were to focus not on the original trials but on sentencing: they would consider inequality in sentencing for similar crimes, undue severity in sentencing, and subsequent developments, including matters relating to age, health, family circumstances, and prison conduct. They could also take account of the effect of release or continued detention on public opinion in any relevant country. Reviewers supposedly would not examine "fresh evidence tending to show that a criminal had been wrongly convicted or that he might have been convicted of a lesser offence." The initial guidelines, however, explicitly stated that when reviewing sentencing, officials should consider the age and rank of the convicted war criminal at the time of the offense and the question of superior orders.[73] Thus, from the beginning of the review process, it was clear that the most junior personnel were to be considered less culpable, as they had been since the first investigations for war crimes were conducted.

Progress on reviews was slow. By July 1953, the British authorities had received one hundred clemency applications, but had examined only twenty-five, and had refused clemency in twenty-one of those cases.[74] In July, the Queen approved the first clemency actions. Four war criminals— a naval chief petty officer and three civilian employees who had been tried together in Singapore for killing two Malay policemen in the days immediately after Japan's surrender—had their sentences of fifteen years reduced to twelve years. With subsequent remission for good conduct, the four would each serve eight years and would be due for release in late 1953. The favorable review was based partly on an assessment that the four accused shared equal guilt for the original crime and on the fact that British sources had testified to the good conduct of three of the four, indicating that "the men were very different from the ordinary run of war criminal who indulged in inhumane maltreatment of prisoners of war." Indeed, forty or so British and Eurasian residents of Singapore had sent in a petition on behalf of one of the accused, Okuda Naotake, at the time of the trial, and further petitions on his behalf were submitted in 1951 and 1953. The Foreign Office was careful to check with the Singapore governor, who confirmed that no adverse reaction from the Malay population was expected if the men were released early, "provided that publicity is kept to a minimum."[75]

In the initial reviews, however, very few decisions were made in the war criminals' favor. At the time of the peace treaty, Sugamo held 116 prisoners convicted in British military courts. By April 1954, that is, two years later, 15 had been released on completion of their sentence, with no clemency granted. Of the remaining 101 prisoners, clemency applications had been reviewed in 46 cases, of which 33 (72 percent) had been rejected. Sentences had been slightly reduced in another 5 cases.[76] In September 1954, Britain was responsible for 93 war criminals but had reviewed clemency applications for only 52. Clemency had led to the release of 8 prisoners by then, with sentence reductions for 2 more, making a total of only 10 clemency actions in the four years since the reviews had begun.[77] The last British-convicted prisoners were not due for release until 1961.[78]

British officials in Tokyo bore the brunt of Japanese impatience.[79] As early as May 1953, they expressed concern at the slow progress: "It is hard for us to explain convincingly to the Japanese why after more than a year not one decision has been transmitted to them." Britain was already lagging behind other governments in releasing war criminals, and Sir Esler Dening, the British ambassador, felt that diplomats in Japan had been placed in "a very invidious position."[80] He perceived a split between politics and legalities when dealing with war criminals and was convinced that the former was more important: "I hope it will not be found in the event that good law makes bad politics."[81] At times the ambassador found the pressure from the Japanese Foreign Ministry "extremely embarrassing," especially in view of the clemency actions of other governments. "Not to put too fine a point on it," he commented through a subordinate, "we do not look forward to finding ourselves in a position of glorious isolation."[82] Dening noted at the end of 1953 that because the U.S. government had paroled a number of war criminals, the British authorities should expect their Japanese counterparts to "turn the heat on us more and more in coming months." In a warning that seems to have struck home to British officials, judging by the fact that it was quoted in several subsequent Foreign Office documents, he added: "Indeed, we must face the prospect that, despite the justice of our position, we are creating for ourselves by our present attitude an incubus of ill will which it may take many years to dissipate."[83] But Foreign Office administrators felt they had their own "politics" to deal with, in the form of potential public reaction in Britain to leniency for war criminals, and did not see "why we should get bullied into granting clemency simply because others have done so."[84]

British officials were aware that from the Japanese point of view, British policy appeared to have got harsher since the peace treaty. Before 1952, the UK government had acted comparatively generously. It had reduced more than one hundred sentences on the recommendation of the 1949 Lynch board; had repatriated all war criminals held overseas to Japan in 1951 on its own initiative, a full two years before prisoners were repatriated by the Philippines and Australia; and had thereby allowed the Supreme Commander for the Allied Powers (SCAP) to parole 127 men before the Occupation ended. In the two and a half years after peace was formally restored, however, only 22 men were freed, 8 by the exercise of clemency. In contrast, China, France, and the Philippines had released everyone. The U.S. government had freed more than 140 men on parole since the treaty and, as we shall see later, had announced in 1954 that prisoners with life sentences would be eligible for parole after ten years.[85] As Colin Crowe of the Foreign Office noted in April 1954, "We are being less lenient than any other country except Australia, and considerably less lenient than the U.S.A."[86] (table 9.1).

Parole was one major issue. SCAP had initiated a parole system during the Occupation, and after the peace treaty, the United States and Netherlands governments also released eligible prisoners conditionally. Britain and the Australian states, however, did not have parole systems. The nearest British domestic equivalent was "release on licence," under which the home secretary could authorize the conditional release of prisoners in certain categories.[87] The Australian government, as we have seen, eventually introduced a short-lived parole system for Japanese war criminals convicted in national tribunals, but the British authorities refused to do so. Officials in London resented being criticized for not paroling Japanese war criminals.[88] In internal correspondence, they pointed out that it would be impossible for British authorities to supervise prisoners on parole in Japan or to ensure the return to prison of someone who violated parole "without risking a crisis in Anglo-Japanese relations." In short, "such merits as the parole system may have had when the Supreme Commander was in a position to enforce its terms, have largely disappeared with the taking over of the custody of the war criminals by the Japanese authorities."[89] In practice, there was little difference between parole and outright release. If there were grounds for clemency, British officials argued, the prisoner should be freed unconditionally.[90] Moreover, because Britain did not have a parole system, public opinion there, they felt,

TABLE 9.1 Clemency Actions in the First Two Years After the
Peace Treaty, by Government

Country	Prisoners on April 28, 1952	Sentences reduced by clemency, April 28, 1952–March 1, 1954	Percentage of remissions to number in prison on April 28, 1952
United States	425	117	27.5
United Kingdom	116	5	4.3
Netherlands	219	29	13.25
France	42	38	90
Australia	184	0	0
Nationalist China	91	91	100
Philippines	52	52	100
Total	1,129	332	29.4

Source: Adapted from table attached to Crowe, "Class 'B' and 'C' Japanese War Criminals,"
April 19, 1954, NA (UK), FO 371/110506.

would not distinguish between release on parole and outright release, and
for that matter, neither would the Japanese public.[91]

Officials also considered that Britain had already acted more liberally
toward Japanese war criminals than had other Allied governments. British
courts had sentenced nearly one-fifth of Japanese personnel convicted
as war criminals. Because many sentences had been reduced in 1949,
however, British-convicted prisoners constituted less than one-tenth of
the total number incarcerated when the peace treaty came into effect. In
September 1954, prisoners convicted by British courts still represented less
than one-seventh of the total then in prison, as British officials observed.
Furthermore, since 1949, life sentences imposed by British military courts
had been fixed at twenty-one years, whereas other governments had maintained the principle of literal life terms and had sentenced many prisoners to terms of thirty or more years. In total, the U.S., Australian, and
Netherlands governments still had 202 life sentences in force in September
1954, according to Foreign Office calculations. As a senior British official

remarked, "The United Kingdom therefore not only convicted a smaller number of the men in gaol than the other allied powers, but [in effect] imposed lighter sentences on them."[92] In addition, generous remissions of sentences had already been applied. In accordance with the practice in ordinary UK prisons for inmates not serving life sentences, war criminals could be granted a remission of one-third of their sentences for good conduct in prison; in practice, this measure was applied universally. When the remission was applied to life sentences fixed at twenty-one years, it meant that no prisoner convicted in a British military court would serve more than fourteen years from date of arrest on suspicion as a war criminal.[93]

British diplomats in Tokyo, who were sensitive to Japanese perceptions of British policy, were unconvinced that parole should be rejected. C. M. James warned in September 1953 that from a Japanese perspective, Britain's rejection of parole would simply look like "legal quibbling":

We fear that by comparison with the Americans, the Dutch and the French we may find ourselves in an isolated and invidious position which would do harm to Anglo-Japanese relations. . . . I doubt very much if the Japanese will be very convinced . . . by the argument . . . that we cannot inaugurate a system of parole because we do not have the same system in the U.K. In Japanese eyes this would seem a legalistic defence for a decision of policy.[94]

As his colleague A. S. Halford added: "Sooner or later the Japanese will either overtly or covertly break the rules and allow parole to the inmates of Sugamo Prison. . . . Any protest which we might then make would merely invite a snub." It would be better, therefore, to "take time by the forelock and condone any such breaches before the act rather than after it."[95] For prisoners convicted in British military courts, however, the UK authorities never did authorize parole.

The Foreign Office's position that Britain was lenient in fixing life sentences at fourteen years after remission for good conduct was undermined in July 1954 when the U.S. president approved a proposal to fix sentences of more than thirty years, including life terms, at ten years.[96] British officials still insisted, however, that political and legal considerations in freeing war criminals remained separate, arguing that release should not be the subject of a "political bargain" but must remain a "judicial" issue. British authorities nevertheless became increasingly defensive about this approach and, in any case, had concluded by the end of 1954 that it was not in British interests to impede the release of Japanese war criminals. In October 1954, the secretary of state told Prime Minister Yoshida that he would review individual cases again, in the hope "that such a review would enable a steady flow of releases to be maintained."[97] This was not an easy strategy to implement. As a London official noted, "We are already down to the hard core of war crimes cases," meaning it was very difficult to find mitigating circumstances to justify a prisoner's release.[98] A general review of sentences early in 1955 found that in sixty cases, British authorities had identified no grounds for reduction.[99] The senior official J. C. O'Dwyer now began to suggest "arbitrary" reductions, rather than case-by-case decisions, "in the interests of Anglo-Japanese relations."[100] In May 1955, the British government accepted the principle that life terms for Japanese war criminals should be reduced from twenty-one to twenty years,[101] to match a similar change recently made for German war criminals. London authorities, however, wanted to keep the decision quiet in both Britain and Japan. In the United Kingdom it was because "a great many people . . . suffered during the war at Japanese hands and there is still a lot of anti-Japanese feeling,"[102] and in Japan the British authorities did not want to encourage their Japanese counterparts to seek further reductions.[103]

By mid-1955, the British authorities were convinced of the need to review existing policy. Japanese war criminals convicted by both the United States and Australia were now theoretically eligible for parole after a maximum of ten years, and British officials believed that both governments were likely to release the prisoners without considering the merits of individual cases. As we have seen, the Australian parole system did not, in fact, work smoothly, but from the vantage point of mid-1955, it appeared to the British authorities that all Australian-convicted prisoners were likely to be released by the middle or end of 1956. If the British government stuck to its existing procedure and the Australians went ahead with the new system, Japanese war criminals sentenced to life imprisonment in British courts might not be released for four or five years after those sentenced to life terms by Australia and the United States. Although British-convicted prisoners would be released unconditionally, whereas those sentenced by American or Australian courts would be subject to parole restrictions, the British authorities were convinced that their Japanese counterparts would not long maintain the conditions of parole.

British officials also considered it unlikely that the Dutch government would be able to hold out against Japanese pressure for leniency. So it seemed very likely that by the end of 1956, the United Kingdom would be the only one of the original prosecuting powers to continue to maintain sentences. In that case, "the United Kingdom would clearly appear to be far more bitter and unforgiving than any other nation," and "this could surely do us no good." At the most senior levels of the British government, the United Kingdom was now thought to be dangerously isolated on the question of war criminals.[104]

In July 1955 the secretary of state proposed to the cabinet that all sentences of more than fifteen years be reduced to fifteen years, with remission of one-third for good behavior, a move that would allow release after ten years.[105] The UK cabinet assented[106] "in view of the attitude adopted by other Allied Governments responsible for the custody of Japanese war criminals."[107] British practice would thus be aligned with the U.S. system and with the supposed Australian practice too, except that Britain did not use parole. There was, however, an important proviso. The cabinet wanted to "reserve right to keep for longer men who were especially brutal."[108] Rather than implementing a rule that stipulated release after ten years, the cabinet thereby retained the principle of individual review of cases, thus preserving the discretion to detain the "worst cases" for "a longer period."[109] The upshot was that in each instance, the Foreign Office still had to make the argument that clemency was warranted, in order to prove that the prisoner in question was not one of the "very worst." Fifty-three of the eighty British-convicted prisoners in Sugamo in July 1955 were serving sentences of between sixteen and twenty years.[110] After the Foreign Office had reviewed the case, the Queen would be asked to reduce each sentence to fifteen years. Officials would then apply the one-third remission and then would apply the new rule of release after ten years. Sugamo rapidly began to empty of British-convicted prisoners. Fifty sentences were terminated between September 1, 1955, and January 1, 1956, including those that had been completed, leaving thirty men convicted by the United Kingdom in prison.[111]

Although Britain had feared being overtaken by U.S. policy, it did not prove easy for American authorities, either, to resolve the question of war criminals. Opinion was divided on what strategy to pursue. Predictably, officials in the U.S. embassy in Tokyo, who were under pressure from the Japanese public, the press, and politicians, had for some time favored prompt action. As early as March 1953, the embassy's Political Division apparently considered the issue a "hot political potato." At this point, embassy staff still believed that cases for clemency should be considered on their individual merits, but they also "strongly recommend[ed] that Washington provide a steady weekly stream of parolees to keep the pressure off the United States" and asked for a change in procedure to speed things up. One of their suggestions was that the president delegate his power to determine clemency to the board, an action that would not only free him of the necessity to decide on each case but would also accelerate paroles.[112]

Opinion within the embassy evidently hardened after the appointment in April 1953 of John Allison as ambassador. Allison had previously been director of the State Department's Office of Northeast Asian Affairs and, before that, had assisted Secretary of State John Foster Dulles in negotiating the Japanese peace treaty. Allison was clearly committed to a strategy that would strengthen Japan's economy and conservative leadership and hence its alliance with the "free world."[113] In January 1954 he recommended to the State Department that a mass pardon or parole of war criminals be authorized or, if that were not possible, that releases by the Clemency and Parole Board speed up. Allison "indicated that the question of war criminals in Japan was becoming a farce in view of the Japanese Government's laxity of control over the prisoners who were permitted to attend baseball games and other activities in Tokyo."[114] Together with some members of the State Department, he favored the rapid release of war criminals for the sake of good relations between the United States and Japan. These officials believed that better relations would encourage the Japanese people to identify with the Western camp in the Cold War and that failure to release war criminals would incite anti-U.S. feeling in Japan and thus would undermine the U.S. global agenda.[115] Allison's view was opposed by gradualists in the State Department, elsewhere in the U.S. government, and on the Clemency and Parole Board. Conrad E. Snow, the board's chairman, defended the board's case-by-case approach, declaring in February 1954 that "a number of cases fell into such a heinous category that the prisoners might never be granted parole or clemency." Other State Department officials felt that "a grant of amnesty would undermine the entire legal basis of the war crime trials in that amnesty or pardon had the effect of wiping out the crime." Parole or clemency, in contrast, "did not necessarily prejudice the legal basis of the trials."[116]

A mass release was never authorized, but in July 1954 President Dwight D. Eisenhower approved a breakthrough measure, following a recommendation by the board. So far, prisoners sentenced by U.S. military tribunals had become eligible for parole after serving one-third of the original term, or fifteen years if they had been sentenced to life imprisonment. Henceforth, war criminals serving thirty years or more, including life terms, would be eligible after ten years.[117] The change affected many war criminals: in January 1954, 175 prisoners in Sugamo sentenced by U.S. military tribunals were serving life terms or thirty years or more.[118] The State Department advised the Clemency and Parole Board that the change of rules "would tend to alleviate an important source of friction between the United States Government and Japan, and help create a psychological climate conducive to Japanese cooperation with the United States." The board was confident that the measure would still allow the continued detention of any prisoner "whose crimes are considered too heinous to permit present release."[119]

Reducing the period before prisoners became eligible for parole, however, did not empty Sugamo of U.S.-convicted prisoners, because the Clemency and Parole Board still had to recommend parole and the president had to approve. In September 1954, according to Japanese records, the U.S. government was responsible for nearly 40 percent of the Sugamo prisoners: 272 out of 694 inmates, of whom 90 percent were serving thirty-five or more years.[120] In early December 1954, there were still 264 left, of whom only 26, or 10 percent, were currently eligible for parole. Some of the 26 had been deemed "unworthy of parole" by the Clemency and Parole Board, while others had been approved by the board but rejected by the president, and about a dozen cases were awaiting action.[121] The board was expected to complete its review of all cases by the end of 1955, and a State Department memo recommended in December 1954 that a mass parole then be implemented.[122] But things did not proceed so smoothly. Not everyone was convinced of the need to clear Sugamo quickly, and by July 1956, the proportion of inmates sentenced by U.S. military courts had risen to more than 50 percent (table 9.2). Ironically, in view of its early role in promoting the release of war criminals, the United States now clearly lagged behind. Although the Australian government was still responsible for 99 prisoners at this point, it was rapidly releasing the war criminals under its control. In fact, if the releases already authorized but not yet effected had been taken into account, Australia's total would have been 87 rather than 99 on July 31, 1956.[123] In July 1956, Britain was responsible for only 7 Sugamo prisoners, and the Netherlands for 1.

Like the UK authorities, U.S. clemency officials were by now attempting to compensate for uneven sentencing in the original trials. The board also took into account "mitigating circumstances found in the record, newly discovered evidence, conduct during confinement, hardship among dependents, and other extenuating information available to the Board." After all of these considerations, however, a substantial number of prisoners would remain. The U.S. authorities now had to face the fact that

TABLE 9.2 Number of War Criminals in Sugamo as on July 31, 1956, Compared with Effective Date of Peace Treaty (April 28, 1952), Categorized by Prosecuting Country

Country	Number of prisoners on April 28, 1952	War criminals added after April 28, 1952	Number of prisoners on July 31, 1956
United States	425	1	115
United Kingdom	116	0	7
France	42	0	0
Netherlands	217	2	1
Australia	23	165 (mostly from Manus Island)	99
Philippines	0	56 (from Muntinlupa)	0
Nationalist China	91	0	0
IMTFE	13	0	0
Total	927	242	222

Note: The prisoner added to the U.S. total after April 1952 served a U.S.-imposed sentence after release by the Republic of China (ROC); the two prisoners added to the Netherlands total had previously been released by Australia from Manus Island. Numbers of French prisoners vary in different sources because of confusion between prisoners considered to be French responsibility and those considered to be Chinese responsibility.

Source: NOPAR, "Statistical Report on War Criminals in Sugamo Prison, Japan (as of 31 July 1956)," NAA 271958, 65.

"the time is approaching when only the most serious cases will be left before the Board." In other words, as officials acknowledged from the end of 1954 onward, they were about to reach the "hard core of bad cases."[124]

The fact that the Clemency and Parole Board was getting down to the most serious cases pointed to a problem concerning the president's power to approve the board's recommendations, a matter that Snow raised with White House staff.[125] Already the president had refused more than a dozen recommendations for parole or reduction of sentence, and it seemed likely that there would be greater difficulties ahead, given that the more straightforward cases had been dealt with. At the end of 1954, President Eisenhower had reportedly "expressed the desire that he be relieved of the necessity of taking action on the individual recommendations of the Board."[126] The White House was initially opposed to the change despite the wishes apparently expressed by the president,[127] but eventually, on May 16, 1955, the board was empowered to reduce sentences and grant parole without the "approval, ratification, or other action by the President."[128] One of the factors slowing the authorization of parole and sentence reduction was thereby removed.

DEALING WITH THE HARD CORE

Pressure increased on Britain and the United States to expedite the release of the remaining prisoners. In addition to the 1956 pardon and repatriation of suspected war criminals by Communist China, discussed in the previous chapter, pressure was heightened by the acceleration of releases by Australia and the steady release of the last prisoners held under Dutch jurisdiction. The Soviet government, too, released more foreign prisoners in 1955–1956, as it sought to adjust its international relations following Josef Stalin's death in 1953.[129] On December 13, 1956, relations between Japan and the Soviet Union were normalized. The Soviet government announced that in view of the formal cessation of war and on humanitarian principles, all Japanese citizens imprisoned in the Soviet Union would be freed and allowed to return home.[130] On December 26, a crowd of 3,000 people met 1,025 Japanese repatriates who arrived in Maizuru on the Red Cross ship *Kōan Maru*. More than 11,000 Japanese believed to have been in the Soviet Union, however, were still unaccounted for.[131]

Pressure for leniency for the Sugamo prisoners continued to be applied from Japan and from humanitarian, pacifist, and Christian international organizations. The moral ground for detaining war criminals was getting shakier. Events subsequent to the Second World War had made it clear that the aim of the war crimes trials to set a standard for future conflicts had not been fulfilled: most pointedly, no war crimes trials resulted from the Korean War. In August 1955, an English-language newspaper in Japan published a letter from George A. Furness, a Boston lawyer who had defended Shigemitsu Mamoru at the IMTFE and had remained in Japan to work as a lawyer and actor in B movies.[132] Furness pointed out that plans for war crimes trials for offenses committed during the Korean War had been dropped, despite preparation for such trials and copious evidence of atrocities. To insist on holding trials had come to be considered "politically unwise," Furness wrote, once it was evident that the conflict would end in "truce, ceasefire, and stalemate," because proceeding with prosecutions would have jeopardized the chances of an armistice. Although Furness supported this stance, he maintained strongly that it contradicted the Allies' attitude toward Japanese war crimes:

> It seems to me that we can no longer insist that our decisions to try the Japanese accused of crimes committed before and during World War II and to punish those found guilty were motivated entirely by a singly minded [sic] passion for justice. Our decisions to try and punish them were political decisions just as the decisions not to attempt to try . . . [war criminals in Korea] were political decisions.

Furness called for the release of the Sugamo prisoners on the basis of justice or politics or both, especially in view of the fact that the United States was asking the Japanese people "to rearm as part of the Free World, and therefore as allies" in the fight against Communist China, whose forces had committed atrocities against American troops during the Korean War: "We cannot, for reasons of policy or justice, justify a policy under which we accord worse treatment to those whom we ask to be our allies than we do to those against whom we ask them to ally."[133]

After several years of reviewing clemency applications, however, American and British officials were well aware that they were left with the "very worst" of the war criminals. Everyone now wanted to clear Sugamo, or at least realized it had to be done, but it proved difficult to work out how to rationalize, justify, and implement the release of the "worst" prisoners while keeping faith with the original desire to dispense stern justice. The arguments used by British officials to justify requests to the Queen to authorize release are explicit in the numerous clemency documents in the Foreign Office files. The minutes of the meetings of the U.S. Clemency and Parole Board do not detail the reasons for authorizing or refusing parole or sentence reduction in each case. Nevertheless, it is clear from the board's deliberations that U.S. officials struggled with the same kinds of issues as their British counterparts and reached broadly similar conclusions.

By December 1954, American and British officials were using the term "hard core" to describe the war criminals guilty of the most heinous crimes.[134] Recognition of such a category was reflected in the British cabinet's decision in July 1955 to allow for the retention of the worst offenders beyond the fifteen years (ten years after remission for good behavior) that would now be the maximum for everyone else.[135] In Washington, the Clemency and Parole Board established a "hard core" category in May 1955. It was subdivided into "permanent hard core," which covered "the most atrocious of the crimes, . . . where there would appear little hope of ever paroling the man under the present standards and procedures," and "temporary hard core," for war criminals who were "not quite as bad" and for whom "parole might be considered at a future date even though it is not considered appropriate to grant them parole now."[136] The aim was to establish an order of priority in dealing with clemency cases, but the main effect was to ensure that the board ended up with a group of prisoners whose behavior was inexcusable.

Throughout the war crimes trial process, from investigation to choice of defendants and then to sentence and confirmation of sentence, British officials had paid attention to the rank of the Japanese military personnel in question and the context in which the crime had been committed. They largely accepted that military necessity, the circumstances of the war, and the imperative for subordinates to obey superiors, as in any army, mitigated the severity of offenses. In clemency reviews, UK officials took serious notice of superior orders when it could be established that such orders had been given and had resulted in a war crime, and of the impediments to humane treatment of POWs or of the people of occupied territories. In March 1954, for example, the Queen was asked to reduce the sentence of former lieutenant Saito Shunkichi, who had been the medical officer in charge of all POWs at camps in the Hong Kong area from January 1942 onward. Large numbers of prisoners had died from diphtheria due to the lack of medicine and delays in treatment. Saito was convicted of neglect and ill-treatment of the prisoners and was sentenced to death. His sentence was subsequently commuted to twenty years. The Queen was now asked to reduce his term further, on the grounds that Saito was "a comparatively junior and inexperienced officer whose authority to take action on his own initiative was limited, and who was compelled to follow the instructions of the Commandant in charge of the prisoner-of-war camps," namely, Colonel Tokunaga Isao, who had been condemned to death but whose sentence had been commuted to twenty-one years. Furthermore, Saito had made efforts to procure anti-diphtheria serum, and senior figures in the Government Medical Services in Hong Kong who knew him well had petitioned for clemency for him. The Queen, as was constitutionally expected of her, authorized the reduction of Saito's sentence from twenty to fifteen years, which, with remission for good behavior, made him eligible for immediate release.[137] Clemency for Kume Matao was recommended in 1954 because officials found fresh evidence that he had objected to an order to execute Burmese civilians without trial and had carried out the execution only on the direct command of his superior officer. Four others who had been convicted of similar crimes against Burmese civilians, however, had their applications for clemency rejected.[138]

In their reviews of the last remaining cases, British officials accepted more and more of the original Japanese defense arguments. By this time, not many really junior soldiers were left in jail. Unless they had been guilty of particular brutality, comparatively few junior personnel had been convicted, and their sentences were often short. So the argument that subordinates were less guilty than their seniors was applied to military personnel of much higher rank, as the soldiers of lowest rank had already been released. Sergeants, sergeant majors, lieutenants, majors, and even a lieutenant colonel could now be described as "subordinate" in rank. Even though Kume had been a colonel in the Kenpeitai, the Foreign Office accepted his argument that he had merely passed on an order from still more senior officers to execute Burmese civilians in Moulmein Prison. In arguments for clemency, it became correspondingly important to stress that the most senior officers, responsible for decision making at the highest operational level, had been severely dealt with at the beginning, that is, had been executed or received life sentences, in order to avoid the impression that crimes had not been sufficiently punished. In a petition for clemency for thirty war criminals submitted in 1955, for example, the Queen was told: "Most of the men were subordinate officials and were guilty of lesser responsibility for the crimes for which they were convicted. The senior officers on whose orders they acted have in most instances paid the death penalty." The thirty war criminals included Matsumoto Meizan, a Korean guard who had committed crimes on the Thailand–Burma Railway, whose case was said to have "no redeeming features" in 1949 and who had been refused clemency in 1953. Another of the thirty was the civil governor of the Andaman Islands, Jochi Ryonosuke, whose crimes were now said to have been the responsibility of the Japanese naval authorities and of six officers who had been executed.[139]

In the end, the British authorities seem to have placed only one war criminal in the "very worst" category. Officials did not wish to recommend clemency for former lieutenant general Kinoshita Eiichi, who, as commander of the Shanghai Kenpeitai, had presided over a regime at Shanghai Bridge House of cruel torture of civilians suspected of insurgency against the Japanese wartime occupation. Officials conducting the clemency review described Kinoshita as "an exceptional case not meriting any degree of clemency"; there were "no mitigating circumstances"; and he was regarded as "fortunate to have escaped the death penalty."[140] Kinoshita had tuberculosis, and it appeared he might die in prison before his release date in 1959. The British authorities did not welcome this possibility, as it seemed likely to "make him a martyr in the eyes of the Japanese."[141] Officials were relieved to be able to avoid political embarrassment when Kinoshita's condition became bad enough to justify freeing him on medical parole in March 1956.[142] Kinoshita was the last remaining British-convicted war criminal when his parole was terminated by an act of clemency in December 1957.[143]

Among the last prisoners convicted by British military courts to leave Sugamo were four former Kenpeitai officers—a lieutenant colonel, a major, a lieutenant, and a reservist major—sentenced to life imprisonment for crimes committed during the February 1942 *sook ching* massacre in Singapore. The British Foreign Office documents recommending clemency for these men are notable for their detailed comments on the very difficult war situation at the time of the offenses, on the comparatively junior rank of the offenders, and on the fact that the offenders had followed their superiors' orders.[144] In accordance with the usual practice, before a final decision was made, the governor of Singapore was asked whether any adverse reaction could be expected there if the men were released. Most unusually, Sir Robert Black asked for a postponement of the decision for at least three months, on the grounds that bitter resentment of the *sook ching* massacre was still alive in Singapore, that the act of clemency could not be kept secret, and that it might be misinterpreted as the British government's disregard of the Singapore Chinese population. The delay in clemency was requested because Singapore was about to pass through a "critical period"—presumably a reference to the April 1956 attempt to negotiate with Britain over self-government.[145] In July 1956, Black notified the secretary of state for the colonies that although anti-Japanese feeling had not entirely dissipated in Singapore, he would no longer object to granting clemency to the four Kenpeitai officers,[146] and the Queen approved clemency in August.[147] At the end of September, only four British-convicted war criminals were left in Sugamo. The last one was released on January 1, 1957, leaving only Kinoshita and one other man technically in British custody but free on medical parole.[148] The Australian and U.S. governments were now the only ones to retain jurisdiction over war criminals in Sugamo.

In Washington, the Clemency and Parole Board worked hard on the cases that offered scope for leniency. Parole was granted to fifty prisoners between August and December 1955 and to another seventy-one in 1956.[149] On April 29, 1957, however, nearly four months after the last war criminal under British jurisdiction was released, the U.S. government was still responsible for another seventy-one war criminals, fifty of whom were serving life terms.[150] Fourteen prisoners convicted by Australia were still incarcerated, but plans had been made to release the last of them over the next two months.[151] Of the seventy-one U.S.-sentenced war criminals, thirty-one had been classed as "permanent hard core." A summary by Snow indicated that their crimes were gruesome (figure 9.1). Nevertheless, the board managed to parole thirty-eight war criminals during 1957.[152] By the end of November 1957, all of the forty-five U.S.-sentenced war criminals remaining in Sugamo were classed as "hard core." Thirty-six had been sentenced to life imprisonment. Very few were from the most junior ranks—of the twenty-seven army personnel, the most junior were five first lieutenants—suggesting that like British officials, the U.S. authorities had already made allowance for junior status and the need to follow superiors' orders (table 9.3). Two related cases accounted for a number of the

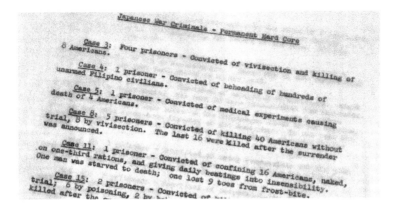

FIGURE 9.1 War criminals classified by U.S. Clemency and Parole Board as "permanent hard core," April 1957. "Chairman's Summary of the Crimes Committed by the 71 Japanese War Criminals Remaining in Sugamo" (ca. April 1957), NARA, RG59, Box 10, folder: 12.2 Japanese War Criminals—Permanent Hard Core (specific cases), 1957.

last war criminals. In May and June 1945, Western Army Headquarters in Fukuoka had turned over eight captured American pilots to Kyūshū Imperial University, where they were subjected to experimental operations and then killed. More than a dozen medical personnel had been convicted as war criminals in the Kyūshū University case, and four were still in custody in 1957. The Western Army case arose from the execution without trial of another thirty-two captured pilots from June to August 1945; several of the perpetrators were among the "hard core" in 1957.[153]

By this time, board members were aware they had reached the limits of the system for which they were responsible. They were not prepared to recommend clemency for the remaining war criminals because of their dreadful crimes, and although they had resisted a "political solution" for years, they now favored such an outcome. George T. Hagen, the board's executive secretary, wrote in sketchy notes that if anything was to be done,

> it should not be under guise of clemency or parole . . . and thus foul our nest . . . and indirectly criticize our own program. . . . It should be done frankly . . . as diplomatic or politic[al] move . . . and without pulling any punches. . . . Can't justify release any other way . . . and only causing trouble.[154]

TABLE 9.3 Ranks of the Last 45 War Criminals in U.S. Jurisdiction, November 1957

Army		Navy		Civilian	
Lieutenant generals	4	Vice admiral	1	Doctors	4
Major generals	3	Captains	2	Prison officials	5
Colonels	7	Warrant officer	1	Guards	3
Lieutenant colonels	2	Chief petty officer	1	Interpreter	1
Majors	4				
Captains	2				
First lieutenants	5				
Total	27		5		13

Source: Clemency and Parole Board to the President, "Report of Clemency and Parole Board for War Criminals (Japanese)," November 27, 1957, NARA, RG220, Box 1, folder: Minutes, CPB, M-81 through M-113.

More formally, as the Clemency and Parole Board wrote to President Eisenhower,

> All of the war criminals remaining in jail were guilty of such heinous offenses that it is becoming difficult to find a basis for further discriminative grants of parole. Accordingly, if there exist political or diplomatic problems that render desirable a termination of the present judicial solution of the war criminal program and the substitution of a political solution, the Board has no objection.[155]

The State Department, however, favored a different outcome: the secretary of state recommended to the president that the board be abolished. The board was indeed abolished by presidential action on December 31, 1957, without taking any further action on the last forty-five war criminals. The secretary of state was now empowered to act on behalf of the U.S. government on matters relating to war criminals. He was instructed to "accept the recommendations of the Government of Japan" on the parole of the remaining prisoners, providing that prior recommendations were made by a "responsible non-political board" that had adequately reviewed each individual case.[156] Hagen commented cynically:

> Plan [is] effort to do in a round-about-way, what they don't want to do on own responsibility. Our plan would accomplish the desired end . . . possibly in about the same time . . . but would require the Dept to take the resp.[responsibility] openly. New plan could be a farce.[157]

The new plan, however, fulfilled its function of delegating the release of war criminals to the Japanese government without requiring the president to admit openly he was doing so. In Japan, the Association to Support the War-Convicted prepared to wind up its operations, as its work was done.[158]

The last 18 Japanese war criminals left Sugamo Prison on parole on May 30, 1958. In the Japanese press, their departure from prison warranted no more than a small article.[159] Technically, the U.S. parolees remained under sentence, as did their counterparts released by the Dutch in 1956. On December 5, 1958, however, the Dutch authorities finally reduced the sentences of their 128 war criminals to time served.[160] The United States followed suit on December 29, and the long process of legal reckoning with Japanese war criminals finally came to an end.

CONCLUSION

Between 1945 and 1951, Allied powers in Asia and the Pacific conducted 2,362 trials of 5,706 men and 1 woman who were accused of carrying out war crimes as members or associates of the Japanese imperial forces. The courts found 4,524 defendants guilty, condemned 1,041 to death, and sentenced the rest to terms of imprisonment. Around 920 were actually executed. A few of those in prison escaped; a number died in captivity (some from suicide); and many were released upon completion of their original sentences. The prison terms of the remainder were truncated in a complex process of granting clemency that reflected a gradual change of mood and shift in judgment on the part of the powers that had brought down the original convictions. During the 1950s, without repudiating the validity of the original verdicts, the convicting powers eventually concluded that no useful moral or political purpose would be served by keeping the convicted men in prison. The last prisoners left Sugamo in May 1958, and the last of the sentences were formally terminated in December 1958.

As we have seen in this book, what began as a simple determination to punish guilty parties quickly developed into a moral, legal, political, and practical tangle.[1] It was a challenge to determine the legal basis for prosecution, to identify and detain suspects, to determine who should be prosecuted, to collect materials that might be presented convincingly as evidence, to run court proceedings that accorded with basic standards of fairness, and, in the longer term, to decide how sentences should be reviewed. Nonetheless, along with their counterpart prosecutions of Nazis in Europe, the trials were a landmark in international criminal law. They punished perpetrators on a scale not seen before or since, and they established new law both in defining war crimes and crimes against peace and in clarifying the specific issues of command responsibility and the defense of superior orders. Although the early release of those convicted might not have been expected when the legal process began, the completion in 1958 of the process of determining and then reviewing sentences appeared overall to have set new and higher standards for legal reckoning with war criminals.

In carrying out trials of individual offenders on such a large scale, the Allies aimed to avoid the long-term political consequences of imputing guilt to the entire Japanese nation. This intention, the outcome of a lesson learned from the perceived failure of the Versailles settlement after the First World War, required that the trials comprehensively prosecute the direct perpetrators of war crimes, so that they, and not the Japanese nation as a whole, would bear guilt and suffer its consequences. In the aftermath of a war that had been marked by savage brutality on both sides, however, the idea that Japan as a nation would not be required to carry the burden of war guilt may have been overoptimistic, and it was undermined from the start by practicalities. Problems of cost and difficulties in presenting appropriate evidence meant that the Allies were, in the end, parsimonious in their prosecution of suspects in the Asia-Pacific theater. Impressive though the scale of the trials was in comparison with previous efforts, the 5,707 people who appeared before the courts represented only a small proportion of those who had at least been suspected of war crimes. Given the public reporting of numerous atrocities, it was evident that the defendants had been selected from among a large number of possibilities. This perception immediately raised the question, especially in Japan, of why particular military personnel had been prosecuted while others had gone free. The realization that the war crimes trials had been selective was exacerbated early on by the political decision of U.S. authorities not to prosecute the Japanese emperor and later by the discovery that those same authorities had also quietly given safe passage to the Japanese perpetrators of hideous medical experiments on prisoners of war and local people in Manchuria, in return for scientific information.

The perception that the trials were incomplete did not prompt widespread demands for more vigorous prosecution. Rather, it cast doubt on the appropriateness even of the prosecutions that had actually been conducted. Particularly in Japan, many people concluded that the Allies had selected defendants arbitrarily and that the convicted men were scapegoats—unfortunate individuals who had been chosen more or less indiscriminately to bear guilt on behalf of the nation. Even among the Allies, many officials felt discomfort over the inconsistencies that stretched from investigation to sentencing in the one international and seven national jurisdictions, leaving aside the Soviet Union and the People's Republic of China (PRC), that were involved in the process of trying war criminals.

It is unrealistic to suggest that the trials would not have been compromised if they had been more, or less, comprehensive. Rather, the very concept of war crimes proved to be extraordinarily difficult to apply in practice, in Japan as it had been in Germany. The legitimacy of the International Military Tribunal for the Far East (IMTFE), in which political and military leaders were arraigned, was undermined by the perception that Japanese leaders were being punished for actions taken in the defense of their national interest and that comparable interventions by Allied powers outside their own borders, during the Second World War and in earlier colonial periods, had not been prosecuted. The Japanese authorities had begun their imperial ventures in Asia highly conscious of the West's record of territorial aggrandizement. Furthermore, the specific international political context of Japan's aggression against China and the West between 1928 and 1945 was ambiguous: Japanese military and political actions, especially in 1940–1941, had been partly a response to economic restrictions imposed by the Allied powers that had had the potential to cripple Japan. There was, therefore, some plausibility in the defense offered by Tōjō Hideki at the IMTFE that Japan had acted in legitimate self-defense. The distinction between the crime of waging aggressive war and the right of states to pursue their legitimate interests by military means was not sharp. In the end, it was the Allies, because they won the war, who had the power to determine who had committed crimes against peace and who had not. These circumstances gave the charge of waging aggressive war that was laid against Tōjō and other Japanese leaders a political cast that clashed with the intention to strengthen universal laws against international aggression.[2] The Tokyo trials thus brought to the fore an issue that remains relevant in international affairs to this day:

to what extent can national leaders be brought to account for actions they have taken according to their judgment of their national interest?[3]

The broad legitimacy of the national trials was not as fragile as that of the Tokyo Trial. Many of the men who were prosecuted had committed terrible acts, including massacre and torture, that were unambiguously considered crimes in most legal systems. Nevertheless, technical questions of legitimacy overshadowed the proceedings. Japan had signed but not ratified the 1929 Geneva Convention governing the treatment of POWs. The legal basis for the prosecution of Japanese military personnel for brutality toward prisoners, therefore, lay in a generalized assertion of what would now be called international humanitarian law, rather than in a specific breach of Japan's international commitments. More important, the legal question of military necessity hung over most of the trials. War is, by its nature, violent: it requires the killing and disabling of enemy forces. War crimes law therefore essentially prohibits only those forms of violence that are deemed unnecessary for military success.[4] This criterion is necessarily vague. Whether the issue was overly harsh discipline for POWs, summary execution of captives, reprisals against civilians, the brutal interrogation of suspects, or the failure to provide livable conditions for detainees, the war crimes courts were commonly confronted with the reality that the imperatives of warfare are very different from those of peacetime. The firebombing of Tokyo in 1945 and the atomic-bombing of Hiroshima and Nagasaki cast doubt on the legitimacy of virtually all war crimes charges against Japanese military personnel, because they suggested that truly extreme actions could be justified by military necessity. By the early 1950s, with other, brutal, wars being fought in Asia and with the Cold War seemingly necessitating a new political alliance with Japan, the argument that a line should be drawn under the atrocities of the Second World War without further, detailed, investigation of what had happened, and that a mechanism should be found for the release of the war criminals who remained in prison, appeared irrefutable.

A similar dynamic was at work in Europe. The overall structure of trials in Europe did not differ greatly from that in Asia. The Tokyo Trial had its counterpart in the International Military Tribunal at Nuremberg, which prosecuted 23 leading Nazis and handed down its verdicts in October 1946. Between December 9, 1946, and April 13, 1949, additional international Nuremberg Military Tribunals (NMT) tried cases that in Asia would have been referred to national jurisdictions. Of the 185 defendants in these trials, 142 were convicted. Charges included participating in the massacre of Jews in Eastern Europe, conducting medical experiments on living humans, and procuring slave labor through concentration camps.[5] Because Nazi record keeping was good, the NMT trials raised fewer problems of evidence than did the Japanese cases, but command responsibility and superior orders produced similar difficulties.

In addition, the Allies established their own national military tribunals to deal with German war crimes. The United States government tried 1,672 German suspects in 489 proceedings, convicting 1,416 of them.[6] Smaller numbers of trials were conducted by British, French, and other Western European authorities. As in Japan, Cold War considerations weakened the Allies' interest in pursuing the trials and contributed to the release of the remaining war criminals. Apart from 3 inmates held jointly by the United States, United Kingdom, France, and the Soviet Union in Spandau Prison in Berlin, and fewer than 30 war criminals still in detention in the Netherlands, France, Belgium, and Italy, the last German war criminals left Landsberg Prison in Bavaria in May 1958, three weeks before their Japanese counterparts left Sugamo Prison in Tokyo.[7] The fact that the last Japanese (except a few still held in the PRC) and almost the last German war criminals were released in the same year was not coincidental: officials in the two areas kept a close eye on each other's policies. Although the scale of the Allied trials in Western Europe was smaller than that of the national trials in Asia, both were dwarfed by the volume of hearings in Eastern Europe, where an estimated 52,721 Germans and Austrians were prosecuted, and by trials in the domestic courts of the two German states, in which about 18,000 people were convicted, most of them before 1950.[8]

As we have seen, in contrast with Europe, no prosecutions took place in the Asia-Pacific region for crimes against humanity.[9] That legal term had been adopted to provide a basis for prosecuting the Nazi genocide of European Jews, an action that had no direct connection with the conduct of the war itself. The Japanese military had carried out no comparable campaign of racial extermination in Asia, and the prosecutions in the Asia-Pacific theater therefore referred exclusively to war crimes, not crimes against humanity. The war crimes trials in Europe wound up at about the same time and for much the same reasons as in Asia, but whereas the conclusion of peace settlements provided both reason and justification for drawing a line under the trials for war crimes, no such implicit statute of limitations applied to crimes against humanity.

The 1958 releases ended the pursuit and detention of war criminals in Asia, but reckoning with wartime atrocities took on new life in Europe in the 1960s with Israel's prosecution of Adolf Eichmann in Jerusalem in 1961 and West Germany's 1963–1965 Frankfurt trial of middle- and lower-ranking officials who had worked in the Auschwitz concentration camp.[10] These prosecutions profoundly transformed the pursuit of war criminals. The trials of the 1940s and early 1950s had been understood primarily as a proper calling to account of German and Japanese perpetrators for their wartime crimes. During this process, the prosecuting powers increasingly recognized that in such reckoning, the desire for revenge should be tempered by mercy, political expediency, and practicalities. The trials of the 1960s and afterward, by contrast, were constructed as a response to unqualified evil, a response that should not be constrained by other considerations. In this era, the Nazi attempt to exterminate European Jews moved to center stage in public and official discourse about the war, and the term "Holocaust" became the accepted label for this attempted extermination.[11] A series of high-profile trials of men accused of crimes against humanity in the Nazi era thus took place: Klaus Barbie in 1983, John Demjanjuk in 1988, Antanas Gecas in 1992, Szymon Serafinowicz (age eighty-five) in 1995, Maurice Papon (age eighty-six) in 1997, and Anthony Sawoniuk in 1999.[12] In 2012, ninety-seven-year-old Laszlo Csatary was arrested in Hungary on charges of assisting in the Holocaust.[13] The German government launched a campaign in July 2013 to track down the very last surviving war criminals, using the slogan "Late, but not too late."[14] Two years later, ninety-four-year-old Oskar Groening was sentenced to four years in prison for complicity in the murder of Jews at Auschwitz, and in June 2016, Reinold Hanning, also a ninety-four-year-old former Auschwitz guard, was convicted of being an accessory to the murder of 170,000 Holocaust victims.[15]

The intellectual foundations for this pursuit had been laid in 1946 by the German thinker Karl Jaspers, in a reflection called *Die Schuldfrage* (*The Question of Guilt*). In that work, he set out what continues to be the major argument concerning war guilt.[16] Writing about Germany, Jaspers identified two broad categories of guilt. On one side were the categories of criminal and political guilt, incurred by those who had directly committed criminal acts or had supported or approved of Nazi policies and programs. These forms of guilt could be erased, he suggested, by a political action, including the purge of former Nazis from positions of influence and prosecution of the perpetrators of actual crimes. Then Jaspers described the two categories he called moral and metaphysical guilt. Moral guilt, he suggested, applied to those who had failed to take action that might have prevented crimes, and metaphysical guilt lay in continuing to share an identity with those who had committed crimes.[17] Jaspers did not suggest that Germans bore collective responsibility for the crimes that their leaders and soldiers had committed during the Second World War. Rather, he argued that individual Germans shared responsibility for what the perpetrators had done because they were willing to share a national identity with the perpetrators without specifically repudiating what their forebears had done. In other words, it was impossible to claim innocence by virtue of not having been involved, or not knowing, or even not having been born at the time.[18]

Jaspers's arguments, published in English in 1947 and subsequently repeated many times, have been highly influential in establishing the belief that the people of a nation bear an enduring moral responsibility for indefensible actions carried out by their forebears.[19] We can catch glimpses of these arguments in Western public and official discussions of the Japanese war crimes trials from as early as 1946, even though the arguments were by no means thoroughly developed at that early stage. Given the perception on both sides that the Pacific War was a struggle between civilization and barbarism, it is hardly surprising that immediately after the conflict ended, many on the Allied side still regarded all the Japanese people as collectively responsible for atrocities, despite the official position that rejected such an approach. Jaspers's argument refined the expression of this belief, which perhaps was atavistic, that failure to avenge a crime leaves the universe morally unsatisfied. It was also read easily as an endorsement of a new concept of collective national guilt.

Bracketed by historical coincidence with Nazi atrocities that in the West have come to represent the greatest collective evil of which humankind has been guilty, the war crimes of the Japanese military—appalling in their own right—came to be portrayed as morally equivalent to the Holocaust and thus deserving of the same relentless prosecution and condemnation. The perception of equivalence was made explicit in the subtitle of Iris Chang's influential book *The Rape of Nanking: The Forgotten Holocaust of World War II*.[20] The widespread rebuke for war crimes proffered by other countries to Japan today focuses principally on the alleged failure of the Japanese nation to apologize sincerely and comprehensively for its war crimes, on its alleged failure to deal honestly with those crimes in school textbooks, and on what have been interpreted as signs of respect paid to the memory of war criminals through official visits to Yasukuni Shrine in Tokyo, where their remains are enshrined.[21] These complaints, though sincere, are analytically and morally shaky.

In 1951, in signing the San Francisco Peace Treaty, the Japanese state formally accepted all legal judgments against convicted war criminals. Although Japanese authorities subsequently worked to mitigate the sentences, no Japanese government ever repudiated or overturned them. The only government to repudiate the judgments of the Asian war crimes trials was that of the Republic of Korea, which in 2006 pardoned eighty-three war criminals of Korean ethnicity.[22] In recent decades, government and nongovernment bodies and individuals in Japan have issued numerous apologies for Japan's wartime conduct.[23]

Negative comments about Japan's supposed failure to apologize adequately for wartime crimes are nevertheless so common as to be virtually routine. Such criticism is based on an implicit assumption that Japan's guilt is somehow greater than that of other countries that have committed atrocities, apart from Germany, where the large majority of war crimes trials since the late 1950s have focused on the unique set of circumstances comprising the Holocaust. Japanese forces did not commit genocide, however great their other wartime offenses. Accordingly, Japanese crimes belong in the same broad category as the massacre and torture of prisoners and local civilians and the recruiting of forced labor by British, French, and American forces in colonial territories and elsewhere, and by rival forces in China's internal political conflicts. Yet, calls for apology for British, French, American, and Chinese offenses or for German actions in the Second World War except in the Holocaust, are comparatively rare. Continuing complaints against Japan for its alleged failure to acknowledge war crimes also are influenced by nationalist agendas in China, Korea, and elsewhere.[24] In this picture, the trials of 1945–1951, especially in the national tribunals, are largely invisible. The nonofficial Women's International Tribunal on Japanese Military Sexual Slavery provides one example. The tribunal convened in Tokyo in 2000 to indict Japanese wartime leaders, including the emperor, for rape, sexual slavery, and other sexual crimes carried out during the war years, evidently ignoring the fact that some of these crimes had been dealt with in the national tribunals convened after the Second World War and were part of the evidence presented at the IMTFE.[25]

In dealing with presumed war guilt, Japan and Asia differed from Germany and Europe in one important respect: Japan did not conduct its own war crimes trials, either immediately after the war or in later years. Whereas the two Germanys undertook thousands of trials after the Allied tribunals had ended, the Japanese authorities never prosecuted their own citizens for crimes committed in the course of the war. This difference arose partly from the absence of Holocaust-like crimes in Asia. The guilt of German Holocaust perpetrators was perceived to be unambiguous in a way that the guilt of Japanese war criminals was not. Moreover, there was no distinct category of Japanese society that could be blamed, legally and morally, for wartime crimes in the way that the Nazis and the SS could be blamed in Germany. The Kenpeitai was the closest equivalent, but it had many fewer members. In consequence, those Japanese military personnel who were prosecuted were more easily seen as scapegoats bearing the burden of national guilt, because they represented a broad cross-section of society, especially given that the military relied heavily on conscription for its recruits. Thus, there was no specific group of culprits to pursue to the end in Japan.

In a simple sense, the lack of Japanese trials has been considered as a sign that Japanese society has not repented its war crimes. It has also had more complex consequences. In Japan, the issue of war guilt was not continually revisited through judicial processes. In Europe, by contrast, each trial provided an opportunity to revise the tangled moral and legal issues of guilt surrounding the atrocities of the Second World War. The proceedings against Eichmann, Barbie, and Papon were presented to the world as the implacable working out of universal principles of justice, but in reality they were important stages in the continuing reworking of those principles. Hannah Arendt initiated a new phase in the understanding of crime and justice, for example, when she introduced the term "banality of evil" in her report on the 1961 Eichmann trial.[26] The absence of trials in Asia after the 1950s meant that, on the public stage at least, a similar reworking could not take place.

In failing to initiate their own trials after 1952, however, the Japanese authorities and the public missed a special moral opportunity. Continuing the prosecutions would have cemented Japan's standing as a country that had accepted internationally endorsed sentences against its own subjects for wartime atrocities. International criticism of Japan would thus have been avoided or lessened. More important, as a major world power,

Japan might have played a leading role in encouraging accountability for war crimes in the conflicts that have occurred since the end of the Second World War. Countless war crimes were committed in the colonial, civil, and international wars of the second half of the twentieth century, but none of them led to international prosecutions until the convening of the International Criminal Tribunal for the former Yugoslavia (ICTY) in 1994. Whether a stronger role by Japan in insisting on accountability could have made a difference is speculative. The ICTY and subsequent tribunals have shown, however, that the global community is willing to contemplate international action on war crimes. It is hard to imagine that such willingness would not have been strengthened if Japan had taken a moral and practical lead.

The immediate initiative after the Second World War to prosecute the individual perpetrators of atrocities rather than settling guilt on whole nations was practically, morally, legally, and politically ambitious. In the face of massive problems of logistics, provision of evidence, and procedure, it was an attempt to bring the cold forensic spirit of the peacetime criminal court into the still barely regulated realm of warfare. Not only was it an attempt to allocate guilt precisely and accurately; it also explicitly aimed to avoid the destructive effects of postwar grievance among the defeated that had contributed to the outbreak of the Second World War in Europe. The trials of Japanese war criminals in Asia fell short of achieving this aim because their scope, although impressive, was not enough to deal with the full weight of the guilt created by wartime crimes. Perhaps inevitably, the trial process was thus inadequate to achieve the far-reaching moral goals of its planners. The process was then overtaken by new developments in the global understanding of guilt, without any fresh proceedings to give voice to these new understandings in an Asian context. In consequence, the business that the war crimes trials began to address has come to seem unfinished.

NOTES

INTRODUCTION

1. See Wojciech Sadurski, *Giving Desert Its Due: Social Justice and Legal Theory* (Dordrecht: Reidel, 1985), 49–56.

2. See International Military Tribunal for the Far East Charter, Tokyo, January 19, 1946, http://www.jus.uio.no/english/services/library/treaties/04/4–06/military-tribunal-far-east.xml.

3. Hayashi suggests on these grounds that the Tokyo trials should be referred to as the AB trials (Hayashi Hirofumi, *Senpan saiban no kenkyū* [Tokyo: Bensei shuppan, 2010], 5–6). For the sole national trial including charges of crimes against peace, see "Trial of Takashi Sakai," United Nations War Crimes Commission, *Law Reports of Trials of War Criminals* (London: HMSO, 1949), 14:1–7; Barak Kushner, *Men to Devils, Devils to Men* (Cambridge, MA: Harvard University, 2015), 148–53.

4. Higurashi Yoshinobu, *Tōkyō saiban* (Tokyo: Kōdansha, 2008), 20–22.

5. Ibid., 28–29. For examples of this misperception in the work of otherwise well-informed observers, see John L. Ginn, *Sugamo Prison, Tokyo* (Jefferson, NC: McFarland, 1992), 33; Philip R. Piccigallo, *The Japanese on Trial* (Austin: University of Texas Press, 1979), 33; Kushner, *Men to Devils, Devils to Men*, 7. See also Kosuge Nobuko, "Kaisetsu 1," in *GHQ Nihon senryōshi*, intro. and trans. Kosuge Nobuko and Nagai Hitoshi (Tokyo: Nihon tosho sentā, 1996), 5:1–4; Utsumi Aiko and Nagai Hitoshi, "Kaisetsu," in *Shinbun shiryō ni miru Tōkyō saiban, BC kyū saiban*, ed. Mainichi shinbun seijibu (Tokyo: Gendai shiryō shuppan, 2000), 1:ix.

6. See, for instance, Yuma Totani, *Justice in Asia and the Pacific Region, 1945–1952* (New York: Cambridge University Press, 2015), 179–81.

7. John W. Dower, *Embracing Defeat* (New York: Norton, 1999), 454.

1. DEFINING WAR CRIMES AND CREATING COURTS

1. Philip Towle, "The Japanese Army and Prisoners of War," in *Japanese Prisoners of War*, ed. Philip Towle, Margaret Kosuge, and Yoichi Kibata (London: Hambledon and London, 2000), 1.

2. Philip R. Piccigallo, *The Japanese on Trial* (Austin: University of Texas Press, 1979), 3; Charles G. Roland, "Allied POWs, Japanese Captors, and the Geneva Convention," *War & Society* 9, no. 2 (1991): 84–85.

3. Hull to American Legation, Bern, "American Interests," December 18, 1941, UK National Archives, Kew (hereafter cited as NA [UK]), WO 325/157; Neil Boister and Robert Cryer, eds., *Documents on the Tokyo International Military Tribunal* (Oxford: Oxford University Press, 2008), 58, 106.

4. See Chris van den Wyngaert and Steven Dewulf, eds., *International Criminal Law* (Leiden: Nijhoff, 2011), 462.

5. Quoted in United Nations War Crimes Commission, *History of the United Nations War Crimes Commission and the Development of the Laws of War* (London: HMSO, 1948), 88.

6. *Punishment for War Crimes* (London: HMSO, 1942), 6, 16; Madoka Futamura, *War Crimes Tribunals and Transitional Justice* (London: Routledge, 2008), 166.

7. Although the Nanjing massacre has been characterized as "forgotten," most notably in Iris Chang's *The Rape of Nanking* (New York: Basic Books, 1997), the atrocities received widespread coverage in the Western press. See, for instance, Hallett Abend, "Japanese Curbing Nanking Excesses," *New York Times*, December 19, 1937, 37, which refers uncompromisingly to "the chaos of looting, raping and killing that has made the Japanese entry into Nanking a national disgrace."

8. "Japanese Atrocities at Hong-Kong: Barbarous Treatment of All Races—Both Civilians and Servicemen," *Manchester Guardian*, March 11, 1942, 3; Cabinet Offices to J. S. M. Washington, October 20, 1945, NA (UK), ADM 116/5664; Sybilla Jane Flower, "British Policymakers and the Prisoner-of-War Issue: Perceptions and Responses," in *The History of Anglo-Japanese Relations 1600–2000*, vol. 3, ed. Ian Gow and Yoichi Hirama (Houndmills: Palgrave Macmillan, 2003), 232–34.

9. Hayashi Hirofumi, "The Battle of Singapore, the Massacre of Chinese and Understanding of the Issue in Postwar Japan," *Asia-Pacific Journal: Japan Focus*, July 13, 2009, http://www.japanfocus.org/-Hayashi-Hirofumi/3187 (accessed February 2, 2013); Wai Keng Kwok, *Justice Done?* (New Haven, CN: Yale University Genocide Studies Program Working Paper no. 18, http://www.yale.edu/gsp/publications/ (accessed February 11, 2014).

10. Betty Jeffrey, *White Coolies* (Sydney: Eden Paperbacks, 1954), 4.

11. Tom Lansford, "Bataan Death March," in *World War II in the Pacific*, ed. Stanley Sandler (New York: Taylor & Francis, 2001), 157–60.

12. Ooi Keat Gin, *The Japanese Occupation of Borneo, 1941–45* (London: Routledge, 2011), 91–98.

13. Bernice Archer, *The Internment of Western Civilians Under the Japanese, 1941–1945* (London: RoutledgeCurzon, 2004), 67–110.

14. Gavan McCormack and Hank Nelson, eds., *The Burma–Thailand Railway* (Sydney: Allen & Unwin, 1993); Gavan Daws, *Prisoners of the Japanese* (Melbourne: Scribe, 1994).

15. On the medical experiments in Manchuria, see Sheldon H. Harris, *Factories of Death* (London: Routledge, 1994).

16. Richard Connaughton, John Pimlott, and Duncan Anderson, *Battle for Manila* (London: Bloomsbury, 1995).

17. Trial of Ichikawa Seigi and others, NA (UK), WO 235/961.

18. For extensive summations and analyses of Japanese war crimes, see Lord Russell of Liverpool, *The Knights of Bushido* (London: Cassell, 1958); Yuki Tanaka, *Hidden Horrors* (Boulder, CO: Westview, 1996).

19. This explanation is commonly found in prisoner of war memoirs and in popular, semischolarly works. See Rohan Rivett, *Behind Bamboo* (Sydney: Angus & Robertson, 1946); and Meirion Harries and Susie Harries, *Soldiers of the Sun* (New York: Random House, 1991). For a thoughtful critique of this approach, see Beatrice Trefalt, "Fanaticism, Japanese Soldiers and the Pacific War, 1937–45," in *Fanaticism and Conflict in the Modern Age*, ed. Matthew Hughes and Gaynor Johnson (Abingdon: Frank Cass, 2005), 33–47.

20. Chang (in *The Rape of Nanking*) and others have explicitly compared Japanese treatment of Chinese in China and elsewhere to the German persecution of Jews, but the extensive Japanese atrocities against Chinese people lacked the intention of racial extermination that characterized the Holocaust. Nor do genocide scholars normally recognize Japanese atrocities as genocidal. See, for instance, Kinue Tokudome, "The Holocaust and Japanese Atrocities," in *Is the Holocaust Unique?*, ed. Alan S. Rosenbaum (Boulder, CO: Westview, 2009), 201–13.

21. John W. Dower, *War Without Mercy* (New York: Pantheon, 1986), 37.

22. International Military Tribunal for the Far East, Judgment, chap. 8, "Conventional War Crimes (Atrocities)," 1003, http://www.legal-tools.org/uploads/tx_ltpdb/JU01-07-a_01.pdf.

23. Daws, *Prisoners of the Japanese*, 295–97.

24. "Grounds for Remission" [April 1953], NA (UK), FO 371/105441.

25. See, for instance, the annotations on photographic evidence submitted in support of later Dutch internee claims for compensation in Diplomatic Record Office, Tokyo (Gaikō shiryōkan), B'-3-1-2-10. On the experience of the European population in the Netherlands Indies during the Occupation, see L. de Jong, *The Collapse of a Colonial Society* (Leiden: KITLV Press, 2002); and Archer, *The Internment of Western Civilians*.

26. "Texts of Statements by Secretary of State Hull on Abuse of U.S. Prisoners by Japanese," *New York Times*, February 12, 1944, 5.

27. "Proclamation by the Heads of Governments, United States, China and the United Kingdom," July 26, 1945, U.S. Department of State, *Foreign Relations of the United States: Diplomatic Papers: The Conference of Berlin (the Potsdam Conference), 1945* (Washington, D.C.: U.S. Government Printing Office, 1945), 2:1476.

28. "Declaration of Amnesty," *American Journal of International Law* 18, no. 2, suppl.: "Official Documents" (April 1924), 92–95. On the Ottoman trials, see Gary Jonathan Bass, *Stay the Hand of Vengeance* (Princeton, NJ: Princeton University Press, 2000), 106–46.

29. Bass, *Stay the Hand of Vengeance,* 58–105; Jürgen Matthäus, "The Lessons of Leipzig: Punishing German War Criminals After the First World War," in *Atrocities on Trial*, ed. Patricia Heberer and Jürgen Matthäus (Lincoln: University of Nebraska Press, 2008), 3–23.

30. Alan Kramer, "The First Wave of International War Crimes Trials: Istanbul and Leipzig," *European Review* 14 (2006): 441–55; Matthäus, "The Lessons of Leipzig."

31. The most influential statement of this argument, and one of the earliest, was John Maynard Keynes, *The Economic Consequences of the Peace* (New York: Harcourt Brace, 1920).

32. For evidence of the enduring impact of the Leipzig failure, see the pamphlet prepared for American soldiers, [U.S.] War Department Education Manual EM 11, G-1 Roundtable ser., "What Shall Be Done with The War Criminals?" 1944, 13–19, in American History Center, Ateneo de Manila University, Manila; War Cabinet, Minute by the Secretary of State for Foreign Affairs, "Treatment of War Criminals," June 22, 1942, 2, NA (UK), CAB 66/25/44; "Punishment of War Criminals," *House of Lords*, October 7, 1942, col. 556–59.

33. *Report of Robert H. Jackson, U.S. Representative to the International Conference on Military Trials, London, 1945* (Washington, D.C.: U.S. Department of State, 1949), 46, 49.

34. International Military Tribunal for the Far East, Transcript of Proceedings, November 12, 1948, 49,749, PURL: https://www.legal-tools.org/doc/9aeof4.

35. Legal Section, Supreme Commander for the Allied Powers (hereafter cited as SCAP), "Trials of Class 'B' and 'C' War Criminals," 38, May 19, 1952, National Archives and Records Administration, College Park, MD (hereafter cited as NARA), RG331, Box 3676.

36. Ibid.

37. See, for example, John W. Dower, *Embracing Defeat* (New York: Norton, 1999); and Mark E. Caprio and Yoneyuki Sugita, "Introduction: The U.S. Occupation of Japan—Innovation, Continuity, and Compromise," in *Democracy in Occupied Japan*, ed. Mark E. Caprio and Yoneyuki Sugita (London: Routledge, 2007), 1–25.

38. See, for instance, "Probe of Jap Plot Started," *Manila Times*, November 23, 1945, 4; "Japan's Evil Spirit," *New York Times*, October 2, 1946, 28.

39.   For discussion of publicity given in Japan by the Occupation authorities to Japanese wartime atrocities, see Dower, *Embracing Defeat*, 506. Allied policies were based on similar considerations in prosecuting German war criminals. See Frank Buscher, *The U.S. War Crimes Trial Program in Germany, 1946–1955* (New York: Greenwood Press, 1989), 7–22.

40.   "Chinese Move to Find Guilty," *Straits Times*, June 8, 1946, 5.

41.   "Yamashita Behind Bars," *New York Times*, September 4, 1945, 4; "Yamashita Shift Asked: Singapore's Chinese Want Him to Stand Trial There," *New York Times*, September 17, 1945, 3. Here and elsewhere, we use the terms "alleged" and "allegedly" to identify persons who might be considered as war criminals but who had not (yet) been determined as criminal in a court of law.

42.   On propaganda on both sides during the Pacific War, see Dower, *War Without Mercy*.

43.   Gavan McCormack, "Apportioning the Blame: Australian Trials for Railway Crimes," in McCormack and Nelson, eds., *The Burma–Thailand Railway*, 89.

44.   Hayashi Hirofumi, *BC-kyū senpan saiban* (Tokyo: Iwanami shoten, 2005), 82; Piccigallo, *The Japanese on Trial*, 84; Beatrice Trefalt, "Japanese War Criminals in Indochina and the French Pursuit of Justice: Local and International Constraints," *Journal of Contemporary History* 49, no. 4 (2014): 729.

45.   See also Yuma Totani, *The Tokyo War Crimes Trial* (Cambridge, MA.: Harvard University Asia Center, 2008), 162; Narrelle Morris, "Justice for 'Asian' Victims: The Australian War Crimes Trials of the Japanese, 1945–51," in *The Hidden Histories of War Crimes Trials*, ed. Kevin Jon Heller and Gerry Simpson (Oxford: Oxford University Press, 2013), 348–66; J. A. Pilcher, "Clemency for Class B and C Japanese War Criminals," September 11, 1953, NA (UK), FO 371/105447.

46.   See A. Gledhill, "Some Aspects of the Operation of International and Military Law in Burma, 1941–1945," *Modern Law Review* 12 (1939): 197.

47.   "Kort verslag over de bespreking van de Procureur-Generaal met enkele Britsche militaire autoriteiten in Singapore, inzake de berechting van oorlogsmisdadigers," December 11 and 13, 1945, Arsip Nasional (Jakarta), Alg. Sec. 288.

48.   See Timothy Brook, *Collaboration* (Cambridge, MA: Harvard University Press, 2004); Han Ming Guang, "Collaboration During the Japanese Occupation" (BA honors thesis, National University of Singapore, 2010), 7–19; Abu Talib Ahmad, *Malay-Muslims, Islam, and the Rising Sun* (Kuala Lumpur: Malaysian Branch of the Royal Asiatic Society, 2003), 91–124; Konrad Mitchell Lawson, "Wartime Atrocities and the Politics of Treason in the Ruins of the Japanese Empire, 1937–1953" (PhD diss., Harvard University, 2012).

49.   "Soekarno Is Quisling: Like Laurel and Bamaw, Says 'Washington Post,'" *Cairns Post*, October 31, 1945, 3. See also Jean Esmein, "Le Juge Henri Bernard au procès de Tōkyō," *Vingtième siècle*, no. 59 (1998): 4.

50.   See Denyse Tessensohn, "The British Military Administration's Treason Trial of Dr Charles Joseph Pemberton Paglar, 1946" (MA thesis, National University of

Singapore, 2007); F. S. V. Donnison, *British Military Administration in the Far East 1943–46* (London: HMSO, 1956), 303.

51.   Teodoro A. Agoncillo, *The Burden of Proof* (Mandaluyong, Metro Manila: University of the Philippines Press, 1984).

52.   George E. Erickson, "United States Navy War Crimes Trials (1945–1949)," *Washburn Law Journal* 5 (1965): 105.

53.   Margherita Zanasi, "Globalizing Hanjian: The Suzhou Trials and the Post–World War II Discourse on Collaboration," *American Historical Review* 113, no. 3 (June 2008): 731–51.

54.   Mas Slamet, *Japanese Souls in Indonesian Bodies* (Batavia: np, 1946).

55.   Lawson, "Wartime Atrocities," 128–64.

56.   Hayashi Hirofumi, "British War Crimes Trials of Japanese," *Nature-People-Society: Science and the Humanities* (Kanto Gakuin University) 31 (July 2001), http://www .geocities.jp/hhhirofumi/eng08.htm (accessed February 14, 2014). See also Morris, "Justice for 'Asian' Victims"; R. John Pritchard, "The Nature and Significance of British Post-War Trials of Japanese War Criminals, 1945–1948," *Proceedings* (British Association for Japanese Studies) 2 (1977): 201.

57.   See Trefalt, "Japanese War Criminals in Indochina," 733–34.

58.   See, for instance, "Hanging Urged for Guilty Japs," *Courier-Mail* (Brisbane), October 5, 1945, 1.

59.   *New York Times*, September 2, 1945, 1; *New York Times*, September 12, 1945, 10; *Newcastle Morning Herald and Miners' Advocate*, January 12, 1946, 4; *Daily News* (Perth), January 15, 1946, 2; *Sydney Morning Herald*, January 16, 1946, 2. See also "Aziatisch barbarisme van de Japanners," *Het vrije volk*, January 31, 1946, 1; "Japanese Cruelty to Prisoners: Evidence of Torture at Singapore," *Scotsman*, September 7, 1945, 5. There are hundreds of such reports.

60.   "Want Japs Executed: Returned Men's Demand," *Newcastle Morning Herald and Miners' Advocate*, January 21, 1946, 4; "Punish Jap Criminals, says R.S.L.," *Mail* (Adelaide), January 26, 1946, 1; "Victims Cry for Revenge," *Examiner* (Launceston, Tas.), January 26, 1946, 1.

61.   "Mercy Is Not Called For," *News* (Adelaide), January 23, 1946, 2.

62.   "Month's Gaol for War Crimes: Ex-Servicemen Protest Darwin Sentences 'Absurd,'" *West Australian*, March 18, 1946, 8; Caroline Pappas, "Law and Politics Australia's War Crimes Trials in the Pacific, 1943–1961" (PhD diss., Australian Defence Force Academy, University of New South Wales, 2001), 52.

63.   "Demands for Sterner Darwin Trials," *Sydney Morning Herald*, March 18, 1946, 3; Dean Aszkielowicz, "After the Surrender: Australia and the Japanese Class B and C War Criminals, 1945–1958" (PhD diss., Murdoch University, 2012), 165.

64.   A. Berriedale Keith, *Wheaton's International Law* (7th ed., 1944), 586, cited in William H. Parks, "Command Responsibility for War Crimes," *Military Law Review* 62 (1973): 16.

65.   Nagai Hitoshi, "Sensō hanzainin ni kansuru seifu seimei an: Higashikuni naikaku ni yoru kakugi kettei no myakuraku," *Nenpō: Nihon gendaishi* 10 (December 2005): 278–80.

66. Gabriella Venturini, "Necessity in the Law of Armed Conflict and in International Criminal Law," *Netherlands Yearbook of International Law* 41 (2010): 51. Among the few exceptions to the idea that military necessity provided overriding justification for military actions taken during hostilities was an objection to perfidy (breaking a promise to act in good faith). Opening fire during an agreed truce, for example, was considered to contravene the laws of war.

67. "Convention with Respect to the Laws and Customs of War on Land" (Hague 2, July 29, 1899), http://avalon.law.yale.edu/19th_century/hague02.asp; "Convention Concerning Bombardment by Naval Forces in Time of War" (Hague 9, October 18, 1907), http://avalon.law.yale.edu/20th_century/hague09.asp.

68. Judith Gail Gardam, *Non-Combatant Immunity as a Norm of International Humanitarian Law* (Dordrecht: Nijhoff, 1993), 16–26.

69. *Violation of the Laws and Customs of War: Reports of Majority and Dissenting Reports of American and Japanese Members of the Commission of Responsibilities, Conference of Paris, 1919* (Oxford: Clarendon, 1919), 17–18.

70. For discussion of this issue, see Gillian Triggs, "Australia's War Crimes Trials: All Pity Choked," in *The Law of War Crimes*, ed. Timothy L. H. McCormack and Gerry J. Simpson (The Hague: Kluwer Law International, 1997), 141.

71. Geneva Convention Relative to the Protection of Civilian Persons in Time of War of 12 August 1949, http://www.icrc.org/eng/assets/files/publications/icrc-002-0173 .pdf.

72. Terrance C. McGovern, Mark A. Berhow, and Chris Taylor, *American Defenses of Corregidor and Manila Bay 1898–1945* (Oxford: Osprey, 2003), 42.

73. See ICRC, Customary IHL, Rule 47. Attacks Against Persons hors de combat, http://www.icrc.org/customary-ihl/eng/docs/v1_rul_rule47#refFn_62_22.

74. Meyer (Admiralty) to Bradshaw (WO), December 15, 1945, NA (UK) ADM 116/5664.

75. Douglas Gillison, *Australia in the War of 1939–1945*, vol. 1, *Royal Australian Air Force 1939–1942*, 3 ser., vol. 1, *Air* (Canberra: Australian War Memorial, 1962), 694–95.

76. "No Jap Survivors of Convoy Holocaust," *Mirror* (Perth), March 6, 1943, 7; George H. Johnston, "Remnants of Jap Convoy Sunk," *Argus* (Melbourne), March 6, 1943, 1.

77. Dower, *War Without Mercy*, 69; Ulrich Straus, *The Anguish of Surrender* (Seattle: University of Washington Press, 2003), 117; Niall Ferguson, "Prisoner Taking and Prisoner Killing in the Age of Total War: Towards a Political Economy of Military Defeat," *War in History* 11, no. 2 (April 2004): 180–82.

78. See N. C. H. Dunbar, "Military Necessity in War Crimes Trials," *British Yearbook of International Law* 29 (1952): 442–52.

79. See Jean-Marie Henckaerts and Louise Doswald-Beck, *Customary International Humanitarian Law*, vol. 1, *Rules* (Cambridge: Cambridge University Press, 2007), 46–50.

80. Günter Hoog and Angela Steinmetz, eds., *International Conventions on Protection of Humanity and Environment* (Berlin: De Gruyter, 1993), 287–89.

81. War Cabinet 34 (44), "Conclusions of a Meeting of the War Cabinet Held at 10 Downing Street, S.W.1, on Monday, 13th March, 1944, at 6.30 p.m.," NA (UK), CAB 65/41/34, 158–59; Arieh J. Kochavi, *Prelude to Nuremberg* (Chapel Hill: University of North Carolina Press, 1998), 63–91. See also War Cabinet, Minute by the Secretary of State for Foreign Affairs [Eden], "Treatment of War Criminals," June 22, 1942, 2–3, NA (UK), CAB 66/25/44.

82. Bradley F. Smith, *The Road to Nuremberg* (New York: Basic Books, 1981), 95–107; Jonathan A. Bush, " 'The Supreme . . . Crime' and Its Origins: The Lost Legislative History of the Crime of Aggressive War," *Columbia Law Review* 102, no. 8 (December 2002): 2324–2424.

83. "General Treaty for Renunciation of War as an Instrument of National Policy, Signed at Paris, August 27, 1928," *Recueil des traités et des engagements internationaux enregistrés par le Secrétariat de la Société des Nations* 94, nos. 1–4 (1929): 57–64.

84. UNWCC, *History of the United Nations War Crimes Commission*, 232–61; *Report of Robert H. Jackson*.

85. See, for instance, James T. Shotwell, "What Is 'War as an Instrument of National Policy?' " *Proceedings of the Academy of Political Science* 13, no. 2 (1929): 25–30.

86. See Chihiro Hosoya, "Miscalculations in Deterrent Policy: Japanese–U.S. Relations, 1938–1941," *Journal of Peace Research* 5, no. 2 (1968): 97–115; Edward S. Miller, *Bankrupting the Enemy* (Annapolis, MD: Naval Institute Press, 2007).

87. UNWCC, *History of the United Nations War Crimes Commission*, 188–220.

88. The name of the commission reflected the wartime characterization of the Allies as the "United Nations." The international organization now known as the United Nations, which came into being on October 24, 1945, was at first commonly referred to as the United Nations Organization (UNO) to distinguish it from the wartime alliance.

89. The UNWCC also had its own separate Pacific and Far Eastern Committee, drawn from the commission's London-based members.

90. J. E. Edmonds and L. Oppenheim, *Land Warfare* (1912), cited in Alan M. Wilner, "Superior Orders as a Defense to Violations of International Criminal Law," *Maryland Law Review* 26, no. 2 (1966): 131–32. See also Gary D. Solis, "Obedience of Orders and the Law of War: Judicial Application in American Forums," *American University International Law Review* 15, no. 2 (1999): 481–526.

91. Wilner, "Superior Orders," 136–37; Aszkielowicz, "After the Surrender," 123–24. See also the discussions in NA (UK), WO 32/11170.

92. Charter of the International Military Tribunal (also known as the London Charter), in M. Cherif Bassiouni, *Crimes Against Humanity* (Cambridge: Cambridge University Press, 2011), 638. Also see the discussion in NA (UK), LCO 53/78.

93. "Imperial Rescript to Soldiers and Sailors 1882," in *Modern Japan*, ed. Arthur E. Tiedemann (Princeton, NJ: Van Nostrand, 1955), 107–12.

94. Article 57, Rikugun keihō, Nakano bunko, http://www.geocities.jp/nakanolib/hou/hm41–46.htm. The Navy Penal Code (Kaigun keihō, 1908) made similar provisions in article 57, http://www.geocities.jp/nakanolib/hou/hm41–48.htm.

95. Edward J. Drea, *Japan's Imperial Army* (Lawrence: University Press of Kansas, 2009), 68, 161.

96. See Coox's discussion of this point in regard to penalties if a commander surrendered to the enemy (Alvin D. Coox, *Nomonhan* [Stanford, CA: Stanford University Press, 1985], 958).

97. Drea, *Japan's Imperial Army*, 259; Clive Emsley, *Soldier, Sailor, Beggarman, Thief* (Oxford: Oxford University Press, 2013), 73.

98. Edward J. Drea, "In the Army Barracks of Imperial Japan," *Armed Forces & Society* 15 (1989): 334.

99. "Sheet 61–66 of Imamura Evidence in Trial of Itsui Hiroshi and Tokoro Kenichi," October 11, 1950, National Archives of Australia (hereafter cited as NAA), 739672. References to the Australian archives in this book give the item's barcode.

100. UNWCC, *History of the United Nations War Crimes Commission*, 435–74.

101. Moscow Conference, October 1943, "Statement on Atrocities, Signed by President Roosevelt, Prime Minister Churchill and Premier Stalin," http://avalon.law.yale.edu/wwii/moscow.asp.

102. See the discussion in NA (UK), WO 32/12640.

103. "Proposed Central War Crimes Agency for Japan," NAA 187951; "Dutch Right to Claim War Crimes Suspects and Hold Them in N.E.I.," D.A.G. to HQ ALFSEA, June 25, 1946, NA (UK), WO 203/6087. See also Simon C. Smith, "Crimes and Punishment: Local Responses to the Trial of Japanese War Criminals in Malaya and Singapore, 1946–48," *South East Asia Research* 5 (March 1997): 43.

104. See map 2, Area Commands Pacific Theater, in Charles W. Bogg, *Marine Aviation in the Philippines* (Washington, D.C.: Historical Division, Headquarters, U.S. Marine Corps, 1951).

105. S. Woodburn Kirby, *The War Against Japan*, vol. 5, *The Surrender of Japan* (London: HMSO, 1969), 225.

106. Ibid., 224; SCAP General Order no. 1, *Political Reorientation of Japan September 1945 to September 1948* (Washington, D.C.: U.S. Government Printing Office, 1949), 2, 442–44; Henry I. Shaw, *The United States Marines in North China, 1945–1949* (Washington, D.C.: Historical Branch, G-3 Division, U.S. Marine Corps, 1968).

107. Eiji Takemae, *Inside GHQ*, trans. Robert Ricketts and Sebastian Swann (London: Continuum, 2002), 53.

108. David G. Marr, *Vietnam 1945* (Berkeley: University of California Press, 1995); Benedict R. O'G. Anderson, *Java in a Time of Revolution* (Ithaca, NY: Cornell University Press, 1972).

109. See Peter Dennis, *Troubled Days of Peace* (New York: St. Martin's Press, 1987).

110. Piccigallo, *The Japanese on Trial*, 83.

111. "French Law Concerning Trials of War Criminals by Military Tribunals and by Military Government Courts in the French Zone of Germany," in United Nations War Crimes Commission, *Law Reports of Trials of War Criminals* (London: HMSO, 1948), 3:93–96; Ordonnance du 28 août 1944 relative à la répression des

crimes de guerre, http://www.legifrance.gouv.fr/affichTexte.do?cidTexte=LEGITE
XT000006070700&dateTexte= .

112.   Royal Warrant—Regulations for the Trial of War Criminals, http://avalon.law.yale.
edu/imt/imtroyal.asp. In practice, British commanders seeking clarification of what
constituted a war crime were referred to the UNWCC list. See Allied Land Forces,
South East Asia, War Crimes Instruction no. 1, November 1945, Arkib Negara
Malaysia, Secretariat Dept/17/91 Legal. War Crimes Instructions.

113.   "United States Law and Practice Concerning Trials of War Criminals by Military
Commissions, Military Government Courts and Military Tribunals," in United
Nations War Crimes Commission, *Law Reports of Trials of War Criminals*,
3:103–4.

114.   Trial of Akiyoshi Hosokawa, Guam, September 12, 1945, NARA, RG 125, research.
archives.gov/description/6997345; trial of Juan Muna, Guam, December 28, 1944,
NARA, RG 125, research.archives.gov/description/6997327.

115.   "United States Law and Practice," in United Nations War Crimes Commission,
Law Reports of Trials of War Criminals, 3:106.

116.   Ibid., 105–7.

117.   "Australian Law Concerning Trials of War Criminals by Military Courts," in
United Nations War Crimes Commission, *Law Reports of Trials of War Criminals*
(London: HMSO, 1948), 5:94–97.

118.   "Netherlands Law Concerning Trials of War Criminals," in United Nations War
Crimes Commission, *Law Reports of Trials of War Criminals* (London: HMSO,
1949), 11:86–102.

119.   "Chinese Law Concerning Trials of War Criminals," in United Nations War Crimes
Commission, *Law Reports of Trials of War Criminals* (London: HMSO, 1949),
14:151–55. Taiwan had been a Japanese colony since 1895. The Taiwanese people were thus Japanese subjects during the war and had never been citizens of the
Republic of China, which had been founded only in 1911. The Chinese government
established its authority on Taiwan in October 1945 and issued a decree on January 12, 1946, retrospectively bestowing Chinese citizenship on Taiwanese people
from October 25, 1945. In prosecuting Taiwanese war crimes suspects, however, all
Allied authorities disregarded this postwar change of status. We thank Lan Shichi
(National Chengchi University) for this information.

120.   William F. Nimmo, *Behind a Curtain of Silence* (Westport, CN: Greenwood Press,
1988); Andrew Barshay, *The Gods Left First* (Berkeley: University of California
Press, 2013); Petra Buchholz, *Vom Teufel zum Menschen* (Munich: Iudicium,
2010).

121.   V. A. Gavrilov and E. L. Katasonova, eds., *Iaponskie voennoplennye v SSSR 1945–
1956* (Moscow: Demokratiia, 2013), 15. We are grateful to David Wells for translat-
ing this source for us.

122.   Ling Yan, "The 1956 Japanese War Crimes Trials in China," in *Historical Origins
of International Criminal Law*, ed. Morten Bergsmo, Cheah Wui Ling, and Yi Ping
(Brussels: Torkel Opsahl Academic EPublisher, 2014), 2:222–23.

123. Piccigallo, *The Japanese on Trial*, 185–87.

124. Ibid., 68–74.

125. Aszkielowicz, "After the Surrender," 90.

126. See Jeanie M. Welch, "Without a Hangman, Without a Rope: Navy War Crimes Trials After World War II," *International Journal of Naval History* 1, no. 1 (April 2002), http://www.ijnhonline.org/wp-content/uploads/2012/01/pdf_welch.pdf (accessed October 1, 2014).

127. U.S. Armed Forces, Pacific, Regulations Governing the Trial of War Criminals (September 24, 1945), cited in Parks, "Command Responsibility for War Crimes," 17; Piccigallo, *The Japanese on Trial*, 188.

128. "Chinese Law Concerning Trials of War Criminals," 151–55.

129. UNWCC, *History of the United Nations War Crimes Commission*, 474; Robert Cribb, "Avoiding Clemency: The Trial and Transfer of Japanese War Criminals in Indonesia, 1946–1949," *Japanese Studies* 31, no. 2 (2011): 153.

130. "French Law Concerning Trials of War Criminals by Military Tribunals and by Military Government Courts in the French Zone of Germany," 93–96; Ordonnance du 28 août 1944 relative à la répression des crimes de guerre.

131. R. John Pritchard, "The Parameters of Justice: The Evolution of British Civil and Military Perspectives on War Crimes Trials and Their Legal Context (1942–1956)," in *International Humanitarian Law*, ed. John Carey, William V. Dunlap, and R. John Pritchard (Leiden: Brill, 2006), 3:295–98.

132. Michael O. Lacey, "Military Commissions: A Historical Survey," *Army Lawyer*, no. 3 (2002): 41–47.

133. See, for instance, David Creed, Moira Raynor, and Sue Rickard, " 'It Will Not Be Bound by the Ordinary Rules of Evidence . . . ,' " *Journal of the Australian War Memorial* 27 (October 1995): 47–53.

134. Dower, *Embracing Defeat*, 475. See also Utsumi Aiko, "Changing Japanese Views of the Allied Occupation of Japan and the War Crimes Trials," *Journal of the Australian War Memorial* 30 (1997), http://www.awm.gov.au/journal/j30/utsumi.asp (accessed August 2, 2015).

135. Nagai, "Sensō hanzainin ni kansuru seifu seimei an," 282–99.

136. [U.S.] War Department Education Manual, "What Shall Be Done with the War Criminals?" 18.

137. Dower, *Embracing Defeat*, 475–77.

138. Le Haut-Commissionaire de France pour l'Indochine (Saigon) to Chef de la mission militaire française (Tokyo), August 27, 1946, and "Affaire d'homicide à Kratie," Archives nationales d'outre-mer, Aix-en-Provence, HCI 122.379. See Trefalt, "Japanese War Criminals," 729.

139. "Jap Sent British Officer to Underground Cell," *Straits Times*, June 27, 1946, 5.

140. "De beul van Tjideng," *Het Dagblad*, November 29, 1945, 2.

141. "War Service Histories of War Criminal Suspects Held at Bangkwang Gaol, Bangkok" [July 1946], 53, NA (UK), FO 371/57570; Peter Davies, *The Man Behind the Bridge* (London: Athlone Press, 1991), 149–50.

142. Peter Lowe, "An Embarrassing Necessity: The Tokyo Trial of Japanese Leaders, 1946–48," in *The Trial in History*, ed. R. A. Melikan (Manchester: Manchester University Press, 2003), 2:139–40; "No Jap Tribunals for War Criminals," *Straits Times*, December 4, 1945, 4.

143. Robert A. Scalapino, *The Japanese Communist Movement, 1920–1966* (Berkeley: University of California Press, 1967), 52.

144. Totani, *The Tokyo War Crimes Trial*, 21–32.

2. INVESTIGATION AND ARREST

1. Memoirs of Captain J. E. Lawson, Imperial War Museum, London, PP/MCR 285 Ts Memoir JEL/1, undated.

2. D. C. S. Sissons, "The Australian War Crimes Trials and Investigations (1942–51)," unpublished manuscript, 4–5, http://www.ocf.berkeley.edu/~changmin/documents /Sissons%20Final%20War%20Crimes%20Text%2018-3-06.pdf.

3. Sir William Webb, "A Report on Japanese Atrocities and Breaches of the Rules of Warfare by Sir William Webb," 1943–1944, National Archives of Australia (hereafter cited as NAA), Canberra, 1580069.

4. Sissons, "The Australian War Crimes Trials," 6.

5. Draft letter to H. G. Wilkie, Chief Secretary to Government of Burma, October 31, 1945, India Office Records (hereafter cited as IOR), IOR/M/4/3038, 184; Chief Secretary of the Government of Burma to L. B. Walsh Atkins (Burma Office), December 21, 1945, IOR/M/4/3038, 170; "Memorandum of a Meeting Held in the Office of the Chief Secretary to the Government of Burma at 11 A.M. on Monday, the 28th November 1945," National Archives of Myanmar (hereafter cited as NAM), accession no. 541, file 4M-8.

6. Deputy Chief of Police, Intelligence, to All SCAOs, 13 July 1945, NAM, accession no. 328, file C-8.

7. HQ 12th Army, SEAC, to 17 Ind Div, 19 Ind Div, North Burma Area, South Burma Dist, 551 Sub Area, December 8, 1945, NAM accession no 541 file 4M-8.

8. Trial of Tsuruoka Shiroo, Singapore, April 1946, UK National Archives (hereafter cited as NA [UK]), WO 235/838.

9. Legal Section, Supreme Commander for the Allied Powers (hereafter cited as SCAP), "Trials of Class 'B' and 'C' War Criminals," 41, May 19, 1952, National Archives and Records Administration, College Park, MD (hereafter cited as NARA), RG331, Box 3676; George E. Erickson, "United States Navy War Crimes Trials (1945–1949)," *Washburn Law Journal* 5 (1965): 94.

10. Sharon Williams Chamberlain, "Justice and Reconciliation" (PhD diss., George Washington University, 2010), 52.

11. State–War–Navy Coordinating Subcommittee for the Far East, "Politico-Military Problems in the Far East: The Apprehension and Punishment of War Criminals," August 9, 1945, NARA, RG165, Box 580.

12. *Staatsblad van Nederlandsch-Indië* 15031, "Toelichting op de ontworpen wetgeving inzake oorlogsmisdrijven," 21–22, Nationaal Archief, The Hague (hereafter cited as NA [NL]), Collectie 584 L. F. de Groot, 1946–1991, toegang 2.21.281.31, inv.nr. 8; L. de Jong, *Het Koninkrijk der Nederlanden in de Tweede Wereldoorlog* (The Hague: SDU, 1988), 870; Iris Heidebrink, "Military Tribunals in the Netherlands Indies," in *Encyclopedia of Indonesia in the Pacific War*, ed. Peter Post et al. (Leiden: Brill, 2010), 411; Peter Dennis, *Troubled Days of Peace* (Manchester: Manchester University Press, 1987), 79.

13. Note pour Monsieur le Secrétaire Général du Comité de l'Indochine, "Objet: a/s de la recherche des crimes de guerre en Indochine," October 30, 1945, Archives nationales d'outre-mer, Aix-en-Provence (hereafter cited as ANOM), INF159/1364. On Roosevelt's attitudes to French Indochina, see Walter LaFeber, "Roosevelt, Churchill, and Indochina: 1942–45," *American Historical Review* 80, no. 5 (December 1975): 1277–95.

14. "Proceedings Against War Criminals (dispatch from Australian representative Chungking)," April 3, 1946, Archives New Zealand (hereafter cited as ANZ), 20106175. On China's involvement with the UNWCC, see Wen-Wei Lai, "China, the Chinese Representative, and the Use of International Law to Counter Japanese Acts of Aggression: China's Standpoint on UNWCC Jurisdiction," *Criminal Law Forum* 25 (2014): 111–32.

15. United Nations War Crimes Commission (UNWCC), *History of the United Nations War Crimes Commission and the Development of the Laws of War* (London: HMSO, 1948), 151–53, 514.

16. See, for instance, the UNWCC's charge prepared in relation to atrocities in Tarawa in the Gilbert Islands, NA (UK), TS 26/830.

17. Dean Aszkielowicz, "After the Surrender: Australia and the Japanese Class B and C War Criminals, 1945–1958" (PhD diss., Murdoch University, 2012), 96.

18. General Headquarters, Far East Command, "Summary of War Crimes Trials," October 19, 1949, 2, National Archives of Japan (hereafter cited as NAJ), 4B-23–5855.

19. "War Crimes: Australian War Crimes Commission and the Apprehension and Trial of Japanese War Criminals," NAA 187951; "Note for Officers Completing Investigation Reports (appendix "A" ALFSEA War Crimes Instr. no. 1)," Arkib Negara Malaysia, Secretariat Dept/17/91.

20. "Kempei Parade in K. Lumpur," *Straits Times*, September 27, 1946, 6; Aszkielowicz, "After the Surrender," 98; Arujunan Narayanan, "Second World War Japanese Atrocities and British Minor War Crimes Trials: The Issue of Fair Trial in Four Selected British Minor War Crimes Trials in Malaya and Singapore in 1946–1947" (PhD diss., University of Wales, Aberystwyth, 2003), 118–19; HQ ALFSEA to C in C HK, December 31, 1945, Public Record Office, Hong Kong (hereafter cited as PRO [HK]), 169-2-147.

21. Quarterly Historical Report of War Crimes, GHQ FARELF (WE 609/1/46) for the quarter ending December 31, 1947, NA (UK), WO 268/104.

22.   See Legal Section, SCAP, "Trials of Class 'B' and 'C' War Criminals," 54; Bridgland (London) to External Affairs, October 31, 1945, NAA 187954; C in C HK to War Office December 18, 1945, PRO (HK), 169–2-147.

23.   List of Suspects, September 26, 1945, and S.E.A.C. Theatre, List of Suspects No. 2, October 1, 1945, NA (UK), TS 26/892.

24.   See nicknames card file in NA (UK), WO 356/23.

25.   "World's Biggest Manhunt in S.E. Asia," *Straits Times* (Sunday ed.), July 14, 1946, 4; Aszkielowicz, "After the Surrender," 97; General Headquarters, Far East Command, "Summary of War Crimes Trials," 2; Erickson, "United States Navy War Crimes Trials," 101–2.

26.   Direk Jayanama, *Thailand and World War II* (Chiang Mai: Silkworm Books, 2008), 294–95; Eastman (Singapore) to War Cabinet, December 14, 1945, NAA 187953.

27.   See A. H. C. Gieben, "Oorlogsmisdaden," March 18, 1946, Arsip Nasional, Jakarta (hereafter cited as ARNAS), Algemene Secretarie 288.

28.   Kirby to Evatt and Dunk, Cablegram 147 [BATAVIA], July 4, 1946, in W. J. Hudson and R. G. Neale, eds., *Documents on Australian Foreign Policy, 1937–49* (Canberra: Australian Government Publishing Service, 1993), 10:22.

29.   "Amendments to S.E.A.C. Theatre Lists of Suspects Nos. 1–23," June 28, 1946, ANZ R20106146.

30.   Monthly summation report of Legal Section, Manila, for the period March 20, 1946, to April 20, 1946, NARA, RG331, Box 893. See also the interrogation reports in NA (NL), Marine en Leger Inlichtingendienst, 2.10.62, inv.nr. 2073.

31.   General Headquarters, Far East Command, "Summary of War Crimes Trials," 2.

32.   "'Magnificent' Jap on Trial," *Manila Times*, October 14, 1945, 2.

33.   Legal Section, SCAP, "Trials of Class 'B' and 'C' War Criminals," 45. See also the many requests for individual service records in Diplomatic Archives, Tokyo (Gaikō shiryōkan), (hereafter cited as GSK), D' 1.3.0.1, 2.

34.   Godwin (2 Aust. War Crimes Sec., Tokyo) to Baxter (NZ), November 23, 1948, ANZ R22439798.

35.   Legal Section, SCAP, "Trials of Class 'B' and 'C' War Criminals"; COMGENCHINA to CINC Hong Kong, September 27, 1945, PRO (HK), 169–2-147; "Brief for C.G.S.: Number of JSP Confined in Civil Jails in S.E.A.," [November 1946], NA (UK), WO 203/6087; "Instruction to Blamey," *Sydney Morning Herald*, September 22, 1945, 3; "Oorlogsmisdadigers op Sumatra," *Het Dagblad*, December 1, 1945, 2.

36.   War Office to C in C Hong Kong, September 12, 1945, PRO (HK), 169–2-147. For typical interrogations, see "Investigation of Atrocities Nauru Island," [September 28, 1945], NAA 187953; "De beul van Tjideng," *Het Dagblad*, November 29, 1945, 2.

37.   "Roster of 40 Ordered Arrested as War Criminals by MacArthur," *New York Times*, September 12, 1945, 3.

38.   Awaya Kentarō, "Selecting Defendants at the Tokyo Trial," in *Beyond Victor's Justice?*, ed. Yuki Tanaka, Tim McCormack, and Gerry Simpson (Leiden: Nijhoff, 2011), 57.

39. Hayashi Hirofumi, *BC-kyū senpan saiban* (Tokyo: Iwanami shoten, 2005), 152–55; Brandon Palmer, "Imperial Japan's Preparations to Conscript Koreans as Soldiers, 1942–1945," *Korean Studies* 31 (2007): 63–78; Brandon Palmer, *Fighting for the Enemy* (Seattle: University of Washington Press, 2013), 166–67; Utsumi Aiko, "Japan's Korean Soldiers in the Pacific War," in *Asian Labor in the Wartime Japanese Empire*, ed. Paul H. Kratoska (Armonk: Sharpe, 2005), 83; Philip S. Jowett, *The Japanese Army, 1931–45* (Oxford: Osprey, 2002), 2:21; Utsumi Aiko, *Kimu wa naze sabakareta no ka* (Tokyo: Asahi shinbun shuppan, 2008); Utsumi Aiko, "The Japanese Army and Its Prisoners: Relevant Documents and Bureaucratic Institutions," http://ajrp.awm.gov.au/AJRP/AJRP2.nsf/50bee6e350d46afoca256b9000002aof /d2e5732b8749d2e04a2567a8007b490c?OpenDocument (accessed February 13, 2014); Utsumi Aiko, "Korean 'Imperial Soldiers': Remembering Colonialism and Crimes Against Allied POWs," in *Perilous Memories*, ed. T. Fujitani, Geoffrey M. White, and Lisa Yoneyama (Durham, NC: Duke University Press, 2001), 203.

40. Utsumi, *Kimu wa naze sabakareta no ka*, 21, 59–66.

41. Trial of Lt-Gen. Ishida Eiguma and four others, Singapore, October–December 1946, NA (UK), WO 235/963, 290.

42. Gavan McCormack, "Apportioning the Blame: Australian Trials for Railway Crimes," in *The Burma-Thailand Railway*, ed. Gavan McCormack and Hank Nelson (Sydney: Allen & Unwin, 1993), 86–87.

43. "Japs Gentlemen Compared with Korean Guards, Says Ex-P.O.W.," *Border Watch* (Mount Gambier, SA), September 16, 1948, 5.

44. "608 A.I.F. Men Drown," *Courier-Mail* (Brisbane), November 18, 1944, 1.

45. McCormack, "Apportioning the Blame," 86–87.

46. SEAC card index, NA (UK), WO 357/5. For a discussion of superior orders in Singapore cases, see David J. Cohen, "The Singapore War Crimes Trials and Their Relevance Today," *Singapore Law Review* 31 (2013): 17–22.

47. John W. Dower, *War Without Mercy* (New York: Pantheon Books, 1986), 297.

48. "Massacre by Japanese: 17 New Zealanders," *Dominion*, October 23, 1944; "Tarawa Massacre: End of Japanese Who Gave Order," *Dominion*, October 24, 1944. See also the card series "Killed in Action or Dead of Natural Causes," NA (UK), WO 357/4.

49. "Jap General Takes Life to Escape Arrest," *Mercury* (Hobart), November 21, 1945, 7; John W. Dower, *Embracing Defeat* (New York: Norton, 1999), 38–39.

50. Ronald H. Spector, "After Hiroshima: Allied Military Occupations and the Fate of Japan's Empire, 1945–1947," *Journal of Military History* 69, no. 4 (October 2005): 1123; Stephen Connor, "Side-Stepping Geneva: Japanese Troops Under British Control, 1945–7," *Journal of Contemporary History* 45, no. 2 (2010): 389–405.

51. Charles A. Willoughby, ed., *Reports of General MacArthur: MacArthur in Japan: The Occupation: Military Phase*, suppl. 1 (Washington, D.C.: U.S. Government Printing Office, 1966), 149–70; Kōseishō, *Engo gojūnen shi* (Tokyo: Gyōsei, 1997), 14.

52. Kōseishō, *Engo gojūnen shi*, 719.

53. Secretary (EA) to Secretary (Army), [December 1945] [typographical errors in original corrected], NAA 187953.

54. Acting Secretary (Army), "Memorandum: War Crimes," November 29, 1945, NAA 187953.

55. Secretary (EA) to Secretary (Army), December 11, 1945, NAA 187953; Forsyth (Washington) to War Cabinet, December 3, 1945, NAA 187953.

56. See, for instance, *United States of America vs. Kajuro Aihara and 27 Others*, 87, http://www.online.uni-marburg.de/icwc/yokohama/Yokohama%20No.%20T290 .pdf; Th. J. van der Peijl, "Verslag van een dienstreis naar Pontianak can 13 tot 20 Maart 1946," March 27, 1946, NA (NL), Proc.-Gen. Hooggerechtshof Ned.-Ind., 2.10.17, inv.nr. 18.

57. Eric Morris, *Corregidor* (New York: Cooper Square Press, 2000), 450.

58. "Wide-Scale Concealment of Evidence by Japanese Charged," May 17, 1948, NAJ, 4B-23-5855.

59. Masanobu Tsuji, *Masanobu Tsuji's "Underground Escape" from Siam After the Japanese Surrender* (Folkstone, Kent: Global Oriental, 2008); "Memorandum for Japanese Government," December 12, 1949, NAJ, 4B-23-5813, 467.

60. Sandra Wilson, "War Criminals in the Post-War World: The Case of Katō Tetsutarō," *War in History* 22, no. 1 (2015): 87–110. See also "Shanghai War Criminals Flee and Not One Has Been Booked," *Manila Times*, September 25, 1945, 2.

61. See Kenichi Gotō, "Life and Death of 'Abdul Rachman' (1906–49): One Aspect of Japanese-Indonesian Relationships," *Indonesia* 22 (1976): 57–68.

62. "Japanese Leaders to Be Arrested," *Manchester Guardian*, September 12, 1945, 5; George E. Jones, "His Suicide Foiled," *New York Times*, September 12, 1945, 1–2.

63. "Suicides" [card index], NA (UK), WO 357/4.

64. On measures to prevent prisoners from committing suicide, see John L. Ginn, *Sugamo Prison, Tokyo* (Jefferson, NC: McFarland, 1992), 211.

65. Chaen Yoshio, "Kaisetsu," in *Nihon senryaku Sugamo purizun shiryō*, ed. Chaen Yoshio (Tokyo: Nihon tosho sentā, 1992), 1:6. See also Higurashi Yoshinobu, contribution to "The Tokyo War Crimes Trial at Sixty: Legacies and Reassessment," Asian Voices Seminar, George Washington University, Washington, D.C., March 23, 2009, 21, spfusa.org/pdfs/2008/Tokyo%20Trial%2003232009.pdf (accessed June 10, 2014). Pritchard suggests that around 10 percent of suspects were brought to trial. If this estimate is accurate, there would have been more than 50,000 suspects in total. See R. John Pritchard, "The International Military Tribunal for the Far East and the Allied National War Crimes Trials in Asia," in *International Criminal Law*, ed. M. Cherif Bassiouni, 2nd ed. (Ardsley, NY: Transnational, 1999), 3:144–45.

66. At its peak in June 1946, the British detention system held 7,500 suspects. See "Brief for C.G.S.: Number of JSP Confined in Civil Jails in S.E.A." [November 1946], NA (UK), WO 203/6087.

67. Central Liaison Office, Tokyo, "Clarification of Status of Former Suspected War Criminals," May 14, 1946, ANZ, R20106154; "Summation of Non-Military Activities in Japan and Korea no. 30," March 1948, NARA, RG331, Box 899; "Summation of Non-Military Activities in Japan and Korea no. 31," April 1948, NARA, RG331, Box 899.

68. General Headquarters, Far East Command, "Summary of War Crimes Trials," October 19, 1949, 2.

69. See, for instance, the detailed paperwork preserved in NA (NL), Vertegenwoordiging Japan, 1946–1954, 2.05.116, inv.nr. 521, and in GSK D' 1.3.0.1, 1.

70. Aida Yūji, *Prisoner of the British*, trans. Hide Ishiguro and Louis Allen (London: Cresset Press, 1966).

71. Dani Botsman, *Punishment and Power in the Making of Modern Japan* (Princeton, NJ: Princeton University Press, 2005), 198; Sandra Wilson, "Prisoners in Sugamo and Their Campaign for Release, 1952–1953," *Japanese Studies* 31, no. 2 (2011): 174.

72. Nagai Hitoshi, "Sensō hanzainin ni kansuru seifu seimei an: Higashikuni naikaku ni yoru kakugi kettei no myakuraku," *Nenpō: Nihon gendaishi* (December 2005): 10:287–88. See Legal Section notices to Japanese liaison office on the cancellation of arrest warrants, Legal Section G-2 Japanese Liaison, September 5, 1947, NAJ 4B-21–5813.

73. "Summation of Non-Military Activities in Japan," September 1946, 28, ANZ, R20106173. For an informal account of the somewhat ramshackle procedures surrounding the exchange of information and the decision to seek the arrest of Japanese suspects, see J. B., "Apprehension and Prosecution of Japanese War Criminals," March 1, 1946, ANZ, R20106173.

74. V. A. Gavrilov and E. L. Katasonova, eds., *Iaponskie voennoplennye v SSSR 1945–1956* (Moscow: Demokratiia, 2013), 17; George Ginsburgs, *The Citizenship Law of the USSR* (The Hague: Nijhoff, 1983), 318. Gavrilov and Katasonova mention an additional 1,058 suspects transferred to China in August 1949, but they provide no further details (16).

75. "De oorlogsmisdadigers," *Het Dagblad*, December 15, 1945, 2.

76. "Trial Records of Military Tribunal—Katayama Hideo (Sub-Lieutenant) and Two Others," February 25–28, 1946, Morotai, NAA 720882; Aszkielowicz, "After the Surrender," 125–35.

77. S-2 Periodic Report no. 3, May 27, 1946, NA (UK), WO 235/1102, 564.

78. See, for example, Carpenter to TK, April 6, 1947, NA (NL), Vertegenwoordiging Japan, 1946–1954, 2.05.116, inv.nr. 521.

79. See Japanese War Crimes: Sworn Affidavits from Former Prisoners-of-War 1946–1949, NA (UK), MEPO 3/2760.

80. EA to Australian Legation, Chungking, September 6, 1945, NAA 187951; Boxer to Yee (Chinese Military Delegation), September 18, 1945, NAA 187954; [EA] to Secretary (Army), November 20, 1945, NAA 187954.

81. Barak Kushner, *Men to Devils, Devils to Men* (Cambridge, MA: Harvard University Press, 2015), 156–57.

82. Beatrice Trefalt, "Japanese War Criminals in Indochina and the French Pursuit of Justice: Local and International Constraints," *Journal of Contemporary History* 49, no. 4 (October 2014): 735.

83. Tsuchihashi Yūitsu, *Gunpuku seikatsu yonjūnen no omoide* (Tokyo: Keisō shuppan, 1985), 588–89.

84. "Rapport de tournée du lieutenant colonel Turck," May 22–31, 1946, ANOM, HCI Conspol/153.

85. Kirsten Sellars, *"Crimes Against Peace" and International Law* (Cambridge: Cambridge University Press, 2013), 68–70; David J. Cohen, "Beyond Nuremberg: Individual Responsibility for War Crimes," in *Human Rights in Political Transitions: Gettysburg to Bosnia*, ed. Carla Hesse and Robert Post (New York: Zone Books, 1999), 59–69.

86. Shirley A. Selz, "Conspiracy Law in Theory and in Practice: Federal Conspiracy Prosecutions in Chicago," *American Journal of Criminal Law* 5 (1977): 37–42.

87. Andrew D. Mitchell, "Failure to Halt, Prevent or Punish: The Doctrine of Command Responsibility for War Crimes," *Sydney Law Review* 22, no. 3 (2000): 383; Laws and Customs of War on Land (Hague IV), annex to the convention, article XLIII, in Leon Friedman, ed., *The Law of War: A Documentary History* (New York: Random House, 1972), 1:321; William H. Parks, "Command Responsibility for War Crimes," *Military Law Review* 62 (1973): 13.

88. John M. Ferren, "General Yamashita and Justice Rutledge," *Journal of Supreme Court History* 28, no. 1 (2003): 58.

89. Richard L. Lael, *The Yamashita Precedent* (Wilmington, DE: Scholarly Resources, 1982), 7–8, 13, 82–83, 86, 97, 137–38. See also A. Frank Reel, *The Case of General Yamashita* (Chicago: University of Chicago Press, 1949); Guénaël Mettraux, *The Law of Command Responsibility* (Oxford: Oxford University Press, 2009), 6–8; Allan A. Ryan, *Yamashita's Ghost* (Lawrence: University Press of Kansas, 2012).

90. See, for example, Stanley Sandler, ed., *World War II in the Pacific* (New York: Garland, 2001), 1063.

91. See, for instance, the brief and cagy discussion in "Trial of General Tomoyuki Yamashita, United States Military Commission, Manila, (8th October–7th December, 1945), and the Supreme Court of the United States (Judgments Delivered on 4th February, 1946)," in United Nations War Crimes Commission, *Law Reports of Trials of War Criminals* (London: HMSO, 1948), 4:84. See also Mettraux, *The Law of Command Responsibility*, 6–8.

92. "Newsmen Het Up Over Unknown Kinks in Trial of Yamashita," *Manila Times*, October 27, 1945, 7.

93. "Trial Records of Military Tribunal—Katayama Hideo (Sub-Lieutenant)," February 25–28, 1946, NAA 720882; JAG Review—Katayama and Others, March 15, 1946, NAA 720882; Emmi Okada, "The Australian Trials of Class B and C Japanese War Crime Suspects, 1945–51," *Australian International Law Journal* 4 (2009): 47–80. In

January 1946, Takasaki was tried for and acquitted of other crimes, committed in northern Sulawesi. Iwakawa suggests that suspects in China, at least, were able to bribe their way out of custody but does not offer specific evidence to support this claim: see Iwakawa Takashi, *Kotō no tsuchi to narutomo* (Tokyo: Kōdansha, 1995), 453–54. For command responsibility in Singapore cases, see Cohen, "The Singapore War Crimes Trials and Their Relevance Today," 7–17.

94. The film *Blood Oath* (also known as *Prisoners of the Sun*), 1990, directed by Stephen Wallace, was based on this case. See also Hank Nelson, "Blood Oath: A Reel History," *Australian Historical Studies* 24, no. 97 (1991): 429–42; Philip Cornford, "The Ghost of Katayama," *Australian*, July 18, 1981 (*Weekend Magazine*, 1–2), July 20, 1981, 7 and July 22, 1981, 7; Aszkielowicz, "After the Surrender," 125–35.

95. Tribunal Militaire Permanent de Saigon, "Ordonnance de non-lieu en l'état," July 22, 1948, Archives du Comité international de la Croix-Rouge (Geneva), B AG G.7/IX 2.

96. Orders from the Supreme Commander for the Allied Powers to the Japanese Government, AG no. 000.5 December 10, 1945, ANZ R20106156.

97. Andrew Roadnight, "Sleeping with the Enemy: Britain, Japanese Troops and the Netherlands East Indies, 1945–46," *History* 87, no. 286 (2002): 245–68; Robert Cribb, "A Revolution Delayed: The Indonesian Republic and the Netherlands Indies, August–November 1945," *Australian Journal of Politics and History* 32, no. 1 (1986): 74–75; Christopher Bayly and Tim Harper, *Forgotten Wars* (London: Allen Lane, 2007), 149.

98. SACSEA to WO, November 18, 1945, NA (UK), ADM 116/5664; Killearn to FO, April 12, 1946, NA (UK), ADM 116/5664.

99. Trial of Fukudome [*sic*] Shigeru and Five Others, Singapore, February 1948, NA (UK), WO 235/1102.

100. Han Bing Siong, "The Secret of Major Kido: The Battle of Semarang, October 15–19, 1945," *Bijdragen Tot de Taal-, Land- en Volkenkunde* 152, no. 3 (1996): 382–428.

101. "Note sur la collusion Nippo-Viet Minh," May 30, 1947, ANOM HCI 57.198. See Christopher E. Goscha, "Belated Allies: The Technical Contributions of Japanese Deserters to the Viêt Minh (1945–1950)," in *A Companion to the Vietnam War*, ed. Marilyn Young and Robert Buzzanco (Malden, MA: Blackwell, 2002), 37–64.

102. From C. K. T. Wheen, "Yamamoto's Nightmare" [1945]; we are grateful to Rear Admiral Wheen for permission to quote this poem.

103. Barak Kushner, "Ghosts of the Japanese Imperial Army: The 'White Group' (*Baituan*) and Early Post-War Sino-Japanese Relations," *Past and Present*, suppl. 8 (2013), 117–50.

104. Awaya, "Selecting Defendants at the Tokyo Trial," 60–61.

105. Robert A. Scalapino, *The Japanese Communist Movement, 1920–1966* (Berkeley: University of California Press, 1967), 52; Sodei Rinjirō, ed., *Dear General MacArthur*, trans. Shizue Matsuda, English ed. edited by John Junkerman (Lanham, MD: Rowman & Littlefield, 2001).

106. General of the Army Douglas MacArthur to the Chief of Staff, United States Army, Dwight Eisenhower, Tokyo, January 25, 1946, *Foreign Relations of the*

United States, VIII (1946), 395–97, quoted in Kiyoko Takeda, *The Dual-Image of the Japanese Emperor* (Houndmills: Macmillan, 1988), 127. See also Stephen S. Large, *Emperor Hirohito and Shōwa Japan* (London: Routledge, 1992), 135; Michael Schaller, *Douglas MacArthur, the Far-Eastern General* (New York: Oxford University Press, 1989), 126. For a contrary view on the nature of the emperor's prewar and wartime exercise of power, see Herbert Bix, *Hirohito and the Making of Modern Japan* (New York: HarperCollins, 2000).

107.   Yuma Totani, *The Tokyo War Crimes Trial* (Cambridge, MA: Harvard University Asia Center, 2008), 43–62; Large, *Emperor Hirohito and Shōwa Japan*, 139.

108.   "Brief for C.G.S.: Number of JSP Confined in Civil Jails in S.E.A" [November 1946], NA (UK), WO 203/6087; Davis to Shapcott, December 5, 1946, NA (UK), WO 311/540.

109.   Trial of Ishida Eiguma and Four Others, Singapore, October–December 1946, NA (UK), WO 235/963.

110.   "Trial Records of Military Tribunal—Katayama Hideo (Sub-Lieutenant)," NAA 720882; JAG Review—Katayama and Others, NAA 720882.

111.   Minutes of Meeting of 16th October [1945], "Policy & Procedure for Dealing with Japanese War Criminals," NA (UK), ADM 116/5664; War Office to BAS Washington, October 20, 1945, NA (UK), ADM 116/5664.

112.   Paul E. Spurlock, "The Yokohama War Crimes Trials: The Truth About a Misunderstood Subject," *American Bar Association Journal* 36, no. 5 (May 1950): 388.

113.   R. John Pritchard, "The Parameters of Justice: The Evolution of British Civil and Military Perspectives on War Crimes Trials and Their Legal Context (1942–1956)," in *International Humanitarian Law*, ed. John Carey, William V. Dunlap, and R. John Pritchard (Leiden: Brill, 2006), 3:302.

114.   Erickson, "United States Navy War Crimes Trials," 105.

115.   Carroll V. Glines, *The Doolittle Raid* (New York: Orion Books, 1988), 178, 209–13; "5 Japanese to Hang for Fliers' Murder," *New York Times*, February 28, 1946, 13.

116.   "Trial of Lieutenant-General Shigeru Sawada and Three Others, United States Military Commission, Shanghai, 27th February, 1946–15th April, 1946," in United Nations War Crimes Commission, *Law Reports of Trials of War Criminals* (London: HMSO, 1948), 5:1–24.

117.   Totani, *The Tokyo War Crimes Trial*; Richard Minear, *Victors' Justice* (Princeton, NJ: Princeton University Press, 1971); Arnold C. Brackman, *The Other Nuremberg* (New York: Morrow, 1987); Neil Boister and Robert Cryer, *The Tokyo International Military Tribunal* (New York: Oxford University Press, 2008). Also useful is Timothy P. Maga, *Judgment at Tokyo* (Lexington: University Press of Kentucky, 2001), but the book is marred by serious errors, such as the suggestion (p. 2) that the IMTFE sat in Yokohama and tried eighty Japanese leaders.

118.   "Trial of Tazaki Takahiko," November 30, 1945, NAA 1348852; Philip R. Piccigallo, *The Japanese on Trial* (Austin: University of Texas Press, 1979), 128.

119. Colin Sleeman, ed., *Trial of Gozawa Sadaichi and Nine Others* (London: William Hodge, 1948).

120. Konrad Mitchell Lawson, "Wartime Atrocities and the Politics of Treason in the Ruins of the Japanese Empire, 1937–1953" (PhD diss., Harvard University, 2012), 46–94.

121. Trial of Ichikawa Seigi and 13 Others, Rangoon, March–April 1946, NA (UK), WO 235/961.

122. Trial of Kenitji Sonei, Temporary Court-Martial, Batavia, 14th August, 1946, UNWCC archive, PURL: https://www.legal-tools.org/doc/fe53b1/.

123. JML Crimes de guerre japonais, Saigon no. 1946/0032, in the digital collection of the Forschungs-und Dokumentationszentrum für Kriegsverbrecherprozesse (ICWC) at the University of Marburg. See also Lt. Gen. Kamori and V. A. Kondo, "Note," September 18, 1945, ANOM HCI.122.379.

124. On these trials, see Kushner, *Men to Devils, Devils to Men*, 137–84. Bob Wakabayashi showed that reports of the contest were largely invented by the Japanese press: Bob Tadashi Wakabayashi, "The Nanking 100-Man Killing Contest Debate: War Guilt Amid Fabricated Illusions, 1971–75," *Journal of Japanese Studies* 26, no. 2 (2000): 307–40.

125. Trial of Akiyoshi Hosokawa, Guam, September 12, 1945, NARA, RG 125, research. archives.gov/description/6997345. Kushner (*Men to Devils, Devils to Men*, 14) refers to a cannibalism trial on Guam on August 20, 1945, but his reference appears to be to the trial of Tachibana Yoshio, which commenced on August 20, 1946.

126. Awaya, "Selecting Defendants at the Tokyo Trial," 58.

3. IN COURT: INDICTMENT, TRIAL, AND SENTENCING

1. L. F. de Groot, "De rechtspraak inzake oorlogsmisdrijven in Nederlands Indië (1947–1949)," *Militair Rechelijk Tijdschrift* 78 (1985): 85; Trial of Motomura Shigeki and 12 Others, Temporary Court-Martial, Macassar, United Nations War Crimes Commission Archive (hereafter cited as UNWCC Archive), File 16422–16440—no. 9, PURL: https://www.legal-tools.org/doc/4da811/.

2. "SCAP Legal Section—Monthly Summation No. 7," April 1946, National Archives and Records Administration, College Park, MD (hereafter cited as NARA), RG331, Box 1389.

3. Record of Military Court (Japanese War Criminals), Trial of Shirozu Wadami and 91 Others, Ambon, January 2, 1946–January 18, 1946, and Morotai, January 25, 1946–February 15, 1946, National Archives of Australia (hereafter cited as NAA), 721016. See also Caroline Pappas, "Law and Politics: Australia's War Crimes Trials in the Pacific, 1943–1961" (PhD diss., University of New South Wales, 1998), 199–209.

4. Trial of Major-General Otsuka Misao and 43 Others, Singapore, August–October 1946, UK National Archives, Kew (hereafter cited as NA [UK]), WO 235/975.

5. Captain Williams to Lt Van Nooten, February 21, 1946, Papers of John Myles Williams (Manuscript), Mitchell Library, Sydney, 1927–1989, MLMSS 5426, Box 3; "Jap Tells of Bayonetting Australian," *Straits Times*, July 13, 1946, 3.

6. The trials were in fact held on the island of Los Negros, which is separated from Manus Island proper by the narrow Loniu Passage. Both the official documents and the public discussion of the time generally refer to Manus Island as the location of the trials, and we have maintained this usage.

7. Judge Advocate General, "War Crimes," April 9, 1951, NAA, 510472.

8. Felicia Yap, "Prisoners of War and Civilian Internees of the Japanese in British Asia: The Similarities and Contrasts of Experience," *Journal of Contemporary History* 47 (2012): 317.

9. Niall Ferguson, "Prisoner Taking and Prisoner Killing in the Age of Total War: Towards a Political Economy of Military Defeat," *War in History* 11, no. 2 (2004): 148–92.

10. For a typical indictment, see Trial of Ideta Wado and Others, Rangoon, May–June 1946, NA (UK), WO 235/930.

11. Jing-Bao Nie, Nanyan Guo, Mark Selden, and Arthur Kleinman, eds., *Japan's Wartime Medical Atrocities* (London: Routledge, 2010).

12. United Nations War Crimes Commission (hereafter cited as UNWCC), *Law Reports of Trials of War Criminals* (London: HMSO, 1949), 14:152–60; "Trial of Takashi Sakai," in UNWCC, *Law Reports of Trials of War Criminals*, 14:1–7; Barak Kushner, *Men to Devils, Devils to Men* (Cambridge, MA: Harvard University Press, 2015), 147–13.

13. V. A. Gavrilov and E. L. Katasonova, eds., *Iaponskie voennoplennye v SSSR 1945–1956* (Moscow: Demokratiia, 2013), 16–17. See also George Ginsburgs, *The Citizenship Law of the USSR* (The Hague: Nijhoff, 1983), 318. It appears that trials also took place in Kazakhstan at around the same time. See Andrew Barshay, *The Gods Left First* (Berkeley: University of California Press, 2013), 139–41.

14. Jing-Bao Nie, "The West's Dismissal of the Khabarovsk Trial as 'Communist Propaganda': Ideology, Evidence and International Bioethics," *Journal of Bioethical Inquiry* 1, no. 1 (2004): 32–42; Boris G. Yudin, "Research on Humans at the Khabarovsk War Crimes Trial," in Nie et al. eds., *Japan's Wartime Medical Atrocities*, 59–78; Adam Cathcart, "'Against Invisible Enemies': Japanese Bacteriological Weapons in China's Cold War, 1949–1952," *Chinese Historical Review* 16, no. 1 (2009): 103–8.

15. See, for instance, *United States of America vs. Kajuro Aihara and 27 Others*, http://www.online.uni-marburg.de/icwc/yokohama/Yokohama%20No.%20T290.pdf. On the Unit 731 experiments and the U.S. decision not to prosecute, see Sheldon H. Harris, *Factories of Death* (London: Routledge, 1994).

16. International Military Tribunal for the Far East, Indictment No. 1, PURL: http://www.legal-tools.org/doc/59771d/. Although "crimes against humanity" are mentioned in the Tokyo indictment, the term is used loosely and is not distinguished from "war crimes."

17.   Changsoo Lee, "The Politics of the Korean Minority in Japan" (PhD diss., University of Maryland, 1971), 12–40; Soon-won Lee, "Korean-Japanese Discord, 1945–1965" (PhD diss., Rutgers University, 1967); Jeong-Chul Kim, "Caricaturing 'Traitors': Communal Reactions to Indigenous Collaboration in Japanese-Occupied Korea," *International Journal of Law, Crime and Justice* 42 (2014): 203–23. Changsoo Lee notes that there was a demand for the prosecution of Japanese responsible for the massacre of Koreans in Japan following the 1923 Kantō earthquake (22).

18.   This number should not be taken as equal to the number of courts. Tribunals from more than one jurisdiction sat in Singapore, Hong Kong, Morotai, Labuan, Shanghai, Ambon, and Tokyo. In the British sphere, more than one court (often up to four) sat in Singapore and Hong Kong, and most of the trials held in small towns in Malaya were conducted by a single circuit court rather than by separately constituted courts.

19.   Australian authorities also commenced one trial in the East Indonesian town of Ambon (Amboina) but shifted to Morotai in mid-January 1946.

20.   Dean Aszkielowicz, "After the Surrender: Australia and the Japanese Class B and C War Criminals, 1945–1958" (PhD diss., Murdoch University, Perth, Australia, 2012), 6.

21.   Trial of Tanaka Hideo, Raub Pahang, July 1946, NA (UK), WO 235/873.

22.   See "Memorie van toelichting op de ontworpen wetgeving inzake oorlogsmisdrijven," [1946], Arsip Nasional, Jakarta (hereafter cited as ARNAS), Alg. Sec. 288.

23.   Yuma Totani, *Justice in Asia and the Pacific Region, 1945–1952* (New York: Cambridge University Press, 2015), 156–78.

24.   Sharon Williams Chamberlain, "Justice and Reconciliation" (PhD diss., George Washington University, 2010), 52.

25.   Raymond Plummer (IWM interview), Imperial War Museum, London, cat. no. 12690.

26.   Trial of Tazumi Motozo and Three Others, Rangoon, June 1946, NA (UK), WO 235/977; Trial of Uyeno Masakaru and Three Others, Rangoon, April 1946, NA (UK), WO 235/1014.

27.   Mark Sweeney, "Letters from Yokohama" (MA thesis, Saint Mary's University, Halifax, Canada, 2008); NOPAR Recommendations, Folder 17, NA (UK), FO 371/105447.

28.   Amendment no. 7 to HQ ALFSEA War Crime Instruction No. 1 (2nd ed.), November 21, 1946, NA (UK), WO 203/6087.

29.   "Qualified Advocates," [September 1945?], Nationaal Archief, The Hague (hereafter cited as NA [NL]), Alg. Sec. 2.10.14, inv.nr. 5176.

30.   Nota voor Mr E. Schokker, [October 1946], ARNAS, Alg. Sec. 288.

31.   "Japanese Defence Counsel & Interpreters: War Crimes Trials" [November 21, 1946], WO 203/6087; George E. Erickson, "United States Navy War Crimes Trials (1945–1949)," *Washburn Law Journal* 5 (1965): 98.

32.   Chamberlain, "Justice and Reconciliation," 60–64.

33.   Nedwarsec Singapore to Regbur Batavia, [March 1946?], NA (NL), Alg. Sec. 2.10.14, inv.nr. 5176; "Oorlogsmisdaden, Japanse tolken en advocaten," April 15, 1947, NA (NL), Alg. Sec. 2.10.14, inv.nr. 5176.

34. Supreme Allied Commander South East Asia, "Procedure for War Criminal Trials in SEAC," November 17, 1945, NA (UK), WO 235/5594.

35. Brig. E. N. Clarke, "Trial of War Criminals," November 19, 1945, NA (UK), WO 235/5594.

36. David Creed, Moira Raynor, and Sue Rickard, "'It Will Not Be Bound by the Ordinary Rules of Evidence . . . ,'" *Journal of the Australian War Memorial* 27 (October 1995): 47–53; Georgina Fitzpatrick, "War Crimes Trials, 'Victor's Justice' and Australian Military Justice in the Aftermath of the Second World War," in *The Hidden Histories of War Crimes Trials*, ed. Kevin Jon Heller and Gerry Simpson (Oxford: Oxford University Press, 2013), 333–34.

37. Robert W. Miller, "War Crimes Trials at Yokohama," *Brooklyn Law Review* 15, no. 2 (1949): 202; Judge Advocate General, "Trial of Japanese War Criminals, Shoji, K. [and 45 Others]," March 4, 1946, NAA, 739151; "No AIF Witnesses for Singapore Trials," *Daily News* (Perth), January 21, 1946, 2.

38. "Lucky People," *Singapore Free Press*, July 4, 1946, 1; "Japs Released: UK Indignation," *Singapore Free Press*, June 30, 1948, 8. See also "Why Some Japs Get Light Sentences," *Straits Times*, July 5, 1946, 2; Laurens van der Post, *The Night of the New Moon* (London: Hogarth, 1970), 151–53.

39. "Shinohara Court Annexure A—Concealment of Evidence by Japanese," March 30, 1946, NAA, 9024319; Tanaka Hiromi, *BCkyū senpan* (Tokyo: Chikuma shobō, 2002), 144–45.

40. Lynette Silver, *Sandakan* (Burra Creek, Australia: Sally Milner Publishing, 1998), 275.

41. Shinji Munemiya, *The Account of Legal Proceedings of Court for War Criminal Suspects* (Tokyo: Horitzu Shinpo Press, 1946) [translation of *Ambontō senpan saihanki* (Tokyo: Hōritsu shinposha, 1946)], 28. See also Narrelle Morris, "Justice for 'Asian' Victims: The Australian War Crimes Trials of the Japanese, 1945–51," in Heller and Simpson, eds., *The Hidden Histories of War Crimes Trials*, 362–63.

42. See Robert Cribb, "Legal Pluralism and Criminal Law in the Dutch Colonial Order," *Indonesia* 90 (2010): 47–66.

43. Report of intercepted letters from POW Fujii Hajime, Case #1486, January 10, 1947, Investigation Reports, 1945–1949, SCAP Legal Section, Investigative Division, NARA RG331, cited in Chamberlain, "Justice and Reconciliation," 47.

44. Chamberlain, "Justice and Reconciliation," 95 (trans. Chamberlain's).

45. Munemiya, *The Account of Legal Proceedings*, 24.

46. See Daniel H. Foote, "Confessions and the Right to Silence in Japan," *Georgia Journal of International and Comparative Law* 21 (1991): 424.

47. General Headquarters, Far East Command, "Summary of War Crimes Trials," October 19, 1949, 2, National Archives of Japan (hereafter cited as NAJ), 4B-23–5855; "Quick Justice at Rabaul," *Sydney Morning Herald*, March 26, 1946, 3.

48. UNWCC, *Law Reports of Trials of War Criminals* (London: HMSO, 1948), 5:1–24. For Sakaba and Suzuki, see Legal Section, Supreme Commander for the Allied

Powers (hereafter cited as SCAP), "Trials of Class 'B' and 'C' War Criminals," 95–96, May 19, 1952, NARA, RG331, Box 3676. For the vivisection case, see ibid., 183–93.

49. Miller, "War Crimes Trials at Yokohama," 202.

50. Munemiya, *The Account of Legal Proceedings*, 9.

51. See, for example, "Proceedings of a Military Court Held at Manus Island on the Eighteenth Day of January, 1951," sheets 5–6, NAA, 720988; Townley to Army HQ, June 26, 1950, NAA, 391800; "Letter from Captain Mackay to Williams," March 31, 1946, Papers of John Myles Williams, MLMSS 5426, Box 1.

52. Trial of Tazumi Motozo and Three Others, Rangoon, June 1946, NA (UK), WO 235/977.

53. "Clemency for Class 'B' and 'C' War Criminals Koigetsu Ueno and Akio Onishi," May 24, 1954, NA (UK), FO 371/110502.

54. Ibid.

55. See IMTFE, Transcript of Proceedings, April 29, 1946, to November 12, 1948, PURL: http://www.legal-tools.org/en/go-to-database/ltfolder/o_28747/#results.

56. R. John Pritchard, "The International Military Tribunal for the Far East and Its Contemporary Resonances," *Military Law Review* 149 (1995): 26–27.

57. On interpreting at the trial, see Kayoko Takeda, *Interpreting the Tokyo War Crimes Tribunal* (Ottawa: University of Ottawa Press, 2010).

58. Trial of Otoda Hiroshi, Alor Star, NA (UK), WO 235/815. In British courts, the presiding judge would order a plea of "guilty" to be replaced with "not guilty" if the charges might lead to the death penalty. In some cases, the plea may have been changed in order to permit the presentation of particular evidence. See, for example, "Singapore Kempei Man Gets 7 Years," *Straits Times*, June 27, 1946, 3.

59. E.g., "Echo of 'Double Tenth,'" *Straits Times*, June 26, 1946, 5.

60. Trial of Motomura Shigeki and 12 Others, Temporary Court-Martial, Macassar, UNWCC Archive, File 16422–16440—no. 9, PURL: https://www.legal-tools.org/doc/4da811/). See also "Allied PoWs Shot During Liberator Raid," *Straits Times*, July 12, 1946, 5.

61. Chamberlain, "Justice and Reconciliation," 73–74, 91–92.

62. Trial of Kirmura [Kimura] Seikon by a Temporary Court Martial at Batavia, September 11, 1946, UNWCC Archive, File 16389–16396—no. 21, PURL: https://www.legal-tools.org/doc/9ffcd1); Trial of Usuki Kishio and 9 Others, Singapore, August 1946, NA (UK), WO 235/918; Trial of Sugasawa Iju, Singapore, December 1946, NA (UK), WO 235/964. See also Arujunan Narayanan, "Second World War Japanese Atrocities and British Minor War Crimes Trials: The Issue of Fair Trial in Four Selected British Minor War Crimes Trials in Malaya and Singapore in 1946–1947" (PhD diss., University of Wales, Aberystwyth, 2003), 219–46; Chamberlain, "Justice and Reconciliation," 77.

63. Trial of Ishida Eiguma and Four Others, Singapore, October–December 1946, NA (UK), WO 235/963.

64. Trial of Yamada Takeo by Temporary Court Martial at Pontianak, November 15, 1946, UNWCC Archive, File 16411–16413—no. 15, PURL: https://www.legal-tools.org/doc/68dc9c/).

65. Trial of Fukudome Shigeru and 5 Others, Singapore, February 1948, NA (UK), WO 235/1102; L. F. de Groot, *Berechting Japanse Oorlogsmisdadigers in Nederlands-Indië, 1946–1949* ('s-Hertogenbosch: Art & Research, 1990), 152.

66. See, for example, "Jailed for Part in Beheading," *Straits Times*, June 6, 1946, 3; SCAP Legal Section, "Rules Covering the Trial of War Criminals," n.d., NARA, RG331, Box 1389. See also discussion in Philip R. Piccigallo, *The Japanese on Trial* (Austin: University of Texas Press, 1979), 125–26, 176, 188.

67. Chamberlain, "Justice and Reconciliation," 91.

68. "Ambon Camp Chief Gives Evidence," *Straits Times*, July 13, 1946, 5; Munemiya, *The Account of Legal Proceedings*, 10–11.

69. Trial of Motomura Shigeki and 12 Others, Temporary Court-Martial, Macassar, UNWCC Archive, File 16422–16440—no. 9, PURL: https://www.legal-tools.org/doc/4da811/; Sandra Wilson, "War Criminals in the Post-War World: The Case of Katō Tetsutarō," *War in History* 22, no. 1 (2015): 87–110.

70. "Korean Guard to Hang," *Straits Times*, June 26, 1946, 5; "Korean Guard Gets 5 Years," *Straits Times*, June 29, 1946, 3; "Jap Sentenced to 5 Yrs.' R.I.," *Straits Times*, July 2, 1946, 3.

71. "Jap Officer Says Least Deaths in Siam," *Straits Times*, June 18, 1946, 5.

72. See, for example, *United States of America v. Ranjo Fujino and 4 Others*, 36, http://www.online.uni-marburg.de/icwc/yokohama/Yokohama%20No.%20T310.pdf.

73. See Cheah Wui Ling, "Post-World War II British 'Hell-Ship' Trials in Singapore: Omissions and the Attribution of Responsibility," *Journal of International Criminal Justice* 8 (2010): 1047; and Trial of Anami Sanso and 12 Others, Singapore, July 1946, NA (UK), WO 235/886.

74. Colin Sleeman, ed., *Trial of Gozawa Sadaichi and Nine Others* (London: William Hodge, 1948); Trial of Kasai Tsuguo and Nine Others, Singapore, October 1946 NA (UK), WO 235/941; "Jap Major Says He 'Could Do Nothing,'" *Straits Times*, June 4, 1946, 3; Utsumi Aiko, "The Korean Guards on the Burma–Thailand Railway," in *The Burma–Thailand Railway*, ed. Gavan McCormack and Hank Nelson (Sydney: Allen & Unwin, 1993), 132; Edward J. Drea, *Japan's Imperial Army* (Lawrence: University Press of Kansas, 2009), 260.

75. Emori, Hidetoshi, 2nd Lieutenant and Camp Commander at Tokyo Area POW Branch Camp No. 1 Kawasaki, Case Synopses from Judge Advocate's Reviews, Yokohama Class B and C War Crimes Trials, http://wcsc.berkeley.edu/wp-content/uploads/Japan/Yokohama/Reviews/Yokohama_Review_Emori.htm.

76. Trial of Takashi Sakai by the Chinese War Crimes Tribunal of the Ministry of National Defence, Nanking, August 27, 1946, 4, UNWCC Archive, PURL: https://www.legal-tools.org/doc/3789a0/.

77. For example, Trial of Ogihara Goro, Temporary Court Martial, Morotai, August 1947, 4, UNWCC Archive, PURL: https://www.legal-tools.org/doc/35b343/.

78. Trial of Ishikawa Hiroyuki, Temporary Court-Martial, Batavia, April 5, 1948, UNWCC Archive, File 16509–16512, PURL: https://www.legal-tools.org/doc /671e79/.

79. "Japanese Says PoWs Were Brave Men," *Straits Times*, July 18, 1946, 5.

80. De Groot, "Rechtspraak inzake oorlogsmisdrijve," 370.

81. Trial of Kudo Hikosaku and 11 Others, Singapore, September–October 1946, NA (UK) WO 235/943; Trial of Hachisuka Kunifusa and 21 Others, Singapore, July– September 1946, NA (UK), WO 235/952. See also "Jap Says PoW's Beating Was Justified," *Straits Times*, July 17, 1946, 5.

82. Trial of Anami Sanso and 12 Others, Singapore, July 1946, NA (UK), WO 235/886; Trial of Kudo Hikosaku and 11 Others, Singapore, September–October 1946, NA (UK), WO 235/943; Honda, Hiroji: Commander of POW Camp 1B Yunoto and 2B Yoshinwara, Case Synopses from Judge Advocate's Reviews, Yokohama Class B and C War Crimes Trials, https://www.ocf.berkeley.edu/~changmin/Japan/Yokohama /Reviews/Yokohama_Reviews.htm.

83. Trial of Kudo Hikosaku and 11 Others, Singapore, September–October 1946, NA (UK), WO 235/943; see also the following Case Synopses from Judge Advocate's Reviews, Yokohama Class B and C War Crimes Trials, https://www.ocf.berkeley .edu/~changmin/Japan/Yokohama/Reviews/Yokohama_Reviews.htm: Hara, Mokichi, Guard, Hiroshima POW Branch Camp No. 1; Imai, Kiyomi, Hokodate [Hakodate] POW Camp; Morita, Hiroyuki, Kobe Branch POW Camp, Osaka Area, Honshu, Japan; Uwamori, Masao, Camp Commander, Tokyo Area Sub-Camp 3-D, 10-D, and 11-D—Yokohama.

84. Jacco van den Heuvel, "Crime and Authority Within Dutch Communities of Intern- ees in Indonesia, 1942–45," in *Forgotten Captives in Japanese-Occupied Asia*, ed. Karl Hack and Kevin Blackburn (London: Routledge, 2008), 193–209.

85. For a rare public discussion of this point, see "Officers Flogged Their Men," *Singapore Free Press*, August 14, 1946, 5; also Wilson, "War Criminals in the Post- War World," 96–97.

86. Trial of Ishikawa Hiroyuki, Temporary Court-Martial, Batavia, April 5, 1948, UNWCC Archive, File 16509–16512, PURL: https://www.legal-tools.org/doc/671e79/.

87. *Law Reports of Trials of War Criminals*, 5:3–4.

88. *United States of America vs. Kajuro Aihara and 27 Others*, 86, http://www.online .uni-marburg.de/icwc/yokohama/Yokohama%20No.%20T290.pdf.

89. Secret cipher telegram no. 453666, 8 July 1944, NA (UK), ADM 116/5664.

90. For example, "Kempitai [*sic*] on 'Shameful' Execution," *Straits Times*, June 1, 1946, 5.

91. See, for example, Australian Manual of Military Law, quoted in "Trial of Captain Eikichi Kato, Australian Military Court, Rabaul, 7th May, 1946," in *Law Reports of Trials of War Criminals*, 5:38.

92. Philip Towle, "The Japanese Army and Prisoners of War," in *Japanese Prisoners of War*, ed. Philip Towle, Margaret Kosuge, and Yoichi Kibata (London: Hambledon and London, 2000), 1–16.

93. Narrelle Morris, "Unexpected Defeat: The Unsuccessful War Crimes Prosecution of Lt Gen Yamawaki Masataka and Others at Manus Island, 1950," *Journal of International Criminal Justice* 11 (2013): 591–613.

94. Trial of Kenitji Sone, Temporary Court-Martial, Batavia, August 14, 1946, UNWCC Archive, File 16397–16410, PURL: https://www.legal-tools.org/doc/fe53b1/.

95. Sleeman, ed., *Trial of Gozawa*; Trial of Fukuei Shinpei, Singapore, February 1946, NA (UK), WO 235/825.

96. On this argument, see Sienho Yee, "The Tu Quoque Argument as a Defence to International Crimes, Prosecution or Punishment," *Chinese Journal of International Law* 3 (2004): 87–134.

97. Review of *United States of America vs. Shintaro Nakagawa and 20 Others*, December 6, 1948, http://www.online.uni-marburg.de/icwc/yokohama/Yokohama%20No.%20T356.pdf.

98. Trial of Takashima Shotaro and Asako Koichi, Singapore, January 1947, NA (UK), WO 235/974. These issues are discussed extensively in Totani, *Justice in Asia and the Pacific Region*, 102–28.

99. "Life Term for Jap Civilian," *Straits Times*, May 10, 1946, 5; "Legal Point to Be Argued in War Trial," *Straits Times*, May 9, 1946, 3; R. John Pritchard, "The Nature and Significance of British Post-War Trials of Japanese War Criminals, 1945–1948," *Proceedings* (British Association for Japanese Studies) 2 (1977): 202, nn. 11 and 12; Trial of Sumida Haruzo and Twenty Others, NA (UK), WO 235/891.

100. Fitzpatrick, "War Crimes Trials, 'Victor's Justice' and Australian Military Justice in the Aftermath of the Second World War," 332.

101. Yuma Totani, *The Tokyo War Crimes Trial* (Cambridge, MA: Harvard University Asia Center, 2008); Neil Boister and Robert Cryer, *The Tokyo International Military Tribunal* (New York: Oxford University Press, 2008).

102. See Suzannah Linton, introduction to *Hong Kong's War Crimes Trials*, ed. Suzannah Linton (Oxford: Oxford University Press, 2013), 1; Totani, *Justice in Asia and the Pacific Region*, 182–83.

103. Trial of Ichikawa Seigi and 13 Others, Rangoon, March–April 1946, NA (UK), WO 235/961.

104. Boister and Cryer, *The Tokyo International Military Tribunal*, 111.

105. See "War Crimes Trials Military Court 1946, Shen-Tse, No. 3," Diplomatic Archives, Tokyo (Gaikō shiryōkan), (hereafter cited as GSK), D' 1.3.0.2–5-1–1; Piccigallo, *The Japanese on Trial*, 175.

106. Trial of Yamada Takeo, Temporary Court-Martial at Pontianak, November 15, 1946, UNWCC Archive, File 16411–16413—no. 15, PURL: https://www.legal-tools.org/doc/68dc9c/).

107. Trial of Kenitji Sone, Temporary Court-Martial, Batavia, August 14, 1946, UNWCC Archive, File 16397–16410, PURL: https://www.legal-tools.org/doc/fe53b1/ (in English).

108. Trial of Itzuki Toshio and 15 Others, Singapore, March 1946, NA (UK), WO 235/834.

109. Trial of Kishi Yasuo and 14 Others, Hong Kong, March–April 1946, NA (UK), WO 235/993; Pritchard, "The Nature and Significance of British Post-War Trials of Japanese War Criminals," 210.

110. Judge Advocate to Admiralty, February 21, 1947, NA (UK), ADM 116/5664.

111. See, for example, Trial of Ogihara Goro, Morotai, August 1947, 4, UNWCC Archive, PURL: https://www.legal-tools.org/doc/35b343/.

112. International Military Tribunal for the Far East, Transcript of Proceedings, November 4, 1948, 48,449–48,451, PURL: http://www.legal-tools.org/doc/629f2b/; Boister and Cryer, *The Tokyo International Military Tribunal*, 154–67.

113. "Jap Major Is Likened to 'a Monster,'" *Straits Times*, June 7, 1946, 5.

114. "Kempei Man to Hang," *Straits Times*, June 27, 1946, 5.

115. "De oorlogsmisdadigers," *Het Dagblad*, March 9, 1946, 2.

116. Trial of Higashigawa Yoshinoru and 34 Others, Penang, NA (UK), WO 235/931.

117. R. John Pritchard, "Lessons from British Proceedings Against Japanese War Criminals," *Human Rights Review* 3, no. 2 (1978): 118.

118. Chamberlain, "Justice and Reconciliation," 73–74.

119. Trial of Banno Hirateru and Six Others, Singapore, September–October 1946, 367, NA (UK), WO 235/1034; Totani, *Justice in Asia and the Pacific Region*, 93–96.

120. J. MacIntosh to Commissioner of Prisons, Singapore, April 6, 1951, NA (UK), FO 371/115290.

121. "Chinese Law Concerning Trials of War Criminals," *Law Reports of Trials of War Criminals*, 14:158.

122. Gavrilov and Katasonova, eds., *Iaponskie voennoplennye v SSSR*, 16.

123. Cabinet Offices to SACSEA, November 11, 1945, Public Record Office, Hong Kong (hereafter cited as PRO [HK]), HKRS 169-2-147; Richard Holmes, *Sahib: The British Soldier in India* (London: Harper Perennial, 2006), 430.

124. Trial of Shimada Chokichi and Four Others, Singapore, January 1947, NA (UK), WO 235/1051.

125. Trial of Chida Sotomatsu and Five Others, NA (UK), WO 235/822; Trial of Matsuo Shinichi and One Other, NA (UK), WO 235/955.

126. Trial of Motomura Shigeki and 12 Others, Temporary Court-Martial, Macassar, May 1947, UNWCC Archive, File 16422–16440—no. 9, PURL, https://www.legal-tools.org/doc/4da811/).

127. On Hirota's career, see Ian Nish, *Japanese Foreign Policy, 1869–1942* (London: Routledge & Kegan Paul, 1977), 197–201. For a vigorous assertion of the injustice of Hirota's conviction, see Dayle Kerry Smith, "The Tokyo War Crimes Trial" (PhD diss., University of Queensland, Brisbane, Australia, 1993).

128. Aszkielowicz, "After the Surrender," 192; Tanaka, *BC-kyū senpan*, 205.

129. For a report of this allegation, see Arujunan Narayanan, "Japanese Atrocities and British Minor War Crimes Trials After World War II in the East," *Jebat* 33 (2006): 12. Narayanan himself concludes (13) that ethnic bias was absent.

130. Narayanan, "Second World War Japanese Atrocities and British Minor War Crimes Trials," 139.

131. The Netherlands Indies military courts continued to try war criminals after the restoration of civil government in November 1946, but sentences had subsequently to be approved by the senior local civil authority (resident or governor).

132. Richard L. Lael, *The Yamashita Precedent* (Wilmington, DE: Scholarly Resources, 1982), 7–13, 82–86, 137–38.

133. UNWCC, Information Concerning Human Rights Arising from Trials of War Criminals (United Nations Economic and Social Council, May 15, 1948), 258–59.

134. See, for example, "Proceedings of a Military Court Held at Manus Island on the Eighteenth Day of January, 1951," sheets 5–6, NAA 720988; Townley to Army HQ, June 2, 1950, NAA, 391800; "Letter from Captain Mackay to Williams," March 31, 1946, Papers of John Myles Williams, MLMSS 5426 Box 1. For discussion of the role of judge advocates, see Piccigallo, *The Japanese on Trial*, 98; Aszkielowicz, "After the Surrender," 102.

135. See, for instance, Tribunal Permanent Militaire de Saigon, no. 3841, December 10, 1947, NAJ 4A17-3 5403.

136. Piccigallo, *The Japanese on Trial*, 37–38, 75.

137. "Staff Judge Advocate Review—Kato Tetsutaro," February 7, 1949, NARA, RG331, Box 9546.

138. Chamberlain, "Justice and Reconciliation," 106.

139. Wilson, "War Criminals in the Post-War World," 90.

140. Confirming Authority, "Military Court, 1st Lt Tazaki, 18 Japanese Army," [December 1945], NAA 1348852.

141. Judge Advocate General, "Trial of Japanese War Criminals, Shoji, K. [and 45 Others]," March 4, 1946, NAA 739151.

142. Aszkielowicz, "After the Surrender," 103, 105.

143. Pritchard, "The Nature and Significance of British Post-War Trials," 209–10.

144. See "Synopsis of Australian Trials," UNWCC Archive, File 21041–21076.

145. For the record of a Dutch review, see the correspondence in ARNAS Alg. Sec. 289.

146. De Groot, "Rechtspraak inzake oorlogsmisdrijven," 88–89, 161, 375–76.

147. Barak Kushner, "Pawns of Empire: Postwar Taiwan, Japan and the Dilemma of War Crimes," *Japanese Studies* 30, no. 1 (2010): 125–26.

148. Piccigallo, *The Japanese on Trial*, 31–32; Boister and Cryer, *The Tokyo International Military Tribunal*, 261–64.

149. Trial of Hara Teizo and Eight Others, Singapore, February–March 1946, NA (UK), WO 235/818; Hara Teizo and Eight Others, Singapore, March–April 1946, NA (UK), WO 235/839.

150. "Judgement on Tanaka Hisakazu," October 18, 1946, PURL, https://www.legal-tools.org/uploads/tx_ltpdb/Guangdong.pdf.

151.   [Australian] Army Headquarters, Melbourne to Headquarters Netherlands East Indies Army, Melbourne, December 3, 1946, NA (NL), Strijdkrachten in Nederlands-Indië 2.13.132, inv.nr. 1445.

152.   Japanese Minor War Criminal, Shimojo, Harukichi, NA (UK), FO 371/105435; Proceedings of Military Tribunal, S/M Shimojo Harukichi, NAA 739439.

153.   "[List of Prisoners in] Outram Road, Singapore," February 1, 1949 (?), NA (UK), FO371/76253, 100; Colonial Secretary's Office to Deputy Commissioner General Colonial Affairs, September 21, 1951, NA (UK), FO371/92379, 65; Commissioner General for the United Kingdom in South East Asia to Foreign Office, November 21, 1951, NA (UK), FO371/92379, 79.

154.   IMTFE, Transcript of Proceedings, June 4, 1946, 337, PURL, https://www.legal -tools.org/doc/436390/.

155.   Trial of Itzuki Toshio and 15 Others, Singapore, March 1946, NA (UK), WO 235/834, cited in Pritchard, "Lessons from British Proceedings," 116.

156.   SACSEA to Cabinet Offices, November 10, 1945, NA (UK), ADM 116/5664; "Manacled Jap Gives Evidence," *Straits Times*, July 8, 1946, 3.

157.   Allied Land Forces South East Asia, Military Courts—War Criminals, Death Warrant, NISHI Yoshinobu, June 26, 1946, Arkib Negara Malaysia (hereafter cited as ANM), R. C. Selangor 511/00155.

158.   Registration of Deaths of Japanese War Criminals, ANM, Malayan Union no. 8331/1947; "Sedatives Given to Japs Before Execution," *Canberra Times*, March 21, 1946, 1.

159.   "Four Burma Japs Hanged," *Straits Times*, July 17, 1946, 3.

160.   See, for example, "Eight Jap War Criminals Are Hanged," *Straits Times*, June 17, 1946, 3.

161.   "Women See 3 Japs Hanged," *Singapore Free Press*, June 26, 1947, 1; "Four Women Watch Hangings," *Straits Times*, June 27, 1947, 1.

162.   Iwakawa Takashi, *Kotō no tsuchi to narutomo* (Tokyo: Kōdansha, 1995), 453; "Jap Death Parade —'Lamentable,'" *Straits Times*, June 19, 1947, 3.

163.   "Japan: Document Detailing War Criminal Execution Procedures Found," June 8, 2013, http://deathpenaltynews.blogspot.de/2013/06/japan-document-detailing-war -criminal.html (accessed October 9, 2014).

164.   John W. Dower, *Embracing Defeat* (New York: Norton, 1999), 449.

165.   "Hair, Fingernails Sent Home," *Singapore Free Press*, September 3, 1948, 3; Shinsho Hanayama, *The Way of Deliverance*, trans. Hideo Suzuki, Eiichi Noda, and James K. Sasaki (London: Victor Gollancz, 1955), 49, 67, 107, 258–59.

166.   Le Capitaine Castagnet à Monsieur le Chef de Bataillon, January 2, 1946, 47, Service historique de la défense, Vincennes, 10H 6038.

167.   SCAP to Chief of French Mission in Japan, January 17, 1947, NARA, RG331, Box 1256.

168.   Saburō Shiroyama, *War Criminal* (Tokyo: Kodansha International, 1977), 1–2.

169.   "Execution of Yamashita," *Sydney Morning Herald*, February 25, 1946, 3.

170.   "Execution of War Criminals," July 26, 1946, and other documents in PRO (HK), HKRS 125-3-146; index cards in NA (UK), WO 357/3.

171.   See, for example, Lt-Gen. R. L. Eichelberger to Mrs Tsuru Yuri, May 17, 1946, NAJ, Justice Ministry, 4B-23-5855; Central Liaison Office to General Headquarters, SCAP, March 5, 1946, GSK D' 1.3.0.1.

172.   "Exhumation and Removal to Japan of Remains of Japanese War Criminals," March–April 1955, National Archives of Singapore, Public Relations Office 19, file 186/55.

173.   "Japanese General Executed," *Sydney Morning Herald*, March 31, 1947, 3.

174.   Index cards in NA (UK), WO 357/3; "Execution of War Criminals," July 26, 1946, PRO (HK), HKRS 125-3-146.

175.   "War Crimes Trials in the Philippines," May 6, 1947, NARA, RG554, Box 495.

176.   "Jap Guards Executed," *Sunday Herald* (Sydney), August 21, 1949, 3; "Jap geëxecuteerd," De Locomotief (Semarang), August 26, 1949, 1.

177.   L. F. Field, "Japanese War Criminals," NA (UK), FO 371/92450; "Hanged War Criminals Buried at Sea," *Sydney Morning Herald*, June 12, 1951, 3.

178.   Richard Minear, *Victors' Justice* (Princeton, NJ: Princeton University Press, 1971).

179.   Application of Homma, 327 U.S. 759 (1946), https://supreme.justia.com/cases/federal/us/327/759/.

180.   "Japs Admit Fairness in War Trials Morotai," *Canberra Times*, February 16, 1946, 1.

4. DILEMMAS OF DETENTION AND THE FIRST MISGIVINGS

1.   SCAP Legal Section, "Allied Land Forces, South East Asia, War Crimes Instruction no. 1, 2nd Edition," May 4, 1946, 9, National Archives and Records Administration, College Park, MD (hereafter cited as NARA), RG331, Box 1429.

2.   Secretariat, Government of the Malayan Union to Inspector of Prisons, Kuala Lumpur, May 16, 1946, Arkib Negara Malaysia (hereafter cited as ANM), Malayan Union no. 970/1946.

3.   HQ Allied Land Forces, South East Asia, to Chief Secretary, Malayan Union Government, May 4, 1946, ANM, Malayan Union no. 970/1946.

4.   Sharon Williams Chamberlain, "Justice and Reconciliation" (PhD diss., George Washington University, 2010), 123; Nagai Hitoshi, *Firipin to taiNichi senpan saiban 1945–1953nen* (Tokyo: Iwanami shoten, 2010), 226.

5.   "Roster Desired by Commanding General," July 2, 1947, NARA, RG338, Box 1049.

6.   "Breakdown of Sugamo Internees," June 18, 1947, NARA, RG331, Box 1360.

7.   "Release of Detained War Crimes Suspects," August 29, 1947, NARA, RG338, Box 1049.

8.   "Roster of Untried Prisoners," October 24, 1947, NARA, RG338, Box 1049.

9. "Employment of All Convicted War Criminals," November 12, 1949, NARA, RG338, Box 1025; "List of Employment at Sugamo," November 12, 1949, NARA, RG338 Box 1025.

10. Marston Logan to L. D. Wakely, February 18, 1948, UK National Archives, Kew (hereafter cited as NA [UK]), WO 311/544.

11. Anthony Reid, "Australia's Hundred Days in South Sulawesi," in *Nineteenth and Twentieth Century Indonesia*, ed. David P. Chandler and M. C. Ricklefs (Clayton, VIC: Southeast Asian Studies, Monash University, 1986), 219.

12. Terence Wesley-Smith, "Australia and New Zealand," in *Tides of History*, ed. K. R. Howe, Robert C. Kiste, and Brij V. Lal (Honolulu: University of Hawai'i Press, 1994), 196.

13. Note, July 8, [1946,] and subsequent correspondence, Public Record Office (Hong Kong) (hereafter cited as PRO [HK]), HKRS 163–1-210, 16. See also J. B. Griffin, "Japanese Sentenced by Military Courts," October 31, 1949, PRO (HK), HKRS 125–3-406.

14. "49th Weekly Meeting—Wednesday the 4th December 1946, War-Time Crimes (Exemption) Bill, 1946," National Archives of Myanmar (hereafter cited as NAM), accession no. 281 File 49G46(8).

15. Secretary of State for Burma to Governor of Burma, December 2, 1947, NA (UK), FO 371/92183.

16. Governor of Burma to Secretary of State for Burma, December 11, 1947, NA (UK), FO 371/92183.

17. Commander Marianas to Commander Eighth Army, June 7, 1947, NARA, RG338, Box 1049, folder: 000.5 (June–December). See also Tim Maga, " 'Away from Tokyo': The Pacific Islands War Crimes Trials, 1945–1949," *Journal of Pacific History*, 36, no. 1 (2001): 37–50.

18. "Headquarters Sugamo Prison," July 2, 1947, NARA, RG338, Box 1049; "War Crimes Trials in the Philippines," May 6, 1947, 6, NARA, RG554, Box 495.

19. Dean Aszkielowicz, "After the Surrender: Australia and the Japanese Class B and C War Criminals, 1945–1958" (PhD diss., Murdoch University, 2012), 172; Richard N. Rosecrance, *Australian Diplomacy and Japan, 1945–1951* (Cambridge: Cambridge University Press, 1962), 55–66; "Manus 'Deserted Junk Heap,'" *Straits Times*, February 21, 1949, 2.

20. "Chief of Legal Section—Memo for Record," February 1950, NARA, RG331, Box 1435.

21. "Treatment of Japanese War Crimes Convicts," February 11, 1947, NA (UK), DO 35/2937.

22. Changi was restored to civilian authority on October 15, 1947. See Logan to Wakely, February 4, 1948, NA (UK), DO 35/2937; "Army Returns Gaol Today," *Straits Times*, October 15, 1947, 5.

23. See Logan to Wakely, February 4, 1948, NA (UK), DO 35/2937. Slightly different figures are provided in HQ Allied Land Forces, South East Asia, to Chief Secretary, Malayan Union Government, May 4, 1946, ANM, Malayan Union no. 970/1946.

24. HQ Allied Land Forces, South East Asia, to Chief Secretary, Malayan Union Government, May 4, 1946, ANM, Malayan Union no. 970/1946. In May 1948, the number of war criminals convicted by Australian courts and held in British colonial prisons was given as 44 (35 in Singapore, 3 in Malaya, and 6 in Hong Kong; see Thompson to Wakely, May 25, 1948, NA [UK], DO 35/2937).

25. Governor Gimson, Singapore, to Arthur Creech-Jones, Colonial Office (hereafter cited as CO), December 11, 1947, NA (UK), DO 35/2937.

26. Note from Commander of Prisons to Colonial Secretary, November 10, 1949, 17, PRO (HK), HKRS 163-1-210.

27. Aszkielowicz, "After the Surrender," 175–76, 179.

28. Alva Carpenter, "Request for Transfer of War Crimes Trials to Japan," July 22, 1948, NARA, RG331, Box 1413; see also Aszkielowicz, "After the Surrender," 181–82.

29. Note pour Monsieur l'Intendant, Chef de l'Intendance, March 8, 1948, Service historique de la défense, Vincennes, 10H 1044; India Office Records (hereafter cited as IOR), IOR/L/E/8/6850, October 1947–July 1948.

30. "Loose Minute," June 9, 1948, PRO (HK), HKRS 163-1-231, 13–14; "D.C.S. from P.A.D.C.S.," June 11, 1948, PRO (HK), HKRS 163-1-231, 15.

31. "Loose Minute," June 9, 1948, 13–14.

32. Telegram from Governor, Hong Kong, to Secretary of State, September 3, 1948, PRO (HK), HKRS 163–1-231, 27.

33. Commissioner of Prisons to F. S., May 19, 1947; and "Summary of Periods for Which the Japanese War Crimes Prisoners Have Been Maintained Up to 31st March, 1950 by Hong Kong," n.d., PRO (HK), HKRS 163-1-231.

34. According to one British source, Japanese convicted war criminals were "in considerable demand" as labor because they were seen as docile. See R. John Pritchard, "The Gift of Clemency Following British War Crimes Trials in the Far East, 1946–1948," *Criminal Law Forum* 7, no. 1 (1996): 21, citing Brief for the Chief of the Imperial General Staff, November 8, 1946, NA (UK), WO 203/6087.

35. Wakely to Logan, March 4, 1948, NA (UK), DO 35/2937; Hampson to Logan, July 15, 1948, NA (UK), DO 35/2937; Hunter to Thompson, August 4, 1948, NA (UK), DO 35/2937.

36. "War Criminals Kill Guards, Escape," *Straits Times*, January 9, 1946, 1.

37. "Condemned Japs Escape from Prison," *Singapore Free Press*, August 10, 1946, 5; "Gaol Break in Kuala Lumpur," *Straits Times*, October 15, 1946, 1.

38. "Le Commissaire du gouvernement près le Tribunal Militaire Permanent de Saigon à Monsieur le Chef des Services de Police et de Sureté de Cochinchine," August 27, 1947, Archives nationales d'outre-mer, Aix-en-Provence (hereafter cited as ANOM), HCI Conspol/270.

39. "Loose Minute," 13–14; "D.C.S. from P.A.D.C.S.," 15.

40. "Report on the Treatment of War Criminal Suspects at Fukuoka Camp by the U.S. Army Personnel," [1946?], Diplomatic Archives, Tokyo (Gaikō shiryōkan) (hereafter cited as GSK), D' 1.3.0.1, 2.

41. Shibata Yaichiro, "Report on Conditions During the Dutch East Indies Area War Crimes Trial," Nationaal Archief, The Hague (hereafter cited as NA [NL]), Vertegenwoordiging Japan, 1946–1954, 2.05.116, inv.nr. 529. See also Alvary Gascoigne to the Governor of Singapore, September 3, 1949, NA (UK), FO 371/76253, 129.

42. "Excerpt from Ai no hikari," January 1952, National Archives of Australia (hereafter cited as NAA), 140815.

43. T. A. Brown, "Report of Enquiry into Treatment of Japanese War Criminals," October 29, 1949, NA (UK), FO 371/84036.

44. Shinji Munemiya and Kazuo Yoshioka, *The Account of Legal Proceedings of Court for War Criminal Suspects* (Tokyo: Horitzu Shinpo Press, 1946), 33.

45. "Stanley Prison: Report Established by the International Committee of the Red Cross on Information Supplied by the Delegate," January 25, 1951, NA (UK), FO 371/92396, 51; see also "Criminels de guerre, suspects et témoins Japonais en Indochine," February 16, 1948, ANOM, INF159/1364.

46. "Report by the Committee of the International Red Cross in Geneva on JSP (Japanese) and P of W Camps in Burma" (based on a visit by H. Frei, May 9–24, 1946), 9, NAM, accession no. 17, 378 D (EA) 46, Box 1, 15–3 (18).

47. "Report by the Committee of the International Red Cross in Geneva of J.S.P. and P.O.W. Camps in Burma" (based on a visit by H. Frei, November 30–December 9, 1946), 13–14, NAM, accession no. 29, File NO. 150 D (EA) 47.

48. "Stanley Prison: Visited on January 25, 1951, by ICRC delegate, Mr F. Bieri," PRO (HK), HKRS 125-3-407.

49. Kawakami Tō, "Sugamo purizun hōkokusho," *Bungei shunjū* (December 1955), quoted in Utsumi Aiko, *Sugamo purizun* (Tokyo: Yoshikawa kōbunkan, 2004), 91–92.

50. See, for example, Sasakawa Ryōichi, *Sugamo Diary*, trans. Ken Hijino (London: Hurst, 2010), 56–61 (entries for early February 1946).

51. Kishi Nobusuke, Yatsugi Kazuo, and Itō Takashi, *Kishi Nobusuke no kaisō* (Tokyo: Bungei shunjū, 1981), 81–82; Paula Daventry, ed., *Sasakawa, the Warrior for Peace, the Global Philanthropist* (Oxford: Pergamon Press, 1981), 45–46.

52. Testimony of Tsukamoto Gorō, Ministry of Foreign Affairs, Kokkai kaigiroku, Sangiin, Hōmu iinkai sensō hanzainin ni taisuru hōteki shochi ni kansuru shōiinkai 1-gō, December 12, 1951, 17. Diet records are available at http://kokkai.ndl.go.jp/.

53. Fukutome Shigeru, witness, ibid., 9. See also Kishi, Yatsugi, and Itō, *Kishi Nobusuke no kaisō*, 80.

54. Gimson, Singapore, to Creech-Jones, CO, December 11, 1947, NA (UK), DO 35/2937.

55. Untitled minute of meeting at CO, February 6, 1948, NA (UK), DO 35/2937.

56. Chaen Yoshio, "Kaisetsu," in *Nihon senryō Sugamo purizun shiryō*, ed. Chaen Yoshio (Tokyo: Nihon tosho sentā, 1992), 1:6; F. G. T. Davis, quoted in Hayashi Hirofumi, "British War Crimes Trials of Japanese," *Nature-People-Society: Science and the Humanities* (Kanto Gakuin University) 31 (July 2001), http://www.geocities.jp/hhhirofumi/engo8.htm#_ednref12.

57. "War Crimes Trials in the Philippines," May 6, 1947, NARA, RG554, Box 495.

58. Higurashi Yoshinobu, "Gasshūkoku to taiNichi senpan saiban no shūketsu," *Shigaku zasshi* 109, no. 11 (November 2000): 18.

59. George F. Kennan, Explanatory notes, March 25, 1948, *Foreign Relations of the United States* (1948): 6:718.

60. Higurashi, "Gasshūkoku to taiNichi senpan saiban no shūketsu," 5–10, 18–21, 23–25; Awaya Kentarō, "Selecting Defendants at the Tokyo Trial," in *Beyond Victor's Justice?*, ed. Yuki Tanaka, Tim McCormack, and Gerry Simpson (Leiden: Nijhoff, 2011), 57; Yuma Totani, *The Tokyo War Crimes Trial* (Cambridge, MA: Harvard University Asia Center, 2008), 68–77; John W. Dower, *Embracing Defeat* (New York: Norton, 1999), 454.

61. "SCAP Legal Section to Department of Army," March 8, 1948, NARA, RG331, Box 1434.

62. For the Kuroda trial, see Yuma Totani, *Justice in Asia and the Pacific Region, 1945–1952* (New York: Cambridge University Press, 2015), 21–24, 46–55.

63. "Chief Legal Section—Release of the Remaining Former Class A Suspects," December 15, 1948, NARA, RG331, Box 1434; Higurashi, "Gasshūkoku to taiNichi senpan saiban no shūketsu," 25.

64. Quoted in R. John Pritchard, "The International Military Tribunal for the Far East and the Allied National War Crimes Trials in Asia," in *International Criminal Law*, ed. M. Cherif Bassiouni, 2nd ed. (Ardsley, NY: Transnational, 999), 3: 133.

65. *The Record of Proceedings in the Trial of U.S.A. vs. Soemu Toyoda* (Tokyo: War Crimes Tribunal, GHQ, SCAP [1949]), 1:1; Higurashi, "Gasshūkoku to taiNichi senpan saiban no shūketsu," 21–25; Totani, *The Tokyo War Crimes Trial*, 75–76; Totani, *Justice in Asia and the Pacific Region, 1945–52*, 156–78.

66. Ann Marie Prévost, "Race and War Crimes: The 1945 War Crimes Trial of General Tomoyuki Yamashita," *Human Rights Quarterly* 14, no. 3 (August 1992): 330–35.

67. "Future Trial of War Criminals," January 17, 1949, NARA, RG338, Box 1060; Philip R. Piccigallo, *The Japanese on Trial* (Austin: University of Texas Press, 1979), 46; Higurashi, "Gasshūkoku to taiNichi senpan saiban no shūketsu," 20.

68. "Chief of Legal Section Weekly Report," November 27, 1951, NARA, RG331, Box 1222.

69. "Japanese Officers (Alleged War Crimes)," House of Commons Debate, June 29, 1948, vol. 452 cc1979–82, available at http://hansard.millbanksystems.com /commons/1948/jun/29/japanese-officers-alleged-war-crimes; Peter Clague, *Bridge House* (Hong Kong: South China Morning Post, 1983), 128–36, 145–51; Trial of Kinoshita Eiichi and Yoshida Bunzo, Hong Kong, October–November 1949, NA (UK), WO 235/1116.

70. Trial of Yokohata Toshiro, NA (UK), WO 235/1117. On British internal discussion over the question of when to halt the trials, see Pritchard, "The Gift of Clemency," 17–20.

71. Pritchard, "The Gift of Clemency," 20. This figure may be inflated. As Pritchard notes, the British had held about 2,000 suspects in 1946, and this number is unlikely to have grown during the following months.

72. Narrelle Morris, "Unexpected Defeat: The Unsuccessful War Crimes Prosecution of Lt Gen Yamawaki Masataka and Others at Manus Island, 1950," *Journal of International Criminal Justice* 11 (2013): 593–94; Dean Aszkielowicz, "Repatriation and the Limits of Resolve: Japanese War Criminals in Australian Custody," *Japanese Studies* 31, no. 2 (2011): 211–28. The number of Manus trials is taken from the Marburg records.

73. It has been reported that 1,058 Japanese suspects were transferred to "Chinese authorities" in August 1949, that is, before the establishment of the PRC. It is likely, but not certain, that these authorities were Communist, since the Chinese Communist Party had already set up functioning administrations in many regions by this time (see V. A. Gavrilov and E. L. Katasonova, eds., *Iaponskie voennoplennye v SSSR 1945–1956* [Moscow: Demokratiia, 2013], 16–17). On the transfers, see Adam Cathcart and Patricia Nash, "War Criminals and the Road to Sino-Japanese Normalization: Zhou Enlai and the Shenyang Trials, 1954–1956," *Twentieth Century China* 34, no. 2 (2009): 93–94.

74. Jing-Bao Nie, "The West's Dismissal of the Khabarovsk Trial as 'Communist Propaganda': Ideology, Evidence and International Bioethics," *Journal of Bioethical Inquiry* 1, no. 1 (2004): 32–42.

75. Higurashi Yoshinobu, *Tōkyō saiban* (Tokyo: Kōdansha, 2008), 316–17.

76. SACSEA to ALFSEA, March 13, 1946, NA (UK), ADM 116/5664.

77. "First Japanese Hanged at K.L.," *Straits Times*, March 13, 1946, 3; "Three Jap War Criminals Hanged in Changi Gaol," *Straits Times*, March 15, 1946, 4.

78. SACSEA to Cabinet Offices, March 14, 1946, NA (UK), ADM 116/5664.

79. SACSEA to Cabinet Offices, October 2, 1945, NA (UK), ADM 116/5664.

80. R. John Pritchard, "The Parameters of Justice: The Evolution of British Civil and Military Perspectives on War Crimes Trials and Their Legal Context (1942–1956)," in *International Humanitarian Law*, ed. John Carey, William V. Dunlap, and R. John Pritchard (Leiden: Brill, 2006), 3:306.

81. Ibid., 306–7.

82. One landmark was U.S. president Abraham Lincoln's 1863 pardoning of Confederate soldiers after the Civil War; see "The Proclamation of Amnesty and Reconstruction by the President of the United States of America," in *Statutes at Large, Treaties, and Proclamations of the United States of America* (Boston, 1866), 13:737–39, available at Freedmen and Southern Society Project, http://www.freedmen.umd.edu /procamn.htm. See also Carolyn Strange, "Mercy and Parole in Anglo-American Criminal Justice Systems, from the Eighteenth to the Twenty-First Century," in *Oxford Handbook of the History of Crime and Criminal Justice*, ed. Paul Knepper and Anja Johansen (Oxford: Oxford University Press, 2016), 573–96; Nasser Hussain and Austin Sarat, "Toward New Theoretical Perspectives on Forgiveness,

Mercy, and Clemency," in *Forgiveness, Mercy and Clemency*, ed. Austin Sarat and Nasser Hussain (Stanford, CA: Stanford University Press, 2007), 1–15.

83. President, Hoofdgerechtshof van Indonesië, "Aftrek preventieve hechtenis m.b.t. oorlogismisdadigers," September 20, 1949, Arsip Nasional, Jakarta, Alg. Sec. 289; "War Criminal List Sentenced by Dutch courts: Sugamo Prison," November 6, 1953, NA (NL), Buitenlandse Zaken / Code-Archief 45–54, 2.05.117, inv.nr. 7703.

84. "Trial of War Criminals (Army Order 31/1945) Review of Sentences," May 6, 1948, NA (UK), LCO 53/101.

85. Shapcott to Lynch, March 4, 1949, NA (UK), WO 311/567. See also Pritchard, "The Parameters of Justice," 308–10.

86. Rogers, "Petitions—Japanese War Criminals," September 14, 1949, NA (UK), WO 311/645.

87. Pritchard, "The Parameters of Justice," 311.

88. Ibid.

89. J. A. Pilcher to Esler Dening, August 21, 1953, NA (UK), FO 371/105446.

90. "Draft Staff Study—Remission of Sentence," February 25, 1949, NA (UK), FO 1060/266; "Remission of Sentence for Good Conduct," February 21, 1949, NA (UK), FO 1060/266.

91. Shapcott to No. 1 War Crimes Sentences Review Board, February 3, 1949, NA (UK), WO 311/567; Brown to Shapcott, November 22, 1949, NA (UK), WO 311/567; Pritchard, "The Parameters of Justice," 310–14.

92. Minute, L. Phillips, January 28, 1953, NA (UK), FO 371/105432.

93. Higurashi, *Tōkyō saiban*, 322–24.

94. "Deduction from Sentences of War Criminals," December 24, 1949, NARA, RG338, Box 1025; Special Assistant [George T. Hagen] to Chief, Legal Section, Liquidation Agency, "Japanese War Criminals Convicted by United States Military or Naval Commissions and by the IMTFE and Still Serving Their Sentences," May 17, 1952, NARA, RG59, Box 25, folder: 5 (Parole Board: SCAP Parole System); SCAP Circular No. 5, "Clemency for War Criminals," March 7, 1950, GSK, D' 1.3.0.1, 3.

95. See, for example, "Temporary Release of Convicted War Criminal," November 30, 1949, NARA, RG338, Box 395.

96. SCAP Circular No. 5, March 7, 1950, NARA, RG59, Box 25. For examples of Parole Board decisions, see "Parole Board Meeting 15/3/51," March 15, 1951, NARA, RG331, Box 1392; "Sakai Sadeo Recommendation for Parole," August 5, 1950, NARA, RG331, Box 1221; John Mendelsohn, "War Crimes Trials and Clemency in Germany and Japan," in *Americans as Proconsuls*, ed. Robert Wolfe (Carbondale: Southern Illinois University Press, 1984), 255–57.

97. [Hagen] to Chief, Legal Section, Liquidation Agency, "Japanese War Criminals."

98. SCAP Public Safety Division, OPARS, "Prison Branch File Copy—Offenders Prevention and Rehabilitation Law," May 23, 1949, NARA, RG331, Box 345; "Law No. 142 Offenders Prevention and Rehabilitation," May 31, 1949, NARA, RG331, Box 1392.

99. "Legal Section to Attorney-General," March 18, 1950, NARA, RG331, Box 1392; "Supervision of War Criminal Parolees," March 20, 1950, NARA, RG331, Box 1392.

100. "Certificate of Parole," NARA, RG59, Box 25.

101. See, for example, "Regular Report on Convicted War Criminal Parolee—Nunonmiya," June 1951, NARA, RG 331, Box 1193.

102. SCAP Public Safety Division, OPARS, "Prison Branch File Copy—Offenders Prevention and Rehabilitation Law"; "Law No. 142 Offenders Prevention and Rehabilitation."

103. "Parole of War Criminals with Parole Destination in Ryukyu Islands," May 25, 1951, NARA, RG554, Box 282.

104. "Cho Sung-Ki—SCAP Legal Section," June 26, 1950, NARA, RG331, Box 1392.

105. [Hagen] to Chief, Legal Section, Liquidation Agency, "Japanese War Criminals."

106. Ivan Morris, *Nationalism and the Right Wing in Japan* (Oxford: Oxford University Press, 1960), 109–10.

107. "Third Japanese Censorship Report, April–June 1949," June 30, 1949, NA (UK), FO 371/76253, 4–7.

108. "Report on the Mentality of Japanese War Criminals in Jail," attached minute, April 7, 1949, NA (UK), FO 371/76251, 101.

109. Creech-Jones to Shinwell, August 31, 1949, NA (UK), DO 35/2937.

110. "Report on the Mentality of Japanese War Criminals in Jail in Singapore and the Federation of Malaya as Deduced from Outgoing Correspondence to Their Families in Japan During the Year 1948," n.d., NA (UK), FO 371/76250, 125. See also F. Tomlinson, "Minutes," February 3, 1949, NA (UK), FO 371/76250.

111. "Trial of Japanese War Criminals," *Dubbo Liberal and Macquarie Advocate* (NSW), January 5, 1946, 2.

112. "Jap Repents with $5 Gift," *Straits Times*, August 15, 1951, 7; see also "Japanese Contrition Seems to Be Superficial," *Sydney Morning Herald*, June 15, 1946, 2.

113. "Trial of War Criminals (Army Order 31/1945) Review of Sentences," May 6, 1948, NA (UK), LCO 53/101.

5. SHIFTING MOOD, SHIFTING LOCATION

1. Katō Hiroko, "Haisha no kikan: Chūgoku kara no fukuin/hikiage mondai no tenkai," *Kokusai seiji* 109 (1995): 110–25; William Nimmo, *Behind a Curtain of Silence* (Westport, CT: Greenwood Press, 1988); Yoshikuni Igarashi, "Belated Homecomings: Japanese Prisoners of War in Siberia and Their Return to Post-War Japan," in *Prisoners of War, Prisoners of Peace*, ed. Bob Moore and Barbara Hately-Broad (Oxford: Berg, 2005), 105–228; Richard Daehler, *Die japanischen und die deutschen Kriegsgefangenen in der Sowjetunion, 1945–1956* (Zurich: LIT, 2007); Lori Watt, *When Empire Comes Home* (Cambridge, MA: Harvard Asia Center, 2009).

2. Rusu kazoku dantai zenkoku kyōgikai shi hankō iinkai, *Ubawareshi ai to jiyū o* (Tokyo: Kyōwatō, 1959), 47–48. On the Association of the Families of the Missing, see Beatrice Trefalt, "A Peace Worth Having: Delayed Repatriations and Domestic Debate Over the San Francisco Peace Treaty," *Japanese Studies* 27, no. 2 (2007): 173, 176–77.

3. Kojima Taisaku, Secretary of Foreign Affairs, Kokkai kaigiroku, Shūgiin, Kaigai dōhō hikiage ni kansuru tokubetsu iinkai (hereafter cited as Shūgiin tokubetsu iinkai) 4-gō, February 20, 1948, 2. Diet records are available at http://kokkai.ndl.go.jp/.

4. The First Demobilization Ministry and the Second Demobilization Ministry were created in December 1945. In a series of administrative changes, the separate ministries were downgraded to become a single Demobilization Agency, and subsequently two bureaus. In December 1948, a combined Demobilization Bureau was created and placed within the Ministry of Welfare. See Watt, *When Empire Comes Home*, 67.

5. Higurashi Yoshinobu, *Tōkyō saiban* (Tokyo: Kōdansha, 2008), 350–51.

6. Kokkai kaigiroku, Sangiin, Zaigai dōhō hikiage mondai ni kansuru tokubetsu iinkai (hereafter cited as Sangiin tokubetsu iinkai) 10-gō, October 16, 1947, 1.

7. Satō Toshihiko, officer of the Diet, presentation of petition no. 234, "Chūgoku tōhoku chiku ni okeru senpansha kyūgo ni kansuru seigan," Kokkai kaigiroku, Shūgiin, Gaimu iinkai (hereafter cited as Shūgiin Gaimu iinkai) 19-gō, November 27, 1947, 6.

8. Shōji Hikō, Shūgiin tokubetsu iinkai 2-gō, February 6, 1948, 3.

9. "Petition for the Acquittal of Ex-MP Warrant Officer Torao Yamamoto, a Member of Jonbell Kempeitai, Who Was Found Guilty by the War Crimes Court in Batavia on November 2, 1948," August 1949, Nationaal Archief, The Hague (hereafter cited as NA [NL]), Vertegenwoordiging Japan, 1946–1954, 2.05.116, inv.nr. 530.

10. Shōji, Shūgiin tokubetsu iinkai 2-gō, February 6, 1948, 3.

11. Mizutani Noboru, Diet member, and Kojima Taisaku, Foreign Ministry official, Shūgiin tokubetsu iinkai 4-gō, February 20, 1948, 2.

12. Wakamatsu Torao, Diet member, Shūgiin Gaimu iinkai 4-gō, April 2, 1949, 1.

13. Nakayama Masa, Diet member, Shūgiin tokubetsu iinkai 5-gō, February 4, 1950, 6.

14. Yamamoto Toshinaga, Diet member, Shūgiin Gaimu iinkai 3-gō, February 8, 1950, 3.

15. Kerstin von Lingen, *Kesselring's Last Battle*, trans. Alexandra Klemm (Lawrence: University Press of Kentucky, 2009), 178–79; Norbert Frei, *Adenauer's Germany and the Nazi Past*, trans. Joel Golb (New York: Columbia University Press, 2002), 147, 152; Jeffrey Herf, *Divided Memory* (Cambridge, MA: Harvard University Press, 1997), 225–26.

16. Frei, *Adenauer's Germany and the Nazi Past*, 116. See also Thomas Alan Schwartz, *America's Germany* (Cambridge, MA: Harvard University Press, 1991), 159.

17. Trial of Fukudome [*sic*] Shigeru and Five Others, Singapore, February 1948, UK National Archives, Kew (hereafter cited as NA [UK]), WO 235/1102.

18. Fukutome Shigeru, "Itsutsu no senpan kangoku ni meguru," *Bungei shunjū* (August 1950): 179.

19. Exchange between Yokota Shintarō and Yano Torio, Diet Secretary for Welfare, Shūgiin tokubetsu iinkai 2-gō, November 11, 1949, 1–2.

20. Gascoigne to Governor of Singapore, September 3, 1949, NA (UK), FO371/76253.

21. Oguri Kazuo and Others to MacArthur, October 3, 1949, NA (NL), Vertegenwoordiging Japan, 1946–1954, 2.05.116, inv.nr. 530.

22. WO 235/834, quoted in R. John Pritchard, "Lessons from British Proceedings Against Japanese War Criminals," *Human Rights Review* 3, no. 2 (1978): 116.

23. "They're Still Savages, Warns Former P.O.W. Could Japs Have Been Reformed in 4 Years?" *News* (Adelaide): April 1, 1950, 4.

24. Yuma Totani, *The Tokyo War Crimes Trial* (Cambridge, MA: Harvard University Asia Center, 2008), 218–20.

25. Studs Terkel, "*The Good War*" (New York: Pantheon, 1984).

26. For a powerful evocation of American understandings of the war as one of good versus evil, see David M. Kennedy, *Freedom from Fear* (New York: Oxford University Press, 1999), 855–56.

27. Robert H. Hamill, *A Just War, or Just Another War* (undated leaflet) (Woodmont, CT: Promoting Enduring Peace, [1960s]).

28. Barak Kushner, *Men to Devils, Devils to Men* (Cambridge, MA: Harvard University Press, 2015), 30.

29. "Report of Proceedings for Carriage of Relief Supplies to P.O.W.s and Civilian Population at Port Blair," September 29, 1945, 3, NA (UK), ADM 1/19341.

30. "Conversation Between Japanese Vice Admiral and Lieut. Comdr. J. F. Bayliss . . . ," [1945], 3, NA (UK), ADM 1/19341.

31. "Louis Allen: In Memoriam," in *Lafcadio Hearn*, ed. Louis Allen and Jean Wilson (Sandgate, Kent: Japan Library, 1992), viii.

32. "Ex-P.O.W. Reader Says, 'Hating the Jap Race Is Unfair,'" *Courier-Mail* (Brisbane), February 7, 1946, 2.

33. "Trial of Japanese War Criminals," *Dubbo Liberal and Macquarie Advocate* (NSW), January 5, 1946, 2.

34. "Recognises Doomed Men in Pictures," *Daily News* (Perth), January 17, 1946, 6.

35. John L. Ginn, *Sugamo Prison, Tokyo* (Jefferson, NC: McFarland, 1992), 34.

36. Basil Archer, *Interpreting Occupied Japan*, ed. and with an introduction by Sandra Wilson (Carlisle, WA: Hesperian Press, 2009), entry for October 29, 1946, 121.

37. Elaine B. Fischel, *Defending the Enemy* (Minneapolis: Bascom Hill Books, 2009), 46.

38. Outis [pseud.], "When War Criminals Have Been Punished—What Then?" *Irish Times Pictorial*, September 1, 1945, 4; "'Bury Hate,' Pleads Higashi-Kuni," *Mercury* (Hobart), September 17, 1945, 2.

39. See "Government Assailed: Speeches in House," *Sydney Morning Herald*, March 8, 1946, 5; "Australian Guilt for Hell-Ship Conditions," *Northern Star* (Lismore, NSW), March 8, 1946, 5; "Jap 'Hell Ship' to Be Inspected in N.G.: Opposition Attack Renewed," *Townsville Daily Bulletin*, March 8, 1946, 1.

40. "Tears of Pity," *Sydney Morning Herald*, March 8, 1946, 2. The reference is to the notorious Nazi concentration camp Bergen-Belsen.

41. " 'Hell Ship' Incident Causes Public Outcry," *Queensland Times* (Ipswich), March 8, 1946, 1.

42. See "Precedent of Indonesians," *Sydney Morning Herald*, March 9, 1946, 4; and "Japanese Hell-Ship," *Sydney Morning Herald*, March 9, 1946, 2.

43. Richard H. Minear, *Victors' Justice* (Princeton, N.J.: Princeton University Press, 1971).

44. The International Prisoner Transfer Program, sponsored by the U.S. government, began in 1977. See Michael Abbell, *International Prisoner Transfer* (Ardsley, NY: Transnational, 2001), 9.

45. "Japan Wants Their War Criminals Sent Home," *Singapore Free Press*, April 12, 1949, 8.

46. "Attention: Relief Committee for Prisoners of War," April 26, 1949, National Archives of Japan, Tokyo (hereafter cited as NAJ), 4B-23–5856.

47. Le Haut-Commissaire en Indochine à Monsieur le Ministre de la France d'Outre-Mer, November 19, 1949, Archives nationales d'outre-mer, Aix-en-Provence, INF159/1364.

48. Commissioner General in South East Asia to Secretary of State for the Colonies, June 20, 1949, NA (UK), DO 35/2937.

49. Kushner, *Men to Devils, Devils to Men*, 174–82.

50. "Tokyo Taking China's Prisoners," *New York Times*, January 31, 1949, 3; Henry R. Lieberman, "New Mao Condition Snags China Talks," *New York Times*, February 6, 1949, 60; "From Tokyo to Foreign Office," December 15, 1949, NA (UK), DO 35/2937, 77; Message from SCAP to Eighth Army, January 22, 1949, National Archives and Records Administration, College Park, MD (hereafter cited as NARA), RG338, Box 1060, folder: 000.5. See also *China Press*, February 1, 1949, quoted in Philip R. Piccigallo, *The Japanese on Trial* (Austin: University of Texas Press, 1949), 170.

51. Lieberman, "New Mao Condition Snags China Talks"; "Peace Terms Must Include the Punishment of Japanese War Criminals and Kuomintang War Criminals: Statement by the Spokesman for the Communist Party of China" (February 5, 1949), in Mao Tse-tung, *Selected Works of Mao Tse-tung* (Beijing: Foreign Languages Press, 1961), 4:333.

52. Robert Cribb, "Avoiding Clemency: The Trial and Transfer of Japanese War Criminals in Indonesia, 1946–1949," *Japanese Studies* 31, no. 2 (2011): 151–70.

53. Commandant en chef des Forces Armées en Extrême Orient, Fiche pour le Haut-Commissaire, août 28, 1948, Service historique de la défense, Vincennes (hereafter cited as SHD), 10H 1044.

54. Beatrice Trefalt, "Japanese War Criminals in Indochina and the French Pursuit of Justice: Local and International Constraints," *Journal of Contemporary History* 49, no. 4 (2014): 738.

55. Note à l'intention de Monsieur le Président de la République, January 9, 1953, Archives nationales, Paris (hereafter cited as AN [F]), 4 AG663.

56. "Plan for Receipt of Japanese War Criminals and Repatriates from French Indo-China," May 31, 1950, NARA, RG338, Box 1041, folder: 000.5, January–August 1950.

57. SHD, 10H 6039.

58. F. S. Tomlinson, FO, minute, July 30, 1949, NA (UK), FO 371/76253, 20. See also Shinwell to Bevin, July 29, 1949, NA (UK), DO 35/2937.

59. Quoted in Creech-Jones, Colonial Office (hereafter cited as CO), to Shinwell, Secretary of State for War, August 31, 1949, NA (UK), FO 371/76253, 39.

60. Tokyo to FO, December 15, 1949, NA (UK), DO 35/2937.

61. CO to FO, January 18, 1950, NA (UK), DO 35/2937.

62. "The Repatriation of Japanese War Criminals from British Colonies and Burma," January 15, 1950, NA (UK), FO 371/92396, 7; FO to CO, January 18, 1951, NA (UK), FO 371/92696, 15; FO to Liaison Mission Tokyo, January 18, 1951, NA (UK), FO 371/92936.

63. "List of Japanese War Criminals Sentenced by Australian Courts," NA (UK), DO 35/2937. Twenty-eight were in Singapore, two in Malaya, and twenty-nine in Stanley Prison in Hong Kong. See also "Extract from the List of Japanese Prisoners," August 25, 1949, NA (UK), DO 35/2937.

64. CRO to Australia (Govt), August 5, 1950, NA (UK), DO 35/2937; CRO to Australia (Govt), December 1, 1950, NA (UK), DO 35/2937; Australia (Govt) to CRO, December 20, 1950, NA (UK), DO 35/2937; "The Repatriation of Japanese War Criminals from British Colonies and Burma," January 15, 1950, NA (UK), FO 371/92396, 7.

65. "[List of Prisoners in] Outram Road, Singapore," February 1, 1949 (?), NA (UK), FO 371/76253, 100; Colonial Secretary's Office to Deputy Commissioner General Colonial Affairs, September 21, 1951, NA (UK), FO 371/92379, 65; Commissioner General for the United Kingdom in South East Asia to FO, November 21, 1951, NA (UK), FO 371/92379, 79.

66. SCAP to UK Liaison Mission in Japan, February 23, 1951, NA (UK), DO 35/2937.

67. "Repatriation of Japanese War Criminals," May 30, 1951, Public Record Office, Hong Kong, HKRS 125–3-408; British Embassy, Rangoon to FO, June 30, 1951, NA (UK), FO 371/92379; British Embassy, Rangoon to British Embassy, Tokyo, July 31, 1951, NA (UK), FO 371/92379; "Early Freedom Expected by War Criminals," *West Australian*, August 15, 1951, 1.

68. British Embassy, Rangoon to Foreign Office, Rangoon, March 21, 1951, National Archives of Myanmar, accession no. 155, 66 FMD 49, Box 8, 15_3 (18).

69. "Reply to the Chinese Mission Protest Regarding SCAP Parole of Japanese War Criminals + Attachment," May 13, 1950, NARA, RG59, Box 3020.

70. "SCAP Circular No. 5, 7/3/50," NARA, RG59, Box 25, folder: 5. Parole Board: SCAP Parole System; for examples of Parole Board decisions, see "Parole Board Meeting 15/3/51," March 15, 1951, NARA, RG331, Box 1392, folder: Meetings of the Parole Board.

71. "Liste nominative des criminels de guerre Japonais condamnés par des Tribunaux Militaires," April 15, 1953, AN (F), 4 AG663.

72. Sharon Williams Chamberlain, "Justice and Reconciliation" (PhD diss., George Washington University, 2010), 123; Nagai Hitoshi, *Firipin to taiNichi senpan saiban 1945–1953 nen* (Tokyo: Iwanami shoten, 2010), 264.

73. Nagai, *Firipin to taiNichi senpan saiban*, 261; Chamberlain, "Justice and Reconciliation," 102, 113.

74. Dean Aszkielowicz, "After the Surrender: Australia and the Japanese Class B and C War Criminals, 1945–1958" (PhD diss., Murdoch University, 2012), 183, 188–90.

75. Mitsuo Nakamura, "General Imamura and the Early Period of Japanese Occupation," *Indonesia* 10 (October 1970): 1–26.

76. "Transfer of Suspected and Convicted War Criminals," February 23, 1950, 3, NARA, RG331, Box 1435. Imamura subsequently claimed that he could have served his sentence in Sugamo but had asked to be transferred to Manus in order to be with his men. See "Unrepentant War Criminals," *Sydney Morning Herald*, August 2, 1953, 9. For a hagiographical account of his request to be transferred to Manus, see "Haruka naru inori: Imamura Hitoshi moto taishō fusai no ai to gisei," *Shufu no tomo* 36, no. 10 (October 1952): 86–94.

77. Higurashi Yoshinobu, contribution to "The Tokyo War Crimes Trial at Sixty: Legacies and Reassessment," Asian Voices Seminar, George Washington University, Washington, D.C., March 23, 2009, 7, spfusa.org/pdfs/2008/Tokyo%20Trial%20 03232009.pdf (accessed June 9, 2014).

78. Higurashi, *Tōkyō saiban*, 350.

79. "Sugamo no naigai: Senpan wa nani o kangaeteiruka," *Shūkan asahi*, February 24, 1952, 10; "Zoku. Sugamo no naigai: Senpan wa dō naru ka," *Shūkan asahi*, cover story, August 16, 1953, 6.

80. "Japs Open Campaign to Save Yamashita," *Deseret News*, December 12, 1945, 2.

81. Suzuki Katsuhiko, "Shingapōru ni tsukaishite," *YMCA nyūsu*, February 5, 1948, 3, NAJ, 4B-23-5856.

82. Tsuji Yutaka, "Nihon yo, shizuka ni, heiwa de are, senpan shikeishu wa inoru," *Shūkan asahi*, February 24, 1952, 12–15. See also Nagai, *Firipin to taiNichi senpan saiban*, 246–47.

83. Tsuji Yutaka, *Montenrupa* (Tokyo: Asahi shinbunsha, 1952), 27–39, 120–21.

84. "Sugamo no naigai," 9.

85. "Senpansha engo dantai renraku kyōgi giji gaiyō," March 22, 1949, NAJ, 4B-23-5855; "Hagen Comments on Japanese War Criminals," September 5, [1952], NAJ, 4B-23-5855.

86. Quoted in Higurashi, *Tōkyō saiban*, 51.

87. Aszkielowicz, "After the Surrender," 174–90, 229–31. The number of trials is taken from the Marburg records.

88. "Trials Conclude at Los Negros," *Sydney Morning Herald*, April 10, 1951, 3.

89. Kōseishō, *In Search of Peace*, August 5, 1953, section 5, Archives du Comité international de la Croix-Rouge, Geneva, B AG 210 000 004–007.

90. Chamberlain, "Justice and Reconciliation," 150–51.

91. Kagao Shūnin, "Ikite iru Hitō senpan," *Kaizō* 32, no. 7 (June 1951): 132.

92. See Nagai, *Firipin to taiNichi senpan saiban*, 245.

93. "Kore ijō shokei o yurushite," *Mainichi shinbun*, February 2, 1951, reproduced in *Mainichi shinbun*, Nagai Hitoshi, and Utsumi Aiko, eds., *Shinbun shiryō ni miru Tōkyō saiban/BC-kyū saiban* (Tokyo: Gendai shiryō shuppan, 2000), 2:130.

94. See examples of petitions from Yamaguchi Prefecture, Aichi Prefecture, Tokyo, Saga Prefecture, March 1951, NAJ 4B-23–6265. See also, for example, the description of petitions by Sakurauchi Tatsurō, Diet member, Kokkai kaigiroku, Sangiin, honkaigi 29-gō, March 24, 1951, 14.

95. Kubota Kan'ichirō, Diet member, Kokkai kaigiroku, Sangiin, Gaimu iinkai 9-gō, March 28, 1951, 6.

6. PEACE AND ARTICLE 11

1. Frederick S. Dunn, *Peace-Making and the Settlement with Japan* (Princeton, NJ: Princeton University Press, 1963), ix, 98.

2. Irie Keishirō, "Heiwa jōyaku sōan no kaisetsu," *Chūō kōron* (September 1951): 196–97.

3. See, for example, Cabinet—Japanese Peace Treaty. Memorandum by the Secretary of State for Foreign Affairs, April 16, 1951, UK National Archives, Kew (hereafter cited as NA (UK)), CAB 129/45, Annex C, 49.

4. Michael M. Yoshitsu, *Japan and the San Francisco Peace Settlement* (New York: Columbia University Press, 1983), 44.

5. Dunn, *Peace-Making and the Settlement with Japan*, 46, 53–59; Michael Schaller, *The American Occupation of Japan* (New York: Oxford University Press, 1985), 95–97.

6. Yoshitsu, *Japan and the San Francisco Peace Settlement*, 1–23, 32–37, 43–48.

7. John M. Allison, *Ambassador from the Prairie, or Allison Wonderland* (Boston: Houghton Mifflin, 1973), 167.

8. Judge Advocate General to Secretary of State for War, March 24, 1948, NA (UK), WO 311/851; Johnson to Dunning, "Effect of Blanket Clemency for Italian War Criminals on NA's Position Regarding Post-Treaty Clemency for Japanese War Criminals," April 5, 1950, National Archives and Records Administration, College Park, MD (hereafter cited as NARA), RG59, Box 3020; Jane L. Garwood-Cutler, "The British War Crimes Trials of Suspected Italian War Criminals, 1945–1947," in

International Humanitarian Law, ed. John Carey, William V. Dunlap, and R. John Pritchard (Ardsley, NY: Transnational, 2003), 1:91, 102.

9.   "Japanese Peace Treaty—General Brief," [1952?], 13, National Archives of Australia (hereafter cited as NAA), 217105.

10.   Draft Treaty of Peace with Japan, August 5, 1947, NARA, RG59, C0044, Reel 8, folder: Japanese Peace Treaty 1947–1948, 1. On the Borton draft, see Schaller, *The American Occupation of Japan*, 98–106.

11.   Dunn, *Peace-Making and the Settlement with Japan*, 67.

12.   "British Commonwealth Conference Ends in Canberra: Agreement on Peace Principles," *Canberra Times*, September 3, 1947, 4.

13.   Japanese Peace Settlement, January 16, 1951, 3, NARA, RG59, Box 1, folder: Japanese Peace Treaty Miscellaneous, 1949–51.

14.   Higurashi Yoshinobu, "Gasshūkoku to taiNichi senpan saiban no shūketsu," *Shigaku zasshi* 109, no. 11 (November 2000): 14–18; Schaller, *The American Occupation of Japan*, 84–85, 122–40, 170–71; John Lewis Gaddis, *George F. Kennan* (New York: Penguin Books, 2011), 286–88, 299–303, 331–32; Dunn, *Peace-Making and the Settlement with Japan*, 59–62, 77–78, 83–84; Takemae Eiji, *Inside GHQ*, ed. and trans. Robert Ricketts and Sebastian Swann (London: Continuum, 2002), 457–68.

15.   Memo by the Secretary of State for Foreign Affairs, December 19, 1950, 2, NA (UK), CAB 129/43.

16.   Japanese Peace Settlement, January 16, 1951, 2–3.

17.   Ibid.; Paper by the United Kingdom Government on the Japanese Peace Treaty, January 2, 1951 (Document 147), in Robin Kay, ed., *Documents on New Zealand External Relations* (Wellington: Historical Publications Branch, Department of Internal Affairs, 1985), 3:426.

18.   Cabinet—Japanese Peace Treaty: General. Memo by the Secretary of State for Foreign Affairs, December 19, 1950, NA (UK), CAB 129/43, Annex A, 5.

19.   Dunn, *Peace-Making and the Settlement with Japan*, 82–83.

20.   Higurashi Yoshinobu, *Tōkyō saiban* (Tokyo: Kōdansha, 2008), 335.

21.   "Commentary on Draft Treaty of Peace with Japan," NARA, RG59, C0044, Reel 9, folder: Peace Treaty Developments Since September 16, 1949. The document is preceded by a handwritten note, "November 1949 Draft and Commentary," but internal evidence indicates the commentary was produced in 1950. This version of the article on war criminals appears to have been shortened and simplified by John Foster Dulles and recirculated on August 9, 1950: see U.S. Department of State, *Foreign Relations of the United States, 1950. East Asia and the Pacific* (Washington, D.C.: U.S. Government Printing Office, 1950), 6:1267–70, http://digital.library.wisc .edu/1711.dl/FRUS.FRUS1950v06.

22.   "Commentary on Draft Treaty of Peace with Japan."

23.   Ibid.

24.   Secretary of State [Dean Acheson] to the President, telegram from Lisbon, February 21, 1952, in U.S. Department of State, *Foreign Relations of the United States,*

1952–1954, vol. 5, *Western European Security, Part 1* (Washington, D.C.: U.S. Government Printing Office, 1983), 82,http://digital.library.wisc.edu/1711.dl/FRUS .FRUS195254v05p1; Lisa Yavnai, "U.S. Army War Crimes Trials in Germany, 1945– 1947," in *Atrocities on Trial*, ed. Patricia Heberer and Jürgen Matthäus (Lincoln: University of Nebraska Press, 2008), 66.

25.   "Commentary on Draft Treaty of Peace with Japan."

26.   Draft of a Peace Treaty with Japan, [Washington], September 11, 1950, in U.S. Department of State, *Foreign Relations of the United States, 1950*, vol. 6, *East Asia and the Pacific* (Washington, D.C.: U.S. Government Printing Office, 1976), 1299– 1300, http://digital.library.wisc.edu/1711.dl/FRUS.FRUS1950v06.

27.   Dunn, *Peace-Making and the Settlement with Japan*, 125.

28.   "Japanese Peace Settlement," January 16, 1951, 1. See also "Report on the Australian–New Zealand Consultations with Dulles at Canberra," March 7, 1951 (Document 231), in Kay, ed., *Documents*, 3:625, 634–35.

29.   Australian Mission to the United Nations, New York, "523. . . . Japanese Peace Settlement," September 22, 1950, Australian War Memorial, Department of Defence— TS Files 1947–51, AWM 263, B/1/12/2.

30.   Dunn, *Peace-Making and the Settlement with Japan*, 99.

31.   Australian Mission to the United Nations, New York, "523. . . . Japanese Peace Settlement."

32.   Dunn, *Peace-Making and the Settlement with Japan*, 121–22.

33.   "Requests for Dealing with War Criminals in the Coming Treaty of Peace," translation of "Heiwa jōyaku teiketsu ni shitagau senpan shori ni kansuru kibō," [late 1950], National Archives of Japan (hereafter cited as NAJ), 4B-23-5835.

34.   "Report on the Australian–New Zealand Consultations with Dulles at Canberra," 648–49. See also Minister of External Affairs to the New Zealand Ambassador, Washington, February 21, 1951 (Document 230), in Kay, ed., *Documents*, 3:624.

35.   See, for example, David Lowe, *Menzies and the "Great World Struggle"* (Sydney: University of New South Wales Press, 1999), 76–80.

36.   Cabinet—Japanese Peace Treaty: General. Memo by the Secretary of State for Foreign Affairs, December 19, 1950, NA (UK), CAB 129/43, 3.

37.   "Quirino Names Security Pact, Reps as Aims," *Manila Times*, August 16, 1951, and "PI Group Wants Japs to Admit War Guilt, Desires Pact Changes," *Manila Times*, May 27, 1951, both in Lopez Memorial Museum newspaper clippings collection, Manila; Nagai Hitoshi, *Firipin to taiNichi senpan saiban 1945–1953 nen* (Tokyo: Iwanami shoten, 2010), 258.

38.   "Report on the Australian–New Zealand Consultations with Dulles at Canberra," 645.

39.   Official Secretary, Office of the High Commissioner for New Zealand, London, to the Secretary of External Affairs, March 6, 1951 (Document 318), in Kay, ed., *Documents*, 3:802–4 (incorporates UK aide-mémoire on peace treaty); Minister of External Affairs to the New Zealand Ambassador, Washington, March 22, 1951 (Document 325), in Kay, ed., *Documents*, 3:835–37; "Changes Made in

Japanese Treaty Draft in Deference to Philippine Representations" [August 1951?],
Quirino Presidential Papers, Filipinas Heritage Library (Ayala Museum), Manila,
B24F4–File010.

40. Official Secretary, Office of the High Commissioner for New Zealand, London,
to the Secretary of External Affairs, March 21, 1951 (Document 323), in Kay, ed.,
Documents, 3:830.

41. New Zealand Ambassador, Washington, to the Minister of External Affairs, April
27, 1951 (Document 347), conveying views of State Department, in Kay, ed., *Documents*, 3:921.

42. Cabinet—Japanese Peace Treaty. Memorandum by the Secretary of State for
Foreign Affairs, April 16, 1951, NA (UK), CAB 129/45, Annex B, 44.

43. "Changes Made in Japanese Treaty Draft in Deference to Philippine Representations"; "War Guilt Is Laid at Door of Ex-Empire," *Manila Times*, August 16, 1951,
in Lopez Memorial Museum newspaper clippings collection.

44. Draft of a Peace Treaty with Japan, [Washington], 1299–1300.

45. Kathleen Dean Moore, *Justice, Mercy, and the Public Interest* (Oxford: Oxford
University Press, 1989), 4–6. We are grateful to Carolyn Strange for guidance on this
point.

46. Cabinet—Japanese Peace Treaty. Memorandum by the Secretary of State for
Foreign Affairs, April 16, 1951, Annex B, 45.

47. Acting High Commissioner for the United Kingdom to the Secretary of External
Affairs, Wellington, May 24, 1951 (Document 360), in Kay, ed., *Documents*, 3:958,
referring to a UK brief of May 3.

48. Minister of External Affairs to the New Zealand Ambassador, Washington, May
25, 1951 (Document 361), in Kay, ed., *Documents*, 3:963; Australian Embassy,
Canada to EA, Canberra, May 23, 1951, NAA 217102; "[Question of?] United
Kingdom Draft Treaty of Peace with Japan," [1951], NAA 140426.

49. The two drafts are reprinted and compared in Cabinet—Japanese Peace Treaty.
Memorandum by the Secretary of State for Foreign Affairs, April 16, 1951.

50. Dunn, *Peace-Making and the Settlement with Japan*, 140.

51. United Kingdom Provisional Draft of Japanese Peace Treaty [April 20, 1951]
(Document 338), in Kay, ed., *Documents*, 3:875–76.

52. Higurashi, *Tōkyō saiban*, 337.

53. Cabinet—Japanese Peace Treaty. Memorandum by the Secretary of State for
Foreign Affairs, April 16, 1951, 2; also Annex B, 45.

54. Acting High Commissioner for the United Kingdom to the Secretary of External Affairs, Wellington, May 11, 1951 (Document 355), in Kay, ed., *Documents*,
3:939.

55. Higurashi, *Tōkyō saiban*, 337–38.

56. Cabinet—Japanese Peace Treaty. Memorandum by the Secretary of State for Foreign
Affairs, June 19, 1951, NA (UK), CAB 129/46, 2. The agreed draft treaty appears as
Annex B of this document. See also Allison, *Ambassador from the Prairie*, 164–65.

57. "Japanese Peace Treaty—War Criminals," Memorandum from Department of External Affairs, Canberra to Department of the Army, Melbourne, September 18, 1951, NAA 388639.

58. "Japanese Peace Treaty—Working Draft and Commentary June 1, 1951," 3, NARA, RG59, Box 2, folder: Japanese Treaty Drafts.

59. "[Question of?] United Kingdom Draft Treaty of Peace with Japan."

60. See the various records in "Discussion and Consideration of the Problem of War Criminals Within the Context of the Japanese Peace Treaty," NA (UK), FO 371/92699; Maurice Pascal Alers Hankey, *Politics, Trials and Errors* (Oxford: Pen-in-Hand, 1950).

61. *The Times*, August 6, 1951, included in "Discussion and Consideration of the Problem of War Criminals."

62. Record of Hankey's visit to Henderson on July 25, 1951, in "Discussion and Consideration of the Problem of War Criminals." On Hankey and his circle, and their efforts on behalf of German and Japanese war criminals, see Kerstin von Lingen, *Kesselring's Last Battle*, trans. Alexandra Klemm (Lawrence: University Press of Kansas, 2009), 160–62.

63. See "'Kōwa jōyaku teiketsu ni shitagau senpan shori ni kansuru' an ni kanshi Burekunī shi to no kaidan gaiyō," February 5, 1951, "Questions [for Blakeney]" [nd], and "Kōwa jōyaku sōanchū no senpansha jōkō ni kanshi Enomoto Shigeharu shi to Burekunī shi to no kaidan yōshi," July 17, 1951, all in NAJ, 4B-23-5835.

64. Letter to Craigie, October 1951, and letters to Sebald, October 1951 and February 1952, NAJ, 4B-23-5835.

65. War Criminals and the Japanese Peace Treaty, Record of Lord Henderson's Verbal Response to Lord Hankey During Hankey's Visit to Henderson on July 25, 1951, to Discuss Article 11, NA (UK), FO 371/92699; Masahiro Yamamoto, "Japan's 'Unsettling' Past: Article 11 of San Francisco Peace Treaty and Its Ramifications," *Journal of US–China Public Administration* 7, no. 5 (May 2010): 6–7.

66. "1951 nen 6 gatsu Arison kōtaishi kaikan kara 1951 nen 7 gatsu 13 nichi heiwa jōyaku an kōhyō ni itaru made no keika chōsho," record by Treaty Bureau Director Nishimura Kumao, July 20, 1951, in Gaimushō, ed., *Nihon gaikō monjo: Heiwa jōyaku no teiketsu ni kansuru chōsho* (Tokyo: Gaimushō, 2003), 3:605.

67. See documents in NAJ, 4B-23-5836.

68. Higurashi, *Tōkyō saiban*, 344–48.

69. Sandra Wilson, "Prisoners in Sugamo and Their Campaign for Release, 1952–1953," *Japanese Studies* 31, no. 2 (September 2011): 171–90.

70. Documents in NAJ, 4B-23-5836.

71. Higurashi, *Tōkyō saiban*, 347–48.

72. Memorandum by Mr. Saito appended to Minutes, October 6, 1952, 2, NARA, RG220, Box 1, folder: Minutes—Clemency and Parole Board for War Criminals, M-1 through M-30.

73. Yoshitsu, *Japan and the San Francisco Peace Settlement*, 44.

74.   [Sugamo fukuekisha no iken], [nd], NAJ, 4B-23–5835.

75.   See, for example, "Kōwa kaigi," *Asahi shinbun*, August 15, 1951, 1; "Final Draft of Japanese Peace Treaty," *Daily Advertiser* (Wagga Wagga, NSW), August 16, 1951, 1.

76.   "Sugamo no naigai," *Shūkan asahi*, February 24, 1952, 9.

77.   Utsumi Aiko, *Sugamo purizun* (Tokyo: Yoshikawa kōbunkan, 2004), 125; and, for example, "Shōwa nijū nana nendo gyōmu yōshi," February 1952, 5, NAJ, 4B-23–5836.

78.   See "The Proclamation of Amnesty and Reconstruction by the President of the United States of America," in United States, *Statutes at Large, Treaties, and Proclamations of the United States of America* (Boston, 1866), 13:737–39, available at Freedmen and Southern Society Project, http://www.freedmen.umd.edu/procamn. htm. For evidence that prominent Japanese figures were aware of the precedent, see Enomoto Shigeharu, quoted in Higurashi, *Tōkyō saiban*, 352–53.

79.   Shimomaki Takeshi, "Gunsai, senpan wa dō naru," *Jurisuto*, May 15, 1952, 14–16.

80.   Ivan Morris, *Nationalism and the Right Wing in Japan* (Oxford: Oxford University Press, 1960), 212.

81.   Sandra Wilson, "War, Soldier and Nation in 1950s Japan," *International Journal of Asian Studies* 5, no. 2 (2008): 194–96.

82.   Hanji Kinoshita, "Echoes of Militarism in Japan," *Pacific Affairs* 26, no. 3 (September 1953): 246 n. 4; Higurashi, *Tōkyō saiban*, 360.

83.   Maruyama Masao, quoted in "Zoku. Sugamo no naigai," *Shūkan asahi*, August 16, 1953, 11. See also 5, 8.

84.   "Sugamo no naigai," 9.

85.   "Condamnés ayant déjà bénéficié d'une grâce individuelle (13)," January 27, 1953, Archives nationales (Paris), 4 AG663; "Sugamo no naigai," 8. See also Le Vice-President du Conseil, Ministre de la Défense Nationale à Monsieur Le Ministre des Affaire étrangères, Direction Asie-Océanie, September 28, 1951, Archives diplomatiques (La Courneuve), Asie Océanie, Japon, 130.

86.   See, for example, the exchange between legal scholar and Diet member Sase Shōzō and Minister of State Ōhashi Takeo, Kokkai kaigiroku, Shūgiin, Hōmu iinkai (hereafter cited as Shūgiin hōmu iinkai) 12-gō, November 14, 1951, 4–7; response to petitions by Takagi Matsukichi, Diet Secretary for Legal Affairs, Shūgiin hōmu iinkai 13-gō, November 15, 1951, 9. Diet records are available at http://kokkai.ndl.go.jp/.

87.   Hasegawa Hiroshi, Diet clerk, Kokkai kaigiroku, Sangiin, Hōmu iinkai (hereafter cited as Sangiin hōmu iinkai) 3-gō, November 15, 1951, 1.

88.   Sangiin hōmu iinkai 4-gō, November 16, 1951, 1.

89.   Onimaru Gisai, Kokkai kaigiroku, Sangiin, Hōmu iinkai sensō hanzainin ni taisuru hōteki shochi ni kansuru shōiinkai (hereafter cited as Sangiin hōmu iinkai shōiinkai) 2-gō, November 27, 1951, 1–2.

90.   Ibid., 1; Sekiguchi Jikō, Sangiin hōmu iinkai shōiinkai 1-gō, December 12, 1951, 7.

91.   Katayama Fumihiko, witness, Sangiin hōmu iinkai shōiinkai 1-gō, December 12, 1951, 3–7.

92. Fukutome Shigeru, witness, Sangiin hōmu iinkai shōiinkai 1-gō, December 12, 1951, 9.

93. Sekiguchi Jikō, witness, Sangiin hōmu iinkai shōiinkai 1-gō, December 12, 1951, 9. See also Noriko Yamaguchi, "Writing New Japan in Sugamo, 1948–1952: The Allied Occupation and Conflicted Democracy," *Prison Journal* 94, no. 1 (March 2014): 60.

94. Imamura Hisako, witness, Sangiin hōmu iinkai shōiinkai 1-gō, December 12, 1951, 2. See list of names of those executed: "Senpan o shokei? Firipin de," *Asahi shinbun*, February 1, 1951, 3.

95. "Sugamo no naigai," 10–11; Sekiguchi, Sangiin hōmu iinkai shōiinkai 1-gō, December 12, 1951, 8.

96. Article 11, Treaty of Peace with Japan, in *Conflict and Tension in the Far East*, ed. John M. Maki (Seattle: University of Washington Press, 1961), 136–37.

97. The number of paroled prisoners originally convicted by Britain was probably 127 rather than 140, with the remaining 13 convicted by Australia. When prisoners convicted by the British were repatriated from Singapore and Hong Kong to Japan in mid-1951, they were accompanied by 23 prisoners who had been convicted by Australian courts in those two venues. SCAP did not distinguish between prisoners sentenced by Britain and by Australia, handing over one consolidated list to the Japanese authorities when Japan took control of Sugamo in April 1952. British officials spent considerable time in 1953 trying to sort out which prisoners had been sentenced by British and which by Australian courts in Singapore and Hong Kong. FO to Chancery, Office of the Commissioner-General in Southeast Asia, Singapore, February 4, 1953, 1, NA (UK), FO371/105438; "Japanese War Criminals Tried by U.K. Military Courts" [October 1954], NA (UK), FO 371/110508.

98. Diplomatic Archives, Tokyo (Gaikō shiryōkan, hereafter cited as GSK), D' 1.3.0.3–1, vol. 2:8.

99. "Release of War Criminals and Its Progress," September 1954, GSK, D' 1.3.0.3–1, vol. 2:39.

7. JAPANESE PRESSURE MOUNTS

1. Frank M. Buscher, *The U.S. War Crimes Trial Program in Germany, 1946–1955* (New York: Greenwood Press, 1989), 72; also 71, 136. See also Kerstin von Lingen, *Kesselring's Last Battle*, trans. Alexandra Klemm (Lawrence: University Press of Kansas, 2009), 173–78; Norbert Frei, *Adenauer's Germany and the Nazi Past*, trans. Joel Golb (New York: Columbia University Press, 2002), 175.

2. Christina Morina, "Instructed Silence, Constructed Memory: The SED and the Return of German Prisoners of War as 'War Criminals' from the Soviet Union to East Germany, 1950–1956," *Contemporary European History* 13, no. 3 (August 2004): 327, 342.

3. Utsumi Aiko, *Sugamo purizun* (Tokyo: Yoshikawa kōbunkan, 2004), 125; and, for example, "Shōwa nijū nananendo gyōmu yōshi," February 1952, 5, National Archives of Japan, Tokyo (hereafter cited as NAJ), 4B-23–5836.

4. Statement by Mr. Saito (described as chief of the Japanese Protection Bureau of Judicial Affairs) attached to Minutes, October 6, 1952, 1, National Records and Archives Administration, College Park, MD (hereafter cited as NARA), RG220, Box 1, folder: Minutes—Clemency and Parole Board for War Criminals (hereafter cited as CPB), M-1 through M-30.

5. L. van Poelgeest, *Japanse Besognes : Nederland en Japan, 1945–1975* (The Hague: SDU, 1999), 207–9, 212.

6. See Yoshida to Stikker, September 8, 1951, Nationaal Archief, The Hague (hereafter cited as NA [NL]), Archief van Dr. L. G. M. Jaquet, 2.21.278, inv.nr. 10.

7. Van Poelgeest, *Japanse Besognes*, 219; British Embassy (hereafter cited as BE), The Hague, to FO, August 21, 1952, UK National Archives, Kew (hereafter cited as NA [UK]), FO 371/99512.

8. Higurashi Yoshinobu, *Tōkyō saiban* (Tokyo: Kōdansha, 2008), 361; "Japan at Peace with Formosa," *The Times*, August 6, 1952, 1; National Offenders' Prevention and Rehabilitation Commission (NOPAR), "Statistical Report on War Criminals in Sugamo Prison, Japan (as of October 31, 1954)," NA (NL), Buitenlandse Zaken (hereafter BuZa)/Code-Archief 45–54, 2.05.117, inv.nr. 7703; "Release of War Criminals and Its Progress," September 1954, Diplomatic Archives, Tokyo (Gaikō shiryōkan, hereafter GSK), D' 1.3.0.3–1, vol. 2:47. According to one of his biographers, the wealthy business-man Sasakawa Ryōichi, who had been imprisoned as a potential defendant in the Tokyo Trial but released without charge at the end of 1948, had petitioned Chiang Kai-shek in 1952 for the release of the prisoners convicted by the Nationalist Chinese (Satō Seizaburō, *Sasakawa Ryoichi*, trans. Hara Fujiko [Norwalk, CT: East Bridge, 2006], 233).

9. Barak Kushner, *Men to Devils, Devils to Men* (Cambridge, MA: Harvard University Press, 2015), 185–219.

10. Dening, BE, Tokyo, to Eden, Secretary of State for Foreign Affairs, August 11, 1952, 1–2, NA (UK), FO 371/99511.

11. *Sugamo no haha*, directed by Adachi Nobuo, 1952.

12. NOPAR, "Decision on Recommendation on Release by Clemency of B and C Class War Criminals," October 20, 1952, 7, NA (UK), FO 371/99513. A similar request was made to free the prisoners tried in the IMTFE: see "Decision on Recommendation on Release by Clemency of A Class War Criminals," October 20, 1952, in, for example, NARA, RG220, Box 1, folder: Working papers 4/28/52–5/31/53 (2).

13. Ono Yoshio (chair of House of Councillors' Legal Committee) to Sugamo Prison administration, August 8, 1952, including attachment "Yōseisho," August 7, 1952, NAJ 4B-21–1707; petitions from some 70 Sugamo prisoners to the U.S. ambassador in Japan and the U.S. president, August 30, 1952, NARA, RG220, Box 4, folder: Clemency Efforts in 1952.

14. "Memorandum for the President. Subject: Recommendations for Parole of War Criminals" [October 20, 1952], NARA, RG59, Box 24, folder: CPB, Chronological 1952–1955 (2).

15. Dening, Tokyo, to FO, June 28, 1952, NA (UK), FO 371/99516.

16. Translation of Supreme Court decision, July 30, 1952, NARA, RG59, Box 3020; Murphy, U.S. Embassy, Tokyo, to Secretary of State, July 31, 1952, NARA, RG 59, Box 3020; Utsumi Aiko, *Kimu wa naze sabakareta no ka* (Tokyo: Asahi shinbun shuppan, 2008), 284–87.

17. [George T. Hagen], "Background Information re Japanese Law 103 of 1952 'Concerning the Enforcement of Sentences, the Granting of Clemency etc. in Accordance with the Provisions of Article 11 of the Treaty of Peace'" [1952/1953], NARA, RG220, Box 2, folder 1.

18. English translations of the text appear in various archival sources. See, for example, Rehabilitation Bureau, Ministry of Justice, Japan, "Laws and Regulations Concerning Japanese War Criminals" (1954), 2–17, NA (NL), BuZa Code-Archief 45–54, 2.05.117, inv.nr. 7703; NA (UK), FO 371/105447.

19. Report to the President of the CPB for War Criminals, January 15, 1953, 2, NARA, RG220, Box 1, folder: Minutes—CPB, M-1 through M-30.

20. [Hagen], "Background Information re Japanese Law 103 of 1952," 8.

21. Turner, American Embassy, Tokyo, to Menzies, Canadian Embassy, Tokyo, December 18, 1952, NARA, RG220, Box 1, folder: Minutes—CPB, M-1 through M-30; summary of statement by Mr. Saito included in Minutes, October 6, 1952, 2, in same folder; "Cabinet Order Concerning Procedure for Liaison Relating to the Recommendation for and Decision on Clemency, Reduction of Sentences, and Parole Provided for in Article 11 of the Treaty of Peace," NA (NL), BuZa Code-Archief 45–54, 2.05.117, inv.nr. 7703.

22. [Hagen], "Background Information re Japanese Law 103 of 1952," 8. See, for example, O'Dwyer, FO, to Pittam, Home Office, February 7, 1953, NA (UK), FO 371/105439; Minutes, September 29, 1952, 2, NARA, RG220, Box 1, folder: Minutes—CPB, M-1 through M-30.

23. Minutes, September 29, 1952, 2; Ambassadeur (Tokio) aan Minister van Buitenlandse Zaken, September 17, 1953, NA (NL), BuZa Code-Archief 45–54, 2.05.117, inv.nr. 7836; Ministère des Affaires étrangères à l'Ambassade d'Australie, August 23, 1952, Archives diplomatiques, La Courneuve (hereafter cited as AD), Asie-Océanie. Japon. 130, 2.

24. "Policy Concerning Japanese War Criminals Sentenced by Australian Military Courts" (Cabinet Agendum No. 347), September 1952, 1, National Archives of Australia (hereafter cited as NAA), 140817; Dean Aszkielowicz, "After the Surrender: Australia and the Japanese Class B and C War Criminals, 1945–1958" (PhD diss., Murdoch University, 2012), 246–48.

25. See, for example, Ministry of Foreign Affairs, Tokyo, Note Verbale to BE, Tokyo, June 24, 1952, NA (UK), FO 371/99511.

26. [Hagen], "Background Information re Japanese Law 103 of 1952," 8.

27. Ministre des Affaires étrangères à l'Ambassade de Washington, August 28, 1952, AD, Asie-Océanie. Japon. 130; "France May Pardon 39 War Criminals," July 18, 1952, NA (UK), DO 35/5797; Beatrice Trefalt, "Japanese War Criminals in Indochina

and the French Pursuit of Justice: Local and International Constraints," *Journal of Contemporary History* 49, no. 4 (October 2014): 740.

28.   Crowe, "Clemency for Class 'B' and 'C' Japanese War Criminals," February 5, 1954, 2, NA (UK), FO 371/110501 (italics in original).

29.   Snow, Department of State, to Legal Adviser, "A Board of Clemency and Parole for War Criminals," May 9, 1952, 2–3, NARA, RG220, Box 1, folder: Working Papers 4/28/52–5/31/53 (1).

30.   Truman, Executive Order 10393, "Establishment of the Clemency and Parole Board for War Criminals," September 4, 1952, NARA, RG220, Box 1, folder: Minutes—CPB, M-1 through M-30.

31.   Report to the President of the CPB for War Criminals, January 15, 1953, 3.

32.   "Memorandum for the President. Subject: Recommendations for Parole of War Criminals" [October 20, 1952], NARA, RG59, Box 24, folder: CPB, Chronological 1952–1955 (2).

33.   [George T. Hagen], "Memo re Clemency for War Criminals," April 4, 1952, NARA, RG220, Box 1, folder: Working Papers 4/28/52–5/31/53 (1).

34.   Minutes, March 16, 1953, and July 6, 1953, NARA, RG220, Box 1, folder: Minutes—CPB, M-1 through M-30.

35.   Minutes, May 10, 1954, July 26, 1954, October 25, 1954, NARA, RG220, Box 1, folder: Minutes, CPB, M-31 through M-80.

36.   Acting Director, Office of Northeast Asian Affairs, State Department, to Parsons, U.S. Embassy, Tokyo, December 2, 1954, NARA, RG59, C0043, Reel 34, folder: M-2.7, War criminals 1954.

37.   Kent to Truman, January 8, 1953, NARA, RG59, Box 24, folder 3.

38.   Kent to Phleger, Legal Adviser, Department of State, March 20, 1953, NARA, RG59, Box 3021, folder 2.

39.   "Report of the Clemency and Parole Board for War Criminals," January 15, 1953, 3–4, NARA, RG220, Box 1, folder: Minutes—CPB, M-1 through M-30.

40.   Eden, Foreign Secretary, to Prime Minister, "Japanese Minor War Criminals and Recommendations for Clemency," August 12, 1952, NA (UK), PREM 11/2580.

41.   Cash, Minute, June 19, 1952, NA (UK), WO 32/15843.

42.   Pilcher, FO, reply to Reading's questions on "Clemency for Japanese War Criminals," May 14, 1953, NA (UK), FO 371/105443.

43.   "Japan at Peace with Formosa" (incorporating "British Seamen Gaoled"), *The Times*, August 6, 1952, 4.

44.   FO, "War Criminals," November 15, 1952, NA (UK), FO 371/99510.

45.   Pilcher, FO, "Japanese War Criminals," November 14, 1952, NA (UK), FO 371/99513.

46.   Crowe, "Clemency for Class 'B' and 'C' Japanese War Criminals: Kakue ISHIYAMA," July 1, 1954, 1, NA (UK), FO 371/110505.

47.   Minute by Pilcher on file, "Japanese War Criminals: Law to Amend Japanese Law No. 103 of 1952," January 30, 1953, NA (UK), FO 371/105439.

48. De la Mare, BE, Tokyo, to Pilcher, FO, July 22, 1952, NA (UK), DO 35/5797; Trefalt, "Japanese War Criminals in Indochina," 740.

49. Van Schravendijk to Hoofd Bureau Oost-Azië en Pacific, December 11, 1952, NA (NL), BuZa Code-Archief 45–54, 2.05.117, inv.nr. 7703.

50. In NA (NL), BuZa Code-Archief 45–54, 2.05.117, inv.nr. 7703; see Hagenaar to Minister van Buitenlandse Zaken, April 18, 1953; Hoofd Bureau Oost-Azië en Pacific, "Japanse oorlogsmisdadigers (vonnissen)," May 20, 1953.

51. American Embassy, Tokyo to Ministry of Foreign Affairs, Tokyo, January 12, 1953, GSK, D' 1.3.0.3–11, vol. 1:298–99.

52. "Memo of Conversation," American Embassy, Tokyo, February 25, 1953, GSK, D' 1.3.0.3–11, vol. 2:500; "Note Verbale" (Australian Embassy, Tokyo to Ministry of Foreign Affairs, Tokyo), March 24, 1953, in same volume, 600; Inukai Takeru, Minister of Justice, to Correction Bureau, Rehabilitation Bureau, Sugamo Prison and NOPAR, January 22, 1953 (in English), in same volume, 573–74. For Britain's similarly hostile reaction, see documents in FO 371/105441.

53. Pilcher to Asakai (Japanese Ambassador, London), November 4, 1953, GSK, D' 1.3.0.3–1-2–1, vol. 2:192–94; Hagen to Snow, "Clemency and Parole of Japanese War Criminals," January 31, 1955, 2, NARA, RG220, Box 5, folder: Working Papers re A, B, and C war criminals 6/1/53–5/31/55 (2).

54. O'Dwyer, "Clemency for Japanese War Criminals: Visit of Mr. Yutaka Tsuchida," October 23, 1953, NA (UK), FO 371/105448.

55. Hiroshi Kitamura, *Screening Enlightenment* (Ithaca, NY: Cornell University Press, 2010), 35–36; John W. Dower, *Embracing Defeat* (New York: Norton, 1999), 405–40.

56. *Sugamo no haha* (*Sugamo Mother*), directed by Adachi Nobuo, 1952; *Araki no naka no haha* (*Mother in the Storm*), directed by Saiki Kiyoshi, 1952; *Montenrupa no yo wa fukete* (*It's Getting Late in Muntinlupa*), directed by Aoyagi Nobuo, 1952; *Haha wa sakebinaku* (*A Mother Calls Tearfully*), directed by Sasaki Keisuke, 1952; *Kabe atsuki heya* (*The Thick-Walled Room*), directed by Kobayashi Masaki, 1953. *The Thick-Walled Room* was not released until 1956, evidently from wariness about how the Americans would react, even after the end of the Occupation. On *Sugamo Mother* and *The Thick-Walled Room*, see Sandra Wilson, "Film and Soldier: Japanese War Movies in the 1950s," *Journal of Contemporary History* 48, no. 3 (2013): 549–51.

57. Aaron Gerow, "Japanese Film and Television," in *Routledge Handbook of Japanese Culture and Society*, ed. Victoria Lyon Bestor, Theodore C. Bestor, and Akiko Yamagata (Abingdon: Routledge, 2011), 219.

58. "Zasshi wa dō yomareteiruka: Zasshi shūkan in yosete," *Shūkan asahi*, June 8, 1952, 14.

59. For example, Iizuka Kōji [Katō Kazuo], ed., *Are kara shichi nen* (Tokyo: Kōbunsha, 1953).

60. Tsuji Yutaka, "Senpan shikeishū wa inoru: 'Nihon yo shizuka ni, heiwa de are,'" *Shūkan asahi*, February 24, 1952, 12–15; Tsuji Yutaka, "Montenrupa kara no 108 nin," *Shūkan asahi*, cover story, August 2, 1953, 4.

61. Readers' letters, *Shūkan asahi*, March 9, 1952, 56.

62. "Sugamo no naigai," *Shūkan asahi*, February 24, 1952, 9.

63. "'Montenrupa no haha': higan kanatta 'koe' no taimen," *Shūkan asahi*, March 2, 1952, 36–37.

64. Ashida Teruichi, "Ima hitotabi no . . . jūnenme, mabuta no otto kaeru Ichinose fujin," *Shūkan asahi*, August 2, 1953, 8–9. On Ichinose Haruo, see Dorothy Minchin-Comm and Dorothy Nelson-Oster, *An Ordered Life* (np: Trafford Publishing, 2010), 105, 138.

65. Tsuji, "Montenrupa kara no 108 nin," 6. On Ueki, see Sharon Williams Chamberlain, "Justice and Reconciliation" (PhD diss., George Washington University, 2010), 136–37, 171–72.

66. Tsuji, "Montenrupa kara no 108 nin," 6; "Kagao Shūnin," *Shūkan asahi*, July 26, 1953, 30. On Kagao, see Chamberlain, "Justice and Reconciliation," 131, 169–71; Beatrice Trefalt, "Hostages to International Relations? The Repatriation of Japanese War Criminals from the Philippines," *Japanese Studies* 31, no. 2 (September 2011): 197–200.

67. Arai Emiko, *Montenrupa no yoake* (Tokyo: Kōjinsha, 2008), 41–42. A version of the song is available at https://www.youtube.com/watch?v=dgDpWBdDcJQ (accessed December 12, 2014).

68. Higurashi, *Tōkyō saiban*, 360.

69. Fukuhara Rintarō, quoted in "Zoku. Sugamo no naigai: Senpan wa dō naru ka," *Shūkan asahi*, August 16, 1953, 10; Hatakeyama Ichirō, "Senpan keishisha no izoku nimo onkyū o: Dai hankyō o yonda onkyūhō no kaisei" (cover story), *Toki no hōrei* 144 (August 1954): 9. See also Jamieson, "War Criminals in Sugamo," cablegram, Australian Embassy, Tokyo, to EA, October 19, 1955, NAA 271960, 380.

70. Takahashi Saburō, *"Senkimono" o yomu* (Kyoto: Akademia shuppankai, 1988), 34–36; Yoshida Yutaka, *Nihonjin no sensōkan* (Tokyo: Iwanami shoten, 1995), 92–93.

71. Higurashi, *Tōkyō saiban*, 360.

72. Hatakeyama, "Senpan keishisha no izoku nimo onkyū o," 9.

73. See, for example, Trial of Chan Eng Thiam and 20 Others, Singapore, NA (UK), WO 235/891. Two defendants were acquitted on grounds of mistaken identity.

74. Tsuji, "Senpan shikeishū wa inoru," 14.

75. "Montenrupa no haha." See also the group interview of prisoners in Usui Yoshimi (chair), "Sugamo BC-kyū senpan no seikatsu to iken: Aru hi no shūdan menkai kara," *Chūō kōron* 779 (September 1953): 160.

76. "Zoku. Sugamo no naigai," 6.

77. Buscher, *The U.S. War Crimes Trial Program in Germany, 1946–1955*, 120, 126, 128 n. 12.

78. See, for example, Usui, "Sugamo BC-kyū senpan no seikatsu to iken," 160–61, 164–65.

79. "Zoku. Sugamo no naigai," 9–10.

80. "Sugamo no naigai," 9–10. It is unlikely that actions that might have won the Order of the Golden Kite were actually treated as war crimes, since the Golden Kite was

awarded for bravery and leadership in battle, and actions taken in battle were outside the definition of war crimes.

81. Usui, "Sugamo BC-kyū senpan no seikatsu to iken," 160–61.

82. "Zoku. Sugamo no naigai," 6.

83. Audrey M. Henty, "Senpan: shikei chokuzen no isho," *Nyū eiji*, February 1952, 25–28.

84. Ōishi Buichi, in "Futatsu no iken," *Shūkan asahi*, April 13, 1952, 10.

85. Tajima Kōbun, quoted in "Zoku. Sugamo no naigai," 8.

86. Usui, "Sugamo BC-kyū senpan no seikatsu to iken," 160.

87. For example, Fukushima Rintarō, quoted in "Zoku. Sugamo no naigai," 10; "Senpan keishisha no izoku ni mo onkyū o," 9.

88. "Zoku. Sugamo no naigai," 10.

89. "Shōwa nijū hachinendo Hōchō kankei gyōmu yōshi," January 1953, 7, NAJ, 4B-23-5836.

90. Ibid.; "Shōwa nijū nananendo gyōmu yōshi," February 1952, 5–6, NAJ, 4B-23-5836.

91. For example, Sanada Hideo, "Hikari sashikomu senpan no mado: Kari shussho, ichijishussho no shikaku, yōken kanwa," *Toki no hōrei* 88, February 1953, 34.

92. Katō Tetsutarō, "Kurueru senpan shikeishū," in Katō Tetsutarō, *Watashi wa kai ni naritai* (Tokyo: Shunjusha, 1994), 26–27. Originally published under the name of Shimura Ikuo in Iizuka, ed., *Are kara shichi nen*. On Katō, see Sandra Wilson, "War Criminals in the Post-War World: The Case of Katō Tetsutarō," *War in History* 22, no. 1 (2015): 87–110.

93. Usui, "Sugamo BC-kyū senpan no seikatsu to iken," 164.

94. Katō, "Kurueru senpan shikeishū," 25–26.

95. "Zoku. Sugamo no naigai," 5.

96. On the establishment of the association, see "Senpan kankeisha no kyūjutsu engo ni kansuru sewa dantai no setsuritsu ni kansuru kōzō," March 1, 1952, NAJ, 4B-23-5882.

97. Sandra Wilson, "War, Soldier and Nation in 1950s Japan," *International Journal of Asian Studies* 5, no. 2 (2008): 194–96.

98. Utsumi, *Sugamo purizun*, 147–48; Higurashi, *Tōkyō saiban*, 351–52; "Issen man en no bokin: sensō jukeisha sewakai sekkyokuteki katsudō e," *Yomiuri shinbun*, June 11, 1952, morning ed., 3.

99. Sensō jukeisha sewakai, "Sensō jukeisha sewakai yakunin meibo," August 1, 1952, NAJ, 4B-23-5882. For a highly favorable account of Imamura's activities on behalf of war criminals' families, see "Haruka naru inori: Imamura Hitoshi moto taishō fusai no ai to gisei," *Shufu no tomo* 36, no. 10 (October 1952): 86–94.

100. Higurashi, *Tōkyō saiban*, 352.

101. Katō Tetsutarō, "Watashitachi wa saigunbi no hikikae kippu de wa nai: senpan shakuhō undō no imi ni tsuite" (first publ. October 1952), in Katō, *Watashi wa kai ni naritai*, 75–76. See also "Senpan boshi: Kishisan ni shakuhō chinjō," *Yomiuri shinbun*, June 15, 1957, evening ed., 5; "Kagoshima ken sensō jukeisha sewakai setsuritsu shuisho," September 1, 1952, NAJ, 4B-23-5882; "Kumamoto ken sensō jukeisha sewakai setsuritsu shuisho," December 1952, NAJ, 4B-23-5882.

102. "Senpan kankeisha no kyūjutsu engo ni kansuru sewa dantai no setsuritsu ni kansuru kōzō ni tsuite," March 1, 1952, NAJ, 4B-23–5882.

103. "Sensō jukeisha sewakai bokin mokuhyō kaku uchiwake," September 9, 1952, NAJ, 4B-23–5882; "Senpan kankeisha no kyūjutsu engo ni kansuru sewa dantai no setsuritsu ni kansuru kōzō ni tsuite."

104. Sensō jukeisha sewakai jimukyoku, "Sensō jukeisha ni dōjō o yoserareru katagata no tame ni," May 31, 1952; Sensō jukeisha sewakai, (no title), November 1952, NAJ, 4B-23–5882.

105. "Shichigatsu mikka sensō jukeisha sewakai renraku kondankai no jōkyō," July 8, 1953, NAJ, 4B-23–5882.

106. Higurashi, Tōkyō saiban, 352.

107. "Kesshoku no yoi 'Sugamo senpan': Bengodan shokaiken. Omoi wa gaichi no dōhō e," Yomiuri shinbun, April 12, 1952, morning ed., 3; "Senpan shakuhō no rōhō aitsugu," Yomiuri shinbun, June 2, 1953, morning ed., 7; Sanada, "Hikari sashikomu senpan no mado," 33; "Zoku. Sugamo no naigai," 7–8; Higurashi, Tōkyō saiban, 352.

108. Higurashi, Tōkyō saiban, 352.

109. Ibid. On Nihon kenseikai and Junkoku seinentai, see Ivan Morris, Nationalism and the Right Wing in Japan (Oxford: Oxford University Press, 1960), 314–15, 323–38.

110. "Sugamo no gokuchū kara senpan shakuhō undō: Kakuku ni kyōryoku o yōsei— dokuritsugo hetta karishakuhō ni fuman no koe," Yomiuri shinbun, July 8, 1953, morning ed., 6. See also Sandra Wilson, "Prisoners in Sugamo and Their Campaign for Release, 1952–1953," Japanese Studies 31, no. 2 (September 2011): 171–90.

111. Sugamo 2 (November 15, 1952), 5 [154]; Sugamo 3 (December 1, 1952), 5 [162], in Chaen Yoshio, ed., Nihon senryaku Sugamo purizun shiryō (Tokyo: Nihon tosho sentā, 1992), vol. 1. Sugamo was a posttreaty newspaper produced in the prison. Ten issues appeared from November 1952 to March 1953. Page numbers in square brackets refer to the facsimile edition published by Chaen.

112. Sugamo 5 (January 1, 1953), 8 [179].

113. Sugamo 3 (December 1, 1952), 8 [165]. This may be the rally described by Utsumi, Sugamo purizun, 144, but she gives no date. According to Utsumi, 70 percent of Sugamo's 927 inmates attended, that is, about 650 people.

114. Sugamo 8 (February 15, 1953), 2 [199].

115. Reprinted as Sugamo hōmu iinkai, ed., Senpan saiban no jissō (Tokyo: Maki shobō, 1981). Utsumi, Sugamo purizun, 114, 129; Utsumi Aiko, "Changing Japanese Views of the Allied Occupation of Japan and the War Crimes Trials," Journal of the Australian War Memorial 30 (April 1997): http://www.awm.gov.au/journal/j30/utsumi. asp (accessed October 24, 2014). See also Chaen Yoshio and Shigematsu Kazuyoshi, eds., Hokan Senpan saiban no jissō (Tokyo: Fuji shuppan, 1987), including Shigematsu Kazuyoshi, "Fukkokuban Senpan saiban no jissō kaidai."

116. Utsumi, Sugamo purizun, 128–32.

117. Wilson, "War, Soldier and Nation in 1950s Japan," 197–99.

118. *Sugamo* 3 (December 1, 1952): 5 [162]; *Sugamo* 4 (December 15, 1952): 4 [169].

119. Memorandum by Mr. Saito attached to Minutes, October 6, 1952, 3, NARA, RG220, Box 1, folder: Minutes—CPB, M-1 through M-30.

120. Figures from *Shūhō*, quoted in Utsumi, *Sugamo purizun*, 147.

121. Kōseishō, *In Search of Peace*, August 5, 1953, Archives du Comité international de la Croix-Rouge (Geneva), B AG 210 000.

122. American Embassy, Tokyo, to Department of State, "War Criminals," October 2, 1952, NARA, RG59, Box 3020.

123. Higurashi, *Tōkyō saiban*, 358–59; documents in NAJ, 4B-23-5836.

124. Okabe Tsune, Diet member, Kokkai kaigiroku, Sangiin, honkaigi 49-gō, June 9, 1952, 3. Diet records are available at http://kokkai.ndl.go.jp/.

125. Iwama Masao, Diet member, Sangiin, honkaigi 49-gō, June 9, 1952, 3.

126. Tago Ichimin and Yamashita Harue, Diet members, Shūgiin, honkaigi 11-gō, December 9, 1952, 1–2.

127. Date Shunzō, Diet member, Shūgiin, honkaigi 11-gō, December 9, 1952, 2.

128. Buscher, *The U.S. War Crimes Trial Program in Germany, 1946–1955*, 140.

129. "Zoku. Sugamo no naigai," 7–9; Utsumi, *Sugamo purizun*, 149.

130. "Zoku. Sugamo no naigai," 7.

131. See, for example, "Senso jukeisha sewakai yakunin taru giin nado kondan no ken," June 24, 1952, NAJ, 4B-21-1707.

132. See, for example, Kōseishō, *In Search of Peace*.

133. Dejean, Tokyo, to Ministre des Affaires étrangères, Direction d'Asie, July 5, 1952, AD, Asie Océanie Japon, 130.

134. De la Mare, BE, Tokyo, to Pilcher, FO, November 18, 1952, NA (UK), FO 371/99513.

135. "Sugamo no naigai," 10; H. Yoshida, "War Criminals," January 21, 1953, NA (UK), FO 262/2085, 12.

136. Yoshida, "War Criminals," January 21, 1953, 12–15.

137. "Onimaru kun, senpan no shakuhō o teiso," *Asahi shinbun*, February 12, 1953, 7; H. Yoshida, "War Criminals," February 2, 1953, NA (UK), FO 262/2086, 3.

138. Sogawa Takeo and Oda Shigeru, *Wagakuni no kokusai hanrei* (Tokyo: Yūkikaku, 1976), 118–19, quoted in Choung Il Chee, "The Alien Registration Law of Japan and the International Covenant on Civil and Political Rights," *Korean Journal of Comparative Law* 15 (1987): 147.

139. See, for example, Hirabayashi Taichi, Diet member, Sangiin, honkaigi 12-gō, June 18, 1953, 8.

8. FINDING A FORMULA FOR RELEASE

1. "Senpan shakuhō no rōhō aitsugu," *Yomiuri shinbun*, June 2, 1953, morning ed., 7.

2. Beatrice Trefalt, "Japanese War Criminals in Indochina and the French Pursuit of Justice: Local and International Constraints," *Journal of Contemporary History* 49, no. 4 (2014): 739.

3. Maurice Dejean, Tokyo, to Ministre des Affaires étrangères, direction d'Asie, July 5, 1952, Archives nationales, Paris (hereafter cited as AN), 4 AG663.

4. Note à l'intention de Monsieur le Président de la République: "Criminels de guerre japonais 1952–1953," January 9, 1953, AN, 4 AG663.

5. Trefalt, "Japanese War Criminals in Indochina," 740–41; "Release of War Criminals and Its Progress," Diplomatic Archives of Japan (Gaikō shiryōkan, hereafter cited as GSK), D' 1 3 0 3–1, vol. 2:48.

6. "Senpan shakuhō no rōhō aitsugu," 7.

7. Stikker, Ministry of Foreign Affairs, The Hague, to Butler, [British Embassy, The Hague], September 1, 1952, UK National Archives, Kew (hereafter cited as NA [UK]), FO 371/99512; British Embassy (hereafter cited as BE), The Hague, to FO, September 4, 1952, NA (UK), FO 371/99512.

8. Van Santen aan DOA/OP, August 5, 1953, Nationaal Archief, The Netherlands (hereafter cited as NA [NL]), Buitenlandse Zaken (hereafter cited as BuZa) / Code-Archief 45–54, 2.05.117, inv.nr. 7703.

9. Note Verbale, August 25, 1953, NA (NL), BuZa Code-Archief 45–54, 2.05.117, inv. nr. 7836.

10. See Minuut, Ministerie van Buitenlandse Zaken, September 17, 1954, and other documents in NA (NL), BuZa Code-Archief 45–54, 2.05.117, inv.nr. 7703.

11. "Osaka Women Mobilize to Help Released Felon," *Asahi Evening News*, February 4, 1954; Dutch translation of article in *Mainichi shinbun*, February 4, 1954; Uittreksel, Hayashi Tetsuo, February 5, 1954, NA (NL), BuZa Code-Archief 45–54, 2.05.117, inv.nr. 7836; "Unlucky Sugamo Prisoner Gets Good News from Netherlands," *Mainichi shinbun*, April 3, 1954, National Archives and Records Administration, College Park, MD (hereafter cited as NARA), RG220, Box 5, folder: Netherlands Government—War Criminals.

12. "Unlucky Sugamo Prisoner Gets Good News from Netherlands."

13. Ambassadeur (Tokio) aan Minister van Buitenlandse Zaken, February 23, 1954, NA (NL), BuZa Code-Archief 45–54, 2.05.117, inv.nr. 7836.

14. "Extract Information of Executing Sentence" [April 3, 1954], NA (NL), BuZa Code-Archief 45–54, 2.05.117, inv.nr. 7836.

15. Application for Parole, April 3, 1954, NA (NL), BuZa Code-Archief 45–54, 2.05.117, inv.nr. 7836.

16. NOPAR, Decision on Recommendation for Parole, April 7, 1954, NA (NL), BuZa Code-Archief 45–54, 2.05.117, inv.nr. 7836; Ambassadeur aan Minister van Buitenlandse Zaken, June 16, 1954, NA (NL), BuZa Code-Archief 45–54, 2.05.117, inv.nr. 7702.

17. Ambassadeur aan Minister van Buitenlandse Zaken, June 16, 1954, NA (NL), BuZa Code-Archief 45–54, 2.05.117, inv.nr. 7702; Note Verbale, Netherlands Ministry of Foreign Affairs to Gaimusho, September 28, 1954, NA (NL), BuZa Code-Archief 45–54, 2.05.117, inv.nr. 7703.

18. J. C. O'Dwyer, "Clemency for Japanese 'B' and 'C' War Criminals: Movements of Criminals After Release," December 3, 1955, NA (UK), FO 371/115293.

19. "Family Situation of War Prisoners in Sugamo Prison" [ca. September 1, 1953], NA (NL), BuZa Code-Archief 45–54, 2.05.117, inv.nr. 7703.

20. For example, Japanese Ministry of Justice, "Statistics of the State of War Criminals in Japan as at October 30th, 1953," NA (NL), BuZa Code-Archief 45–54, 2.05.117, inv.nr. 7703.

21. See, for example, "Report on Prison Conduct and Labour Rating of Criminals of War Who Were Convicted by Netherlands Authorities and Are Serving in Sugamo Prison," December 31, 1955, NA (NL), BuZa Code-Archief 45–54, 2.05.117, inv.nr. 7703.

22. Decision re addition of materials for recommendation: Kasai Heijiro, April 11, 1955, and Decision re addition of materials for recommendation: Mori Shohachiro, July 21, 1955, both in NA (NL), BuZa Code-Archief 45–54, 2.05.117, inv. nr. 7703.

23. "Quirino Explains Aim in Pardoning Japs," *Daily Mirror*, July 6, 1953, in newspaper clippings collection, Lopez Museum and Library, Manila (hereafter cited as LM).

24. "[Australia] to Free 173 Japan War Criminals," *Manila Chronicle*, July 8, 1953, 4.

25. "Jap Turnover Slated Today," *Manila Chronicle*, July 15, 1953, 1; "Jap Prisoners Off for Yokohama," *Manila Chronicle*, July 16, 1953, 1. Formally, 108 prisoners were handed over, but in fact 2 prisoners, one of whom was ill, had been sent home earlier. Different sources cite slightly different numbers of prisoners repatriated at this point. For an explanation, see Sharon Williams Chamberlain, "Justice and Reconciliation" (PhD diss., George Washington University, 2010), 182.

26. "Zoku. Sugamo no naigai: Senpan wa dō naru ka," *Shūkan asahi*, August 16, 1953, 4.

27. "Hitō tokusha no hitobito kaeru," *Mainichi shinbun*, July 22, 1953, reproduced in *Mainichi shinbun*, Nagai Hitoshi, and Utsumi Aiko, eds., *Shinbun shiryō ni miru Tōkyō saiban / BC-kyū saiban*, 2 (Tokyo: Gendai shiryō shuppan, 2000), 181.

28. Quoted in Toru Nakagawa, "Japan-Philippine Relations," *Fookien Times Yearbook* (Manila, 1953), 80.

29. Henry Raymont, "Remove Ulcer Tonight," *Daily Mirror*, July 8, 1953, in LM.

30. "Quirino Explains Aim in Pardoning Japs."

31. Nagai Hitoshi, *Firipin to taiNichi senpan saiban 1945–1953 nen* (Tokyo: Iwanami shoten, 2010), 263–64.

32. Ikehata Setsuho, "The Japanese Occupation Period in Philippine History," in *The Philippines Under Japan*, ed. Ikehata Setsuho and Ricardo Jose (Manila: Ateneo de Manila University Press, 1999), 1, 17–18; John W. Dower, *Embracing Defeat* (New York: Norton, 1999), 506; General Headquarters, United States Army Forces, Pacific, "Typical Japanese Atrocities During the Liberation of the Philippines," September 12, 1945, GSK, D' 1-3-0-1-13, vol. 4:443–50.

33. Moises B. Bautista, "Nihonjin e no hageshii zōo—Nihon wa Firipin de nani o shitaka," *Shinchō* 564 (April 1952): 11, quoted in Nagai, *Firipin to taiNichi senpan saiban*, 266.

34. Chamberlain, "Justice and Reconciliation," 180–81; Beatrice Trefalt, "Hostages to International Relations? The Repatriation of Japanese War Criminals from the Philippines," *Japanese Studies* 31, no. 2 (September 2011): 204–5.

35. "Changes Made in Japanese Treaty Draft in Deference to Philippine Representations," B24F4—File010, Quirino Presidential Papers (hereafter cited as QPP), Filipinas Heritage Library (Ayala Museum), Manila (hereafter cited as AM); Roger Dingman, "The Diplomacy of Dependency: The Philippines and Peacemaking with Japan, 1945–52," *Journal of Southeast Asian Studies* 17, no. 2 (September 1986): 307–21; K. V. Kesavan, "The Attitude of the Philippines Towards the Japanese Peace Treaty," *International Studies* 12, no. 2 (1973): 222–50.

36. "To Swap Jap POWs for Rep," *Daily Mirror*, January 3, 1953, in LM.

37. Reported in "NPs Seek Cash Taken by Japs," *Manila Times*, January 5, 1953, in LM.

38. For example, "Not Ungrateful," editorial, *Nippon Times*, August 31, 1953, 8.

39. Nagai, *Firipin to taiNichi senpan saiban*, 290–93. See also Trefalt, "Hostages to International Relations?" 204.

40. Republic of the Philippines, *Official Gazette* (Manila: n. publ.) 49 nos. 10–12, clxxxv, December 28, 1953.

41. "Kankei kakkoku no genjō," September 28, 1953, GSK, D' 1 3 0 3–1, vol. 2:33.

42. For example, "Hikoku, Sugamo no senpan o shamen fukuekichū no zen'in gojūni mei," *Asahi shinbun*, December 29, 1953, 1.

43. Carlos Quirino, *Apo Lakay* (Makati, Metro Manila: Total Book World, 1987), 117.

44. David Wurfel, "The Philippines," *Journal of Politics* 25, no. 4 (November 1963): 758.

45. Republic Act No. 842, "An Act Providing for Compensation and Automatic Salary Increases for Public School Officials, Teachers, and Other School Personnel of the Government of the Philippines" (1953), Chan Robles Virtual Law Library, Republic Acts, http://www.chanrobles.com/republicacts/republicactno842.html#. VJgkz6DAPA (accessed December 24, 2014).

46. Wurfel, "The Philippines," 760.

47. Quirino, *Apo Lakay*, 117.

48. Elizalde to Quirino, November 29, 1952, B24F6-File006, QPP, AM.

49. "EQ Asked to Explain Pardons," newspaper article (source not given), April 30, 1954, in B129F4—File016, QPP, AM.

50. Republic of the Philippines: Congressional Record—Senate. Third Congress of the Republic, First Session, 1, No. 23, February 24, 1954, 309–10, and 1, No. 24, February 25, 1954, 329, in B129F4—File002, QPP, AM.

51. Resolution No. 6 of the Senate, adopted March 4, 1954, Third Congress of the Republic of the Philippines, First Session. B129F4—File 021, QPP, AM.

52. Senators Cea and Delgado, Republic of the Philippines: Congressional Record—Senate. Third Congress of the Republic, First Session, 1, No. 23, February 24, 1954, 311–12, QPP, AM.

53. "EQ Asked to Explain Pardons."

54. "Says Body Exceeding Law Limits," *Daily Mirror* [May 7, 1954], in LM.

55. "President Drops Plans to Nullify Pardons to Goons," *Daily Bulletin*, February 5, 1954, in Magsaysay Library, Manila.

56. "Who really won?" *Philippines Free Press*, December 3, 1949, in Laurel Library, Manila; Russell H. Fifield, "The Challenge to Magsaysay," *Foreign Affairs* 33, no. 1 (October 1954): 149.

57. Dingman, "The Diplomacy of Dependency," 311.

58. "Foreign News: The Philippines—The Lonely Election," *Time*, November 21, 1949, 31.

59. Ma. Concepcion P. Alfiler, "Administrative Measures Against Bureaucratic Corruption: The Philippine Experience," *Philippine Journal of Public Administration* 23, nos. 3–4 (July–October 1979): 323, quoted in Jon S. T. Quah, "Curbing Corruption in the Philippines: Is This an Impossible Dream?" *Philippine Journal of Public Administration* 54, nos. 1–2 (January–December 2010): 3. Conversely, Raissa Pinosa-Nobles claims that Quirino "has been dismissed by contemporary foreign writers in one word—'corrupt' "—because they relied on assessments by U.S. State Department officials, "all of whom wanted a more malleable and cooperative Philippine Chief Executive" (Raissa Pinosa-Nobles, *To Fight Without End* [Makati, Metro Manila: Ayala Foundation Inc., 1990], 10).

60. "Sensō jukeisha sewakai bokin mokuhyō kaku uchiwake," September 8, 1952, National Archives of Japan, Tokyo (hereafter cited as NAJ), 4B-23–5882.

61. Satō Seizaburō, *Sasakawa Ryoichi*, trans. Hara Fujiko (Norwalk CT: East Bridge, 2006), 133, 143–46; Itō Takashi, "Kaisetsu," in *Senpansha o sukue*, ed. Itō Takashi (Tokyo: Chūō kōronsha, 2008), 56–63; Katō Miyoko, *Akumyō no hitsugi* (Tokyo: Gentōsha, 2010), 252–67.

62. Nagai, *Firipin to taiNichi senpan saiban*, 287 and 417–18, n. 516; on numerous unofficial meetings between Japanese representatives and Filipino officials about the prisoners' release, see 279–84.

63. See the following documents in QPP, AM: Collás, President's Private Secretary, to Imperial, Tokyo, August 17, 1953 (passing on Quirino's thanks for gifts from Federation of Mothers of Wakamatsu City, Kyushu), B27F2-File 029; Kasai, Director, Philippine Society of Japan, to Quirino, April 16, 1955, B129F4-File 001; Fujiwara, Social Democratic Party of Japan, to Quirino, December 29, [1953?], B129F4-File 009; Yamaji, President, Women's Association of Kagoshima, June 1, 1955, B129-F4-File011.

64. Jimbo [*sic*] to Quirino, February 17, 1954, B129F4-File 020, QPP, AM.

65. Halsford, BE, Tokyo, to Pilcher, FO, July 10, 1953, NA (UK), FO 371/105445.

66. Currie, Third Secretary, Australian Embassy, Tokyo, to Secretary, External Affairs (hereafter cited as EA), Canberra, September 6, 1952, National Archives of Australia (hereafter cited as NAA), 140817, quoted in Dean Aszkielowicz, "After the Surrender: Australia and the Japanese Class B and C War Criminals, 1945–1958" (PhD diss., Murdoch University, 2012), 260–61.

67. Dean Aszkielowicz, "Repatriation and the Limits of Resolve: Japanese War Criminals in Australian Custody," *Japanese Studies* 31, no. 2 (September 2011): 212, 219–25; Aszkielowicz, "After the Surrender," 286–87.

68. "Zoku. Sugamo no naigai," 4.

69. "Fukaki kansha no atsumai," *Asahi shinbun*, September 9, 1953, evening ed., 3.

70. "Senpan shakuhō ni chomei undō," *Asahi shinbun*, November 5, 1953, 7.

71. "Kaimu jōkoku narabi ni kaikei jōkoku," May 1, 1953–April 30, 1954 [nd], NAJ, 4B-23-5882, 8. On the 30 million signatures, see also Toyoda Kumao, letter with no addressee, July 1954, NAJ, 4B-23-5855.

72. See, for example, Kokkai kaigiroku, Shūgiin, Hōmu iinkai 3-gō, February 2, 1954, 1; Shūgiin, Hōmu iinkai 10-gō, February 24, 1954. On May 29, 1954, 92 of 111 petitions listed in the records of the Committee on Legal Affairs demanded the release of war criminals (Shūgiin, Hōmu iinkai 65-gō, May 29, 1954, 1–4). Diet records are available at http://kokkai.ndl.go.jp.

73. Franziska Seraphim, *War Memory and Social Politics in Japan, 1945–2005* (Cambridge, MA: Harvard University Asia Center, 2006), 125; Beatrice Trefalt, "Remnants of Empire in the Cold War: How Post-War Repatriation to Japan Occasionally Kept Open the 'Bamboo Curtain,'" in *Globalisation, Localization, and Japanese Studies in the Asia Pacific Region*, ed. James Baxter (Kyoto: International Research Centre for Japanese Studies, 2010), 155–70.

74. Andreas Hilger and Jörg Morré, "SMT-Verurteilte als Problem der Entstalinisierung. Die Entlassungen Tribunalverurteilter aus sowjetischer und deutscher Haft," in *Sowjetische Militärtribunale*, ed. Andreas Hilger, Mike Schmeitzner, and Ute Schmidt (Cologne: Böhlau, 2003), 2:697–708.

75. "The Development on Negotiations on Repatriation in Moscow" (Japanese report), November 2, 1953, NA (UK), FO 371/105448.

76. See, for example, "Kōan maru jōsensha: Yonhyakunijūmei no shimei wakaru: Soren dainiji hikiage," *Asahi shinbun*, March 19, 1954, 3; "Hiki gomogomo no rusu kazoku: Soren dainiji hikiage," *Asahi shinbun*, March 19, 1954, 7; "Jap. Prisoners Repatriated," *Recorder* (Port Pirie, South Australia), December 2, 1953, 1; "Japanese Prisoners Freed by Russia," *Advertiser* (Adelaide), March 22, 1954, 16; "Jōsen daihyō o tsurekomu," *Asahi shinbun*, July 8, 1953, 7.

77. Soviet Section, F.O.R.D. [Foreign Office Research Department], "The Soviet Union and the Problem of Prisoners of War," October 1955, 7 (also numbered as 9), NA (UK), FO 371/115283. According to this report, Japanese authorities estimated in June 1955 that 12,642 prisoners were still unaccounted for. In the same month, Soviet officials put the number still in detention at 1,365, of whom 1,011 were former soldiers. Soviet officials named the prisoners for the first time in June 1955 (7).

78. Shimazu Tadatsugu, head of Japan Red Cross, Kokkai kaigiroku, Shūgiin, Kaigai dōhō hikiage oyobi ikazoku engo ni kansuru chōsa tokubetsu iinkai 12-gō, June 10, 1954, 1.

79. Ling Yan, "The 1956 Japanese War Crimes Trials in China," in *Historical Origins of International Criminal Law*, ed. Morten Bergsmo, Cheah Wui Ling, and Yi Ping (Brussels: Torkel Opsahl Academic EPublisher, 2014), 2:218; Barak Kushner, *Men to Devils, Devils to Men* (Cambridge, MA: Harvard University Press, 2015), 258–59; Adam Cathcart and Patricia Nash, "War Criminals and the Road to Sino-Japanese Normalization: Zhou Enlai and the Shenyang Trials, 1954–1956," *Twentieth-Century China* 34, no. 2 (April 2009), 95; "ChūSo seimei: Kokunai no hankyō," *Asahi shinbun*, October 13, 1954, 1; Shigemitsu Mamoru, Foreign Minister, Kokkai kaigiroku, Sangiin, Gaimu iinkai 4-gō, December 19, 1954, 2. See also Sensō jukeisha sewakai, "Kaimu jōkoku narabi ni kaikei jōkoku dainikai," April 30, 1954, 9, NAJ, 4B-23–5882.

80. Shigemitsu Mamoru, "Rijikai giji keika hōkoku: Besshi dai ni," September 30, 1955, NAJ, 4B-23–5882.

81. Sensō jukeisha sewakai, "Kaimu jōkoku narabi ni kaikei jōkoku daisankai," April 30, 1955, 9, NAJ, 4B-23–5882.

82. "Sensō jukeisha sewakai zenkoku kyōgikai no jōkyō," July 20, 1955, 1, NAJ, 4A-22–7306.

83. Department of State, Intelligence Report No. 7271, "Japanese Sentiment for Release of War Criminals," June 14, 1956, 2, NARA, RG220, Box 6, folder: Working papers re A, B, & C war criminals, 6/1/55–12/31/56 (2).

84. Hirose Hisadata, Diet member, Kokkai kaigiroku, Sangiin, Yosan iinkai 3-gō, March 29, 1955, 10.

85. See, for example, "Sugamo senpan zen'in no shakuhō o konomu: Shasetsu," *Asahi shinbun*, September 26, 1956, 2; "BC-kyū senpan no shakuhō o konomu: Shasetsu," *Asahi shinbun*, June 17, 1957, 2.

86. "Itsu kieru senpan no mei," *Asahi shinbun*, December 18, 1956, 7.

87. Treaty of Peace with Japan, in *Conflict and Tension in the Far East*, ed. John M. Maki (Seattle: University of Washington Press, 1961), 136–37, 144–45. Notwithstanding Article 25, Korea and China were entitled to specific, limited benefits under the treaty, as provided in Article 21.

88. Draft reply to Indian government attached to McPetrie to Fitzmaurice, FO, May 19, 1953, p. 2, NA (UK), DO 35/5799.

89. Telegram, UK High Commissioner in India (Acting) to CRO, "Japanese War Criminals," April 9, 1952, NA (UK), FO 371/99509.

90. Telegram, CRO to UK High Commissioner in India, May 9, 1953, NA (UK), DO 35/5799.

91. Quotation from Anderson to Bishop, May 21, 1953, NA (UK), DO 35/5799. Also Anderson, CRO, to Cole, New Delhi, "Exercise of Clemency Under Article 11 of the Japanese Peace Treaty," August 5, 1954, NA (UK), DO 35/5801; "Exercise of Clemency for Class 'A' Japanese War Criminals Under Article 11 of the Japanese Peace Treaty—Claim of India to Participate in Discussions," NA (UK), DO 35/5801.

92. See, for example, the papers in NA (UK), DO 35/5799.

93. Telegram, BE, Washington to FO, "Japanese Major War Criminals," June 29, 1952, NA (UK), DO 35/5797. The U.S. government wished to consult Nationalist China only "in principle"; in practice, no consultation would be necessary, since Taibei had renounced any interest in war criminals when it signed a peace treaty with Japan.

94. Telegram, BE, Washington to FO, "Japanese Major War Criminals," June 16, 1952, NA (UK), DO 35/5797.

95. Thomas, CRO, to Gandee, Ottawa, May 23, 1952, NA (UK), DO 35/5797.

96. Telegram, FO to BE, Washington, June 25, 1952, NA (UK), DO 35/5797.

97. Telegram, BE, Washington, to FO, April 29, 1953, NA (UK), DO 35/5799.

98. Telegram, BE, Tokyo, to FO, December 7, 1952, NA (UK), DO 35/5798; Anderson, CRO, to Emery, New Delhi, April 14, 1953, NA (UK), DO 35/5799.

99. Telegram, FO to BE, Washington, May 4, 1953, NA (UK), DO 35/5799.

100. Minute appended to O'Dwyer, "Japanese Major War Criminals," January 27, 1953, NA (UK), FO 371/105450. See extensive discussion of the relevant issues in NA (UK), DO 35/5799.

101. Marten, FO, to Tomlinson, BE, Washington, February 9, 1953, NA (UK), FO 371/105450.

102. Tomlinson to Marten, January 19, 1953, NA (UK), FO 371/105450; Pilcher, "Procedure for Dealing with Applications for Clemency by the Japanese Government to Japanese Major War Criminals," January 27, 1953, NA (UK), FO 371/105450.

103. "Summary of Meeting February 19, 1953, of Representatives of Interested Governments on Procedure to Deal with Class 'A' War Criminals," 1–2, NARA, RG220, Box 1, folder: Working Papers 4/28/52–5/31/53 (2).

104. [NOPAR], "Decision on Recommendation on Release by Clemency of A Class War Criminals," October 20, 1952, NARA, RG220, Box 1, folder: Working Papers 4/28/52–5/31/53 (2).

105. Turner, U.S. Embassy, Tokyo, to Department of State, "Applications for Clemency of Class A War Criminals," April 21, 1953, NARA, RG220, Box 1, folder: Working Papers 4/28/52–5/31/53 (3); "Clemency for Class 'A' Japanese War Criminals: Summary of the Present Position," 1, August 20, 1954, NA (UK), DO 35/5801.

106. Telegram, Department of State to U.S. Embassy, Tokyo, December 30, 1953, NARA, RG220, Box 5, folder: Working Papers re A, B & C war criminals, 6/1/53–5/31/55; C. T. Crowe, "Clemency for Japanese Class 'A' War Criminals: Araki, Hata and Minami," February 9, 1954, 1, NA (UK), FO 371/110509.

107. Telegram, Allison, Tokyo, to Secretary of State, December 23, 1953, NARA, RG220, Box 5, folder: Working Papers re A, B & C war criminals, 6/1/53–5/31/55.

108. Higurashi, Tōkyō saiban, 371–72.

109. "Sensō jukeisha sewakai zenkoku kyōgikai no jōkyō," July 20, 1955, 2, NAJ, 4A-22-7306.

110. Robert Trumbull, "Japan Urges U.S. Free War Guilty," New York Times, June 21, 1955, 11.

111. "Telegram from the Embassy in Japan to the Department of State," January 6, 1955, in *Foreign Relations of the United States, 1955–1957*, vol. 23, part 1 (Washington, D.C.: Department of State, 1991), 3; "Memorandum of a Conversation, Department of State, Washington, January 28, 1955," in same vol., 15.

112. Mayall, [Report of interview with Mr Shigemitsu], January 7, 1955, NA (UK), FO 371/115288.

113. "Memorandum of a Conversation, Department of State, Washington, August 31, 1955, 10 a.m.," in *Foreign Relations of the United States, 1955–1957*, vol. 23, part 1, 107.

114. Kokkai kaigiroku, Shūgiin, honkaigi 43-gō, July 19, 1955, 1. Quotation is from the English translation sent to foreign governments: "Resolution Requesting an Immediate Release of War Criminals," GSK, D' 1.3.0.3-9-1, 359.

115. Nakayama Tadanori, Kokkai kaigiroku, Shūgiin, honkaigi 43-gō, July 19, 1955, 1.

116. "Decision on a Recommendation for General Release of War Criminals," July 25, 1955, GSK, D' 1.3.0.3–9-1, 361–364.

117. Submission: "Japanese Major War Criminals: Araki," [nd], 1, NA (UK), DO 35/5800.

118. Telegram, CRO to High Commissioners, March 9, 1954, 2, NA (UK), DO 35/5800.

119. "Sensō jukeisha sewakai zenkoku kyōgikai no jōkyō," September 20, 1955, 2, NAJ, 4A-22–7306; Joy, BE, Washington, to Marten, FO, February 16, 1954, NA (UK), DO 35/5800; Joy to Marten, March 19, 1954, NA (UK), DO 35/5801.

120. Laking, New Zealand Embassy, Washington, to External Affairs, Wellington, "Japanese War Criminals," February 23, 1954, NA (UK), DO 35/5800.

121. Marten, FO, to Joy, BE, Washington, March 1954, NA (UK), DO 35/5800. See marginal note on 2. Also Joy to Marten, March 19, 1954, NA (UK), DO 35/5801.

122. Joy to Marten, March 19, 1954.

123. Crowe, FO, to Scott, BE, Washington, May 5, 1955, NA (UK), FO 371/115294; Telegram, BE, Washington, to FO, June 7, 1955 NA (UK), FO 371/115295; BE, Washington, to FO, June 15, 1955, NA (UK), FO 371/115295.

124. Soviet Section, F.O.R.D., "The Soviet Union and the Problem of Prisoners of War," 7; Ling, "The 1956 Japanese War Crimes Trials in China," 218; Cathcart and Nash, "War Criminals and the Road to Sino-Japanese Normalization," 95.

125. "Telegram from the Embassy in Japan to the Department of State," January 6, 1955, in *Foreign Relations of the United States, 1955–1957*, vol. 23, part 1, 3.

126. Pelletier to Dunning, Department of State, October 4, 1954, NA (UK), FO 371/110512.

127. "Clemency for Class 'A' Japanese War Criminals: Summary of the Present Position," 2, August 20, 1954, NA (UK), DO 35/5801.

128. [Memorandum to Japanese Government Authorizing Release on Special Medical Parole of Hata and Oka], October 26, 1954, NA (UK), FO 371/110512.

129. Telegram, BE, Washington, to FO, March 28, 1955, NA (UK), FO 371/115294.

130. New Zealand Department of External Affairs, Aide-Memoire, March 1954, NA (UK), DO 35/5801.

131. Dunning, Department of State, to Parsons, BE, Washington, October 11, 1954, NA (UK), DO 35/5801.

132. Memorandum, "Clemency for Japanese War Criminals: Views and Practice of the Various Powers Concerned in the Exercise of Clemency," [late 1954], NA (UK), FO 371/110512.

133. Crowe, "Clemency for Class 'A' Japanese War Criminals," December 8, 1954, NA (UK), FO 371/110512.

134. Reading, December 16, 1954, NA (UK), FO 371/110512.

135. This passage was included in a draft of the Crowe document: see "Clemency for Class 'A' Japanese War Criminals," NA (UK), FO 371/110512.

136. Crowe, "Clemency for Class 'A' Japanese War Criminals," December 8, 1954.

137. Joy, BE, Washington, to Crowe, FO, June 1, 1955, NA (UK), FO 371/115294.

138. Joy to Crowe, February 10, 1955, NA (UK), FO 371/115294.

139. Casey, Minister for External Affairs, and Cramer, Minister for the Army, Cabinet submission: "Japanese Minor War Criminals," [April–May 1956], NAA 271958, 288.

140. Crowe, FO to Makins, British Ambassador, Washington, July 6, 1955, NA (UK), FO 371/115295.

141. "Cabinet: Conclusions of a Meeting of the Cabinet Held at 10 Downing Street, S.W.1, on Thursday, 28th July, 1955, at 2.30 p.m.," 6, NA (UK), CAB 128/29.

142. BE, Washington, to FO, September 7, 1955, NA (UK), FO 371/115295.

143. Minutes, December 19, 1955, NARA, RG220, Box 1, folder: Minutes—Clemency and Parole Board for War Criminals, M-81 through M-113.

144. Cathcart and Nash, "War Criminals and the Road to Sino-Japanese Normalization," 93–94; Kushner, Men to Devils, Devils to Men, 258–66; Jing Chen, "The Trial of Japanese War Criminals in China: The Paradox of Leniency," China Information 23 (2009): 452–62.

145. Chu Hua (1951), quoted and translated in Justin Jacobs, "Preparing the People for Mass Clemency: The 1956 Japanese War Crimes Trials in Shenyang and Taiyuan," China Quarterly 205 (March 2011): 161. On early postwar discourse in China on Japanese war crimes, see Jacobs, 156–62.

146. Cathcart and Nash, "War Criminals and the Road to Sino-Japanese Normalization," 99–100, 107–8; Jacobs, "Preparing the People for Mass Clemency," 153–54, 155; Chen, "The Trial of Japanese War Criminals in China," 450–51; Ling, "The 1956 Japanese War Crimes Trials in China," 233–34; Adam Cathcart and Patricia Nash, " 'To Serve Revenge for the Dead': Chinese Communist Responses to Japanese War Crimes in the PRC Foreign Ministry Archive, 1949–1956," China Quarterly 200 (December 2009): 1068.

147. An uncertain, but large, number of suspected war criminals also were executed in unofficial, summary trials; see Iwakawa Takashi, Kotō no tsuchi to narutomo (Tokyo: Kōdansha, 1995), 80; and Kushner, Men to Devils, Devils to Men, 249.

148. Ling, "The 1956 Japanese War Crimes Trials in China," 225, 234–35.

149. Kushner, Men to Devils, Devils to Men, 281–93; Cathcart and Nash, "War Criminals and the Road to Sino-Japanese Normalization," 102–6 ; Zhang Tianshu,

"The Forgotten Legacy: China's Post-Second World War Trials of Japanese War Criminals, 1945–1956," in Bergsmo, Cheah, and Yi, eds., *Historical Origins of International Criminal Law*, 2:287–96.

150. Telegram, John Moore Allison, Tokyo, to Secretary of State, June 30, 1956, NARA, RG220, Box 6, folder: Working papers re A, B, & C war criminals, 6/1/55–12/31/56 (2).

151. "Statistical Report on War Criminals in Sugamo Prison, Japan (as at 31 March 1956)," 390. Numbers vary slightly across the different archives, most commonly because there was a gap between the authorization of parole and the actual release.

9. THE RACE TO CLEAR SUGAMO

1. State Department Memo, "Disposition of Japanese War Criminal Problem," December 13, 1954, U.S. National Archives and Records Administration, College Park, MD (hereafter NARA), RG59, Box 23, folder: Japanese War Criminals Disposition.

2. Leonard Cooper, "Rhyming Prophecy for a New Year," in *The Faber Book of Comic Verse*, ed. Michael Roberts (London: Faber & Faber, 1974), 383. "Australian Test team" refers to the sport of cricket.

3. See also Sandra Wilson, "The Sentence Is Only Half the Story: From Stern Justice to Clemency for Japanese War Criminals, 1945–1958," *Journal of International Criminal Justice* 13, no. 4 (2015): 745–61.

4. Kazuhiko Tōgō, *Japan's Foreign Policy, 1945–2009* (Leiden: Brill, 2010), 196.

5. "Opening van de besprekingen inzake Yoshida-Stikker agreement op maandag 10 October te 2h30 namiddags," Nationaal Archief, The Hague (hereafter NA [NL]), Ambassade in Japan (1941–1974), 2.05.196, inv.nr. 382; L. van Poelgeest, *Japanse Besognes: Nederland en Japan, 1945–1975* (The Hague: SDU, 1999), 272–77.

6. "Protocol Between the Government of the Kingdom of the Netherlands and the Government of Japan Relating to Settlement of the Problem Concerning Certain Types of Private Claims of Netherlands Nationals," March 13, 1956, NA (NL), Ambassade in Japan (1941–1974), 2.05.196, inv. nr. 383; "Netherlands Claim in Japan Is Settled," *New York Times*, January 31, 1956, 7.

7. Chef Directie Oosten aan Ambassadeur (Tokyo), May 15, 1956, NA (NL), Ambassade in Japan (1941–1974), 2.05.196, inv.nr. 381.

8. See the following documents in NA (NL), Ambassade in Japan (1941–1974), 2.05.196, inv.nr. 381: Gaimushō, Note Verbale 37/EA5, 19 April 1956; Minister van Buitenlandse Zaken, Beschikking, May 16, 1956; Gaimushō, Notes Verbales 71/EA5, 96/EA5 and 118/EA5, June 15, July 23, and August 18, 1956; Gaimushō, Note Verbale 133/EA5, 12 September 1956.

9. Minute by GTH [Hagen], March 30, 1956, NARA, RG220, Box 5, folder: Netherlands Government—War Criminals.

10. Minister for External Affairs and Minister for the Army, draft cabinet submission, "Japanese Minor War Criminals," March 7, 1956, National Archives of Australia

(hereafter NAA), 271960, 40–41; Casey, Minister for External Affairs (hereafter EA), and Cramer, Minister for the Army, cabinet submission: "Japanese Minor War Criminals" (April–May 1956), NAA 271958, 288–90.

11. EA, "Japanese Minor War Criminals," January 4, 1956, NAA 271960, 179; Jamieson, Australian Embassy, Tokyo, to EA, "Release on Parole of Minor War Criminals," October 6, 1955, NAA 271960, 402.

12. See the following documents in NARA, RG220, Box 6, folder: Working Papers re A, B, & C War Criminals, 6/1/55–12/31/56 (2): "Release of Minor War Criminals in 1954, 1955 and Up to 31st March, 1956"; Peterson, "Accelerated Parole by Australia of Class B and C War Criminals," telegram, U.S. Embassy, Canberra, to Department of State, May 16, 1956. The numbers given in the cabinet submission discussed here conflate all Australian releases, giving the figure for 1955 as 14, without noting that 7 were prisoners who had completed their terms (290).

13. Casey and Cramer, cabinet submission: "Japanese Minor War Criminals."

14. Ministers for EA and Army, draft cabinet submission, "Japanese Minor War Criminals," 41.

15. Plimsoll, Assistant Secretary, EA, "Japanese Minor War Criminals," February 25, 1956, NAA 271960, 78.

16. H. Yoshida, "War Criminals" (report of conversation with Sugamo inmates), January 21, [1953], UK National Archives, Kew (hereafter cited as NA [UK]), FO 262/2085. See also Iwakawa Takashi, *Kotō no tsuchi to narutomo* (Tokyo: Kōdansha, 1995), 257.

17. Handwritten minute on EA, Memo for the Minister, "Japanese Minor War Criminals," May 15, 1956, NAA 271958, 294.

18. Casey and Cramer, cabinet submission: "Japanese Minor War Criminals," 290–92.

19. Cabinet Minute, Canberra, May 18, 1956, Decision No. 197, NAA 271958, 286; EA, Press release, "Japanese War Criminals," July 3, 1956, NAA 271958, 180; Loomes, EA, "Japanese War Criminals," June 28, 1956, NAA 271958, 222. A first draft of the cabinet submission appears to have been forwarded by EA to the Department of the Army as early as January 13, 1956: Tange, Secretary, EA, to Department of the Army, Melbourne, April 10, 1956, NAA 217958, 412.

20. Secretary, Department of Army, Melbourne, to Secretary, EA, Canberra, "Japanese War Criminals," June 21, 1956, NAA 271958, 250; Loomes, EA, to Australian Embassy, Tokyo, "Japanese War Criminals," June 27, 1956, NAA 271958, 226.

21. EA, Record of Visit of Japanese Ambassador, May 14, 1956, NAA 271958, 368.

22. EA, Record of Conversation with Japanese Ambassador to Canberra, February 10, 1956, NAA 271960, 94.

23. EA, Record of Conversation with Mr. T. Suzuki, Japanese Ambassador to Canberra, July 2, 1956, NAA 271958, 187.

24. "Japs Pay for War Crimes," *Argus* (Melbourne), September 29, 1956, 2. One of the "Japs" was a Korean and another was a Taiwanese.

25. Secretary, Department of Army, Melbourne, to Secretary, EA, Canberra, "Japanese War Criminals," June 21, 1956.

26. Percival, EA, "Japanese War Criminal—Yasusaka Masaji," July 31, 1957, NAA 271963, 12.

27. Telegram, Allison, Tokyo, to Secretary of State, June 30, 1956, NARA, RG220, Box 6, folder: Working Papers re A, B, & C war criminals, 6/1/55–12/31/56 (2).

28. Press Statement by Director of Public Affairs and Cultural Affairs Bureau, Japanese Ministry of Foreign Affairs, July 4, 1956 (official translation), NAA 217958, 143.

29. Telegram, Allison, Tokyo, to Secretary of State, June 30, 1956.

30. *Japan Times*, July 28, 1956, in NAA 271958, 109.

31. Telegram, Allison, Tokyo, to Secretary of State, June 30, 1956.

32. British Embassy (hereafter BE), Tokyo, to FO, June 30, 1953, NA (UK), FO 371/105444.

33. "Memorandum to U.S. Board of Clemency and Parole for War Criminals: Summary of Case for Clemency in Behalf of the National Council for Prevention of War by Frederick J. Libby and James Finucane of the NCPW Staff, November 3, 1952," NARA, RG220, Box 1, folder: Minutes, Clemency and Parole Board for War Criminals (hereafter CPB), M-1 through M-30.

34. Bradley to Snow, April 27, 1954, NARA, RG220, Box 5, folder: Working Papers re A, B & C War Criminals 6/1/53–5/31/55 (2).

35. Kerstin von Lingen, *Kesselring's Last Battle*, trans. Alexandra Klemm (Lawrence: University Press of Kansas, 2009), 160–62, 261–63, 299.

36. Hankey to Reading, August 6, 1954, NA (UK), FO 371/110506.

37. Hankey to Reading, October 15, 1954, NA (UK), FO 371/110506.

38. House of Commons, Debate on the Address, June 15, 1956, *Hansard 1803–2005*, 637–42, http://hansard.millbanksystems.com/commons/1955/jun/15/debate-on-the-address#S5CV0542P0_19550615_HOC_255 (accessed April 8, 2014). See also, for example, G. Godfrey Buxton to Lord Kilmuir, "Japanese War Criminals," November 13, 1956, NA (UK), LCO 2/3001.

39. Marten, Record of Reading's Meeting on September 18, 1953, with Arita and Yamashita, September 23, 1953, NA (UK), FO 371/105447.

40. Pilcher, "Visit of Mr. Tsuchida," November 10, 1953, NA (UK), FO 371/105448; Minutes, October 28, 1953, NARA, RG220, Box 1, folder: Minutes, CPB, M-31 through M-80.

41. Marten, Record of Reading's Meeting on September 18, 1953, with Arita and Yamashita; Allen, Minute, November 14, 1953 on file "Clemency for Japanese War Criminals," NA (UK), FO 371/105448.

42. Crowe, "Clemency for Class 'B' and 'C' Japanese War Criminals," February 5, 1954, NA (UK), FO 371/110501.

43. Pilcher, "Clemency for Class B and C Japanese War Criminals," September 11, 1953, 3, NA (UK), FO 371/105447.

44. Pilcher, FO, to Dening, BE, Tokyo, February 6, 1952, NA (UK), FO 371/99509.

45. Marginal note by Marten on "Clemency for Japanese War Criminals" [ca. July 1954], NA (UK), FO 371/110508.

46.   Minute, September 3, 1953, NA (UK), FO 262/2092.

47.   Draft submission, "General Review of Sentences of Class 'B' and 'C' Japanese War Criminals" [ca. February 1955], NA (UK), FO 371/115292.

48.   Dean Aszkielowicz, "Repatriation and the Limits of Resolve: Japanese War Criminals in Australian Custody," *Japanese Studies* 31, no. 2 (September 2011): 214, 225; Marcy, First Secretary, U.S. Embassy, The Hague, to Department of State, "Dutch-Japanese Relations: War Criminals and Civilian Internees," January 5, 1955, NARA, RG220, Box 5, folder: Working Papers re A, B & C War Criminals 6/1/53–5/31/55 (2).

49.   McIntyre to CPB [August 1956], NARA, RG220, Box 6, folder: Working Papers re A, B & C War Criminals 6/1/55–12/31/56 (2).

50.   Quoted in Higurashi Yoshinobu, *Tōkyō saiban* (Tokyo: Kōdansha, 2008), 374.

51.   Miyagi Kenshū, *Sengo, sensō no eigashi* (Tokyo: Bokutō shinjūsha, 1991), 147; John W. Dower, *Embracing Defeat* (New York: Norton, 1999), 514. According to Dower, these figures apply to the single year of 1952, but neither Miyagi nor Dower gives a source.

52.   Sandra Wilson, "Prisoners in Sugamo and Their Campaign for Release," *Japanese Studies* 31, no. 2 (September 2011): 179–81.

53.   De la Mare, BE, Tokyo to Pilcher, FO, December 2, 1952, and Pilcher to De la Mare, January 14, 1953, NA (UK), FO 371/99514.

54.   H. Yoshida, "Diet on War Criminals," December 26, [1952], NA (UK), FO 262/2085.

55.   Ibid.

56.   "Sugamo keimusho de okonowareta 'shogai sagyō' no jittai ni tsuite," September 15, 1960, [3], National Archives of Japan (hereafter cited as NAJ), 4B-23–7320.

57.   Higurashi, *Tōkyō saiban*, 374.

58.   Pemmerenke to CPB, Washington, D.C., July 15, 1954, and Telegram, Allison, Tokyo to Secretary of State, September 1, 1954, both in NARA, RG220, Box 5, folder: Working Papers re A, B & C War Criminals 6/1/53–5/31/55 (2).

59.   "War Criminals Working Secretly Outside Gaols," *Central Queensland Herald* (Rockhampton), October 20, 1955, 27. See also Cablegram, Jamieson, Australian Embassy, Tokyo to EA, "War Criminals in Sugamo," October 19, 1955, NAA 271960, 379–81.

60.   "129 War Criminals Absent from Prison," *Asahi Evening News*, October 14, 1955, NAA 271960, 370.

61.   "Recollections of My Life in Sugamo Prison. By Sadao Araki, Former General of the Defunct Imperial Japanese Army," NAA 271960, 306. See also, for example, "Recollections of My Life in Sugamo Prison," NARA, RG220, Box 6, folder: Working Papers re A, B & C War Criminals 6/1/55–12/31/56 (1).

62.   "Sugamo Prison 'Freedom' Hit," *Asahi Evening News*, October 13, 1955, NAA 271960, 369.

63.   Translations of some Japanese press reactions are contained in NAA 271960, 365–68. See also, for example, Secretary, Department of Army to Secretary, Department of EA, October 24, 1955, NAA 271960, 378.

64. "Felon Story Repudiated by Gaimusho," *Nippon Times*, October 16, 1955, NAA 271960, 372.

65. Hōmushō, "Iwayuru 'Araki hōgen' mondai," nd, NAJ, 4B-23–7369.

66. Sensō jukeisha sewakai (hereafter SJS), "Kaimu hōkoku narabi ni kaikei hōkoku, dai san kai [1954–1955]," 6, NAJ, 4A-22–7275.

67. Ibid., 10–11;"The Quiet Life," *Manchester Guardian*, December 30, 1954, NA (UK), FO 371/110514.

68. O'Dwyer, Minute, December 30, 1954, NA (UK), FO 371/110514.

69. SJS, "Kaimu hōkoku narabi ni kaikei hōkoku, dai san kai," 11; SJS, "Onegai," [1955], NAJ, 4B-23–7369; Utsumi Aiko, *Kimu wa naze sabakaretanoka* (Tokyo: Asahi shinbun shuppan, 2008), 289–90.

70. Utsumi, *Kimu wa naze sabakaretanoka*, 290, 292. See also Morikawa Kenji, "Sugamo no daisankokujin senpan," *Asahi shinbun*, January 17, 1955, 3; "Sugamo karishussho kotowaru—daisankokujin seikatsu shikin yokoseto—shōgai," *Asahi shinbun*, December 29, 1954, evening ed., 3; " 'Seikatsu dekinu' to momeru—Sugamo shussho no Taiwanjin senpan," *Asahi shinbun*, January 8, 1955, evening ed., 3.

71. SJS, "Kaimu hōkoku narabi ni kaikei hōkoku, dai san kai," 12; Franziska Seraphim, *War Memory and Social Politics in Japan, 1945–2005* (Cambridge, MA: Harvard University Asia Center, 2006), 79.

72. SJS, "Kaimu hōkoku narabi ni kaikei hōkoku, dai san kai"; SJS, "Kaimu hōkoku narabi ni kaikei hōkoku, dai yon kai [1954–1956]," NAJ, 4A-22–7275.

73. See drafts of "Considerations to Be Taken Into Account in Examining Applications for Clemency on Behalf of Japanese War-Criminals," February 1953, NA (UK), FO 371/105440.

74. FO to Coleman, July 8, 1953, NA (UK), FO 371/105444; Marten, "Clemency for Class B and C Japanese War Criminals: Yaokichi AMARI, Naotake OKUDA, Masayoshi ISAMO, Keisuke YOSHII, War Office Trial No. 84/J," July 3, 1953, NA (UK), FO 371/105445.

75. O'Dwyer, Minute, July 29, 1953, NA (UK), FO 371/105445; Marten, "Clemency for Class B and C Japanese War Criminals: Yaokichi AMARI, Naotake OKUDA, Masayoshi ISAMO, Keisuke YOSHII."

76. Crowe, "Class 'B' and 'C' Japanese War Criminals," April 10, 1954, NA (UK), FO 371/110506.

77. O'Dwyer, "Clemency for Class 'B' and 'C' Japanese War Criminals: Progress of Foreign Office Review of Appeals," September 15, 1954, NA (UK), FO 371/110507.

78. "Japanese War Criminals Tried by U.K. Military Courts," table attached to O'Dwyer, "Clemency for Class 'B' and 'C' Japanese War Criminals," October 28, 1954, NA (UK), FO 371/110508.

79. For example, de la Mare, BE, Tokyo, to Pilcher, FO, March 18, 1953, and reply, Pilcher to de la Mare, March 27, 1953, NA (UK), FO 371/105441.

80. Dening, BE, Tokyo to Scott, FO, May 12, 1953, NA (UK), FO 371/105443.

81. Dening, BE, Tokyo to Allen, FO, June 3, 1953, NA (UK), FO 371/105444.

82. Halford, BE, Tokyo to Pilcher, FO, August 5, 1953, NA (UK), FO 371/105446. Halford stated that he wrote under Dening's instructions.

83. Telegram, Dening, BE, Tokyo, to FO, "Japan: Fortnightly Summary. Period December 21, 1953–January 3, 1954," 2, NA (UK), FO 371/110501.

84. Pilcher, Minute, June 15, 1953, NA (UK), FO 371/105444.

85. See the following documents in NA (UK), FO 371/110508: "Clemency for Class 'B' and 'C' Japanese War Criminals," [ca. September 1954]; table, "Japanese War Criminals Tried by U.K. Military Courts," attached to O'Dwyer, "Clemency for Class 'B' and 'C' Japanese War Criminals," October 28, 1954.

86. Crowe, "Class 'B' and 'C' Japanese War Criminals," April 10, 1954, NA (UK), FO 371/110506.

87. Nigel Walker, *Crime and Punishment in Britain*, rev. ed. (Edinburgh: Edinburgh University Press, 1968), 152–54; Terence Morris, *Crime and Criminal Justice Since 1945* (Oxford: Blackwell, 1989), 116. Parole was introduced in England and Wales in 1968, and in the Australian states from 1956 onward. Before the 1967 legal changes, the term "parole" was used in Britain to mean temporary release for a special purpose; colloquially, it also referred to conditional release on license.

88. For an example of Japanese pressure on the British government to employ a system of parole, see "Present Condition of the Japanese War Criminals Sentenced by the British Military Courts (Condition as of September 15, 1954)," Diplomatic Archives of Japan (Gaikō shiryōkan; hereafter GSK), D' 1.3.0.3–1-2–1, 390–94.

89. O'Dwyer, "Japanese War Criminals: Procedure for Dealing with Applications for Clemency," April 10, 1953, NA (UK), FO 371/105441.

90. O'Dwyer, "Clemency for Class 'B' and 'C' Japanese War Criminals: Men Serving Long Sentences," September 8, 1954, NA (UK), FO 371/110507.

91. Pilcher to Dening, Tokyo, August 21, 1953, NA (UK), FO 371/105446.

92. O'Dwyer, "Clemency for Class 'B' and 'C' Japanese War Criminals: Men Serving Long Sentences."

93. Draper, War Office, to O'Dwyer, FO, "Clemency in Respect of Japanese War Criminals," February 19, 1953, NA (UK), FO 371/105440.

94. James, Minute, September 2, 1953, NA (UK), FO 262/2092.

95. Halford, Minute, September 3, 1953, NA (UK), FO 262/2092.

96. Telegram, Department of State to U.S. Embassy, Tokyo, July 16, 1954, NARA, RG220, Box 5, folder: Working Papers re A, B, & C War Criminals 6/1/53–5/31/55 (2).

97. Crowe, "Clemency for Class 'B' and 'C' Japanese War Criminals: Masazo FUJINO," December 17, 1954, NA (UK), FO 371/110508.

98. Allen, Minute, December 20, 1954, on Crowe, "Clemency for Class 'B' and 'C' Japanese War Criminals: Masazo FUJINO."

99. O'Dwyer, "General Review of Sentences on Class 'B' and 'C' Japanese War Criminals," January 25, 1955, NA (UK), FO 371/115292.

100. O'Dwyer, Minute, February 16, 1955; "General Review of Sentences of Class 'B' and 'C' Japanese War Criminals," undated (earlier draft of submission), NA (UK), FO 371/115292.

101.   O'Dwyer, "Clemency for Japanese War Criminals," May 10, 1955, NA (UK), FO 371/115290.

102.   Mayall, Minute, May 12, 1955, on O'Dwyer, "Clemency for Japanese War Criminals," NA (UK), FO 371/115290.

103.   Crowe, "Clemency for Japanese War Criminals Convicted by British Military Courts," May 7, 1955, NA (UK), FO 371/115290.

104.   "Clemency for Class 'B' and 'C' Japanese War Criminals" (undated) and "Japanese War Criminals," June 25, 1955, NA (UK), FO 371/115292.

105.   "Japanese War Criminals: Memorandum by the Secretary of State for Foreign Affairs," July 13, 1955, NA (UK), CAB 129/76.

106.   "Conclusions of a Meeting of the Cabinet Held at 10 Downing Street, S.W. 1, on Thursday, 28th July, 1955, at 2.30 p.m.," NA (UK), CAB 128/29.

107.   Crowe, "Clemency for Class 'B' and 'C' Japanese War Criminals," August 23, 1955, NA (UK), FO 371/115292.

108.   Cabinet Notebook, July 28, 1955, NA (UK), CAB 195/14, 35.

109.   "Conclusions of a Meeting of the Cabinet Held at 10 Downing Street, S.W. 1, on Thursday, 28th July, 1955, at 2.30 p.m."

110.   Crowe, "Clemency for Japanese War Criminals," July 7, 1955, NA (UK), FO 371/115292.

111.   R. John Pritchard, "The Gift of Clemency Following British War Crimes Trials in the Far East, 1946–1948," *Criminal Law Forum* 7, no. 1 (1996): 48.

112.   Young to Snow, March 24, 1953, NARA, RG 220, Box 1, folder: Working Papers 4/28/52–5/31/53 (3).

113.   John M. Allison, *Ambassador from the Prairie, or Allison Wonderland* (Boston: Houghton Mifflin, 1973), 222–92.

114.   "General Amnesty for Japanese War Criminals," February 16, 1954, NARA, RG220, Box 5, folder: Working Papers re A, B, & C War Criminals, 6/1/53–5/31/55 (2).

115.   Higurashi, *Tōkyō saiban*, 364.

116.   "General Amnesty for Japanese War Criminals."

117.   Telegram, Dulles, Department of State to U.S. Embassy, Tokyo, July 16, 1954, NARA, RG220, Box 5, folder: Working Papers re A, B, & C War Criminals, 6/1/53–5/31/55 (2).

118.   Snow, "Memorandum for Mr. William J. Hopkins, the White House. Subject: Recommendation Relative to War Criminals," June 22, 1954, NARA, RG220, Box 5, in same folder.

119.   Ibid.

120.   Ministry of Justice, Japan, "Release of War Criminals and Its Progress," September 1954, GSK, D' 1.3.0.3–1, vol. 2:50.

121.   Snow to Phleger, "Ultimate Disposal of Japanese War Criminal Problem," December 8, 1954, NARA, RG220, Box 5, folder: Working Papers re A, B, & C War Criminals, 6/1/53–5/31/55 (2).

122.   Robertson to Phleger, "Disposition of Japanese War Criminal Problem," December 13, 1954, NARA, RG59, Box 23, folder: State Department Legal Adviser—Japanese War Criminals Disposition.

123. Percival, EA, to Nishimiya, Japanese Embassy, Canberra, July 26, 1956, NAA 271958, 116.

124. Snow to Phleger, "Ultimate Disposal of Japanese War Criminal Problem."

125. Minutes, November 29, 1954, NARA, RG220, Box 1, folder: Minutes, CPB, M-31 through M-80.

126. Minutes, December 13, 1954, in same folder.

127. Minutes, January 10, 1955, in same folder.

128. Eisenhower, "Amendment of Executive Order No. 10393 of September 4, 1952, Establishing the Clemency and Parole Board for War Criminals," May 16, 1955, NARA, RG220, Box 5, folder: Working Papers re A, B, & C War Criminals, 6/1/53–5/31/33 (3).

129. Andreas Hilger and Jörg Morré, "SMT-Verurteilte als Problem der Entstalinisierung. Die Entlassungen Tribunalverurteilter aus sowjetischer und deutscher Haft," in *Sowjetische Militärtribunale*, ed. Andreas Hilger, Mike Schmeitzner, and Ute Schmidt (Cologne: Böhlau, 2003), 2:714–37.

130. "Japan's Divided Sympathies," *The Times*, December 14, 1956, 8.

131. "Kōan maru Maizuru nyūkō—sennjūgonin ga kaeru—Soren hikiage," *Asahi shinbun*, December 26, 1956, evening ed., 1; "News in Brief: Russians Repatriate 1,025 Japanese," *The Times*, December 27, 1956, 5.

132. Furness also played IMTFE president William Webb in two television series, in 1976 and 1977: see South Toranomon Law Offices, http://www.s-tora.com/en/overview/?PHPSESSID=4b5sjsndbkk3p4d4hnd37n28l6 (accessed October 8, 2015).

133. Furness to Editor, "Release of Sugamo Prisoners," *Nippon Times*, August 21, 1955, NARA, RG59, C0043, Reel 34, folder: M-2.7 War Criminals 1955.

134. Allen, Minute, December 20, 1954, on Crowe, "Clemency for Class 'B' and 'C' Japanese War Criminals: Masazo FUJINO," NA (UK), FO 371/110508; Snow to Phleger, "Ultimate Disposal of Japanese War Criminal Problem."

135. "Conclusions of a Meeting of the Cabinet Held at 10 Downing Street, S.W. 1, on Thursday, 28th July, 1955, at 2.30 p.m."

136. Minutes, May 2, 1955, NARA, RG220, Box 1, folder: Minutes, CPB, M-31 through M-80; Raymond to MacArthur, January 4, 1957, "Japanese War Criminals," NARA, RG59, Box 10, folder: 12.2 Japanese War Criminals—Permanent Hard Core (specific cases) 1957.

137. Eden, Secretary of State for Foreign Affairs, Petition to the Queen for Clemency for Shunkichi Saito, March 8, 1954 (marked as approved by the Queen), NA (UK), FO 371/110502.

138. "Clemency for Class 'B' and 'C' Japanese War Criminals: Japanese Request for Clemency for Five Prisoners Convicted of Crimes Against Residents of Burma," [June 1954], NA (UK), FO 371/110502; Trial of Kume Matao and 17 Others, Rangoon, August–September 1947, NA (UK), WO 235/1064.

139. Macmillan, Secretary of State for Foreign Affairs, Petition to the Queen for Clemency for 30 Japanese War Criminals, August 23, 1955 (marked as approved by the Queen), NA (UK), FO 371/115292.

140. Crowe, "Clemency for Class 'B' and 'C' Japanese War Criminals: Ryosaburo TANAKA," April 18, 1956, NA (UK), FO 371/121082; Crowe, "Clemency for Class 'B' and 'C' Japanese War Criminals," February 28, 1956, NA (UK), FO 371/121081; Bushe-Fox, Minute, October 26, 1955, on O'Dwyer, "Clemency for Class 'B' and 'C' Japanese War Criminals: Cases of KINOSHITA and YOKOHATA," October 14, 1955, NA (UK), FO 371/115293.

141. "Clemency for Class 'B' and 'C' Japanese War Criminals: Eiichi KINOSHITA" [nd], NA (UK), FO 371/115293.

142. Bushe-Fox, Minute, October 26, 1955; Ministry for Foreign Affairs, Japan, Note Verbale, March 28, 1956, NA (UK), FO 371/121081.

143. Telegram, CRO to High Commissioners, "Japanese War Criminals," April 4, 1958, NA (UK), FO 371/133632.

144. Crowe, "Clemency for Class 'B' and 'C' Japanese War Criminals," February 22, 1956, NA (UK), FO 371/121081.

145. Telegram, Black to Secretary of State for the Colonies, March 21, 1956, NA (UK), FO 371/121081.

146. Telegram, Governor, Singapore to Secretary of State for the Colonies, July 19, 1956, NA (UK), FO 371/121081.

147. Lloyd, Secretary of State for Foreign Affairs, Petition to Queen (marked as approved by the Queen), [August 1956], NA (UK), FO 371/121083.

148. NOPAR, "Statistical Report on War Criminals in Sugamo Prison, Japan (as at 30 September 1956)," table 1, NA (UK), FO 371/121086; FO to Dening, BE, Tokyo, September 22, 1956, NA (UK), FO 371/121083; Selby, BE, Tokyo, to Crowe, FO, October 12, 1956, NA (UK), FO 371/121083.

149. Hagen Note, NARA, RG220, Box 2, folder: General Work File, B & C War Criminals (2).

150. "Chairman's Summary of the Crimes Committed by the 71 Japanese War Criminals Remaining in Sugamo," NARA, RG59, Box 10, folder: 12.2 Japanese War Criminals—Permanent Hard Core (specific cases) 1957.

151. "Monthly Information of Sugamo Prison Inmate [sic] Sentenced by Australian Military Courts (for April 1957)," NAA 271962, 5; Quinn, EA, to Jamieson, "Japanese War Criminals," May 21, 1957, NAA 271962, 32.

152. Hagen Note, NARA, RG220, Box 2, folder: General Work File, B & C War Criminals (2).

153. CPB to the President, "Report of Clemency and Parole Board for War Criminals (Japanese)," November 27, 1957, NARA, RG220, Box 1, folder: Minutes, CPB, M-81 through M-113.

154. Hagen Notes, February 11, 1957 (ellipses in original), NARA, RG220, Box 2, folder: General Work File, B & C War Criminals (3). See also Hagen Note, December 9, 1957, NARA, RG220, Box 2, folder: General Work File, B & C War Criminals (2).

155. CPB to the President, "Report of Clemency and Parole Board for War Criminals (Japanese)," November 27, 1957, NARA, RG220, Box 1, folder: Minutes, CPB, M-81 through M-113.

156.   Executive Order 10747, *Federal Register* 23, no. 2 (January 3, 1958), NARA, RG220, Box 1, in same folder.

157.   Hagen Note, February 25, 1957, NARA, RG220, Box 2, folder: General Work File, B & C War Criminals (2).

158.   SJS jimukyoku to directors, "Sensō jukeisha shakuhō sokushin to tōkai no shōrai ni tsuite," February 20, 1958, NAJ, 4A-22–7306.

159.   "Saigo no senpan—BC kyū jūhachinin shussho—Sugamo purizun misejimai," *Asahi shinbun*, May 30, 1958, 5.

160.   Washington to The Hague, September 30, 1958, and "List of Parolees Whose Penal Terms Were Expired by Reduction of Sentence" [February 7, 1959], NA (NL), Ambassade in Japan (1941–1974), 2.05.196, inv.nr. 381.

CONCLUSION

1.   See also Robert Cribb, "How Finished Business Became Unfinished: Legal, Moral and Political Dimensions of the Class 'B' and 'C' War Crimes Trials in Asia and the Pacific," in *The Pacific War*, ed. Christina Twomey and Ernest Koh (Abingdon: Routledge, 2015), 91–109.

2.   In his *Victors' Justice* (Tokyo: Tuttle, 1972), Richard H. Minear argues systematically that the trial of Japanese leaders was not sound under principles of international law, partly because of procedural issues and partly because the legitimate concern for national defense was at least an element in their policymaking. On this last point, see 34–73.

3.   See, for instance, Christopher Hitchens's speculative polemic, *The Trial of Henry Kissinger* (London: Verso, 2001).

4.   Christopher Greenwood, "Current Issues in the Law of Armed Conflict: Weapons, Targets and International Criminal Liability," *Singapore Journal of International & Comparative Law* 1 (1997): 441–67.

5.   Kevin Jon Heller, *The Nuremberg Military Tribunals and the Origins of International Law* (Oxford: Oxford University Press, 2011).

6.   Frank M. Buscher, *The U.S. War Crimes Trial Program in Germany, 1946–1955* (New York: Greenwood Press, 1989), 31, 51.

7.   Norbert Frei, *Adenauer's Germany and the Nazi Past*, trans. Joel Golb (New York: Columbia University Press, 2002), 229–30.

8.   Devin Pendas, "Putting the Holocaust on Trial in the Two Germanies, 1945–1989," in *The Routledge History of the Holocaust*, ed. Jonathan C. Friedman (Abingdon: Routledge, 2011), 425–28.

9.   Sakai Takashi was charged with "crimes against humanity" by the Chinese authorities, but the term was used loosely and was not distinguished from "war crimes," for which he was also charged. See Trial of Takashi Sakai by the Chinese War

Crimes Tribunal of the Ministry of National Defence, Nanking, August 27, 1946, 4, UNWCC Archive, PURL: https://www.legal-tools .org/doc/3789a0/.

10. Hannah Arendt, *Eichmann in Jerusalem* (New York: Viking Press, 1963); Devin O. Pendas, *The Frankfurt Auschwitz Trial, 1963–1965* (Cambridge: Cambridge University Press, 2006).

11. Michael Marrus, *The Holocaust in History* (New York: Meridian, 1987), 3.

12. On Papon and Barbie, see Richard J. Golsan, *The Papon Affair* (New York: Routledge, 2000).

13. "Hungary: Alleged Nazi War Criminal Laszlo Csatary, 97, Arrested," July 18, 2012, http://www.cbsnews.com/8301-202_162-57475167/hungary-alleged-nazi-war-criminal-laszlo-csatary-97-arrested/ (accessed November 8, 2012).

14. "Germany Launches Poster Appeal to Find Last Remaining Nazi War Criminals," *Guardian*, July 24, 2013, http://www.theguardian.com/world/2013/jul/23/germany-poster-appeal-nazi-war-criminals-wiesenthal (accessed August 14, 2013).

15. "Oskar Groening, 'Book-Keeper of Auschwitz,'" July 15, 2015, www.bbc.com/news/world-europe-32336353 (accessed August 9, 2015); Elke Ahlswede, "Ex-Auschwitz Guard Convicted in Holocaust Murder Trial," *Huffington Post*, June 17, 2016, http://www.huffingtonpost.com/entry/reinhold-hanning-auschwitz-guilty_us_5763ec86e4bofbbc8be9fad7 (accessed August 15, 2016).

16. Karl Jaspers, *Die Schuldfrage* (Heidelberg: Lambert Schneider, 1946).

17. Jaspers's argument is explicated by Gregory Mellema, *Collective Responsibility* (Amsterdam: Rodopi, 1997); and Tracy Isaacs, "Accountability for Collective Wrongdoing" in *Accountability for Collective Wrongdoing*, ed. Tracy Isaacs and Richard Vernon (Cambridge: Cambridge University Press, 2011), 3–5.

18. See also Michael J. Sandel, *Justice* (New York: Farrar, Straus & Giroux, 2009), 225–30, which argues that responsibility for dark elements in the past is the obverse of the pride that individuals take in the achievements of those groups to which they belong.

19. Karl Jaspers, *The Question of German Guilt* (New York: Dial Press, 1947); Lutz R. Reuter, "How Germany Has Coped: Four Decades Later," in *Transitional Justice*, ed. Neil J. Kritz (Washington, D.C.: U.S. Institute of Peace Press, 1995), 2:64.

20. Iris Chang, *The Rape of Nanking* (New York: Basic Books, 1997). Factual and philosophical problems in portraying Japanese atrocities such as the Nanjing massacre as equivalent to the Holocaust are discussed in David B. MacDonald, *Identity Politics in the Age of Genocide* (Abingdon: Routledge, 2008), 144–54.

21. For a survey of the issues, see Onuma Yasuaki, "Japanese War Guilt and Postwar Responsibilities of Japan," *Berkeley Journal of International Law* 20, no. 3 (2003): 600–620.

22. "83 Koreans Wrongfully Accused of War Crimes: Gov't," November 13, 2006, http://english.hani.co.kr/arti/english_edition/e_national/171442.html (accessed October 8, 2015).

23. Alexis Dudden, *Troubled Apologies Among Japan, Korea, and the United States* (New York: Columbia University Press, 2008).

24. Wakabayashi offers a sensitive analysis of the sequence of events that put Japanese war crimes back on the agenda of allegedly unfinished business. See Bob Tadashi Wakabayashi, "The Messiness of Historical Reality," in *The Nanking Atrocity*, ed. Bob Tadashi Wakabayashi (New York: Berghahn, 2007), 3–28.

25. [Christine M. Chinkin], "Women's International Tribunal on Japanese Military Sexual Slavery," *American Journal of International Law* 95, no. 2 (April 2001): 335–40; Helen Durham and Narrelle Morris, "Women's Bodies and International Criminal Law: From Tokyo to Rabaul," in *Beyond Victor's Justice?*, ed. Yuki Tanaka, Tim McCormack, and Gerry J. Simpson (Leiden: Nijhoff, 2011), 283–90.

26. Arendt, *Eichmann in Jerusalem*, 135.

BIBLIOGRAPHY

1. ARCHIVES

AUSTRALIA

National Archives of Australia, Canberra and Melbourne (NAA)

Commission of Inquiry into Japanese Atrocities (Series A10943). File: a Report on Japanese Atrocities and Breaches of the Rules of Warfare by Sir William Webb, 1580069

Department of the Army, Central Office (Series MP742/1). File: Reps by Sir William Webb on Sacrifices, etc., 391800

Department of Defence (Series A471). Files: 510472, 721016, 720962, 720988, 739151, 739439, 739672, 1348852, 510467–510472

Department of External Affairs (Series A4311). File: Procedure for Dealing with Japanese War Criminals—March 1946–1949, 9024319

Department of External Affairs Central Office (Series A1066). Files: 187951, 187953, 187954

Department of External Affairs, Correspondence Files, 1948–1989 (Series A1838). Files: 140817, 271958, 271960, 271962, 271963

Mitchell Library, Sydney

Papers of John Myles Williams (Manuscript), 1927–1989, MLMSS 5426

FRANCE

Archives diplomatiques, La Courneuve (AD)

Asie Océanie Japon, 130. Affaires militaires et criminels de guerre. Février 1945–Octobre 1954

Archives nationales, Paris (AN [F])

4 AG663. Criminels de guerre japonais, 1952–1953

Archives nationales d'outre-mer, Aix-en-Provence (ANOM)

Conspol 57.198. Japonais–Vietminh
Conspol 153. 1944–1946. Recherche et préparations pour la répression des crimes de guerre
Conspol 270. Criminels de guerre 1946–1948
Fonds du Haut-commissariat à l'Indochine (HCI)
Indochine nouveaux fonds (INF) 159/1364
122.379. Tokyo: Affaires françaises, 1947–1951

Service historique de la défense, Vincennes (SHD)

10H 1044. Prisonniers de guerre Japonais, 1948
10H 6038. États des exécutions capitales en Indochine (1947, 1948)
10H 6039. Exécutions Poulo Condore 1950–1951

HONG KONG

Public Record Office, Hong Kong (PRO [HK])

HKRS 125–3-146, Execution of War Criminals and Prisoners Convicted of High Treason
HKRS 125–3-406, Japanese War Criminals and Political Prisoners, Authority for Control of
HKRS 125–3-407, Japanese War Criminals and Political Prisoners, Miscellaneous Correspondences Relating to
HKRS 163–1-210, Japanese War Criminals. 1. Question of Legal Position re Hanging and Detention of . . . by the Civil Govt; 2. Legislation to Provide for Detention of . . . After Conclusion of Peace Treaty
HKRS 163–1-231, Subsistence and Repatriation of War Criminals. Question of Whether . . . Should Be Borne by the M.A. or the Civil Government
HKRS 169–2-147, War Criminals and Crimes

INDONESIA

Arsip Nasional, Jakarta (ARNAS)

Algemene Secretarie te Batavia
Arsip Delegasi Indonesia

JAPAN

Gaikō shiryōkan (Diplomatic Record Office), Tokyo (GSK)

B'-3–1-2–10: Oranda kokumin no aru shu no shiteki seikyūken mondai kaiketsu ni kansuru NichiRankan giteisho kankei ikken

D' 1 3 0 1, 2: Honpō sensō hanzainin kankei zakken dainikan

D' 1.3.0.1, 3: Honpō sensō hanzainin kankei zakken daisankan

D' 1 3 0 1–13: Honpō sensō hanzainin kankei zakken: Chōsho, shiryō kankei (shinbun kirinuki o fukumu) daiikkan

D' 1 3 0 2–5-1-1: Honpō senpan saiban kankei zakken: Gaichi ni okeru honpōjin no gunji saiban kankei—Chūgoku no bu (hanketsubun). Tsuzuri daiikkan

D' 1 3 0 3–1: Kōwa jōyaku hakkōgo ni okeru honpōjin senpan toriatsukai kankei zakken: Kakkoku no taido narabi ni sochi kankei dainikan

D' 1 3 0 3–1-2–1: Kōwa jōyaku hakkōgo ni okeru honpōjin senpan toriatsukai kankei zakken: Kakkoku no taido narabi ni sochi kankei—Eirenpō no bu, Eikoku daiyonkan

D' 1 3 0 3–9-1: Kōwa jōyaku hakkōgo ni okeru honpōjin senpan toriatsukai kankei zakken: shamen kankoku kankei: Eikoku no bu

D' 1 3 0 3–11: Kōwa jōyaku hakkōgo ni okeru honpōjin senpan toriatsukai kankei zakken: Hōritsu "daihyakusangō" kankei daiikkan

National Archives of Japan, Tokyo (NAJ)
(all files produced by Ministry of Justice, Japan)

4A 17 3 5403: BC-kyū (Furansu saiban kankei). Saigon saiban/dai 38 gō jiken (sanmei)

4A 22 7275: Sensō jukeisha sewakai, Kaimu hōkoku narabi ni kaikei hōkoku

4A 22 7306: Senpan kankei

4B 21 1707: Sensō jukeisha sewakai tsuzuri

4B 21 5813: Sensō saiban sankō shiryō—Rengōgun tsūchi sono san (isō naikan shakuhō taihō rei sakujo)

4B 23 5835: Sensō saiban kankei shiryō: Kōwa jōyaku kankei

4B 23 5836: Sensō saiban sankō shiryō: Hōmu kankei gyōmu shori yōkō (Ichi, Ni fuku kyōdō kenkyū no mono)

4B 23 5855: Sensō saiban zatsu sankō shiryō

4B 23 5856: Sensō saiban sankō shiryō—gaichi fukuekisha kyūjutsu kankei

4B 23 5882: Sensō jukeisha sewakai kankei

4B 23 6265: Senpan ni kansuru zatsu tsuzuri

4B 23 7320: Sugamo keimusho

4B 23 7369: Sensō saiban no jissō sono ta

MALAYSIA
Arkib Negara Malaysia, Kuala Lumpur (ANM)

Malayan Union no. 8331/1947

Malayan Union no. 970/1946

R. C. Selangor 511/00155

Secretariat Dept/17/91 Legal. War Crimes Instructions

MYANMAR

National Archives of Myanmar, Yangon (NAM)

Accession no. 17, 378 D (EA) 46, Box 1, 15–3 (18)
Accession no. 29, File No. 150 D (EA) 47
Accession no. 281 File 49G46(8)
Accession no. 328, File C-8 War Crimes
Accession no. 541, File 4M-8 War Crimes

THE NETHERLANDS

Nationaal Archief, The Hague (NA [NL])

Algemene Secretarie van de Nederlands-Indische Regering (1944–1950), 2.10.14
Ambassade in Japan (1941–1974), 2.05.196
Buitenlandse Zaken/Code-Archief 45–54 (1945–1954), 2.05.117
Dr. L. G. M. Jaquet (1936–1990), 2.21.278
L. F. de Groot (1946–1991), Collectie 584, 2.21.281.31
Marine en Leger Inlichtingendienst, 2.10.62
Procureur-Generaal bij het Hooggerechtshof van Nederlands-Indië, 2.10.17
Strijdkrachten in Nederlands-Indië 2.13.132
Vertegenwoordiging Japan (1946–1954), 2.05.116

NEW ZEALAND

Archives New Zealand, Wellington (ANZ)

R20106146 [ACIE 8798 EA2/163], R20106154 [ACIE 8798 EA2/167] Law and Justice—War crimes—Apprehension and Lists of Far East War Criminals
R20106173 [ACIE 8798 EA2/173], R20106175 [ACIE 8798 EA2/174] Law and Justice—War Crimes—Japanese War Crimes
R22439798 [AAYS 8638 AD1/1403] Casualties—War Crimes—Far East Appointments of NZ Staff to War Crimes Tribunal

THE PHILIPPINES

American History Center, Ateneo de Manila University, Manila
Filipinas Heritage Library (Ayala Museum), Manila (AM)

Quirino Presidential Papers

Jose P. Laurel Library and Museum, Manila
Lopez Museum and Library, Manila (LM)
Magsaysay Library, Manila

Newspaper clippings collection

SINGAPORE

National Archives of Singapore, Singapore

Public Relations Office 19, file 186/55

SWITZERLAND

Archives du Comité international de la Croix-Rouge, Geneva (ACICR)

B AG G.7/IX 2 Criminels de guerre généralités, 1945–1950
B AG 210 000 Rapatriements 004–007
BG3. 78.2 Delegation de Singapour, Juin 1946–Juin 1947, Correspondance envoyée

UNITED KINGDOM

Imperial War Museum, London

Memoirs of Captain J. E. Lawson, PP/MCR 285 Ts Memoir JEL/1
Raymond Plummer (IWM interview), cat. no. 12690

India Office Records, London (IOR)

IOR/L/E/8/6850 Costs of Maintenance of Japanese War Criminals
IOR/M/4/3038 Japanese War Criminals: Trials in Burma

National Archives, Kew, United Kingdom (NA [UK])

ADM 1, Admiralty, and Ministry of Defence, Navy Department: Correspondence and Papers
ADM 116, Admiralty: Record Office: Cases
CAB 65, War Cabinet and Cabinet: Minutes (WM and CM Series)
CAB 66, War Cabinet and Cabinet: Memoranda (WP and CP Series)
CAB 128, Cabinet: Minutes (CM and CC Series)
CAB 129, Cabinet: Memoranda (CP and C Series)
CAB 195, Cabinet Secretary's Notebooks
DO 35, Dominions Office and Commonwealth Relations Office: Original Correspondence
FO 262, Foreign Office and Foreign and Commonwealth Office: Embassy and Consulates, Japan: General Correspondence
FO 371, Foreign Office: Political Departments: General Correspondence from 1906–1966
FO 1060, Control Office for Germany and Austria and Foreign Office: Control Commission for Germany (British Element), Legal Division, and UK High Commission, Legal Division: Correspondence, Case Files, and Court Registers
LCO 2, Lord Chancellor's Office and Lord Chancellor's Department: Registered Files
LCO 53, War Office and Lord Chancellor's Office: Judge Advocate General's Office: Administration Files
MEPO 3, Metropolitan Police: Office of the Commissioner: Correspondence and Papers, Special Series

PREM 11, Prime Minister's Office: Correspondence and Papers, 1951–1964

TS 26, Treasury Solicitor and HM Procurator General: War Crimes Papers

WO 32, War Office and Successors: Registered Files (General Series)

WO 172, War Office: British and Allied Land Forces, South East Asia: War Diaries, Second World War

WO 203, War Office: South East Asia Command: Military Headquarters Papers, Second World War

WO 235, Judge Advocate General's Office: War Crimes Case Files, Second World War

WO 268, War Office: Far East Land Forces: Quarterly Historical Reports

WO 311, Judge Advocate General's Office, Military Deputy's Department, and War Office, Directorates of Army Legal Services and Personal Services: War Crimes Files (MO/JAG/FS and other series)

WO 325, War Office: General Headquarters, Allied Land Forces, (South East Asia) War Crimes Group: Investigation Files

WO 356, War Office: Judge Advocate General's Office, Military Deputy's Department: War Crimes, South East Asia, Card Indexes, Second World War

WO 357, War Office: South East Asia Command, War Crimes Branch: Record Cards

UNITED STATES

National Archives and Records Administration, College Park, MD (NARA)

RG 43 International Conferences, Commissions, and Expositions

Box 1, Records of Far Eastern Commission Committees, Committee V, War Criminals, General Records, March 1946–March 1949.

RG 59 Department of State Records, Central Files 1910–January 1963

Boxes 1–2, Japanese Peace Treaty Files, 1946–1960

Box 10, Japan Subject Files, 1954–1959: War Crimes and Criminals

Boxes 23–25, Records of the Legal Adviser Relating to War Crimes

Box 3020, Central Decimal File 1950–54, from 694.0011/4—651 to 694.0026/6—2652

Box 3021, Central Decimal File 1950–54, from 694.0026/7—252 to 694.0026/6—3053

C0043, Reel 34, Japan Subject Files, 1945–1956, War Criminals

C0044, Reel 8, Japanese Peace Treaty, 1947–1948

C0044, Reel 9, Peace Treaty Developments Since September 16, 1949

RG 165 Records of the War Department General and Special Staffs

Box 580, Security-Classified Papers of the Army Member of the Combined Civil Affairs Committee (CCAC), January 1942–June 1949, SFE Agenda to 109/7

RG 220 Records of Temporary Committees, Commissions, and Boards

Boxes 1, 2, 4, 5, 6, Clemency and Parole Board for War Criminals Japan

RG 331 Records of Allied Operational and Occupation Headquarters, World War II

Box 345, SCAP Public Safety Division, Prison Branch, Subject File 1945–52, Nagoya District to OPARS

Box 893, SCAP Legal Section, Miscellaneous Files 1942–1951, FIB Permits to Miscellaneous Reference Material

Box 1193, SCAP Legal Section, POW 201 File 1945–52, Nunomiya to Ohta

Box 1221, SCAP Legal Section, Parole Completed File, 1950–52, 1 to 4

Box 1222, SCAP Legal Section, Miscellaneous Subject File 1945–52, List of Officials to U.S. Army Stockade

Box 1256, SCAP Legal Section, Decimal File 1945–52, 091 to 091.311

Box 1360, SCAP Legal Section, Sugamo Prison File 1945–51, Daily Reports

Box 1389, SCAP Legal Section, Miscellaneous File 1945–48, Japanese Surnames to Miscellaneous Folder

Box 1392, SCAP Legal Section, Parole Board Documents 1946–51, Chinese, Dutch, and American Convictions to Parole Office Memo

Box 1413, SCAP Legal Section, Decimal File, 1945–1951

Box 1429, SCAP Legal Section, Miscellaneous File 1946–49, Czechoslovakia to Scap Circulars

Box 1434, SCAP Legal Section, Miscellaneous Classified File 1945–52, Index to Miscellaneous Secret Files to 1754, Vol. 1

Box 1435, SCAP Legal Section, Miscellaneous Classified File 1945–52, Bunka POW Camp Files to Confidential List of POW Camps

Box 3676, Civil Property Custodian, Legal Section

Box 9546, SCAP Judge Advocate Section, Records of Trial File 1945–49, Case Docket nos. 360 to 365

RG 338 Army Commands, 1942–

Box 395, Eighth Army, Adjutant General Section, General Correspondence 1949, 000.1 to 000.8

Box 982, Eighth Army, Adjutant General Section, "Occupation File" 1948, 000.5 (January) to 000.5 (April)

Box 1025, Eighth Army, Adjutant General Section, "Occupation File" 1949, 000.5 to 000.8

Box 1041, Eighth Army, Adjutant General Section, "Occupation File" 1950, 000.5 to 110.01

Box 1049, Eighth Army, Adjutant General Section, Security-Classified "Occupation File" 1947, 000.5 to 061

Box 1060, Eighth Army, Adjutant General Section, Security-Classified "Occupation File" 1949, 000.5 to 293

RG 554 Records of General Headquarters, Far East Command, Supreme Commander Allied Powers, and United Nations Command

Box 282, Adjutant General's Section, General Correspondence 1951, 000.3 to 000.92

Box 495, Adjutant General's Section, Secret General Correspondence 1947, 000.0 to 091.71

2. ONLINE LEGAL ARCHIVES

INTERNATIONAL CONVENTIONS AND AGREEMENTS

Convention Concerning Bombardment by Naval Forces in Time of War (Hague 9, October 18, 1907), http://avalon.law.yale.edu/20th_century/hague09.asp (accessed October 19, 2014).

Convention with Respect to the Laws and Customs of War on Land (Hague 2, July 29, 1899), http://avalon.law.yale.edu/19th_century/hague02.asp (accessed October 18, 2014).

Geneva Convention Relative to the Protection of Civilian Persons in Time of War of 12 August 1949, http://www.icrc.org/eng/assets/files/publications/icrc-002-0173.pdf (accessed November 4, 2012).

ICRC, Customary IHL, Rule 47. Attacks Against Persons hors de combat, http://www.icrc.org/customary-ihl/eng/docs/v1_rul_rule47#refFn_62_22 (accessed November 10, 2013).

Moscow Conference, October 1943, "Statement on Atrocities, Signed by President Roosevelt, Prime Minister Churchill and Premier Stalin," http://avalon.law.yale.edu/wwii/moscow.asp (accessed July 22, 2013).

NATIONAL LEGISLATION AND REGULATIONS

France

Ordonnance du 28 août 1944 relative à la répression des crimes de guerre, http://www.legifrance.gouv.fr/affichTexte.do?cidTexte=LEGITEXT000006070700&dateTexte.

Japan

Kaigun keihō, 1908, Nakano bunko, http://www.geocities.jp/nakanolib/hou/hm41–48.htm.

Rikugun keihō, 1908, Nakano bunko, http://www.geocities.jp/nakanolib/hou/hm41–46.htm.

United Kingdom

Royal Warrant—Regulations for the Trial of War Criminals, http://avalon.law.yale.edu/imt/imtroyal.asp.

NATIONAL TRIALS

Australia

"Synopsis of Australian Trials," UNWCC Archive, File 21041–21076.

China

Judgement on Tanaka Hisakazu, October 18, 1946, PURL: https://www.legal-tools.org/uploads/tx_ltpdb/Guangdong.pdf.

Trial of Takashi Sakai by the Chinese War Crimes Tribunal of the Ministry of National Defence, Nanking, August 27, 1946, 4, UNWCC Archive, PURL: https://www.legal-tools.org/doc/3789ao/.

France

Trial of Wada Keiji and 10 Others, Saigon, February 2, 1948, JML_crimes de guerre japonais, Saigon, no. 0022 in the digital collection of the Forschungs-und Dokumentationszentrum für Kriegsverbrecherprozesse (ICWC) at the University of Marburg.

The Netherlands

Trial of Ishikawa Hiroyuki, Temporary Court-Martial at Batavia, April 5, 1948, UNWCC Archive, File 16509–16512, PURL: https://www.legal-tools.org/doc/671e79/.

Trial of Kenitji Sone, Temporary Court-Martial at Batavia, August 14, 1946, UNWCC Archive, File 16397–16410, PURL: https://www.legal-tools.org/doc/fe53b1/.

Trial of Kirmura [Kimura] Seikon, Temporary Court-Martial at Batavia, September 11, 1946, UNWCC Archive, File 16389–16396, no. 21, PURL: https://www.legal-tools.org/doc/9ffcd1.

Trial of Mizuo Katsuno, Temporary Court-Martial at Medan, May 7, 1947, UNWCC Archive, File 16465–16469—18, PURL: https://www.legal-tools.org/doc/2bf8e6/.

Trial of Motomura Shigeki and 12 Others, Temporary Court-Martial at Macassar, July 18, 1947, UNWCC Archive, File 16422–16440—no. 9, PURL: https://www.legal-tools.org/doc/4da811/.

Trial of Ogihara Goro, Temporary Court-Martial at Morotai, August 1947, 4, UNWCC Archive, PURL: https://www.legal-tools.org/doc/35b343/.

Trial of Yamada Takeo, Temporary Court Martial at Pontianak, November 15, 1946, UNWCC Archive, File 16411–16413, no. 15, PURL: https://www.legal-tools.org/doc/68dc9c/.

The Philippines

Indictment, no. 1, PURL: http://www.legal-tools.org/doc/59771d/.

International Military Tribunal for the Far East (IMTFE) Charter, Tokyo, January 19, 1946, http://www.jus.uio.no/english/services/library/treaties/04/4-06/military-tribunal-far-east.xml.

Judgment, chap. 8, Conventional War Crimes (Atrocities), 1003, http://www.legal-tools.org/uploads/tx_ltpdb/JU01-07-a_01.pdf.

Republic Act, no. 842, An Act Providing for Compensation and Automatic Salary Increases for Public School Officials, Teachers, and Other School Personnel of the Government of the Philippines (1953), Chan Robles Virtual Law Library, Republic Acts, http://www.chanrobles.com/republicacts/republicactno842.html#.VJgkz6DAPA.

Transcript of Proceedings, April 29, 1946, to November 12, 1948, PURL: http://www.legal-tools.org/en/go-to-database/ltfolder/0_28747/#results.

Transcript of Proceedings, June 4, 1946, 337, PURL: https://www.legal-tools.org/doc /436390/.

Transcript of Proceedings, November 4, 1948, PURL: http://www.legal-tools.org/doc /629f2b/.

Transcript of Proceedings, November 12, 1948, PURL: https://www.legal-tools.org/doc /9aeof4.

United Nations War Crimes Commission Records

Final Report of the Far Eastern and Pacific Sub-Commission of the UNWCC, September 17, 1947, 6, UNWCC Archive, PURL: https://www.legal-tools.org/doc/5016fa/.

UNWCC, Far Eastern and Pacific Sub-Commission, Minutes of the Twenty-Second Meeting (March 8, 1946), PURL: https://www.legal-tools.org/uploads/tx_ltpdb/File_2826 –2827_01.pdf.

United States

Application of Homma, 327 U.S. 759 (1946) https://supreme.justia.com/cases/federal/us /327/759/.

Case Synopses from Judge Advocate's Reviews, Yokohama Class B and C War Crimes Trials, https://www.ocf.berkeley.edu/~changmin/Japan/Yokohama/Reviews/Yokohama _Reviews.htm: Hara, Mokichi, Guard, Hiroshima POW Branch Camp, no 1; Imai, Kiyomi, Hokodate [Hakodate] POW Camp; Morita, Hiroyuki, Kobe Branch POW Camp, Osaka Area, Honshu, Japan; Uwamori, Masao, Camp Commander, Tokyo Area Sub-Camp 3-D, 10-D, and 11-D—Yokohama.

Emori, Hidetoshi, Second Lieutenant and Camp Commander at Tokyo Area POW Branch Camp, no. 1 Kawasaki, Case Synopses from Judge Advocate's Reviews, Yokohama Class B and C War Crimes Trials, http://wcsc.berkeley.edu/wp-content/uploads/Japan/Yokohama /Reviews/Yokohama_Review_Emori.htm.

Honda, Hiroji: Commander of POW Camp 1B Yunoto and 2B Yoshinwara, Case Synopses from Judge Advocate's Reviews, Yokohama Class B and C War Crimes Trials, https:// www.ocf.berkeley.edu/~changmin/Japan/Yokohama/Reviews/Yokohama_Reviews.htm.

Review of *United States of America vs. Shintaro Nakagawa and 20 Others*, December 6, 1948, http://www.online.uni-marburg.de/icwc/yokohama/Yokohama%20No.%20T356.pdf.

Trial of Akiyoshi Hosokawa, Guam, September 12, 1945, NARA, RG 125, research.archives. gov/description/6997345.

Trial of Asano Yukio, Yokohama, May 1947, http://wcsc.berkeley.edu/wp-content/uploads /Japan/Yokohama/Reviews/Yokohama_Review_Asano.htm.

Trial of Juan Muna, Guam, December 28, 1944, NARA, RG 125, research.archives.gov /description/6997327.

United States of America vs. Kajuro Aihara and 27 Others, 87, http://www.online.uni -marburg.de/icwc/yokohama/Yokohama%20No.%20T290.pdf.

United States of America vs. Ranjo Fujino and 4 Others, 36, http://www.online.uni-marburg .de/icwc/yokohama/Yokohama%20No.%20T310.pdf.

3. ONLINE PARLIAMENTARY RECORDS

HOUSE OF COMMONS (UNITED KINGDOM)

Debate on the Address, June 15, 1956, *Hansard 1803–2005*, 637–642, http://hansard. millbanksystems.com/commons/1955/jun/15/debate-on-the-address#S5CV0542P0 _19550615_HOC_255.

House of Commons Debate, June 29, 1948, vol. 452, ca. 1979–1982, http://hansard.mill banksystems.com/commons/1948/jun/29/japanese-officers-alleged-war-crimes.

HOUSE OF LORDS (UNITED KINGDOM)

"Punishment of War Criminals," October 7, 1942, cols. 555–594, http://hansard.mill banksystems.com/lords/1942/oct/07/punishment-of-war-criminals#S5LV0124P0 _19421007_HOL_8.

JAPANESE DIET (HTTP://KOKKAI.NDL.GO.JP/)

Shūgiin (House of Representatives)

Gaimu iinkai, November 27, 1947–February 4, 1950.

Hōmu iinkai, February 2, 1954–May 29, 1954.

Honkaigi, December 9, 1952–July 19, 1955.

Kaigai dōhō hikiage ni kansuru tokubetsu iinkai, February 6, 1948–February 4, 1950.

Kaigai dōhō hikiage oyobi ikazoku engo ni kansuru chōsa tokubetsu iinkai, July 14, 1953– June 10, 1954.

Sangiin (House of Councillors)

Gaimu iinkai, March 28, 1951–December 19, 1954.

Hōmu iinkai sensō hanzainin ni taisuru hōteki shochi ni kansuru shōiinkai, November 27, 1951–December 12, 1951.

Honkaigi, March 24, 1951–June 18, 1953.

Yosan iinkai, March 29, 1955.

Zaigai dōhō hikiage mondai ni kansuru tokubetsu iinkai, October 16, 1947–February 20, 1948.

4. NEWSPAPER ARTICLES

"Aanstoot-gevende Jappen." *Het Dagblad*, November 29, 1945, 1.

Abend, Hallett. "Japanese Curbing Nanking Excesses." *New York Times*, December 19, 1937, 37.

Ahlswede, Elke. "Ex-Auschwitz Guard Convicted in Holocaust Murder Trial." *Huffington Post*, June 17, 2016, http://www.huffingtonpost.com/entry/reinhold-hanning-auschwitz -guilty_us_5763ec86e4b0fbbc8be9fad7 (accessed August 15, 2016).

"Allied PoWs Shot During Liberator Raid." *Straits Times*, July 12, 1946, 5.

"All Japs Leave Rempang by July 8." *Straits Times*, July 5, 1946, 5.

"Ambon Camp Chief Gives Evidence." *Straits Times*, July 13, 1946, 5.

"Army Returns Gaol Today." *Straits Times*, October 15, 1947, 5.

Ashida Teruichi. "Ima hitotabi no . . . jūnenme, mabuta no otto kaeru Ichinose fujin." *Shūkan asahi*, August 2, 1953, 8–9.

"[Australia] to Free 173 Japan War Criminals." *Manila Chronicle*, July 8, 1953, 4.

"Australian Guilt for Hell-Ship Conditions." *Northern Star* (Lismore, NSW), March 8, 1946, 5.

"Aziatisch barbarisme van de Japanners." *Het vrije volk*, January 31, 1946, 1.

"BC-kyū senpan no shakuhō o konomu: shasetsu." *Asahi shinbun*, June 17, 1957, 2.

" 'Bury Hate,' Pleads Higashi-Kuni." *Mercury* (Hobart), September 17, 1945, 2.

"Chinese Move to Find Guilty." *Straits Times*, June 8, 1946, 5.

"ChūSo seimei: kokunai no hankyō." *Asahi shinbun*, October 13, 1954, 1.

"Condemned Japs Escape from Prison." *Singapore Free Press*, August 10, 1946, 5.

"De beul van Tjideng." *Het Dagblad*, November 29, 1945, 2.

"Demands for Sterner Darwin Trials." *Sydney Morning Herald*, March 18, 1946, 3.

"De oorlogsmisdadigers." *Het Dagblad*, March 9, 1946, 2.

"Early Freedom Expected by War Criminals." *West Australian*, August 15, 1951, 1.

"Echo of 'Double Tenth.' " *Straits Times*, June 26, 1946, 5.

"Eight Jap War Criminals Are Hanged." *Straits Times* June, 17, 1946, 3.

"83 Koreans Wrongfully Accused of War Crimes: Gov't." November 13, 2006, http://english .hani.co.kr/arti/english_edition/e_national/171442.html (accessed October 8, 2015).

"Enemy Tortured Dying Americans with Sadist Medical Experiments." *New York Times*, September 2, 1945, 1.

"Execution of Yamashita." *Sydney Morning Herald*, February 25, 1946, 3.

"Ex-P.O.W. Reader Says, 'Hating the Jap Race Is Unfair.' " *Courier-Mail* (Brisbane), February 7, 1946, 2.

"First Japanese Hanged at K.L." *Straits Times*, March 13, 1946, 3.

"Foreign News: The Philippines—The Lonely Election." *Time*, November 21, 1949, 31.

"Four Burma Japs Hanged." *Straits Times*, July 17, 1946, 3.

"Four Women Watch Hangings." *Straits Times*, June 27, 1947, 1.

"Fukaki kansha no atsumai." *Asahi shinbun*, September 9, 1953, evening ed., 3.

"Futatsu no iken." *Shūkan asahi*, April 13, 1952, 10–11.

"Gaol Break in Kuala Lumpur." *Straits Times*, October 15, 1946, 1.

"Germany Launches Poster Appeal to Find Last Remaining Nazi War Criminals." *Guardian*, July 24, 2013, http://www.theguardian.com/world/2013/jul/23/germany-poster-appeal -nazi-war-criminals-wiesenthal (accessed August 14, 2013).

"Government Assailed: Speeches in House." *Sydney Morning Herald*, March 8, 1946, 5.

"The Grim Record of Japan's Brutal Gestapo." *Sydney Morning Herald*, January 16, 1946, 2.

"Hair, Fingernails Sent Home." *Singapore Free Press*, September 3, 1948, 3.

"Hanged War Criminals Buried at Sea." *Sydney Morning Herald*, June 12, 1951, 3.

"Hanging Urged for Guilty Japs." *Courier-Mail* (Brisbane), October 5, 1945, 1.

" 'Hell Ship' Incident Causes Public Outcry." *Queensland Times* (Ipswich), March 8, 1946, 1.

"Hiki gomogomo no rusu kazoku: Soren dainiji hikiage." *Asahi shinbun*, March 19, 1954, 7.

"Hikoku, Sugamo no senpan o shamen fukuekichū no zen'in gojūni mei." *Asahi shinbun*, December 29, 1953, 1.

"Hungary: Alleged Nazi War Criminal Laszlo Csatary, 97, Arrested." July 18, 2012, http:// www.cbsnews.com/8301-202_162-57475167/hungary-alleged-nazi-war-criminal-laszlo -csatary-97-arrested/ (accessed November 8, 2012).

"Instruction to Blamey." *Sydney Morning Herald*, September 22, 1945, 3.

"Issen man en no bokin: sensō jukeisha sewakai sekkyokuteki katsudō e." *Yomiuri shinbun*, June 11, 1952, morning ed., 3.

"Itsu kieru senpan no mei." *Asahi shinbun*, December 18, 1956, 7.

"Jailed for Part in Beheading." *Straits Times*, June 6, 1946, 3.

"Japan at Peace with Formosa" (incorporating "British Seamen Gaoled"), *The Times*, August 6, 1952, 1, 4.

"Japan: Document Detailing War Criminal Execution Procedures Found." June 8, 2013, http://deathpenaltynews.blogspot.de/2013/06/japan-document-detailing-war-criminal .html (accessed October 9, 2014).

"Japan's Divided Sympathies." *The Times*, December 14, 1956, 8.

"Japan's Evil Spirit." *New York Times*, October 2, 1946, 28.

"Japan Wants Their War Criminals Sent Home." *Singapore Free Press*, April 12, 1949, 8.

"Japanese Atrocities at Hong-Kong: Barbarous Treatment of All Races—Both Civilians and Servicemen." *Manchester Guardian*, March 11, 1942, 3.

"Japanese Contrition Seems to Be Superficial." *Sydney Morning Herald*, June 15, 1946, 2.

"Japanese Cruelty Described by Nisei: Prisoners Used as 'Guinea Pigs' in Samurai Sword Practice, Former Sergeant Says." *New York Times*, September 12, 1945, 10.

"Japanese Cruelty to Prisoners: Evidence of Torture at Singapore." *Scotsman*, September 7, 1945, 5.

"Japanese General Executed." *Sydney Morning Herald*, March 31, 1947, 3.

"Japanese Hell-Ship." *Sydney Morning Herald*, March 9, 1946, 2.

"Japanese Leaders to Be Arrested." *Manchester Guardian*, September 12, 1945, 5

"Japanese Prisoners Freed by Russia." *Advertiser* (Adelaide), March 22, 1954, 16.

"Japanese Says PoWs Were Brave Men." *Straits Times*, July 18, 1946, 5.

"Jap Captain Charged with Deaths of 2390 Men." *Newcastle Morning Herald and Miners' Advocate*, January 12, 1946, 4.

"Jap Death Parade—'Lamentable.' " *Straits Times*, June 19, 1947, 3.

"Jap geëxecuteerd." *De Locomotief* (Semarang), August 26, 1949, 1.

"Jap General Takes Life to Escape Arrest." *Mercury* (Hobart), November 21, 1945, 7.

"Jap Guards Executed." *Sunday Herald* (Sydney), August 21, 1949, 3.

"Jap 'Hell Ship' to Be Inspected in N.G.: Opposition Attack Renewed." *Townsville Daily Bulletin*, March 8, 1946, 1.

"Jap Jungle Camps Bad." *Courier-Mail* (Brisbane), November 18, 1944, 1.

"Jap Major Is Likened to 'a Monster.' " *Straits Times*, June 7, 1946, 5.

"Jap Major Says He 'Could Do Nothing.' " *Straits Times*, June 4, 1946, 3.

"Jap Officer Says Least Deaths in Siam." *Straits Times*, June 18, 1946, 5.

"Jap Prisoners Off for Yokohama." *Manila Chronicle*, July 16, 1953, 1.

"Jap. Prisoners Repatriated." *Recorder* (Port Pirie, SA), December 2, 1953, 1.

"Jap Repents with $5 Gift." *Straits Times*, August 15, 1951, 7.

"Japs Admit Fairness in War Trials." *Canberra Times*, February 16, 1946, 1.

"Jap Says PoW's Beating Was Justified." *Straits Times*, July 17, 1946, 5.

"Jap Sent British Officer to Underground Cell." *Straits Times*, June 27, 1946, 5.

"Jap Sentenced to 5 Yrs.' R.I." *Straits Times*, July 2, 1946, 3.

"Jap Tells of Bayonetting Australian." *Straits Times*, July 13, 1946, 3.

"Jap Turnover Slated Today." *Manila Chronicle*, July 15, 1953, 1.

"Jap War Criminals in Condemned Compound." *Daily News* (Perth), January 16, 1946, 5.

"Japs Gentlemen Compared with Korean Guards, Says Ex-P.O.W." *Border Watch* (Mount Gambier, SA), September 16, 1948, 5.

"Japs Open Campaign to Save Yamashita." *Deseret News*, December 12, 1945, 2.

"Japs Pay for War Crimes." *Argus* (Melbourne), September 29, 1956, 2.

"Japs Released: UK Indignation." *Singapore Free Press*, June 30, 1948, 8.

"Japs Tried to Freeze Soldiers to Death." *Daily News* (Perth), January 15, 1946, 2.

Johnston, George H. "Remnants of Jap Convoy Sunk." *Argus* (Melbourne), March 6, 1943, 1.

Jones, George E. "His Suicide Foiled." *New York Times*, September 12, 1945, 1–2.

"Jōsen daihyō o tsurekomu." *Asahi shinbun*, July 8, 1953, 7.

"Kagao Shūnin." *Shūkan asahi*, July 26, 1953, 30.

"Kempei Man to Hang." *Straits Times*, June 27, 1946, 5.

"Kempei Parade in K. Lumpur." *Straits Times*, September 27, 1946, 6.

"Kempitai [*sic*] on 'Shameful' Execution." *Straits Times*, June 1, 1946, 5.

"Kesshoku no yoi 'Sugamo senpan': Bengodan shokaiken. Omoi wa gaichi no dōhō e." *Yomiuri shinbun*, April 12, 1952, morning ed., 3.

"Kōan maru jōsensha: Yonhyakunijūmei no shimei wakaru: Soren dainiji hikiage." *Asahi shinbun*, March 19, 1954, 3.

"Kōan maru Maizuru nyūkō—sennijūgonin ga kaeru—Soren hikiage." *Asahi shinbun*, December 26, 1956, evening ed., 1.

"Korean Guard Gets 5 Years." *Straits Times*, June 29, 1946, 3.

"Korean Guard to Hang." *Straits Times*, June 26, 1946, 5.

"Legal Point to Be Argued in War Trial." *Straits Times*, May 9, 1946, 3.

Lieberman, Henry R. "New Mao Condition Snags China Talks." *New York Times*, February 6, 1949, 60.

"Life Term for Jap Civilian." *Straits Times*, May 10, 1946, 5.

"Lucky People." *Singapore Free Press*, July 4, 1946, 1.

"'Magnificent' Jap on Trial." *Manila Times*, October 14, 1945, 2.

"Manacled Jap Gives Evidence." *Straits Times*, July 8, 1946, 3.

"Manus 'Deserted Junk Heap.'" *Straits Times*, February 21, 1949, 2.

"Massacre by Japanese: 17 New Zealanders." *Dominion*, October 23, 1944.

"Mercy Is Not Called For." *News* (Adelaide), January 23, 1946, 2.

Miller, Harry. "A Sime Roader Looks at Rempang." *Straits Times*, July 8, 1946, 4.

"'Montenrupa no haha': higan kanatta 'koe' no taimen." *Shūkan asahi*, March 2, 1952, 36–37.

"Month's Gaol for War Crimes: Ex-Servicemen Protest Darwin Sentences 'Absurd.'" *West Australian*, March 18, 1946, 8.

Morikawa Kenji. "Sugamo no daisankokujin senpan." *Asahi shinbun*, January 17, 1955, 3.

"Netherlands Claim in Japan Is Settled." *New York Times*, January 31, 1956, 7.

"News in Brief: Russians Repatriate 1,025 Japanese." *The Times*, December 27, 1956, 5.

"No AIF Witnesses for Singapore Trials." *Daily News* (Perth), January 21, 1946, 2.

"No Jap Survivors of Convoy Holocaust." *Mirror* (Perth), March 6, 1943, 7.

"No Jap Tribunals for War Criminals." *Straits Times*, December 4, 1945, 4.

"Not Ungrateful." Editorial, *Nippon Times*, August 31, 1953, 8.

"Officers Flogged Their Men." *Singapore Free Press*, August 14, 1946, 5.

"Onimarukun, senpan no shakuhō o teiso." *Asahi shinbun*, February 12, 1953, 7.

"Oorlogsmisdadigers op Sumatra." *Het Dagblad*, December 1, 1945, 2.

"Oskar Groening, 'Book-Keeper of Auschwitz.'" July 15, 2015, www.bbc.com/news/world-europe-32336353 (accessed August 9, 2015).

Outis [pseud.]. "When War Criminals Have Been Punished—What Then?" *Irish Times Pictorial*, September 1, 1945, 4.

"Precedent of Indonesians." *Sydney Morning Herald*, March 9, 1946, 4.

"Probe of Jap Plot Started." *Manila Times*, November 23, 1945, 4.

"Punish Jap Criminals, Says R.S.L." *Mail* (Adelaide), January 26, 1946, 1.

"Quick Justice at Rabaul." *Sydney Morning Herald*, March 26, 1946, 3.

"Recognises Doomed Men in Pictures." *Daily News* (Perth), January 17, 1946, 6.

"The Roles Are Changed in Indo-China." *West Australian*, March 19, 1946, 5.

"Roster of 40 Ordered Arrested as War Criminals by MacArthur." *New York Times*, September 12, 1945, 3.

"Saigo no senpan—BC kyū jūhachinin shussho—Sugamo purizun misejimai." *Asahi shinbun*, May 30, 1958, 5.

"Sedatives Given to Japs Before Execution." *Canberra Times*, March 21, 1946, 1.

"'Seikatsu dekinu' to momeru—Sugamo shussho no Taiwanjin senpan." *Asahi shinbun*, January 8, 1955, evening ed., 3.

"Senpan boshi: Kishisan ni shakuhō chinjō." *Yomiuri shinbun*, June 15, 1957, evening ed., 5.

"Senpan shakuhō ni chomei undō." *Asahi shinbun*, November 5, 1953, 7.

"Senpan shakuhō no rōhō aitsugu." *Yomiuri shinbun*, June 2, 1953, morning ed., 7.

"Shanghai War Criminals Flee and Not One Has Been Booked." *Manila Times*, September 25, 1945, 2.

"Singapore Kempei Man Gets 7 Years." *Straits Times*, June 27, 1946, 3.

"Soekarno Is Quisling: Like Laurel and Bamaw, Says 'Washington Post.'" *Cairns Post*, October 31, 1945, 3.

"Sugamo karishussho kotowaru—daisankokujin seikatsu shikin yokoseto—shōgai." *Asahi shinbun*, December 29, 1954, evening ed., 3.

"Sugamo no gokuchū kara senpan shakuhō undō: Kakuku ni kyōryoku o yōsei—dokuritsugo hetta karishakuhō ni fuman no koe." *Yomiuri shinbun*, July 8, 1953, morning ed., 6.

"Sugamo no naigai: Senpan wa nani o kangaeteiruka." *Shūkan asahi*, February 24, 1952, 3–11.

"Sugamo senpan zen'in no shakuhō o konomu: Shasetsu." *Asahi shinbun*, September 26, 1956, 2.

Suzuki Katsuhiko. "Shingapōru ni tsukaishite." *YMCA nyūsu*, February 5, 1948, 3, NAJ, 4B 23 5856.

"Tarawa Massacre: End of Japanese Who Gave Order." *Dominion*, October 24, 1944.

"Tears of Pity." *Sydney Morning Herald*, March 8, 1946, 2.

"Texts of Statements by Secretary of State Hull on Abuse of U.S. Prisoners by Japanese." *New York Times*, February 12, 1944, 5.

"They're Still Savages, Warns Former P.O.W. Could Japs Have Been Reformed in 4 Years?" *News* (Adelaide), April 1, 1950, 4.

"Three Jap War Criminals Hanged in Changi Gaol." *Straits Times*, March 15, 1946, 4.

"Tokyo Taking China's Prisoners." *New York Times*, January 31, 1949, 3.

"Trial of Japanese War Criminals." *Dubbo Liberal and Macquarie Advocate* (NSW), January 5, 1946, 2.

"Trials Conclude at Los Negros." *Sydney Morning Herald*, April 10, 1951, 3.

Trumbull, Robert. "Japan Urges U.S. Free War Guilty." *New York Times*, June 21, 1955, 11.

Tsuji Yutaka. "Montenrupa kara no 108 nin." *Shūkan asahi*, August 2, 1953, 3–8.

——. "Senpan shikeishū wa inoru: 'Nihon yo shizuka ni, heiwa de are.'" *Shūkan asahi*, February 24, 1952, 12–15.

"Unrepentant War Criminals." *Sydney Morning Herald*, August 2, 1953, 9.

"Victims Cry for Revenge." *Examiner* (Launceston, TAS), January 26, 1946, 1.

"Want Japs Executed: Returned Men's Demand." *Newcastle Morning Herald and Miners' Advocate*, January 21, 1946, 4.

"War Criminals." *Straits Times*, August 16, 1948, 1.

"War Criminals Kill Guards, Escape." *Straits Times*, January 9, 1946, 1.

"War Criminals Working Secretly Outside Gaols." *Central Queensland Herald* (Rockhampton), October 20, 1955, 27.

"Why Some Japs Get Light Sentences." *Straits Times*, July 5, 1946, 2.

"Women See 3 Japs Hanged." *Singapore Free Press*, June 26, 1947, 1.

"World's Biggest Manhunt in S.E. Asia." *Straits Times*, July 14, 1946, 4.

"Yamashita Behind Bars." *New York Times*, September 4, 1945, 4.

"Yamashita Shift Asked: Singapore's Chinese Want Him to Stand Trial There." *New York Times*, September 17, 1945, 3.

"Zasshi wa dō yomareteiruka: Zasshi shūkan in yosete." *Shūkan asahi*, June 8, 1952, 14–17.

"Zoku. Sugamo no naigai: Senpan wa dō naru ka." *Shūkan asahi*, August 16, 1953, 3–11.

5. BOOKS, ARTICLES, CHAPTERS, AND DISSERTATIONS

Abbell, Michael. *International Prisoner Transfer*. Ardsley, NY: Transnational, 2001.

Afiler, Ma. Concepcion P. "Administrative Measures Against Bureaucratic Corruption: The Philippine Experience." *Philippine Journal of Public Administration* 23, nos. 3–4 (July–October 1979), 321–49.

Agoncillo, Teodoro A. *The Burden of Proof: The Vargas-Laurel Collaboration Case*. Mandaluyong, Metro Manila: University of the Philippines Press, 1984.

Ahmad, Abu Talib. *Malay-Muslims, Islam, and the Rising Sun: 1941–1945*. Kuala Lumpur: Malaysian Branch of the Royal Asiatic Society, 2003.

Aida Yūji. *Prisoner of the British: A Japanese Soldier's Experience in Burma*. Trans. Hide Ishiguro and Louis Allen. London: Cresset Press, 1966.

Allison, John M. *Ambassador from the Prairie, or Allison Wonderland*. Boston: Houghton Mifflin, 1973.

Anderson, Benedict R. O'G. *Java in a Time of Revolution: Occupation and Resistance, 1944–1946*. Ithaca, NY: Cornell University Press, 1972.

Arai Emiko. *Montenrupa no yoake: BC-kyū senpan no inochi o sukutta uta o tsukutta hitobito*. Tokyo: Kōjinsha, 2008.

Archer, Basil. *Interpreting Occupied Japan: The Diary of an Australian Soldier, 1945–1946*, ed. and with an introduction by Sandra Wilson. Carlisle, WA: Hesperian Press, 2009.

Archer, Bernice. *The Internment of Western Civilians Under the Japanese, 1941–1945: A Patchwork of Internment*. London: RoutledgeCurzon, 2004.

Arendt, Hannah. *Eichmann in Jerusalem: A Report on the Banality of Evil*. New York: Viking Press, 1963.

Aszkielowicz, Dean Michael. "After the Surrender: Australia and the Japanese Class B and C War Criminals, 1945–1958." PhD diss., Murdoch University, 2012.

——. *The Australian Pursuit of Japanese War Criminals, 1943–1958: From Foe to Friend*. Hong Kong: Hong Kong University Press, 2017.

——. "Repatriation and the Limits of Resolve: Japanese War Criminals in Australian Custody." *Japanese Studies* 31, no. 2 (September 2011): 211–28.

Awaya Kentarō. "Selecting Defendants at the Tokyo Trial." In *Beyond Victor's Justice? The Tokyo War Crimes Trial Revisited*, ed. Yuki Tanaka, Tim McCormack, and Gerry J. Simpson, 57–62. Leiden: Nijhoff, 2011.

Barshay, Andrew. *The Gods Left First: The Captivity and Repatriation of Japanese POWs in Northeast Asia*. Berkeley: University of California Press, 2013.

Bass, Gary Jonathan. *Stay the Hand of Vengeance: The Politics of War Crimes Tribunals*. Princeton, NJ: Princeton University Press, 2000.

Bassiouni, M. Cherif. *Crimes Against Humanity: Historical Evolution and Contemporary Application*. Cambridge: Cambridge University Press, 2011.

Bayly, Christopher, and Tim Harper. *Forgotten Wars: The End of Britain's Asian Empire*. London: Allen Lane, 2007.

Bix, Herbert. *Hirohito and the Making of Modern Japan*. New York: HarperCollins, 2000.

Bogg, Charles W. *Marine Aviation in the Philippines*. Washington, D.C.: Historical Division, Headquarters, U.S. Marine Corps, 1951.

Boister, Neil, and Robert Cryer. *The Tokyo International Military Tribunal: A Reappraisal*. New York: Oxford University Press, 2008.

——, eds. *Documents on the Tokyo International Military Tribunal: Charter, Indictment and Judgments*. Oxford: Oxford University Press, 2008.

Botsman, Dani. *Punishment and Power in the Making of Modern Japan*. Princeton, NJ: Princeton University Press, 2005.

Brackman, Arnold C. *The Other Nuremberg: The Untold Story of the Tokyo War Crimes Trials*. New York: Morrow, 1987.

Brook, Timothy. *Collaboration: Japanese Agents and Local Elites in Wartime China*. Cambridge, MA: Harvard University Press, 2004.

Buchholz, Petra. *Vom Teufel zum Menschen: Die Geschichte der Chinaheimkehrer in Selbstzeugnissen*. Munich: Iudicium, 2010.

Buscher, Frank. *The U.S. War Crimes Trial Program in Germany, 1946–1955*. New York: Greenwood Press, 1989.

Bush, Jonathan A. " 'The Supreme . . . Crime' and Its Origins: The Lost Legislative History of the Crime of Aggressive War." *Columbia Law Review* 102, no. 8 (December 2002): 2324–2424.

Caprio, Mark E., and Yoneyuki Sugita. "Introduction: The U.S. Occupation of Japan—Innovation, Continuity, and Compromise." In *Democracy in Occupied Japan: The U.S. Occupation and Japanese Politics and Society*, ed. Mark E. Caprio and Yoneyuki Sugita, 1–25. London: Routledge, 2007.

Cathcart, Adam. " 'Against Invisible Enemies': Japanese Bacteriological Weapons in China's Cold War, 1949–1952." *Chinese Historical Review* 16, no. 1 (2009), 103–8.

Cathcart, Adam, and Patricia Nash. " 'To Serve Revenge for the Dead': Chinese Communist Responses to Japanese War Crimes in the PRC Foreign Ministry Archive, 1949–1956." *China Quarterly* 200 (December 2009): 1053–69.

——. "War Criminals and the Road to Sino-Japanese Normalization: Zhou Enlai and the Shenyang Trials, 1954–1956." *Twentieth Century China* 34, no. 2 (2009): 89–111.

Chaen Yoshio. *BC-kyū senpan Chūgoku Fukkoku saiban shiryō*. Tokyo: Fuji shuppan, 1992.

——. "Kaisetsu." In Chaen Yoshio, ed., *Nihon senryaku Sugamo purizun shiryō 1: Zenteiki hakkanshi* (jō), 5–8. Tokyo: Nihon tosho sentā, 1992.

——, ed. Introduction to *Nihon BC-kyū senpan shiryō*. Tokyo: Fuji shuppan, 1983.

——, ed. *Nihon senryaku Sugamo purizun shiryō 1: Zenteiki hakkanshi* (jō). Tokyo: Nihon tosho sentā, 1992.

Chaen Yoshio, and Shigematsu Kazuyoshi, eds. *Hokan Senpan saiban no jissō*. Tokyo: Fuji shuppan, 1987.

Chamberlain, Sharon Williams. "Justice and Reconciliation: Postwar Philippine Trials of Japanese War Criminals in History and Memory." PhD diss., George Washington University, 2010.

Chang, Iris. *The Rape of Nanking: The Forgotten Holocaust of World War II*. New York: Basic Books, 1997.

Cheah Wui Ling. "Post-World War II British 'Hell-Ship' Trials in Singapore: Omissions and the Attribution of Responsibility." *Journal of International Criminal Justice* 8 (2010): 1035–58.

Chen, Jing. "The Trial of Japanese War Criminals in China: The Paradox of Leniency." *China Information* 23 (2009): 447–72.

[Chinkin, Christine M.] "Women's International Tribunal on Japanese Military Sexual Slavery." *American Journal of International Law* 95, no. 2 (April 2001): 335–40.

Choung Il Chee. "The Alien Registration Law of Japan and the International Covenant on Civil and Political Rights." *Korean Journal of Comparative Law* 15 (1987): 105–58.

Clague, Peter. *Bridge House*. Hong Kong: South China Morning Post, 1983.

Cohen, David J. "Beyond Nuremberg: Individual Responsibility for War Crimes." In *Human Rights in Political Transitions: Gettysburg to Bosnia*, ed. Carla Hesse and Robert Post, 53–92. New York: Zone Books, 1999.

——. "The Singapore War Crimes Trials and Their Relevance Today." *Singapore Law Review* 31 (2013): 3–38.

Connaughton, Richard, John Pimlott, and Duncan Anderson. *Battle for Manila*. London: Bloomsbury, 1995.

Connor, Stephen. "Side-Stepping Geneva: Japanese Troops Under British Control, 1945–7." *Journal of Contemporary History* 45, no. 2 (2010): 389–405.

Cooper, Leonard. "Rhyming Prophecy for a New Year." In *The Faber Book of Comic Verse*, ed. Michael Roberts, 383–84. London: Faber & Faber, 1974.

Coox, Alvin D. *Nomonhan: Japan Against Russia, 1939*. Stanford, CA: Stanford University Press, 1985.

Creed, David, Moira Raynor, and Sue Rickard. " 'It Will Not Be Bound by the Ordinary Rules of Evidence. . . . ' " *Journal of the Australian War Memorial* 27 (October 1995): 47–53.

Cribb, Robert. "A Revolution Delayed: The Indonesian Republic and the Netherlands Indies, August–November 1945." *Australian Journal of Politics and History* 32, no. 1 (1986): 72–85.

——. "Avoiding Clemency: The Trial and Transfer of Japanese War Criminals in Indonesia, 1946–1949." *Japanese Studies* 31, no. 2 (2011): 151–70.

——. "How Finished Business Became Unfinished: Legal, Moral and Political Dimensions of the Class 'B' and 'C' War Crimes Trials in Asia and the Pacific." In *The Pacific War: Aftermaths, Remembrance and Culture*, ed. Christina Twomey and Ernest Koh, 91–109. Abingdon: Routledge, 2015.

——. "Legal Pluralism and Criminal Law in the Dutch Colonial Order." *Indonesia* 90 (2010): 47–66.

Daehler, Richard. *Die japanischen und die deutschen Kriegsgefangenen in der Sowjetunion, 1945–1956: Vergleich von Erlebnissen*. Zurich: LIT, 2007.

Daventry, Paula, ed. *Sasakawa, the Warrior for Peace, the Global Philanthropist*. Oxford: Pergamon Press, 1981.

Davies, Peter. *The Man Behind the Bridge: Colonel Toosey and the River Kwai*. London: Athlone, 1991.

Daws, Gavan. *Prisoners of the Japanese: POWs of World War II in the Pacific*. Melbourne: Scribe, 1994.

Declaration of Amnesty. *American Journal of International Law* 18, no. 2, suppl.: Official Documents (April 1924): 92–95.

Dennis, Peter. *Troubled Days of Peace: Mountbatten and South East Asia Command, 1945–46*. New York: St. Martin's Press, 1987.

Dingman, Roger. "The Diplomacy of Dependency: The Philippines and Peacemaking with Japan, 1945–52." *Journal of Southeast Asian Studies* 17, no. 2 (September 1986): 307–21.

Donnison, F. S. V. *British Military Administration in the Far East 1943–46*. London: HMSO, 1956.

Dower, John W. *Embracing Defeat: Japan in the Wake of World War II*. New York: Norton, 1999.

——. *War Without Mercy: Race and Power in the Pacific War*. New York: Pantheon, 1986.

Drea, Edward J. "In the Army Barracks of Imperial Japan." *Armed Forces & Society* 15 (1989): 329–48.

——. *Japan's Imperial Army: Its Rise and Fall, 1853–1945*. Lawrence: University Press of Kansas, 2009.

Dudden, Alexis. *Troubled Apologies Among Japan, Korea, and the United States*. New York: Columbia University Press, 2008.

Dunbar, N. C. H. "Military Necessity in War Crimes Trials." *British Yearbook of International Law* 29 (1952): 442–52.

Dunn, Frederick S. *Peace-Making and the Settlement with Japan*. Princeton, NJ: Princeton University Press, 1963.

Durham, Helen, and Narrelle Morris. "Women's Bodies and International Criminal Law: From Tokyo to Rabaul." In *Beyond Victor's Justice? The Tokyo War Crimes Trial Revisited*, ed. Yuki Tanaka, Tim McCormack, and Gerry J. Simpson, 283–90. Leiden: Nijhoff, 2011.

Emsley, Clive. *Soldier, Sailor, Beggarman, Thief: Crime and the British Armed Services Since 1914*. Oxford: Oxford University Press, 2013.

Erickson, George E. "United States Navy War Crimes Trials (1945–1949)." *Washburn Law Journal* 5 (1965): 89–111.

Esmein, Jean. "Le Juge Henri Bernard au procès de Tōkyō." *Vingtième siècle*, no. 59 (1998): 3–14.

Ferguson, Niall. "Prisoner Taking and Prisoner Killing in the Age of Total War: Towards a Political Economy of Military Defeat." *War in History* 11, no. 2 (April 2004): 148–92.

Ferren, John M. "General Yamashita and Justice Rutledge." *Journal of Supreme Court History* 28, no. 1 (2003): 54–80.

Fifield, Russell H. "The Challenge to Magsaysay." *Foreign Affairs* 33, no. 1 (October 1954): 149–54.

Fischel, Elaine B. *Defending the Enemy: Justice for the WWII Japanese War Criminals.* Minneapolis: Bascom Hill Books, 2009.

Fitzpatrick, Georgina. "War Crimes Trials, 'Victor's Justice' and Australian Military Justice in the Aftermath of the Second World War." In *The Hidden Histories of War Crimes Trials,* ed. Kevin Jon Heller and Gerry Simpson, 327–47. Oxford: Oxford University Press, 2013.

Flower, Sybilla Jane. "British Policymakers and the Prisoner-of-War Issue: Perceptions and Responses." In *The History of Anglo-Japanese Relations 1600–2000, III: The Military Dimension,* ed. Ian Gow and Yoichi Hirama, 232–41. Houndmills: Palgrave Macmillan, 2003.

Foote, Daniel H. "Confessions and the Right to Silence in Japan." *Georgia Journal of International and Comparative Law* 21 (1991): 415–88.

Frei, Norbert. *Adenauer's Germany and the Nazi Past: The Politics of Amnesty and Integration.* Trans. Joel Golb. New York: Columbia University Press, 2002.

Friedman, Leon, ed. *The Law of War: A Documentary History.* Vol. 1. New York: Random House, 1972.

Fukutome Shigeru. "Itsutsu no senpan kangoku ni meguru." *Bungei shunjū* (August 1950): 176–85.

Futamura, Madoka. *War Crimes Tribunals and Transitional Justice: The Tokyo Trial and the Nuremberg Legacy.* London: Routledge, 2008.

Gaddis, John Lewis. *George F. Kennan: An American Life.* New York: Penguin Books, 2011.

Gaimushō, ed. *Nihon gaikō monjo: Heiwa jōyaku no teiketsu ni kansuru chōsho.* Vol. 3. Tokyo: Gaimushō, 2003.

Gardam, Judith Gail. *Non-Combatant Immunity as a Norm of International Humanitarian Law.* Dordrecht: Nijhoff, 1993.

Garwood-Cutler, Jane L. "The British War Crimes Trials of Suspected Italian War Criminals, 1945–1947." In *International Humanitarian Law: Origins, Challenges, Prospects.* Vol. 1, *Origins,* ed. John Carey, William V. Dunlap, and R. John Pritchard, 89–103. Ardsley, NY: Transnational, 2003.

Gavrilov, V. A., and E. L. Katasonova, eds. *Iaponskie voennoplennye v SSSR 1945–1956.* Moscow: Demokratiia, 2013.

General Treaty for Renunciation of War as an Instrument of National Policy, Signed at Paris, August 27, 1928. *Recueil des traités et des engagements internationaux enregistrés par le Secrétariat de la Société des Nations* 94, nos. 1–4 (1929): 57–64.

Gerow, Aaron. "Japanese Film and Television." In *Routledge Handbook of Japanese Culture and Society,* ed. Victoria Lyon Bestor, Theodore C. Bestor, and Akiko Yamagata, 213–25. Abingdon: Routledge, 2011.

Gillison, Douglas. *Australia in the War of 1939–1945.* Vol. 1, *Royal Australian Air Force 1939–1942.* 3 ser., vol. 1, *Air.* Canberra: Australian War Memorial, 1962.

Ginn, John L. *Sugamo Prison, Tokyo: An Account of the Trial and Sentencing of Japanese War Criminals in 1948, by a U.S. Participant.* Jefferson, NC: McFarland, 1992.

Ginsburgs, George. *The Citizenship Law of the USSR.* The Hague: Nijhoff, 1983.

Gledhill, A. "Some Aspects of the Operation of International and Military Law in Burma, 1941–1945." *Modern Law Review* 12 (1939): 191–204.

Glines, Carroll V. *The Doolittle Raid: America's Daring First Strike Against Japan.* New York: Orion Books, 1988.

Golsan, Richard J. *The Papon Affair: Memory and Justice on Trial.* New York: Routledge, 2000.

Goscha, Christopher E. "Belated Allies: The Technical Contributions of Japanese Deserters to the Viêt Minh (1945–1950)." In *A Companion to the Vietnam War,* ed. Marilyn Young and Robert Buzzanco, 37–64. Malden, MA: Blackwell, 2002.

Gotō, Kenichi. "Life and Death of 'Abdul Rachman' (1906–49): One Aspect of Japanese–Indonesian Relationships." *Indonesia* 22 (1976): 57–68.

Greenwood, Christopher. "Current Issues in the Law of Armed Conflict: Weapons, Targets and International Criminal Liability." *Singapore Journal of International & Comparative Law* 1 (1997): 441–67.

Groot, L. F. de. *Berechting Japanse Oorlogsmisdadigers in Nederlands-Indië, 1946–1949: Temporaire Krijgsraad Batavia.* 's-Hertogenbosch: Art & Research, 1990.

——. "De rechtspraak inzake oorlogsmisdrijven in Nederlands Indië (1947–1949)." *Militair Rechtelijk Tijdschrift* 78 (1985): 81–90, 161–72, 248–57, 361–76.

Hamill, Robert H. *A Just War, or Just Another War* (undated leaflet). Woodmont, CT: Promoting Enduring Peace, [1960s].

Hanayama, Shinsho. *The Way of Deliverance: Three Years with the Condemned Japanese War Criminals.* Trans. Hideo Suzuki, Eiichi Noda, and James K. Sasaki. London: Victor Gollancz, 1955.

Han Bing Siong. "The Secret of Major Kido: The Battle of Semarang, 15–19 October 1945." *Bijdragen tot de Taal-, Land- en Volkenkunde* 152, no. 3 (1996): 382–428.

Han Ming Guang. "Collaboration During the Japanese Occupation: Issues and Problems Focusing on the Chinese Community." BA honors thesis, National University of Singapore, 2010.

Hankey, Maurice Pascal Alers. *Politics, Trials and Errors.* Oxford: Pen-in-Hand, 1950.

Harries, Meirion, and Susie Harries. *Soldiers of the Sun: The Rise and Fall of the Imperial Japanese Army.* New York: Random House, 1991.

Harris, Sheldon H. *Factories of Death: Japanese Biological Warfare, 1932–45, and the American Cover-up.* London: Routledge, 1994.

"Haruka naru inori: Imamura Hitoshi moto taishō fusai no ai to gisei." *Shufu no tomo* 36, no. 10 (October 1952): 86–94.

Hatakeyama Ichirō. "Senpan keishisha no izoku nimo onkyū o: Dai hankyō o yonda onkyūhō no kaisei." *Toki no hōrei* 144 (August 1954): 1–11.

Hayashi Hirofumi. "The Battle of Singapore, the Massacre of Chinese and Understanding of the Issue in Postwar Japan." *Asia-Pacific Journal: Japan Focus,* 28-4-09, July 13, 2009, http://www.japanfocus.org/-Hayashi-Hirofumi/3187 (accessed February 2, 2013).

——. *BC-kyū senpan saiban.* Tokyo: Iwanami shoten, 2005.

——. "British War Crimes Trials of Japanese." *Nature-People-Society: Science and the Humanities* (Kanto Gakuin University) 31 (July 2001): http://www.geocities.jp/hhhirofumi/eng08.htm#_ednref12.

——. *Senpan saiban no kenkyū: senpan saiban seisaku no keisei kara Tōkyō saiban, BC-kyū saiban made.* Tokyō: Bensei shuppan, 2010.

Heidebrink, Iris. "Military Tribunals in the Netherlands Indies." In *Encyclopedia of Indonesia in the Pacific War*, ed. Peter Post et al., 411–16. Leiden: Brill, 2010.

Heller, Kevin Jon. *The Nuremberg Military Tribunals and the Origins of International Law.* Oxford: Oxford University Press, 2011.

Henckaerts, Jean-Marie, and Louise Doswald-Beck. *Customary International Humanitarian Law.* Vol. 1, *Rules.* Cambridge: Cambridge University Press, 2007.

Henty, Audrey M. "Senpan: shikei chokuzen no isho." *Nyū eiji*, February 1952, 25–28.

Herf, Jeffrey. *Divided Memory: The Nazi Past in the Two Germanys.* Cambridge, MA: Harvard University Press, 1997.

Heuvel, Jacco van den. "Crime and Authority Within Dutch Communities of Internees in Indonesia, 1942–45." In *Forgotten Captives in Japanese-Occupied Asia*, ed. Karl Hack and Kevin Blackburn, 193–209. London: Routledge, 2008.

Higurashi Yoshinobu. Contribution to "The Tokyo War Crimes Trial at Sixty: Legacies and Reassessment." Asian Voices Seminar, George Washington University, Washington, D.C., March 23, 2009, 21, spfusa.org/pdfs/2008/Tokyo%20Trial%2003232009.pdf (accessed June 10, 2014).

——. "Gasshūkoku to taiNichi senpan saiban no shūketsu." *Shigaku zasshi* 109, no. 11 (November 2000): 1–34.

——. *Tōkyō saiban.* Tokyo: Kōdansha, 2008.

Hilger, Andreas, and Jörg Morré. "SMT-Verurteilte als Problem der Entstalinisierung. Die Entlassungen Tribunalverurteilter aus sowjetischer und deutscher Haft." In *Sowjetische Militärtribunale.* Vol. 2, *Die Verurteilung deutscher Zivilisten 1945–1955*, ed. Andreas Hilger, Mike Schmeitzner, and Ute Schmidt, 685–756. Cologne: Böhlau, 2003.

Hitchens, Christopher. *The Trial of Henry Kissinger.* London: Verso, 2001.

Holmes, Richard. *Sahib: The British Soldier in India.* London: Harper Perennial, 2006.

Hōmu daijin kanbō shihō hōsei chōsabu. *Sensō hanzai saiban gaishi yō.* Tokyo: Hōmu daijin kanbō shihō hōsei chōsabu, 1973.

Hoog, Günter, and Angela Steinmetz, eds. *International Conventions on Protection of Humanity and Environment.* Berlin: De Gruyter, 1993.

Hosoya, Chihiro. "Miscalculations in Deterrent Policy: Japanese-U.S. Relations, 1938–1941." *Journal of Peace Research* 5, no. 2 (1968): 97–115.

Hudson, W. J., and R. G. Neale, eds. *Documents on Australian Foreign Policy, 1937–49, 10, July–December 1946.* Canberra: Australian Government Publishing Service, 1993.

Hussain, Nasser, and Austin Sarat. "Toward New Theoretical Perspectives on Forgiveness, Mercy and Clemency." In *Forgiveness, Mercy and Clemency*, ed. Austin Sarat and Nasser Hussain, 1–15. Stanford, CA: Stanford University Press, 2007.

Igarashi, Yoshikuni. "Belated Homecomings: Japanese Prisoners of War in Siberia and Their Return to Post-War Japan." In *Prisoners of War, Prisoners of Peace: Captivity, Homecoming and Memory in World War II*, ed. Bob Moore and Barbara Hately-Broad, 105–228. Oxford: Berg, 2005.

Iizuka Kōji [Katō Kazuo], ed. *Are kara shichi nen: Gakuto senpan no gokuchū kara no tegami*. Tokyo: Kōbunsha, 1953.

Ikehata Setsuho. "The Japanese Occupation Period in Philippine History." In *The Philippines Under Japan: Occupation Policy and Reaction*, ed. Ikehata Setsuho and Ricardo Jose, 1–20. Manila: Ateneo de Manila University Press, 1999.

Irie Keishirō. "Heiwa jōyaku sōan no kaisetsu." *Chūō kōron* (September 1951): 183–209.

Isaacs, Tracy. "Accountability for Collective Wrongdoing." In *Accountability for Collective Wrongdoing*, ed. Tracy Isaacs and Richard Vernon, 1–20. Cambridge: Cambridge University Press, 2011.

Itō Takashi. "Kaisetsu." In *Senpansha o sukue: Sasakawa Ryōichi to Tōkyō saiban*. Vol. 2, ed. Itō Takashi, 5–78. Tokyo: Chūō kōronsha, 2008.

——, ed. *Senpansha o sukue: Sasakawa Ryōichi to Tōkyō saiban*. Vol. 2. Tokyo: Chūō kōronsha, 2008.

Iwakawa Takashi. *Kotō no tsuchi to narutomo—BC-kyu senpan saiban*. Tokyo: Kōdansha, 1995.

Jacobs, Justin. "Preparing the People for Mass Clemency: The 1956 Japanese War Crimes Trials in Shenyang and Taiyuan." *China Quarterly* 205 (March 2011): 152–72.

Jaspers, Karl. *The Question of German Guilt*. New York: Dial Press, 1947.

——. *Die Schuldfrage*. Heidelberg: Lambert Schneider, 1946.

Jayanama, Direk. *Thailand and World War II*. Chiang Mai: Silkworm Books, 2008.

Jeffrey, Betty. *White Coolies*. Sydney: Eden Paperbacks, 1954.

Jong, L. de. *The Collapse of a Colonial Society: The Dutch in Indonesia During the Second World War*. Leiden: KITLV Press, 2002.

——. *Het Koninkrijk der Nederlanden in de Tweede Wereldoorlog: Deel 12, Epiloog, tweede helft*. The Hague: SDU, 1988.

Jowett, Philip S. *The Japanese Army 1931–45*. Vol. 2, *1942–45*. Oxford: Osprey, 2002.

Kagao Shūnin. "Ikiteiru Hitō senpan." *Kaizō* 32, no. 7 (June 1951): 132–37.

Katō Hiroko. "Haisha no kikan: Chūgoku kara no fukuin/hikiage mondai no tenkai." *Kokusai seiji* 109 (1995): 110–25.

Katō Miyoko. *Akumyō no hitsugi: Sasakawa Ryōichi den*. Tokyo: Gentōsha, 2010.

Katō Tetsutarō. *Watashi wa kai ni naritai: Aru BC kyū senpan no sakebi*. Tokyo: Shunjusha, 1994.

Kay, Robin, ed. *Documents on New Zealand External Relations*. Vol. 3, *The ANZUS Pact and the Treaty of Peace with Japan*. Wellington: Historical Publications Branch, Department of Internal Affairs, 1985.

Kennedy, David M. *Freedom from Fear: The American People in Depression and War, 1929–1945*. New York: Oxford University Press, 1999.

Kesavan, K. V. "The Attitude of the Philippines Towards the Japanese Peace Treaty." *International Studies* 12, no. 2 (1973): 222–50.

Keynes, John Maynard. *The Economic Consequences of the Peace*. New York: Harcourt Brace, 1920.

Kim, Jeong-Chul. "Caricaturing 'Traitors': Communal Reactions to Indigenous Collaboration in Japanese-Occupied Korea." *International Journal of Law, Crime and Justice* 42 (2014): 203–23.

Kinoshita, Hanji. "Echoes of Militarism in Japan." *Pacific Affairs* 26, no. 3 (September 1953): 244–51.

Kirby, S. Woodburn. *The War Against Japan*. Vol. 5, *The Surrender of Japan*. London: HMSO, 1969.

Kishi Nobusuke, Yatsugi Kazuo, and Itō Takashi. *Kishi Nobusuke no kaisō*. Tokyo: Bungei shunjū, 1981.

Kitamura, Hiroshi. *Screening Enlightenment: Hollywood and the Cultural Reconstruction of Defeated Japan*. Ithaca, NY: Cornell University Press, 2010.

Kochavi, Arieh J. *Prelude to Nuremberg: Allied War Crimes Policy and the Question of Punishment*. Chapel Hill: University of North Carolina Press, 1998.

Kōseishō. *Engo gojūnen shi*. Tokyo: Gyōsei, 1997.

Kōseishō hikiage engokyoku hōmu chōsashitsu hen, Tanaka Hiromi kaisetsu. *Sensō saiban to shotaisaku narabini kaigai ni okeru senpan jukeisha no hikiage*. Tokyo: Ryokuin shobō, 2011.

Kosuge Nobuko. "Kaisetsu 1." In *GHQ Nihon senryōshi*. Vol. 5, *BC kyū sensō hanzai saiban*. Trans. and introduction by Kosuge Nobuko and Nagai Hitoshi, 1–10. Tokyo: Nihon tosho sentā, 1996.

Kramer, Alan. "The First Wave of International War Crimes Trials: Istanbul and Leipzig." *European Review* 14 (2006): 441–55.

Kushner, Barak. "Ghosts of the Japanese Imperial Army: The 'White Group' (*Baituan*) and Early Post-War Sino-Japanese Relations." *Past and Present*, suppl. 8 (2013): 117–50.

——. *Men to Devils, Devils to Men: Japanese War Crimes and Chinese Justice*. Cambridge, MA: Harvard University Press, 2015.

——. "Pawns of Empire: Postwar Taiwan, Japan and the Dilemma of War Crimes." *Japanese Studies* 30, no. 1 (2010): 111–33.

Lacey, Michael O. "Military Commissions: A Historical Survey." *Army Lawyer*, no. 3 (2002): 41–47.

Lael, Richard L. *The Yamashita Precedent: War Crimes and Command Responsibility*. Wilmington, DE: Scholarly Resources, 1982.

LaFeber, Walter. "Roosevelt, Churchill, and Indochina: 1942–45." *American Historical Review* 80, no. 5 (December 1975): 1277–95.

Lai, Wen-Wei. "China, the Chinese Representative, and the Use of International Law to Counter Japanese Acts of Aggression: China's Standpoint on UNWCC Jurisdiction." *Criminal Law Forum* 25 (2014): 111–32.

Lansford, Tom. "Bataan Death March." In *World War II in the Pacific: An Encyclopedia*, ed. Stanley Sandler, 157–60. New York: Taylor & Francis, 2001.

Large, Stephen S. *Emperor Hirohito and Shōwa Japan: A Political Biography*. London: Routledge, 1992.

Lawson, Konrad Mitchell. "Wartime Atrocities and the Politics of Treason in the Ruins of the Japanese Empire, 1937–1953." PhD diss., Harvard University, 2012.

Lee, Changsoo. "The Politics of the Korean Minority in Japan." PhD diss., University of Maryland, 1971.

Lee, Soon-won. "Korean–Japanese Discord, 1945–1965." PhD diss., Rutgers University, 1967.

Ling Yan. "The 1956 Japanese War Crimes Trials in China." In *Historical Origins of International Criminal Law*, ed. Morten Bergsmo, Cheah Wui Ling, and Yi Ping. Vol. 2, 215–41. Brussels: Torkel Opsahl Academic EPublisher, 2014.

Lingen, Kerstin von. *Kesselring's Last Battle: War Crimes Trials and Cold War Politics, 1945–1960*. Trans. Alexandra Klemm. Lawrence: University Press of Kansas: 2009.

Linton, Suzannah. Introduction to *Hong Kong's War Crimes Trials*, ed. Suzannah Linton, 1–11. Oxford: Oxford University Press, 2013.

"Louis Allen: In Memoriam." In *Lafcadio Hearn: Japan's Great Interpreter: A New Anthology of His Writings, 1894–1904*. ed. Louis Allen and Jean Wilson, vii–x. Sandgate, Kent: Japan Library, 1992.

Lowe, David. *Menzies and the "Great World Struggle": Australia's Cold War, 1948–1954*. Sydney: University of New South Wales Press, 1999.

Lowe, Peter. "An Embarrassing Necessity: The Tokyo Trial of Japanese Leaders, 1946–48." In *The Trial in History*. Vol. 2, *Domestic and International Trials, 1700–2000*, ed. R. A. Melikan, 137–56. Manchester: Manchester University Press, 2003.

MacDonald, David B. *Identity Politics in the Age of Genocide: The Holocaust and Historical Representation*. Abingdon: Routledge, 2008.

Maga, Timothy P. "'Away from Tokyo': The Pacific Islands War Crimes Trials, 1945–1949." *Journal of Pacific History* 36, no. 1 (2001): 37–50.

——. *Judgment at Tokyo: The Japanese War Crimes Trials*. Lexington: University Press of Kentucky, 2001.

Mainichi shinbun, Nagai Hitoshi, and Utsumi Aiko, eds. *Shinbun shiryō ni miru Tōkyō saiban/BC-kyū saiban*. Vol. 2. Tokyo: Gendai shiryō shuppan, 2000.

Mainichi shinbunsha. *Ichiokunin no Shōwashi: Nihon senryō*. Vol. 2. Tokyo: Mainichi shinbunsha, 1980.

Maki, John M., ed. *Conflict and Tension in the Far East: Key Documents, 1894–1960*. Seattle: University of Washington Press, 1961.

Mao Tse-tung. *Selected Works of Mao Tse-tung* 4. Beijing: Foreign Languages Press, 1961.

Marr, David G. *Vietnam 1945: The Quest for Power*. Berkeley: University of California Press, 1995.

Marrus, Michael. *The Holocaust in History*. New York: Meridian, 1987.

Matthäus, Jürgen. "The Lessons of Leipzig: Punishing German War Criminals After the First World War." In *Atrocities on Trial: Historical Perspectives on the Politics of Prosecuting War Crimes*, ed. Patricia Heberer and Jürgen Matthäus, 3–23. Lincoln: University of Nebraska Press, 2008.

McCormack, Gavan. "Apportioning the Blame: Australian Trials for Railway Crimes." In *The Burma–Thailand Railway: Memory and History*, ed. Gavan McCormack and Hank Nelson, 85–115. Sydney: Allen & Unwin, 1993.

McCormack, Gavan, and Hank Nelson, eds. *The Burma–Thailand Railway: Memory and History*. Sydney: Allen & Unwin, 1993.

McGovern, Terrance C., Mark A. Berhow, and Chris Taylor. *American Defenses of Corregidor and Manila Bay, 1898–1945*. Oxford: Osprey, 2003.

Mellema, Gregory. *Collective Responsibility*. Amsterdam: Rodopi, 1997.

Mendelsohn, John. "War Crimes Trials and Clemency in Germany and Japan." In *Americans as Proconsuls: United States Military Government in Germany and Japan, 1944–1952*, ed. Robert Wolfe, 26–259. Carbondale: Southern Illinois University Press, 1984.

Mettraux, Guénaël. *The Law of Command Responsibility*. Oxford: Oxford University Press, 2009.

Miller, Edward S. *Bankrupting the Enemy: The U.S. Financial Siege of Japan Before Pearl Harbor*. Annapolis, MD: Naval Institute Press, 2007.

Miller, Robert W. "War Crimes Trials at Yokohama." *Brooklyn Law Review* 15, no. 2 (1949): 191–209.

Minchin-Comm, Dorothy, and Dorothy Nelson-Oster. *An Ordered Life: The Andrew N. Nelson Story*. Np: Trafford Publishing, 2010.

Minear, Richard H. *Victors' Justice: The Tokyo War Crimes Trial*. Princeton, NJ: Princeton University Press, 1971.

Mitchell, Andrew D. "Failure to Halt, Prevent or Punish: The Doctrine of Command Responsibility for War Crimes." *Sydney Law Review* 22, no. 3 (2000): 381–410.

Miyagi Kenshū. *Sengo, sensō no eigashi*. Tokyo: Bokutō shinjūsha, 1991.

Moore, Kathleen Dean. *Justice, Mercy, and the Public Interest*. Oxford: Oxford University Press, 1989.

Morina, Christina. "Instructed Silence, Constructed Memory: The SED and the Return of German Prisoners of War as 'War Criminals' from the Soviet Union to East Germany, 1950–1956." *Contemporary European History* 13, no. 3 (August 2004): 323–43.

Morris, Eric. *Corregidor: The American Alamo of World War II*. New York: Cooper Square Press, 2000.

Morris, Ivan. *Nationalism and the Right Wing in Japan: A Study of Post-War Trends*. Oxford: Oxford University Press, 1960.

Morris, Narrelle. "Justice for 'Asian' Victims: The Australian War Crimes Trials of the Japanese, 1945–51." In *The Hidden Histories of War Crimes Trials*, ed. Kevin Jon Heller and Gerry Simpson, 348–66. Oxford: Oxford University Press, 2013.

——. "Unexpected Defeat: The Unsuccessful War Crimes Prosecution of Lt Gen Yamawaki Masataka and Others at Manus Island, 1950." *Journal of International Criminal Justice* 11 (2013): 591–613.

Morris, Terence. *Crime and Criminal Justice Since 1945*. Oxford: Blackwell, 1989.

Munemiya, Shinji, and Kazuo Yoshioka. *The Account of Legal Proceedings of Court for War Criminal Suspects*. Tokyo: Horitzu Shinpo Press, 1946.

Nagai Hitoshi. *Firipin to taiNichi senpan saiban: 1945–1953 nen*. Tokyo: Iwanami shoten, 2010.

——. "Sensō hanzainin ni kansuru seifu seimei an: Higashikuni naikaku ni yoru kakugi kettei no myakuraku." *Nenpō: Nihon gendaishi* 10 (December 2005): 277–321.

Nakagawa, Toru. "Japan–Philippine Relations." In *Fookien Times Yearbook*, 73–74, 80. Manila, 1953.

Nakamura, Mitsuo. "General Imamura and the Early Period of Japanese Occupation." *Indonesia* 10 (October 1970): 1–26.

Narayanan, Arujunan, "Japanese Atrocities and British Minor War Crimes Trials After World War II in the East." *Jebat* 33 (2006): 1–28.

——. "Second World War Japanese Atrocities and British Minor War Crimes Trials: The Issue of Fair Trial in Four Selected British Minor War Crimes Trials in Malaya and Singapore in 1946–1947." PhD diss., University of Wales, Aberystwyth, 2003.

Nie, Jing-Bao. "The West's Dismissal of the Khabarovsk Trial as 'Communist Propaganda': Ideology, Evidence and International Bioethics." *Journal of Bioethical Inquiry* 1, no. 1 (2004): 32–42.

Nie, Jing-Bao, Nanyan Guo, Mark Selden, and Arthur Kleinman, eds. *Japan's Wartime Medical Atrocities: Comparative Inquiries in Science, History, and Ethics*. London: Routledge, 2010.

Nimmo, William F. *Behind a Curtain of Silence: Japanese in Soviet Custody, 1945–1956*. Westport, CT: Greenwood Press, 1988.

Nish, Ian. *Japanese Foreign Policy, 1869–1942: Kasumigaseki to Miyakezaka*. London: Routledge & Kegan Paul, 1977.

Okada, Emmi. "The Australian Trials of Class B and C Japanese War Crime Suspects, 1945–51." *Australian International Law Journal* 4 (2009): 47–80.

Onuma Yasuaki. "Japanese War Guilt and Postwar Responsibilities of Japan." *Berkeley Journal of International Law* 20, no. 3 (2003): 600–620.

Ooi Keat Gin. *The Japanese Occupation of Borneo, 1941–45*. London: Routledge, 2011.

Palmer, Brandon. *Fighting for the Enemy: Koreans in Japan's War, 1937–1945*. Seattle: University of Washington Press, 2013.

——. "Imperial Japan's Preparations to Conscript Koreans as Soldiers, 1942–1945." *Korean Studies* 31 (2007): 63–78.

Pappas, Caroline. "Law and Politics: Australia's War Crimes Trials in the Pacific, 1943–1961." PhD diss., Australian Defence Force Academy, University of New South Wales, 2001.

Parks, William H. "Command Responsibility for War Crimes." *Military Law Review* 62 (1973): 1–104.

Pendas, Devin O. *The Frankfurt Auschwitz Trial, 1963–1965: Genocide, History, and the Limits of the Law*. Cambridge: Cambridge University Press, 2006.

——. "Putting the Holocaust on Trial in the Two Germanies, 1945–1989." In *The Routledge History of the Holocaust*, ed. Jonathan C. Friedman, 425–28. Abingdon: Routledge, 2011.

Piccigallo, Philip R. *The Japanese on Trial: Allied War Crimes Operations in the East, 1945–1951*. Austin: University of Texas Press, 1979.

Pinosa-Nobles, Raissa. *To Fight Without End: The Story of a Misunderstood President*. Makati, Metro Manila: Ayala Foundation, 1990.

Poelgeest, L. van. *Japanse Besognes: Nederland en Japan 1945–1975*. The Hague: SDU, 1999.

Political Reorientation of Japan September 1945 to September 1948: Report of Government Section, Supreme Commander for the Allied Powers. Washington, D.C.: U.S. Government Printing Office, 1949.

Post, Laurens van der. *The Night of the New Moon*. London: Hogarth, 1970.

Prévost, Ann Marie. "Race and War Crimes: The 1945 War Crimes Trial of General Tomoyuki Yamashita." *Human Rights Quarterly* 14, no. 3 (August 1992): 303–38.

Pritchard, R. John. "The Gift of Clemency Following British War Crimes Trials in the Far East, 1946–1948." *Criminal Law Forum* 7, no. 1 (1996): 15–50.

——. "The International Military Tribunal for the Far East and Its Contemporary Resonances." *Military Law Review* 149 (1995): 25–35.

——. "The International Military Tribunal for the Far East and the Allied National War Crimes Trials in Asia." In *International Criminal Law*. Vol. 3, *Enforcement*, ed. M. Cherif Bassiouni, 109–69. 2nd ed. Ardsley, NY: Transnational, 1999.

——. "Lessons from British Proceedings Against Japanese War Criminals." *Human Rights Review* 3, no. 2 (1978): 104–21.

——. "The Nature and Significance of British Post-War Trials of Japanese War Criminals, 1945–1948." *Proceedings* (British Association for Japanese Studies) 2 (1977): 189–219.

——. "The Parameters of Justice: The Evolution of British Civil and Military Perspectives on War Crimes Trials and Their Legal Context (1942–1956)." In *International Humanitarian Law*. Vol. 3, *Origins, Challenges and Prospects*, ed. John Carey, William V. Dunlap, and R. John Pritchard, 277–326. Leiden: Brill, 2006.

"The Proclamation of Amnesty and Reconstruction by the President of the United States of America." In *Statutes at Large, Treaties, and Proclamations of the United States of America* 13 (1866): 737–39.

Punishment for War Crimes: The Inter-Allied Declaration Signed at St James's Palace London on 13 January 1942, and Relevant Documents. London: HMSO, 1942.

Quah, Jon S. T. "Curbing Corruption in the Philippines: Is This an Impossible Dream?" *Philippine Journal of Public Administration* 54, nos. 1–2 (January–December 2010): 1–43.

Quirino, Carlos. *Apo Lakay: The Biography of President Elpidio Quirino of the Philippines*. Makati, Metro Manila: Total Book World, 1987.

Record of Proceedings in the Trial of *U.S.A. v. Soemu Toyoda*. Vol. 1. Tokyo: War Crimes Tribunal, GHQ, SCAP [1949].

Reel, A. Frank. *The Case of General Yamashita*. Chicago: University of Chicago Press, 1949.

Reid, Anthony. "Australia's Hundred Days in South Sulawesi." In *Nineteenth and Twentieth Century Indonesia: Essays in Honour of Professor J. D. Legge*, ed. David P. Chandler and M.C. Ricklefs, 210–24. Clayton, VIC: Southeast Asian Studies, Monash University, 1986.

Report of Robert H. Jackson, U.S. Representative to the International Conference on Military Trials, London, 1945. Washington, D.C.: U.S. Department of State, 1949.

Republic of the Philippines. *Official Gazette* 49, nos. 10–12. Manila: n. publ., 1953.

Reuter, Lutz R. "How Germany Has Coped: Four Decades Later." In *Transitional Justice: How Emerging Democracies Reckon with Former Regimes*. Vol. 2, *Country Studies*, ed. Neil J. Kritz, 63–69. Washington, D.C.: U.S. Institute of Peace Press, 1995.

Rivett, Rohan. *Behind Bamboo: An Inside Story of the Japanese Prison Camps*. Sydney: Angus & Robertson, 1946.

Roadnight, Andrew. "Sleeping with the Enemy: Britain, Japanese Troops and the Netherlands East Indies, 1945–46." *History* 87, no. 286 (2002): 245–68.

Roland, Charles G., "Allied POWs, Japanese Captors and the Geneva Convention." *War & Society* 9, no. 2 (1991): 83–101.

Rosecrance, Richard N. *Australian Diplomacy and Japan, 1945–1951*. Cambridge: Cambridge University Press, 1962.

Russell of Liverpool, Lord. *The Knights of Bushido*. London: Cassell, 1958.

Rusu kazoku dantai zenkoku kyōgikai shi hankō iinkai. *Ubawareshi ai to jiyū o . . . hikiage sokushin undō no kiroku*. Tokyo: Kyōwatō, 1959.

Ryan, Allan A. *Yamashita's Ghost: War Crimes, MacArthur's Justice, and Command Accountability*. Lawrence: University Press of Kansas, 2012.

Sadurski, Wojciech. *Giving Desert Its Due: Social Justice and Legal Theory*. Dordrecht: Reidel, 1985.

Sanada Hideo. "Hikari sashikomu senpan no mado: Kari shussho, ichijishussho no shikaku, yōken kanwa." *Toki no hōrei* 88 (February 1953): 32–34.

Sandel, Michael J. *Justice: What's the Right Thing to Do?* New York: Farrar, Straus & Giroux, 2009.

Sandler, Stanley, ed. *World War II in the Pacific: An Encyclopedia*. New York: Garland, 2001.

Sasakawa Ryōichi. *Sugamo Diary*. Trans. Ken Hijino. London: Hurst, 2010.

Satō Seizaburō. *Sasakawa Ryoichi: A Life*. Trans. Hara Fujiko. Norwalk, CT: East Bridge, 2006.

Scalapino, Robert A. *The Japanese Communist Movement, 1920–1966*. Berkeley: University of California Press, 1967.

Schaller, Michael. *The American Occupation of Japan: The Origins of the Cold War in Asia*. New York: Oxford University Press, 1985.

——. *Douglas MacArthur, the Far-Eastern General*. New York: Oxford University Press, 1989.

Schwartz, Thomas Alan. *America's Germany: John J. McCloy and the Federal Republic of Germany*. Cambridge, MA: Harvard University Press, 1991.

Sellars, Kirsten. *"Crimes Against Peace" and International Law*. Cambridge: Cambridge University Press, 2013.

Selz, Shirley A. "Conspiracy Law in Theory and in Practice: Federal Conspiracy Prosecutions in Chicago." *American Journal of Criminal Law* 5 (1977): 35–71.

Seraphim, Franziska. *War Memory and Social Politics in Japan, 1945–2005*. Cambridge, MA: Harvard University Asia Center, 2006.

Shaw, Henry I. *The United States Marines in North China, 1945–1949*. Washington, D.C.: Historical Branch, G-3 Division, U.S. Marine Corps, 1968.

Shimomaki Takeshi. "Gunsai, senpan wa dō naru." *Jurisuto*, May 15, 1952, 14–16.

Shiroyama, Saburō. *War Criminal: The Life and Death of Hirota Kōki*. Tokyo: Kodansha International, 1977.

Shotwell, James T. "What Is 'War as an Instrument of National Policy?'" *Proceedings of the Academy of Political Science* 13, no. 2 (1929): 25–30.

Sienho Yee. "The Tu Quoque Argument as a Defence to International Crimes, Prosecution or Punishment." *Chinese Journal of International Law* 3 (2004): 87–134.

Silver, Lynette. *Sandakan: A Conspiracy of Silence*. Burra Creek, NSW: Sally Milner, 1998.

Sissons, D. C. S. "The Australian War Crimes Trials and Investigations (1942–51)." Unpublished manuscript, Boxes 4 and 5, http://www.ocf.berkeley.edu/~changmin/documents/Sissons%20Final%20War%20Crimes%20Text%2018-3-06.pdf (accessed July 21, 2013).

Slamet, Mas. *Japanese Souls in Indonesian Bodies*. Batavia: np, 1946.

Sleeman, Colin, ed. *Trial of Gozawa Sadaichi and Nine Others*. London: William Hodge, 1948.

Smith, Bradley F. *The Road to Nuremberg*. New York: Basic Books, 1981.

Smith, Dayle Kerry. "The Tokyo War Crimes Trial: U.S.A. & o'rs v Koki Hirota & o'rs." PhD diss., University of Queensland, 1993.

Smith, Simon C. "Crimes and Punishment: Local Responses to the Trial of Japanese War Criminals in Malaya and Singapore, 1946–48." *South East Asia Research* 5 (March 1997): 41–56.

Sodei Rinjirō, ed. *Dear General MacArthur: Letters from the Japanese During the American Occupation*. Trans. Shizue Matsuda. English edition edited by John Junkerman. Lanham, MD: Rowman & Littlefield, 2001.

Sogawa Takeo, and Oda Shigeru. *Wagakuni no kokusai hanrei*. Tokyo: Yūhikaku, 1976.

Solis, Gary D. "Obedience of Orders and the Law of War: Judicial Application in American Forums." *American University International Law Review* 15, no. 2 (1999): 481–526.

South Toranomon Law Offices. http://www.s-tora.com/en/overview/?PHPSESSID=4b5sjsndbkk3p4d4hnd37n28l6 (accessed October 8, 2015).

Spector, Ronald H. "After Hiroshima: Allied Military Occupations and the Fate of Japan's Empire, 1945–1947." *Journal of Military History* 69, no. 4 (October 2005): 1121–36.

——. *In the Ruins of Empire: The Japanese Surrender and the Battle for Postwar Asia*. New York: Random House, 2007.

Spurlock, Paul E. "The Yokohama War Crimes Trials: The Truth About a Misunderstood Subject." *American Bar Association Journal* 36, no. 5 (May 1950): 387–89, 436–37.

Strange, Carolyn. "Mercy and Parole in Anglo-American Criminal Justice Systems, from the Eighteenth to the Twenty-First Century." In *Oxford Handbook of the History of Crime and Criminal Justice*, ed. Paul Knepper and Anja Johansen, 573–96. Oxford: Oxford University Press, 2016.

Straus, Ulrich. *The Anguish of Surrender: Japanese POWs of World War II*. Seattle: University of Washington Press, 2003.

Sugamo hōmu iinkai, ed. *Senpan saiban no jissō*. Tokyo: Maki shobō, 1981.

Sweeney, Mark. "Letters from Yokohama: Major John Dickey and the Prosecution of Japanese Class 'B' and 'C' War Crimes." MA thesis, Saint Mary's University, Halifax, Nova Scotia, 2008.

Takahashi Saburō. *"Senkimono" o yomu: Sensō taiken to sengo Nihon shakai*. Kyoto: Akademia shuppankai, 1988.

Takeda, Kayoko. *Interpreting the Tokyo War Crimes Tribunal: A Sociopolitical Analysis*. Ottawa: University of Ottawa Press, 2010.

Takeda, Kiyoko. *The Dual-Image of the Japanese Emperor*. Houndmills: Macmillan, 1988.

Takemae, Eiji. *Inside GHQ: The Allied Occupation of Japan and Its Legacy*. Trans. Robert Ricketts and Sebastian Swann. London: Continuum, 2002.

Tanaka Hiromi. *BCkyū senpan*. Tokyo: Chikuma shobō, 2002.

Tanaka, Yuki. *Hidden Horrors: Japanese War Crimes in World War II*. Boulder, CO: Westview, 1996.

Terkel, Studs. *"The Good War": An Oral History of World War Two*. New York: Pantheon, 1984.

Tessensohn, Denyse. "The British Military Administration's Treason Trial of Dr Charles Joseph Pemberton Paglar, 1946." MA thesis, National University of Singapore, 2007.

Tiedemann, Arthur E., ed. *Modern Japan: A Brief History*. Princeton, NJ: Van Nostrand, 1955.

Tōgō, Kazuhiko. *Japan's Foreign Policy, 1945–2009: The Quest for a Proactive Policy*. Leiden: Brill, 2010.

Tokudome, Kinue. "The Holocaust and Japanese Atrocities." In *Is the Holocaust Unique? Perspectives on Comparative Genocide*, ed. Alan S. Rosenbaum, 201–13. Boulder, CO: Westview, 2009.

Totani, Yuma. *Justice in Asia and the Pacific Region, 1945–1952: Allied War Crimes Prosecutions*. New York: Cambridge University Press, 2015.

——. *The Tokyo War Crimes Trial: The Pursuit of Justice in the Wake of World War Two*. Cambridge, MA: Harvard University Asia Center, 2008.

Towle, Philip. "The Japanese Army and Prisoners of War." In *Japanese Prisoners of War*, ed. Philip Towle, Margaret Kosuge, and Yoichi Kibata, 1–16. London: Hambledon and London, 2000.

Trefalt, Beatrice. "Fanaticism, Japanese Soldiers and the Pacific War, 1937–45." In *Fanaticism and Conflict in the Modern Age*, ed. Matthew Hughes and Gaynor Johnson, 33–47. Abingdon: Frank Cass, 2005.

———. "Hostages to International Relations? The Repatriation of Japanese War Criminals from the Philippines." *Japanese Studies* 31, no. 2 (September 2011): 191–209.

———. "Japanese War Criminals in Indochina and the French Pursuit of Justice: Local and International Constraints." *Journal of Contemporary History* 49, no. 4 (October 2014): 727–42.

———. "A Peace Worth Having: Delayed Repatriations and Domestic Debate Over the San Francisco Peace Treaty." *Japanese Studies* 27, no. 2 (2007): 173–87.

Triggs, Gillian. "Australia's War Crimes Trials: All Pity Choked." In *The Law of War Crimes: National and International Approaches*, ed. Timothy L. H. McCormack and Gerry J. Simpson, 123–49. The Hague: Kluwer Law International, 1997.

Tsuchihashi Yūitsu. *Gunpuku seikatsu yonjūnen no omoide.* Tokyo: Keisō shuppan, 1985.

Tsuji, Masanobu. *Masanobu Tsuji's "Underground Escape" from Siam After the Japanese Surrender.* Folkstone, Kent: Global Oriental, 2008.

Tsuji Yutaka. *Montenrupa: Hitō yūshū no kiroku.* Tokyo: Asahi shinbunsha, 1952.

United Nations War Crimes Commission. *History of the United Nations War Crimes Commission and the Development of the Laws of War.* London: HMSO, 1948.

———. *Information Concerning Human Rights Arising from Trials of War Criminals.* New York: United Nations Economic and Social Council, May 15, 1948.

———. *Law Reports of Trials of War Criminals.* Vols. 3, 4, 5, 11, 14. London: HMSO, 1948–1949.

United States Department of State. *Foreign Relations of the United States: Diplomatic Papers, 1945.* Vol. 2, *The Conference of Berlin (the Potsdam Conference).* Washington, D.C.: U.S. Government Printing Office, 1945.

———. *Foreign Relations of the United States: Diplomatic Papers, 1945.* Vol. 6, *The British Commonwealth, the Far East.* Washington, D.C.: U.S. Government Printing Office, 1969.

———. *Foreign Relations of the United States, 1948.* Vol. 6, *The Far East and Australasia.* Washington, D.C.: U.S. Government Printing Office, 1948.

———. *Foreign Relations of the United States, 1950.* Vol. 6, *East Asia and the Pacific.* Washington, D.C.: U.S. Government Printing Office, 1950.

———. *Foreign Relations of the United States, 1952–1954.* Vol. 5, part 1: *Western European Security.* Washington, D.C.: U.S. Government Printing Office, 1983.

———. *Foreign Relations of the United States, 1955–1957.* Vol. 23, part 1: *Japan.* Washington, D.C.: U.S. Government Printing Office, 1991.

Usui Yoshimi (chair). "Sugamo BC-kyū senpan no seikatsu to iken: Aru hi no shūdan menkai kara." *Chūō kōron* 779 (September 1953): 160–69.

Utsumi, Aiko. "Changing Japanese Views of the Allied Occupation of Japan and the War Crimes Trials." *Journal of the Australian War Memorial* 30, April 1997, http://www.awm.gov.au/journal/j30/utsumi.asp (accessed October 24, 2014).

———. "The Japanese Army and Its Prisoners: Relevant Documents and Bureaucratic Institutions." http://ajrp.awm.gov.au/AJRP/AJRP2.nsf/50bee6e350d46afoca256b9000002aof/d2e5732b8749d2e04a2567a8007b490c?OpenDocument (accessed February 13, 2014).

——. "Japan's Korean Soldiers in the Pacific War." In *Asian Labor in the Wartime Japanese Empire: Unknown Histories*, ed. Paul H. Kratoska, 81–89. Armonk, NY: Sharpe, 2005.

——. *Kimu wa naze sabakareta no ka: Chōsenjin BC-kyū senpan no kiseki*. Tokyo: Asahi shinbun shuppan, 2008.

——. "The Korean Guards on the Burma–Thailand Railway." In *The Burma–Thailand Railway: Memory and History*, ed. Gavan McCormack and Hank Nelson, 127–39. Sydney: Allen & Unwin, 1993.

——. "Korean 'Imperial Soldiers': Remembering Colonialism and Crimes Against Allied POWs." In *Perilous Memories: The Asia-Pacific War*, ed. T. Fujitani, Geoffrey M. White, and Lisa Yoneyama, 199–217. Durham, NC: Duke University Press, 2001.

——. *Sugamo purizun: senpantachi no heiwa undō*. Tokyo: Yoshikawa kōbunkan, 2004.

Utsumi Aiko and Nagai Hitoshi. "Kaisetsu." In *Shinbun shiryō ni miru Tōkyō saiban, BC kyū saiban*. Vol. 1, *Tōkyō saiban*, ed. Mainichi shinbun seijibu, iii–xxv. Tokyo: Gendai shiryō shuppan, 2000.

Venturini, Gabriella. "Necessity in the Law of Armed Conflict and in International Criminal Law." *Netherlands Yearbook of International Law* 41 (2010): 45–78.

Violation of the Laws and Customs of War: Reports of Majority and Dissenting Reports of American and Japanese Members of the Commission of Responsibilities, Conference of Paris, 1919. Oxford: Clarendon, 1919.

Wai Keng Kwok. *Justice Done? Criminal and Moral Responsibility Issues in the Chinese Massacres Trial, Singapore 1947*. New Haven, CT: Yale University Genocide Studies Program Working Paper no. 18, http://www.yale.edu/gsp/publications/) (accessed February 11, 2014).

Wakabayashi, Bob Tadashi. "The Messiness of Historical Reality." In *The Nanking Atrocity: Complicating the Picture*, ed. Bob Tadashi Wakabayashi, 3–28. New York: Berghahn, 2007.

——. "The Nanking 100-Man Killing Contest Debate: War Guilt Amid Fabricated Illusions, 1971–75." *Journal of Japanese Studies* 26, no. 2 (2000): 307–40.

Walker, Nigel. *Crime and Punishment in Britain: The Penal System in Theory, Law, and Practice*. Rev. ed. Edinburgh: Edinburgh University Press, 1968.

Watt, Lori. *When Empire Comes Home: Repatriation and Reintegration in Post-War Japan*. Cambridge, MA: Harvard Asia Center, 2009.

Welch, Jeanie M. "Without a Hangman, Without a Rope: Navy War Crimes Trials After World War II." *International Journal of Naval History* 1, no. 1 (April 2002): http://www.ijnhonline.org/wp-content/uploads/2012/01/pdf_welch.pdf (accessed October 1, 2014).

Wesley-Smith, Terence. "Australia and New Zealand." In *Tides of History: The Pacific Islands in the Twentieth Century*, ed. K. R. Howe, Robert C. Kiste, and Brij V. Lal, 195–226. Honolulu: University of Hawai'i Press, 1994.

Willoughby, Charles A., ed. *Reports of General MacArthur: MacArthur in Japan: The Occupation: Military Phase*. Suppl. 1. Washington, D.C.: U.S. Government Printing Office, 1966.

Wilner, Alan M. "Superior Orders as a Defense to Violations of International Criminal Law." *Maryland Law Review* 26, no. 2 (1966): 127–42.

Wilson, Sandra. "Film and Soldier: Japanese War Movies in the 1950s." *Journal of Contemporary History* 48, no. 3 (2013): 537–55.

——. "Prisoners in Sugamo and Their Campaign for Release, 1952–1953." *Japanese Studies* 31, no. 2 (September 2011): 171–90.

——. "The Sentence Is Only Half the Story: From Stern Justice to Clemency for Japanese War Criminals, 1945–1958." *Journal of International Criminal Justice* 13, no. 4 (2015): 745–61.

——. "War Criminals in the Post-War World: The Case of Katō Tetsutarō." *War in History* 22, no. 1 (2015): 87–110.

——. "War, Soldier and Nation in 1950s Japan." *International Journal of Asian Studies* 5, no. 2 (2008): 187–218.

Wurfel, David. "The Philippines." *Journal of Politics* 25, no. 4 (November 1963): 757–73.

Wyngaert, Chris van den, and Steven Dewulf, eds. *International Criminal Law: A Collection of International and Regional Instruments.* Leiden: Nijhoff, 2011.

Yamaguchi, Noriko. "Writing New Japan in Sugamo, 1948–1952: The Allied Occupation and Conflicted Democracy." *Prison Journal* 94, no. 1 (March 2014): 52–74.

Yamamoto, Masahiro. "Japan's 'Unsettling' Past: Article 11 of San Francisco Peace Treaty and Its Ramifications." *Journal of US–China Public Administration*, 7, no. 5 (May 2010): 1–16.

Yap, Felicia. "Prisoners of War and Civilian Internees of the Japanese in British Asia: The Similarities and Contrasts of Experience." *Journal of Contemporary History* 47 (2012): 317–46.

Yavnai, Lisa. "U.S. Army War Crimes Trials in Germany, 1945–1947." In *Atrocities on Trial: Historical Perspectives on the Politics of Prosecuting War Crimes*, ed. Patricia Heberer and Jürgen Matthäus, 49–71. Lincoln: University of Nebraska Press, 2008.

Yoshida Yutaka. *Nihonjin no sensōkan: Rekishi no naka no hen'yō.* Tokyo: Iwanami shoten, 1995.

Yoshitsu, Michael M. *Japan and the San Francisco Peace Settlement.* New York: Columbia University Press, 1983.

Yudin, Boris G. "Research on Humans at the Khabarovsk War Crimes Trial." In *Japan's Wartime Medical Atrocities: Comparative Inquiries in Science, History, and Ethics*, ed. Jing-Bao Nie, Nanyan Guo, Mark Selden, and Arthur Kleinman, 59–78. London: Routledge, 2010.

Zanasi, Margherita. "Globalizing Hanjian: The Suzhou Trials and the Post–World War II Discourse on Collaboration." *American Historical Review* 113, no. 3 (June 2008): 731–51.

Zhang Tianshu. "The Forgotten Legacy: China's Post-Second World War Trials of Japanese War Criminals, 1945–1956." In *Historical Origins of International Criminal Law*, ed. Morten Bergsmo, Cheah Wui Ling, and Yi Ping. Vol. 2, 267–300. Brussels: Torkel Opsahl Academic EPublisher, 2014.

6. FILMS

Araki no naka no haha, directed by Saiki Kiyoshi, 1952.
Haha wa sakebinaku, directed by Sasaki Keisuke, 1952.
Kabe atsuki heya, directed by Kobayashi Masaki, 1953.
Montenrupa no yo wa fukete, directed by Aoyagi Nobuo, 1952.
Sugamo no haha, directed by Adachi Nobuo, 1952.
Yesterday's Enemy, directed by Val Guest, 1959.

INDEX